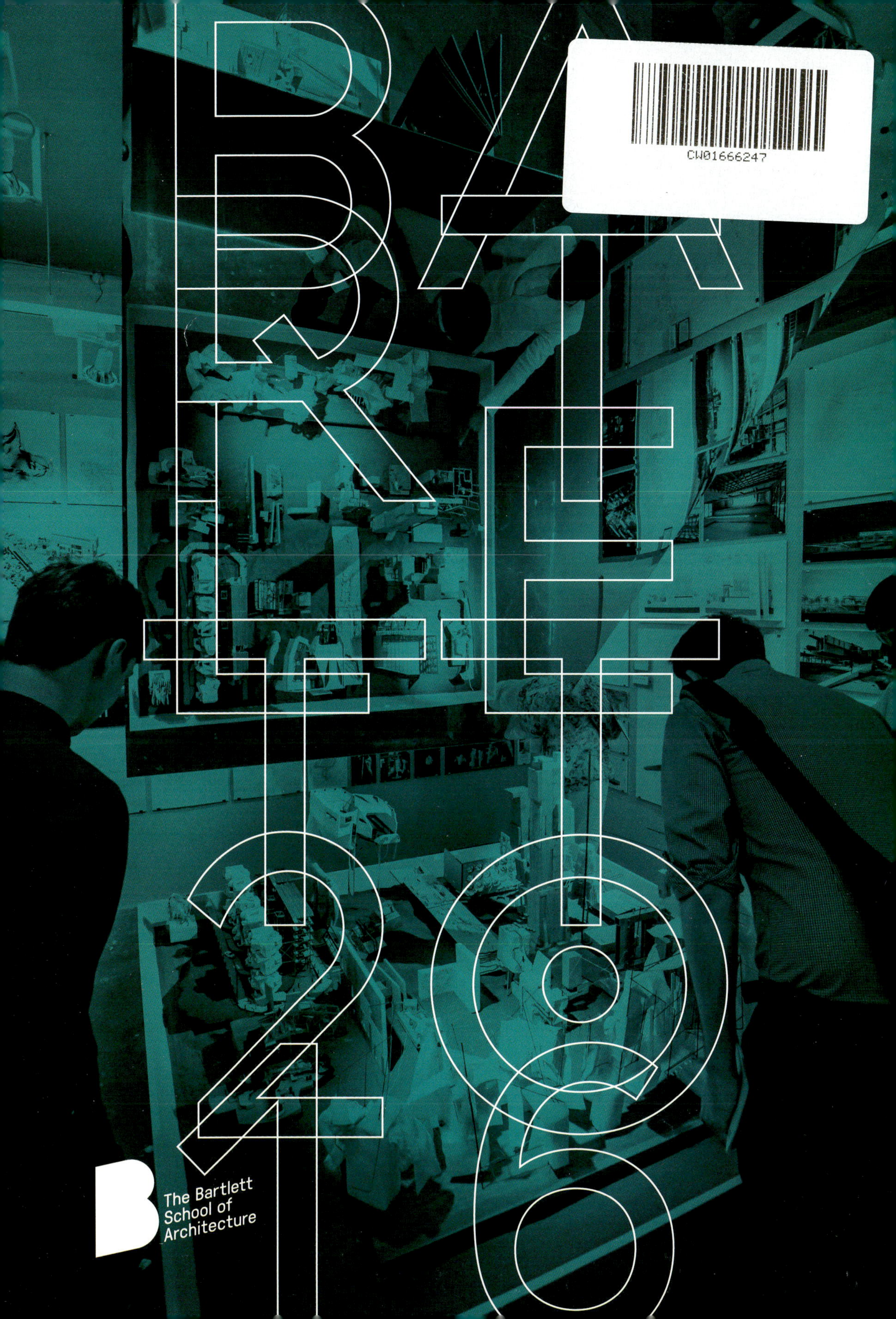

BARTLETT 2016

The Bartlett School of Architecture

ALLFORD HALL MONAGHAN MORRIS

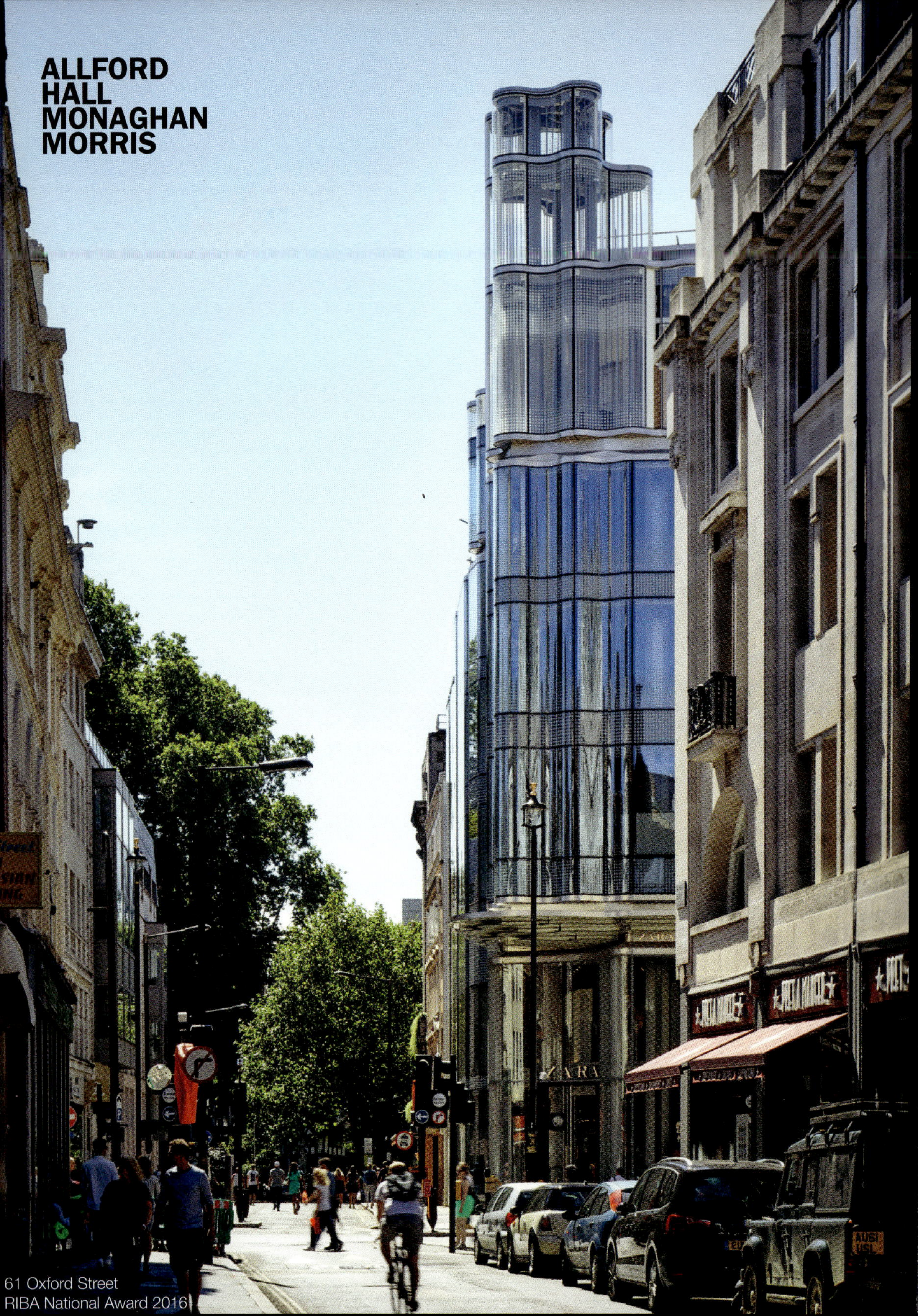

61 Oxford Street
RIBA National Award 2016

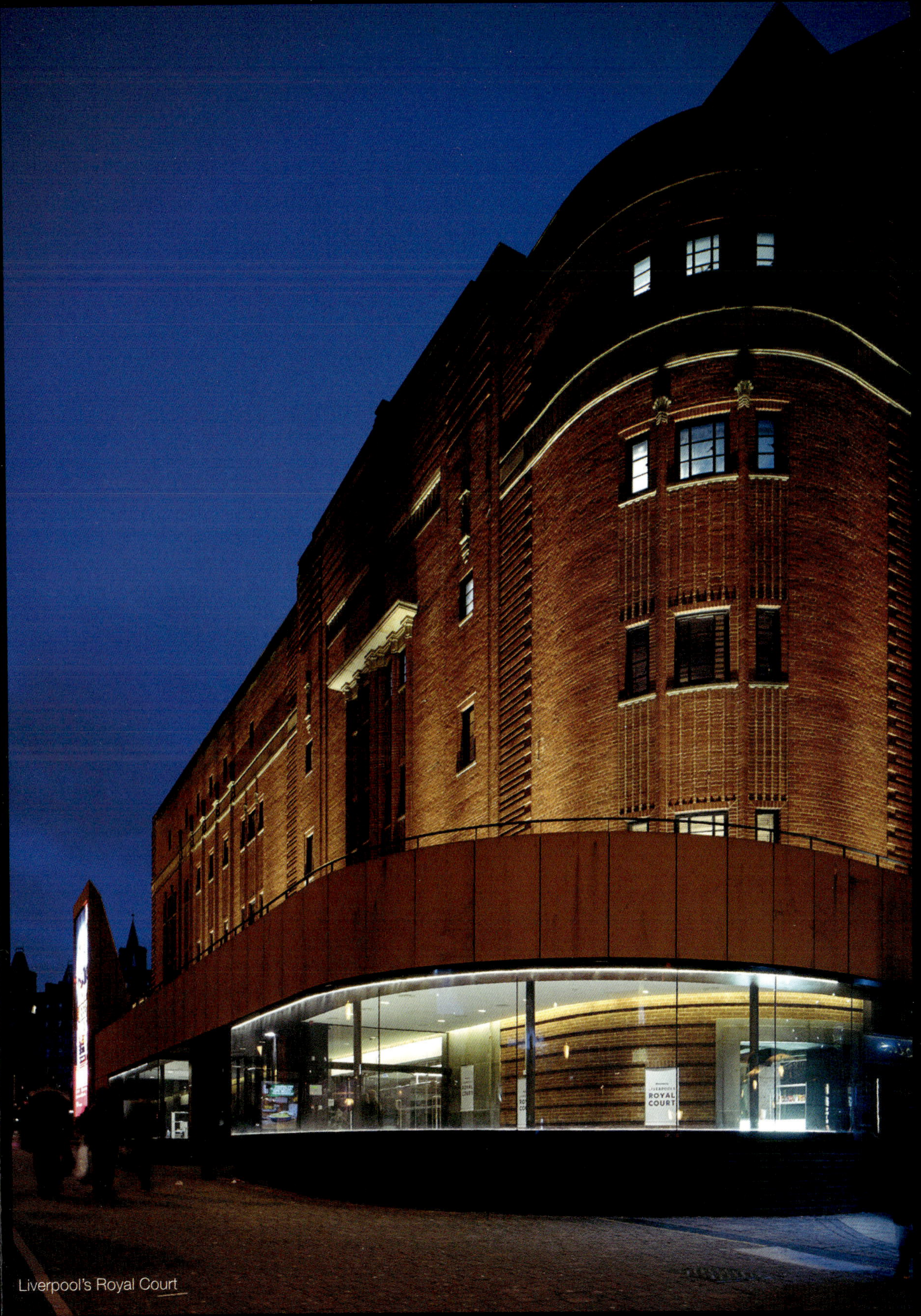

Liverpool's Royal Court

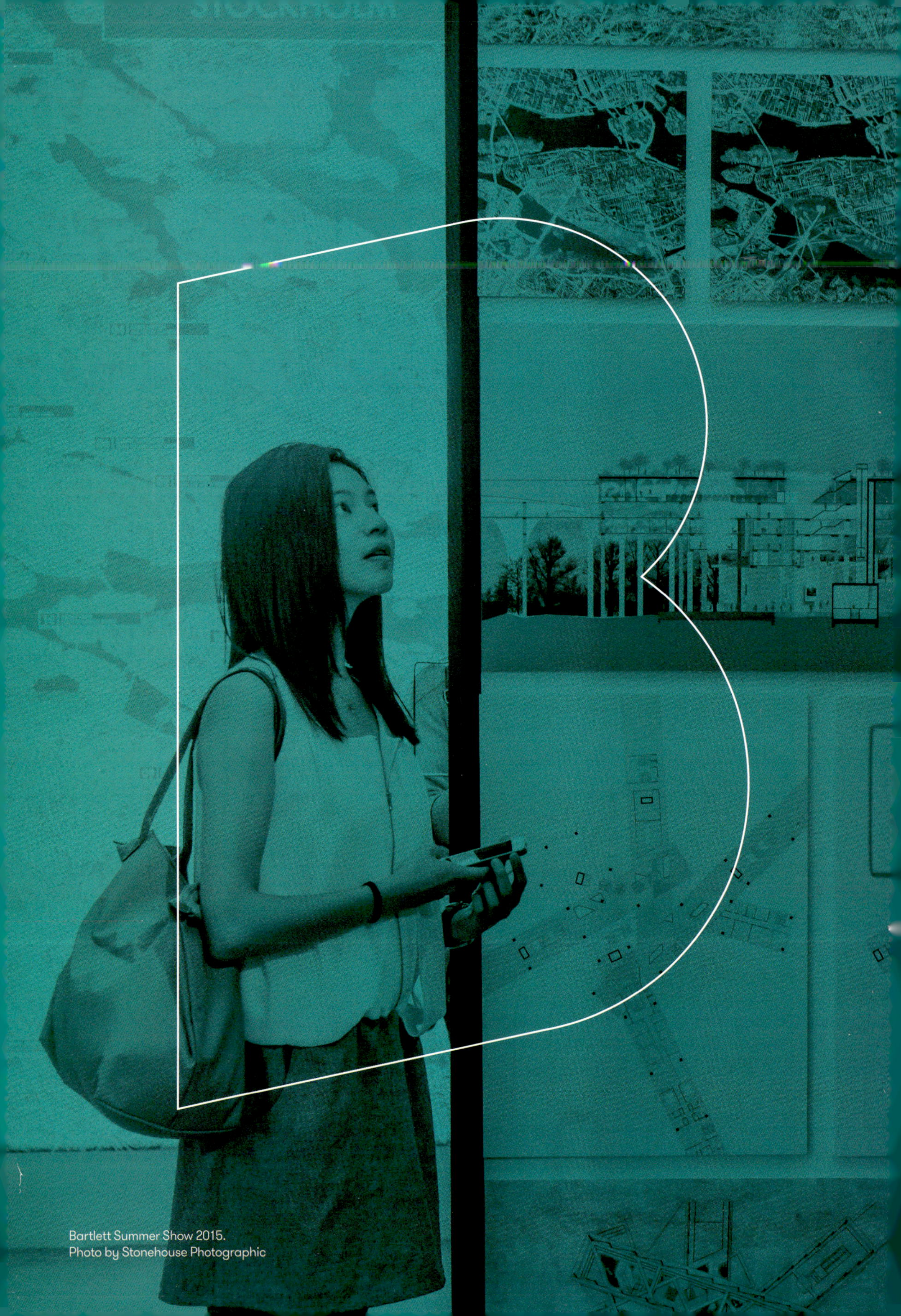

Bartlett Summer Show 2015.
Photo by Stonehouse Photographic

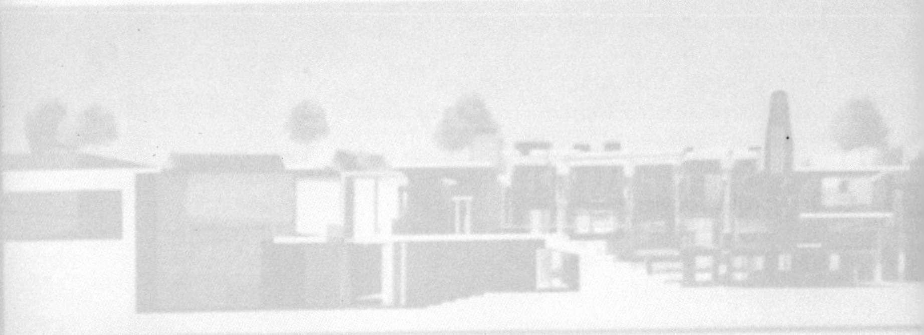
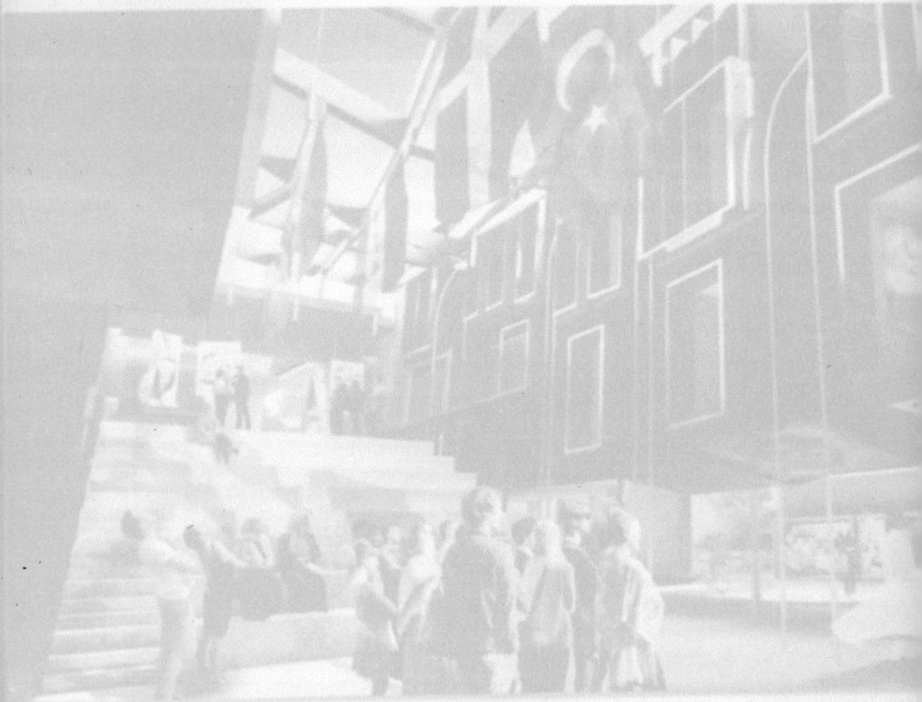
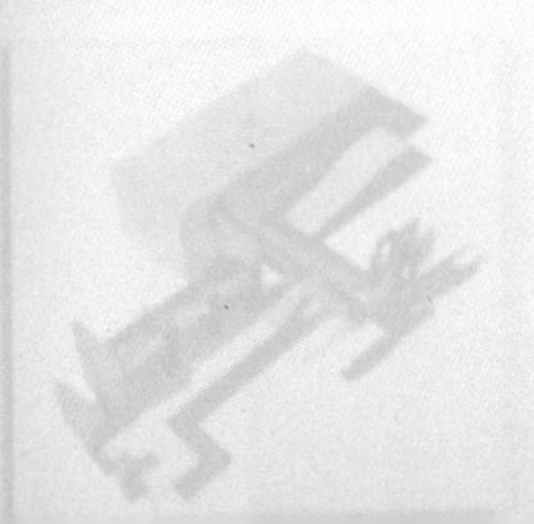

Contents

THE BARTLETT 2016

Introduction

Welcome to The Bartlett School of Architecture's Summer Show catalogue, a celebration of our students' 2015-16 work from the BSc Architecture (ARB/RIBA Part 1), BSc Architecture and Interdisciplinary Studies, and the MArch Architecture (ARB/RIBA Part 2) programmes. In these pages we can only present a sample of the best work by the more than 500 students in these programmes, over 200 of whom are graduating this year. It's well-known, however, that many of our students could easily fill half a catalogue with their own work alone, and indeed, many of our design units are publishing end-of-year pamphlets to tell more of the story behind their projects. Our students have an extraordinary range of toolsets at their disposal to develop, produce and disseminate their work, either in physical or animated form, and by hand, digitally and in print. Nonetheless, it never ceases to amaze us how they overcome this potentially overwhelming abundance and defy an increasingly exponential learning curve to continue to effortlessly raise the stakes. This year is no exception, and it's no wonder that these catalogues end up all over the world, pored over by everyone from those still at school, university students and recent graduates to academics, teachers and professionals of all ages and backgrounds. It's deeply inspiring material, and on behalf of all our staff, we thank every student for the imagination and commitment they bring to it.

——2015-16 has been a special time for both the School and University College London (UCL). A hundred years ago, in 1915-16, Gertrude Leverkus became the first female student to fully enrol onto the architecture undergraduate programme, just a few years before the School was named in honour of its benefactor Henry Herbert Bartlett. 175 years ago (in 1841), UCL appointed Thomas Leverton Donaldson as its first Professor of Architecture. A founder of the Royal Institute of British Architects (established in 1834), his appointment to UCL (founded in 1826) signified that architecture was recognised as a central point of enquiry of the institution, and was foundational to its radical ethos and roots. We celebrated this in 2016 with a 'Bartlett 175' publication in collaboration with *The Architectural Review*, which explores the school's distant and recent past, as well as its future trajectory. Other special events this year have included the launch of a new annual Donaldson Lecture, fabulously delivered by the artist Grayson Perry in January, the Open Crits; a PhD conference and retrospective exhibition; a presentation at RIBA by our Bronze Medal winner Boon Yik Chung; the launch of the UCL 'Think Space' forum; and a provocative and inspiring conference on 'Research-Based Education' hosted for the association of architectural educators (aae). There's a lot more to come before these celebrations conclude this December, so do keep an eye on our event listings.

——Many will know that we will soon return to 22 Gordon Street (formerly Wates House) where the School has stood since 1975. The greatly expanded and upgraded facilities that await us, at the very heart of UCL's Bloomsbury campus, and featuring an exciting new exhibition space, have been a long time coming. Together with the additional shared facilities opening at Here East in Hackney Wick in 2017-18, The Bartlett School of Architecture and the Bartlett Faculty are at a once-in-a-generation turning point, enabling us to expand our capacity within existing programmes and introduce four pioneering new programmes. As a larger school, we will build on our established strengths in design, critical thinking, experimentation and research to tackle the global challenges of the twenty-first century. We will achieve this by broadening the scale of our engagement with social and environmental issues, bridging the disciplines of engineering and craft, developing exchange between theory and practice, as well as between innovations in computation and media, intercultural interactions, the evolution of cities, building design, and building use. Bridging these territories, and more besides, are the keystones of architectural education, research and enterprise – the fundamental building blocks of the school.

——We must not forget, however, that it is the people here who make us what we are; not only the staff and students on the programmes celebrated in this book, but all who participate in making The Bartlett School of Architecture such a challenging, fascinating and exciting place to work, to visit, and to know. One such person was lost this year – our facilities manager Graeme Kennett, who died unexpectedly. His loss was a shock and we extend our deepest sympathy to his friends and family. Another tragic loss this year was that of Dame Zaha Hadid, an icon of world architecture, an inspiration to countless students, practitioners, friends and colleagues, and a regular visitor to the school in times past.

——On this vital note of people and their critical importance to The Bartlett, one of the most rewarding achievements in this anniversary year has been the strengthening of ties between the school and its alumni, a bond explored more fully in the final article in our 'Bartlett 175' magazine. Throughout the year, a number of alumni gatherings were held, from Singapore to Shoreditch, which gave many the taste for more. We are very pleased therefore to announce that later this year we will launch 'Friends of The Bartlett School of Architecture,' an organisation that will offer students, staff, former staff, alumni, supporters and visitors a means to create and maintain a global network that keeps us all in touch. In support of this initiative, we will be also opening a FBSA Members' Room on the 6th floor of 22 Gordon Street, and we look forward to seeing you there.

Professor Frédéric Migayrou
Chair, Bartlett Professor of Architecture

Professor Bob Sheil
Director of The Bartlett School of Architecture

Prizes 2015 – 16

Bartlett School of Architecture Medal

For students averaging 80% or higher in professional programmes

BSc Architecture
Calvin Po, UG6

MArch Architecture
Finbarr Fallon, Unit 24
Robin Farmer, Unit 11
Chun Ting (Sam) Ki, Unit 10
Fergus Knox, Unit 11
Andreas Körner Unit 20
Adam Lampon, Unit 11
Ting-Jui (Brook) Lin, Unit 24
Luke Lupton, Unit 23
Luke Scott, Unit 12
Angeline Wee, Unit 21
Eric Wong, Unit 10

BSc Architecture Year 1

Herbert Batsford Prize
Oscar Henry Maguire

BSc Architecture Year 2

Victor Kite Prize for Design Technology, sponsored by AHMM
Claudia Walton, UG9

BSc Architecture Year 3

Distinguished Work in History and Theory
Rachel Yemitan, UG1

Environmental Design Prize
Ben Sykes-Thompson, UG0

Fitzroy Robinson Drawing Prize
Xin Hao (Jerome) Ng, UG6

Making Buildings Prize
Tae Woo (Freddie) Hong, UG8

iGuzzini Light First Prize
Issui Shioura, UG9

Professional Studies Prize
Jack Leather, UG1

BSc Architectural & Interdisciplinary Studies

Distinguished Work in History and Theory
Thomas Visscher

MArch Architecture Year 4

History and Theory Prize
Joshua Toh, Unit 19
Kirsty McMullan, Unit 23

Kohn Pedersen Fox Associates Bursary
Vanessa Lafoy, Unit 11

Rogers Stirk Harbour + Partners Bursary
Patrick Mawson, Unit 20

Imagination Bursaries
Amani Radeef, Unit 16
Ivo Tedbury, Unit 19
Matthew Lucraft, Unit 24

Saint-Gobain Innovation Award
Jonathan Davis, Unit 21
Joshua Honeysett, Unit 16
Matthew Lucraft, Unit 24
Agostino Nickl, Unit 11
Amani Radeff, Unit 16

MArch Architecture Year 5

Ambrose Poynter Prize
Luke Scott, Unit 12

Fitzroy Robinson Drawing Prize
Eric Wong, Unit 10

Max Fordham Environmental Design Prize
Andreas Körner, Unit 20

Sir Andrew Taylor Prize
Luke Lupton, Unit 23

Sir Banister Fletcher Medal
Eric Wong, Unit 10

Postgraduate Diploma in Professional Practice & Management in Architecture (ARB/RIBA Part 3)

Ross Jamieson Memorial Prize
Sara L'Espérance
Adam Hiles

2015 RIBA Medals

Bronze President's Medal for Best Design Project at Part 1
Boon Yik Chung,
BSc Architecture UG8

Bronze President's Medal High Commendation & SOM Foundation Fellowship for Part I
Douglas Miller,
BSc Architecture UG7

Silver President's Medal Serjeant Award for Excellence in Drawing & SOM Foundation Fellowship for Part II
Benjamin Ferns,
MArch Architecture Unit 12

President's Award for Outstanding Master's Degree Thesis
Christopher Purpura

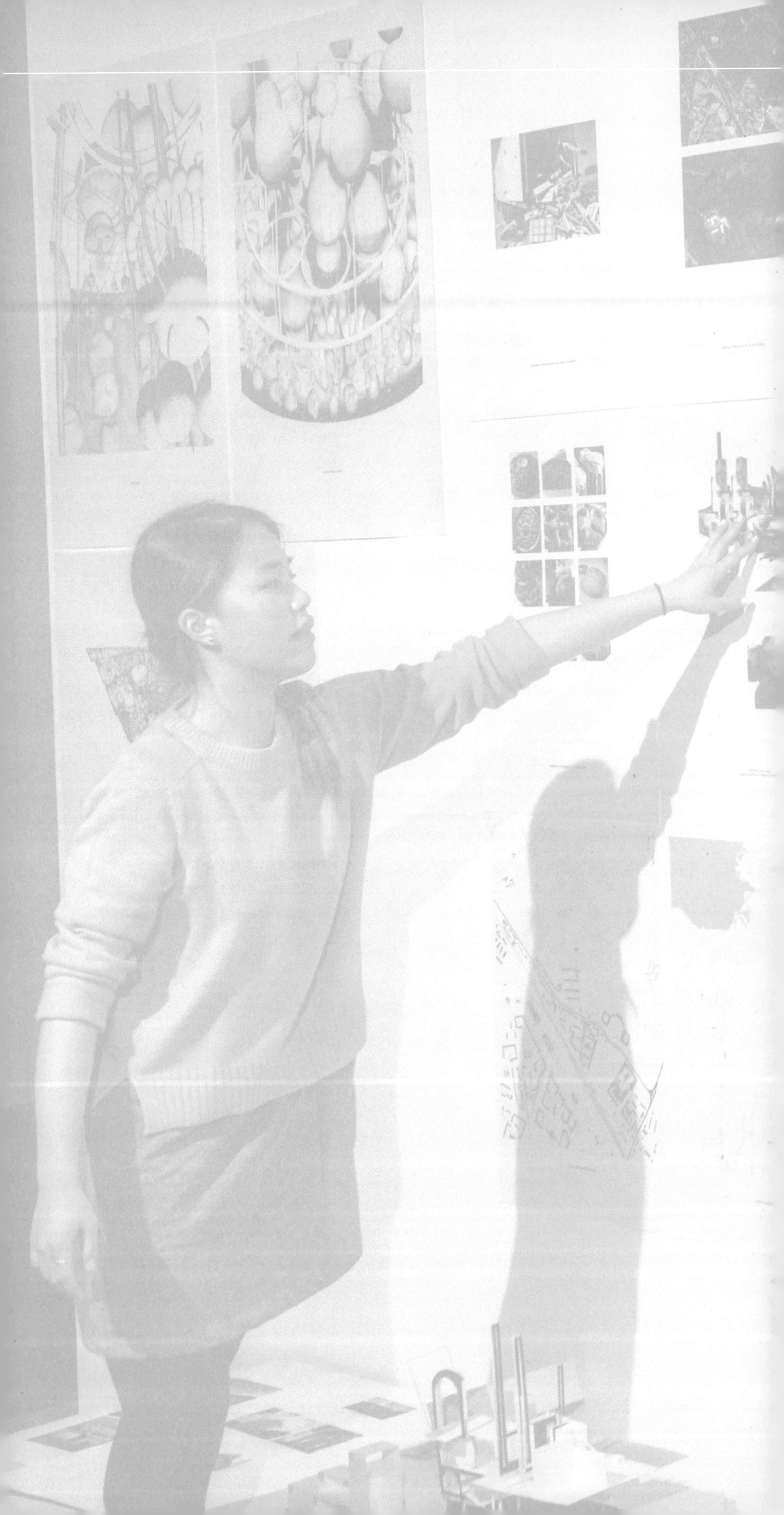

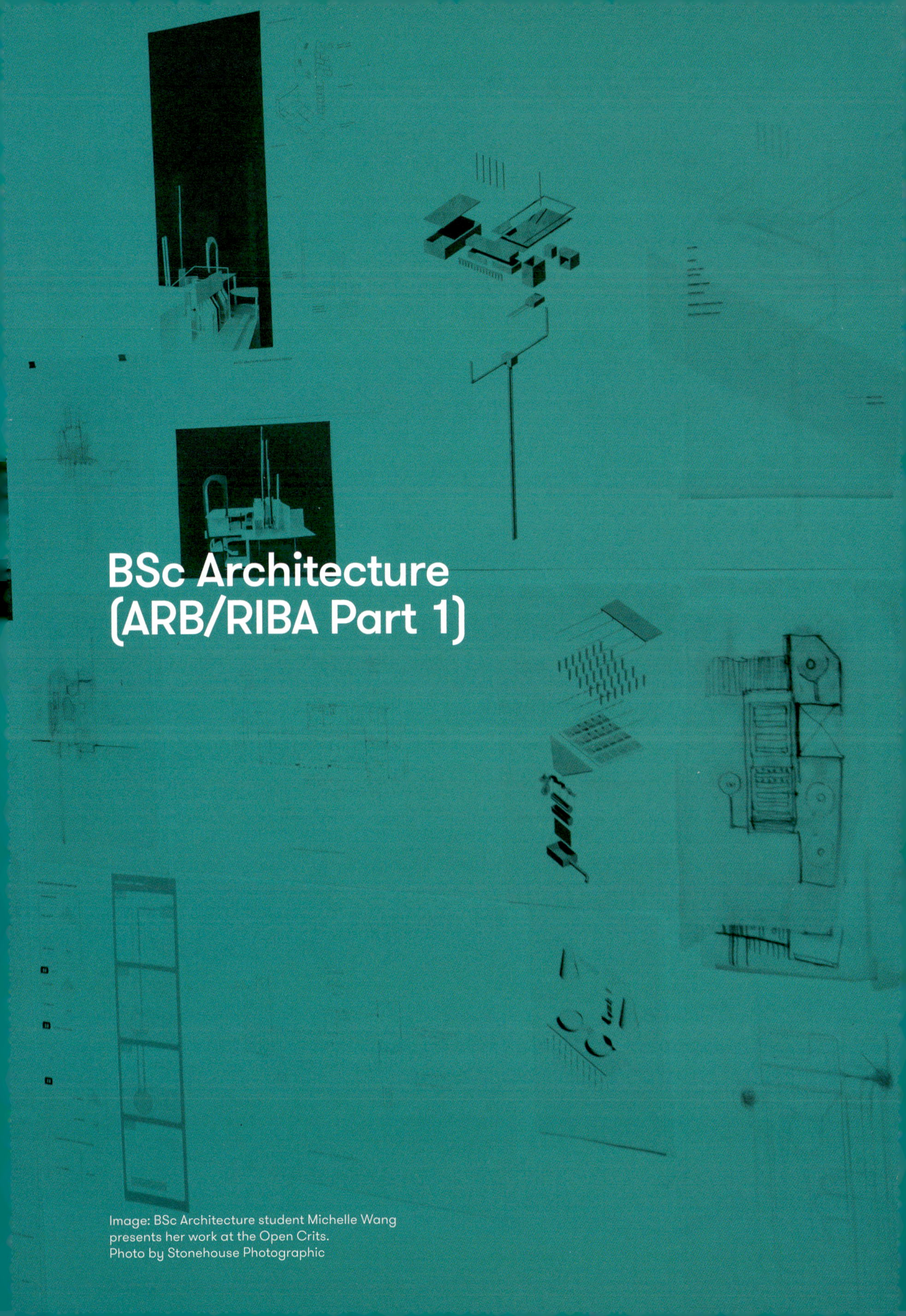

BSc Architecture (ARB/RIBA Part 1)

Image: BSc Architecture student Michelle Wang presents her work at the Open Crits.
Photo by Stonehouse Photographic

BSc Architecture (ARB/RIBA Part 1)

Programme Directors: Matthew Butcher, Mollie Claypool

Year 1 Design Directors
Nat Chard, Carlos Jiménez Cenamor

Year 1 Design Tutors
Lucy Leonard, Ifigenia Liangi, Emma-Kate Matthews, Frederik Petersen, Eva Ravnborg, Gavin Robotham, Emmanouil Stavrakakis, Catrina Stewart, Umut Yamac, Nick Westby

Year 2 & 3 Design Tutors
UG0
Murray Fraser, Justin C.K. Lau, Sara Shafiei
UG1
Francesca Hughes, Gergely Kovács
UG2
Damjan Iliev, Javier Ruiz Rodriguez
UG3
Luke Olsen, Graeme Williamson
UG4
Ana Monrabal-Cook, Luke Pearson
UG5
Julia Backhaus, Pedro Font Alba, Martin Tang
UG6
Christine Hawley, Paolo Zaide
UG7
Pascal Bronner, Thomas Hillier
UG8
Colin Herperger, Thomas Pearce
UG9
Jessica In, Chee-Kit Lai
UG10
Tamsin Hanke, Guan Lee
UG11
James Hampton, Sofia Krimizi

This programme concentrates on providing extensive general knowledge and understanding about what architecture is as a subject, a discipline and a practice, with a distinct emphasis on architectural design through research-based education. It aims to establish the student's core knowledge, critical ability and skills through drawing and making (both analogue and digital), technology (including environmental design, sustainability and computation), history and theory, and professional studies. The Year 1 cohort is organised as a single group, and a vertical unit system begins in Year 2. A core ethos of the entire BSc programme is that students relate their design projects to all other taught modules on an incremental basis. This culminates in Year 3 where design and technology are developed in synthesis, augmented by complementary self-selected themes in history and theory, and professional studies.

Year 1

Year 1 is a 'contextual' year where core architectural expertise and knowledge around cities, buildings and practice is developed through diverse experimentation and exploration, including drawing, making, writing and film. The 'History of Cities and their Architecture' module is shared with fellow Bartlett BSc students of Planning, and the 'Making Cities' module is shared with fellow Bartlett BSc students of Planning, and Construction and Project Management. In this latter module students from all schools work in groups of 10 to produce films for the final submission, which has now started to involve the Survey of London. The final building design project evolves in parallel to separate coursework in other modules – it finishes the year with a common springboard into Year 2.

Year 2

Year 2 centres on 'diversity', which is exemplified by the unit system in design as well as seminar groups in history and theory. Although distinct from one another, units deliver a common set of principles that include: spatial organisation, communication, culture, critique, context, and environmental and social impact. In tandem with the final building design project, the technology module requires strategic and detailed technical investigations, including how fragments of the project could be built. This presents a tactile introduction to architectural design, its relationship to construction techniques and associated disciplines, and the challenge of making information for making buildings. Elsewhere in the year, students must demonstrate understanding of a selected theme in architectural history, as well as core skills in computing.

Year 3

Year 3 centres on 'synthesis' between architectural design, critical understanding, core skills, professional practice and creative exploration. Design projects evolve as an individual response to the unit brief through innovative research in tandem with a comprehensive technical dissertation. Projects are rooted in core principles of spatial and physical design, supported by an extensive network of practice-based consultants. Students are also encouraged to speculate on conventional boundaries of architectural production and architectural representation. In 2014-15, one unit ran a live project in King's Cross, where one structure by a Year 2 student subsequently won the 2016 AJ Small Projects Award. In the same year, a Year 3 project, entitled 'Space as the Third Teacher', won the RIBA Bronze Medal. Year 3 also includes modules in architectural history and theory, and professional practice.

Year Out

Increasingly, students are taking a further year out whilst remaining engaged, bringing the cohort to around 200. The course focuses on practice management, business and enterprise through a series of talks and seminars based on five recall days followed by informal networking events, tutorials and PEDR monitoring. Students write an end-of-year essay on a topic of interest related to contemporary practice or architectural education.

Year 1

Constructing Your Practice

Nat Chard, Carlos Jiménez Cenamor

Year 1 Staff
Lucy Leonard, Ifigenia Liangi, Emma-Kate Matthews, Frederik Petersen, Eva Ravnborg, Gavin Robotham, Emmanouil Stavrakakis, Catrina Stewart, Umut Yamac, Nick Westby

Architectural Media Studies Tutor
Joel Cady, Danielle Hodgson

Year 1 Coordinator
Emmanouil Stavrakakis

Year 1 Administrator
Izzy Blackburn

We would like to thank The Bartlett School of Architecture and the Architecture Research Fund (ARF) for their constant support of and care for Year 1.

We would like to thank Emma Flynn, CJ Lim, Hina Lad, Christine Hawley, Gergerly Kovács, Luke Pearson, Mollie Claypool, Matthew Butcher, Sara Shafei, Steve Johnson, Damjan Iliev, Blanche Cameron, Caroline Rabourdin, Joel Cady, Murray Fraser, Javier Ruiz Rodrigez, Chee-Kit Lai, Thomas Pearce, Dimitri Argyros, Danielle Wilkinson, Danielle Hodgson, Francesca Hughes, Regner Ramos, Jessica In, Sofia Krimizi, Paolo Zaide, Bernadette Devilat and Paz, Afra van 't Land, James Sale, Luke Olsen, Graeme Williamson, Natasha Sandmeier, Elizabeth Dow, B-made, ScanLAB Projects, Brian O'Reilly, Bob Sheil and the irreplaceable Frosso Pimenides.

The Bartlett Architecture Office, with Emer Girling and Izzy Blackburn on the steering wheel, has made the year possible. Thank you so much!

Year 1 is a very special moment in every architect's career – the time in which our creativity, passion and dedication meet a new challenge: to define the environment that nurtures the social context in which we all develop our lives. It is not a simple task, since it addresses all scales from furniture to urban design, from permanent to temporary constructions; and so perhaps our most important responsibility is to have an integral vision of reality. With this purpose we train our students to observe, analyse and respond through a series of projects. The outcome of these design questions will combine their radical creativity, their uniqueness and the technical expertise acquired in conversations with tutors, consultants and experts.

——This year students were asked how they might construct their practice. An introductory project teased out the personal knowledge they had already accrued about architecture from inhabiting it all their lives. This work also probed how the process of drawing might be particular to the content that was being discussed, a theme that was developed in the second project. Four groups of students invented and built a variety of drawing boards (or surfaces) imbued with 'opinions', and the rest of the students built idea-specific drawing tools that were related to at least one of the boards. The project related the processes of making and drawing as content-led media, putting students in control of the materials and processes through which they would be thinking about their work. To help this we spent a day drawing aircraft and their components at the aeroplane museum at Duxford – an opportunity to use drawing to carefully observe how precise artefacts can be made.

——In January we travelled to Madrid and drew on Carlos Jiménez's wide range of contacts in the city. We visited and 3D scanned buildings by Izaskun Chinchilla Moreno, Andrés Jaque, Mi5 Architects, Langarita Navarro and Zuloark, architects who have forged a range of new types of practice during the recession.

——These encounters set the scene for the building project, set on a range of sites along the Regent's Canal. A workshop at the start of the project helped each student set up their own framework for how they would practice. This introduction encouraged an experimental approach to the work, which was taken in different directions by the eight first year studios. The building projects also provided a vehicle for the students' technical studies.

——Early in the year there was a strong emphasis on developing hand-drawing skills as well as the connection between what was being drawn, and how. In the second half of the year we introduced digital modelling, 3D scanning and offered a 3D printing workshop. The goal of Year 1's digital implementation aims to facilitate the combination of analogue and digital thinking as complementary design methodologies and languages in order to trigger students' contemporary creative thinking.

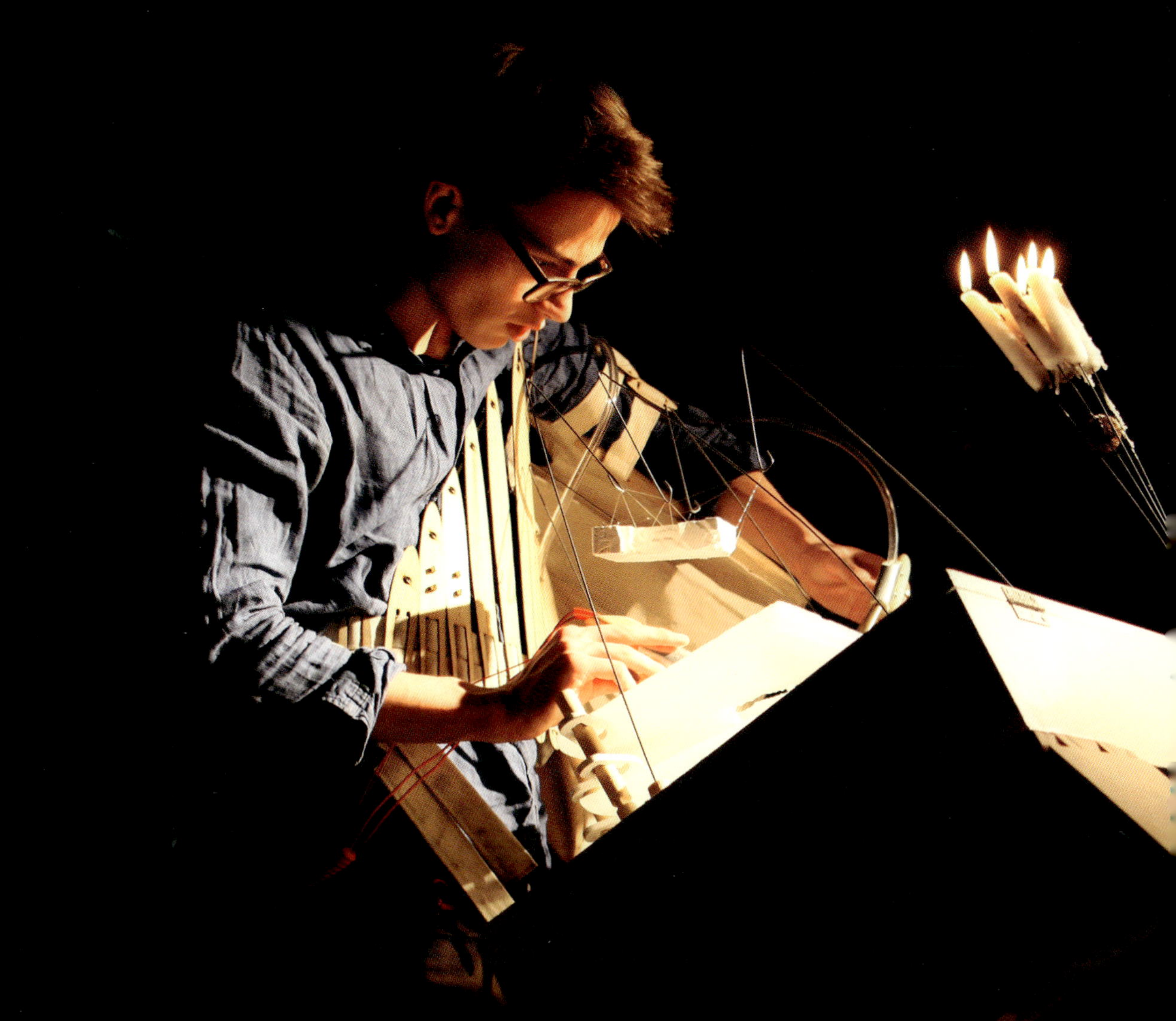

Students
Gunel Aliyeva, Assankhan Amirov Oliver Ansell, Kofi Arthur, Elizabeth Atherton, Moe Atsumeda, Jack Barnett, Grant Beaumont, Poppy Becke, Daniel Boran, Theo Brader-Tan, George Brazier, Paul Brooke, Liana Buttigieg, Yuqi Cai, James Carden, Teresa Carmelita, Yung Chan, Lauren Childs, Annette Choy De Leon, Wei Chung, Yoojin Chung, Theo Clarke, James Cook, Helen Cope, Bryn Davies, Caitlin Davies, Xavier De La Roche, Aleksy Dojnow, Joe Douglas, Hao Du, Camille Dunlop, Eleanor Evason, Sebastian Fathi, Mengzi Fu, Maxim Goldau, Gabriele Grassi, Millicent Green, Grey Grierson, Lola Haines, Alys Hargreaves, Zachariah Harper Le Petevin Dit Le Roux, Florence Hemmings, Shu Hoe, Yo Hosoyamada, Joe Johnson, Daniel Johnston, Sarah Jones, Kyuri Kim, Rusna Kohli, Katarina Krajciova, Jie Yi Kuek, Dagyung Lee, Jiyoon Lee, Thomas Leggatt, Victor Leung, Yee Liang, Chi Ka Lo, Felix Loftus, Harrison Long, Yingying Lou, Oscar Maguire, Megan Makinson, Linggezi Man, Samuel Martin, John Mathers, Joanna Mclean, Lauren Mcnicoll, Nur Mohamad Adzlee, Anna O'leary, Patrycja Panek, Agnes Parker, Chandni Patel, Maya Patel, Jolanta Piotrowska, Lingyun Qian, Katherine Ramchand, James Robinson, Silje Seim, Hanmo Shen, Justine Shirley, Negar Taatizadeh, Edward Taft, Kenji Tang, An-Ni Teng, Jarron Tham, Emily Thomas, Giselle Thong, Olivia Trinder, Andreea-Ioana Vihristencu, George Wallis, Gabriella Watkins, Chun Wong, Hon Wong, Chloe Woodhead, Rupert Woods, Jun Yap, Yuk Yip, Renzhi Zeng, Yurou Zhang and Yanmin Zhang

Figs. Y1.1 – 1.5 'The Drawing Room'. **Fig. Y1.1 Camille Dunlop, Grey Grierson, Arthur Wong**, 'Waxing', installation project. This drawing tool uses wax and candlelight to project the shadow of an object from which the formwork of a sculpture is created. The tool is comprised of a costume that holds two sculpting pens, one that provides heat and the other that cools down the wax. The wax is placed in layers so that the offcuts are not thrown away but instead create the negative of the sculpture while it's being made. **Fig. Y1.2 Theo Brader-Tan, Sebastian Fathi, Teresa Carmelita**, 'The Drawing Pause', installation project. The drawing instrument allows the wearer to pause during moments of transition and draw onto the surface of the suit. **Fig. Y1.3 Jarron Tham, Victor Leung, Justine Shirley, Yo Hosoymada, James Carden, Renzhi Zeng**, 'Piloti', installation project. This collaborative drawing tool is inspired by the plans of Le Corbusier's Villa Savoye. **Fig. Y1.4** Installation project, **Xavier De La Roche, Joe Jonston, Jie Kuek, Lauren Mcnicoll**, 'Ambidextrous Simultaneous'. This drawing device allows one to draw with both hands simultaneously. The vertical drawing surface enhances the method of this tool while it allows one hand to be guided by the other in the process of drawing. **Fig. Y1.5 Rusna Kohli, Chun (Dereck) Wong, Joanna Mclean**, 'Skin Tool'. This drawing tool is composed of two parts: the costume which has stitches representing an invented measuring system whose units relate to the body; and a series of stencils that are again designed from body curvatures and help to guide the hand to draw.

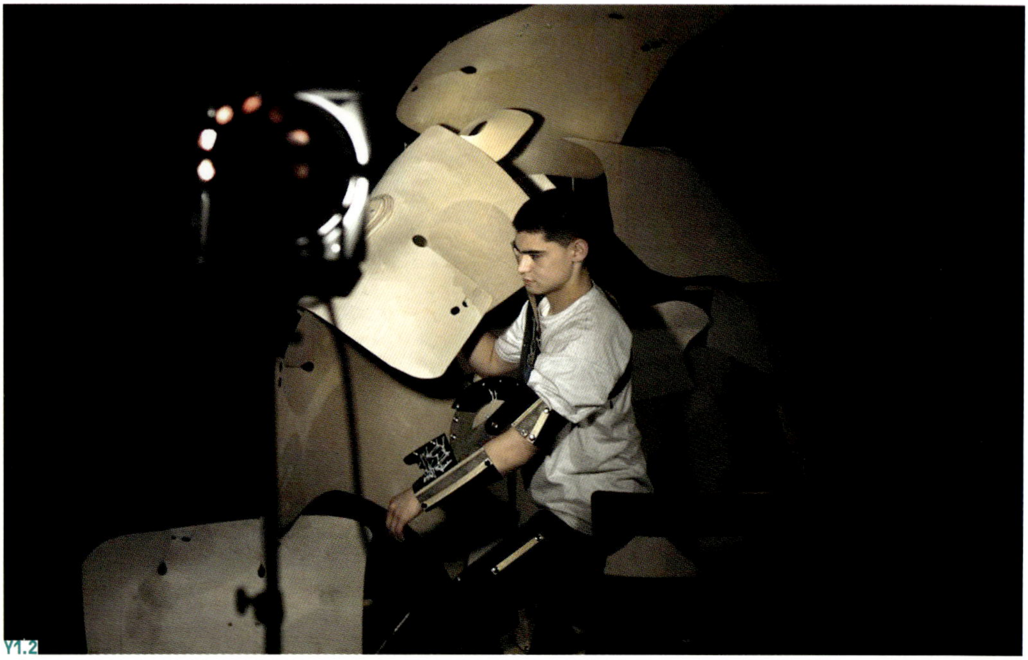

Y1.2

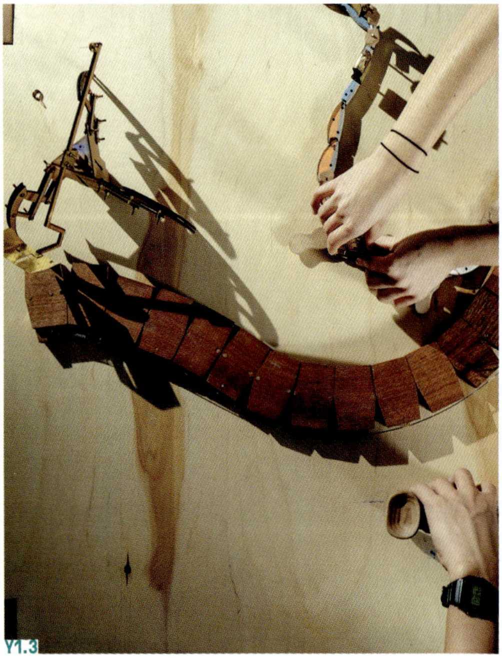

Y1.3

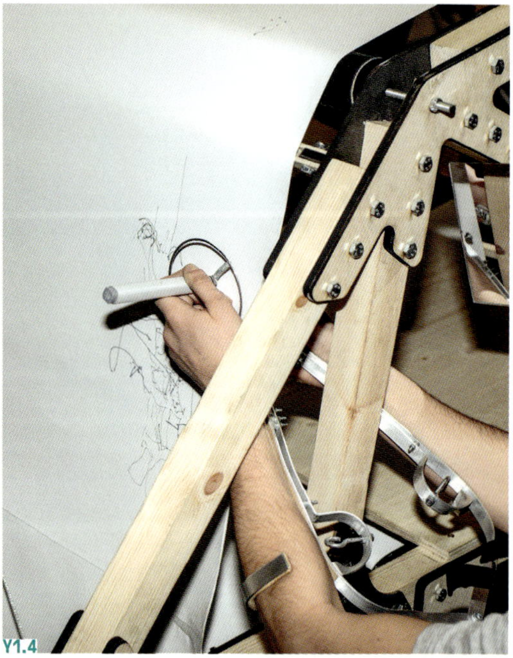

Y1.4

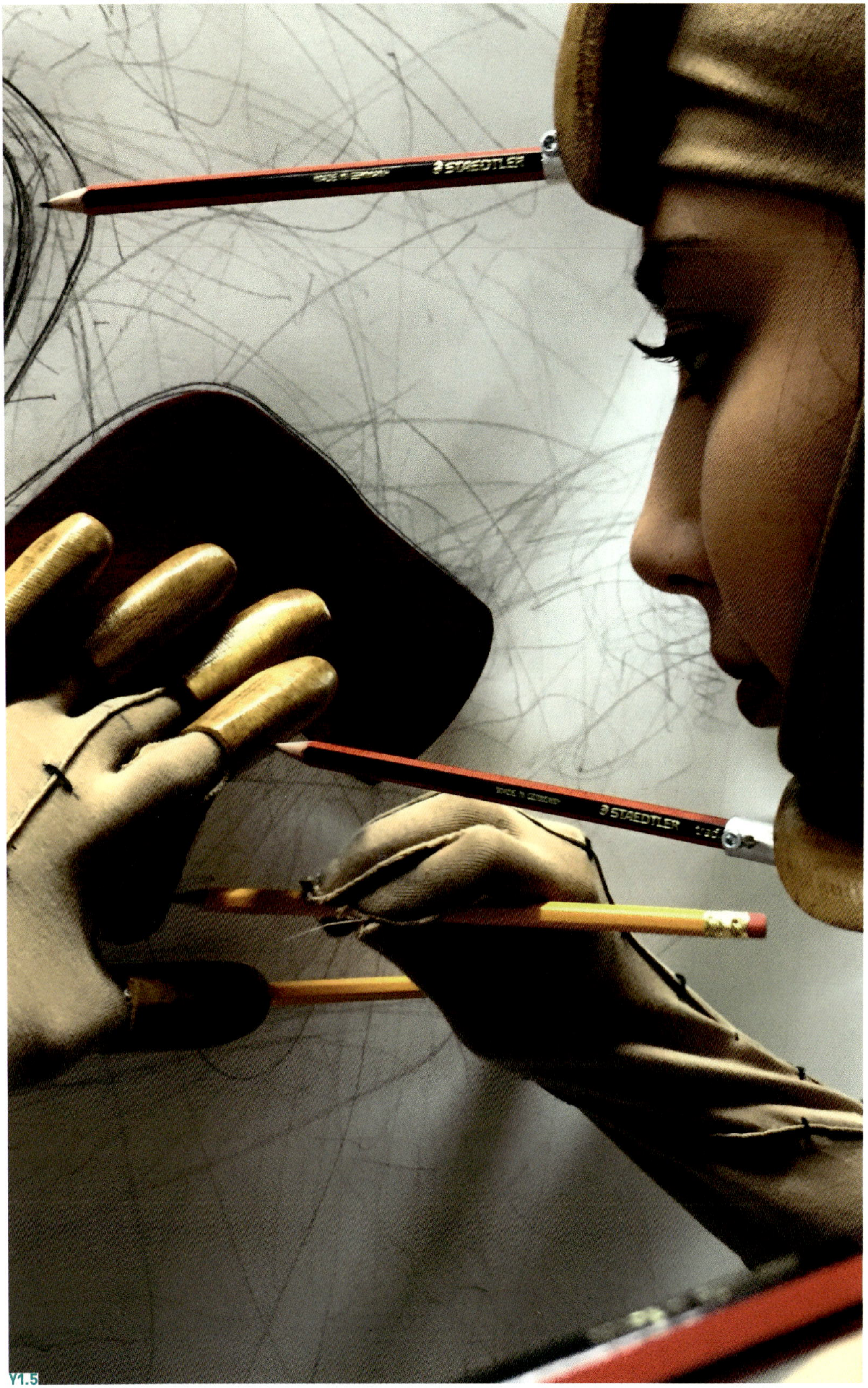

Y1.5

Fig. Y1.6 Jack Barnett, 'A Plumber and his Water Purification Temple'. This house sits on the canalside and collects the water for a pool, purifying it through a series of organic filters. **Fig. Y1.7 Max Shen**, 'An attempt to capture the moment of falling asleep'. The project discusses the moment of falling asleep through a series of drawings which try to capture the threshold between being awake and falling asleep. **Fig. Y1.8 Lingyun Qian**, 'Mario and his Mushroom Farm'. The project develops from a series of bird origami which are redesigned to fit inside one other. **Y1.9 Megan Makinson**, 'A Ruined House for a Cello Teacher'. The house is composed of a series of walls which are assembled by the ruins of bombarded London. A collection of the teacher's memories are displayed within the structure, organising an emotional and functional promenade.

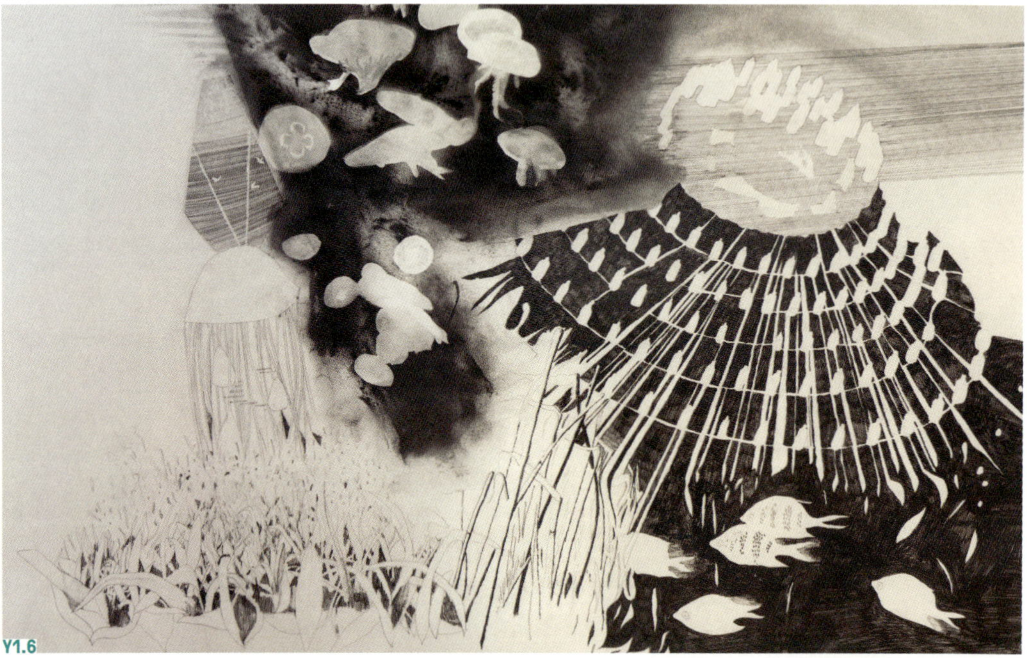

Y1.6

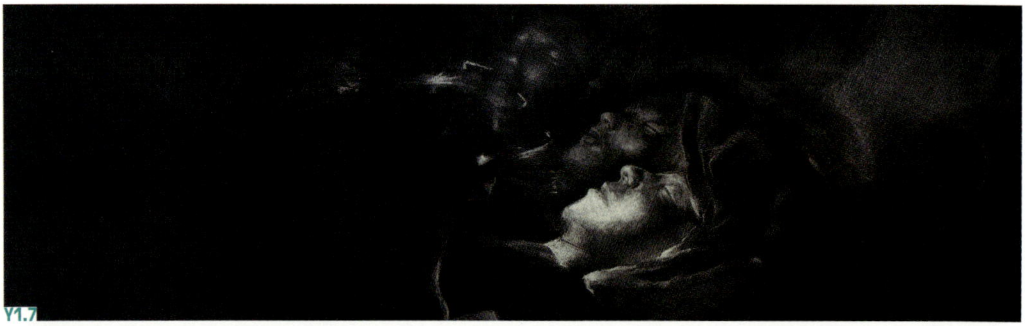

Y1.7

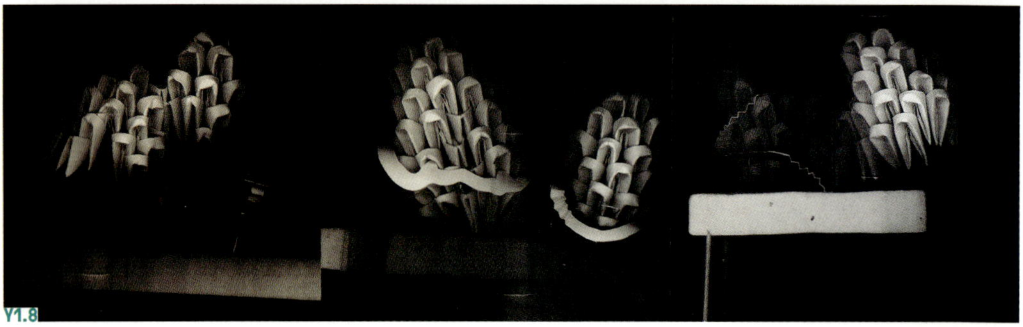

Y1.8

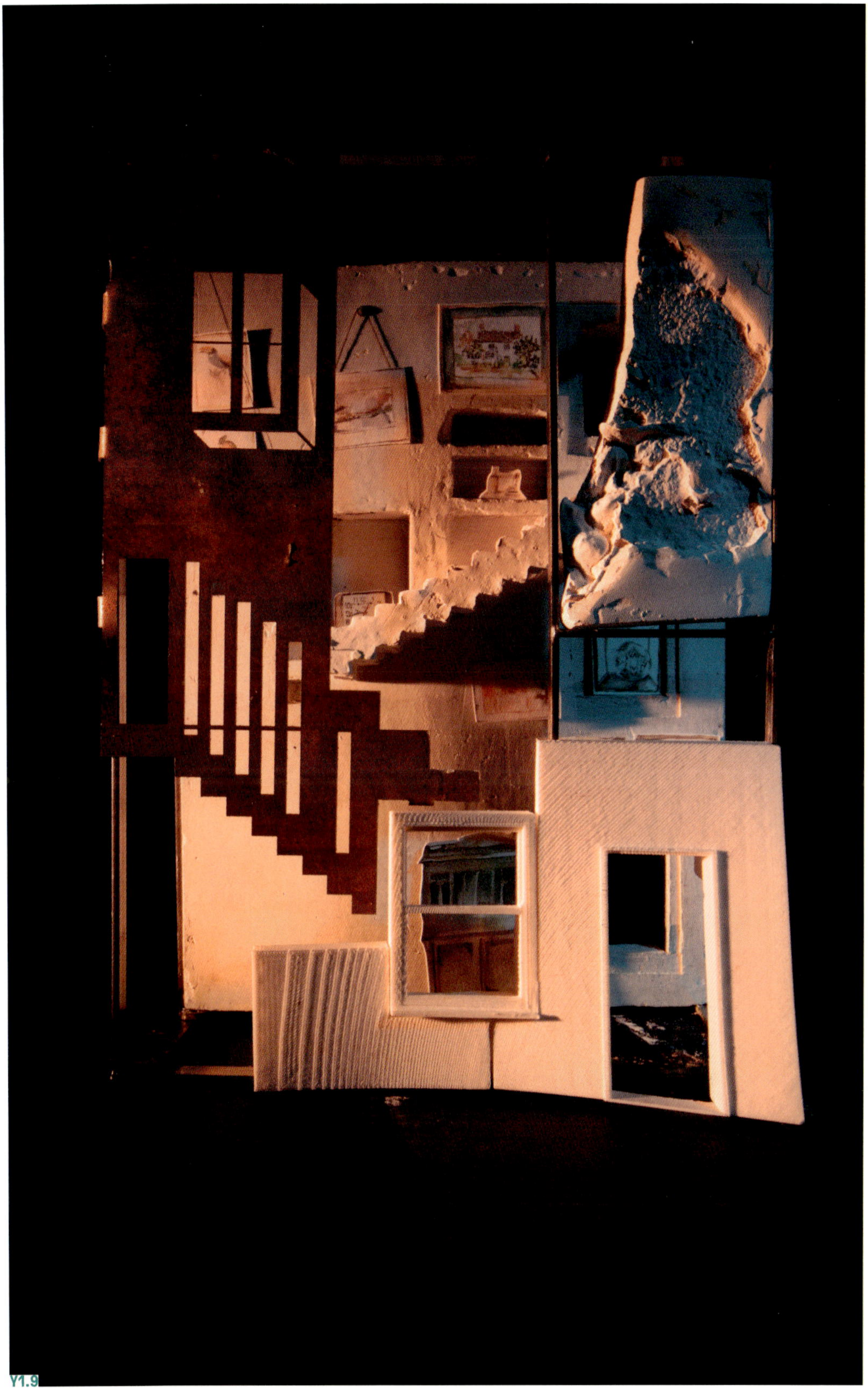

Y1.9

Fig. Y1.10 Daniel Boran, Yoojin Chung, Zak Harper Le Petevin Dit Le Roux, Eeda Lee, Oscar Maguire, Maya Patel, 'The Hug Plane'. An immersive drawing surface which offers a range of curvatures to accept each of the drawing tools. **Fig. Y1.11 Maya Patel**, 'Nettle House.' Owned by a couple, this house comprises a foraging shop in which customers 'forage' for the products. The couple sell nettle pesto and also have an underground experimental herbal medicine project. **Fig. Y1.12 Olivia Trinder**, 'The Afternoon Jamboree House'. A house that celebrates British traditions, where teas are served and fruits are dried, strained and pressed to make the perfect jam. The stains left upon the stretched skin of the building will be in constant transition, reflecting the fruits of the seasons. The customers can sail in to collect their orders whilst the fruit produce filters through the roof structure. **Fig. Y1.13 Lola Haines**, 'Tessie's Vegetable Performance'. A little house in Mile End where Tessie makes puppets out of fruit and vegetables. A Victorian façade disguises the performance world which opens itself to the public only once they have decided to enter the grocery shop.

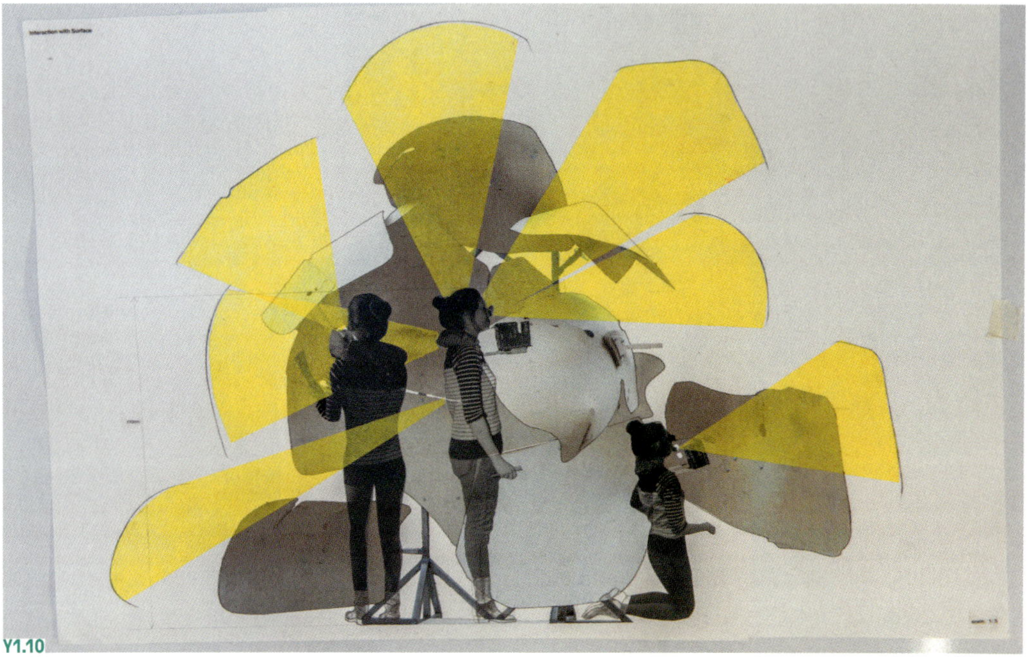

Y1.10

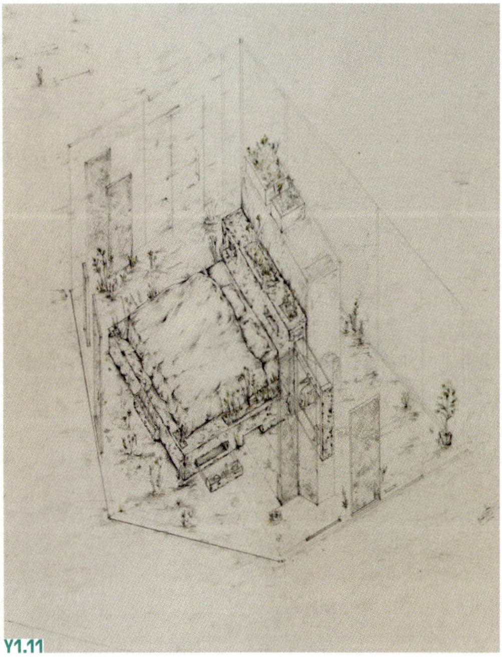

Y1.11

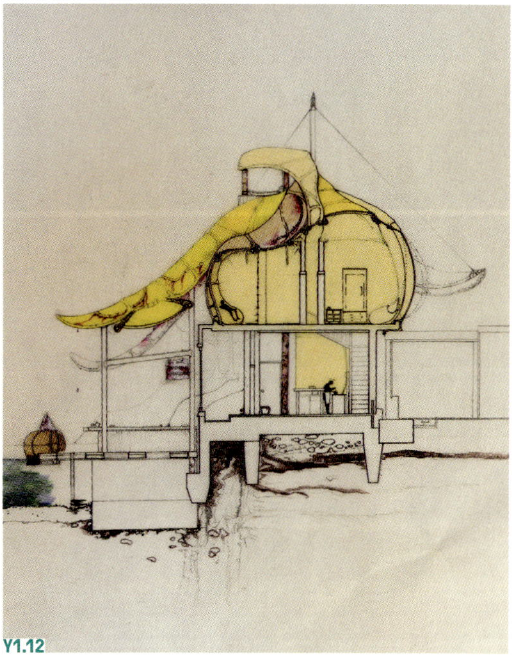

Y1.12

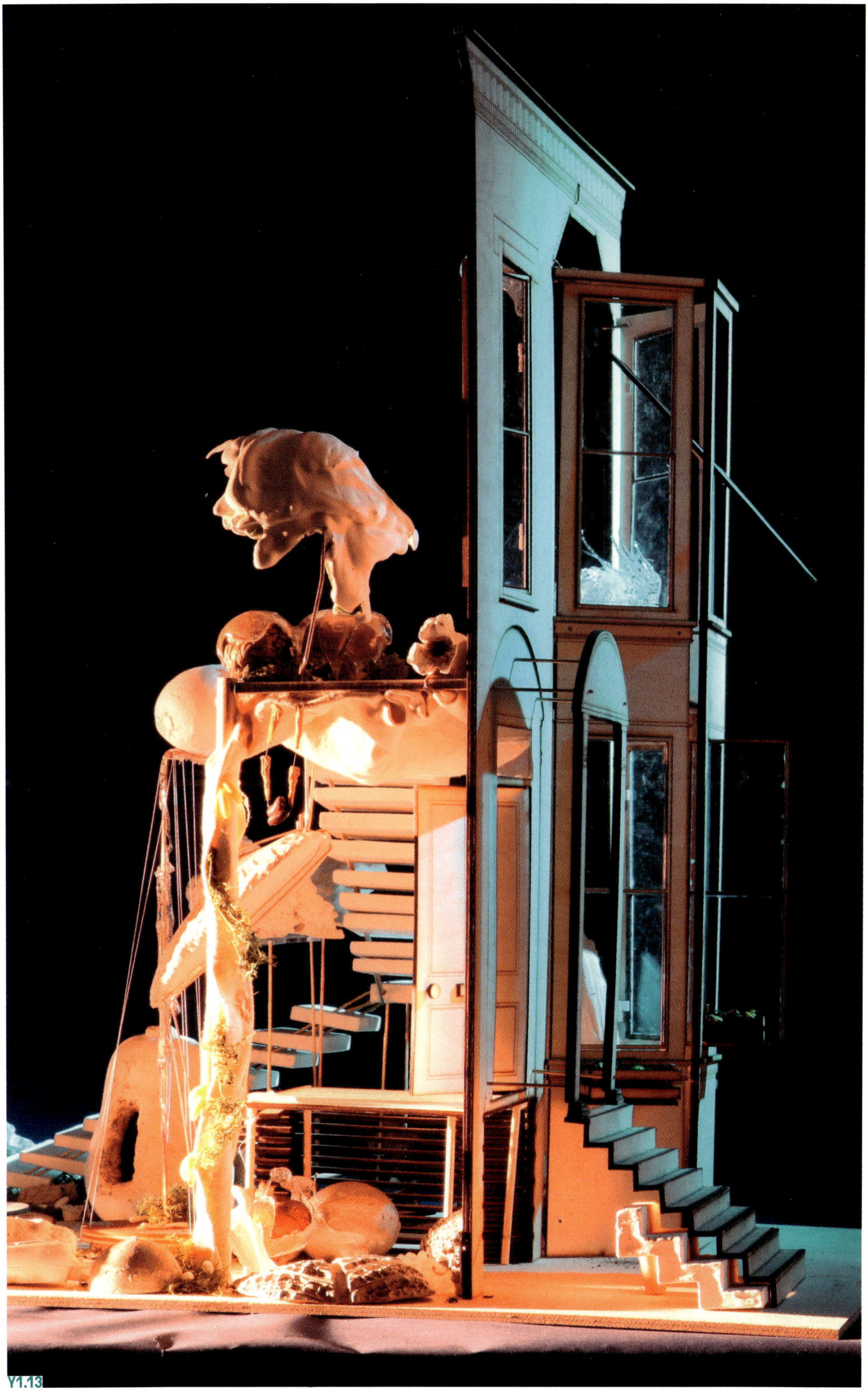

Y1.13

Fig. Y1.14 Enoch Liang, 'Clinic for Sleep Disorder'. A place that provides diverse types of spaces for various sleeping patterns. These spaces channel sounds from the animals around the canal, whilst the architecture allows for the growth of lavender, which enhances relaxation. **Fig. Y1.15 Victor Leung**, 'The Percussionist's House'. A public space and private residence that acts as an interactive aural experience that showcases the client's vast percussion collection. The building also engages and links its residents and visitors through its musical ecosystem. **Fig. Y1.16 Olivia Trinder**, 'The Afternoon Jamboree House'. **Fig. Y1.17 Moe Atsumeda**, 'A Japanese-inspired teahouse'. A weaver's studio and consultation space and a small house for the Mile End community.

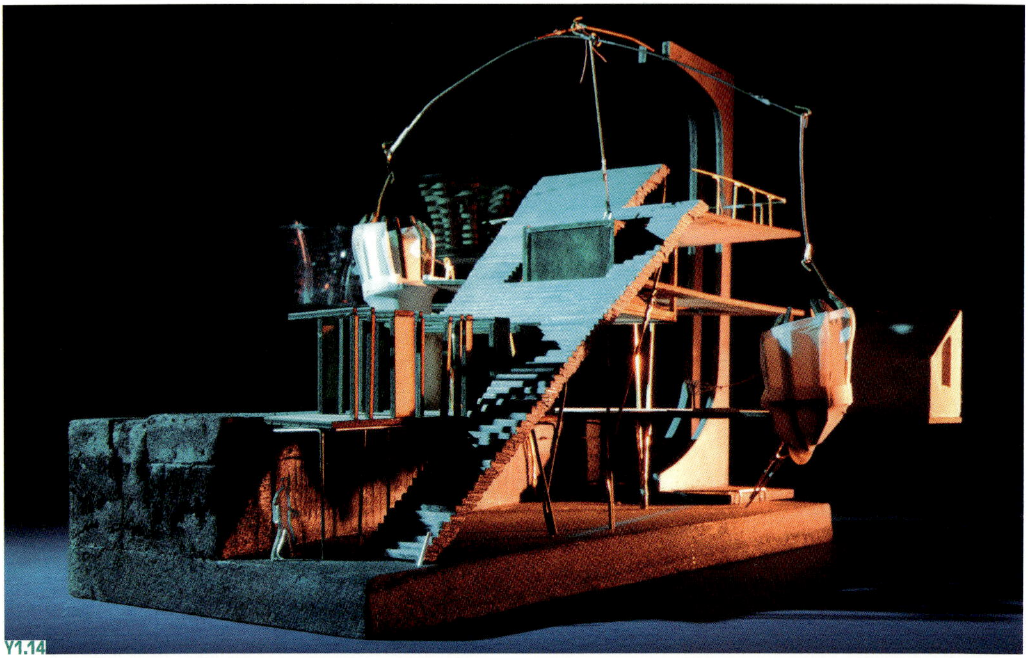

Y1.14

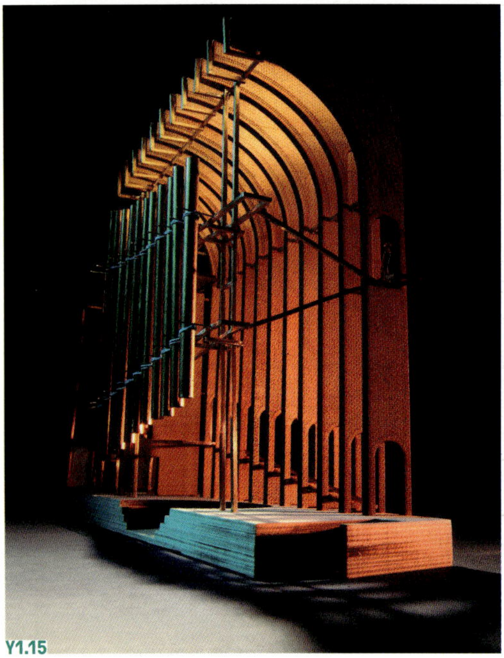

Y1.15

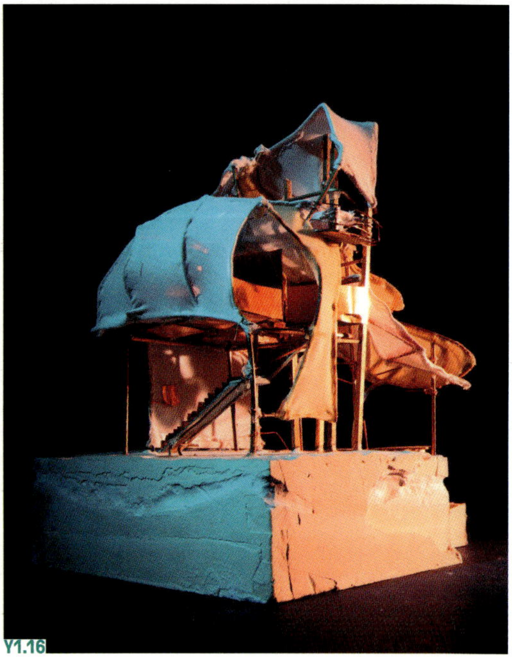

Y1.16

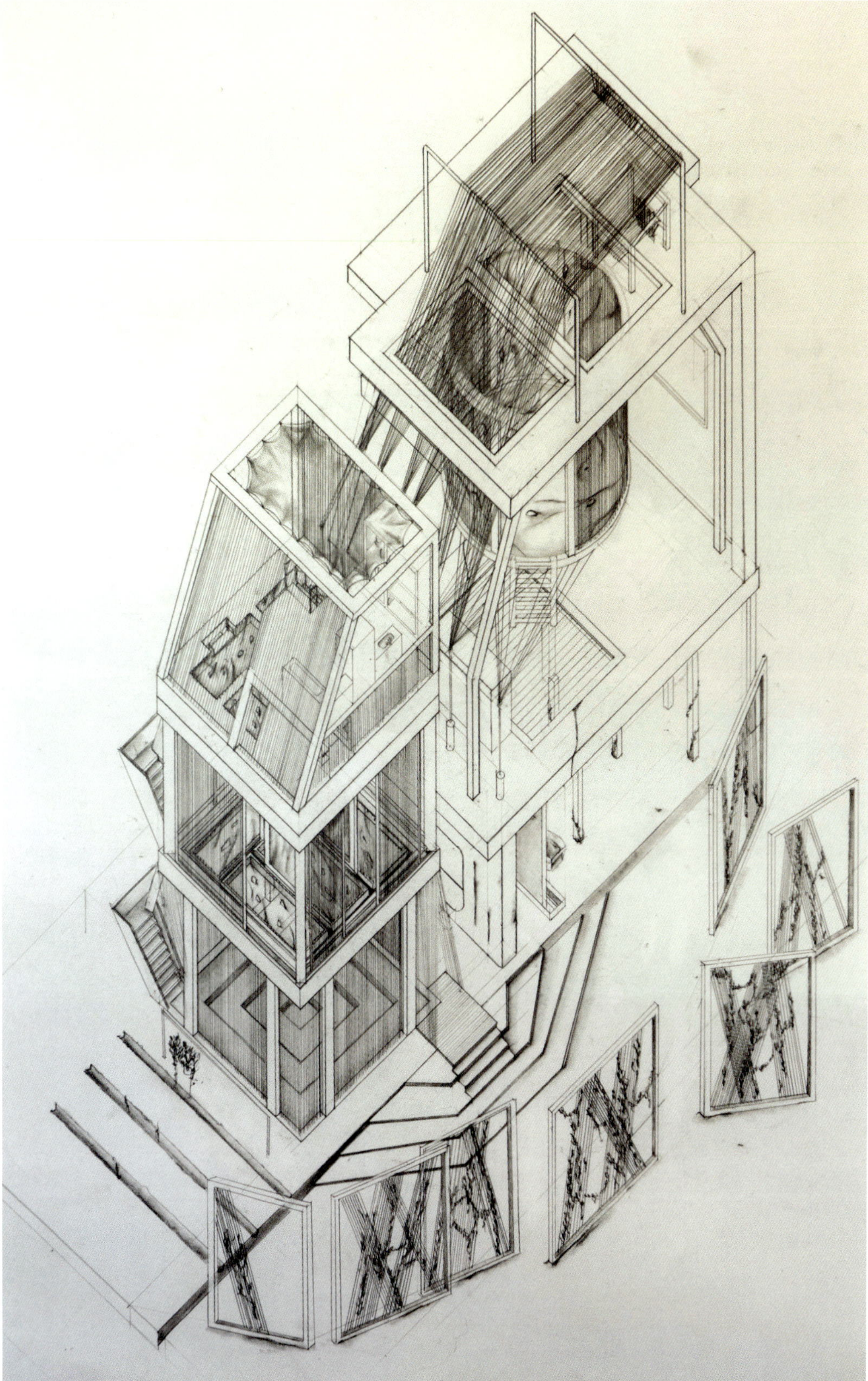

Y1.17

UGO

Soft City

Murray Fraser, Justin C.K. Lau, Sara Shafiei

Year 2
Peter Davies, Qi (Nichole) Ho, Simina Marin, Carolina Mondragon, Rosie Murphy, Elena Real-Davies, Louise Rymell, Felix Sagar

Year 3
Linzi Ai, Angus Iles, Cheuk Wang (Chaplin) Ko, Ka Wing (Clarence) Ku, Maryna Omelchenko, Achilleas Papakyriakou, Sophie Percival, Bethan Ring, Ben Sykes-Thompson

Thanks to our consultants and critics: Julia Backhaus, Tim Barwell, Anthony Boulanger, Eva Branscome, Matthew Butcher, Mollie Claypool, Pierre D'Avoine, George Epolito, Pedro Font-Alba, Stephen Gage, Penelope Haralambidou, Ewa Hazla, Jonathan Hill, Johan Hybschmann, Tim Ireland, Mary Johnson, Hazel McGregor, Martin Manfai, Roy Nash, Jack Newton, Justin Nicholls, Luke Olsen, Stuart Piercy, Aleksandra Rizova, Bob Sheil, Matthew Springett, Ben Stringer, Michiko Sumi, Richard Townend, Graeme Williamson

Thanks to our sponsors Bean Buro

The theme of the unit for this year was the 'soft city'. Students were asked to investigate ways of looking differently at a major global city such as London, seeing it not as a harsh or alienating environment, or as existing only in the realm of economics and other systems, but rather as an open and fluid entity that allows for many readings of 'softness'. This term could be understood literally, in terms of the relative density/hardness of the materials which are used to create buildings and urban spaces; or else more metaphorically in terms of the flows and interactions of human bodies, energies, weather patterns, trees, plants and animal species within the city; or else poetically through the expression of feelings such as love, warmth, openness and communality. How can designing the spatial practices and physical qualities of softness contribute to our urban experience, including the enhancement of sensations such as health and wellbeing? How might softness and hardness be designed together, whether in opposition or symbiosis, or indeed as some complex hybrid form?

——To start the year, students were asked to investigate their personal understanding of London through an artefact, or perhaps a series of artefacts, which explored ideas of softness in relation to a specific area of the city. The aim of designing and/or making this artefact(s) was to introduce a diverse set of sensibilities and ideas about London as a 'soft city'. These investigations then fed into the main design project for each student, in which they developed their own particular theme on a site of their own choosing within London in order to engage more substantively with ideas of softness in metropolitan life. These projects were asked to deal with aspects of social and cultural life (eating, sleeping, congregating, etc); economic exchange (business, shops, markets, etc); ritualised ceremonies (religion, shopping, education, etc); urban performances (media, theatre, sport, etc); or environmental conditions (parks, gardening, seasonal activities, etc).

——Our unit field trip, from late November to early December, was to northern India, during which we visited the cities of Delhi/New Delhi, Chandigarh, Jaipur, Jodhpur and Agra. There we encountered very different cultural attitudes and traditions towards issues of softness/hardness, openness/closure, official/unofficial within the city, and this in turn greatly enriched the projects that students designed this year.

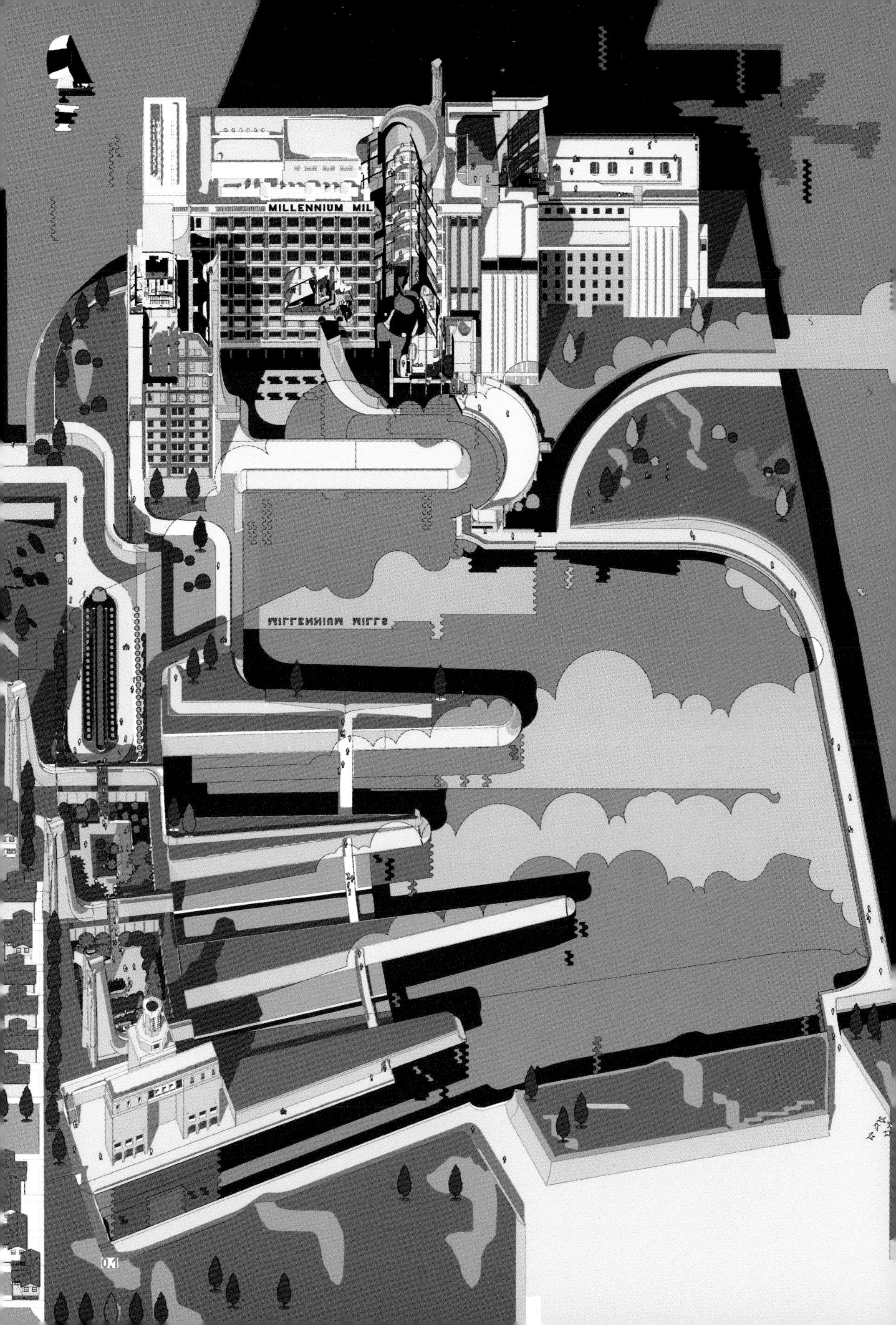

0.1

Fig. 0.1 **Ben Sykes-Thompson** Y3, 'Sensing Silvertown, Millennium Mills', Rayleigh Road, E16. Geometric projection of entire scheme. A disused flour mill in the Royal Docks is turned into a sensory park based upon sight, sound and smell. In part of the older tradition of parks providing repose within the city, here that is accentuated by inserting new facilities through which citizens can self-diagnose early-stage problems developing in their eyes, ears and noses. As a landscape project and a creative reuse of a powerful existing building, a novel community-distributed model of healthcare is promoted. **Figs. 0.2 – 0.3** **Ben Sykes-Thompson** Y3, 'Memory Mapping'. Folded section; physical model. We understand cities not through maps or fixed notions of time, but by individual journeys through the urban continuum. In doing so, we link together seemingly disparate places based on our durations of travel and occupation, as shown by a series of models and folded drawings. **Fig. 0.4** **Rosie Murphy** Y2, 'Centre for Slow Sports', Finsbury Square, EC2. Basement plan; time-stretched basement plan. Urban workers need places to escape the frantic pace of London, so a slow sports centre in the City of London offers a chance to engage in time-honoured pursuits like bowls, chess, tiddlywinks, and staring contests. Sunk into a basement car park below an urban square, sensations of time are investigated graphically in sliced and extended drawings.

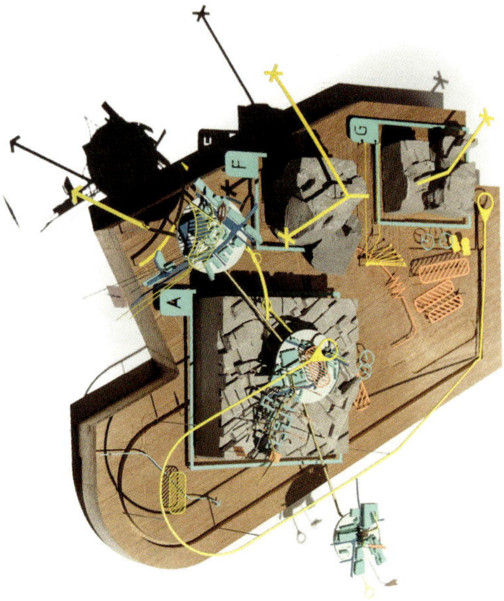

0.2

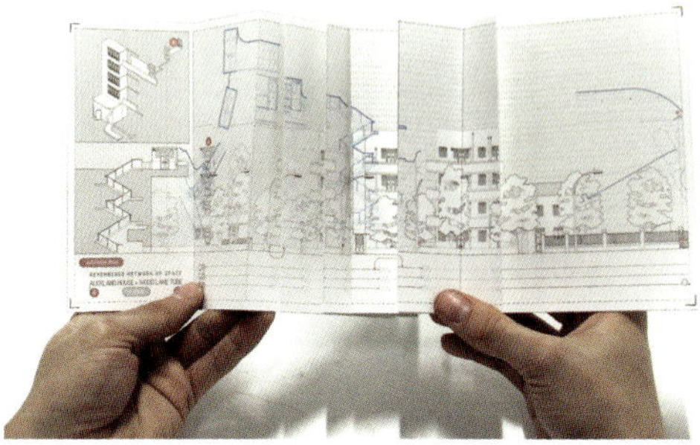

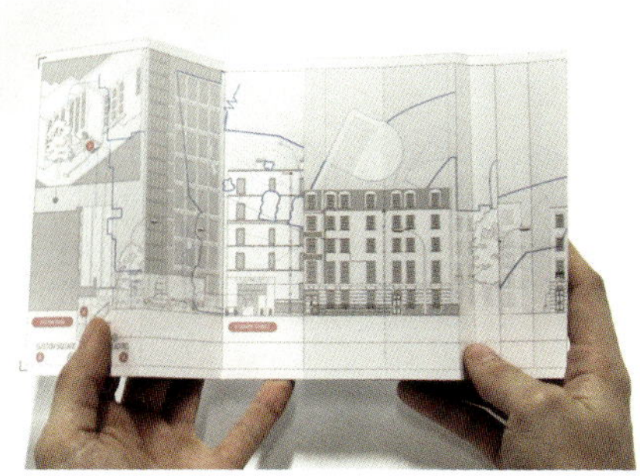

0.3

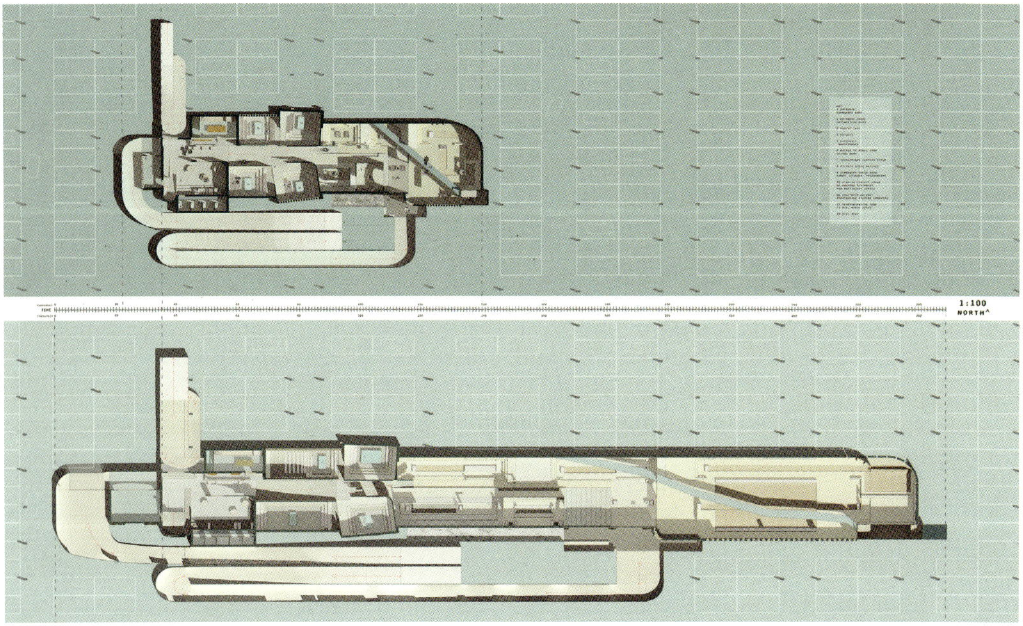

0.4

Fig. 0.5 **Simina Marin** Y2, 'Edible Eden', Camley Street Natural Park, King's Cross, N1. Physical model. In the much-loved but much-threatened Camley Street park, an innovative strategy aims to resist the gentrification and displacement of the King's Cross redevelopment by building a nutrition school for local children. By introducing them to the processes involved in growing and cooking food, the revised park will stimulate play, physical pleasure, and a healthier diet for these children.

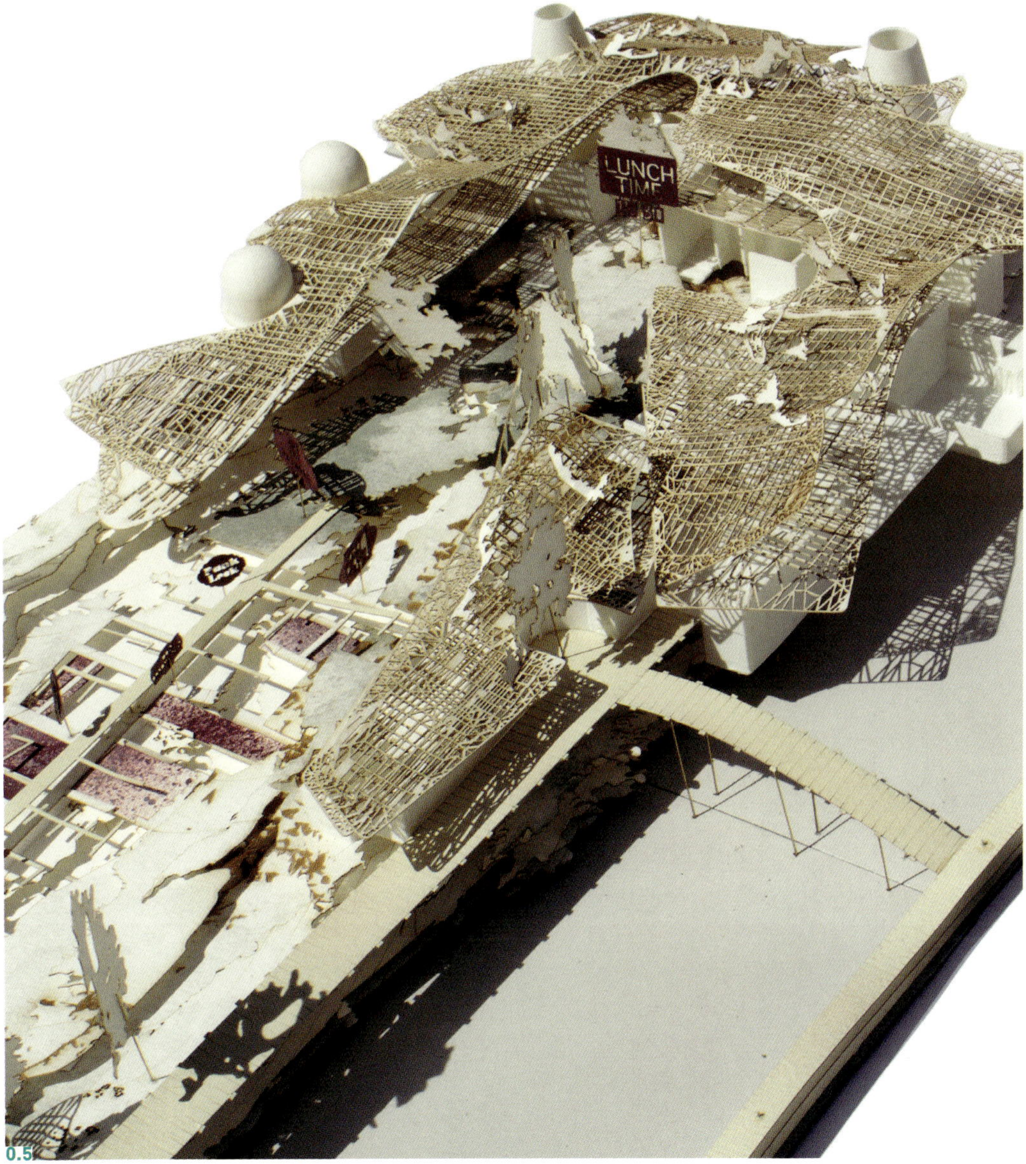

0.5

Fig. 0.6 Peter Davies Y2, 'Softening Brutalism', Barbican Estate, EC2. Physical model; render; general projection showing lines of views. Examining Brutalism's legacy, it is clear that the clichéd views about its harshness and inhumanity are grossly exaggerated. By careful analysis of the Barbican Estate through light and colour, a softer and more nuanced appreciation is derived. **Fig. 0.7 Felix Sagar** Y2, 'Psychological Thresholds', Prince Albert Road, Regent's Park, NW1. Geometric projection. The boundary edges of Regent's Park offer scant preparation or protection for those who suffer from psychological conditions like agoraphobia, and find its open spaces terrifying. A new after-school centre and playground helps children with such anxieties to develop a happier relationship with this loveliest of Royal Parks.

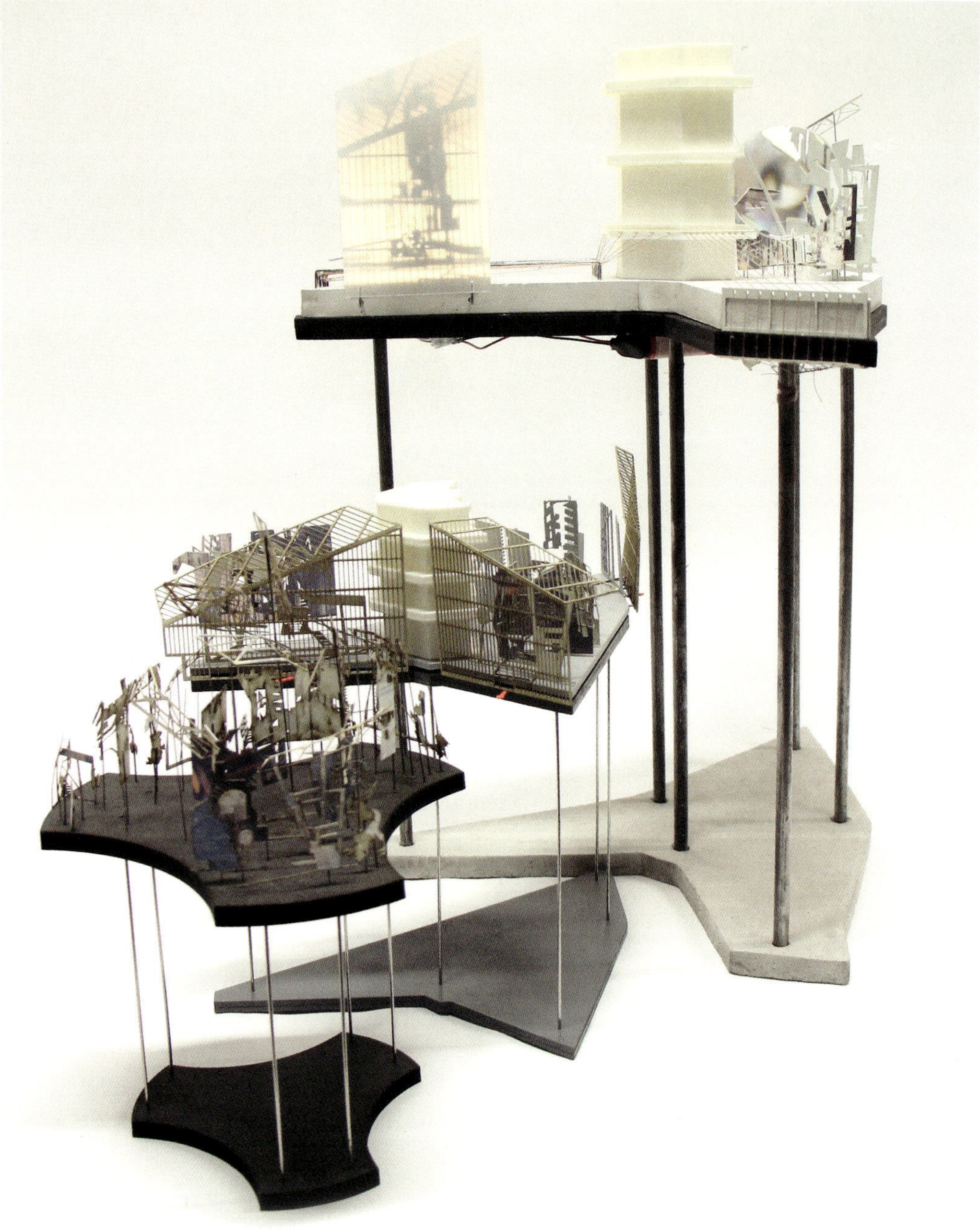

0.6

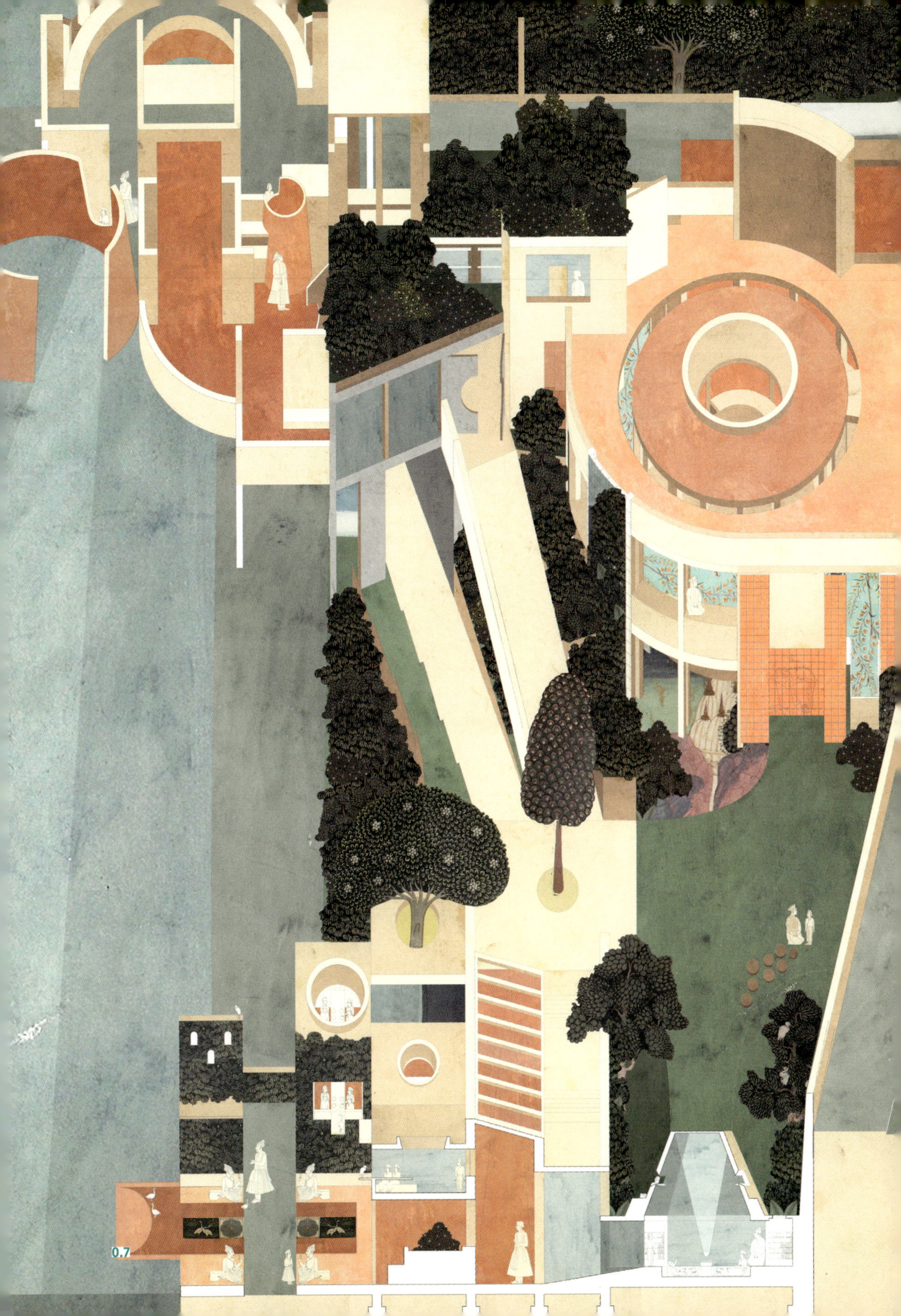
0.7

Fig. 0.8 Carolina Mondragon Y2, 'Incendiary Institute', Bethnal Green, E1. Physical model. In a dense urban site near Brick Lane, a test facility is created for experimental new materials being developed by the digital artisanal culture now developing in that area. Visitors can walk around and enjoy the burning of materials to experience the softness of ashes, probably the softest of all our urban materials. **Fig. 0.9 Cheuk Wang (Chaplin) Ko** Y3, 'Prisoners of Knowledge', Camden Road, Holloway, N7. Physical model. In this twist on the 'halfway houses' used to re-introduce prisoners to society, here the emphasis is on rehousing/training those who worked as prison librarians. Deep shade and bright light highlight the book displays that are open to the public, especially local children. **Fig. 0.10 Linzi Ai** Y3, 'The Snug', Princess Louise Pub, Holborn, WC1. Embossed drawing. Within the toughness of Victorian London, the city's pubs offered decorative oases of rest and indulgence, made especially soft in the snug bars of the Princess Louise and other pubs. Now this sense of material and decoration can be reused to design places of drinking in contemporary London. **Fig. 0.11 Ka Wu (Clarence) Ku** Y3, 'Flying Breakfast', City Airport, Hartmann Road, E16. Test models. Flight crews coming in and out of the increasingly internationalised City Airport are provided with a special hotel where they can stop over, and above all, enjoy wondrous 'Full English' breakfasts that incorporate bacon, eggs and other produce grown on site.

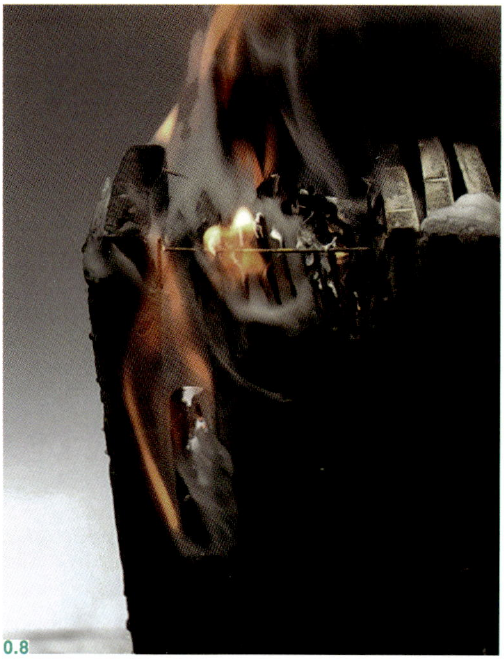

0.8

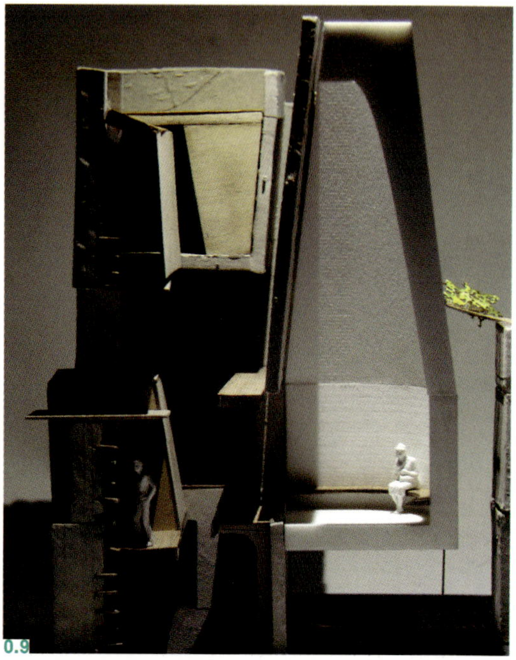

0.9

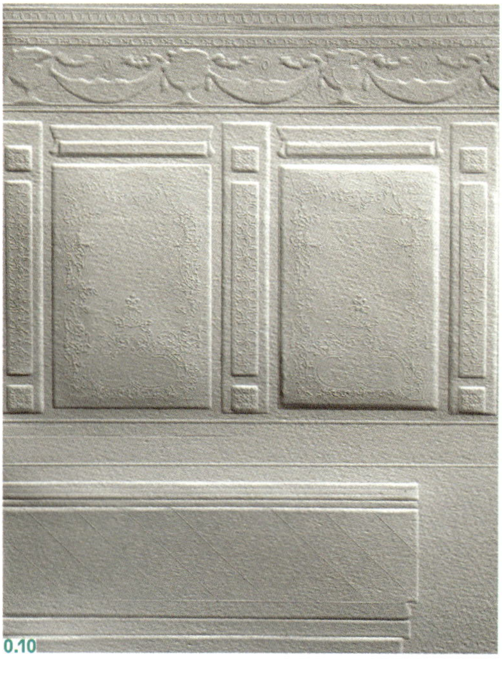

0.10

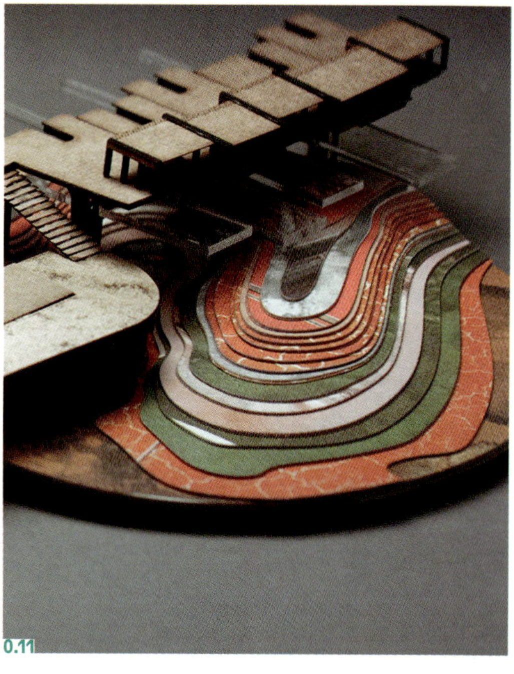

0.11

Fig. 0.12 Maryna Omelchenko Y3, 'Farm/Temple of Falling Water', Commercial Road, Limehouse, E14. Geometric projection. In gritty Limehouse, close to the canal basin, a new urban farm is inserted that also serves as a place of contemplation for those who wish to walk through it. Aeroponic tubes are fed with water that is collected on a large disused railway bridge, thereby linking the local environment directly to the building's programme. **Fig. 0.13 Elena Real-Davies** Y2, 'The Museum of Impermanence', Rochester Square, Camden, NW1. Poster. Housing rights in London are being eroded through escalating prices and punitive legislation, so in a Camden square a group of squatters take action. A political campaign to defend their occupation is then turned into a museum that occupies the square and local houses, and which records the displacement of people and their possessions from London over time. **Figs. 0.14 – 0.15 Bethan Ring** Y3, 'Lund Point Mash-Up', Carpenters Estate, Stratford, E15. Geometric projection, pattern book construction sheets. Stratford is one of London's development hotspots but this is leading to the erasure of the communities that once lived there. So, rather than demolishing a tower block on the Carpenters Estate, this design strips it back to basics and provides facilities for a diverse mixture of users: allotments for existing residents, live/work studio spaces for artists, digital fabrication laboratories for UCL students, and a rooftop vantage point for West Ham football fans.

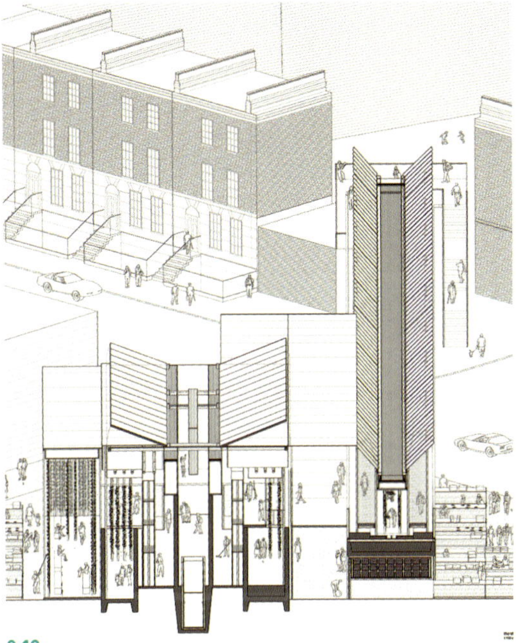

0.12

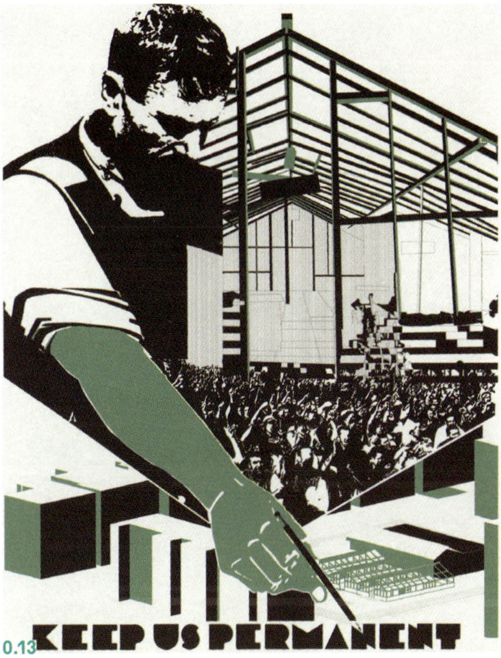

0.13

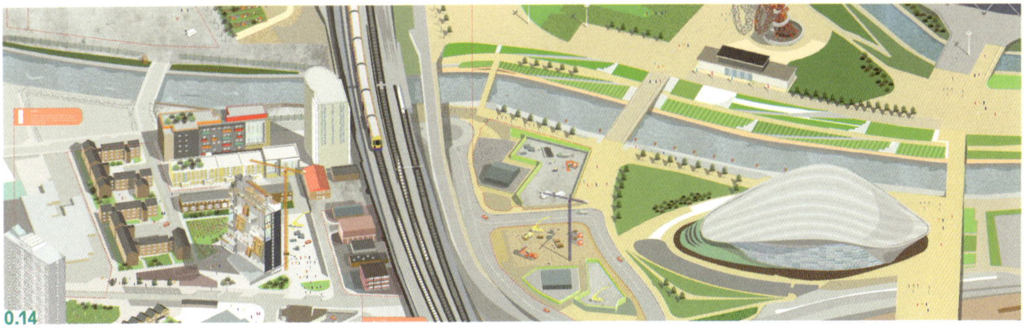

0.14

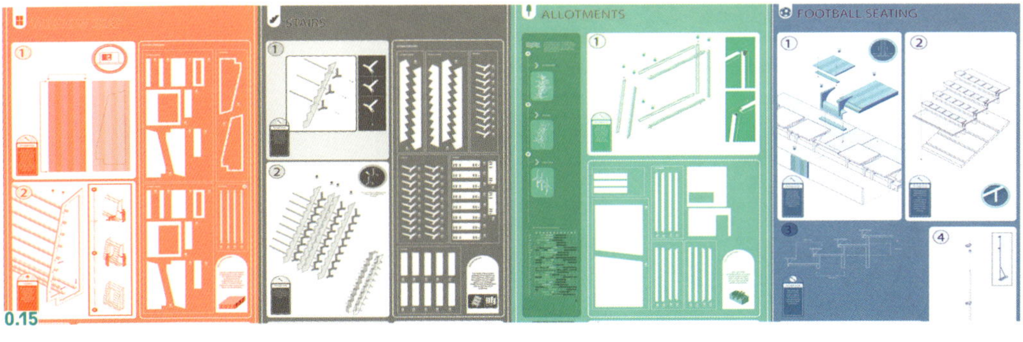

0.15

Figs. 0.16 – 0.18 Sophie Percival Y3, 'Holly-Burb-Land', Hampstead Garden Suburb, NW11. Physical models of bricks; section; ground-floor plan. So successful has Hampstead Garden Suburb been in defying change that it has become perhaps what it was always destined to be, a television and film set for endless Edwardian class-based dramas. Here a few existing houses are stealthily tuned into studios by peeling back walls, inserting luminous pink bricks, and hiding camera positions into the ubiquitous hedges that line the estate.
Fig. 0.19 Achilleas Papakyriakou Y3, 'Asclepeion by the Thames', Doon Street, South Bank Centre, London SE1. Ground-floor plan; section. In Ancient Greece, those experiencing mental health issues could retire for a while to an asclepeion, a retreat that included bathing pools, theatres, libraries, and other places to sit and think and recover. Using the Greek-inspired Olivier Theatre and the cultural facilities of the South Bank as its trigger, this scheme offers sumptuous relaxing baths to citizens on what is currently a grungy car park.

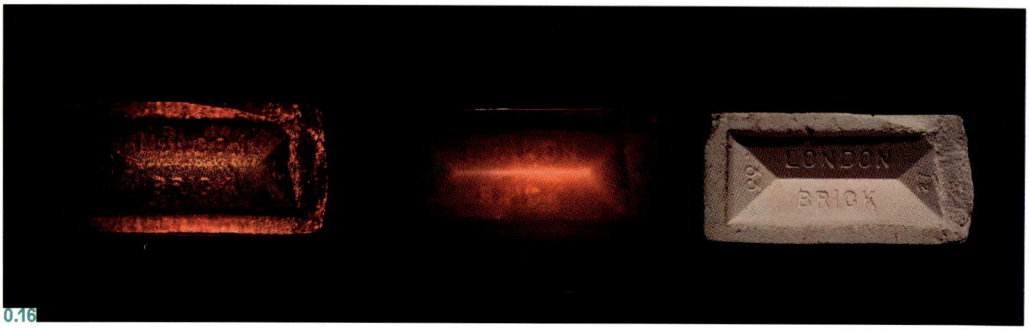

0.16

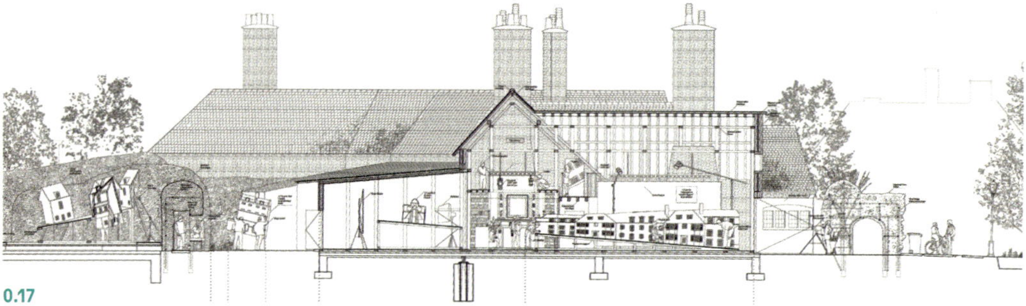

0.17

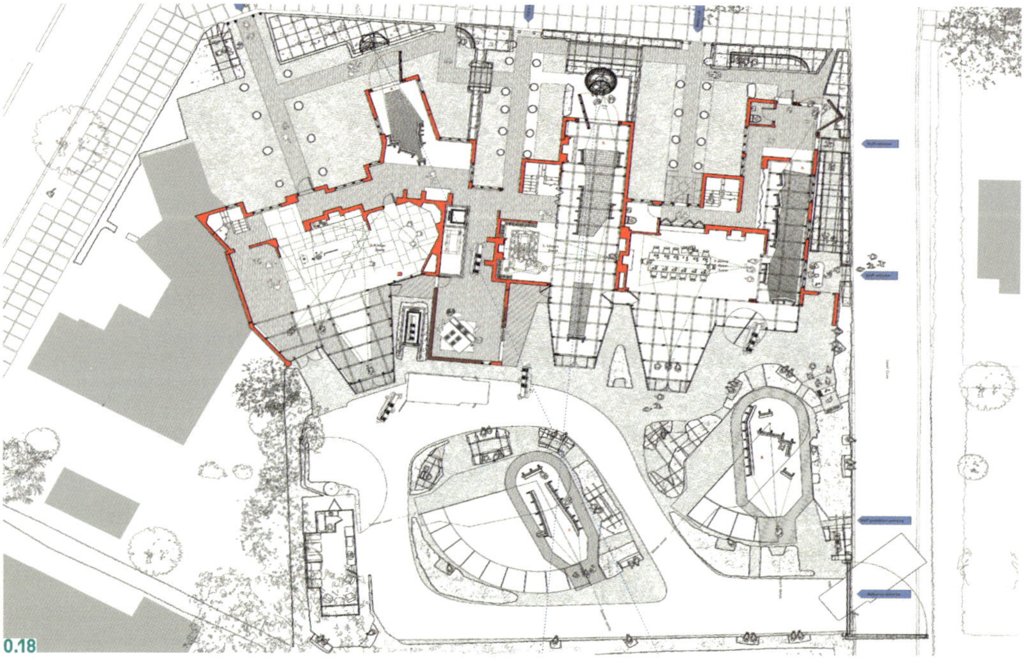

0.18

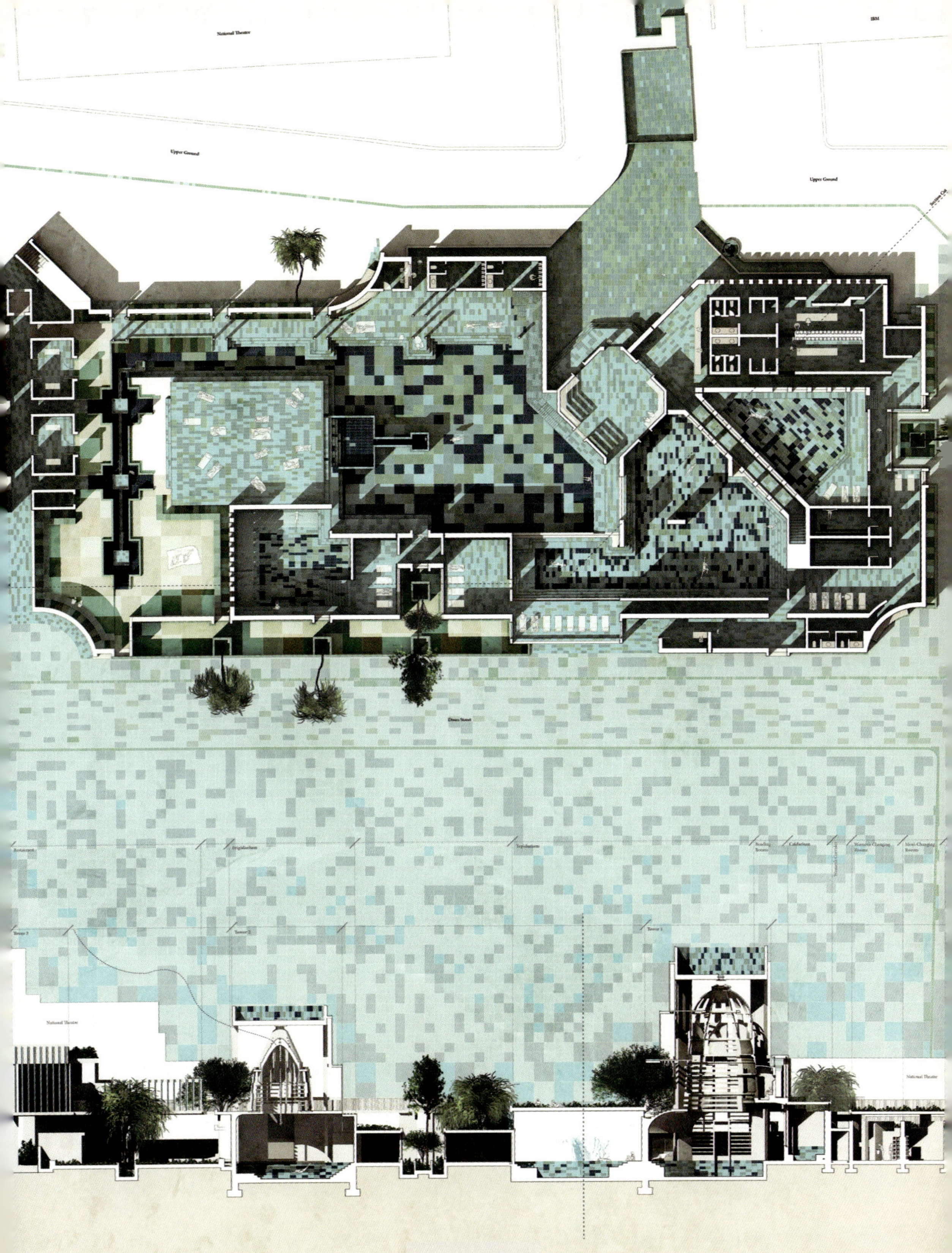
National Theatre
IBM
Upper Ground
Upper Ground
Restaurant
Frigidarium
Tepidarium
Caldarium
Women's Changing Rooms
Men's Changing Rooms
National Theatre
National Theatre

UG1

Invisible Infrastructures: the unHousing of Science

Francesca Hughes, Gergely Kovács

Year 2
Richard Aina, Seowon (Sharon) Change, Nikhil Cherian, Wai (Tiffany) Chong, Olga Karchevska, Divesh Mayaramani, Kevin (Hyun Sik) Yoon

Year 3
Hoi (Christy) Chan, Jack Cox, Lucca Ferrarese, Jack Leather, Xiao Ma, Nihal Tamang, Rachel Yemitan, Yinong Zhang

Thanks to our Technical Tutor Matthew Wells

In contrast with the positivism of science, architecture is often cast as 'knowledge'. But what, we might ask, of architecture's periodic positivism, or of the scientist's quiet wielding of knowledge? Mechanical objectivity, the view from the machine – Nagel's "view from nowhere" – is still a view from somewhere. Falsely revered as an uncorrupted preserve of the rational, fetishized or treated with suspicion, architecture's relations to the domain of technology are not simply complex but also complicated. In the architect's many seminal flirtations with the authority of science – think of Le Corbusier's love song to the sleek autonomy of the aircraft – we often find that what is being addressed is precisely not science, rather a desired something else that technology has become a cipher for. Simply put, from Konrad Waschmann to Greg Lynn, when architects say they are talking about technology, they are usually not.

——With this in mind we started our own talking this year with the Science Museum, a conversation we shared with some 34,118 technological artefacts in their Wroughton Large Object Store, each a mute witness to the convolutions of progress and obsolescence. Focusing on the objects that belonged to their Physical Infrastructure Collections, the essentially invisible systems that underpin architecture and urbanism (gas and electricity distribution, sewerage and sanitation, transport and telecommunications, civil engineering and construction) we exploited architecture's ability to strategically mediate not only between the scale of the object and the vast scale of the infrastructural, but also between the domain of culture and the domain of science: both conceptual 'infrastructures' of thought in themselves.

——What emerged from this mediation is a curious set of micro-infrastructures, architectural proposals that in the addressing of essentially infrastructural questions perform a reterritorialisation of scalar jurisdictions. Rather than unconsciously hook up to the infrastructural they resist and subvert its requirement to conform: Rachel voluptuously exposes the intersection between our fear of shit and the designed failure of infrastructure. Nihal questions both the trust in the machine and idealization of the natural in the purification of the water we daily drink. Lucca's catalogue of seminal failed construction details takes us to 1970s Boston where the failure of a glazing detail notionally rewrites the space of risk in the shadow of the John Hancock Tower. Kevin returns Tesla and Edison's AC versus DC battle, science at its quintessentially most irrational, to Holborn Viaduct, the nascent site of electrical infrastructure. Jack C treats Alberti's perspective as our ultimate infrastructure of spatial distribution and, in the footsteps of Palladio's Vicenza experiments in virtuality, reconfigures the city as theatre fly-tower. Meanwhile, Jack L locks himself in Wroughton and unravels the infrastructure of the object store to its ultimate conclusion: the entropic endgame of obsolescence.

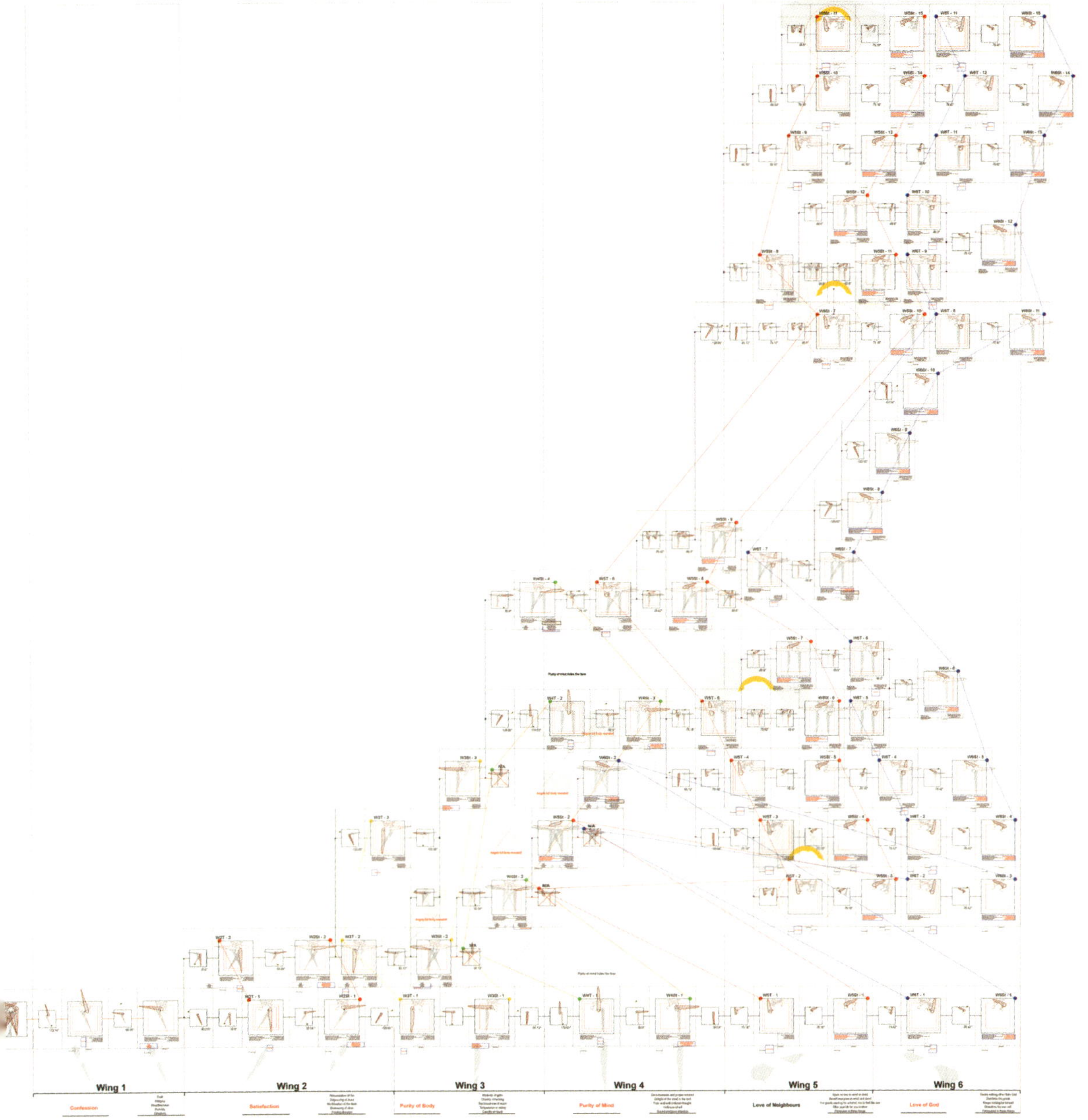
Wing 1
Confession
Wing 2
Satisfaction
Wing 3
Purity of Body
Wing 4
Purity of Mind
Wing 5
Love of Neighbours
Wing 6
Love of God

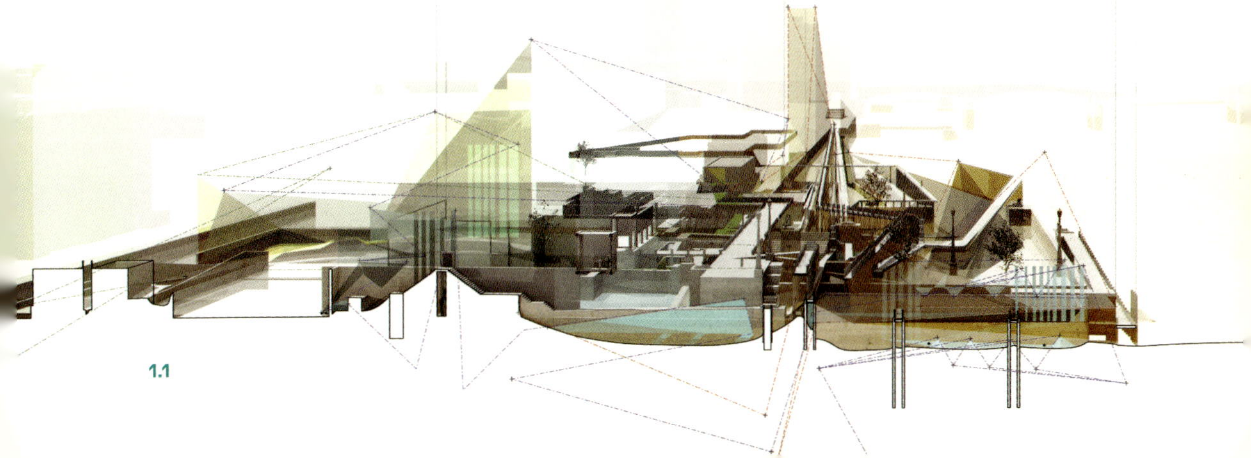

1.1

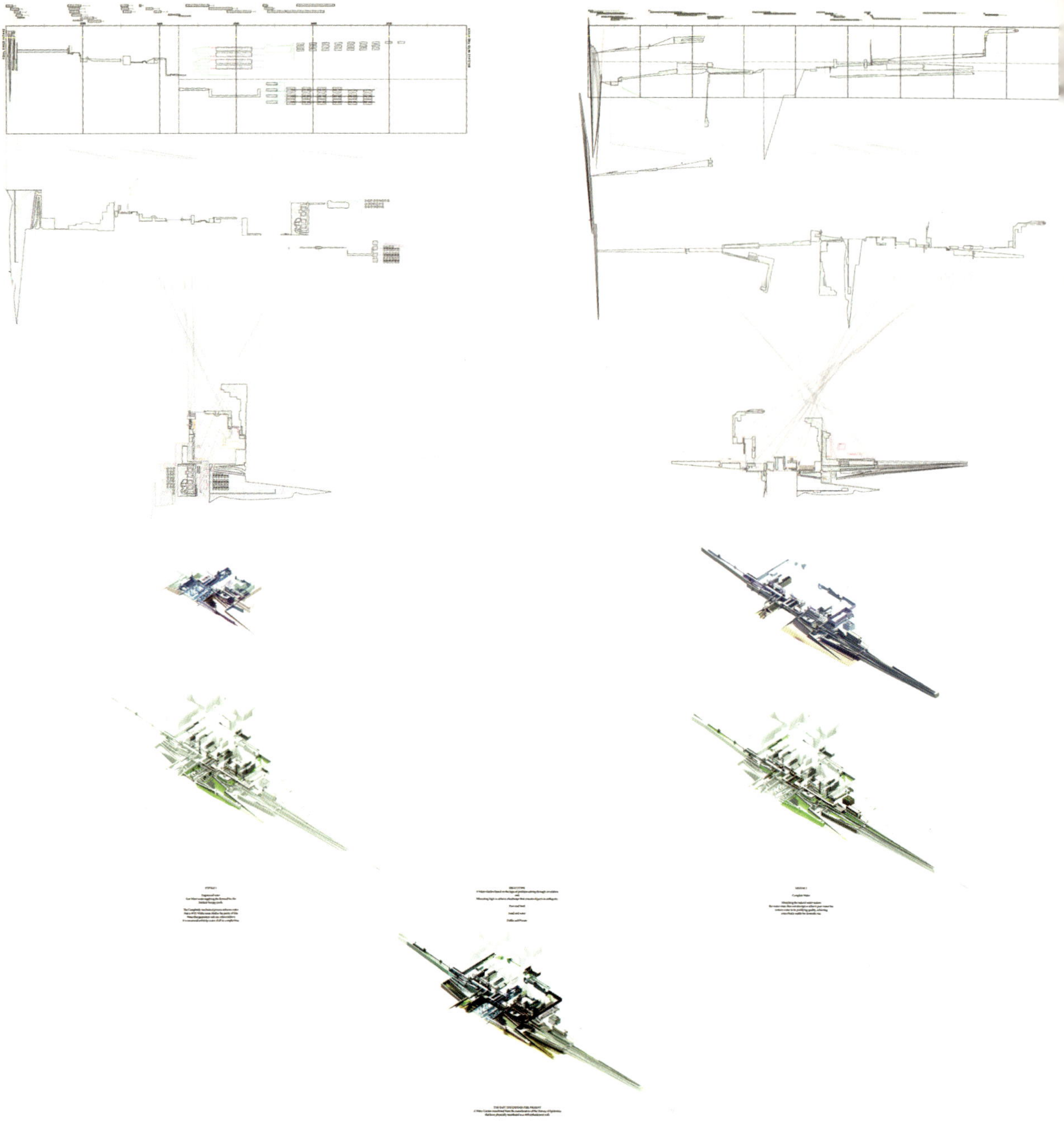

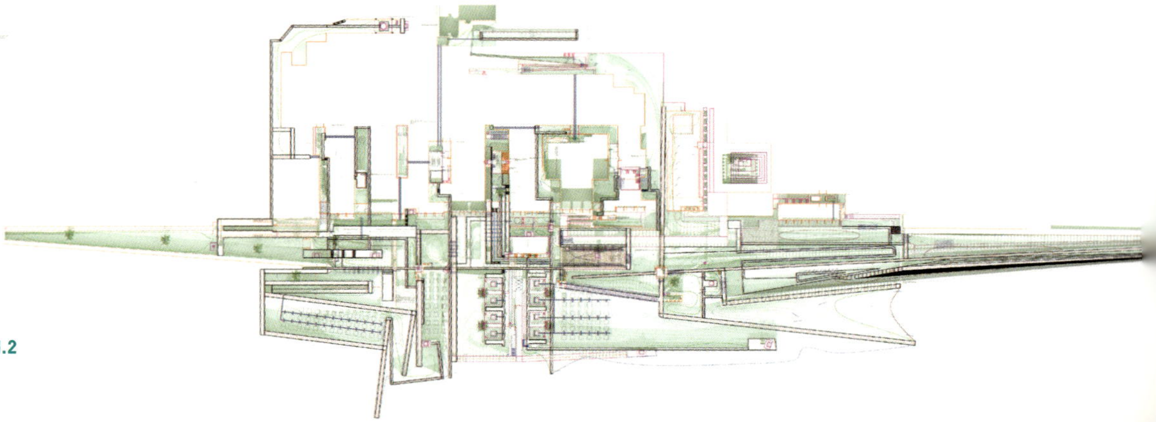

1.2

Figs. 1.1 – 1.2 Nihal Tamang Y3, 'The Engineering of Purity'. Central to the idea of infrastructure is the fiction of efficiency and its control, not least over the natural. This proposal is a micro-infrastructure that interlaces machined and natural water purification systems between St Thomas' Hospital and the Thames. Both purification systems are a measure of time. Here fluctuations in the tidal cycle produce spillovers and the mingling of different water bodies. Within this engineered landscape the same pool is sometimes pure and sometimes foul, confronting Londoners with their fear of the river. Only the system's logic revealed through its full set of iterations lends order to what appears disorientating and disorderly.
Fig. 1.3 Jack Leather Y3, 'Decay by Design: the Archive of the Never Lost'. As the Science Museum moves the entire contents of its Blythe House store to join the store in Wroughton, where it will double the footprint of objects, this project asks: what is the endgame of the archive? When is a technological artifact obsolete in its archival life also? The 'Archive of the Never Lost' harnesses and amplifies the decay agents in the Wiltshire landscape to accelerate the entropic degradation of the terminally obsolete artifact. Deploying an array of macro and micro decay delivery infrastructures (weather-catchers, cold-bridges, drainage prevention details) the landscape houses a set of pavilion-like tombs customised to the artefacts they must destroy.

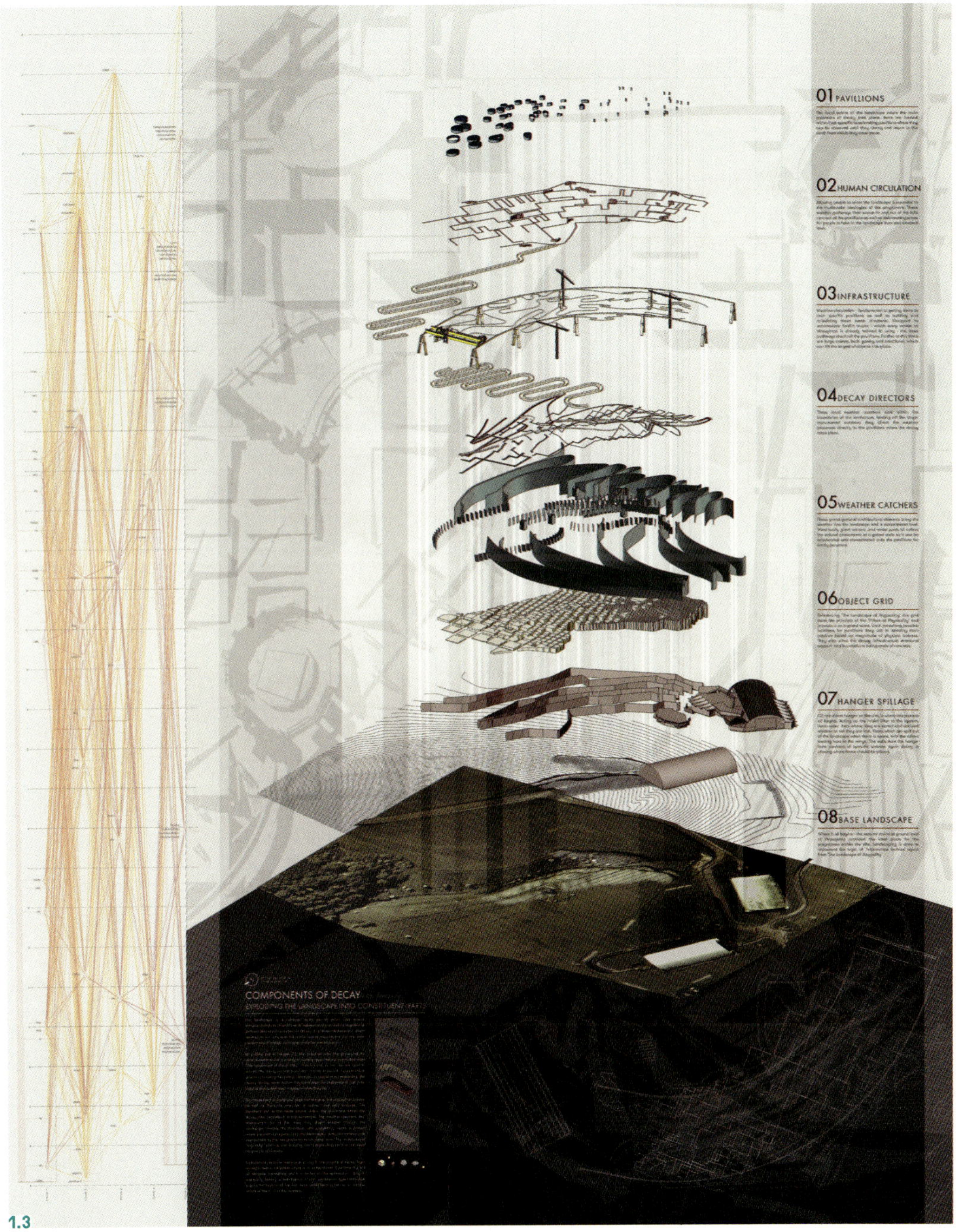

1.3

Fig. 1.4 Jack Cox Y3, 'Teatro Viale - the City as Fly-Tower'. Palladio and Scamozzi's extraordinary experiments in virtuality, manifest in Teatro Olympico's extruded streets whose false perspective notionally projects into Vicenza's fabric, remind us that the virtual was once not simply digital, nor simply dumb. 'Teatro Viale' similarly treats Vicenza as its fly-tower – this time literally. In pursuit of Josef Svoboda's Total Theatre of 'psycho-plastic space, elastic in its scope and alterable in its quality' this proposal, with its infrastructure of rails and grip men, physically cuts, edits and relocates elements of the cityscape as performative actors in themselves. As street and theatre merge within this new theatrical corporeality the public is never quite sure which side of the proscenium arch, the invisible 'skin' between artifice and the real, they are on.

Fig. 1.5 Lucca Ferrarese Y3, 'Perpetual Monument to Failed Details'. Ronan Point's H2 joint, which not only brought down half of the tower but also 1960's high rise-housing in general, illustrates the power of the failed detail to rewrite the city. This anti-monument to Hancock Tower proposes a public space of risk in which the spectacle of erratically failing gaskets and falling glazing can be observed as it is endlessly reharvested, recast and resituated on the façade only to fail again.
The staging of perpetual failure and its denial of completion interrogates architecture's uneasy relations to failure, not least in its more heroic moments. **Fig. 1.6 Rachel Yemitan** Y3, 'The Authorship of Shit: Sewage and Seduction'. Some things prefer to remain anonymous. When the Thames Tideway tunnel is complete it still won't stop raw sewage overflowing into the

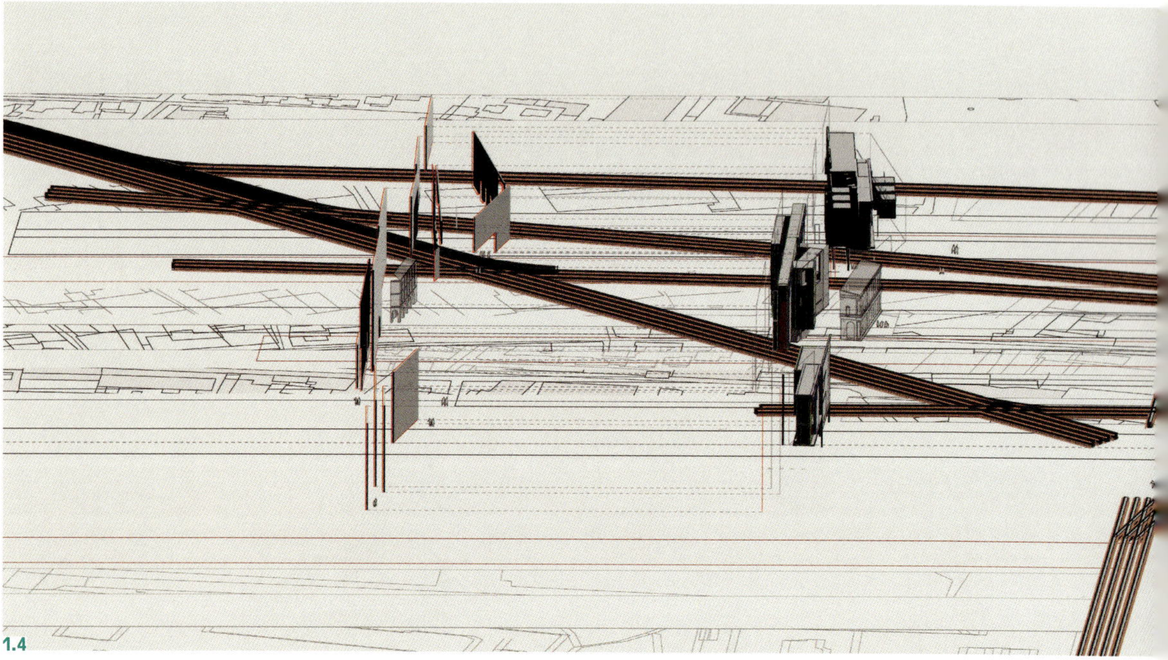

1.4

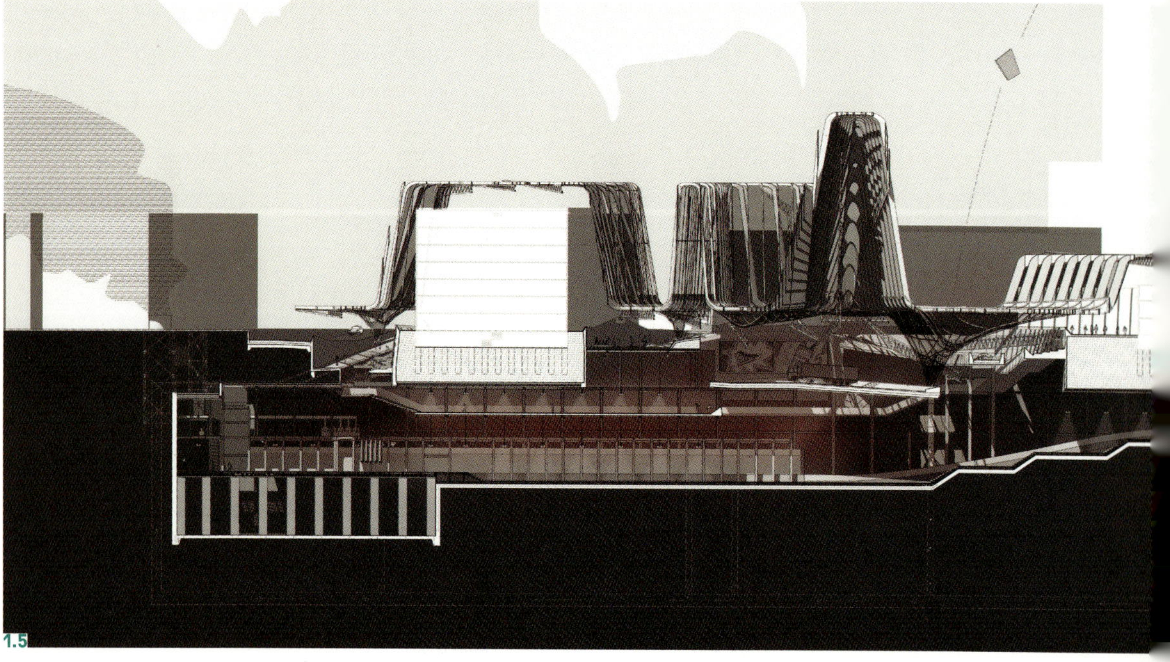

1.5

river on a regular basis. This scatalogical archive exploits the strategic indeterminacy of authorship and waste in order to confront the city with its horror of effluent by stealthy seduction as the overflow inflates a voluptuous riverside palace of shit. **Fig. 1.7** **Richard Aina** Y2, 'Robert Fludd's Balloon Burst Chamber'. This typological parody treats the technology of particle collision/observation chambers (cloud chambers, bubble chambers) as belonging to the same tradition as Robert Fludd's 1617 memory theatre: a space whose surfaces are able to serially record and delete (or forget) the events which they contain: Here, the pantomime gesture of bursting an ink-filled balloon whose splatter is registered by Fludd's rusticated masonry. **Fig. 1.8** **Kevin (Hyun Sik) Yoon** Y2, 'The Housing of Infrastructure'. As we become increasingly reliant on battery powered devices this project revisits the case for D.C. electrical supply via a speculative rewriting of space in two historic sites central to Thomas Edison's failed endeavour in his battle with Tesla's A.C.: Pearl Street's now demolished 1882 Power Station in central Manhattan and the palatial substructure of Holborn Viaduct – Edison's trial location for the first electrical infrastructure. The first is notionally reconfigured using Aron's Clock Meter in which two pendulums measure time and consumption, only to clash if there is a surge in the latter; the second, using the continuous measure of a conveyor belt of traders orbiting an internet exchange for optimised dealing from their D.C. underworld.

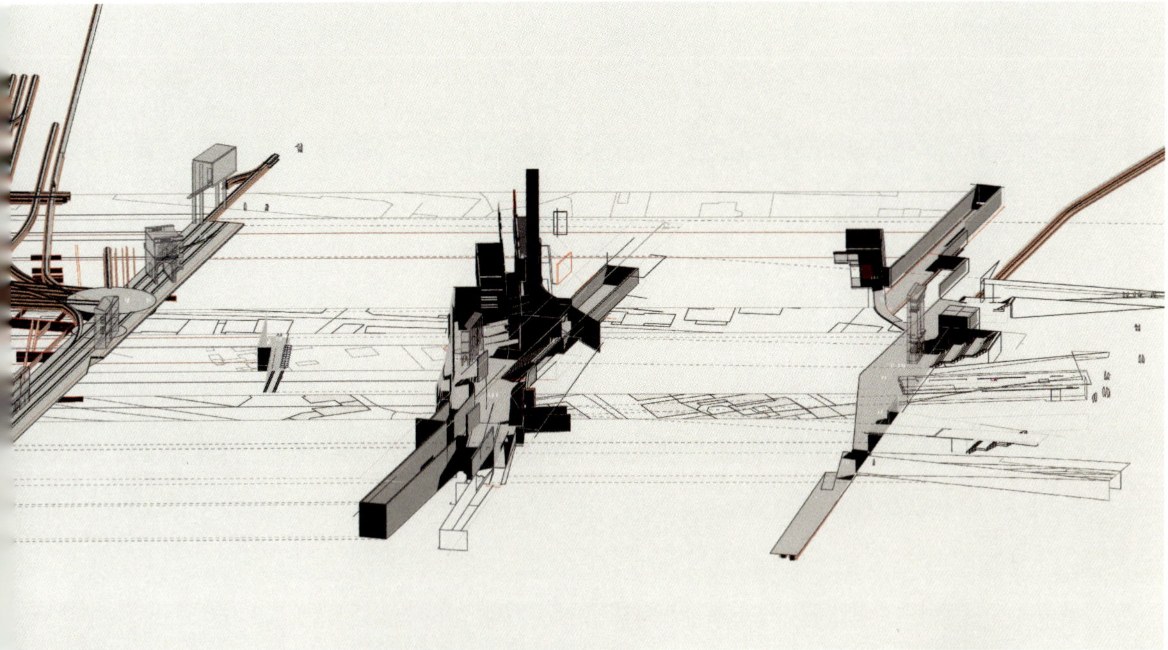

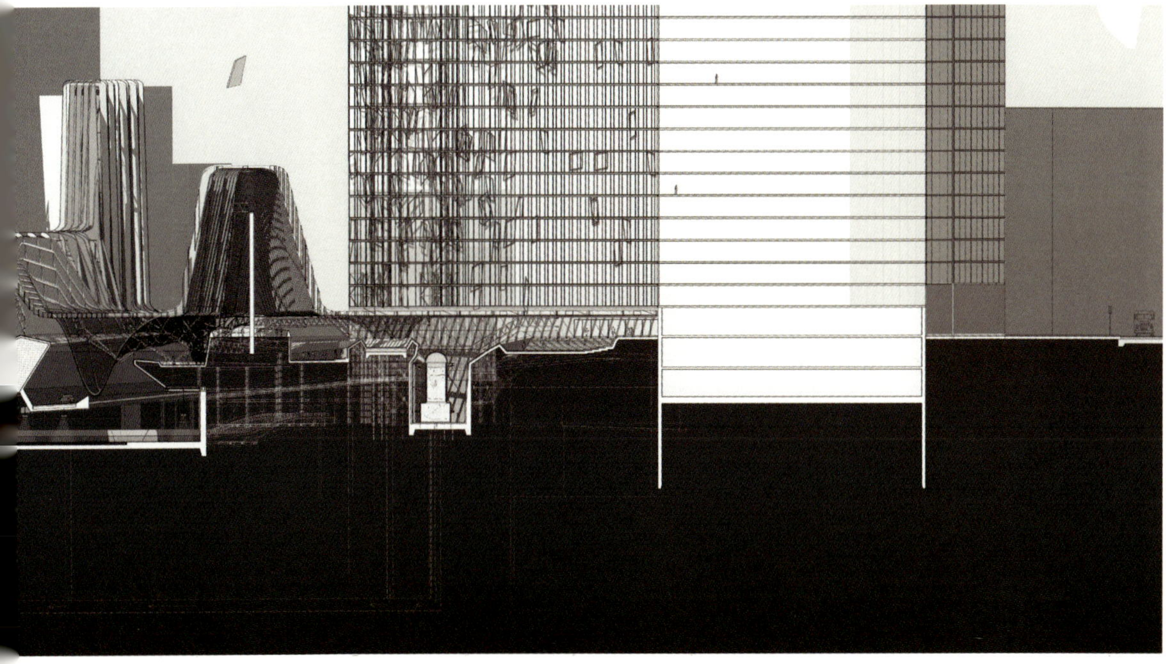

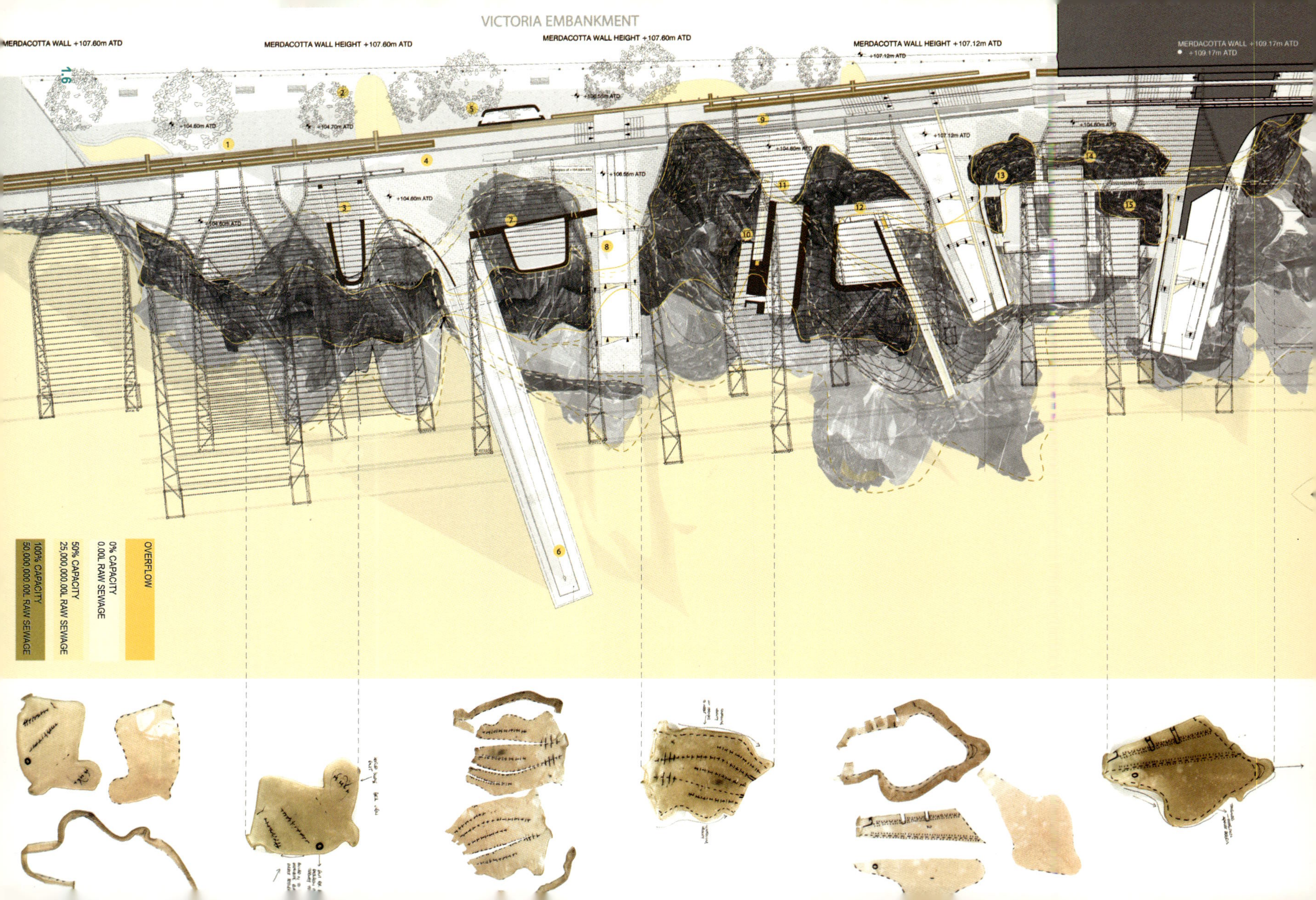
VICTORIA EMBANKMENT
MERDACOTTA WALL +107.60m ATD
MERDACOTTA WALL HEIGHT +107.60m ATD
MERDACOTTA WALL HEIGHT +107.60m ATD
MERDACOTTA WALL HEIGHT +107.12m ATD
MERDACOTTA WALL +109.17m ATD
+109.17m ATD
+104.60m ATD
+104.70m ATD
+106.56m ATD
+107.12m ATD
+104.60m ATD
OVERFLOW
0% CAPACITY
0.00L RAW SEWAGE
50% CAPACITY
25,000,000.00L RAW SEWAGE
100% CAPACITY
50,000,000.00L RAW SEWAGE

1.6

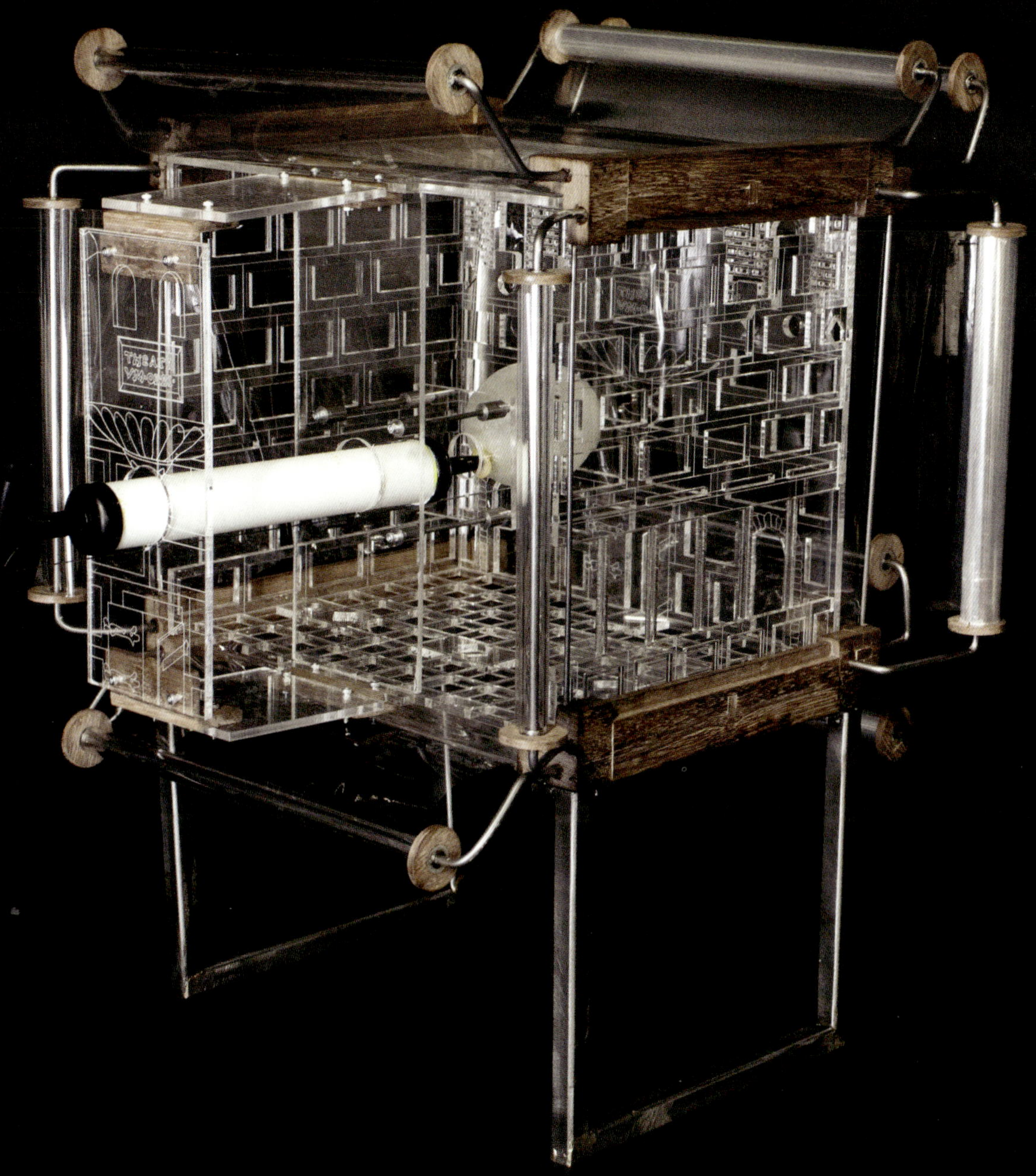

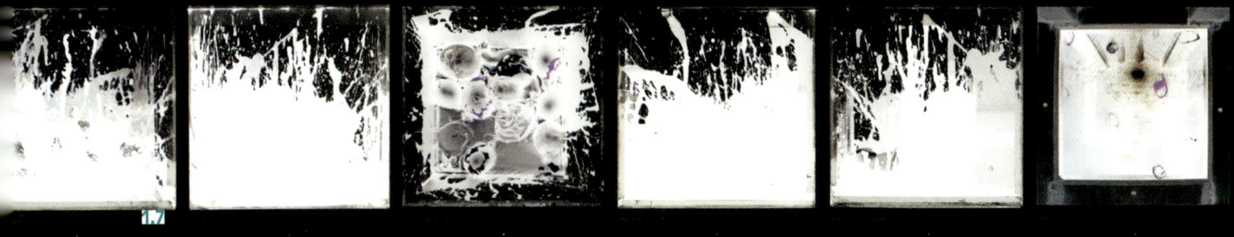

1.7

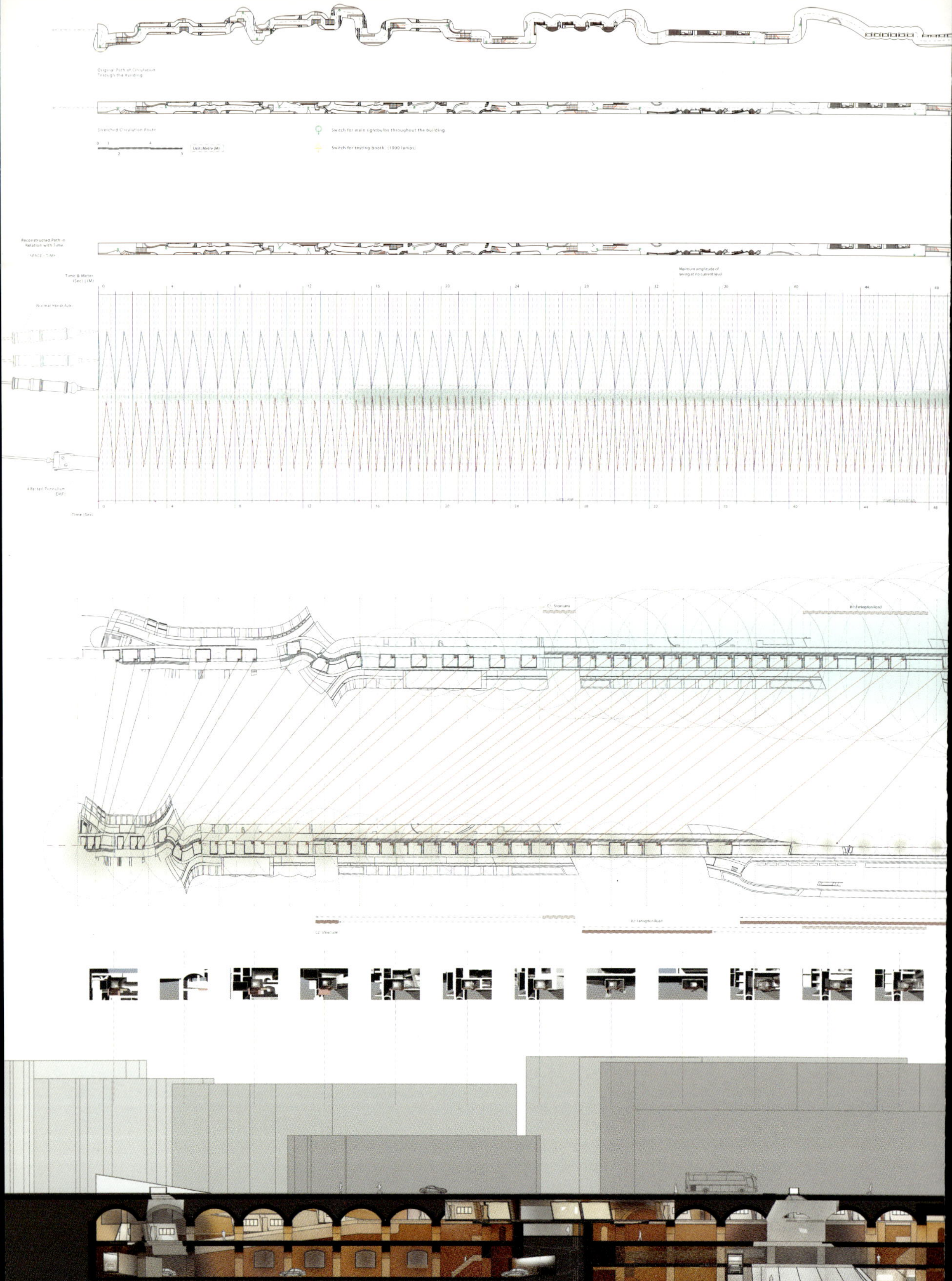
Original Path of Circulation
Through the Building
Stretched Circulation Route
Switch for main lightbulbs throughout the building
Switch for testing booth. (1000 lamps)
Unit: Metre (M)
Reconstructed Path in
Relation with Time
SPACE - TIME
Time & Meter
(Sec) | (M)
Maximum amplitude of
swing at no current level
Normal Pendulum
Affected Pendulum
EMF
Time (Sec)

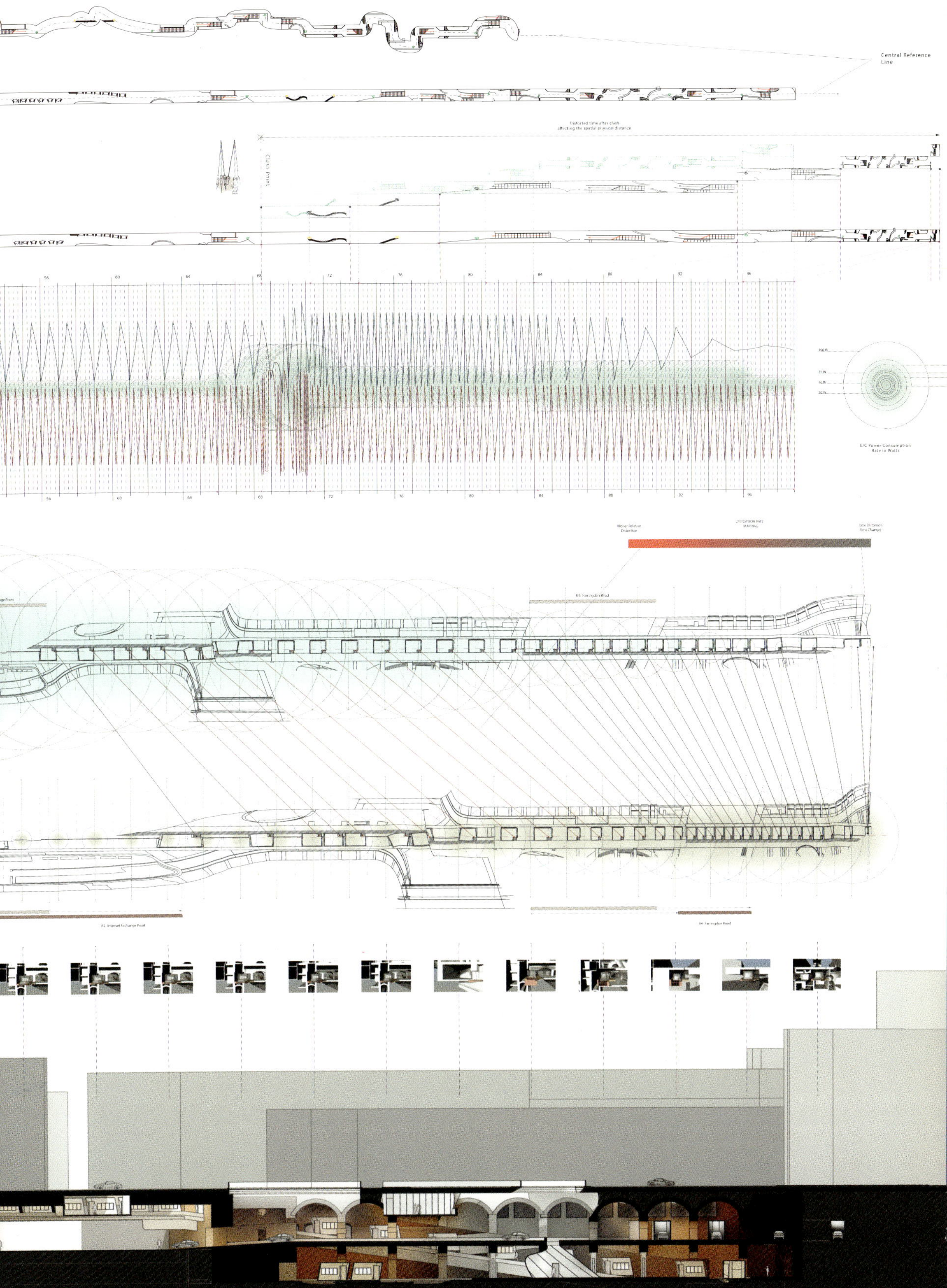
Central Reference Line
Distorted time after clash affecting the spatial physical distance
Clash Point
56
60
64
68
72
76
80
84
88
92
96
100 W
75 W
50 W
30 W
E/C Power Consumption Rate in Watts
Higher Relative Distortion
DISTORTION RATE MAPPING
Low Distortion (Less Change)
A2. Internet Exchange Point

UG2

Sprezzatura

Damjan Iliev, Javier Ruiz

Year 2
Yihan (Zara) Chen, Wing (Melody) Chu, Hanadi Izzuddin, Jaejun Kim, Aleksandra Kugacka, Rachel Lee, Niraj Shah, Ziyuan (Oliver) Zhu

Year 3
Yan Ho (Brian) Cheung, Hilda Hiong, Ning (Yi) Lui , Minesh Patel, Tobias Petyt, Sze (Viola) Poon, Joanna Rzewuska, Meng (Tony) Zhao

Thank you to our consultants and critics: Richard Beckett, Isaïe Bloch, Harry Bucknall, Mathew Butcher, Marjan Colletti, Mollie Claypool, Manuel Jimenez Garcia, Yael Riesner, Bob Sheil, David Storring and Barry Wark

One must avoid affectation and practice in all things a certain sprezzatura, disdain or carelessness, so as to conceal art, and make whatever is done or said appear to be without effort and almost without any thought about it.
The Book of the Courtier, Baldassare Castiglione, 1528

This year UG2 explored spaces for living and socialising in the future using time-based tools and advanced 3D modelling computation techniques driven by emergent paradigms in digital design. We emphasised the use of *Sprezzatura*, a courtier's most valuable skill, also defined as nonchalance, studied carelessness or well- rehearsed naturalness. The focus was on demonstrating how the perfect courtier, in order to behave with *Sprezzatura*, uses strategies of rhetoric and deceit and how these behavioural strategies and techniques can be reconfigured to drive a contemporary design methodology using advanced digital tools.

From Form to Formation

In Term 1, we familiarised ourselves with the concept of *Sprezzatura* through a series of task-specific workshops which investigated parallel digital and spatial design strategies in architecture. We decoded the underlining principles of this socio-cultural behaviour and used them to inform and customise specific computational techniques to explore concepts such as intricacy, redundancy, exuberance and excess. The design task was to propose a series of inhabitable spaces/fragments in Rome. The function and context of our proposals were dependent on individual preference, however, they all needed to exemplify the tension that *Sprezzatura* provides such as: complex vs. simple; extravagant vs. plain; redundant vs. essential; eccentric vs. balanced; intricate vs. smooth; explicit vs. ambiguous; formed vs. amorphous. At the same time we discussed the contemporary confrontation between design mediums (manual, intuitive) and automatic tools (algorithmic).

From Formation to Ecosystem

During Terms 2 and 3 we designed a public Villa hybridised with additional programmes sited in Rome, Venice or Florence. The design process began by criticising the typology of the Villa and proposing new radical possibilities of inhabitation. We re-examined housing as a body of formal and behavioural possibilities, triggering new and innovative opportunities for the design of living and socialising spaces. The control, rigour and precision of some of our techniques would interlock with the redundancy, vagueness and ambiguity that others produce. *Sprezzatura*, by nature, is an art of dissimulation and a process of communication whose extreme application will hyper-polarise the output, from which will emerge a new 'ego', or in our case, a new architectural typology; an emergent architectural persona.

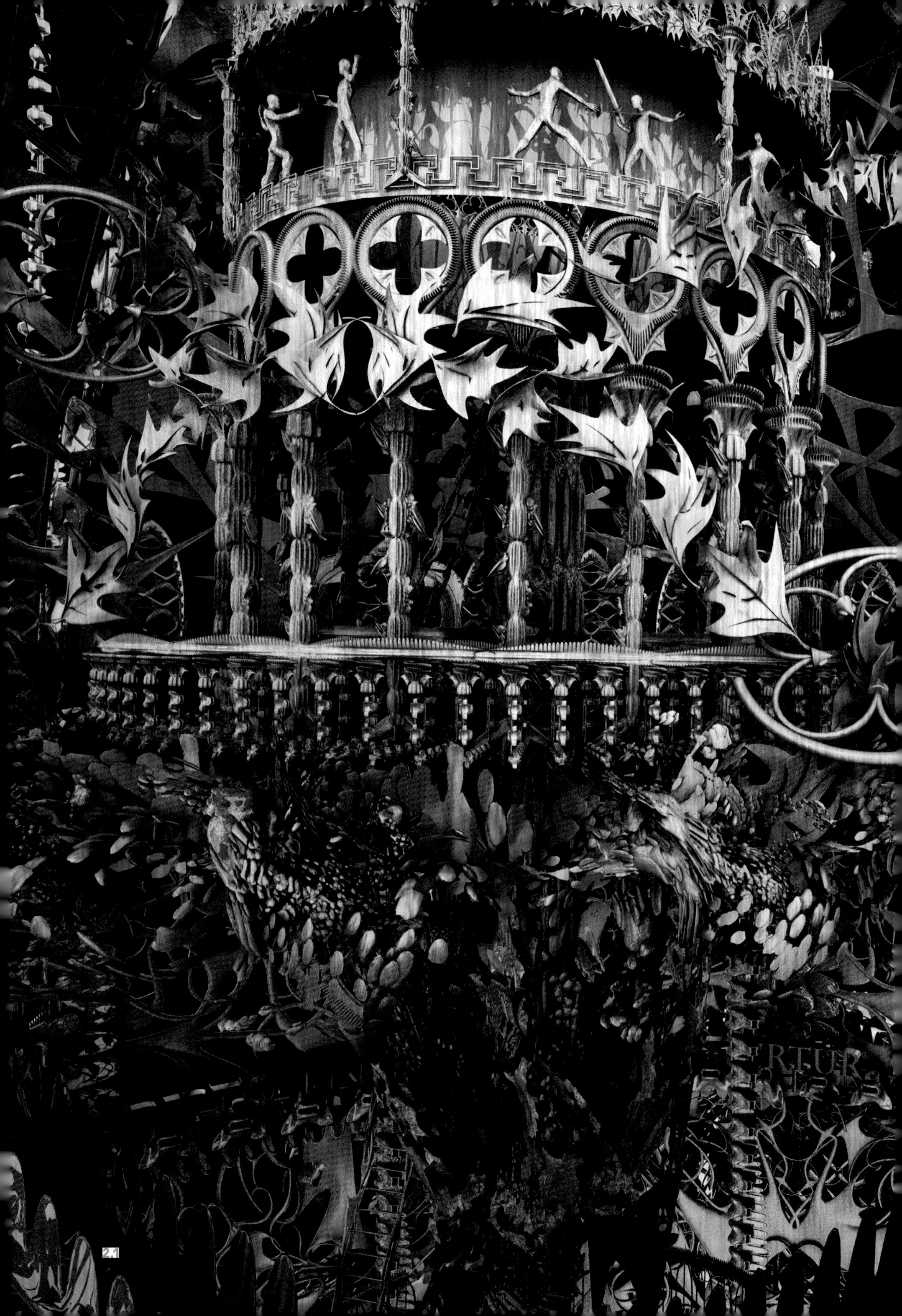
RTUR
2.1

Fig. 2.1 Ning (Yi) Lui Y3, 'Tough Love', Wedding Venue Obstacle Course, Venice. Typically the altar and dome of a cathedral represent heaven, and in this project this place of holy matrimony has been reinvented. The wedding venue creates an engaging, and more realistic representation of communal union, whilst providing visitors with a picturesque and romantic setting. **Fig. 2.2 Ning (Yi) Lui** Y3, 'Tough Love', Wedding Venue Obstacle Course, Venice. The cathedral draws on typical Gothic elements, as gargoyles adorn the facades. The carved grotesques prevent rainwater damage, as water spouts theatrically from their mouths. The functional and highly ornamental nature of this is quintessentially Gothic. **Figs. 2.3 & 2.5 Hanadi Izzuddin** Y2, 'Birdwatching Pavilion', Rome. The project explores a transition in formal condition through three architectural components that mediate between states of solidity, fibrosity and porosity: a bench, a staircase and three birdwatching pods. The formal state is varied to inform functionality, such as the creation of a porous artificial nest where the figure is able to materialise and dematerialise as one transits into the realm of the birds. **Fig. 2.4 Minesh Patel** Y3, 'Private Members Club', Rome. Situated on Tiber Island, the building provides facilities for creatives and media artists working and traveling through the city. The proposal investigates various notions of privacy and voyeurism by accentuating topographic characteristics of the site to influence movement patterns and visual permeability throughout the building.

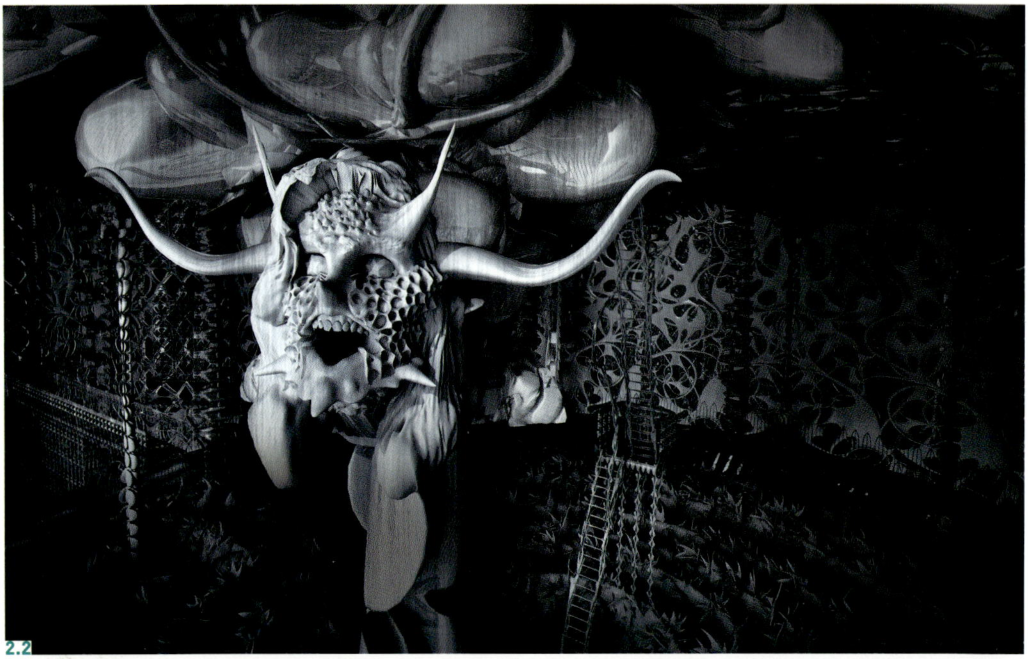

2.2

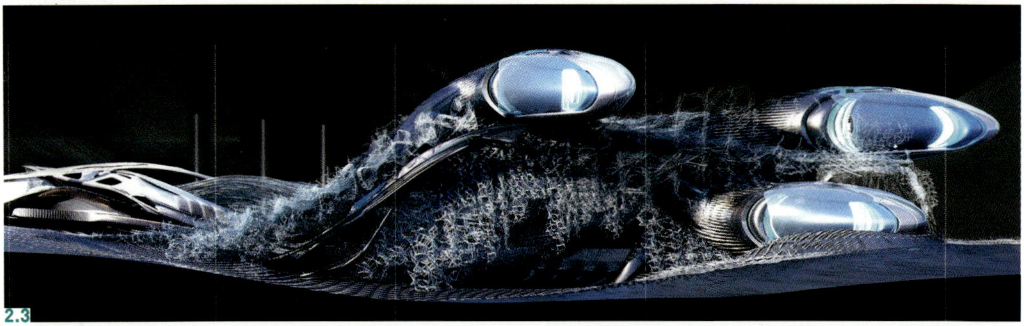

2.3

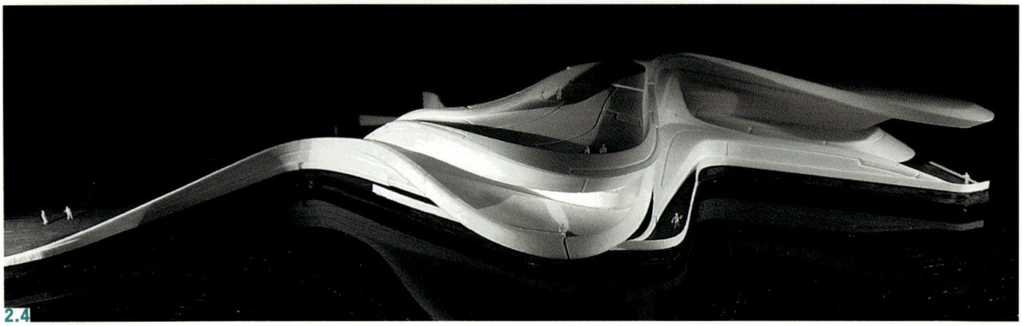

2.4

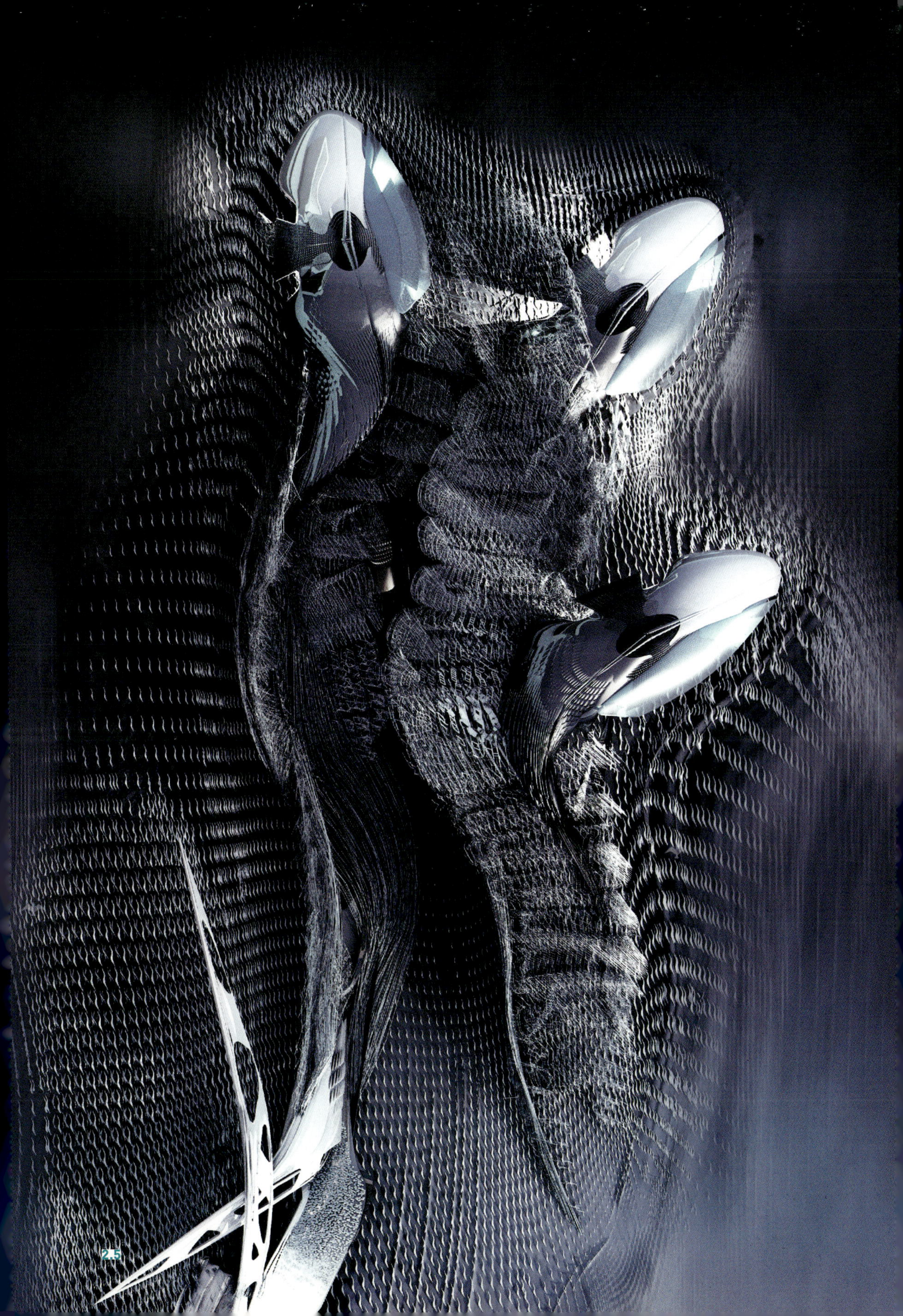

2.5

Fig. 2.6 Tobias Petyt Y3, 'Steampunk Villa-Cum-Workshop Residence', Rome. This project takes the original purpose of the Italian renaissance villa as an agricultural farmhouse and re-interpreted it within an urban industrial context. The project combines the domestic value of a villa with the output qualities of a factory to create a completely self-automated building reminiscent of Rome's industrial past intertwined with Italian Renaissance flamboyance. **Fig. 2.7 Hilda Hiong** Y3, 'Villa for Gymnast', Rome. Ornamentation is re-appropriated as an architectural device embedded with gymnastics exercising equipment for people to practice and develop physio-motoric skills. The wall also acts as a perforated interstitial space filtering air and facilitating natural ventilation throughout the building. **Fig 2.8 Tobias Petyt** Y3, 'Dystopian Prosthesis', Venice. Derived from interpretations of Sprezzatura, the design focused around developing a mecha-organic prosthetic set in a Venetian dystopian future. Out of this intervention developed the programme of a clockmaker character in pursuit of rebuilding his home on an abandoned classic Venetian façade repaired with leftover metal pieces, clockwork mechanical elements intertwined with Gothic Renaissance architecture. **Fig. 2.9 Yan Ho (Brian) Cheung** Y3, 'Bath House Villa', Tuscany. Situated next to a natural hot spring, the building pumps mineral-rich water into an aggregation of outdoor bath pools embedded into the slope of the landscape. The topography of the baths will evolve over time as a consequence of the precipitation of the water into calcium concretions.

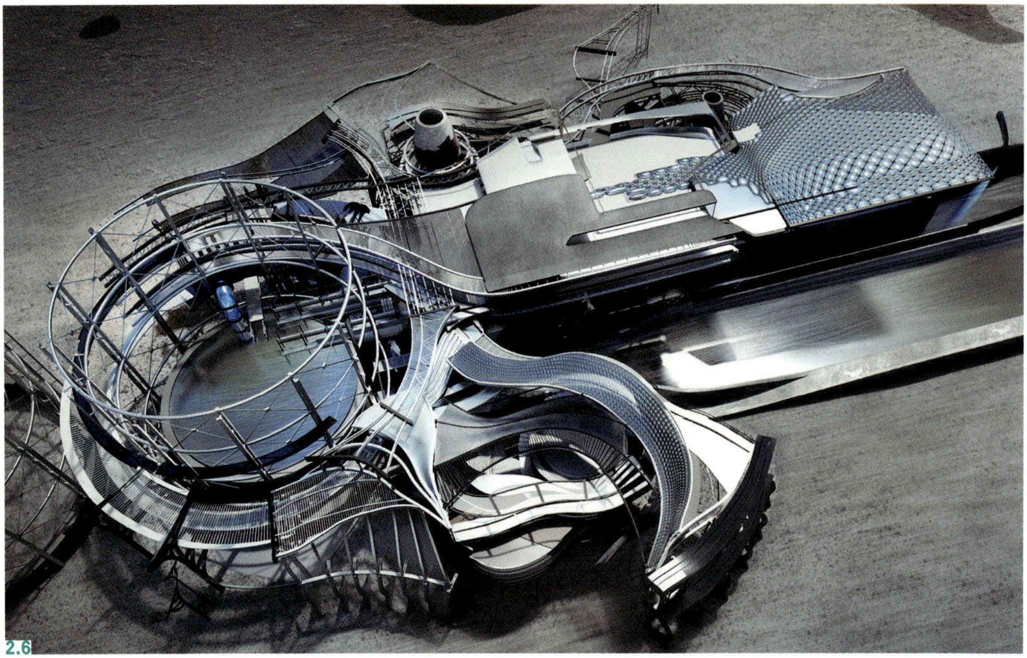

2.6

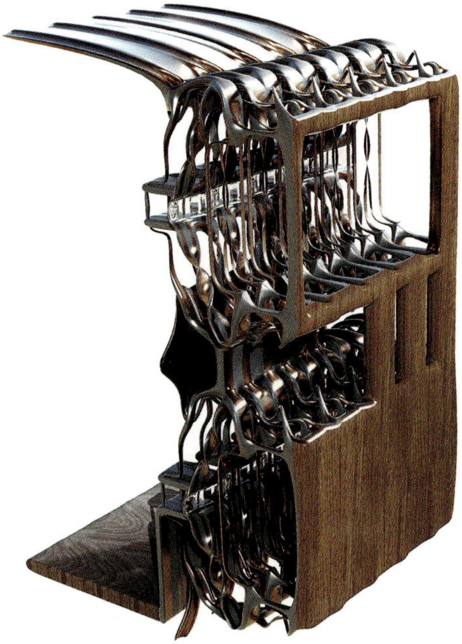

2.7

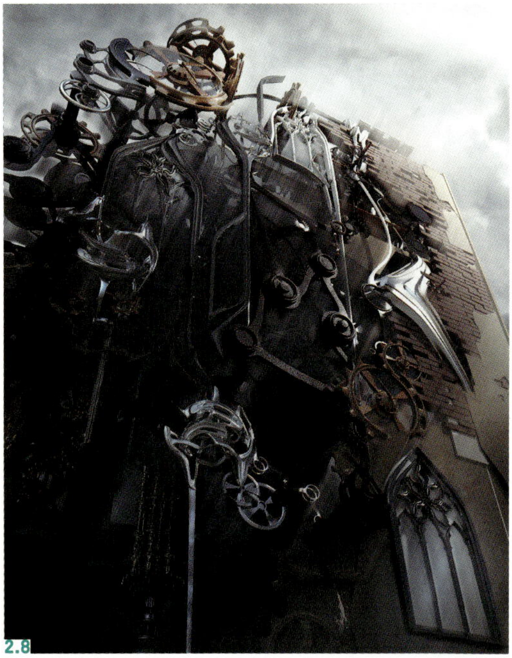

2.8

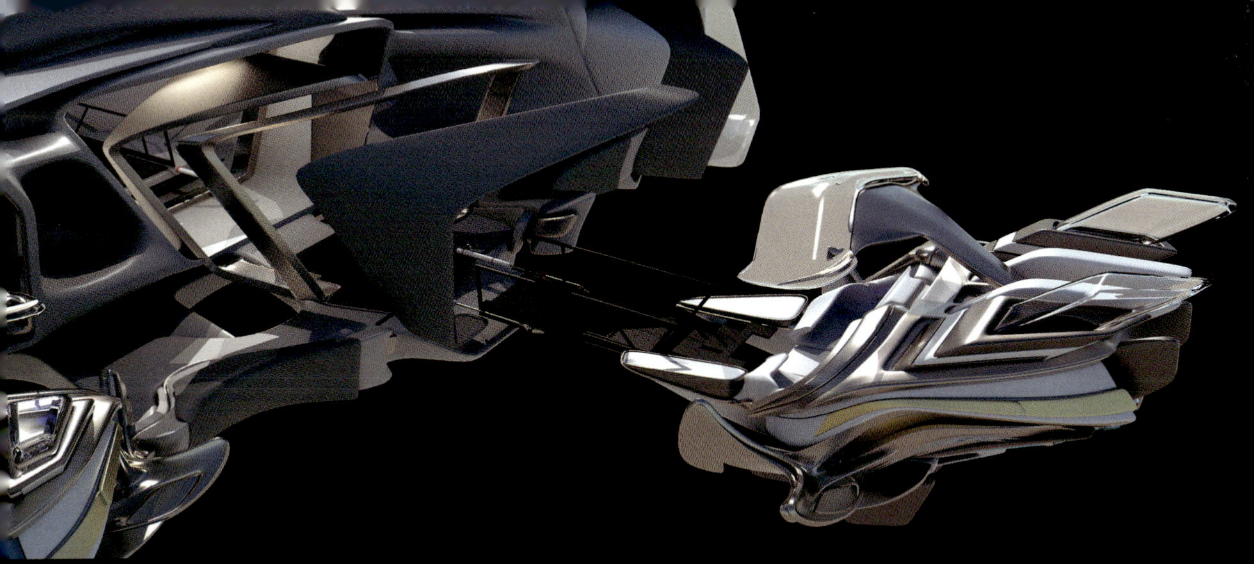

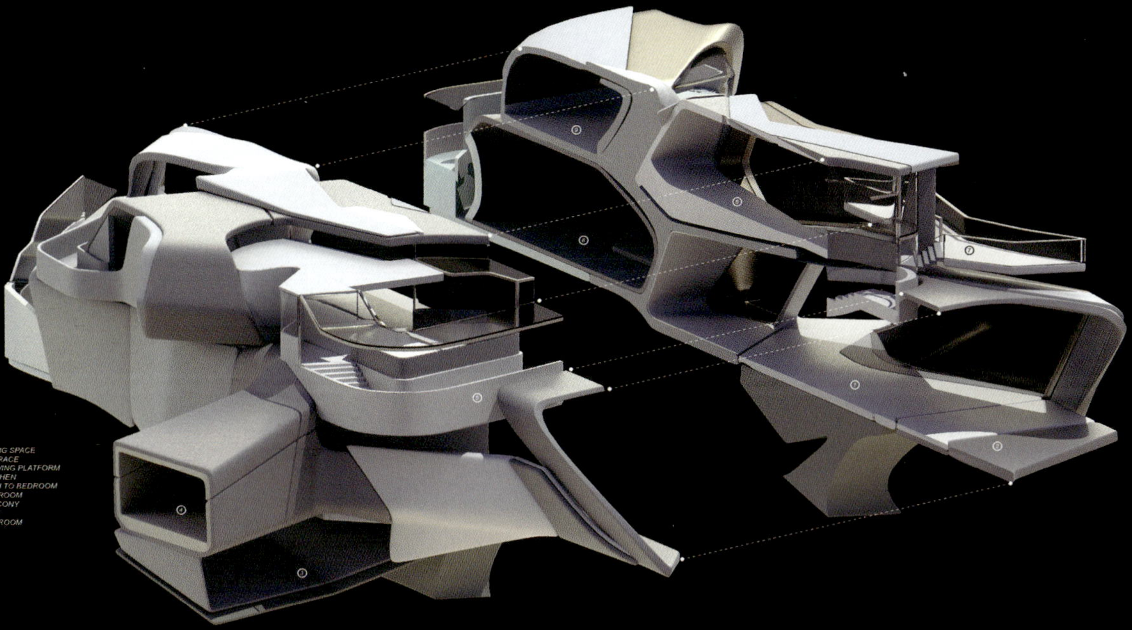

1. LIVING SPACE
2. TERRACE
3. VIEWING PLATFORM
4. KITCHEN
5. PATH TO BEDROOM
6. BEDROOM
7. BALCONY
8. GYM
9. BEDROOM

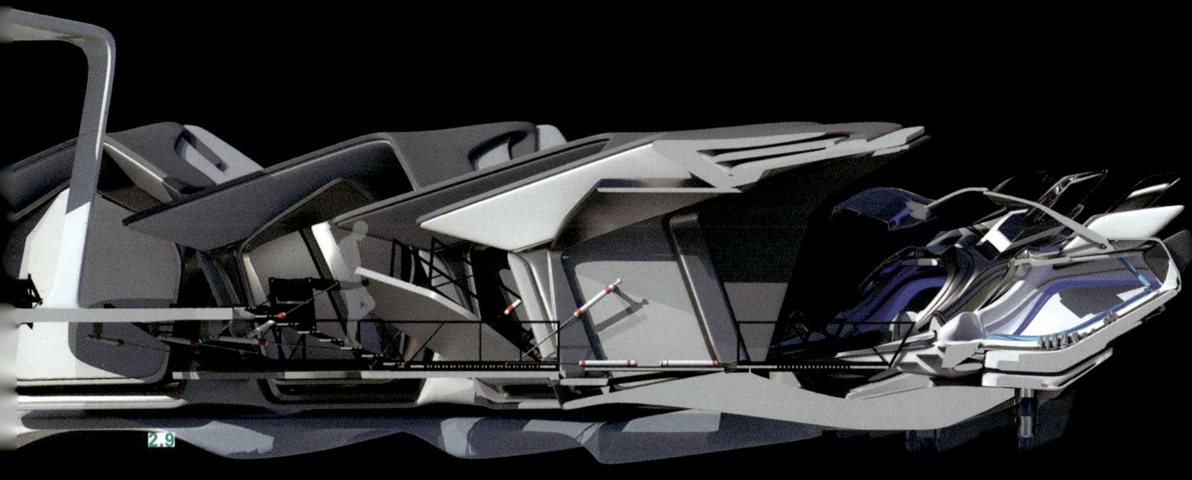

Fig. 2.10 Jaejun Kim Y2, 'Inhabitable Bridge', Venice. Jaejun's project investigates the possibility of a multi-directional inhabitable bridge which would link a number cul-de-sacs disconnected by the Venetian canals whilst also providing space for leisure and public gatherings. **Fig. 2.11 Jaejun Kim** Y2, 'Villa + Glassblowing Workshop', Murano Island, Venice. Physical Model. Expressing chemical bond changes in glass molecules through intense heat, the overall building structure and façade envelope is developed to represent a delicate artefact referential to its immediate context. **Fig. 2.12 Niraj Shah** Y2, 'Advanced Material Laboratory and Residence', Modena. Based near Italy's illustrious 'Motor Valley', this building is inspired by automotive and aviation technologies, materials and manufacture process. The proposal embeds Modena's car culture in Parco Enzo Ferrari, as well as being the luxury residence of the owner. **Fig. 2.13 Tony Zhao** Y3, 'Film Studio Villa', Venice. The project borrows from futuristic scenarios of science-fiction filmography, as well as contemporary technologies in fabrication, to propose a home for a movie director. Situated on Lido Island near the Venice Film Festival, the villa represents an assemblage of technological interventions, controlled underwater cooling systems and audio-visual equipment.

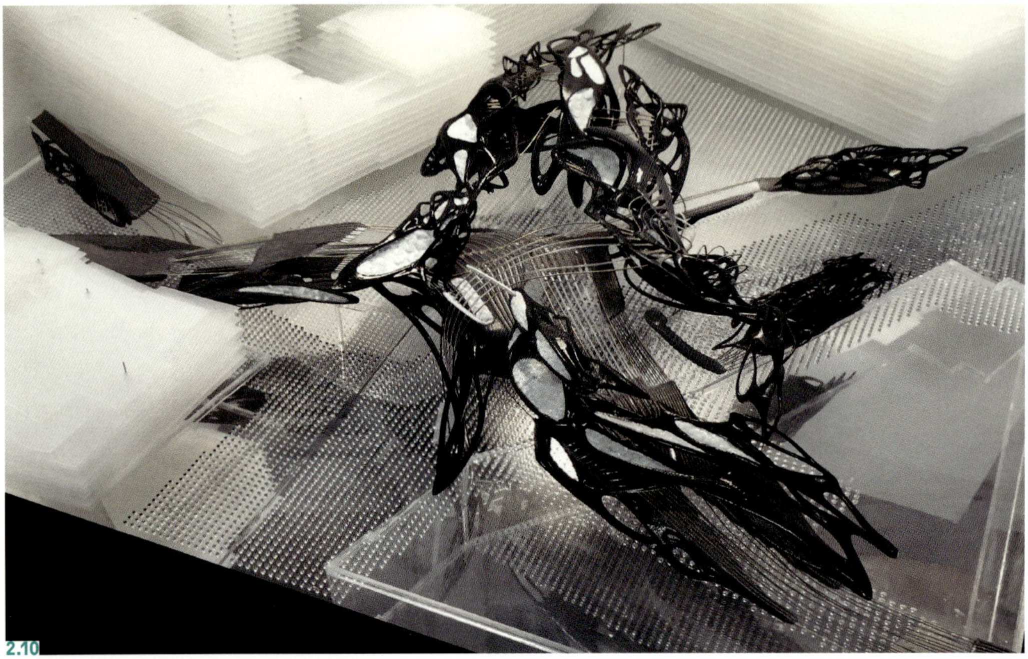

2.10

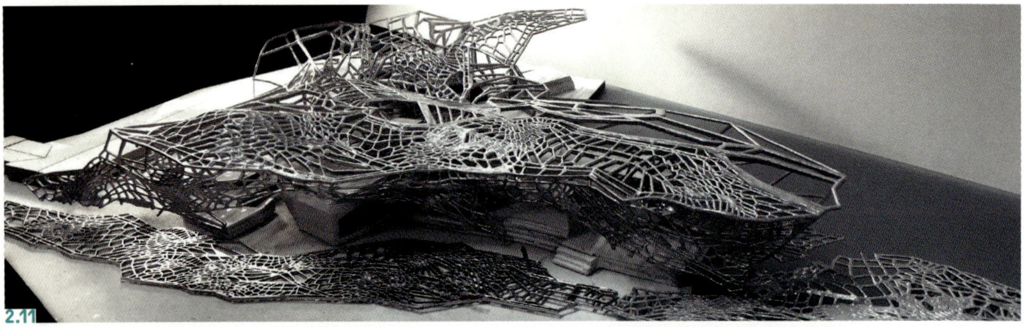

2.11

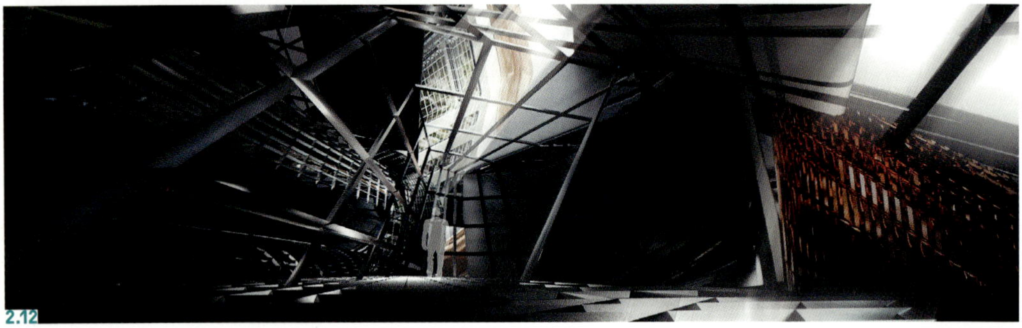

2.12

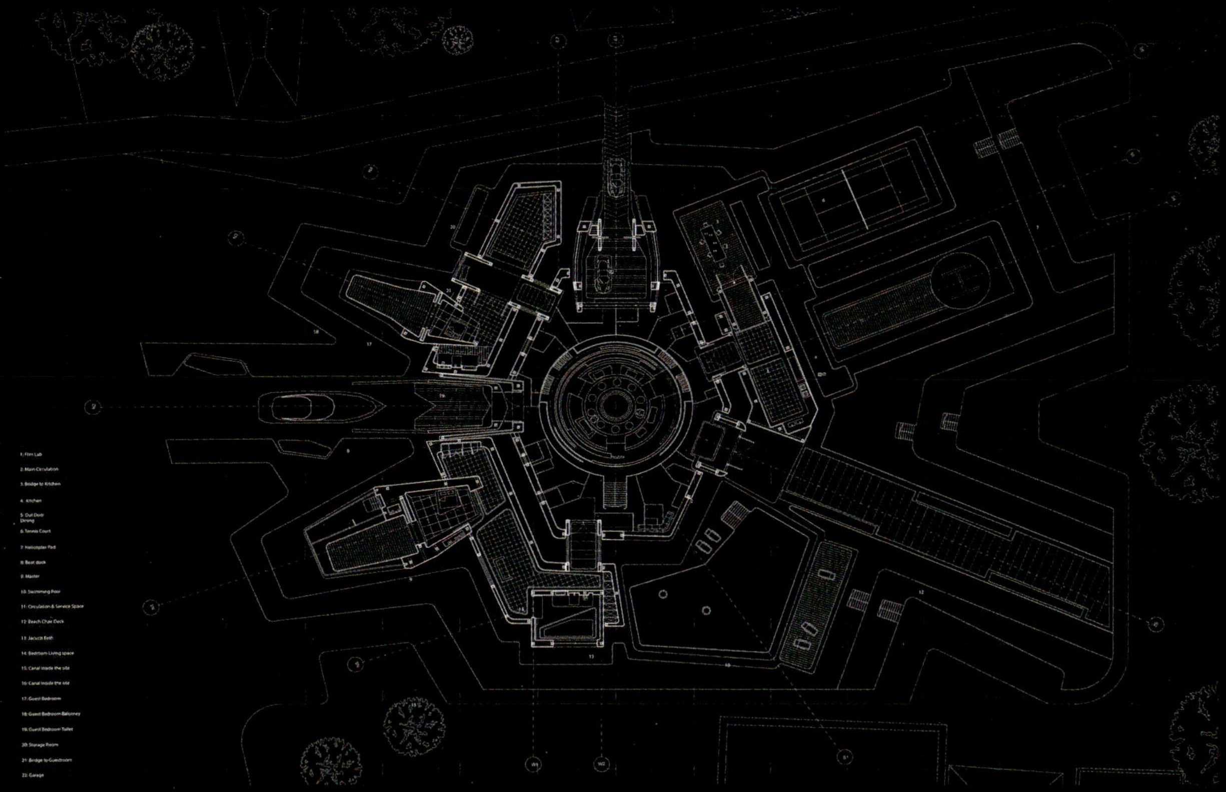
1: Film Lab
2: Main Circulation
3. Bridge to Kitchen
4. Kitchen
5. Out Door Dining
6. Tennis Court
7. Helicopter Pad
8. Boat dock
9. Master
10. Swimming Pool
11: Circulation & Service Space
12: Beach Chair Deck
13: Jacuzzi Bath
14: Bedroom Living space
15. Canal inside the site
16: Canal inside the site
17: Guest Bedroom
18: Guest Bedroom Balconey
19: Guest Bedroom Toilet
20: Storage Room
21: Bridge to Guestroom
22: Garage

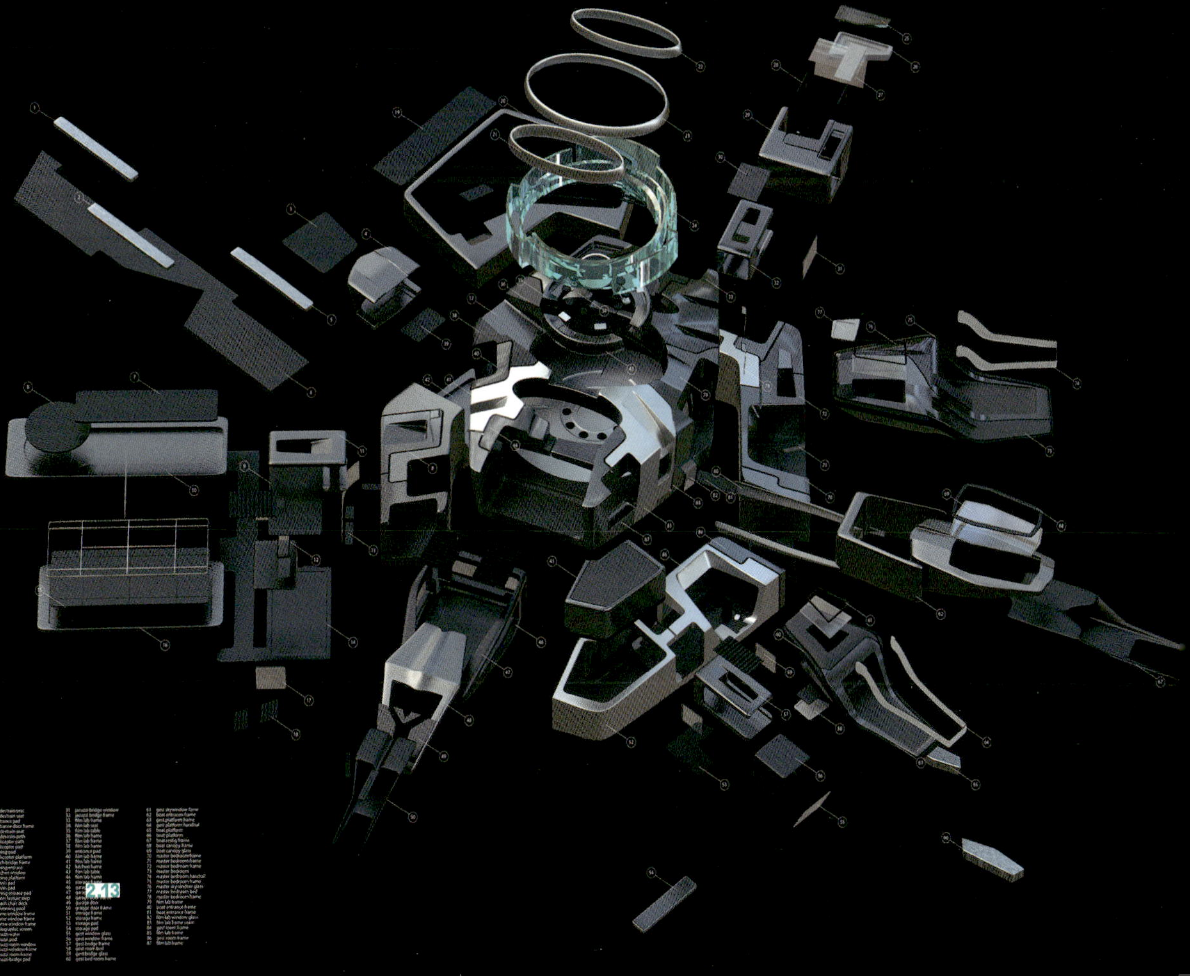

2.13

Fig. 2.14 Aleksandra Kugacka Y2, 'Aroma Villa', Rome. Wall fragment and ceiling detail.The project was driven by the investigation on materialising the evanescent quality of smell. It plays on the notion of seduction and attraction through blurring the line between open and closed spaces. The villa undertakes a sensory journey which leads from the herbal gardens through the distillation of essential oils to the experience in the aromatherapy chambers. The exuberant factory identity of the building that produces smells make visitors reconnect with their senses in order to produce a strong and lasting image of architecture. **Fig. 2.15 Sze (Viola) Poon** Y3, 'Retreat Villa Borghese', Rome. Stair detail. The building provides a retreat from the busy park and city life where visitors are guided through the infrastructure with the movement of water. A series of inhabitable spaces and reconstructed public parks aims to raise awareness of the current water situation through investigation of the integration of ecology and infrastructure, while providing multiple platforms for interaction with the aquatic world. **Fig. 2.16 Ning (Yi) Lui** Y3, 'Tough Love', A Wedding Venue Obstacle Course, Venice. Extravagant, daring and excessive in form, this cathedral allows all the passion that love entails to come alive. Marriage and companionship are celebrated for what they really are; beautiful, spectacular and undoubtedly tough.

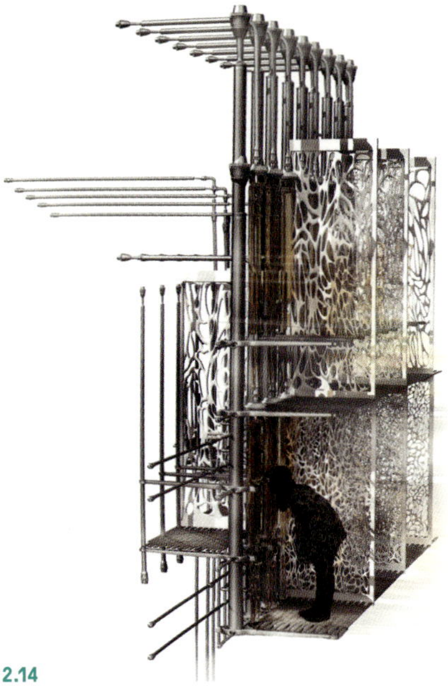

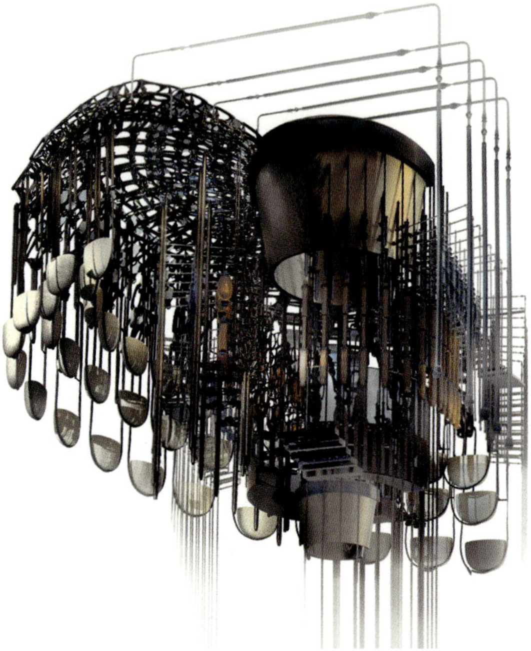

2.14

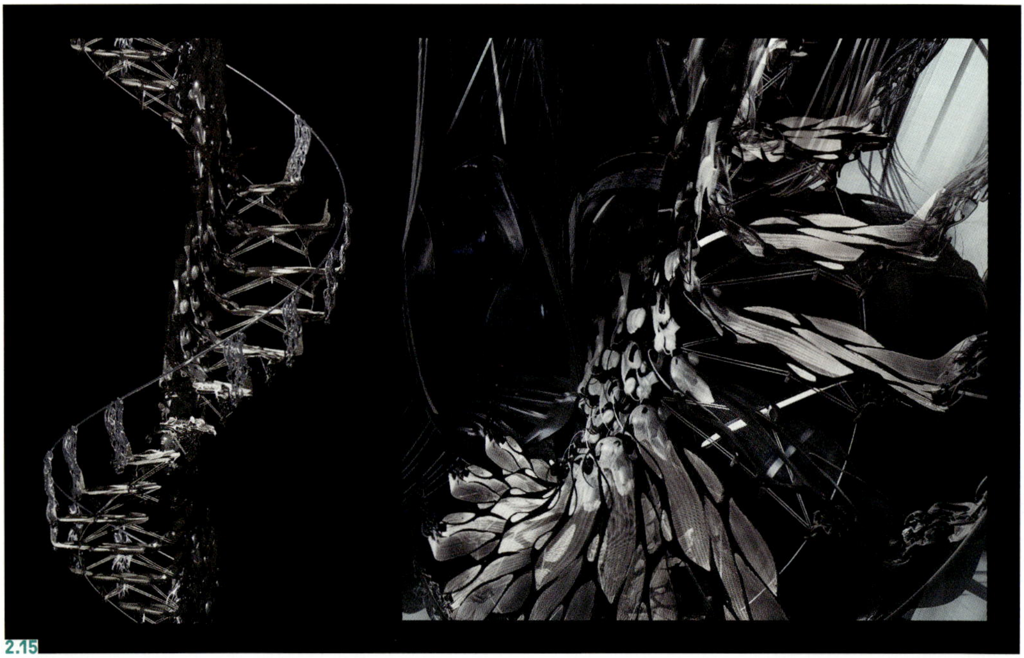

2.15

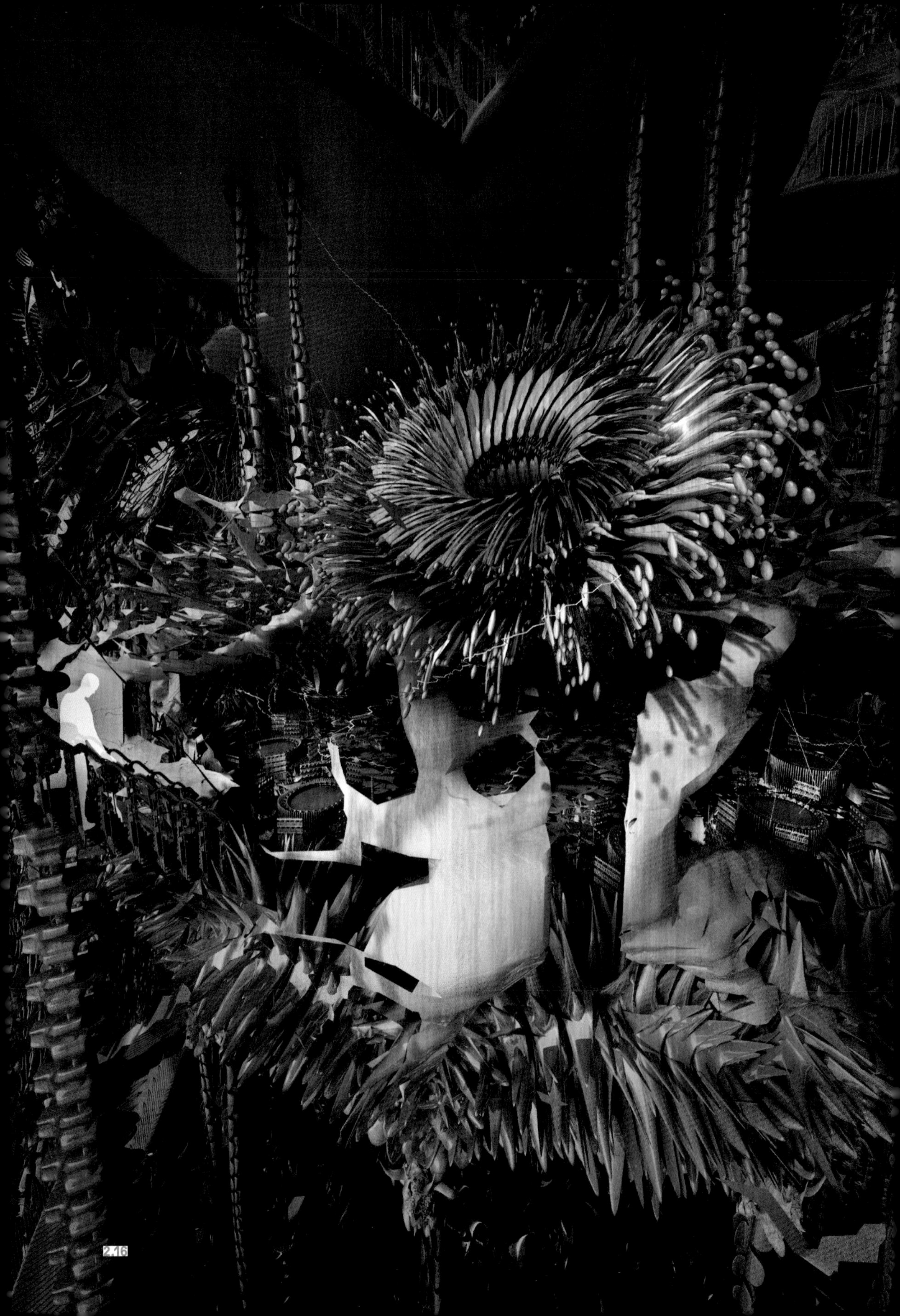

UG3

Atlas of Remote Islands

Luke Olsen, Graeme Williamson

Year 2
Freya Bolton, Jade Chao, Hanna Idziak, Georgia Jaeckle, Holly Moore, Elliot Nash, Edie Parfitt, Harry Pizzey

Year 3
Jooyoung Cho, Maria Marysia Chodzen, Conor Clarke, Peter Feehily, Subin Koo, Samuel Napleton, Shona Sharma, Yuanchu Yi

With sincere thanks to Bob Sheil, Stephen Gage, Gabby Shawcross at Westminster and SOCA, Chris Roberts at David Morley Architects, James Wignall at aLL design, Roz Barr at Roz Barr Architects, Jack Hosea at Threefold Architects, Rupert Scott at Open Practice Architects, Susanne Isa at Greenwich, Leon Chew at Modern Parallax, Simon Withers, Nicole Salnicov at Venturi & Scott Brown, Wayne Urquart at A&E Networks, Oliviu-Lugojan at Universal Assembly Unit and Ed Pearce at Foster + Partners

An epic journey such as this begins with a simple question – ours was to find 'remoteness' in a world of global connectedness, exchange and auto-accessibility. We began our search in the epicentre of London, tracing an ever-changing line out to the furthest reaches of Great Britain, beyond the Outer Hebrides, towards a land where people evolved in tangential directions, and the sky, sea and land were biblical in proportion. En route to this elusive destination we unearthed remoteness on the islands of Skye, Harris and the uninhabited and mystical Isles of Shiant.

——In term one, we made provocative and evocative films that explored the idea of remoteness within the city. These were premièred at the world-famous Curzon Cinema in Soho in full 5.1 Dolby immersion. We then extended this inquiry through to craft, visuals and assemblage over the course of our island odyssey. Architecture was forged through the meditation between the made and the illusory, the tactile and the imagined, the artefact and the allegory, and the haptic and the lucid. Buildings that enhance the genius loci were cultured and proposed through this dialogue.

——Our Year 3 students invented their islands, architecture and inhabitants. Our Year 2 students proposed buildings on the Isle of Shiant – an island gifted to a boy on his 21st birthday to live on for the past 21 years. The emergent building propositions are experienced through drawings, images, relics, instruments, junctions, soundscapes, episodes, details, crops, scenes and moments. UG3 posits an architecture that is fragmentary and implicit rather than whole and explicit. To guide us on this adventure we ran masterclasses in Premiere Pro, After Effects, Avid Pro Tools, Auditions, Microstation 3D and other beasts such as Rhino and Grasshopper. We brought in rolling conversations with experts in the field. We would like to thank sincerely all the critics, designers and guiding lights for their elegant ideas, vision and generous input across the year.

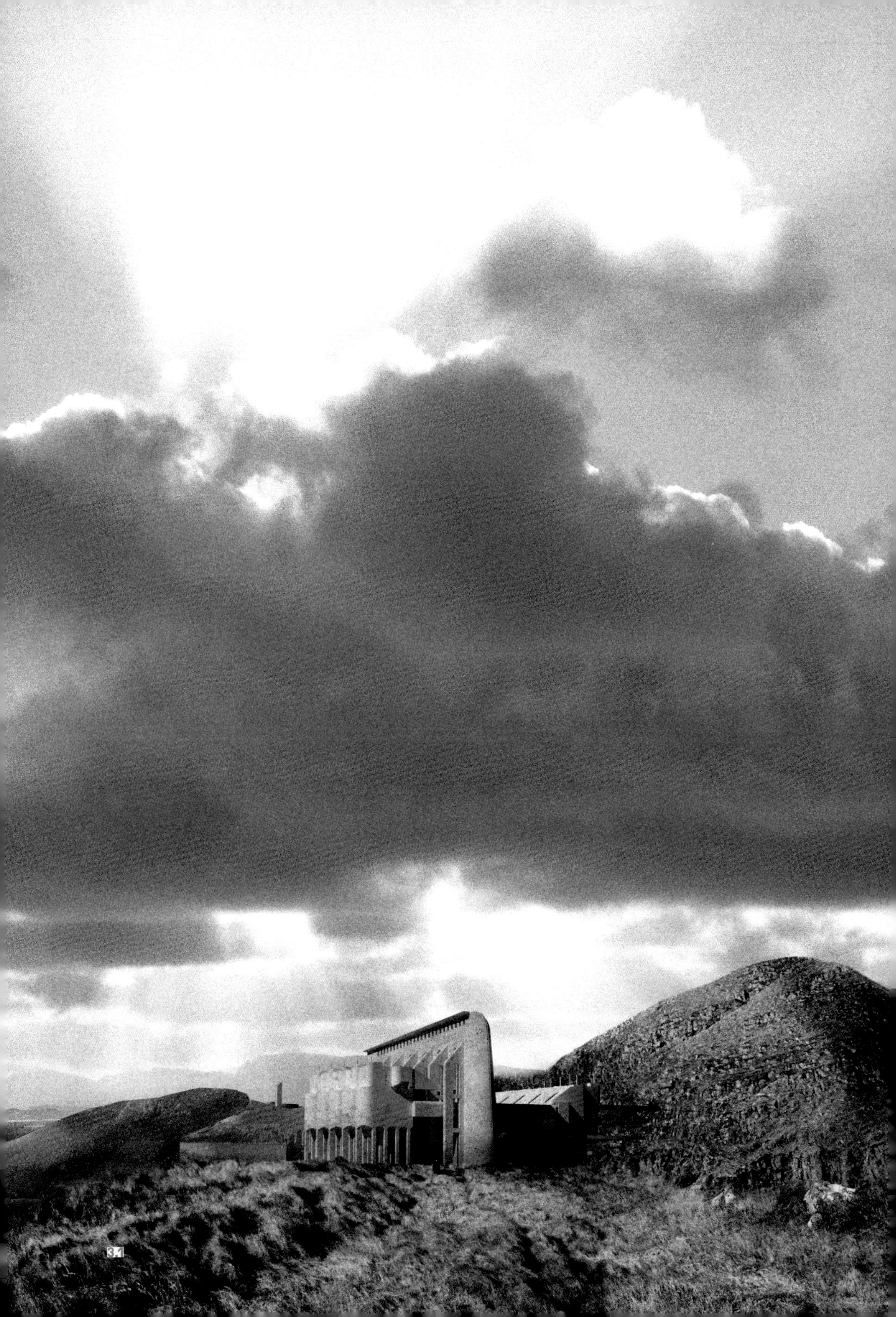

3.1

Figs. 3.1 – 3.6 Elliot Nash Y2, 'Charterhouse for the Carthusian Nuns', The Shiant Isles, Outer Hebrides. Solitude in Community: A Charterhouse for the Shiant Isles'. Followers of the Carthusian order lead the strictest eremitic life, dedicating their time to absolute prayer. The canonical hours govern the rhythm and rituals of the sisterhood. The project adapts these hours to rules of architecture, and aims to create the sense of the superfluity of nuns without the need for visual encounters, allowing a pure, worshipful dedication. The architecture celebrates the biblical Hebridean light as a monument of the basalt rock, a site for pilgrimage for the Carthusian commitment.

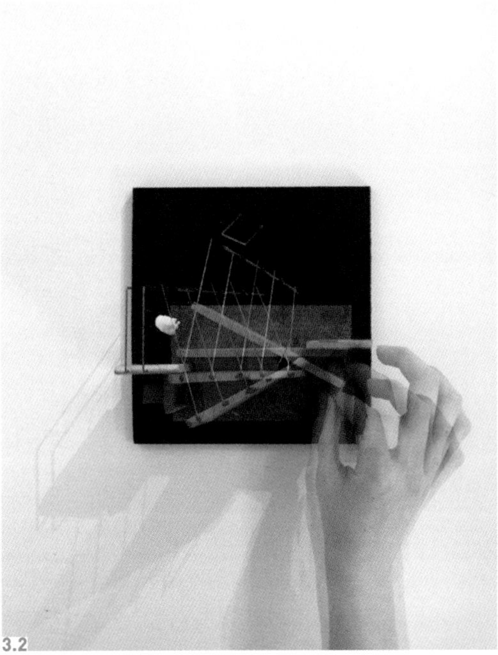
3.2

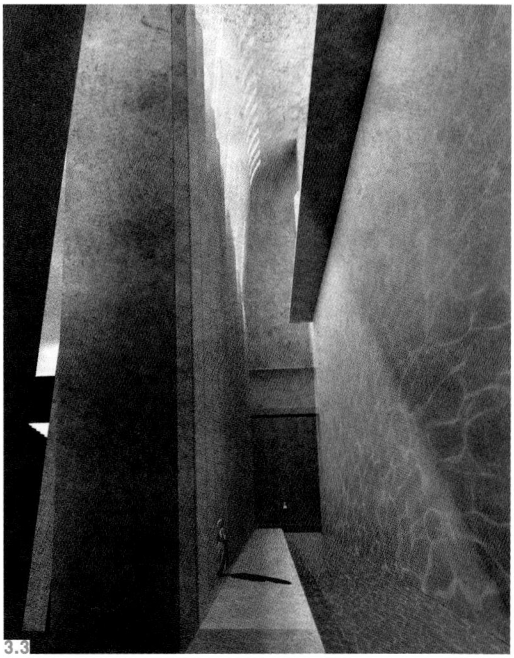
3.3

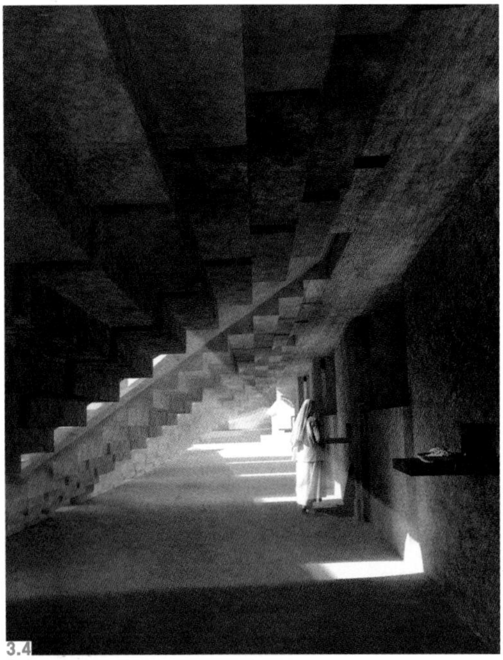
3.4

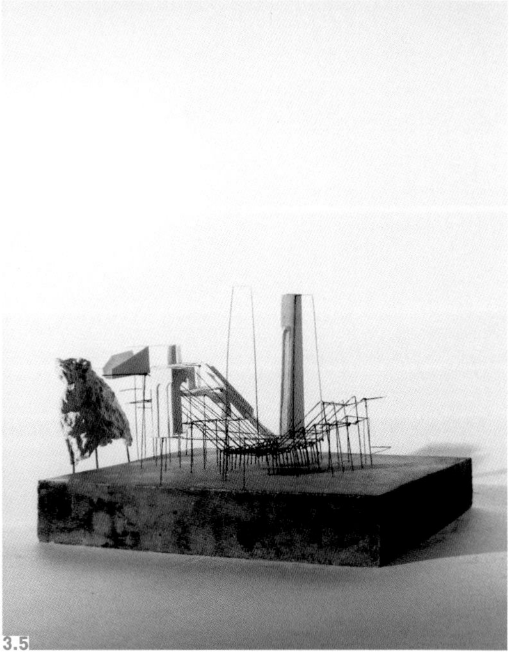
3.5

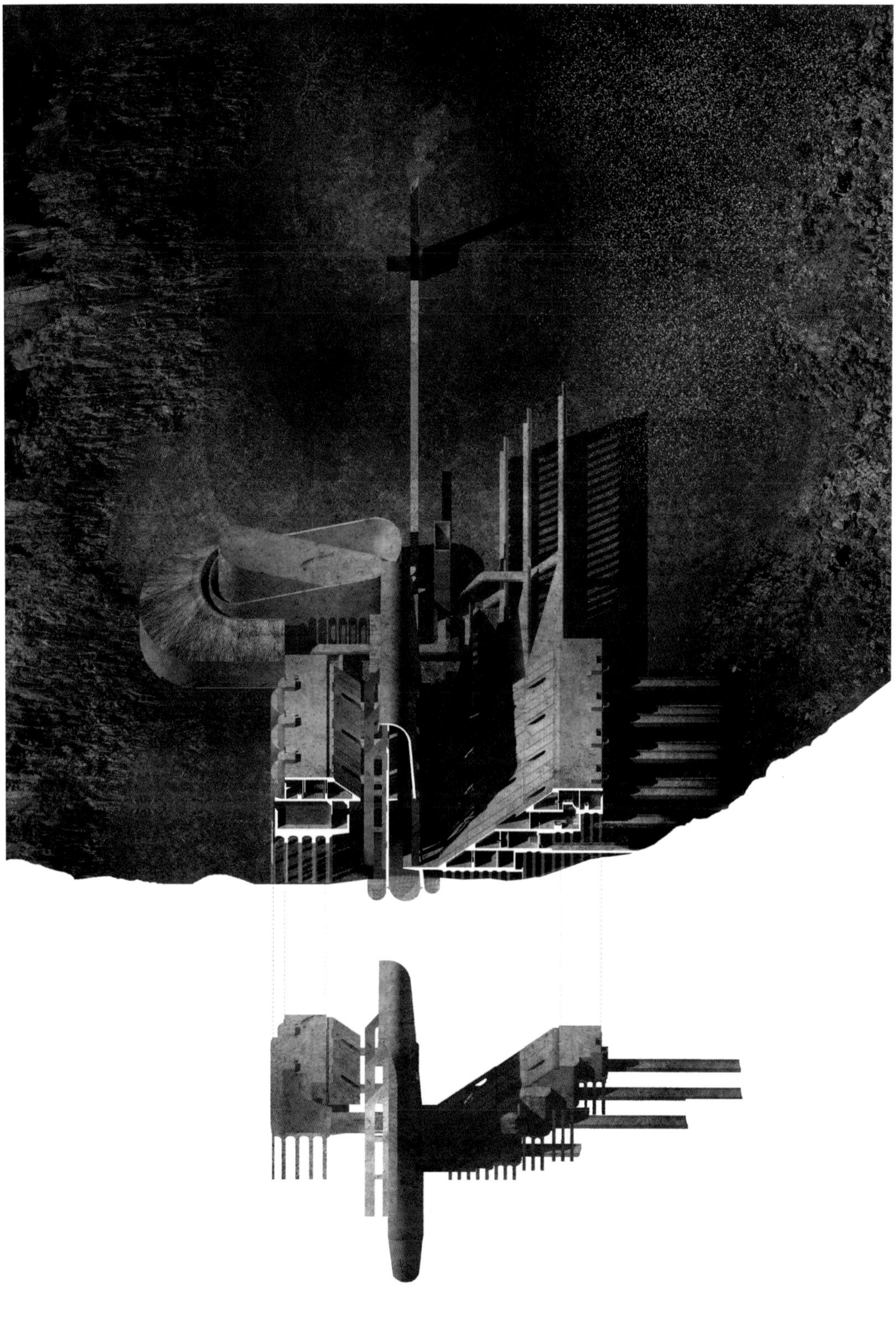

3.6

Fig. 3.7 Marysia Chodzen Y3 'Terra Creatura Masonry Institute', The Shiant Isles, Outer Hebrides. An apprentice's summer school in basalt masonry. **Fig.3.8 Peter Feehily** Y3 'The Illuminatus Coniculum', Isle of Skye. Country house and global headquarters for the Illuminati. The project explores ideas of power control and deception housing an archive, debating chamber and accommodation. **Fig. 3.9 Harry Pizzey** Y2 'Infectious Diseases Vault', The Shiant Isles, Outer Hebrides. A facility holding the last samples of eradicated diseases such as Smallpox. **Fig. 3.10 Georgia May Jaeckle** Y2 'Film : Thresholds YXZ'. A uniquely abstract study of the Barbican complex in London, this three-minute film was a mesmerising and saturated exploration into spatiality, time and vector. **Figs. 3.11 – 3.13 Yuanchu Yi** Y3 'A Micronation on The Shiant Isles', Outer Hebrides. An illusory film set creating the impression of a larger organisation through carefully positioned camera views.

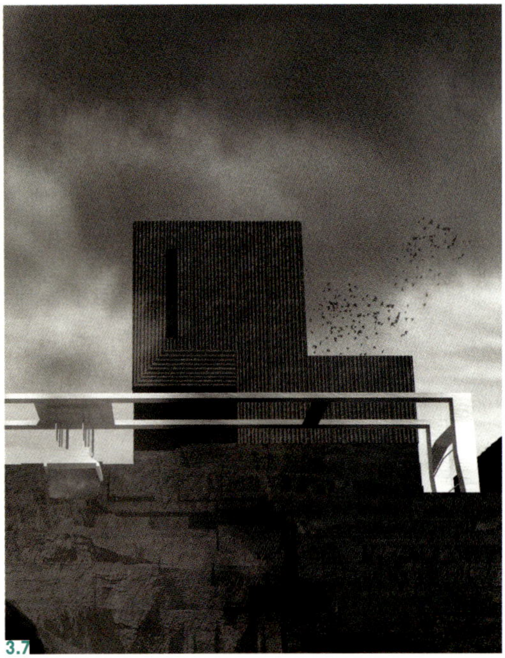

3.7

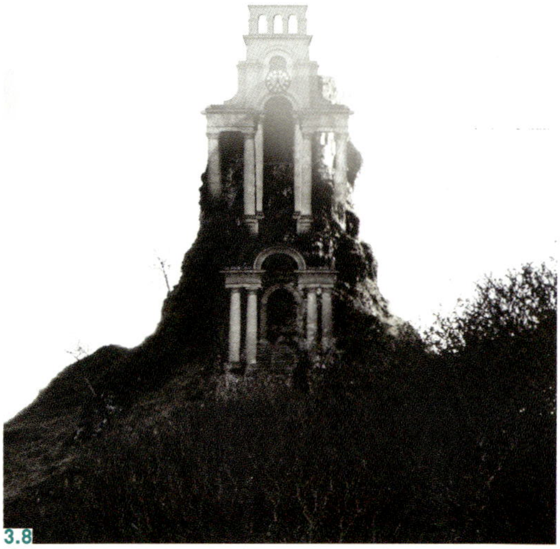

3.8

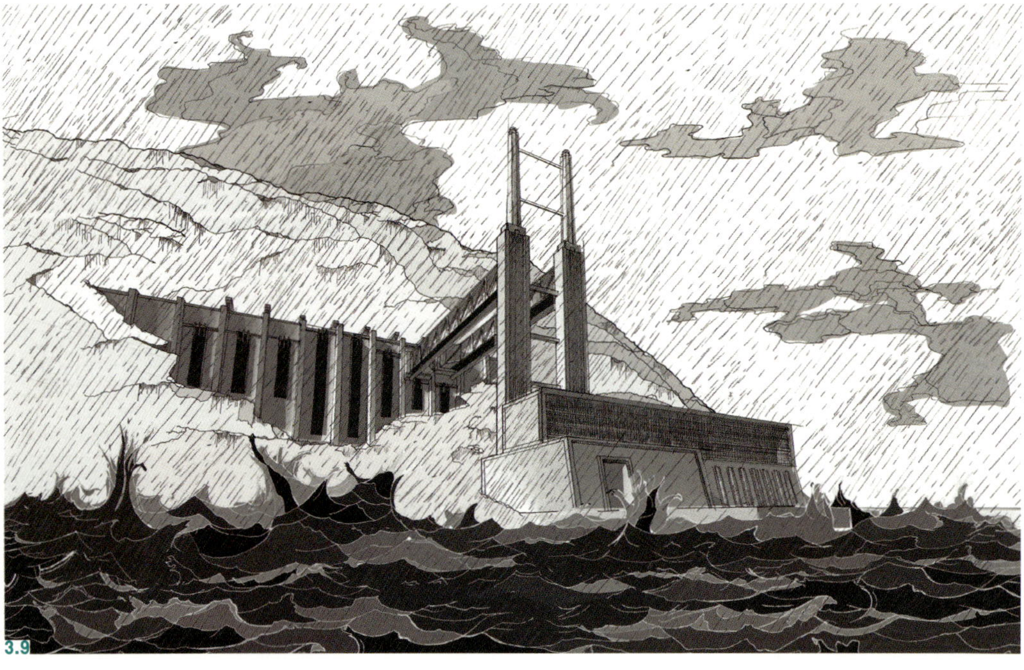

3.9

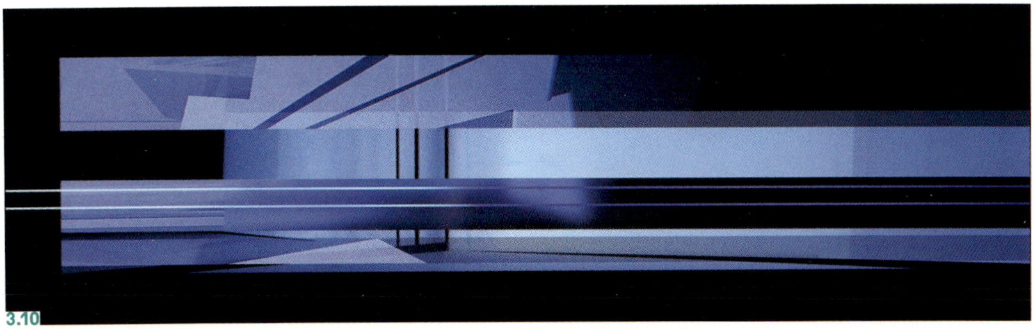
3.10

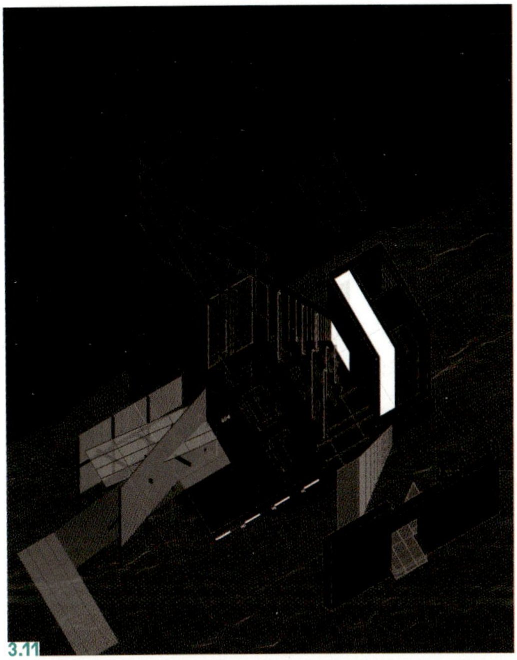
3.11

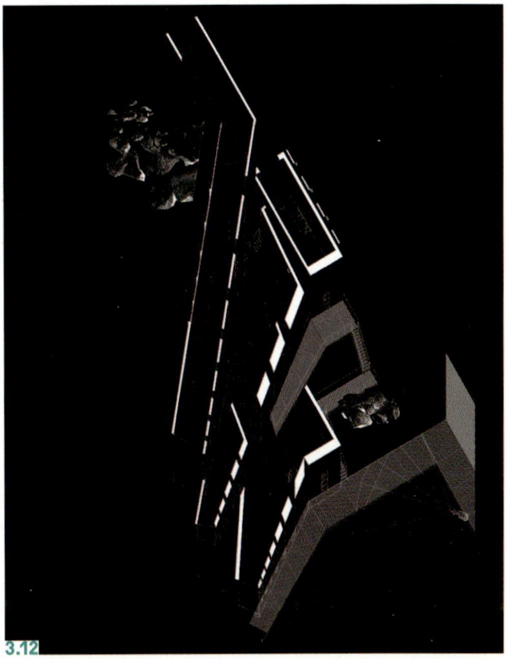
3.12

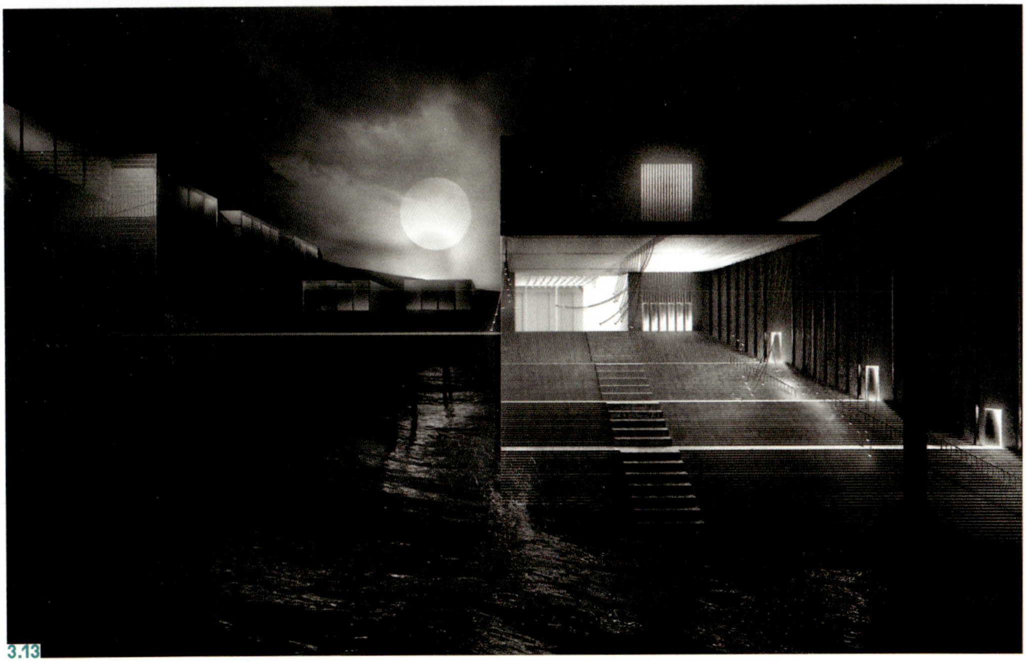
3.13

Figs. 3.14 – 3.18 Shona Sharma Y3 '24-Hour Theatre', Uig, Isle of Skye. An engaging investigation into kinetic architecture creates a shifting backdrop for a theatre that adapts and responds to the changing lives of its occupants/actors. The play tells a story of a couple's life trajectory, from being happily married, the introduction of children, infidelity, infirmity and finally death. As an interpretation of Lifetime Homes Standards the project posits an alternate view of how an adaptable dwelling may respond to different periods of life experience in an activated sequence of four houses or sets. The audience are drawn through each house under, over and within the walls as if eavesdropping, taken over rotting timber foundations to the ending sequence of hovering above the death bed.

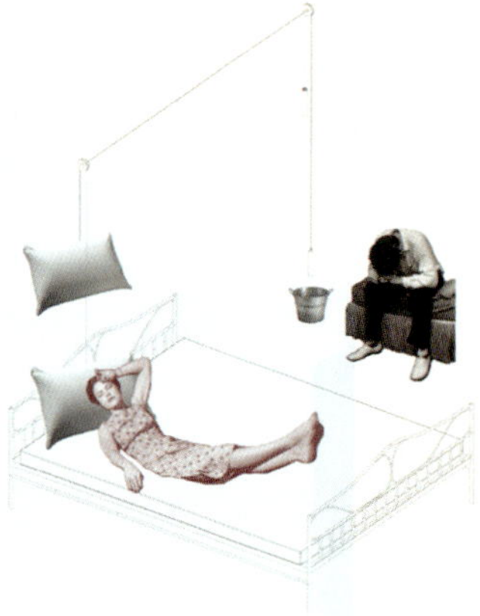

3.14

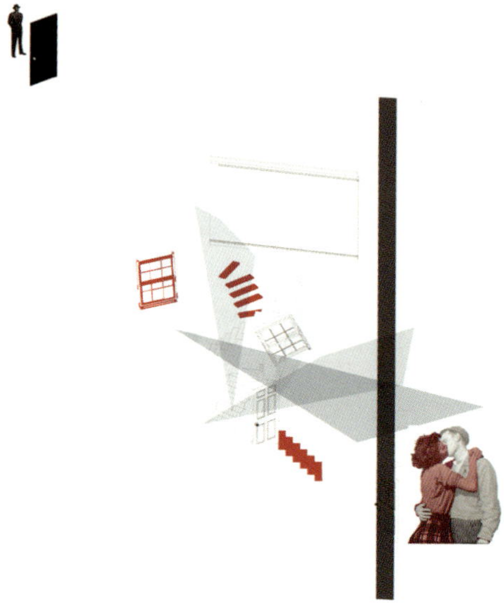

3.15

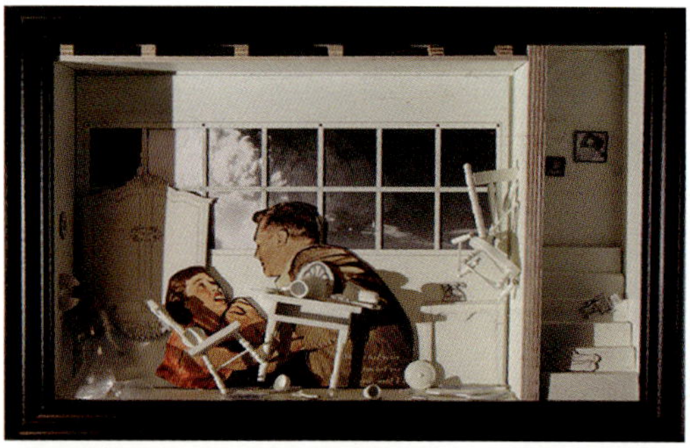

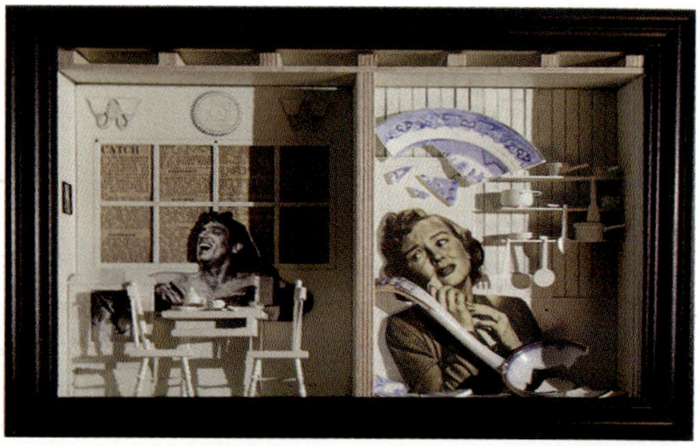

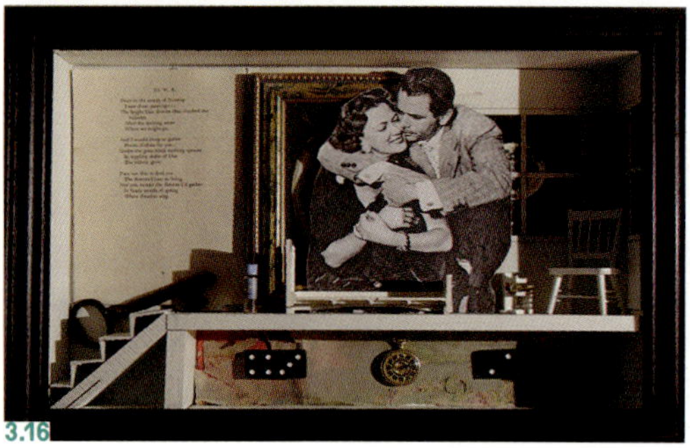

3.16

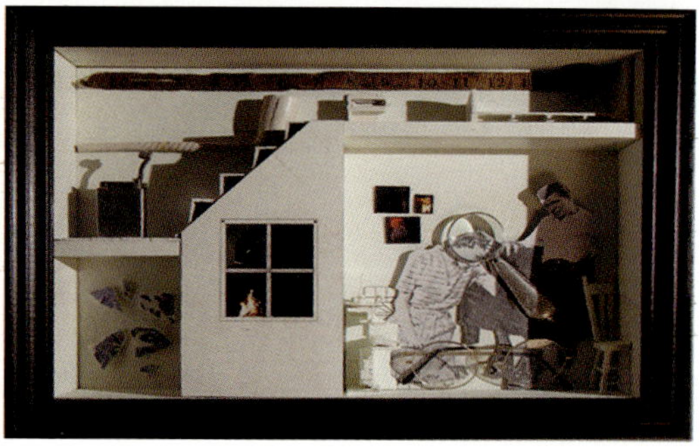

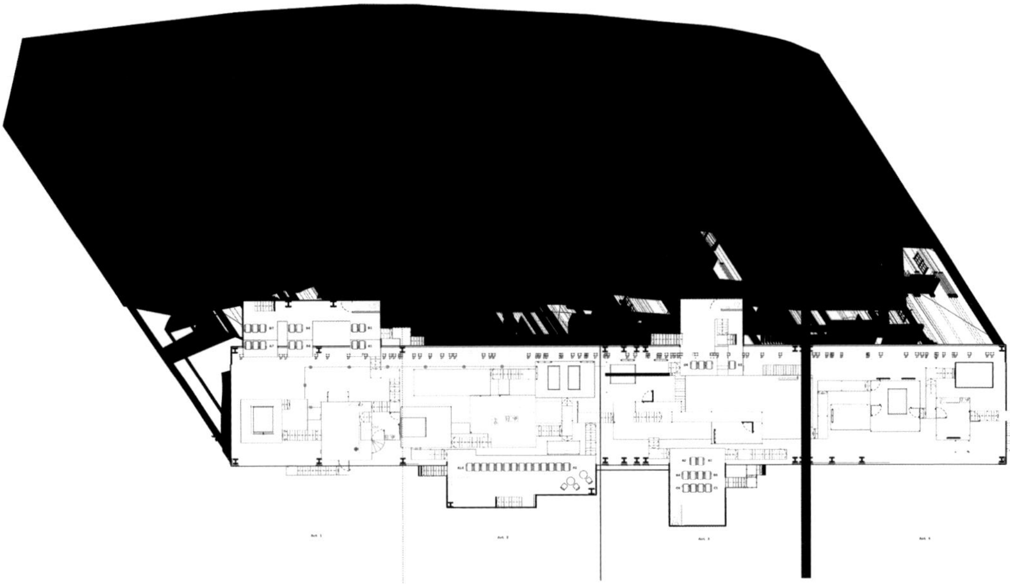

3.17

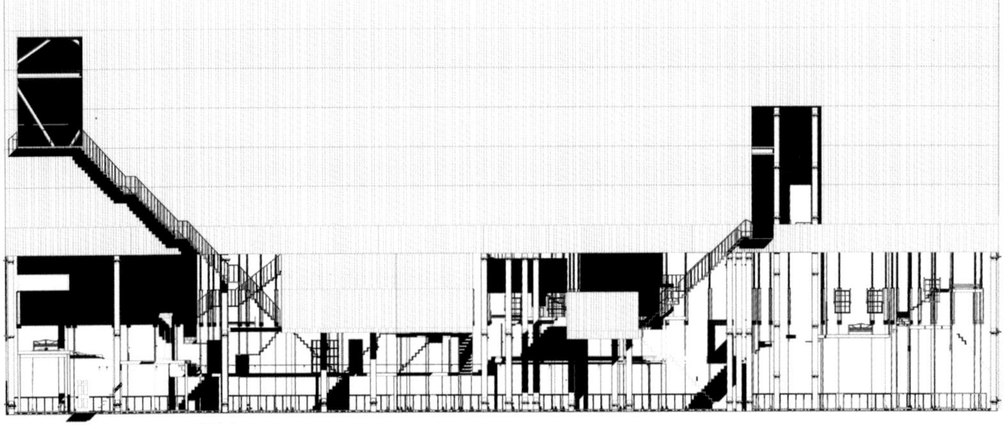

3.18

Fig. 3.19 Freya Bolton Y2 'Shiant Tweed Factory Housing', the Shiant Isles, Outer Hebrides. The project evolves the cottage industry of Harris Tweed to an industrial scale to explore relationships between communal living, domesticity and workplace. The programme was explored through a sequence of digitally stitched vignettes and drawings. **Figs. 3.20 – 3.21 Conor Clarke** Y3 'Cryogenics Institute', Isle of Pabbay, Outer Hebrides. The facility creates a landscape of remembrance for loved ones and descendants through engagement with projected holographic sequences of those held in stasis below ground. **Figs. 3.22 – 3.23 Georgia Jaeckle** Y2 'Foundation for Walter De Maria', The Shiant Isles, Outer Hebrides. As a series of connected galleries built around principal works by the artists, the programme generates a sequential experience collaged against landscape, horizon and light. **Fig. 3.24 Samuel Napleton** 'Offshore Dwellings', no specific site. The project speculates on future offshore inhabitation as a result of extreme rises in sea level.

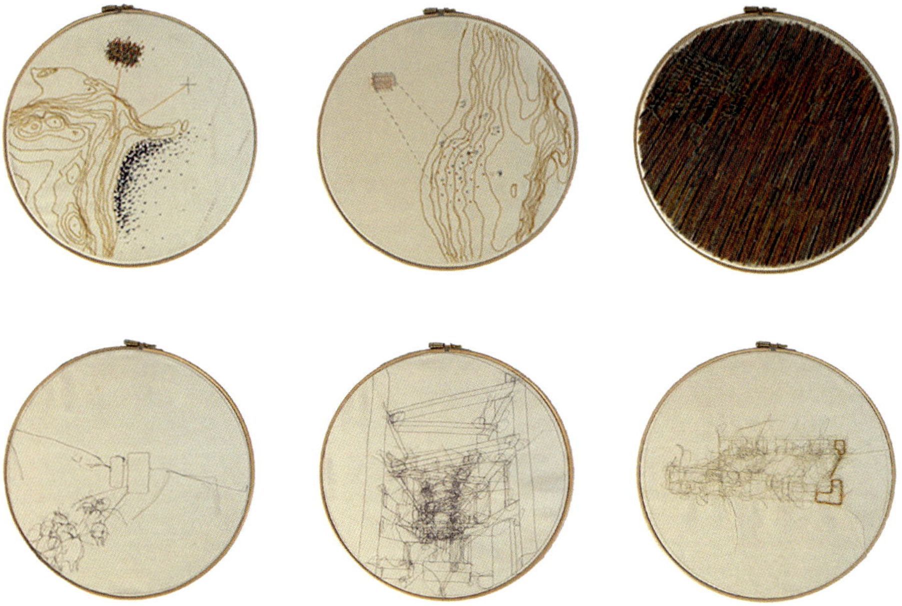

3.19

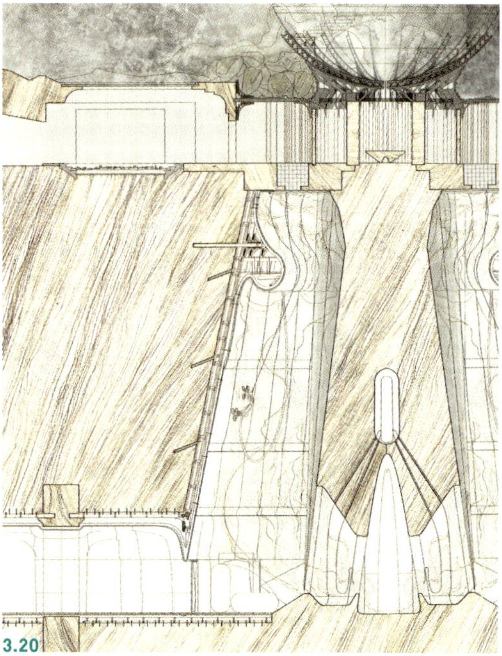

3.20

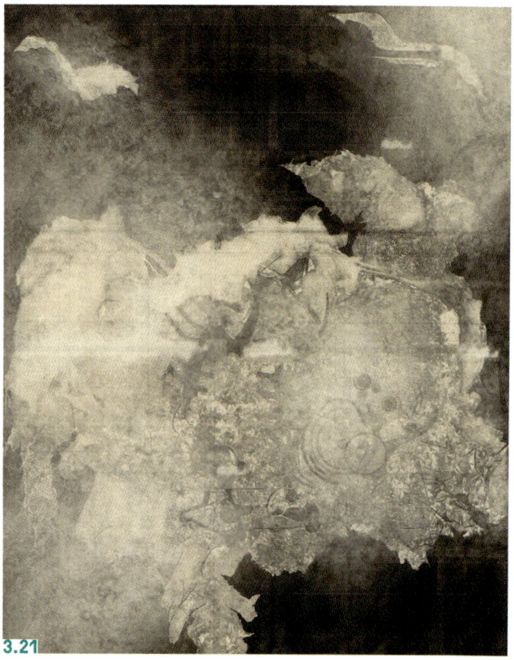

3.21

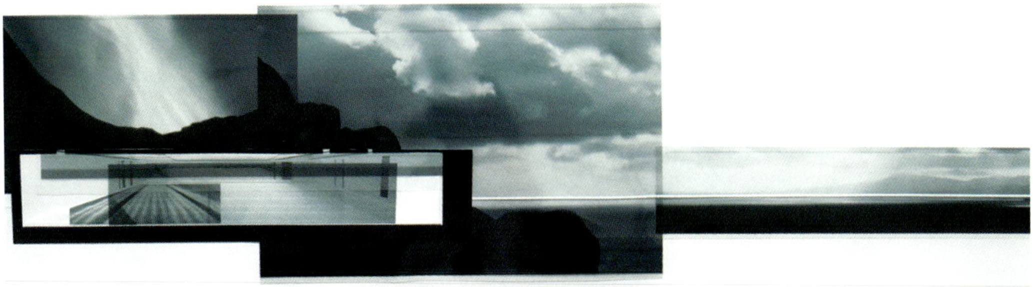

3.22

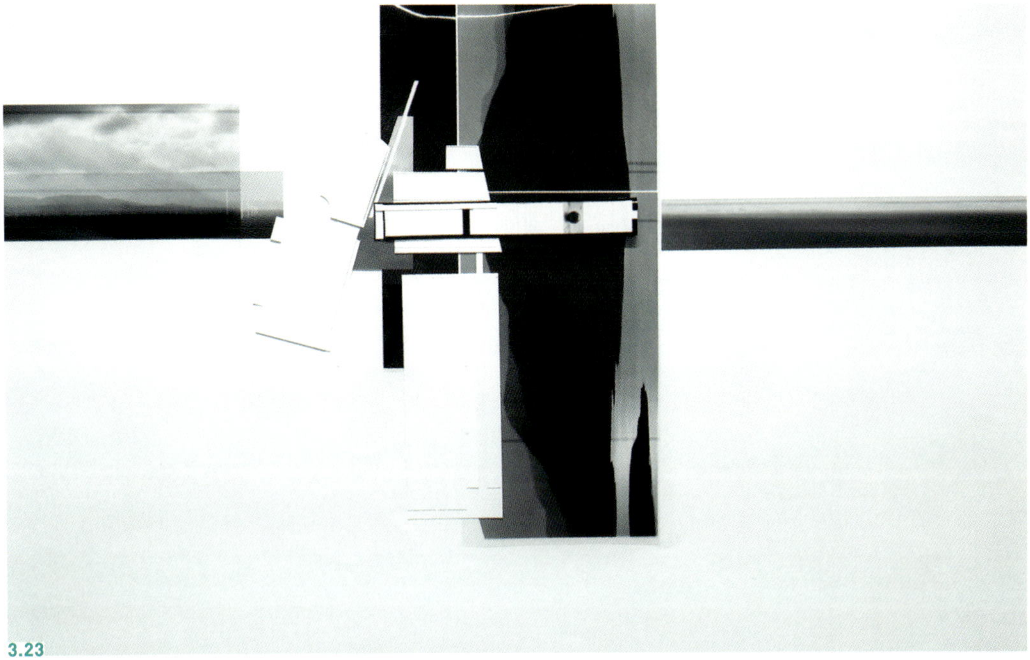

3.23

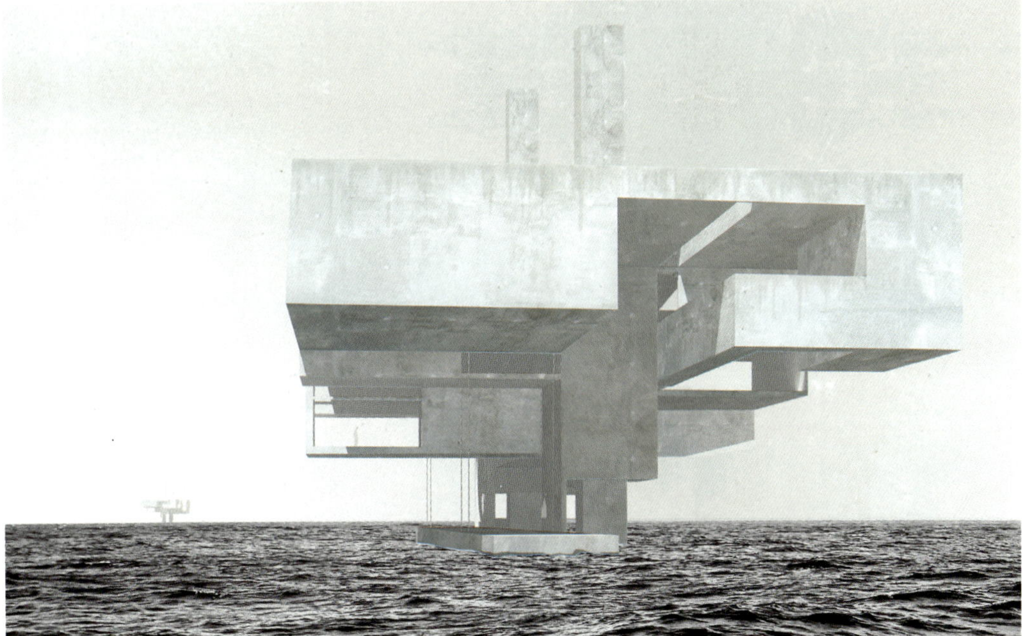

3.24

UG4

Otakutecture

Ana-Monrabal Cook, Luke Pearson

Year 2
Hohgun Choi, Nicholas Chrysostomou, Arthur Harmsworth, Will Kirkby, Jimmy Liu, Oliver Mitchell, Aikawa Mok, Luke Sanders, Sarmad Suhail

Year 3
Milly Black, Sam Davies, Alex Findley, Emma Jurczynski, Adam Moqrane, Afrodite Moustroufis, Andrew Riddell

Many thanks to Gavin Hutchison for his continued help and advice as our technical tutor. And to German Casado, Greg Kythreotis (Shedworks Interactive) and Sam McGill (Studio Archetype) for their media workshops and support

Thanks to our critics: Laura Allen, Elisa Bertoja, Matthew Butcher, Ian Chalk, Tom Coward, Stephen Gage, Penelope Haralambidou, Gavin Hutchison, Will Jefferies, Carlos Jiménez Cenamor, Diony Kypraiou, Ifigeneia Liangi, Sam McGill, Christopher Pierce, Dan Scoulding, Bob Sheil, and Sandra Youkhana

Special thanks to: Akihiko Niiho, Keigo Kobayashi and all at Waseda University, Momoyo Homma (Arakawa + Gins Tokyo Office) and Massimo Baracco (Prada Japan) for their hospitality and guidance during our trip to Tokyo

From *Godzilla* to *Blade Runner*, Tokyo is often held as an architectural synecdoche of the future, a city symbolising the relationship between technology and the metropolis – both seductive and uneasy. Nowhere is this tension more present than in the culture of *otaku*. As a term roughly translating into 'nerd', Japan's otaku population throw themselves into pop culture proliferated by technology, obsessing over virtual anime pop stars, manga, videogame worlds, trains, modified cars or even the recreation of historical Japanese periods. Cultural critic Hiroki Azuma argues that otaku creativity is both heir to Edo-era Japanese aesthetics, and a Japanese domestication of Americanised pop culture. At best such passion drives the country's creativity and economy, at worst it is symptomatic of a population withdrawing from the reality of modern Japan, betraying the fragility of the nation's identity.

——Otaku also means 'your home' and is a polite form of 'you' – equating a person with their architectural space of residence. Otaku's multiple identities remind us of the weird and wonderful bastardisations of culture that sit just beneath the city's surface. Otaku culture challenges boundaries between actual and virtual, fact and fiction, and author versus consumer. As *Otakutects* we applied these tensions and distortions in the design of new architectural typologies.

——UG4 questions the status of architecture in our image-saturated digital world. This year we challenged the boundaries of architectural media through workshops with professionals from the visualisation, animation and videogame industries. Exposing relationships between modern technology and their historical precedents, we blended real, fictional, technological and historical approaches. Projects collapsed distinctions between architecture, craft, nature and super-nature. Otaku approaches saw students embody the qualities of gods in videogames, turn bedrooms into landscapes of scrolling parallax drawings, create spatiotemporal comics, design foldable buildings for slot sites, machine pavilion-scale Noh masks and plan post-apocalyptic playgrounds.

——By extending these obsessions and idiosyncrasies into the design of a building, students worked towards synthesising a piece of true *Otakutecture*. Research methodologies developed in term one were carried into the production of unique building projects that questioned the nature of obsession in design, becoming transcriptions of our fascinations – from crystallising the typology of Tokyo's police kobans, through a museum that becomes a secret pilgrimage for a cult, to an artificial landscape containing hidden spaces for Tokyo's women to break their cultural bonds.

——Embracing technology, obsession, tradition, perversion and malfunction, we jumped into the symbolic overload of the modern city and emerged as Otakutects!

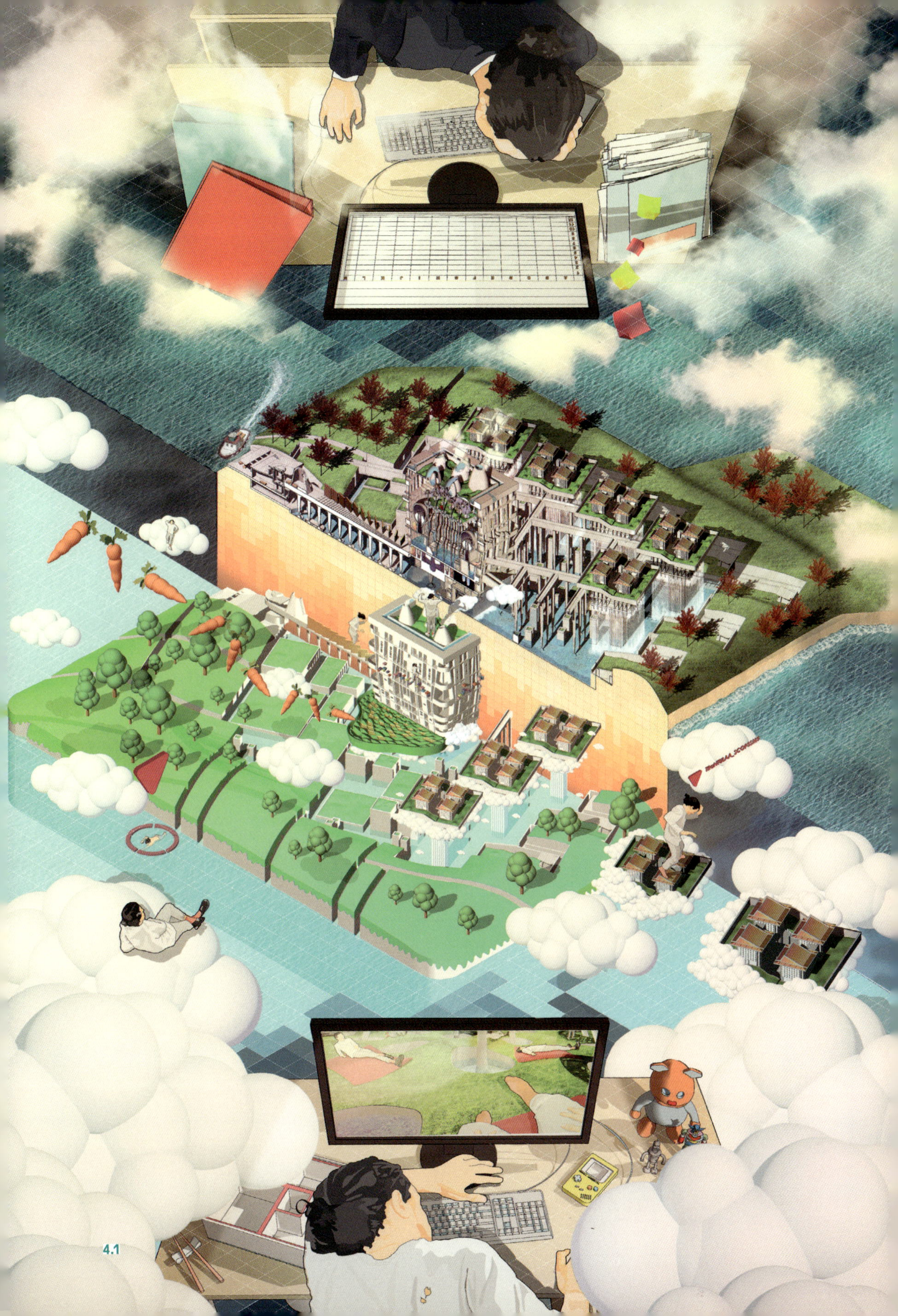

4.1

Fig. 4.1 Alexander Findley Y3, 'Habitat AFK'. The project explores 'hikikomori,' homebound videogame and manga addicts, numbering over one million in Japan. It aims to reintegrate the Hikikomori as functional members of society through the appliance of hyperstimulation, gamification and other escapist techniques to create architectures. **Fig. 4.2 Afrodite Moustroufis** Y3, 'The Sounds of Kyudo'. Designed for the 2020 Tokyo Olympics, the project is a public pavilion exhibiting Kyudo, a traditional form of Japanese archery with an emphasis on the sound of the shot. The building becomes a sonic landscape framing the archers. **Figs. 4.3 – 4.4 Adam Moqrane** Y3, 'Muology'. Drawn from 'Mu' theory, the project investigates breaking the city down into components of urbanism, before redistributing them along urban rules developed in the Unity game engine. **Fig. 4.5 Emma Jurczynski** Y3, 'The Hashigakari Noh School'. Sited in Shibuya, the building is based around five elements of Noh performance; acting, instrumental music, chorus, mask carving and costumes and stagecraft. Through its environmental mediations it recreates the open-air Noh stages of Miyajima island. **Fig. 4.6 Emma Jurczynski** Y3, 'Noh-ify'. This project uses the protocols of the emotionless Noh mask to explore architectural façades. As Noh actors tilt their heads to make emotions through light and shadow, so the façades communicate emotion through the sun's passage across the course of a day. These CNC milled masks allow one to become an architectural Noh character.

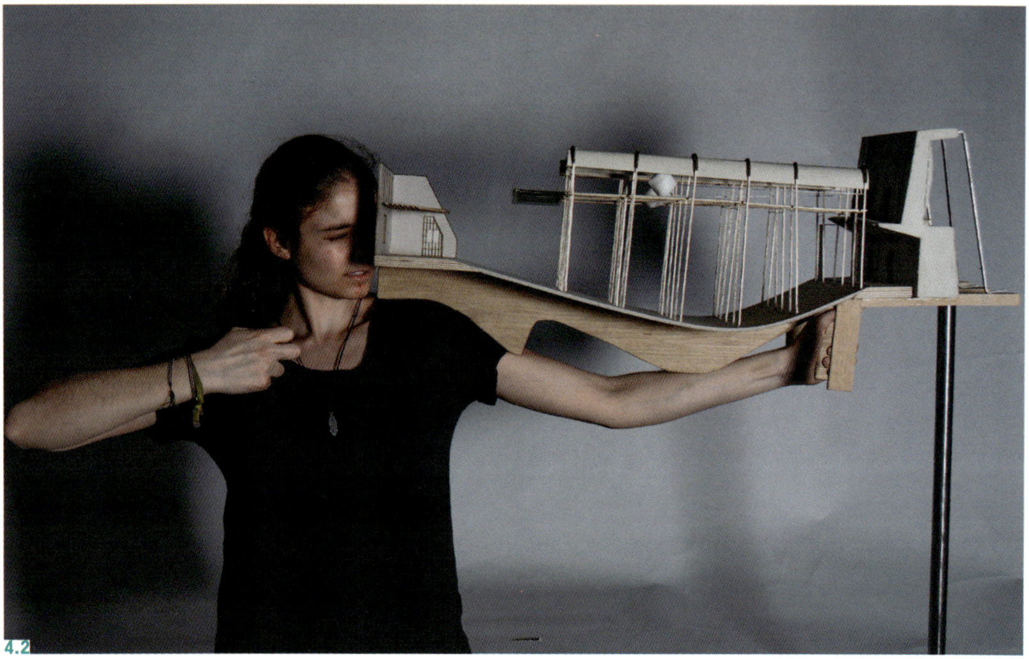

4.2

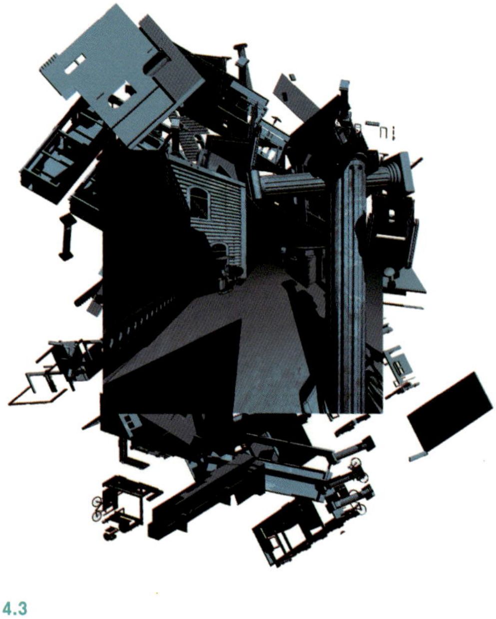

4.3

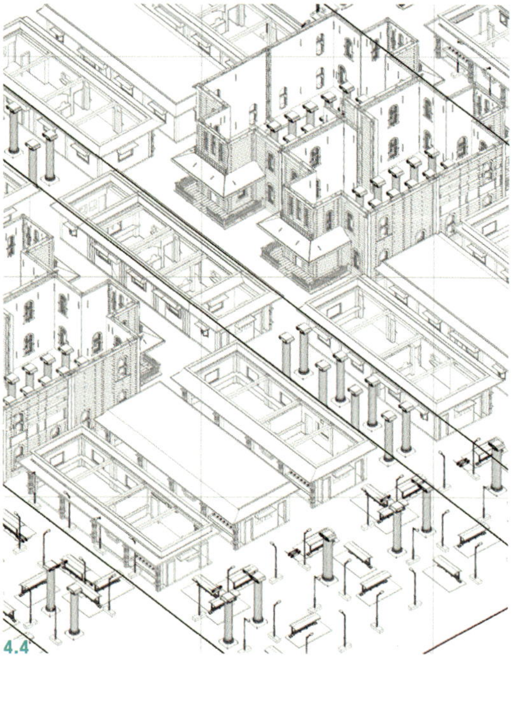

4.4

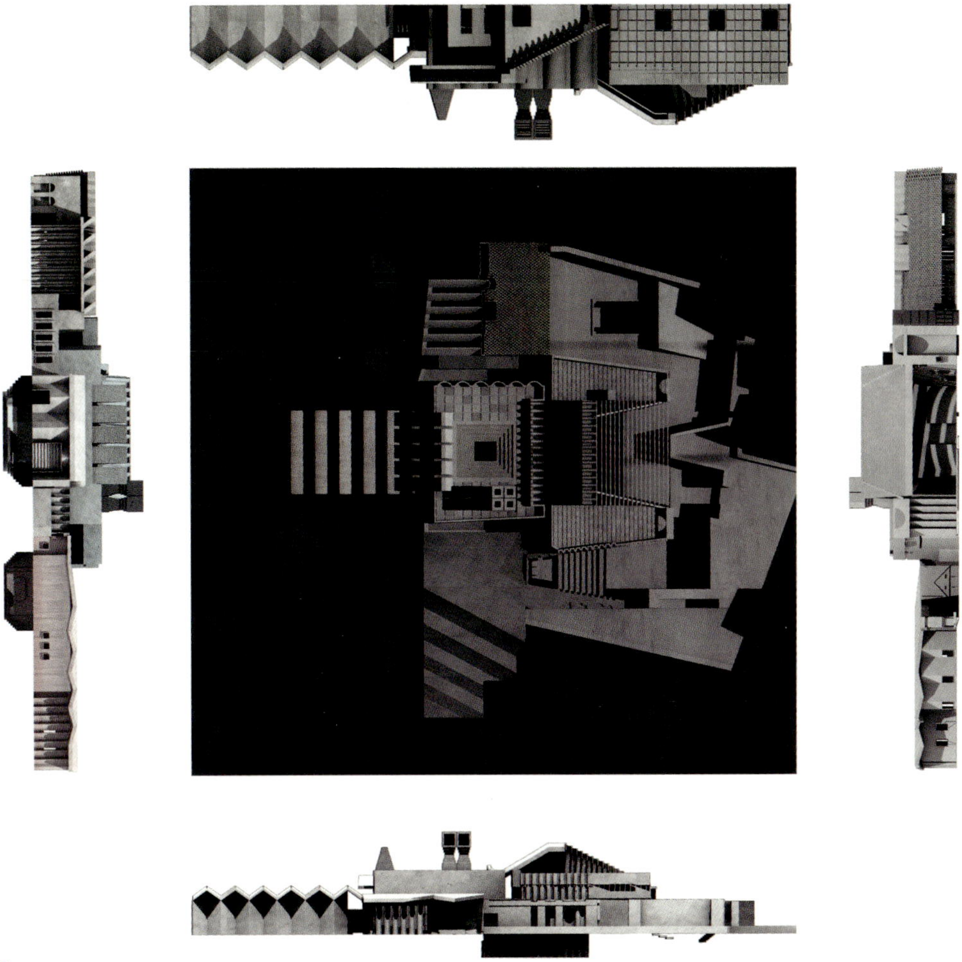

4.5

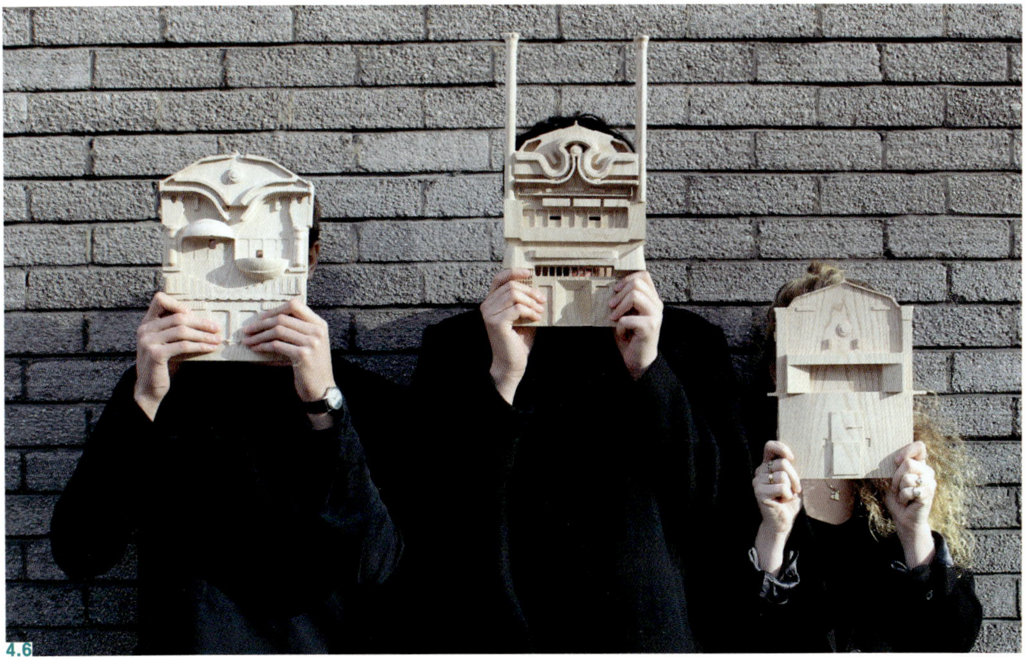

4.6

Fig. 4.7 Andrew Riddell Y3, 'Baby Bunker'. The building is designed in response to the crisis of birth rates in Japan and children becoming a scarce 'natural resource'. Inspired by Froebel Block toys, the daycare centre reinforces Japanese educational attitudes that teach children to respect, and even love, seismic activity as an experience. Constructed from hybrid concrete and silicon materials, under tremors the building will crack to reveal luminous colurful and soft materials, augmenting a playscape of blocks at a smaller scale. **Fig. 4.8 Nicholas Chrysostomou** Y2, 'Tenkei's Natural History Museum'. Yamato-No-Miya is a Japanese cult founded by Ajiki Tenkei which is preoccupied with saving humanity through purifying the environment, finding deities in stones, water and trees. The project provides a safe place of worship for the followers of Yamato-No-Miya protecting them from public prejudice. The museum is a forest of columns containing discrete pavilions, each showcasing one of the Yamato-No-Miya deities hidden in plain sight amongst other similar objects. **Figs. 4.9 – 4.11 Aikawa Mok** Y2, 'Meido Dance House'. A dance school for Butoh, a form of contemporary Japanese dance that emphasises non-Western aesthetics, taboo subjects and bizarre settings. Sited in westernised Roppongi, the building becomes an embodiment of the seven trials of Meido – the Buddhist 'purgatory'. It is designed through a series of choreographic and symbolic transcriptions of the trials of Meido. These trials are translated into articulated spaces to create an architecture that augments the body in different ways as a physical manifestation of Butoh.

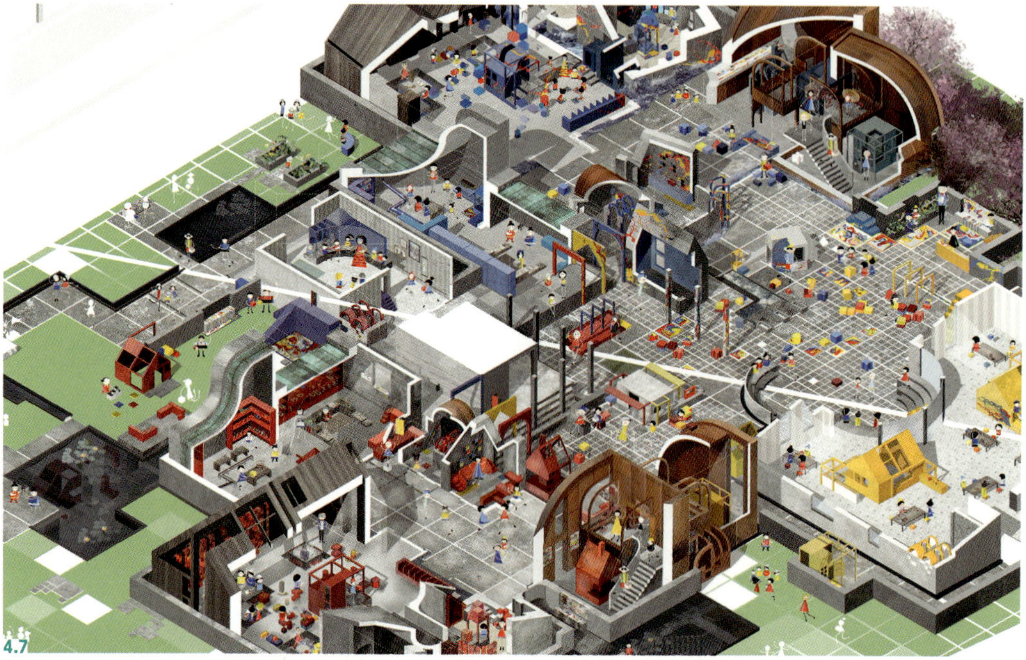

4.7

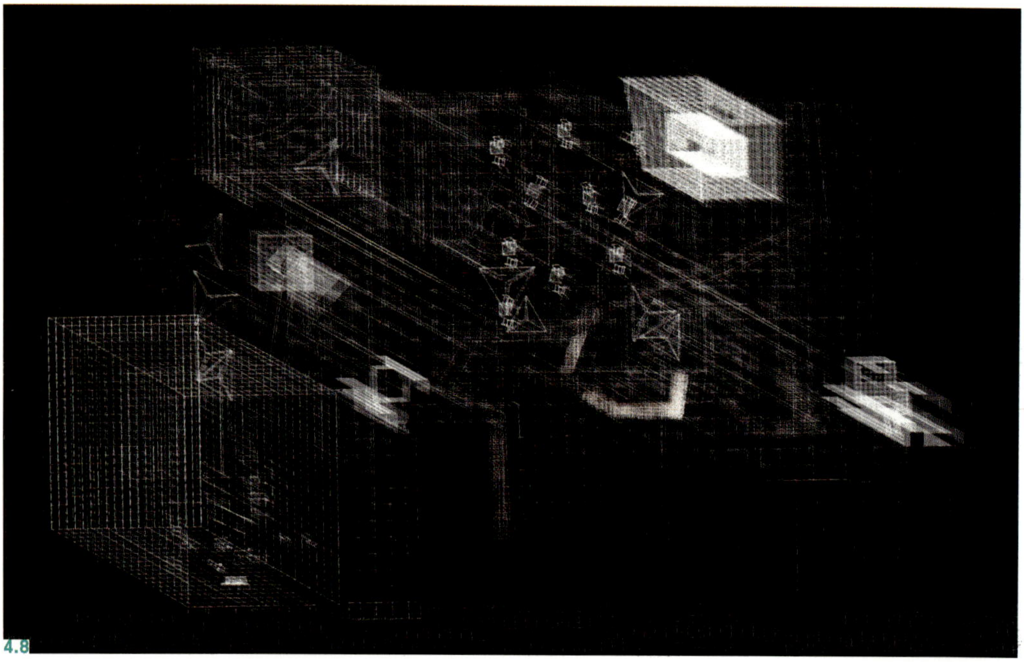

4.8

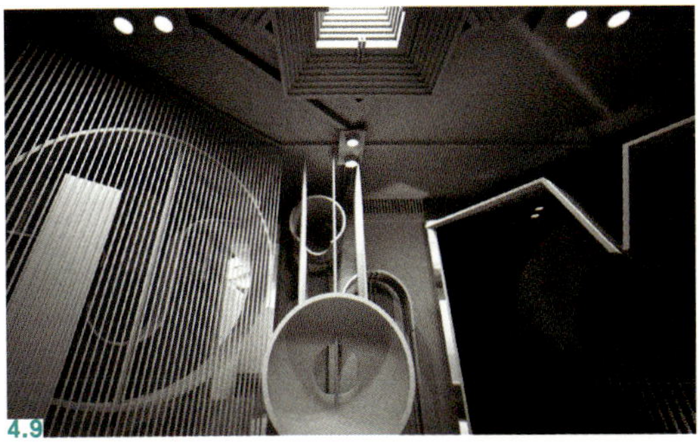

4.9

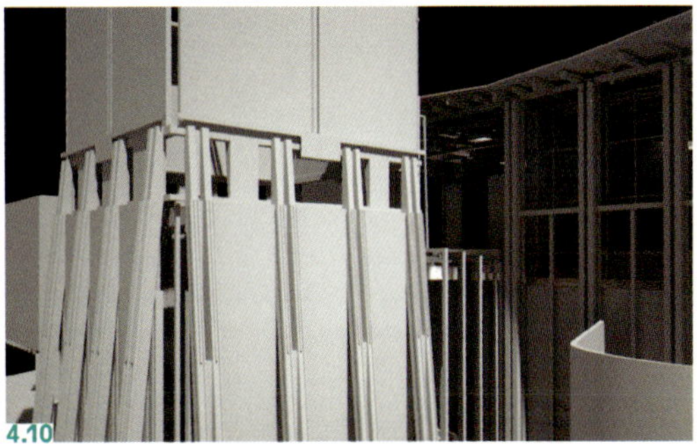

4.10

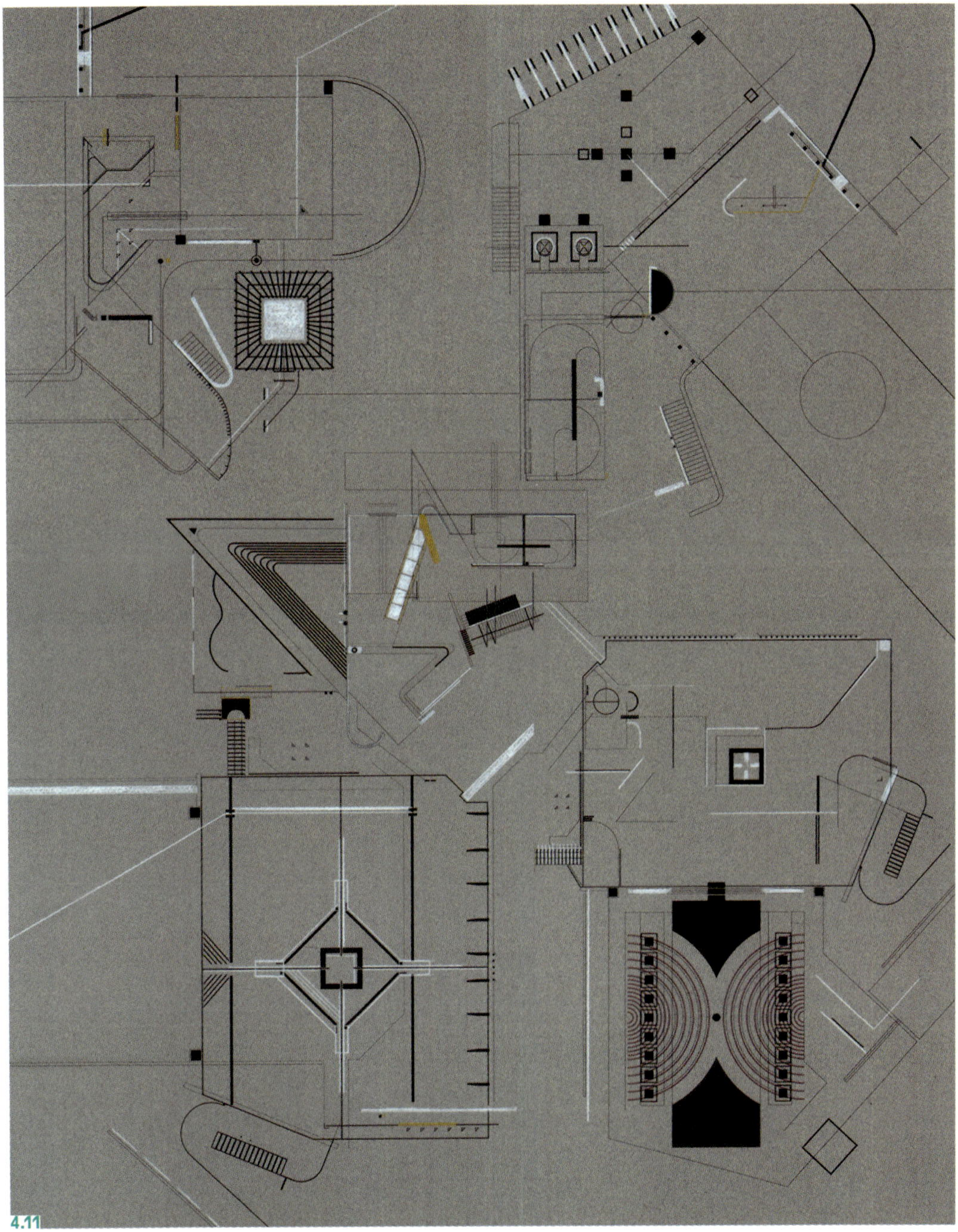

4.11

Figs. 4.12 – 4.13 Sarmad Suhail Y2, 'Tokyo Ritsuban Training Facility'. The project draws from the eclectic typology of Tokyo's Police Kobans (public information cabins). Police officers are retrained in the seven orders of the Bushido code of honour through Kobans that encourage and symbolise Loyalty, Honesty, Courage, Respect, Kindness, Politeness and Integrity. Each Koban is designed externally to reflect contextual themes based on a specific value of Bushido, and internally conditioned to reinforce this value on each of its four resident officers. **Fig. 4.14 Arthur Harmsworth** Y2, 'Studio Arukadia'. An animation studio located in Tama. Through structural 'trees' and squeaking nightingale floors, the building becomes an internalised environment to fire the imaginations of the animators. **Fig. 4.15 Luke Sanders** Y2, 'Tokyo Netsuke Collection'. A collection of 15 3D printed Japanese miniatures called netsuke. Traditionally netsuke represented places and experiences of their owner. These contemporary figurines collectively form a journey through modern Tokyo, defining it as a series of miniature territories. **Fig. 4.16 Samuel Davies** Y3, 'NDL Tsundoku'. An extension to the National Library of Japan to deal with the pressures of digitisation. The project frames and architecturally exaggerates the inefficiency of the digitisation process into a celebratory procession. Taking cues from cultural Japanese case studies, the project looks towards architecture that accepts its own eventual redundancy. Through scale model tests, a scheme of designed demolition is devised; a transient flurry of analogue activity that accentuates the physical at the outset of the digital age.

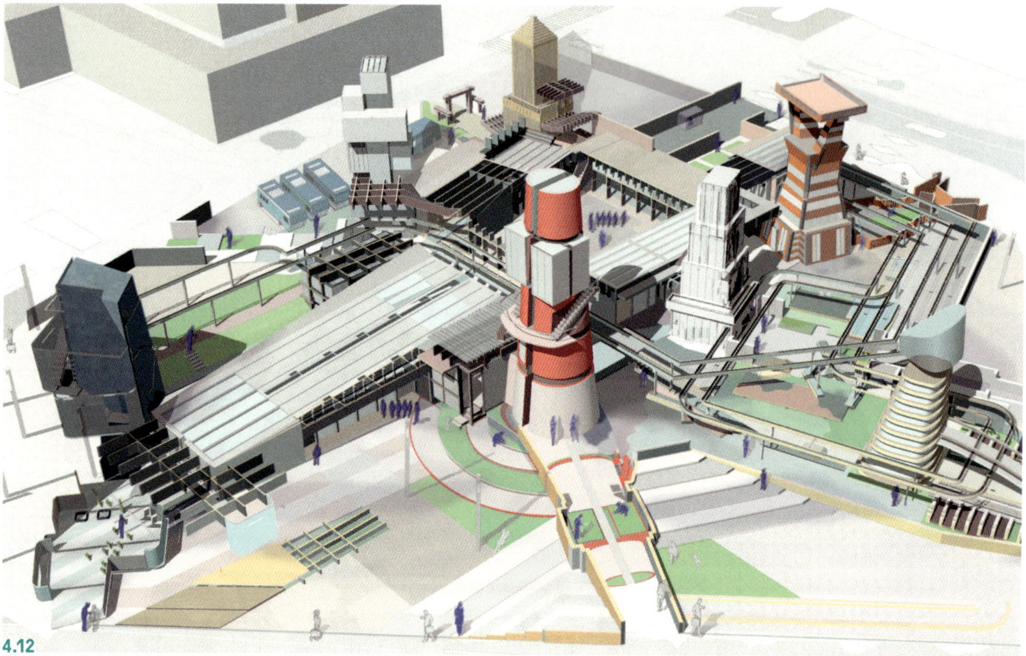

4.12

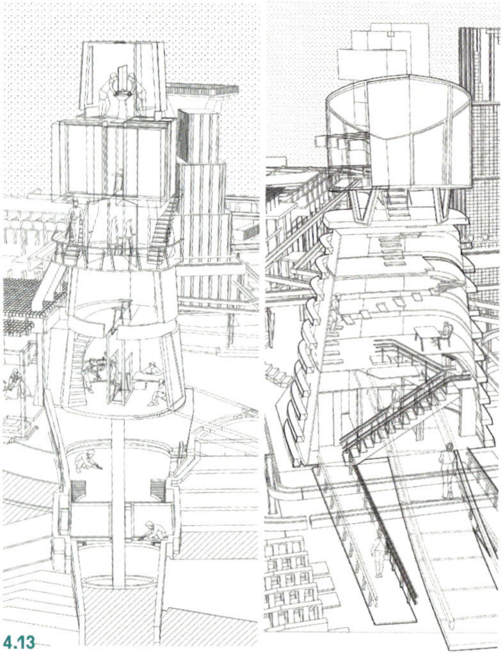

4.13

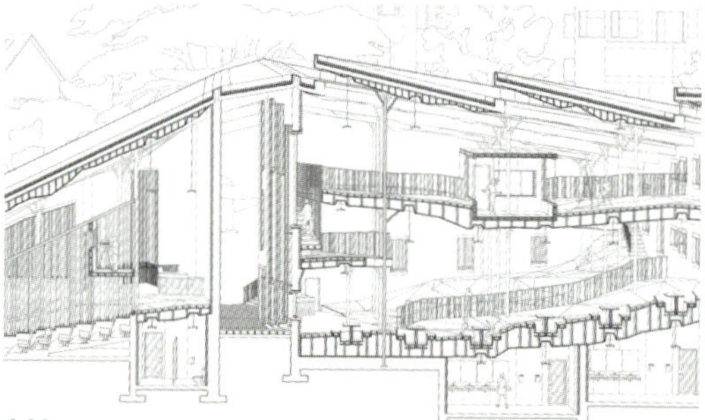

4.14

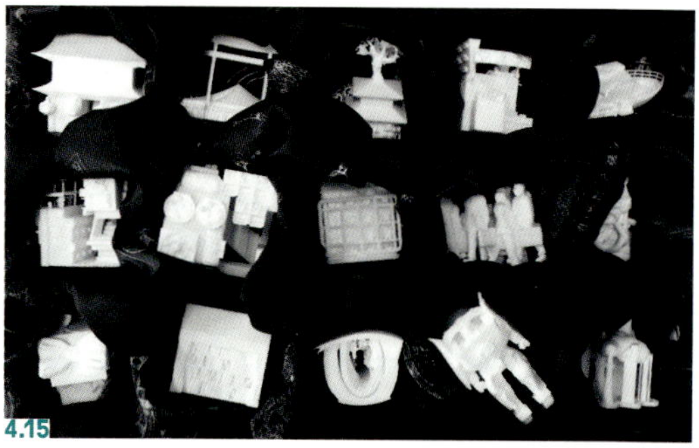

4.15

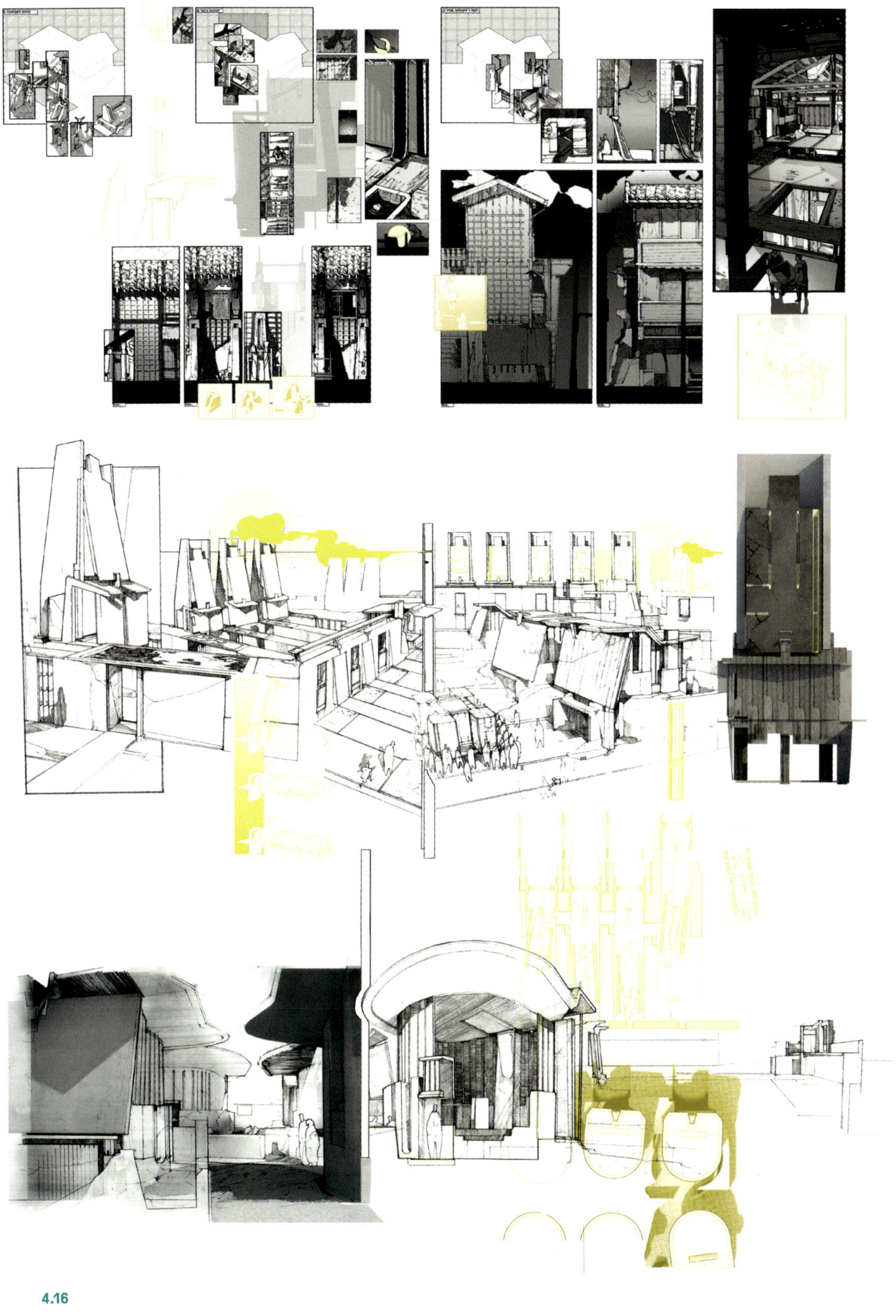

4.16

Fig. 4.17 Hohgun Choi Y2, 'Tsukiji Fishslice'. A hotel for the post-relocation Tsukiji fish market district. Like the market, the building uses an auctioning system – as a method of booking hotel rooms, where guests inspect slices of a hotel room like a dealer assessing a tuna. Each slice becomes a sample of the room's metaphorical fat content, quality and character. **Fig. 4.18 Jimmy Liu** Y2, 'Nihonbashi Totem'. A structure puncturing the layers of Tokyo around the famous Nihonbashi Bridge. The architecture striates the historical layers of the city and protocols of Japanese art from Edo to contemporary Tokyo. **Fig. 4.19 Jimmy Liu** Y2, 'Superflat Sando'. Inspired by Takashi Murakami's 'Superflat' Japanese pop art movement, the project proposes a studio for young artists that blurs the boundary between architecture and its image, becoming a form of inhabitable artwork. **Figs. 4.20 – 4.21 Milly Black** Y3, 'Kyokai Park'. Despite being an advanced global economy, Japan maintains a traditional cultural identity that often restricts the rights and actions of women. The project focuses on the creation of a spa that offers a sanctuary from exclusion, inspired by ritual cleansing that takes place at temples and shrines. The building is divided into the public domain, private pavilions and the thresholds between them. Excavated into the ground, the building embodies the concept of the Low-City, with private spaces, drawing inspiration from Origami as a method of concealment. Folded beneath a roofscape of cleansing boundaries, it offers a place of retreat and support that ultimately lifts women up (figuratively speaking) above their recognised social position.

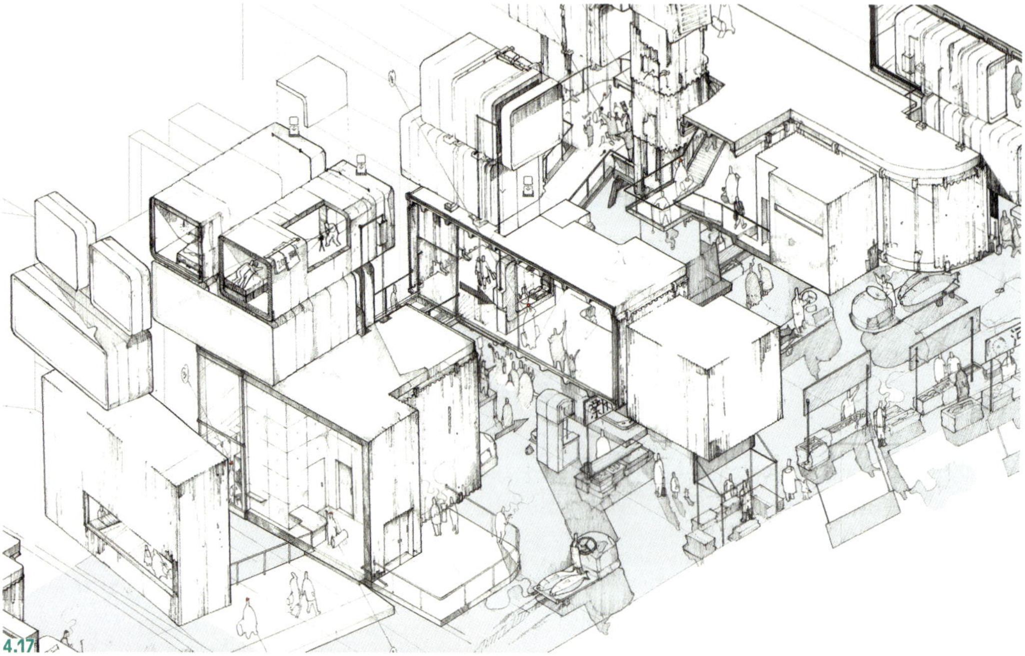

4.17

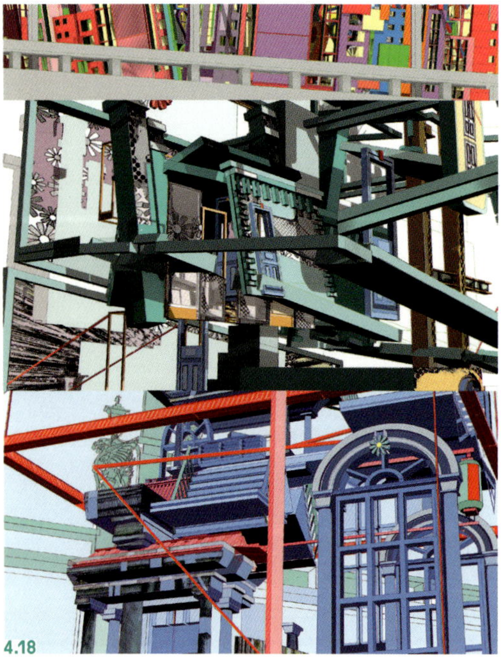

4.18

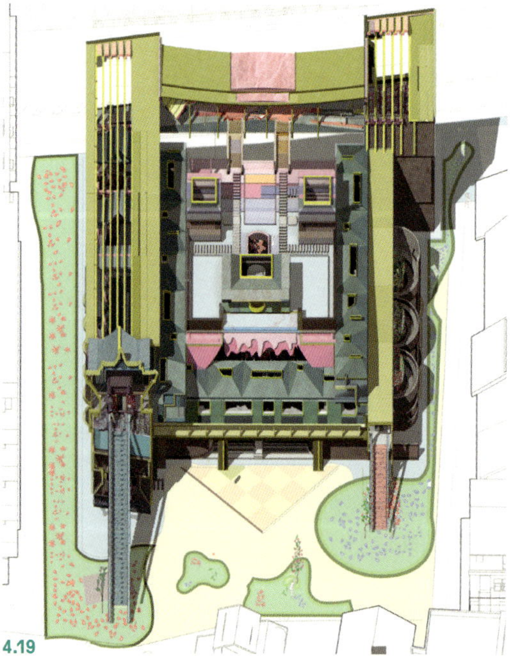

4.19

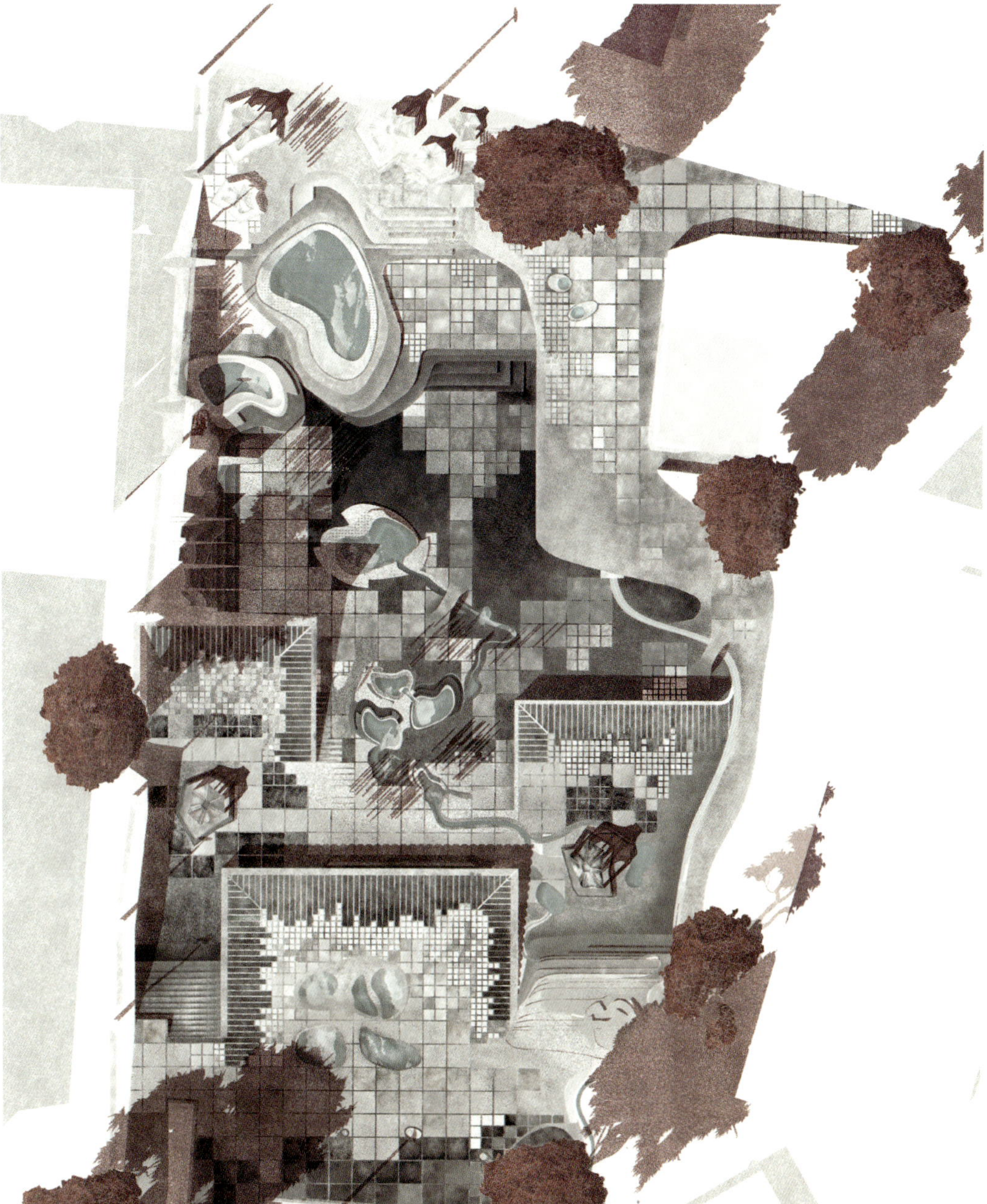

4.20

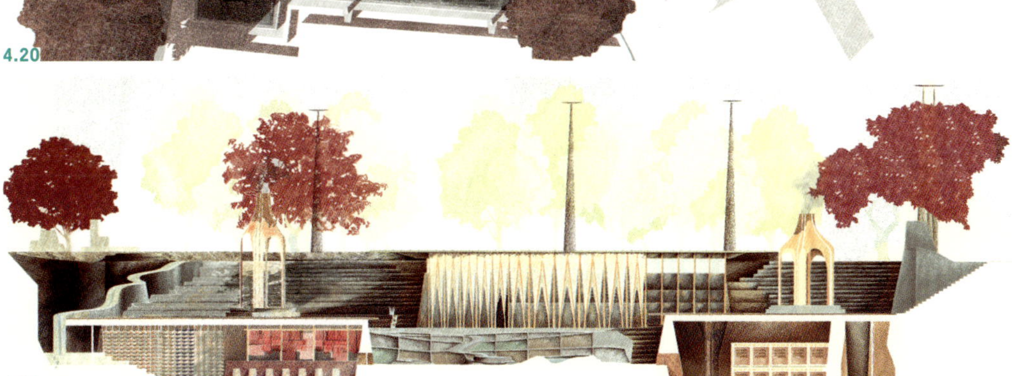

4.21

UG5

Restless Ground

Julia Backhaus, Pedro Font Alba & Martin Tang

Year 2
Kelly Au, Gabriel Beard, Christina Garbi, Kaizer Hud, Hannah Lewis, Yidong (Isabel) Li, Minghan (Tom) Lin, Jack Spence, William Stephens

Year 3
Yangzi (Cherry) Guo, Niema Jafari, Karolina Kielb, Benjamin Mehigan, Rachael Taylor, Olufunto Thompson, Kate Woodcock-Fowles, Yehan Zheng

Many thanks to our technical tutors Dimitris Argyros and Mick Brundle

Special thanks to our critics: Luísa Alpalhão, Abigail Ashton, Laura Allen, Pascal Bronner, Tina di Carlo, Salvador Cejudo, Carlos Jiménez Cenamor, Mollie Claypool, Diego Delas, Max Dewdney, Murray Fraser, Stephen Gage, Thomas Hillier Justin C.K Lau, Adriana Laura Massidda, Tania Sengupta, Sarah Shafiei, Bob Sheil, Sabine Storp, Michiko Sumi and Patrick Weber

Our unit continues to explore the relationship between land use, technology and science and the synthesis of inherent cultural identity. This year Tokyo became the test bed for our investigations.

——In the 60's a group of apprentice Japanese architects dreamed of an alternative future for cities and defined a new architectural vocabulary, giving birth to an architectural movement called 'Metabolism'. The name, taken from the biological concept, derived from the idea that architecture and cities, like living organisms, share the ability to grow, reproduce, transform and respond to their specific environment. Their ideas were grand and surprising. They combined philosophical references with new discoveries in science; for example, interweaving ideas about the structure of DNA with elements of Buddhist thinking on change and growth, resulting in profoundly poetic and radical visions. Now, at a time when Japan is experiencing the aftermath of the 2011 earthquake, a stagnant economy and a significant shift in demographics, and where over 70% of the area is mountainous and notoriously difficult to inhabit, what are the lessons we can learn from the Metabolists today?

——Cities, generally considered resilient to rapidly transient conditions, are in constant flux, exposed to their own geo-dynamics, shifting patterns of behaviour and demographics. As a unit, we are interested in exploring an architecture that is open-ended and not a finished product; architectural propositions that can adapt, mutate and respond to the dynamic nature of the restless urban landscape; a socially benevolent edict, where creativity and daring leads to fantastical but perfectly possible futures.

——We started the year in the workshop: 'Dreamland' was a model-based project that became a miniature surrogate of the city, super-specific yet a siteless urban landscape in constant flux, encapsulating its past and present as a foundation for its future. We approached the unit's work as an 'Expo', an experimental assembly of the individual works into a whole that depicted an intensified and forward-thinking version of the city of today. Our main building project started with the field trip to Tokyo and Kyoto. Here, we experienced a city that Bognat describes as an endless agglomeration of many cities and villages – a hundred different cities smashed into one, remaining a 'dream machine', where the parts are more in focus than the whole. Both Tokyo and Kyoto offered an opportunity and fertile ground to critically rethink the concepts of permanence, impermanence and genius loci.

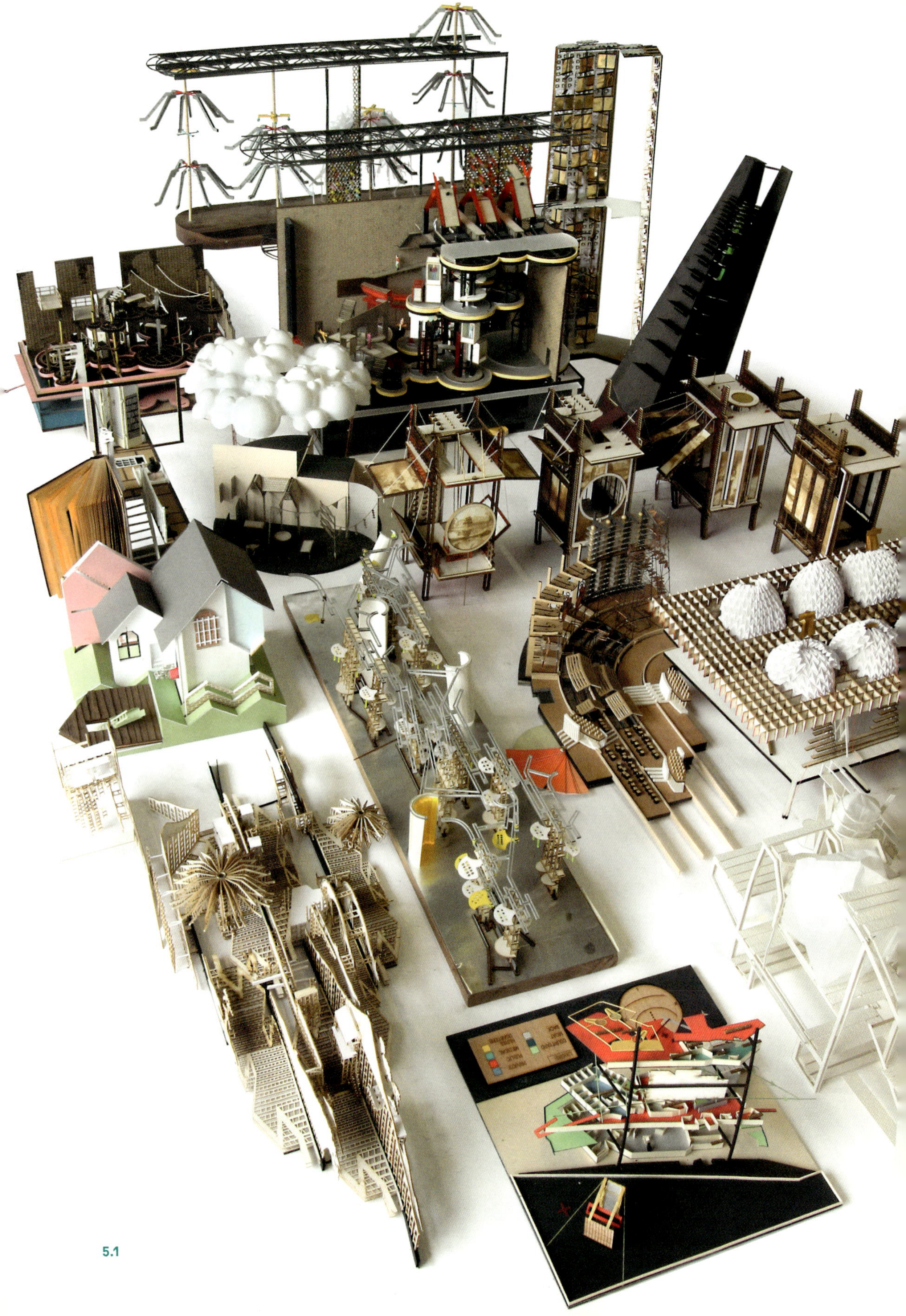

5.1

Fig. 5.1 Group Project Y2&3, 'Dreamland'. An experimental assembly of the individual works depicting an intensified and forward-thinking version of Japan. **Fig. 5.2 Hannah Lewis** Y2, 'Loneliness, Otaku and Rehabilitation in Contemporary Kyoto'. The Otaku Centre offers a place for people to reform their obsessive behaviour. Located on the outskirts of Kyoto, the resort provides a solution to improve the lives of the nation's social outcasts. **Fig. 5.3 Benjamin Mehigan** Y3, 'The Nakasendo Villages: A Pre- and Post- Earthquake Proposal'. Located on the outskirts of Kyoto with direct train links to Tokyo, the Nakasendo village investigates adaptive architecture. Predominantly existing as a rural retreat, the village is designed to transform into a place of refuge for Tokyo's inhabitants. **Fig. 5.4 Jack Spence** Y2, 'Shinobazu Open Theatre'. Situated on Shinobazu Pond, the theatre stages illusionary performances against the backdrop of Ueno Park and the Tokyo Skyline. Floating modular stages and seating provide a versatile set for a range of performances that can take place across the vast expanse of the pond.

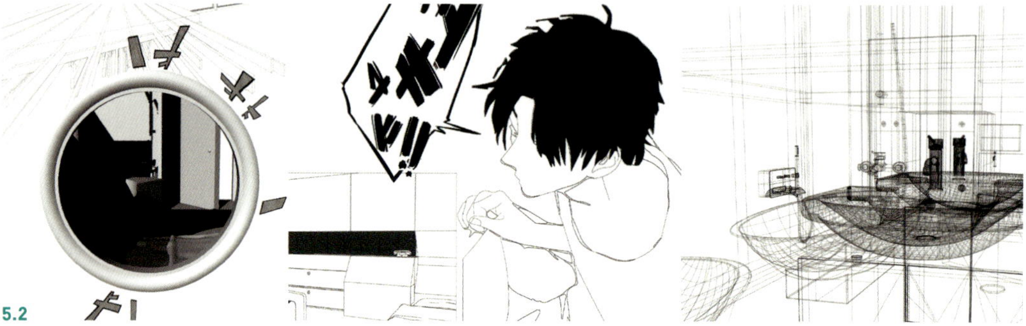

5.2

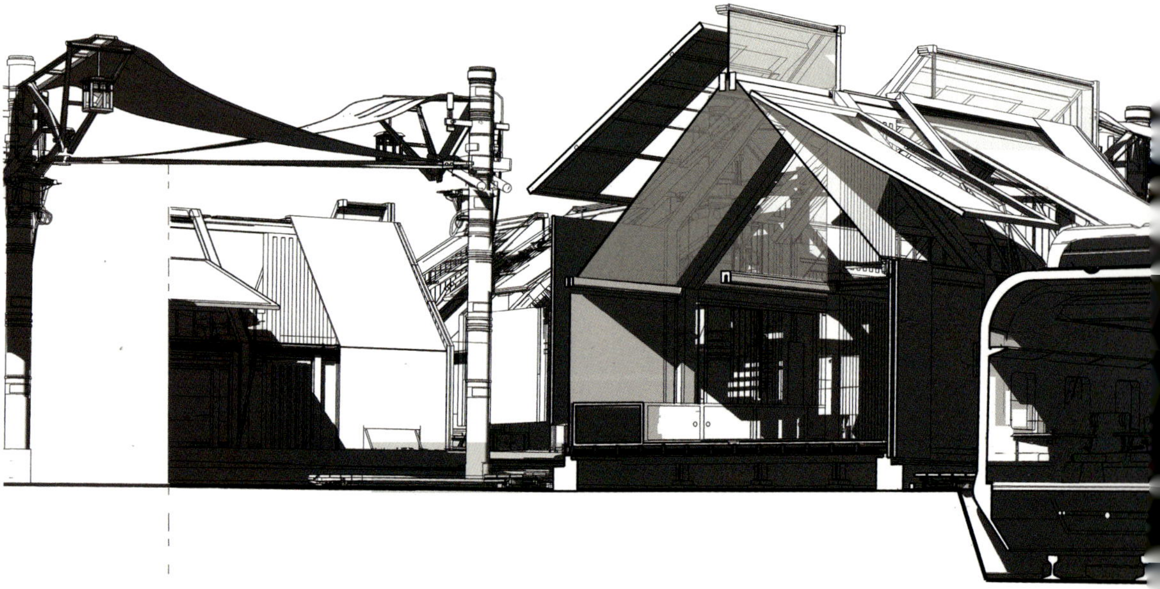

5.3

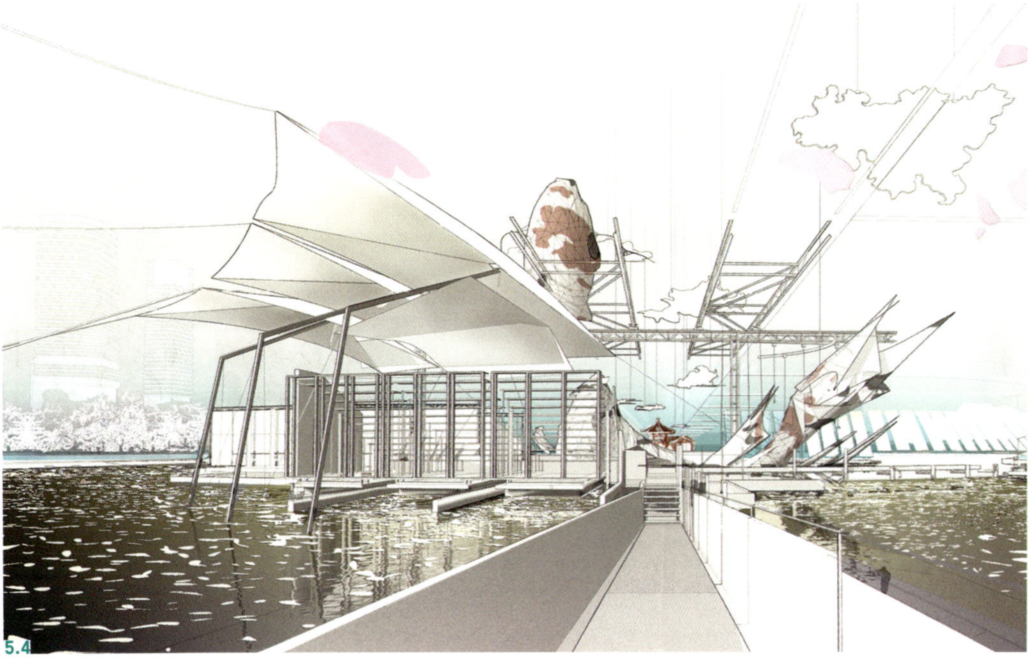

5.4

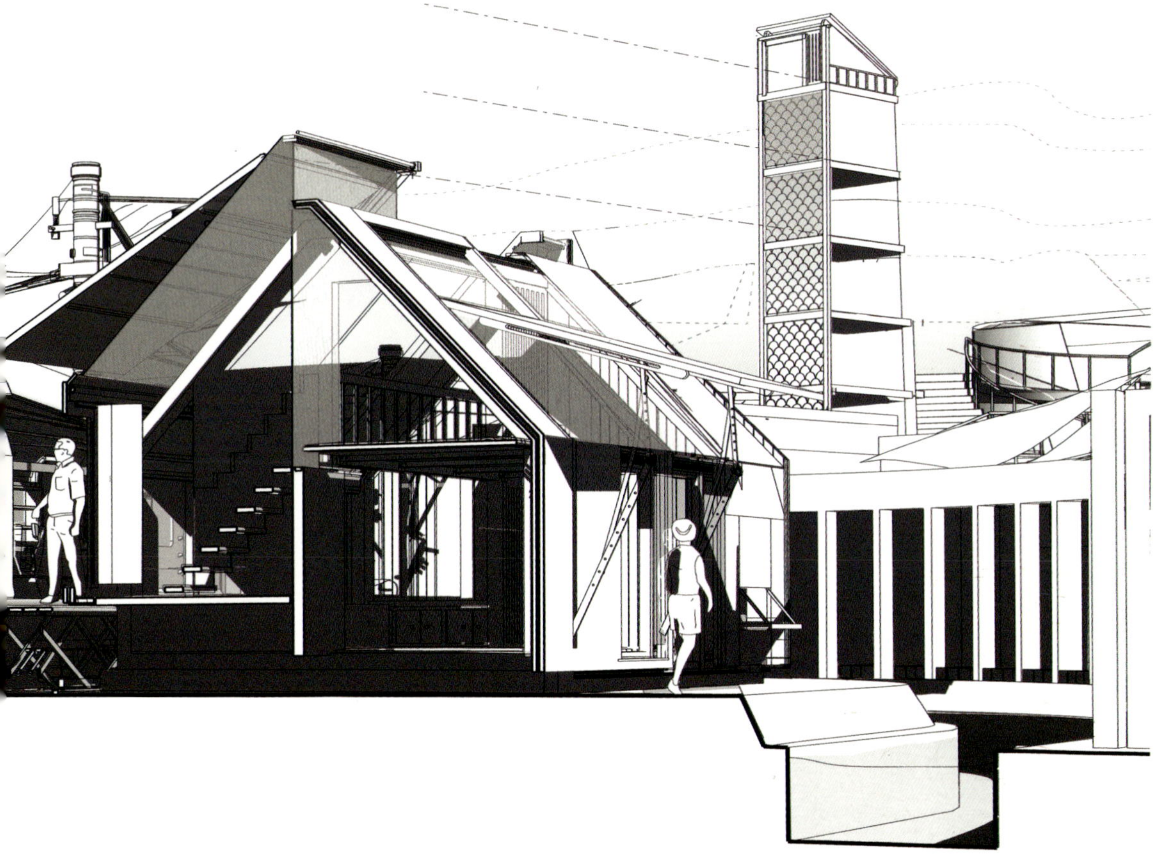

Fig. 5.5 Kate Woodcock-Fowles Y3, 'The Thomasson House and Archive'. A Japanese artist coined the name 'Thomasson' to describe the many obsolete pieces of infrastructure he found around Tokyo. By putting Thomassons back into use and manipulating some of the city's building laws, this project comments on the problems facing modern-day Tokyo. **Fig. 5.6 Kelly Au** Y2, 'Urban Offerings'. The 'flying dwellings' attached to the electrical poles are designed to provide shelter, warmth, food and water for the homeless in Ueno, Tokyo. They plug into the existing infrastructure of Ameyoko Street and the Tokudaiji Temple (flying temple), providing offerings and comforts. **Fig. 5.7 Christina Garbi** Y2, 'Utakai Hajime Poem Competition Writing Pods'. This project proposes a collection of writing pods inspired by the thresholds that exist within the Forbidden Gardens of Tokyo. Located around the city, the pods broadcast images of the Gardens as a source of inspiration for writers entering the annual Utakai Hajime. Each pod corresponds to one of the four seasons and reflects the Japanese art of Ikebana (flower arranging).

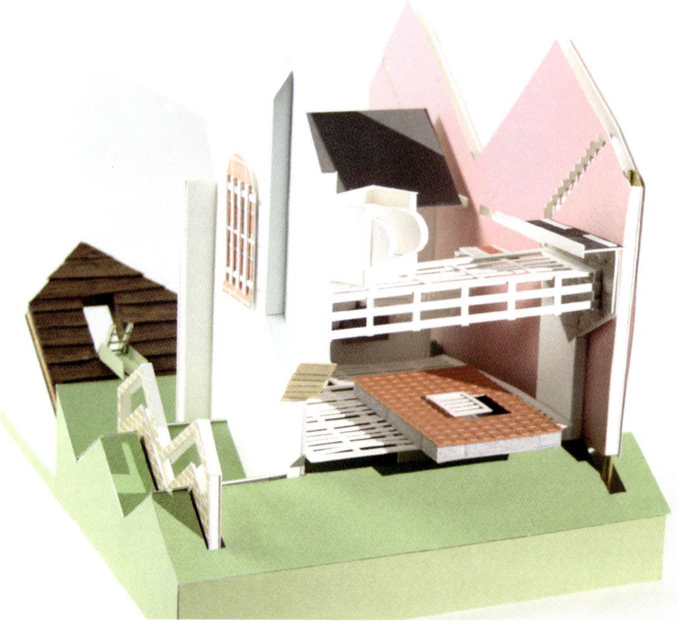

5.5

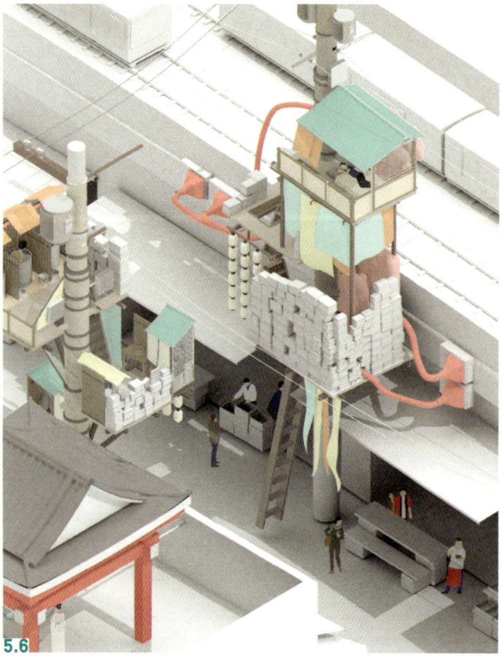

5.6

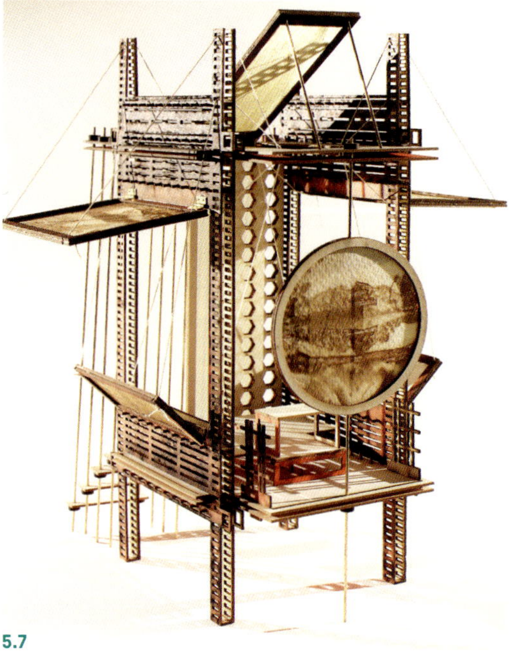

5.7

Fig. 5.8 Karolina Kielb Y3, 'Kyoto Paper Matsuri'. In response to Kyoto's over-consumption of paper, the building recycles and reproduces traditional Japanese paper which is turned into large-scale paper structures that are released into the air and river as a form of celebration and appreciation for paper.
Fig. 5.9 Olufunto Thompson Y3, 'Replanting the Shinto Forest'. Situated on the holiest site in Japan, the Ise Grand Shrine is religiously reconstructed every 20 years. This sacred tradition is extremely wasteful, with 14,000 cypress trees used for construction and material from the previous shrine going to waste. This project proposes symbolically re-planting the Shinto forest by creating a spiritual architecture from reclaimed timber.

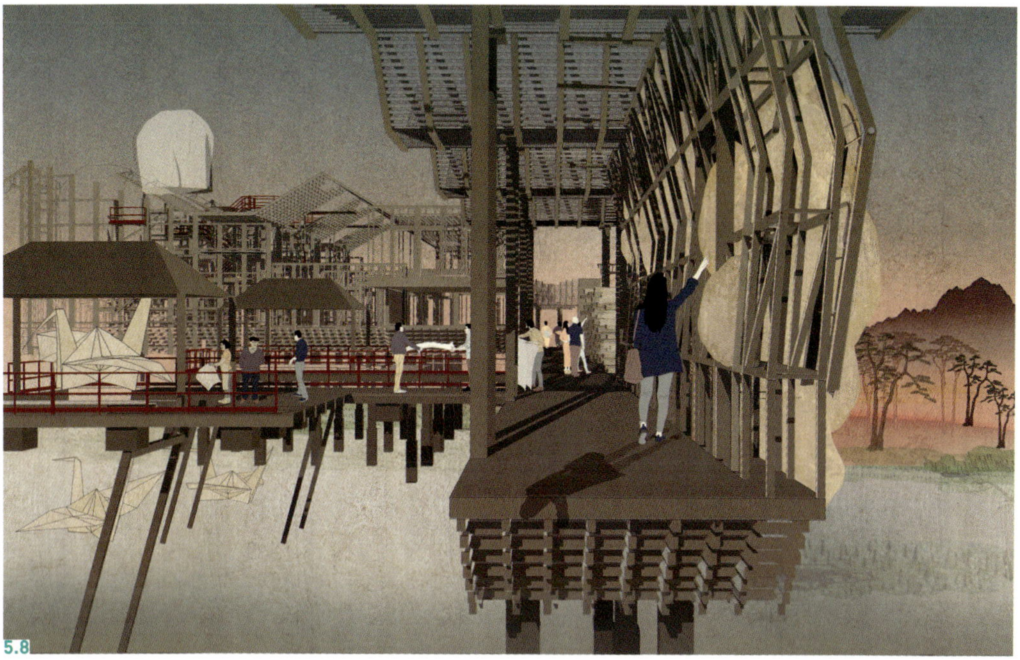

5.8

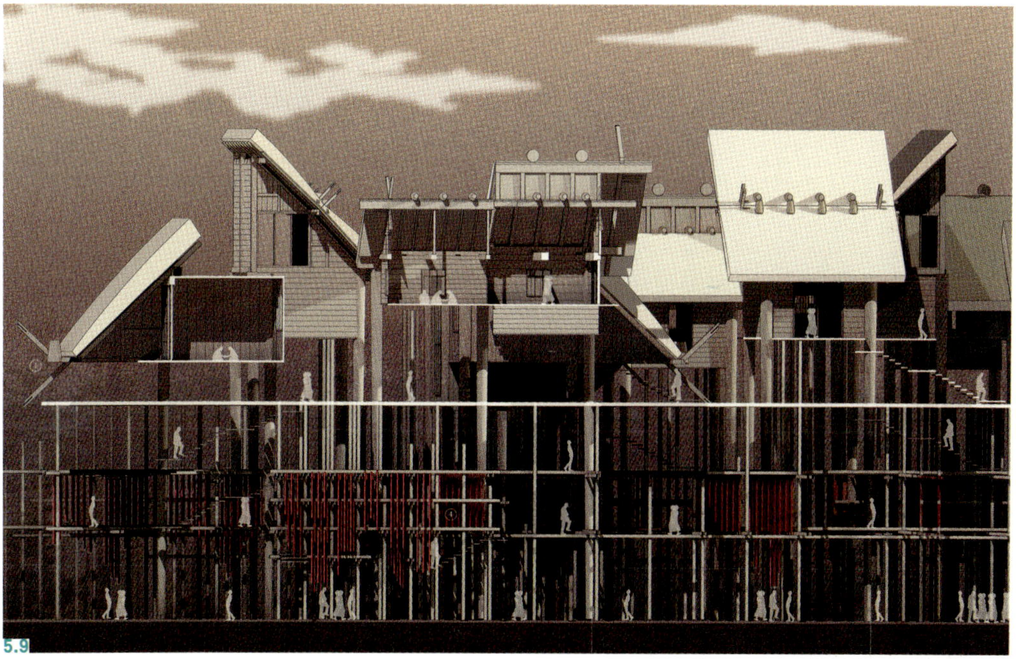

5.9

Fig. 5.10 **Kaizer Hud** Y2, 'Food for Thought: Ritualizing Information'. An informational landscape investigating Japan's unsustainable food production practices. The model is interactive, requiring the user to perform a sushi eating ritual to understand. Each step becomes a learning ritual in which the user's action reflects a piece of information. **Fig. 5.11** **Tom Lin** Y2, 'Tokyo Bay Urban Battery'.**Fig. 5.12** **Will Stephens** Y2, 'SONY Exhibition Centre Façade'. The façade creates an image of a 'greener' SONY, encouraging people to recycle electronic items. **Fig. 5.13** **Yangzi (Cherry) Guo** Y3, 'Third Harvest Market Place'. Food sold in Japanese supermarkets has the shortest shelf life in the world, based on a regulation called the 1/3 rule. The project proposes a new typology of marketplace that would collect fruit/veg from nearby restaurants and supermarkets in Tokyo, and preserve it in order to extend shelf life for re-consumption. **Fig. 5.14** **Rachael Taylor** Y3, 'Architectural Salvage Centre'. Architectural heritage is of little significance in Tokyo. The salvage centre collects fragments of iconic buildings for resale in order to preserve parts of the lost city. **Fig. 5.15** **Gabriel Beard** Y2, 'Tokyo Bay Traffic Cone Storage and Leisure Facility'. **Fig. 5.16** **Isabel Li** Y2, 'Porous Engawa – Fabric Reseach Center'. A catwalk provides circulation around the fabric research centre where visitors are encouraged to create their own clothes and style. The façade plays with the visual interaction between interior and exterior by controlling what people can see; which contributes to the marketing effect of the whole building.

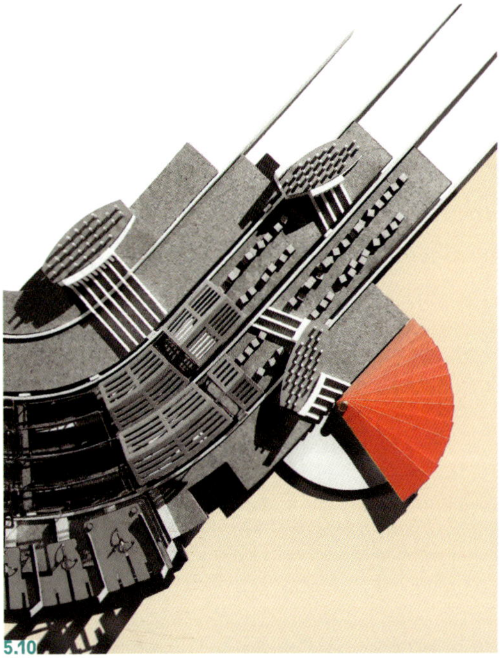

5.10

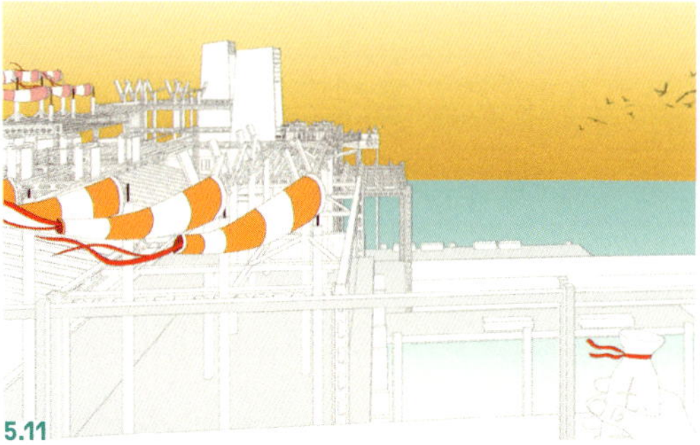

5.11

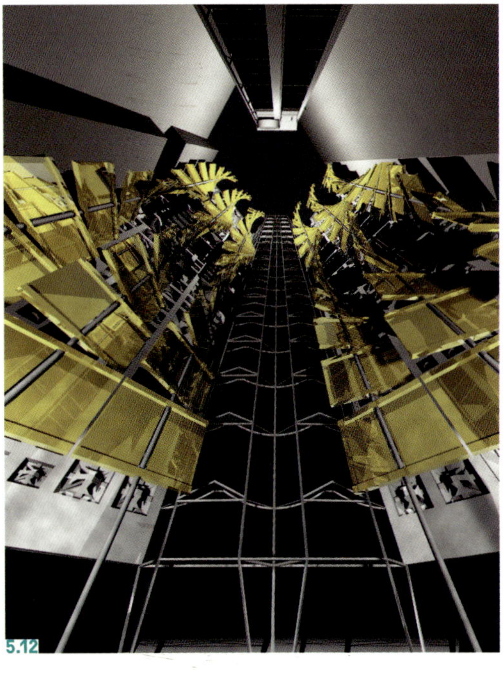

5.12

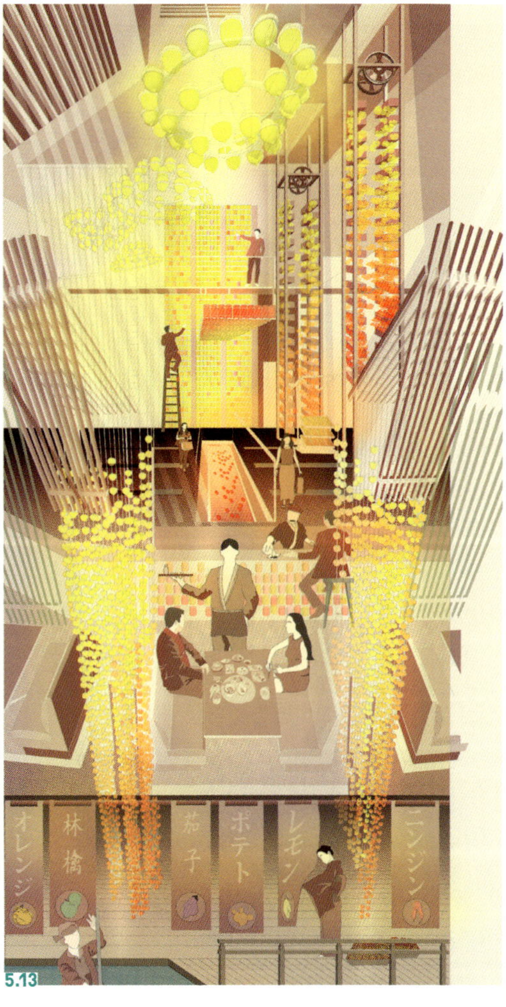

5.13

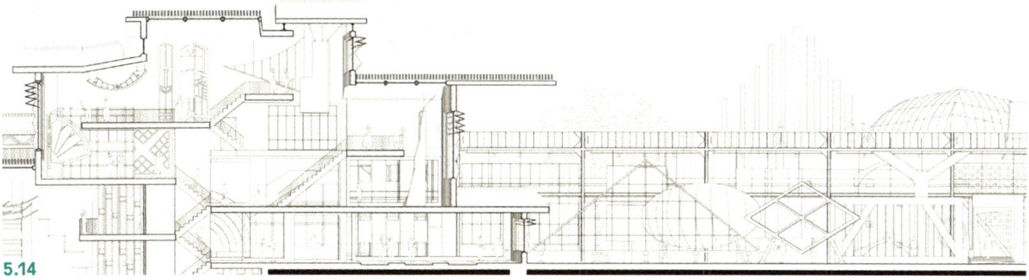
5.14

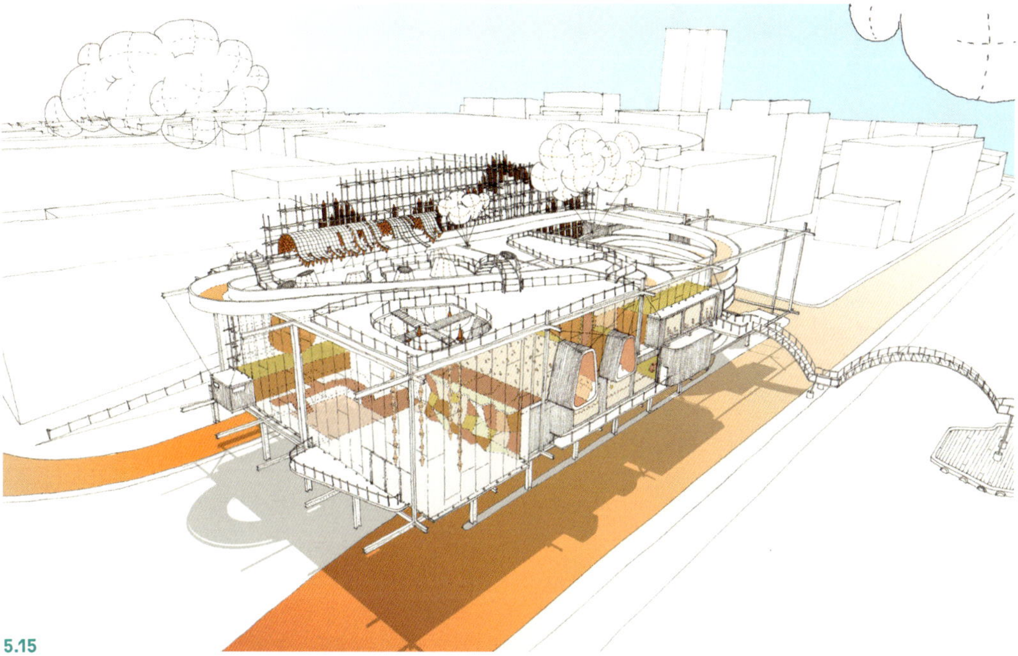
5.15

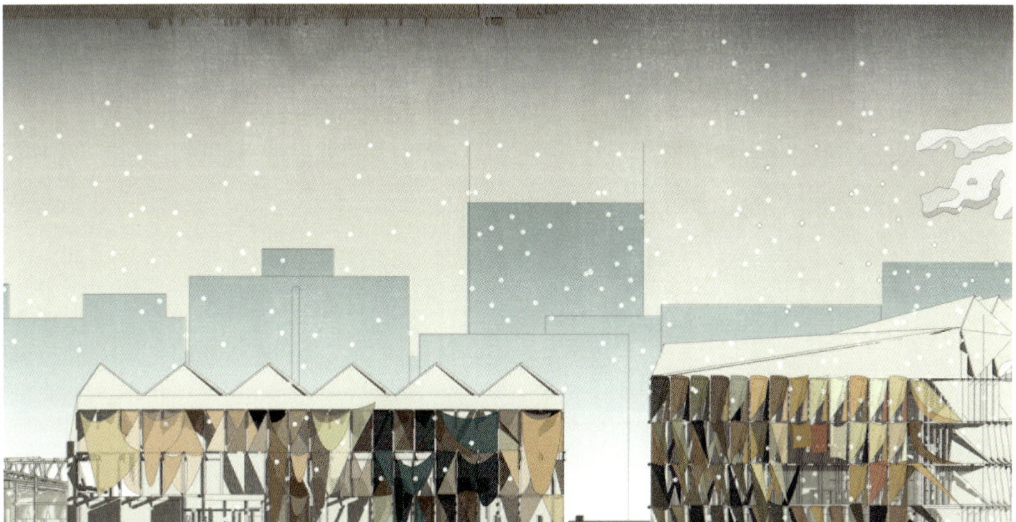
5.16

Fig. 5.17 Jack Spence Y2, 'Apartment Of Deception'. Creating virtual extensions of the apartment in order to create illusions both of and within the inhabitable space through day-to-day life. **Fig. 5.18 Gabriel Beard** Y2, 'Tokyo Bay Traffic Cone Storage and Leisure Facility'. **Fig. 5.19 Zheng Yehan** Y3, 'Kyoto Dementia Respite Centre'. The Kyoto Dementia Respite Centre provides short term care for mid-stage patients who are coming to grips with the rapid decline of present cognitive ability, but who are still physically able. By celebrating memory and reality, the programme takes a fresh approach to dementia care.

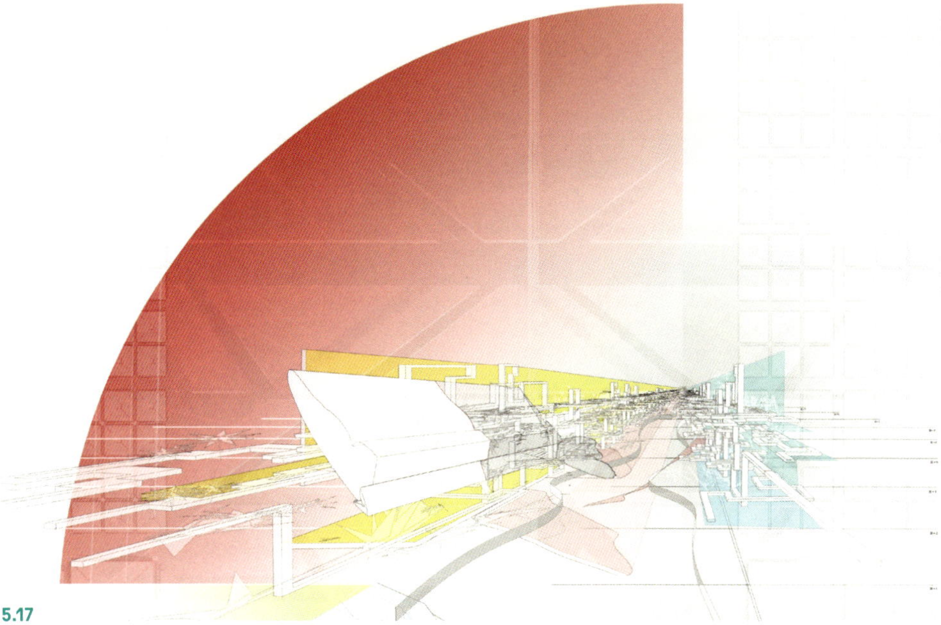

5.17

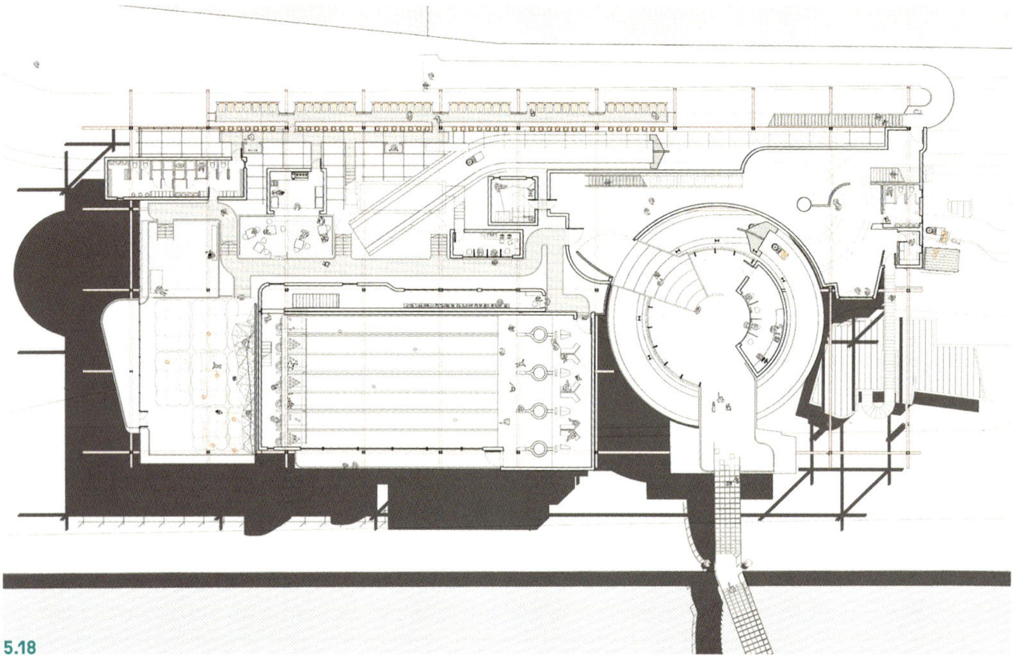

5.18

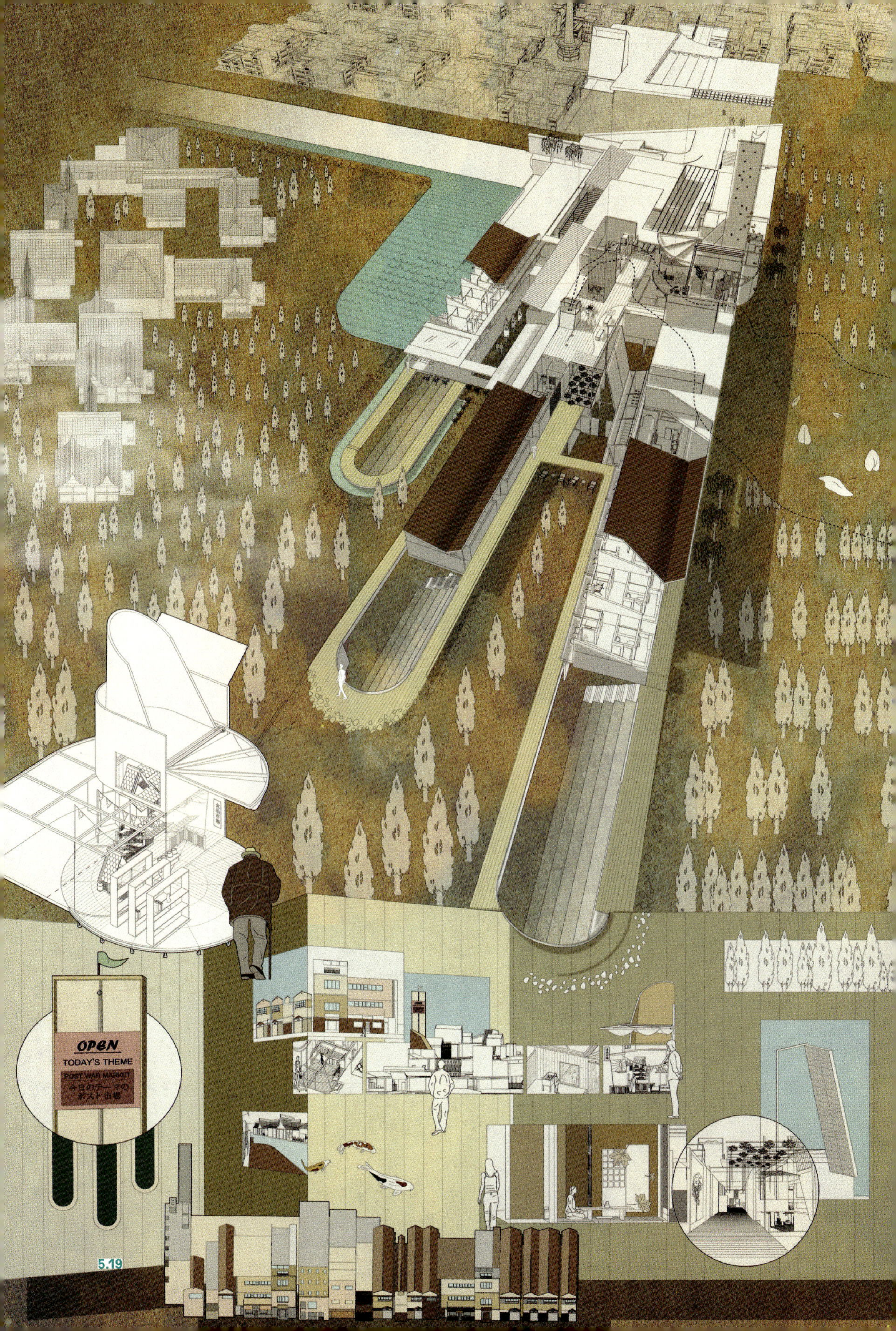

5.19

UG6

Indian Nose Reconstruction

Christine Hawley, Paolo Zaide

Year 2
Alex Desov, Ashleigh-Paige Fielding, Dustin May, Edward Sear, Fan (Lisa) Wu

Year 3
Lester Tian-Lang Cheung, Deedee Pun Tik Chung, Ching Kuo, Xin Hao (Jerome) Ng, Hoi Lai (Kerry) Ngan, Yuchen Pan, Calvin Po, Yip Wing Siu, York Tsing (Nerissa) Yeung

UG6 would like to thank our friends and critics: Bartek Arendt, Abigail Ashton, Paul Bailey, Peter Bishop, Max Butler, Stephen Gage, Jamie Hignett, Alex Julyan, Jens Kongstad, CJ Lim, Anu and Shilpa Mridul, Tim Norman, Emily Priest, Sabine Storp, Joe Travers-Jones, Patrick Weber, Ivor Williams

Special thanks to our technical tutors Matt Springett and Clyde Watson

This year UG6 approached the issue of health from a cultural perspective, looking at both the clinical models of the West and the natural 'life balance', which is the more popular alternative across Asian continents. Health is currently a topical subject that, within the UK, can make or destroy political parties as current NHS provision becomes increasingly inadequate. A demographic change will challenge our understanding of conventional medicine and perhaps raise interesting discussions about alternative approaches.

——This subject is not just an issue for politicians and the medical community but also for designers; history has shown that groundbreaking design can provide innovative care decades ahead of its time. In 1926 the holistic medical philosophy pioneered by Drs George Scott Williamson and Innes Hope Pearse was offered at the Peckham Health Centre. Both the building and the clinical support radically challenged the tradition of reactive medicine; it emphasised the importance of a socially, mentally and physically balanced lifestyle; it is only now that the wisdom and efficacy of their approach offers a concept that we should consider, if contrasted against the costly science of modern medicine.

——In November the Unit travelled to India where we observed attitudes to health and traditional medicine that promote certain similarities to the Peckham Experiment through ideas of holistic well-being, where the body, the mind and lifestyle have to be in balance. Joseph Carpue, born in 1764 in London, studied plastic surgery in India for twenty years and was the first to perform 'rhinoplasty' or, as it was known then, 'Indian nose reconstruction'. What do these medical cultures share and what might they offer us today? And is some of this thinking relevant to the health provision of the future?

——The brief challenges concepts of collective and civic health and its place in the contemporary city. The students explored an alternative to the modern primary care centre, currently offering a service that responds only to illness and not to well-being. Why and when do we need medical advice and prescription and how can this be minimised? Set in future Peckham, the projects explored ideas about health and lifestyle that comments on all aspects of what we do, whether it be work, recreation or simply doing nothing.

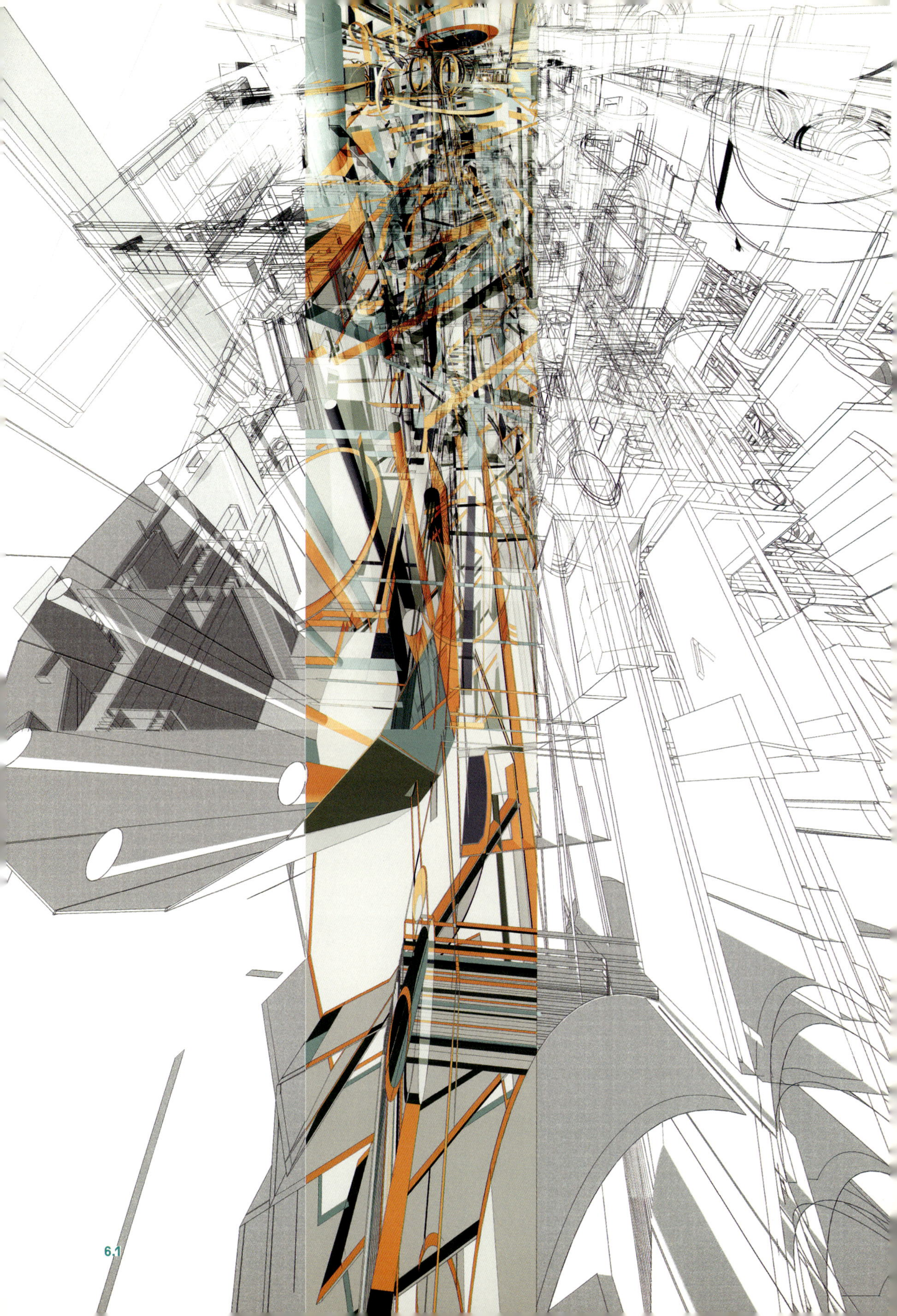

6.1

Fig. 6.1 Deedee Pun Tik Chung Y3, 'Hydro-Rehabilitation Centre'. This project incorporates hydrotherapy as a remedial treatment for both sports injury prevention and rehabilitation. Situated adjacent to the Peckham Library, the project offers a platform to host events and celebrations in Peckham. It includes diverse suspended water elements which promote mental and social wellbeing. **Fig. 6.2 Dustin May** Y2, 'Peckham Food Centre'. Society has become disconnected with the food it eats. The project educates Peckham's community on the food industry; from cultivation and growing to culinary classes and wider environmental impacts. **Fig. 6.3 Fan (Lisa) Wu** Y2, Peckham Convalescent Home'. The NHS is under high pressure due to the lack of continuity in social care facilities. Many argue that the current hospital environment is disempowering for patients, resulting in a slower recovery time. Therefore an intermediary recovery centre is crucial for the community of Peckham. **Figs. 6.4 – 6.5 Ashleigh-Paige Fielding** Y2, 'Peckham Hydro-Health Centre'. Over the next fifty years, London will increasingly become a stressful environment. This project aims to weave in moments of tranquility into the urban fabric. The Peckham Hydro-Health Centre becomes the extension of Peckham Square, exposing the forgotten Surrey Canal. The issue of mental health is approached by a series of sensory moments suspended above a sculpted landscape, connected through the overarching theme of water.

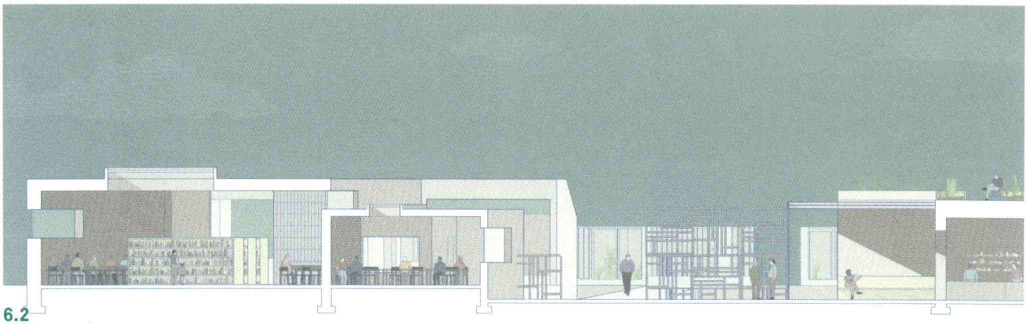

6.2

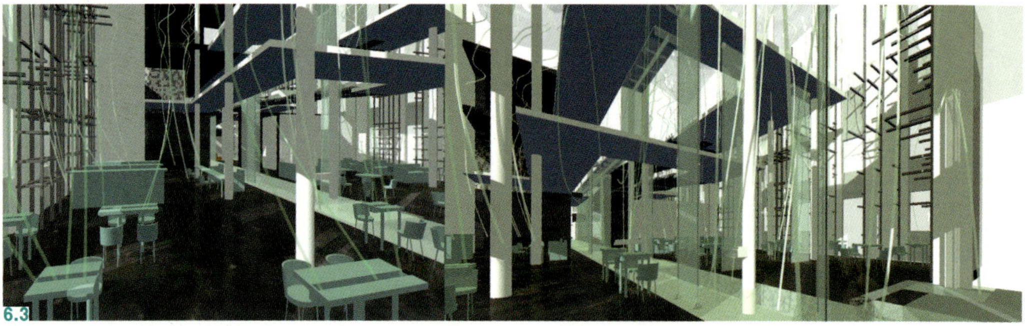

6.3

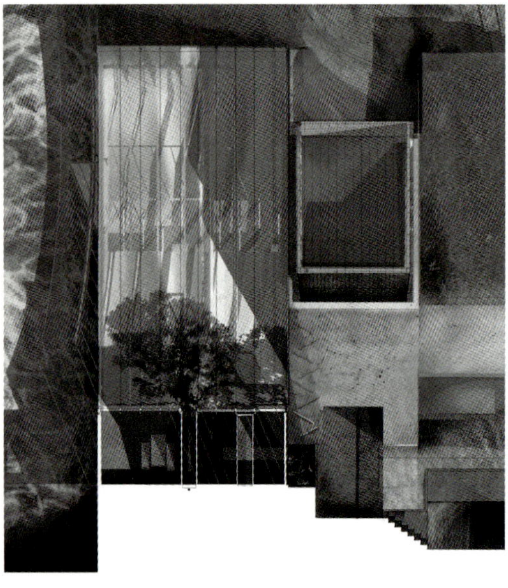

6.4

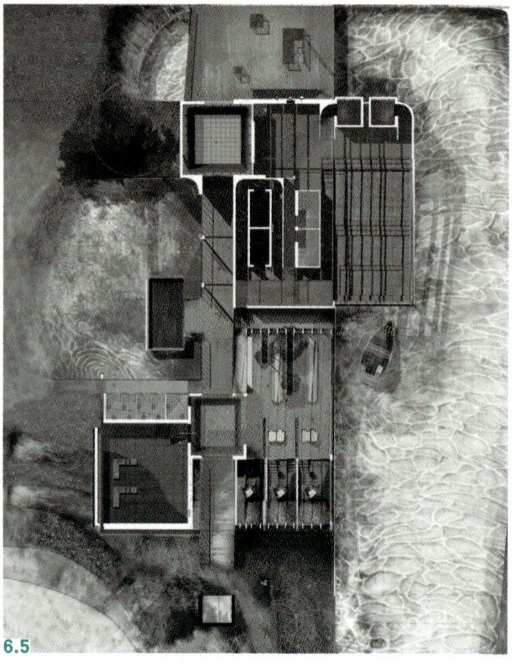

6.5

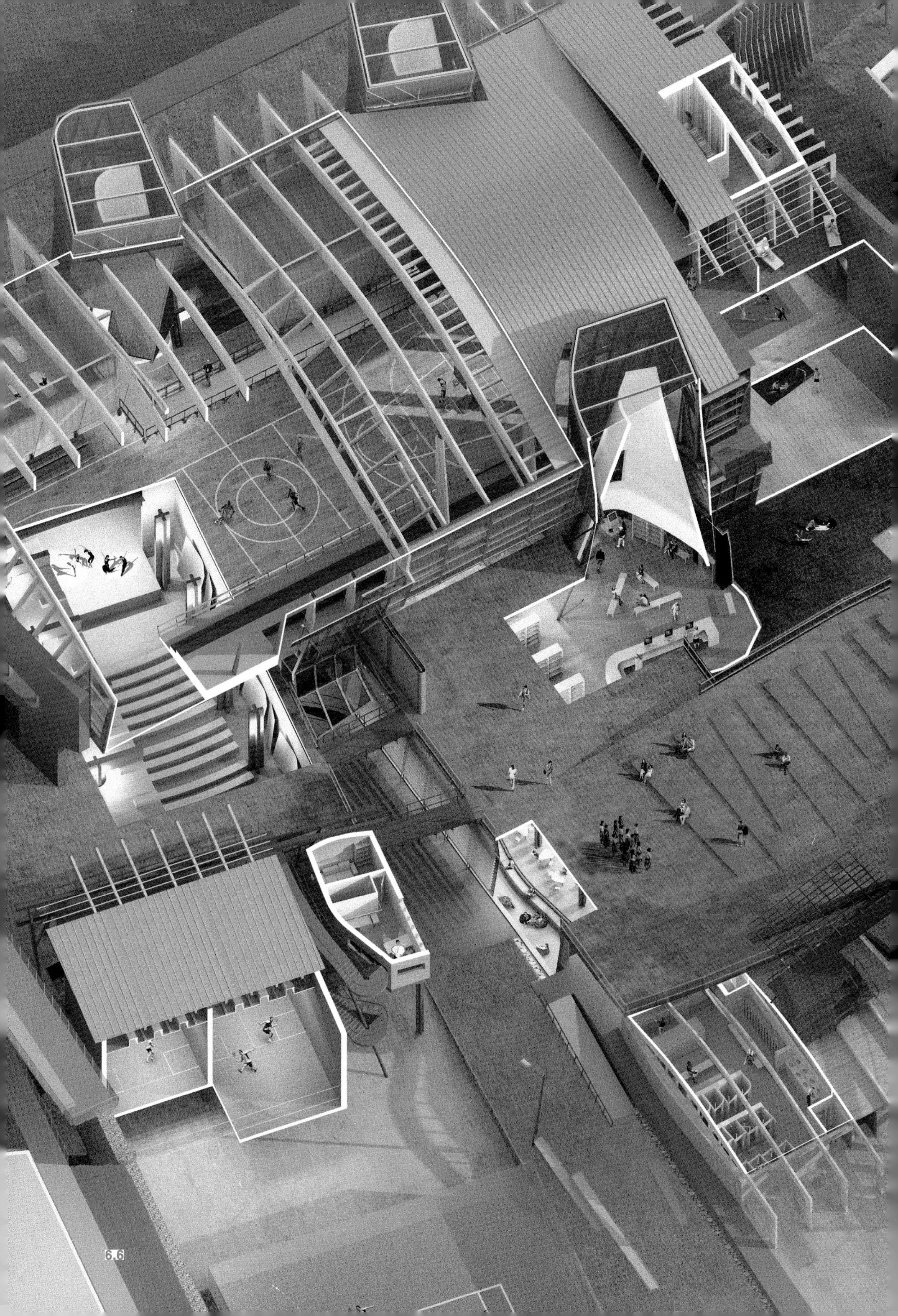
6.6

Fig. 6.6 Calvin Po Y3, 'Peckham Health Common'. This project re-examines the contemporary relevance of 'common land' as an intersection of communities and a common site for the shared concern for health. It reinterprets the Peckham Experiment's holistic, preventative approach in the context of healthcare's present and future, combining sport, community life, leisure and medicine, acknowledging health as not only an absence of illness but a consequence of all aspects of living. **Fig. 6.7 Xin Hao (Jerome) Ng** Y3, 'Peckham Hospice Care Home'. Situated in a Grade II listed building, the Hospice home provides care for people, enabling them to live the remainder of their lives to the full. Each unit offers views of the garden through the use of periscopes and movable façades and includes an additional room for family members.

Figs. 6.8 – 6.9 York Tsing (Nerissa) Yeung Y3, 'Peckham Wellbeing Sports Centre'. Situated within the existing multi-storey carpark in Peckham, this project is an interpretation of the 1930s Peckham Experiment with additional cultural and recreation facilities. The building consists of transformable catalysts at varying scales which incrementally change this urban site into a vibrant centre for the community. **Figs. 6.10 – 6.11 Lester Tian-Lang Cheung** Y3, 'Blind Community Centre'. The proposal aims to enrich the lives of the visually impaired by providing an environment for social integration and personal growth. The use of tactile surfaces and sound devices become the guiding principles to navigate through the building.

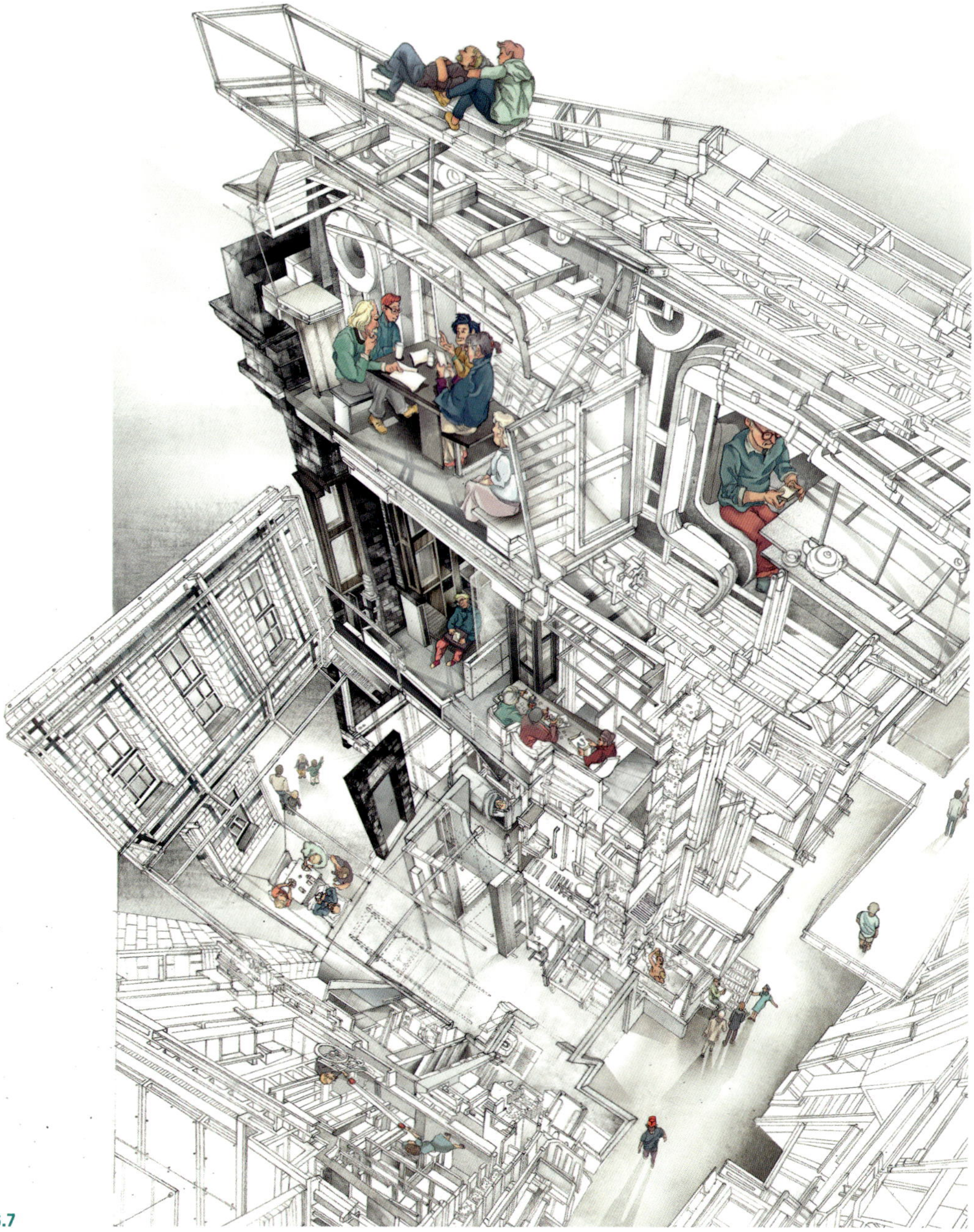

6.7

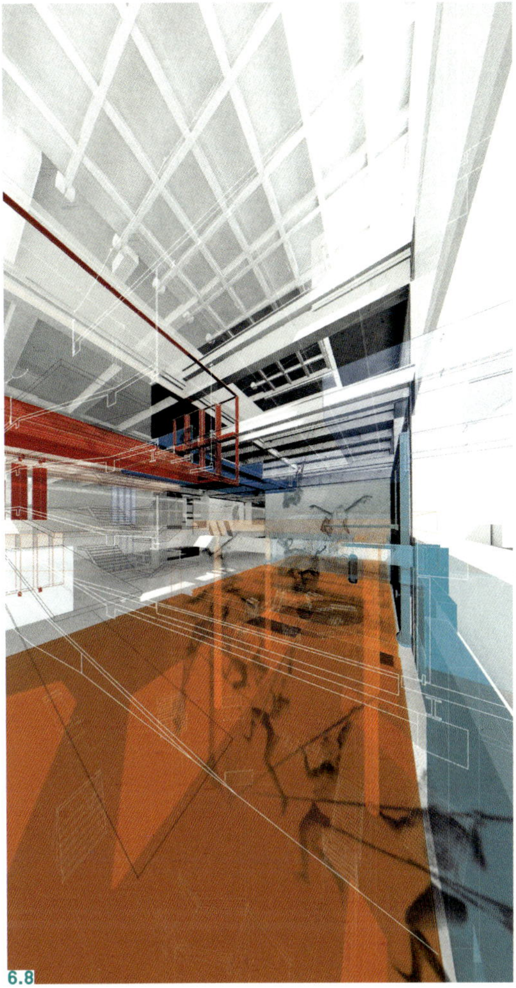
6.8

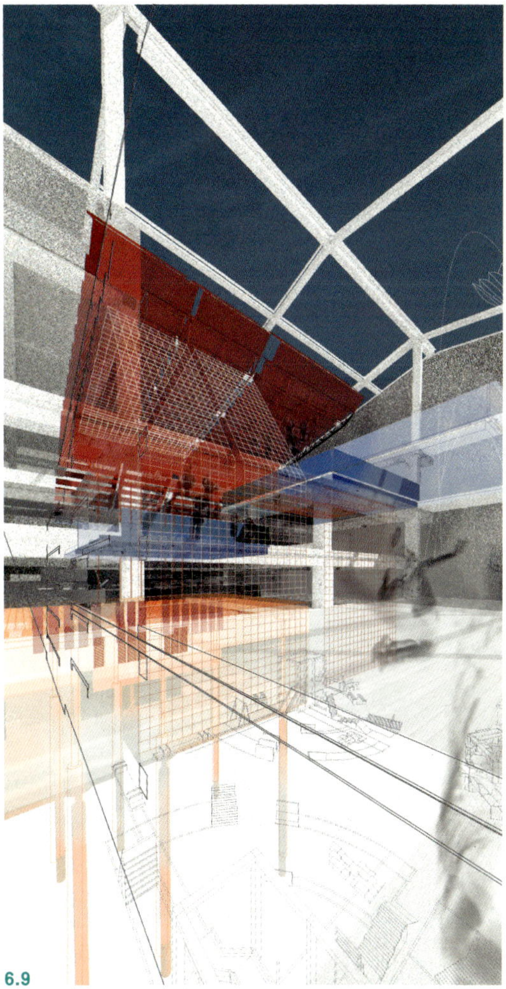
6.9

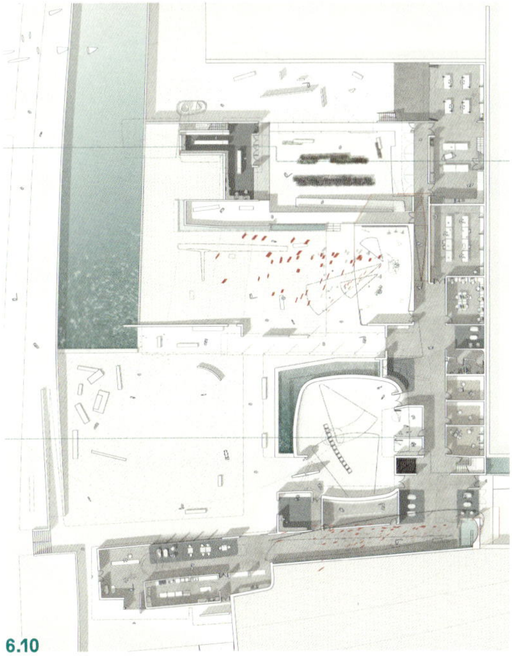
6.10

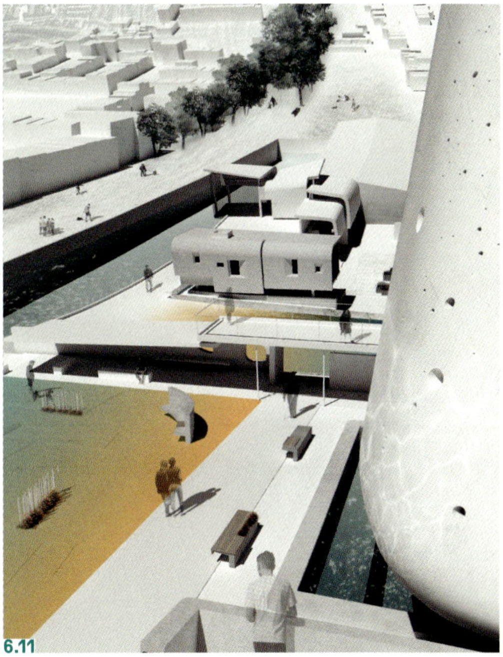
6.11

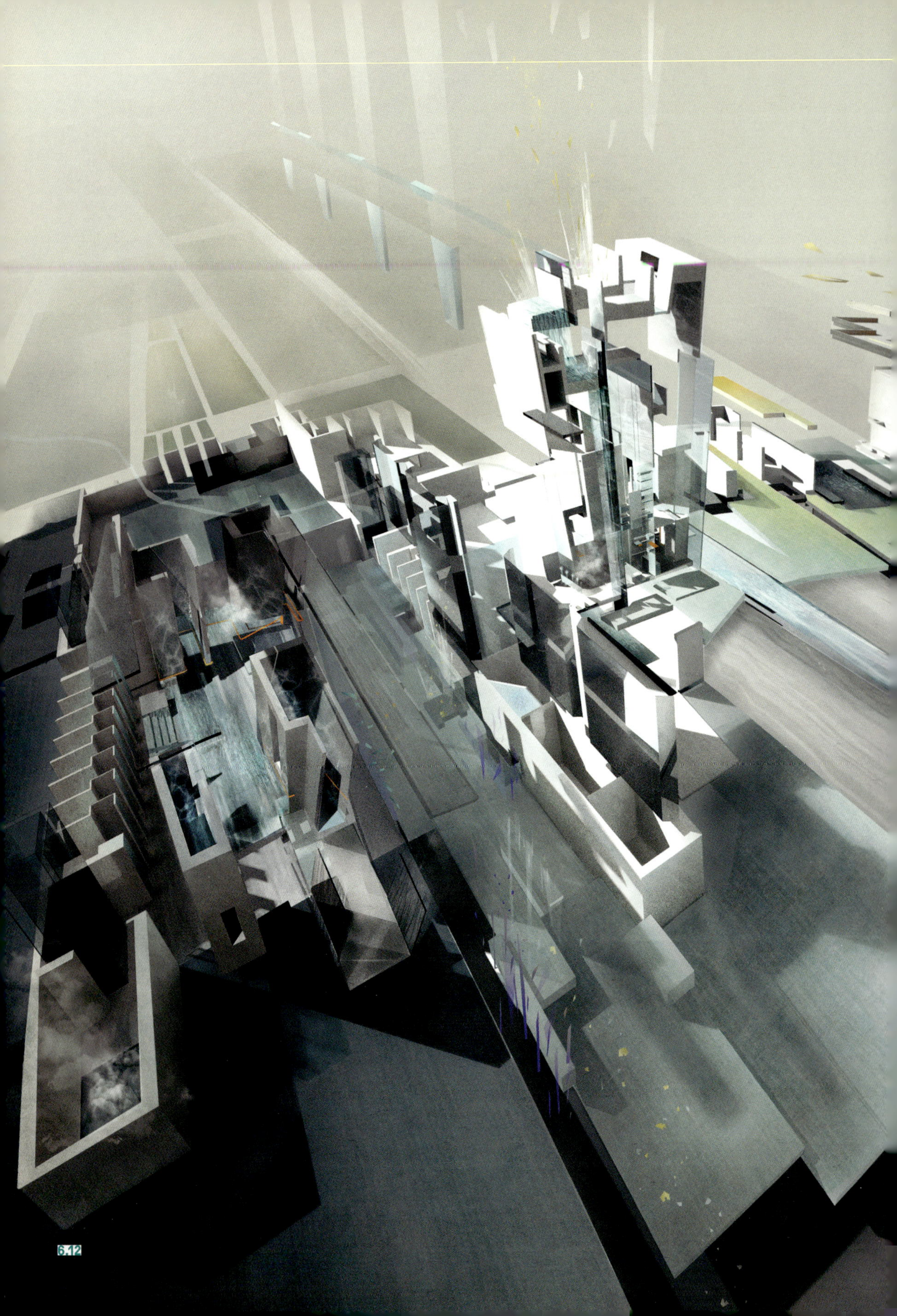

6.12

Fig. 6.12 Hoi Lai (Kerry) Ngan Y3, 'Peckham Horizon'. The project responds to the needs of dementia patients through the sensitive use of landscape. SItuated next to the River Peck, the building becomes a repository of personal and historical memories. Pockets of garden and waterscape exude a tranquil and calming environment for the patient, caretakers and visting families with spaces arranged around common courtyards and personal rain rooms. **Fig. 6.13 Alex Desov** Y2, 'Multicultural Healing Garden'. The project is a vibrant garden that brings together the diverse backgrounds and traditions that exist in Peckham's dynamic streetscape. The garden combines a spiritual healing centre and museum, exhibiting a range of seeds, plants and natural environments. The building becomes a celebration of different beliefs and cultures.

Fig. 6.14 Edward Sear Y2, 'The Spike Community Centre'. With social interaction and community spirit key to maintaining mental health and wellbeing, the Spike Community Centre accommodates and employs the homeless people of Peckham. The programme focuses on breaking the users' self-destructive cycles, through vocational training and fostering community activities. Holding regular events such as street parties, markets, pop-up cinema nights and arts/crafts workshops, the centre serves as a platform for the communities of Peckham to converge and flourish.

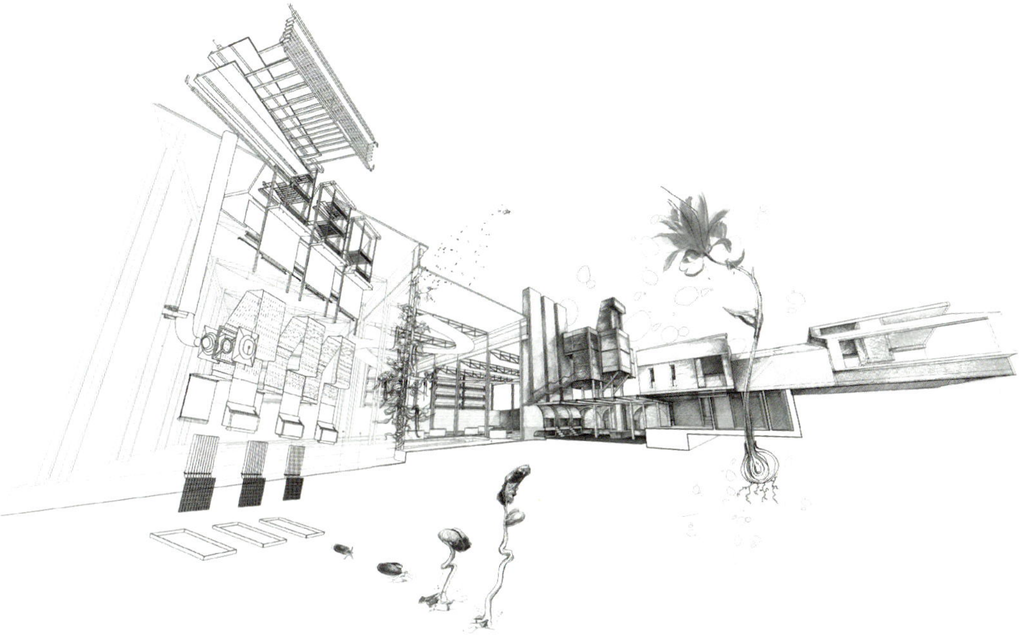

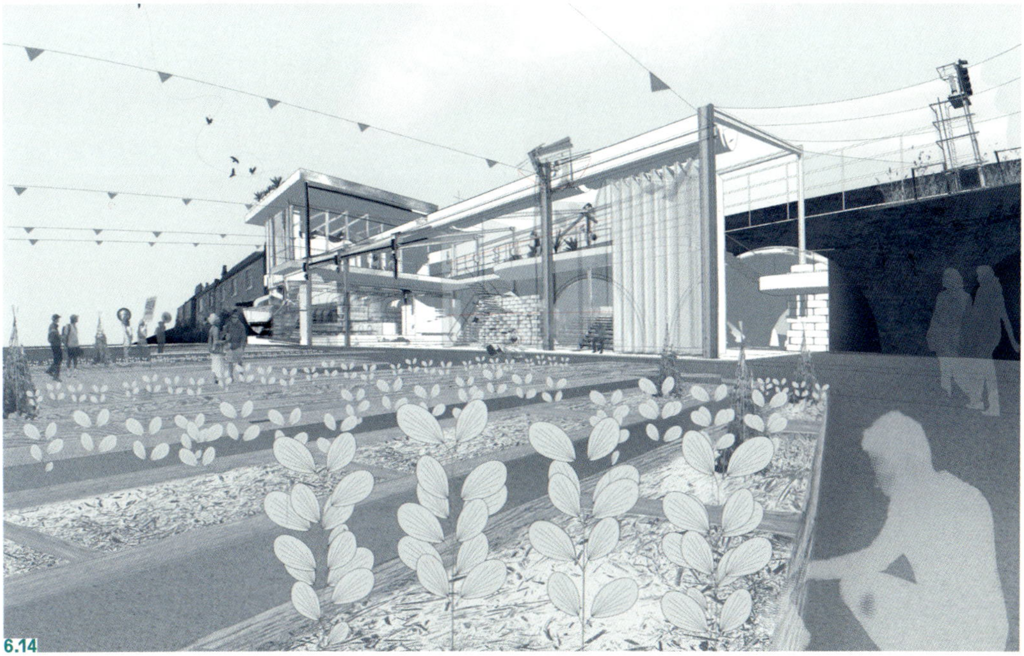

6.14

Fig. 6.15 Ching Kuo Y3, 'Peckham Urban Farm'. This scheme redevelops a disused multi-storey car park into a series of horticultural spaces for educational purposes and recreation. The design seeks to demonstrate different growing conditions throughout the building, allowing people to understand a wider range of growing methods in the food production cycle.
Fig. 6.16 Yuchen Pan Y3, 'Asthmatic Clinic Centre For Children'. Located in a Grade II listed site, the project addresses the demands of children sufferring from asthma. Providing facilities and accomodation, alongside therapeutic environments, the building helps reduce the recurrance of asthma attacks. The insertion of different lightweight elements, indoor gardens and towers create a unique environment filled with light and air. **Figs. 6.17 – 6.19 Yip-Wing Siu** Y3, 'The Super-Able Housing, CIC'. With an ageing population expected to rise by 46% in 2029, the requirements of a rapidly shifting demographic applied on the NHS, social infrastructure and the built environment must be addressed. Sited in Peckham, this masterplan tackles London's ageing demographic and shortage of public housing by promoting socio-physical wellbeing and community cohesion through an integrated agricultural social enterprise. Key to the proposal is the development of a 'Lifetime Home' which adapts to the four life stages that evolve to suit the needs of the young through to the old.

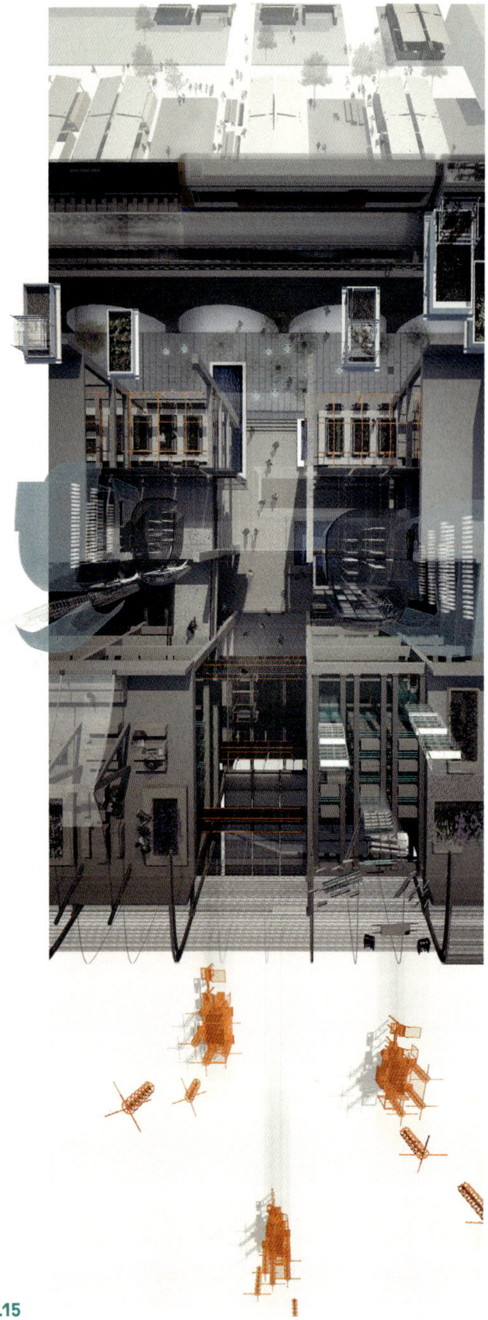

6.15

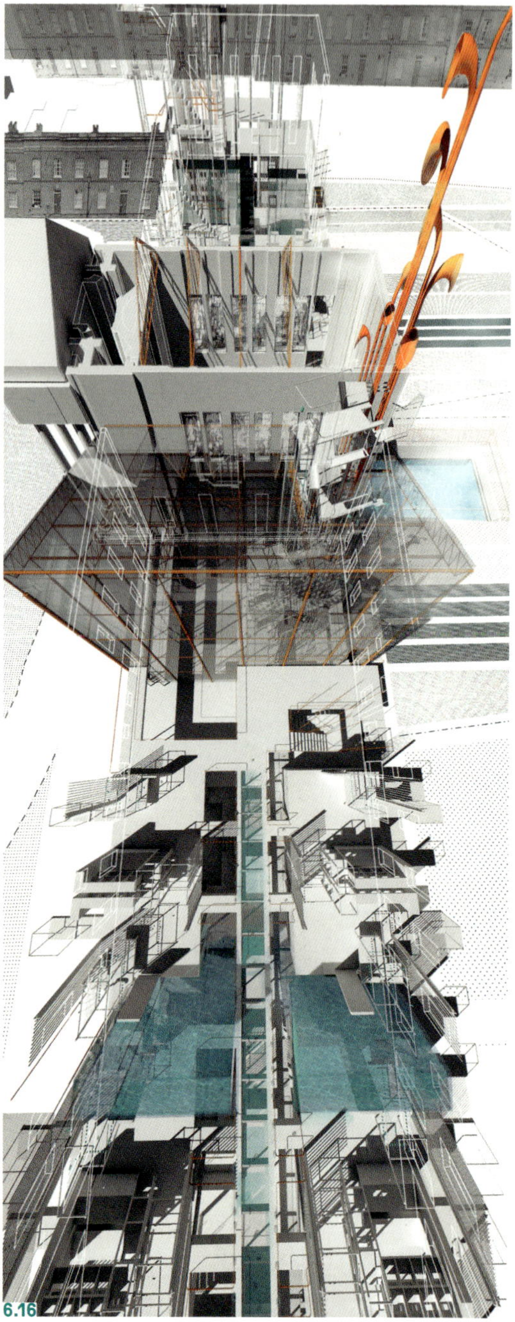

6.16

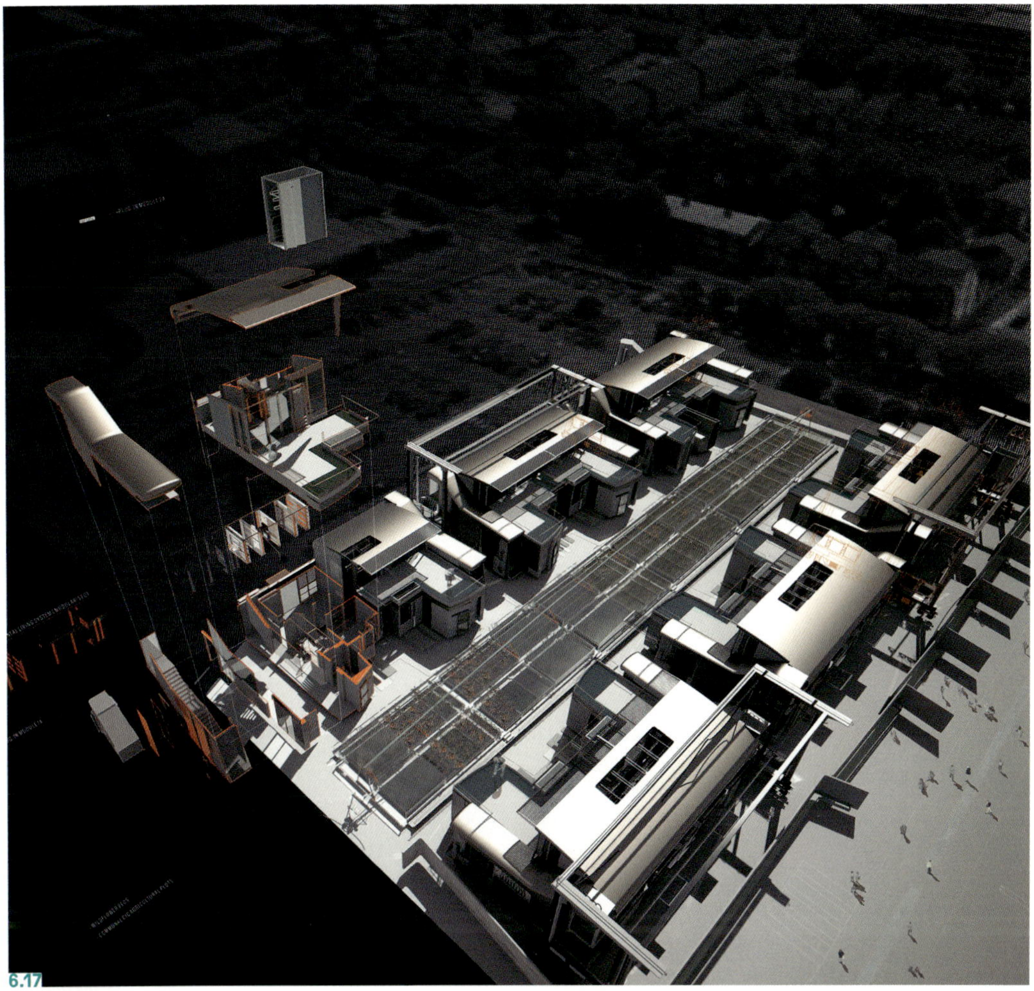

6.17

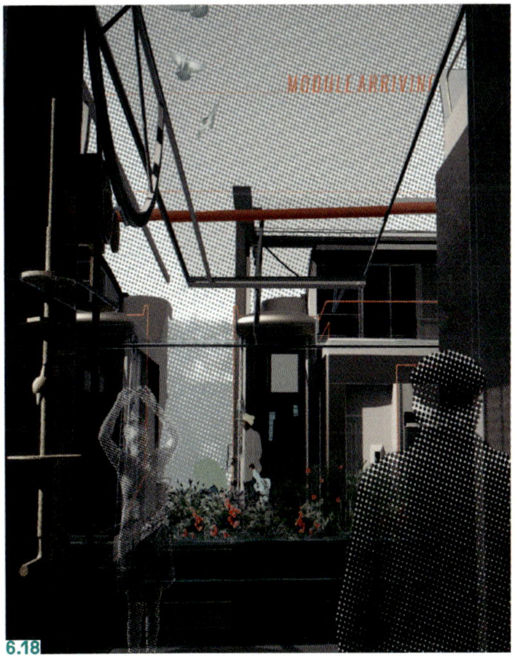

6.18

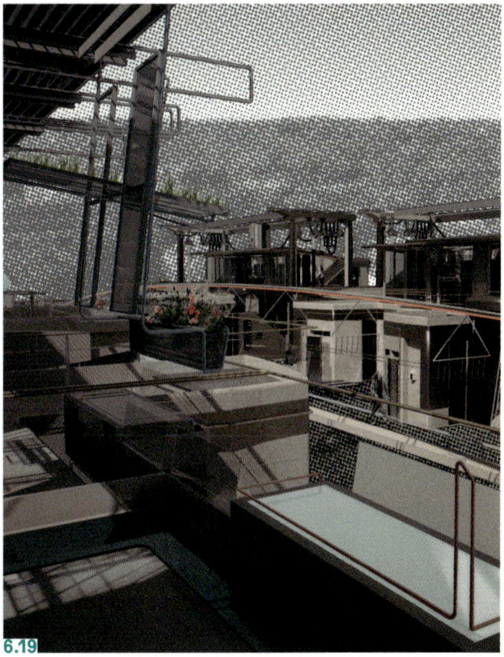

6.19

UG7

Time goes, you say? Ah no, alas, time stays, we go

Pascal Bronner, Thomas Hillier

Year 2
Ella Adu, Se (Elva) Choi, Lap (Justin) Chow, Joanna Hobbs, Ka Law, Alvin Lim, Margarita Marsheva, Ella Wragg, Douglas Yang

Year 3
Iman Raisa Datoo, Stefan Florescu, Klaudia Kapinska, Liam Merrigan, Iman Mohd Hadzhalie, Panagiotis Tzannetakis, Michelle Wang

We would like to thank our technical tutor Nick Westby and our critics throughout the year: Julia Backhaus, Scott Batty, Matthew Butcher, Ed Clark, Mollie Claypool, Tina Di Carlo, Pedro Font-Alba, James Hampton, Bill Hodgson, Sofia Krimizi, Dionysia Kypraiou, CJ Lim, Tim Lucas, Adriana Massidda, Regner Ramos, Bob Sheil

During the Age of Enlightenment, French philosopher Denis Diderot co-founded, edited and compiled the first volume of his *Universal Dictionary of Arts and Sciences*, cataloguing the cutting edge of contemporary technologies and 'mechanical arts' of the time. In his wildest dreams he could not have foreseen that, 250 years later, mankind would be living out a large part of its collective life inside virtual machines and electronic devices. As we enter the third generation of the Digital Revolution, we must ask ourselves if we are losing our affinity with the analogue, the physical, the crafted and the tangible.

These questions were explored through the typology of the 'archive' in order to examine the value of our physical existence in an increasingly digital world. The notion of the archive is incredibly diverse and ever-evolving, be it the Svalbard Global Seed Vault in Norway, often called the 'Doomsday Vault' or the mass art reproduction factories of Dafen Village in Shenzhen, China, where thousands of classic western paintings are reproduced on a daily basis. The artist Joseph Cornell, who rarely ventured beyond his home in New York State, created an archive in his basement comprising thousands of objects he called his dossiers of paper ephemera 'explorations', which took him, his imagination and his work around the world – a route to armchair travelling.

Disassemble

The unit travelled to and through Russia, visiting Moscow and Saint Petersburg, both famed for their cultural history and deep tradition in technological innovation. Before this journey, and in preparation for it, the students were asked to research, discover and disassemble a historical object from Russia's past, present or (hypothesised) future and archive it in an inventive way. Taking inspiration from *Diderot's Dictionary of Arts and Sciences*, they classified, catalogued, drew and described everything about this artifact, creating a new architectural assemblage that was used as a research tool to help them discover their programme, site and brief for the rest of the year.

Assemble

Informed by their disassembled archive-architectures and field trip investigations in Russia, the students proposed buildings that aimed to question the meaning of the archive in the digital age, challenge the conventions of drawn architecture and speculate on the relationships between old and new technologies and their cause-and-effect on the built environment. They did this whilst utilising Russia's dialogue between historical tradition and its thirst for technological advancement.

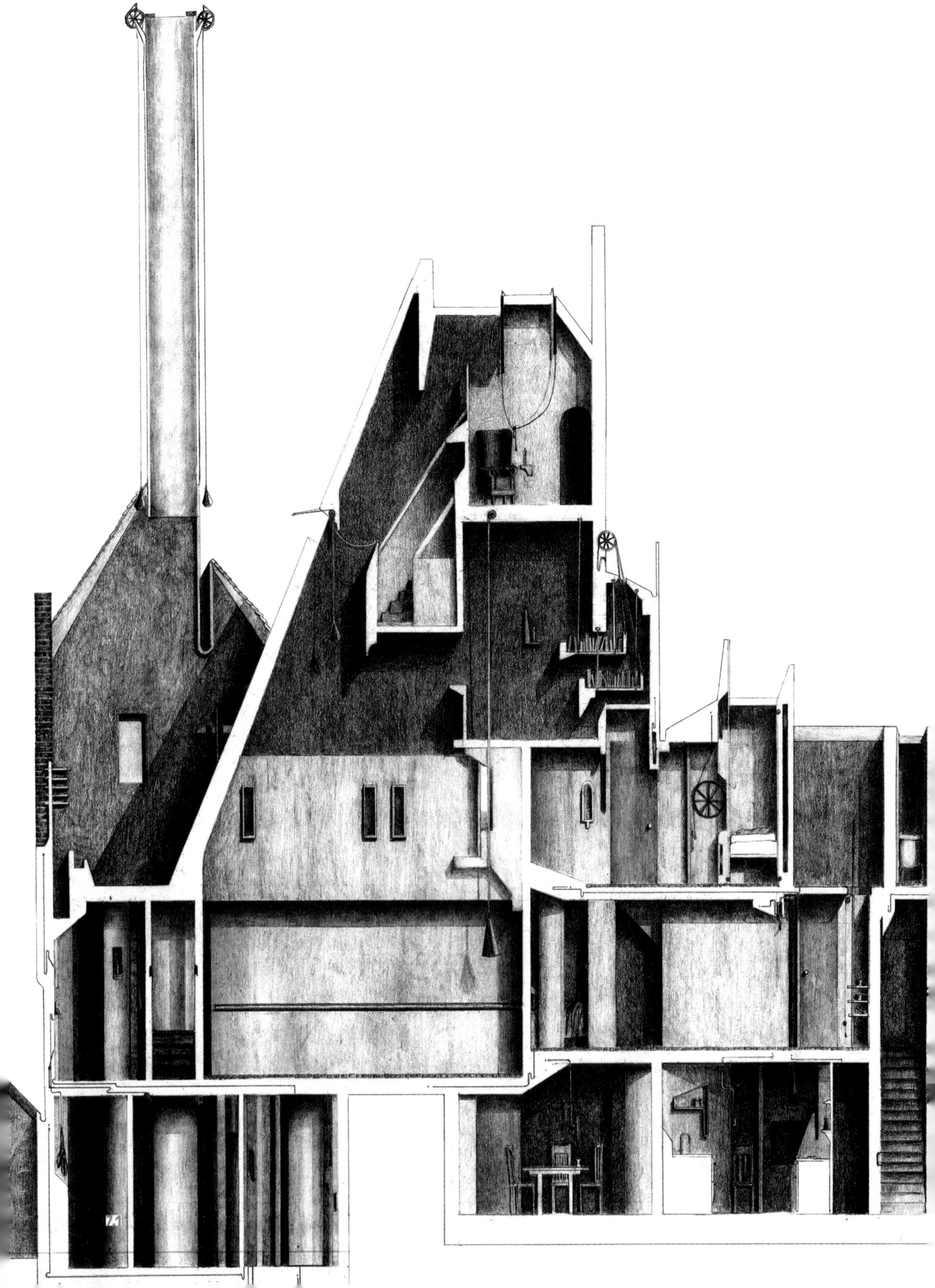

Fig. 7.1 Joanna Hobbs Y2, 'The Choreographer's Home'. Caught between two love affairs, Vaslav Nijinsky, often claimed to be the greatest male dancer of the early 20th century, is banished from the Ballet Russe and forbidden to dance. Forced to pursue his passion in complete secrecy, his home, located in close proximity to the Mariinsky Theatre, becomes a finely tuned map of moments allowing his family to conceal his movements to the watchful world outside. **Fig. 7.2 Iman Mohd Hadzhalie** Y3, 'The Archive of Lost Russian Treasures'. Sunken within the Alexander Nevsky Monastery of St. Petersburg lies a choreographed landscape of water, myth and buried treasure. These moat-protected archives, research and exhibition spaces wait in anticipation for the famous '10 lost treasures of Russia to fill their halls. As each treasure is found and exhibited, the architecture and surrounding landscape evolves in celebration through a series of water-powered devices, but all is not what it seems as below this undulating landscape lies the real treasures which are secretly removed, replaced and replicated creating a secret underground archive for the Russian elite. **Fig. 7.3 Stefan Florescu** Y3, 'The 1961 Space Race Egg'. With a profound and poetic Russian soul, Fabergé's works of art, like the stories they tell, continue to exert a powerful fascination as hypnotic today as it ever was. As with all of Faberge's eggs this one aims to archive one of the most astonishing events in human history, the first human space flight. This miniature world aims to encapsulate and express architectonically what people felt when they found out that man had entered the unknown.

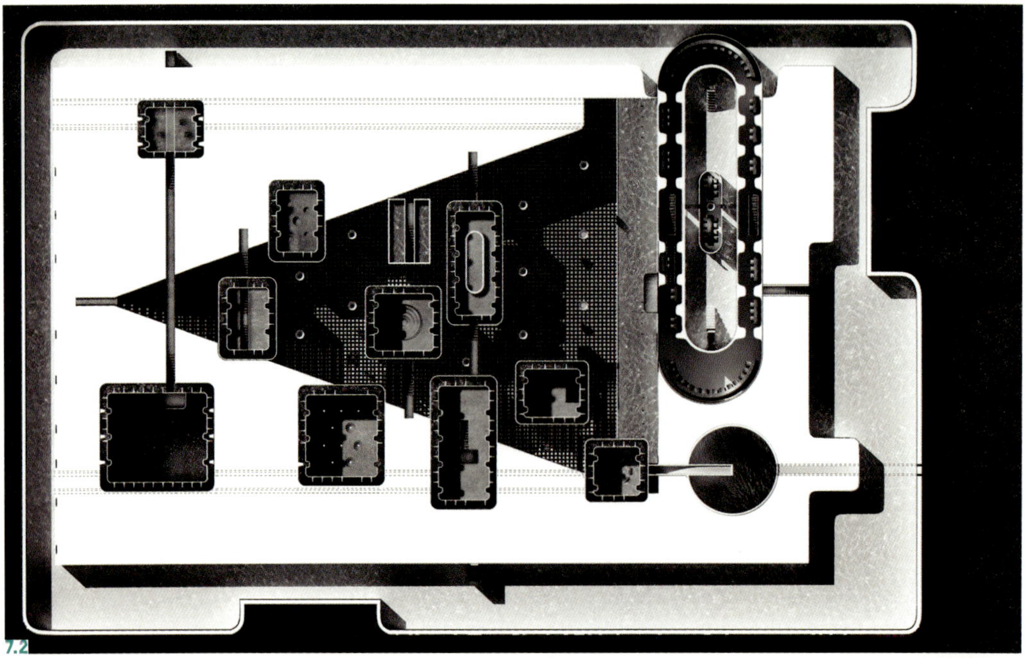

7.2

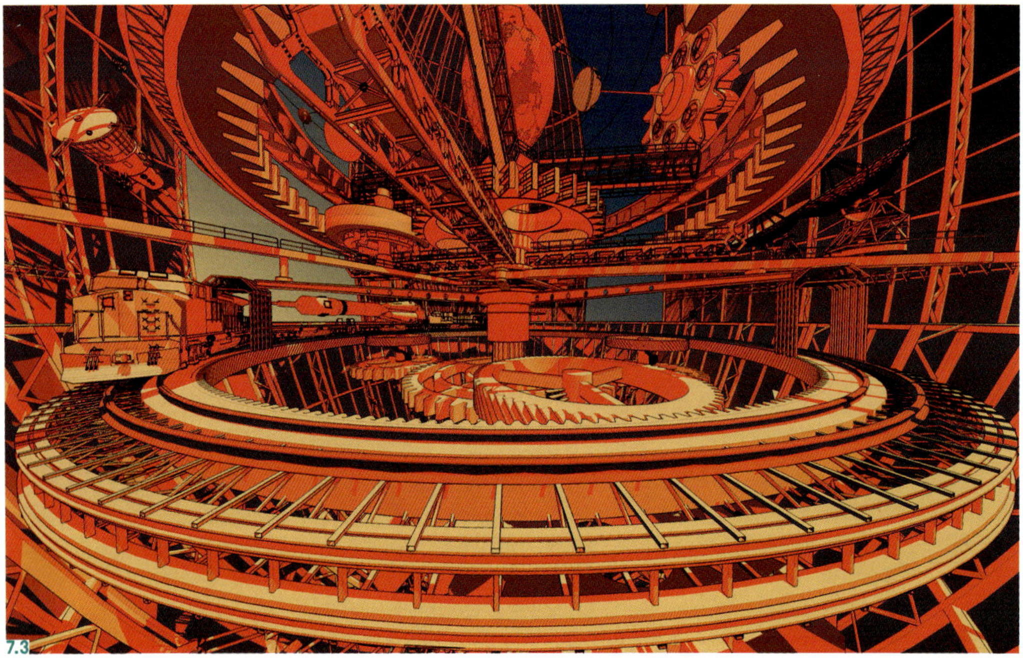

7.3

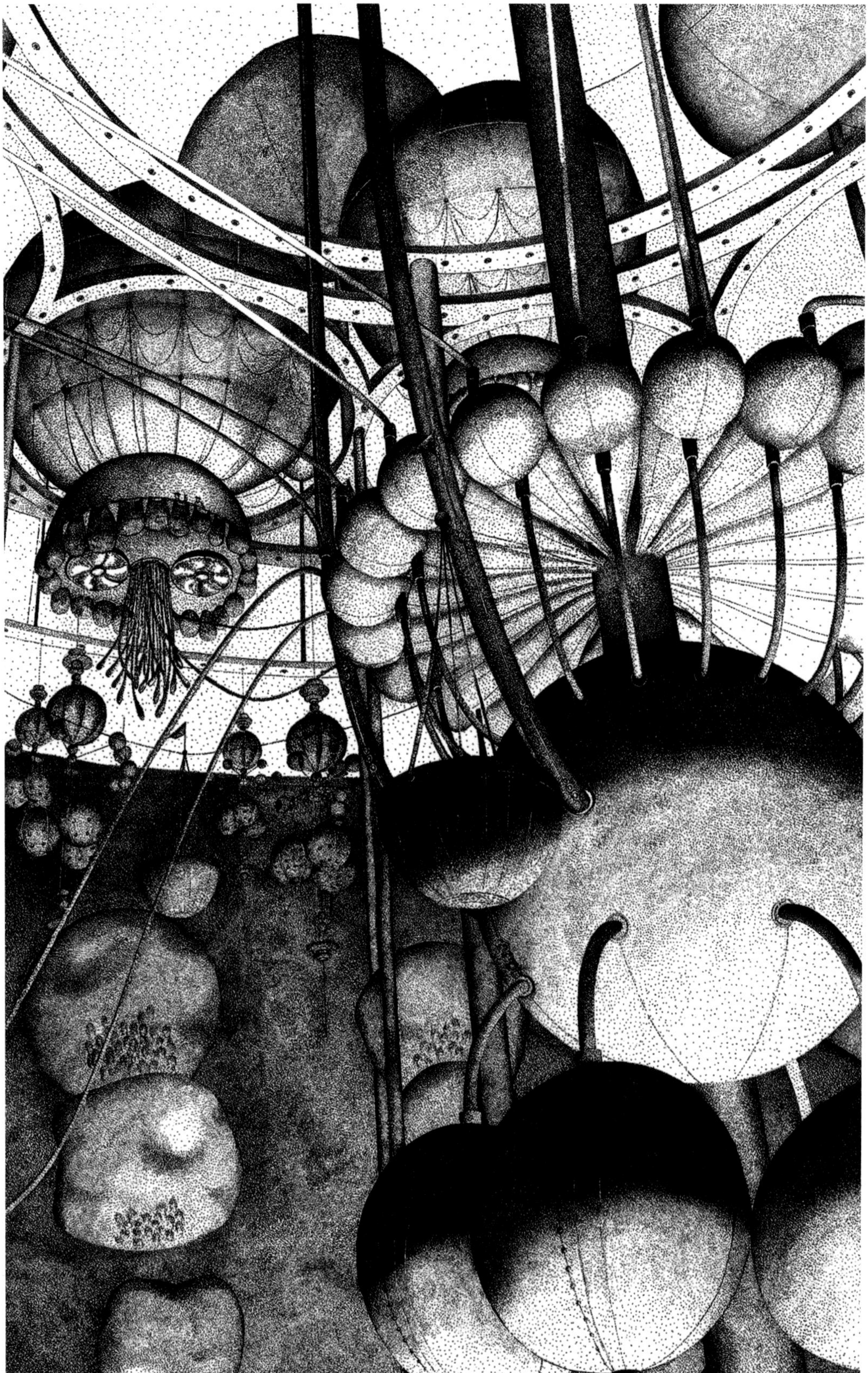

7.4

Fig. 7.4 Michelle Wang Y3, 'The Mirny Buttery'. Influenced by Russia's controversial import embargo on food in relation to the Ukraine crisis. The project speculates on the future of Russian food production by reintroducing the once thriving butter industry into a disused diamond mine in Eastern Siberia. Utilising the extreme weather and environmental conditions of this – the second-largest excavated hole in the world – to create an underground buttery of gigantic proportions. This alien landscape creates a new datum line within this abandoned environment which is filled with a series of methane-powered floating islands that include grazing land for dairy cows and dairy production and storage facilities. The project acts as a piece of architectural propaganda illustrating Russian self-reliance.

Fig. 7.5 Klaudia Kapinska Y3, 'The Amber Extraction Instrument'. This device proposes the reconstruction of the now lost Amber Room of Catherine's Palace in Tsarskoye Selo near St Petersburg, which until its disappearance during World War II was considered the 'Eighth Wonder of the World'. Tree resin, used as a substitute for pure amber, is slowly and meticulously collected via a series of resin extraction machines that are mechanically attached to a set of pine trees in the grounds of the Palace. Across one year exactly 270 litres of resin is extracted, heated using a constant flow of warm water and constantly set in motion across the instrument, turning the mechanism itself into one of the lost panels of this world famous chamber.

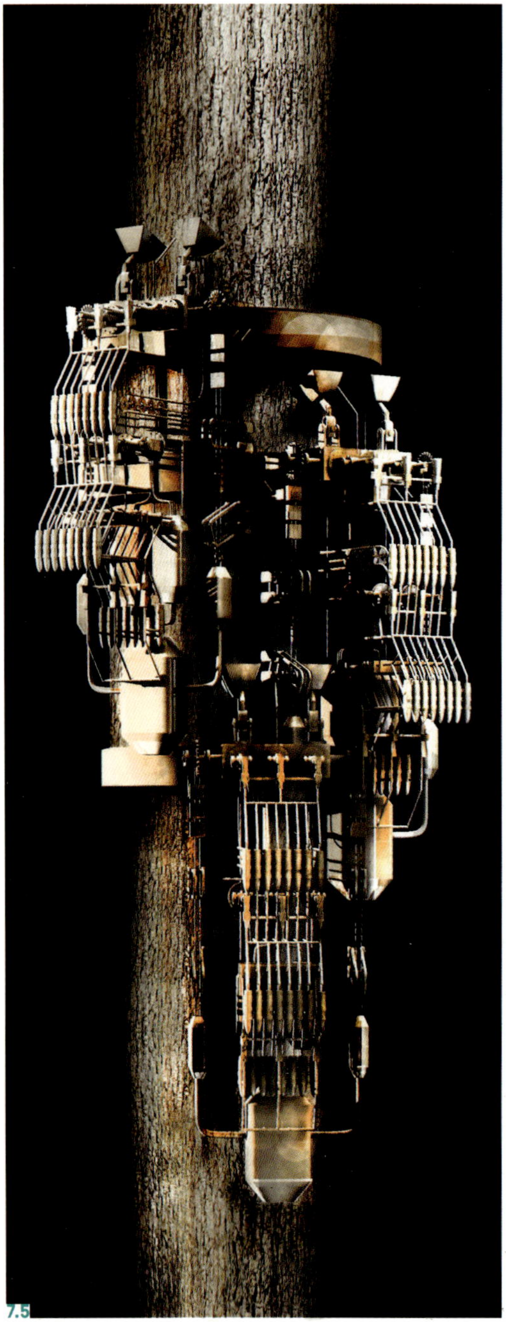

7.5

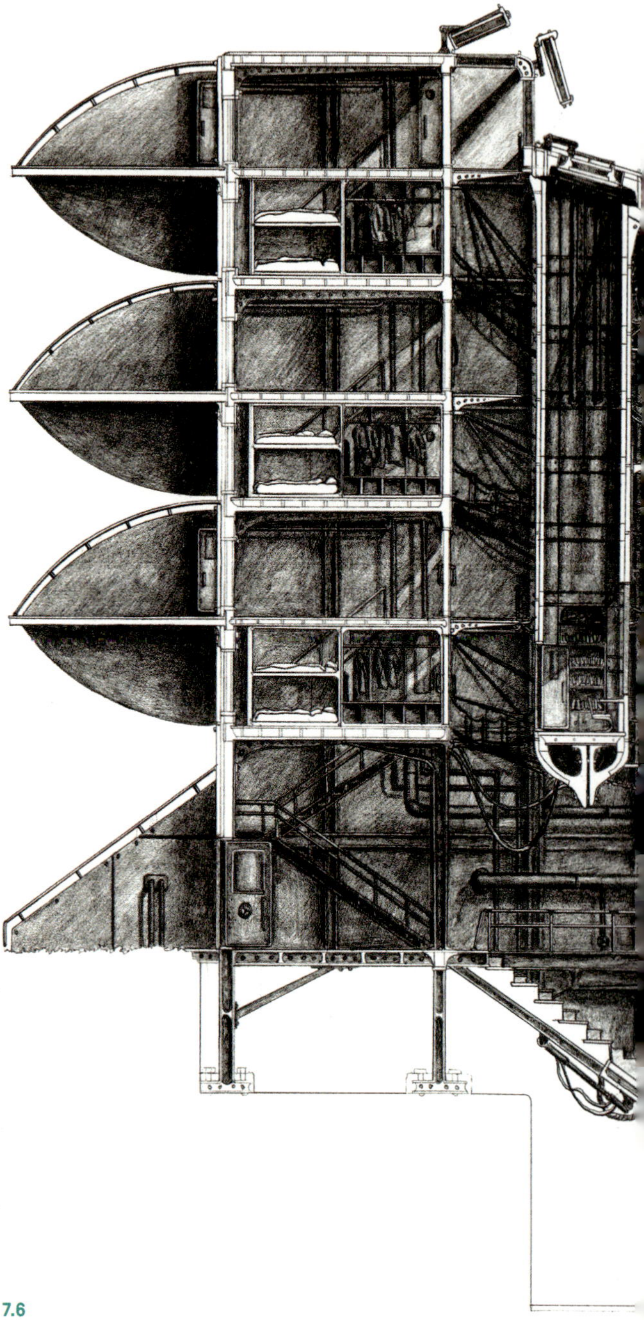

7.6

Fig. 7.6 **Douglas Yang** Y2, 'Ekateringof Science Fiction Writers Commune'. Established by the Russian government in the year 2142, an ancient theatre, a relic from the past, is used as a portal to another world. Located within an abandoned theme park in the historic Ekateringof Park in St Petersburg, this concrete monolith, inspired by Arthur C. Clarke's 'Space Odyssey', is designed to look as though it 'landed' within this abandoned and barren landscape. Inside and hung from its ceiling are a series of bespoke writing modules, all of which give the writer a unique view of both the surrounding landscape and the infinite underground library of science fiction that continues to grow with every new writer that enters this brave new world.

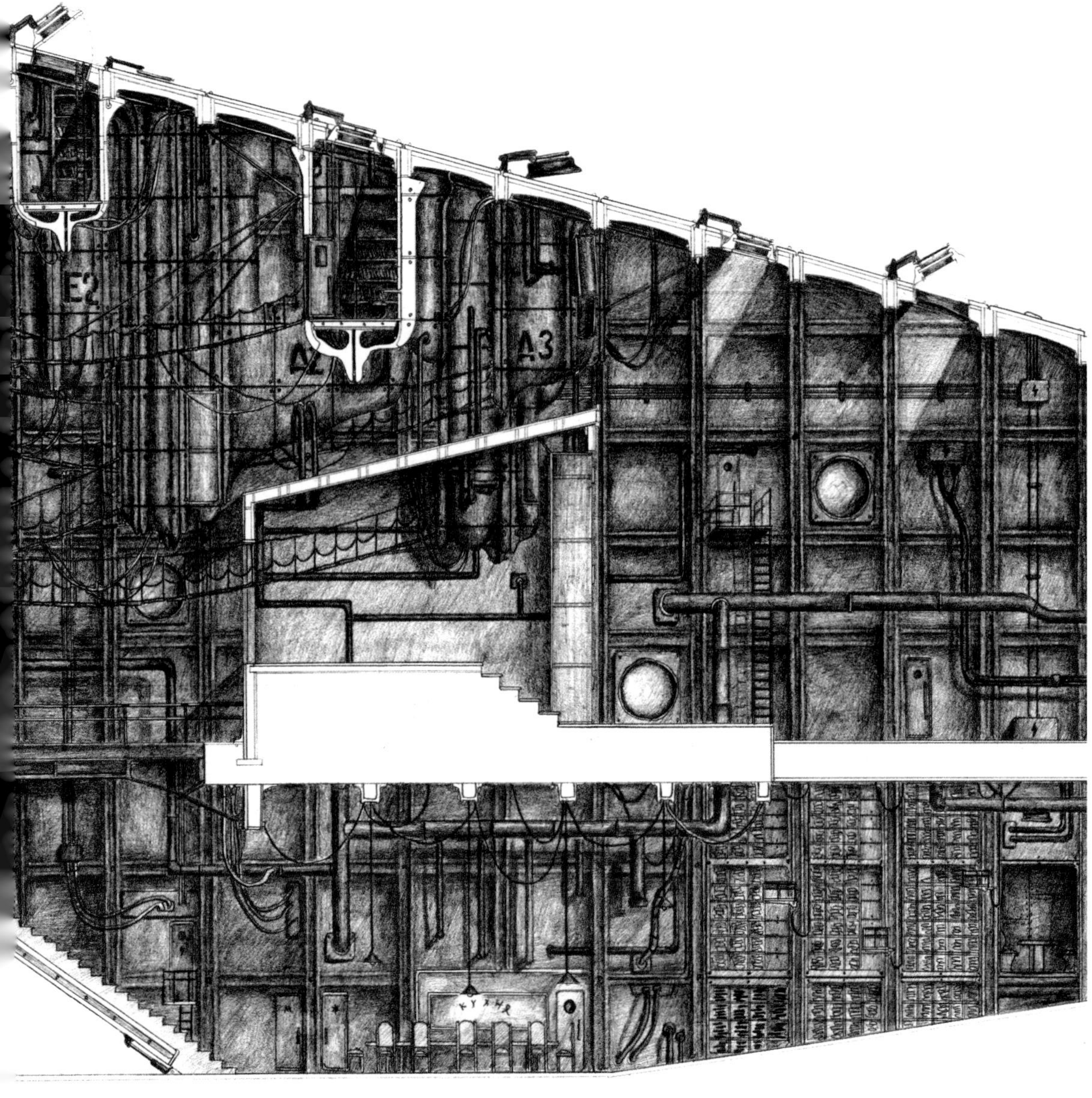

Fig. 7.7 Alvin Lim Y2, 'The Mariinsky Monastery'. Set on the abandoned marine fortress of Kronsholt, 30 kilometers due west from St Petersburg's preeminent ballet company, the Mariinsky Theatre, lies this ballet dance academy which is inspired by the intense symmetry and repetition of Russian ballet. The building is composed of monastical accommodation and ballet rehearsal spaces, each individually tailored to different elements of ballet and a reconstruction of the actual Mariinsky stage that is constantly watched over by the 'clapping' tectonic audience. The dancers who dwell here are devoted to the recreation of the original 1876 Tchaikovsky score of Swan Lake, which was deemed too difficult and agonising to accomplish, with the aim to better their bitter rival, the Bolshoi Theatre in Moscow.

Fig. 7.8 Lap (Justin) Chow Y2, 'Living on Mars: A Catalogue of Everyday Items'. The project posits a fictional timeline where England colonises Mars, in the 1970s. To this end, a series of bespoke and eccentric domestic mechanisms were designed for use inside the 'Arcadia Holiday Resort', a popular holiday destination located within Mars Arcadia Planitia. Tourists visiting the resort would relish unproductive forms of entertainment and luxury that back on earth people would find normal.

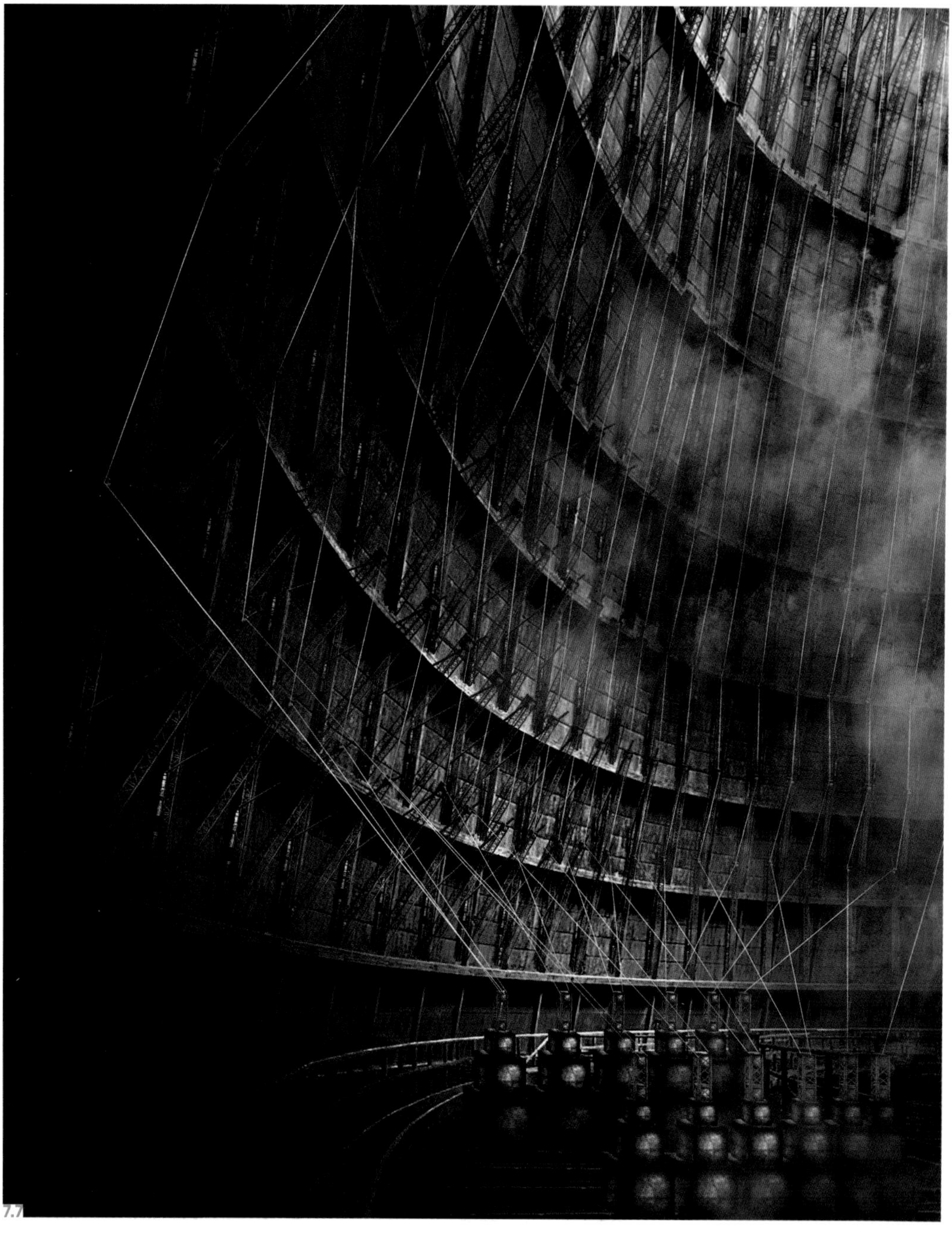

7.7

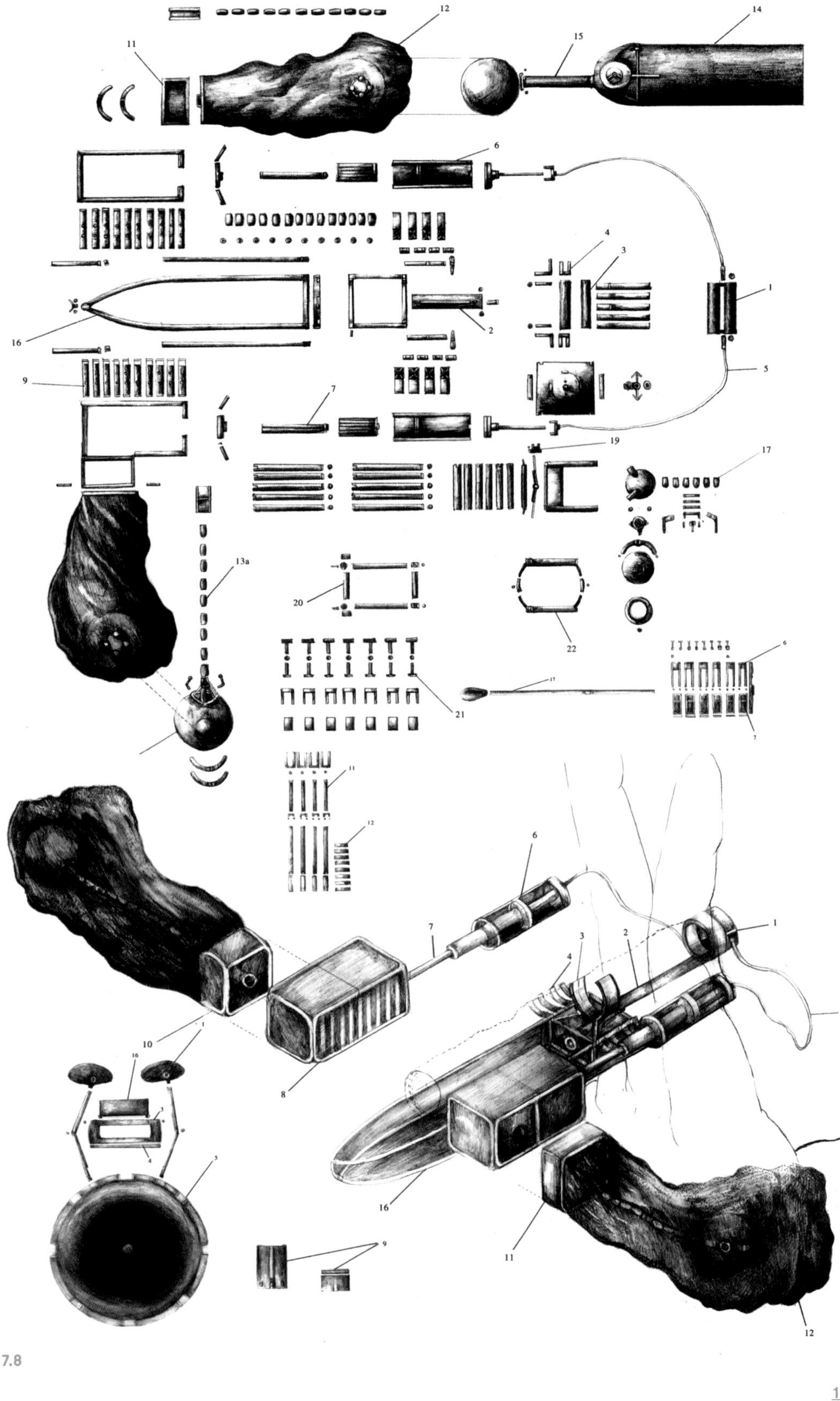

7.8

Fig. 7.9 Ka Law Y2, 'Snail Island'. Inspired by the mysterious Buyan Island of Russian folklore, Snail Island is a water quality monitoring facility inhabited and operated solely by African Giant Snails whose unique shells are used as a barometer of water cleanliness. Surrouded by lettuce fields and a fibre optic copper-tipped boundary, used as a snail defense mechanism, this artificial island floats across the severely polluted Neva Bay in St. Petersburg, leaving in its wake a trail of clean water. **Fig. 7.10 Liam Merrigan** Y3, 'COPM-4'. 2020: The Russian Federation's COPM protocol (System for Operative Investigative Activities) extends beyond monitoring digital media. COPM-4 intrudes upon Moscow. A fleet of airborne probes indiscriminately survey citizens from above, functioning more as a tool of propaganda than law enforcement. Infrastructure underpinning the scheme is deliberately monumental. An array of aerostatic platforms cover the city, surveillance data being therefore assimilated by a new typology of supercomputer housed within an imposing steel edifice. **Fig. 7.11 Elva Choi** Y2, 'The Chairmakers Guild'. In response to Plato's theory of forms on 'what makes a chair a chair' and society's recommendation of a perfect sitting position, the Chairmakers Guild provides students an opportunity to design and make chairs free from ideology. As each chair is made, it is immediately archived in the surrounding gridded landscape, ensuring no one inside the building can see them, to encourage designs to be forever original and experimental.

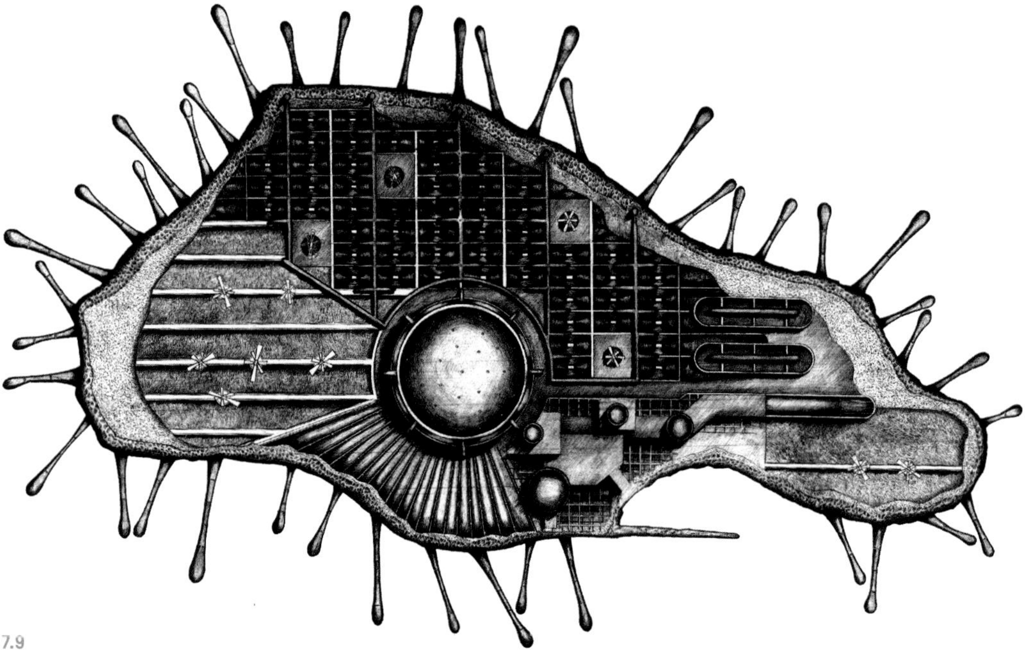

7.9

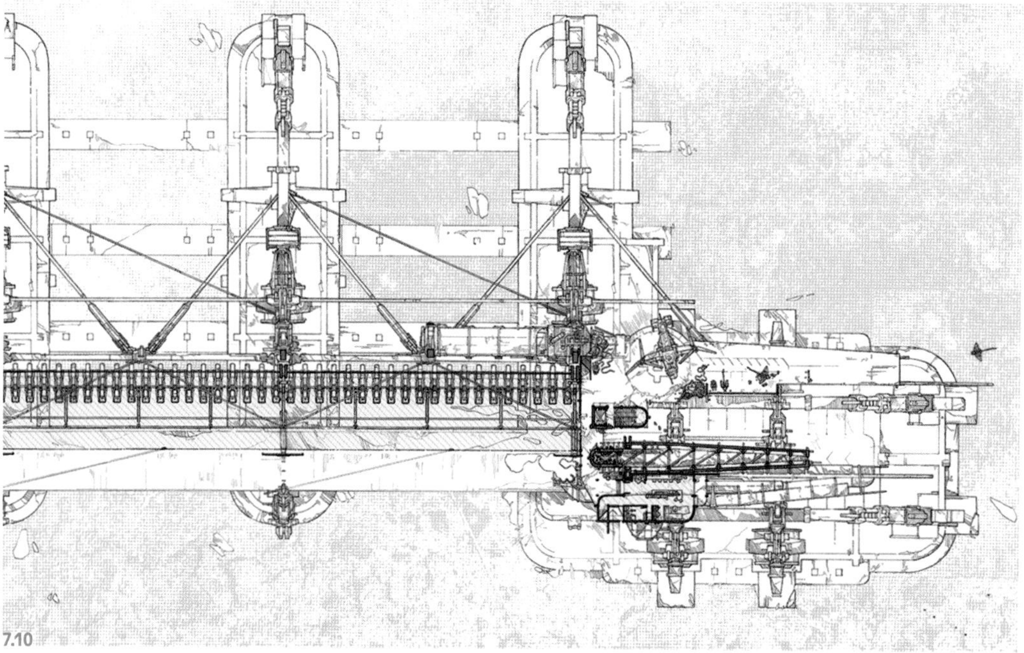

7.10

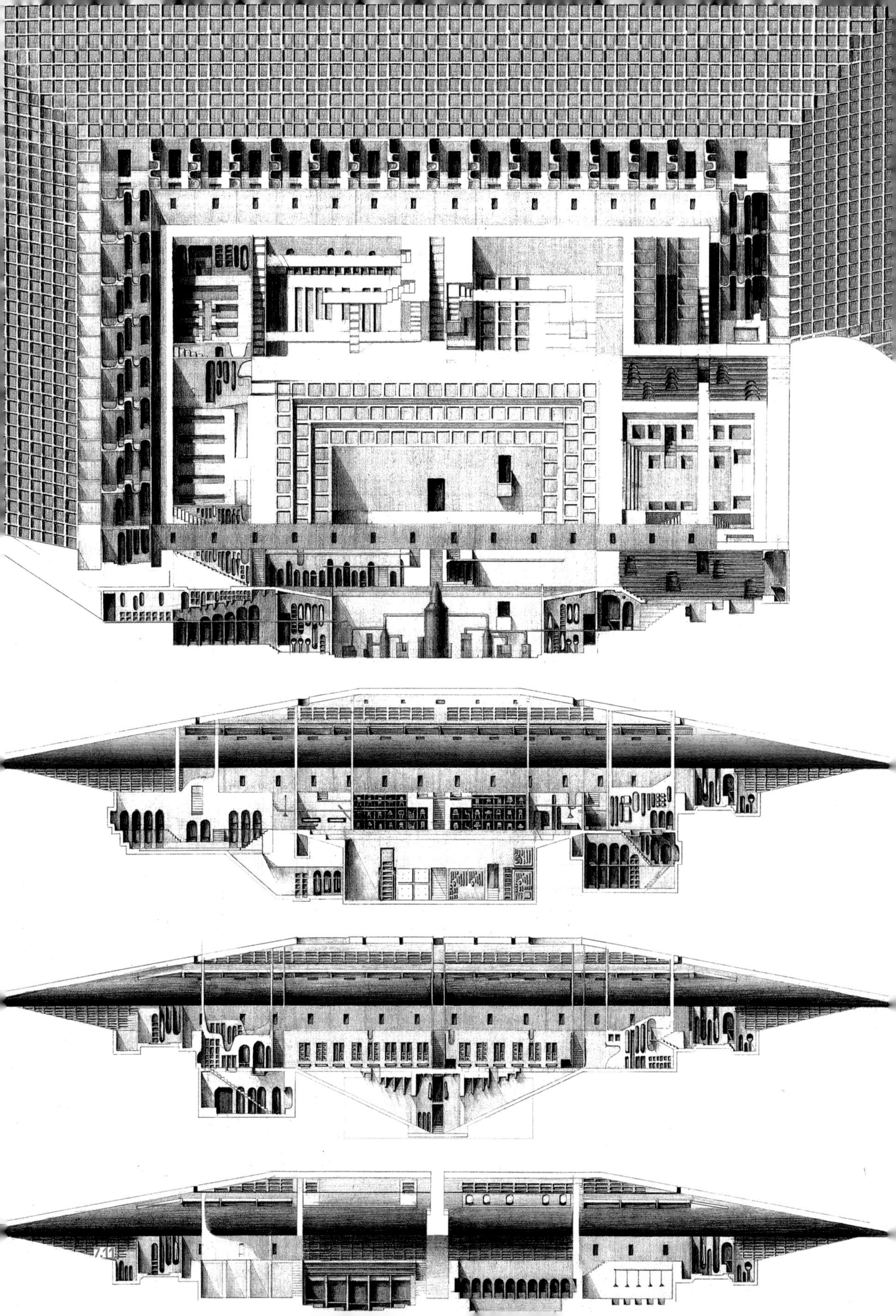

7.11

UG8

Souvenirs and Foreign Ghosts

Colin Herperger, Thomas Pearce

Year 2
Ella Caldicott, Jun Chan, Krina Christopoulou, Morgan Hamel de Monchenault, James Hepper, Janis Ho, Rory Noble-Turner, Daniel Pope, Ryan Walsh

Year 3
James Bradford, Danny Dimbleby, Tae Woo (Freddy) Hong, Charles Redman, Isaac Simpson, Matthew Taylor, Minh Tran

Special thanks to our technical tutor Scott Batty and to Soma Sato. Thanks to our critics and speakers Charles Arsène-Henry, Alessandro Ayuso, Amy Begg, William Bondin, Tom Budd, Alastair Browning, Matthew Butcher, Nat Chard, Max Dewdney, Patch Dobson-Pérez, Gary Edwards, Stephen Gage, Penelope Haralambidou, Niki-Marie Jansson, Carlos Jiménez, Mara Kanthak, Felipe Lanuza Rilling, Ifigeneia Liangi, Anna Liu, Luke Lupton, Johanna Maierski, Shaun Murray, Ian Ng, Davide Sacconi, Peter Scully, Greg Storrar, Tom Svilans, Mohammed Syafiq Jubri, Josh Toh, William Trossell, Athanasios Varnavas, Emmanuel Vercruysse, Boon Yik Chung and Simon Withers

Thank you as well to our sponsors: Harlequin Floors, Fernox, & ScanLAB Projects

Max Ernst paints a garden. When he has finished the picture, he sees that he has forgotten to paint a tree. He immediately has the tree cut down.
Jean Baudrillard (1997)

Souvenir is a verb. To remember (*se souvenir*) is to construct, repair, erase, project, extend, consolidate, extract, mystify. Memory is a tool of invention as well as a repository of truth. This year UG8 investigated how memory and mistranslation can play an active role in creative practice.

——We set out to refashion (the) Souvenir as a complex and subjective material practice of physical and mental construction, oscillating between the stubborn materiality of the physical artefact and an active notion of memory. Preferring the German-English mistranslation "to make a picture" to the more passive English "to take a picture", we followed Max Ernst into his garden and started to edit reality driven by the shadows, gaps, outcasts, eccentricities, aberrations and off-cuts of memories, hidden between the cracks of consciousness and the seams of London's urban fabric.

——Our field trip lead us to Japan, the theatre of conflicting mnemonic practices of ritual remembering and constructive forgetting, where the re-enactment of architectural craftsmanship outlives the western obsession with the so-called 'original' object or building. Our own building projects were then conceived as 'Foreign Ghosts', which enjoyed the opportunity of being foreign within the familiar context of London. Following in the footsteps of architects like Bruno Taut or Frank Lloyd Wright, who architecturally absorbed 'Japan-ness' through the lens of their own ambitions, we devised architectural strategies that deployed our imported memories while leaving space for creative (mis)translation, constructive forgetting, selective amnesia, fabricated origins and the ever-shifting re-inventions of the verb *se souvenir*.

——In UG8, we like to make disobedient things and find curiosity within challenging ideas. This is delightfully hard but is nurtured within the studio through creative practice – a focused learning of architectural craft and technique through repeated prediction, attempt, reflection and iteration. This allows for the development of an intuitive ability to become precise in a manner that does not hold responsibility to prove, but more importantly the will to find out. We seek pleasure in the precision of the unresolved.

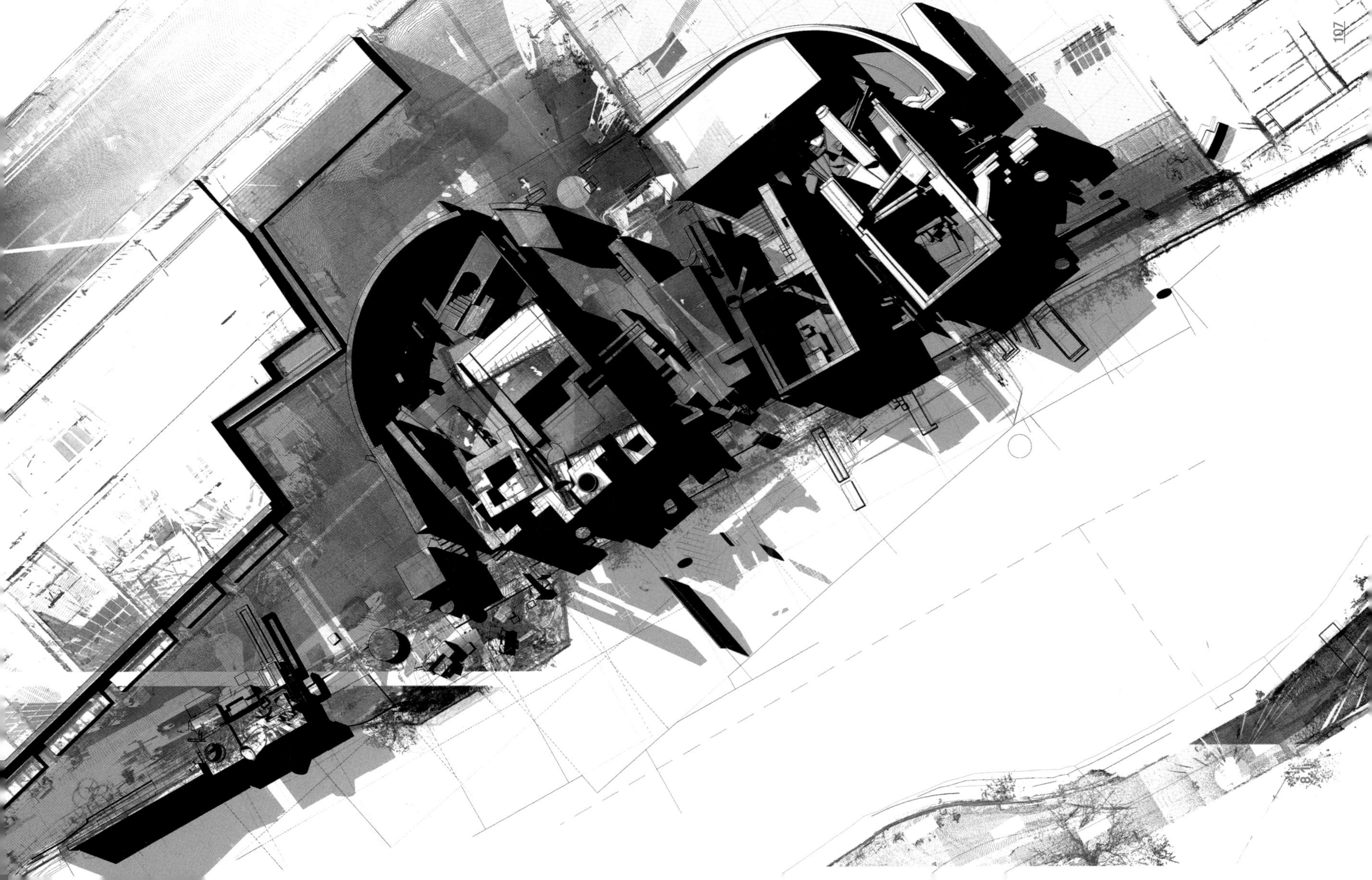

8.1

Fig. 8.1 Isaac Nanabeyin Simpson Y3, 'Discovered Misreadings'. A host for the production, conservation and dissemination of the Survey of London, the building is constructed as a palimpsest of conflicting cartographic systems that encourages conversations between architecture, people and how we read and make the city. **Figs. 8.2 & 8.4 James Hepper** Y2, 'Inhabiting the Space of Desire'. The promenade of tiny bars occupies a deep façade, masking and subverting the existing elevation through a series of drawn, written and fabricated Perecian operations that use confabulated memory, obsessive observation, erasure and inversion as sources of re-invention. **Fig. 8.3 Morgan Hamel De Monchenault** Y2, 'Kingsland Mooring Spa'. The vertical spa occupies the interlocking solids within a refined play of suspended volumes – scaled-up mistranslations of the geometrical rules of Japanese joinery and the spatial qualities of its interstitial voids. **Figs. 8.5 – 8.6 Jun Hao Chan** Y2, 'Weather – Negotiating the Boundary'. Reading the weather not just as a subject matter but also as a co-author of JMW Turner's paintings, the proposal for a house, public library and garden incorporates it as an active element of architectural design, allowing users to experience the intimate variations in the weather of the exterior, interior and transitional.

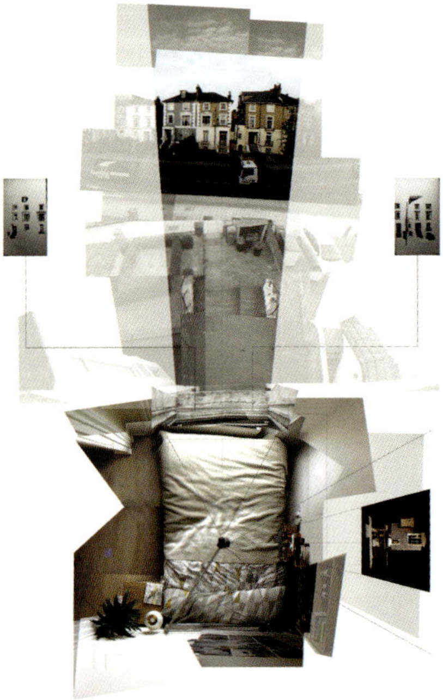
8.2

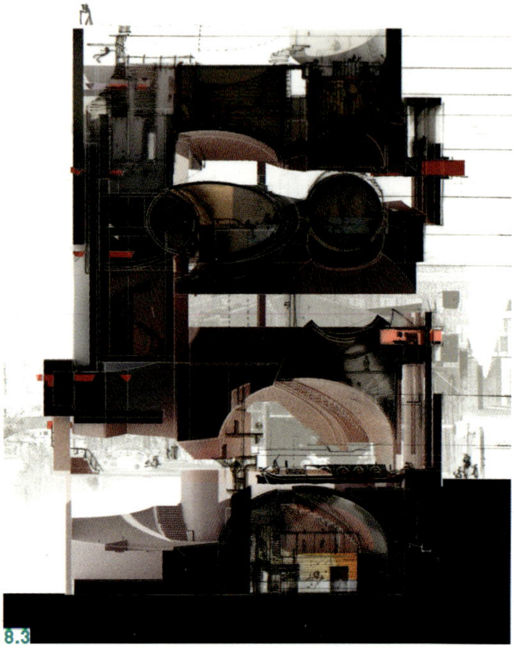
8.3

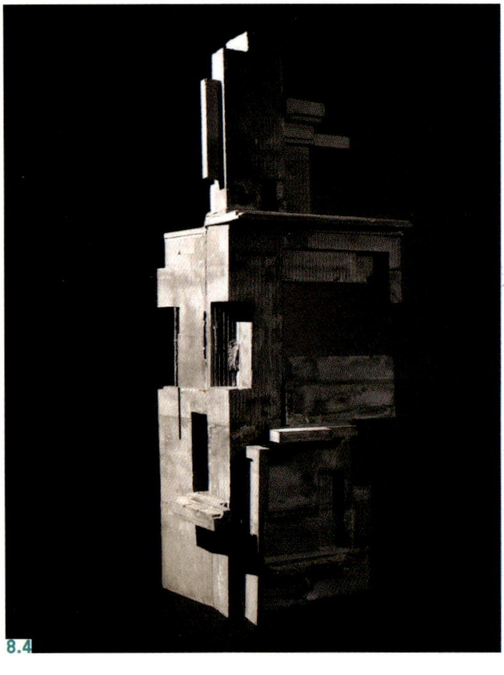
8.4

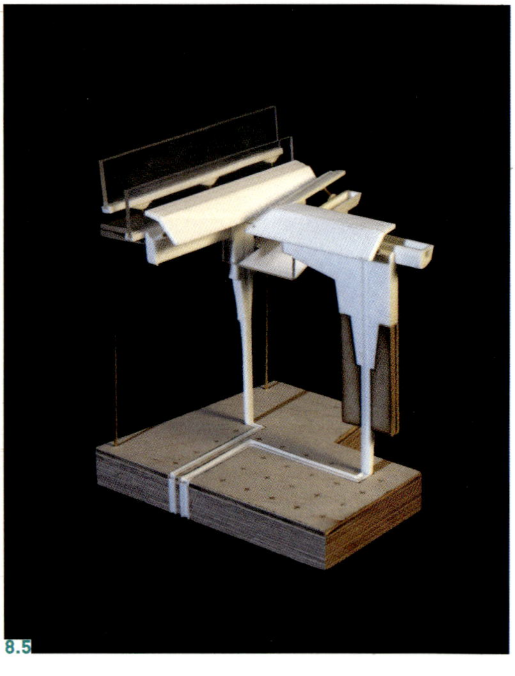
8.5

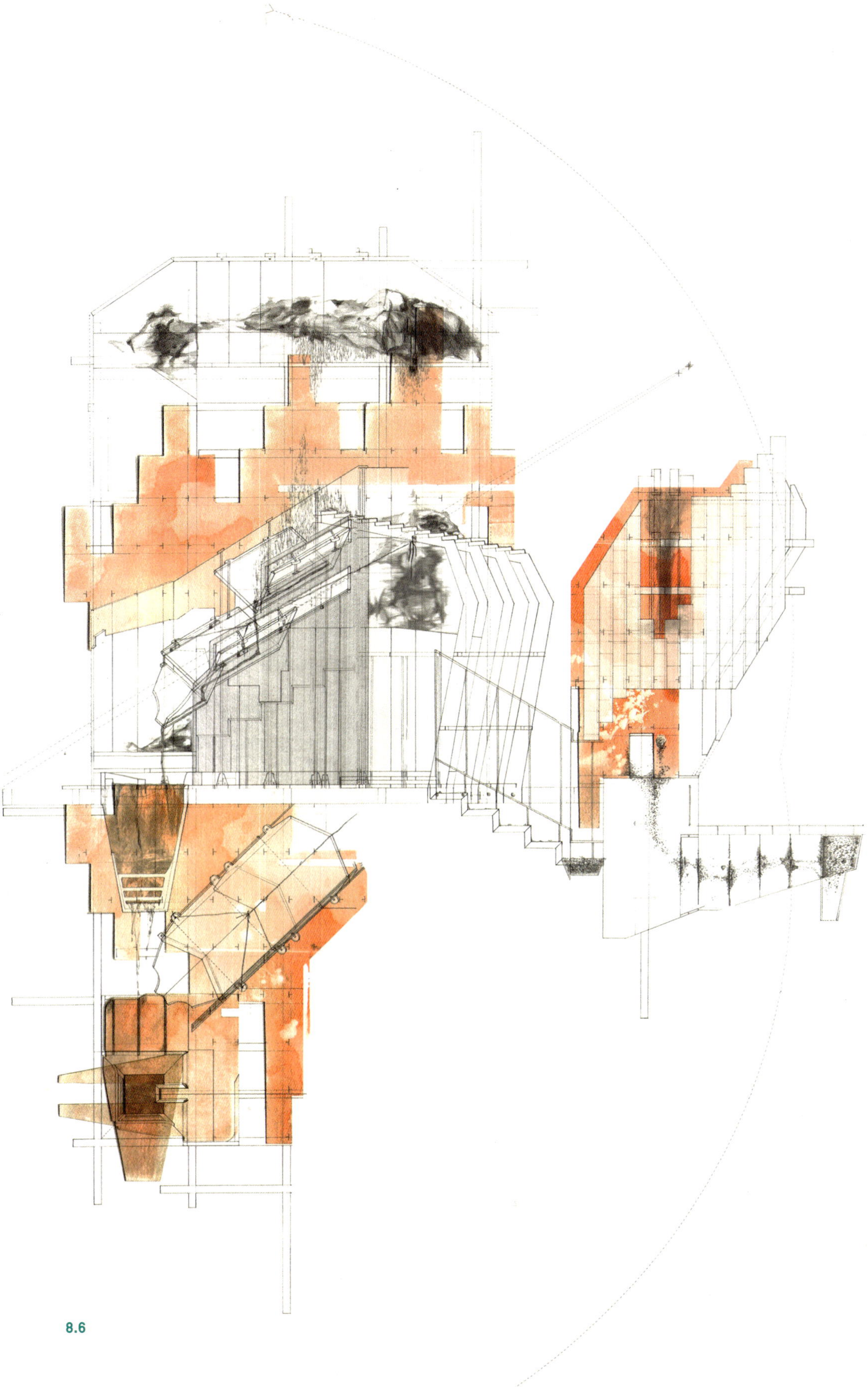

8.6

Figs. 8.7 – 8.8 Tae Woo (Freddie) Hong Y3, 'A Bath of Mnemonic Vectors'. A reterritorialised Japanese bathhouse in Hoxton translating the symmetries and asymmetries of shared memories into measurable architectural units. These memories are diagrammed, encoded and re-staged by masked actors, then digitally captured and algorithmically translated to be 3D printed live in a performative procession of mistranslation. The baths stretch along a central inhabited service wall which separates genders but modulates the desire and projection of the assumed symmetry between the two halves. **Fig. 8.9 Janis Ho** Y2, '24hrs Microcosm'. An exploration of osmotic architectural skins negotiating and staging seduction between a nightclub, convenience store and capsule hotel. The architecture addresses the negotiation between spaces, programmes and people through the deceptive and subtle movement of surfaces. **Fig. 8.10 Ella Caldicott** Y2, 'The Lichen Zoo'. Creating a symbiotic relationship between human and non-human inhabitants on the canalside site – a careful negotiation with the environment allows for the growth, harvesting and processing of lichen products. **Fig. 8.11 Rory Noble-Turner** Y2, 'Caravaggio Dreams of Sushi'. A restaurant etched out from the darkness of the void, an architecture in honour of the art of sushi. It constructs an atmosphere of darkness and curiosity through the careful engineering of light in order to recreate the dramatic world present within Caravaggio's paintings.

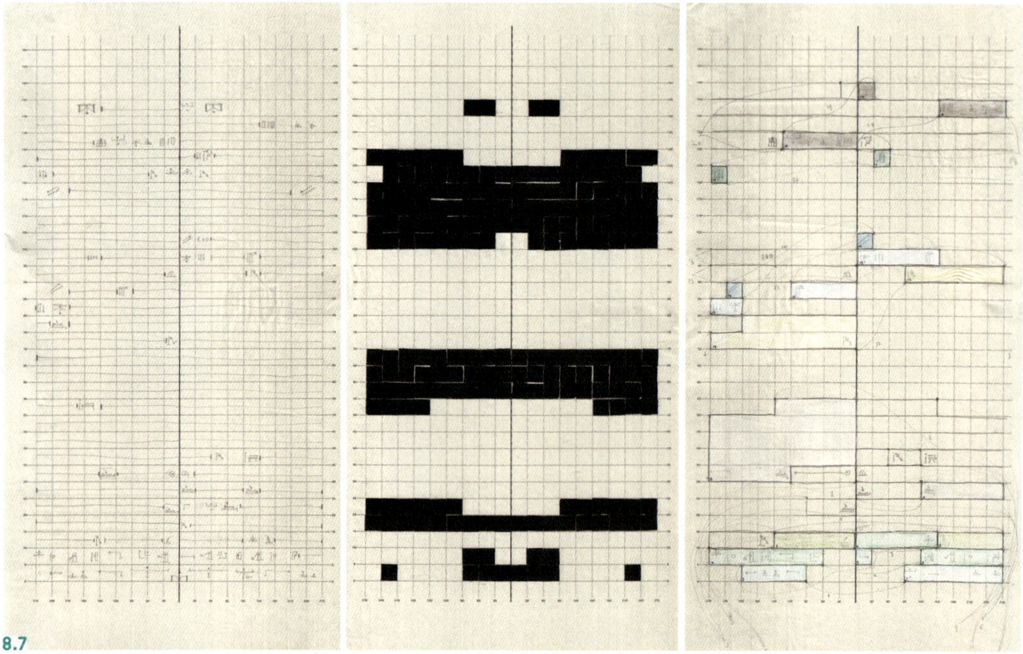

8.7

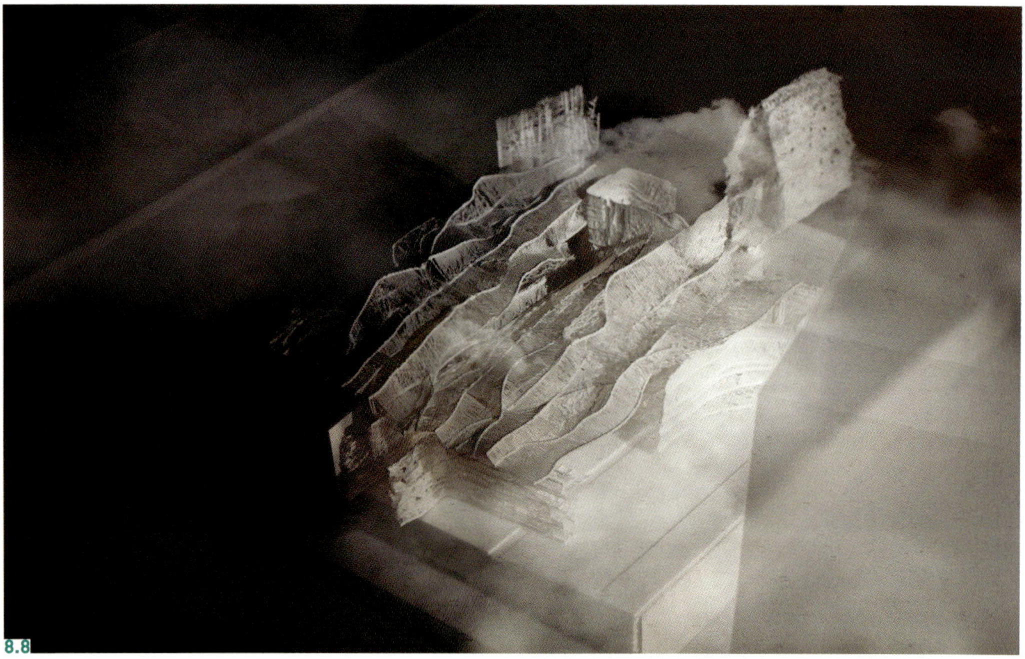

8.8

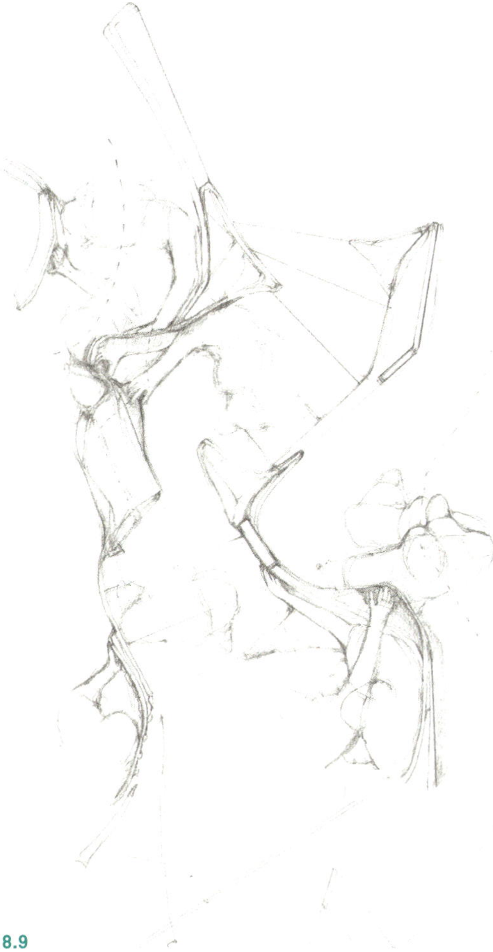

8.9

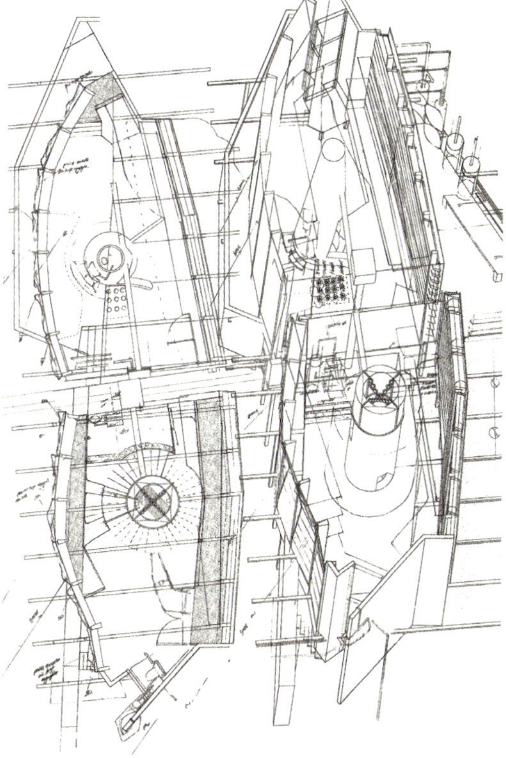

8.10

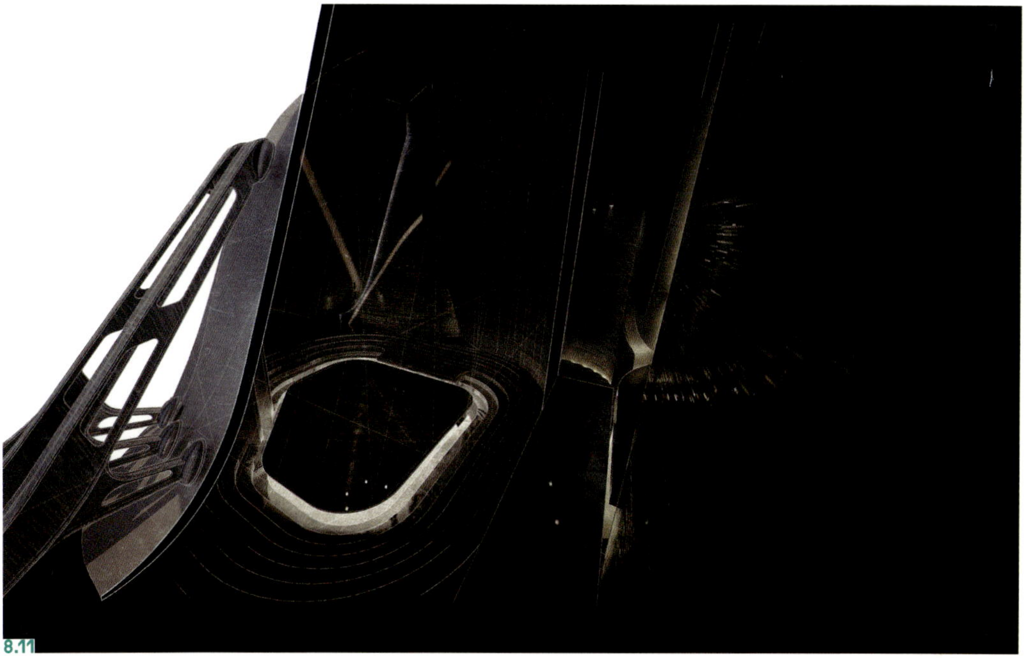

8.11

Fig. 8.12 James Bradford Y3, 'Hoxton Country House'. Seducing the visitor into buying and consuming rural products, the house architecturally re-interprets techniques of the English landscape garden to create a sense of spatial opulence within London's urban fabric. **Figs. 8.13 & 8.17 Minh Ngoc Tran** Y3, 'Gerontosonic Grand Palace'. A destination for elderly people where a Winter and a Summer Palace break the psychological boundaries between companionship and solitude by manipulating the architectural boundaries of acoustics. **Fig. 8.14 Krina Christopoulou** Y2, 'Staging Deception'. The theatre challenges conventions of stage and auditorium to embrace notions of choice and chance – both within the experience of the plays and within the building's design, which is generated through digital and analogue translations of rule-based folds. **Fig. 8.15 Danny Dimbleby** Y3, 'Hotel Derivé'. A Situationist answer to Airbnb, Hotel Derivé forms unique hyper-real narratives that playfully quote scenes and deconstruct cinematic techniques, borrowing scenery such as an architectural Japanese garden. Hotel Derivé flourishes through its users' discussion of 'experience'. **Fig. 8.16 Matthew Taylor** Y3, 'Empowering Focus Through Light'. The calligraphy school uses the ruled geometries of delicate concrete cast shells to modulate light and redefine the perceived boundaries and scale of a hallucinogenic architecture. **Fig. 8.18 Dan Pope** Y2, 'Redrawing Conventions'. A live drawing school collapsing the hierarchy between the object and subject of perspectival drawing, a prosthetic to the body of the site and the body of the drawer.

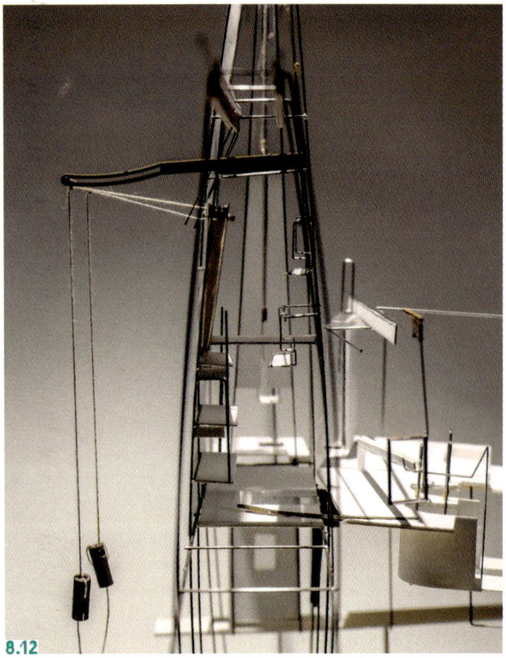

8.12

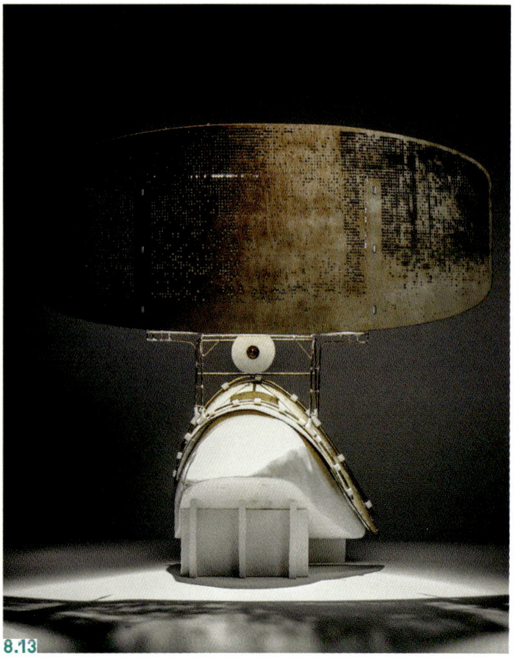

8.13

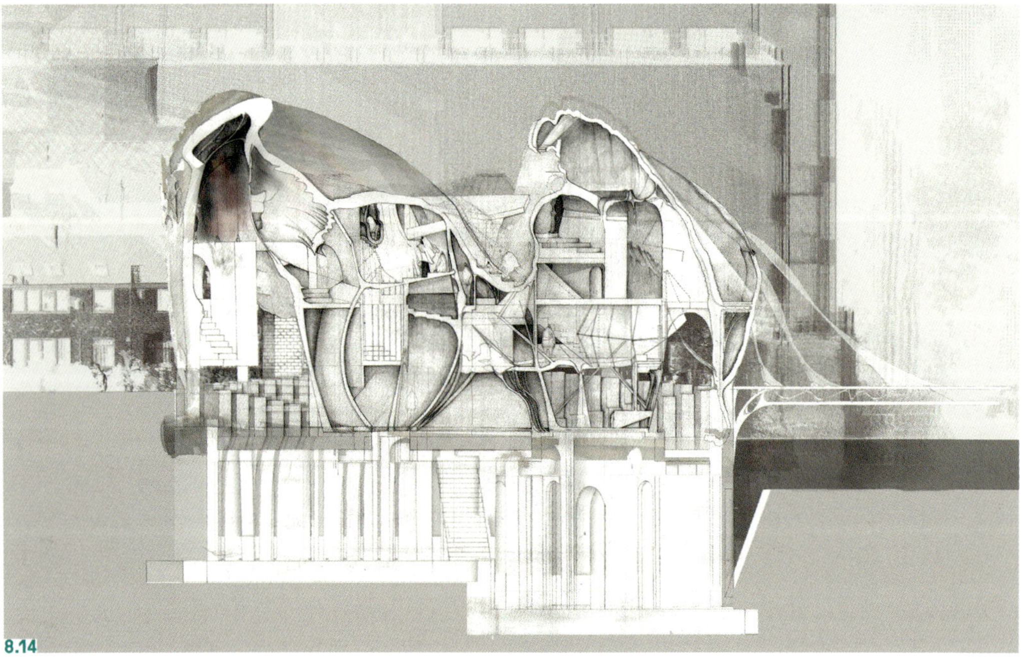

8.14

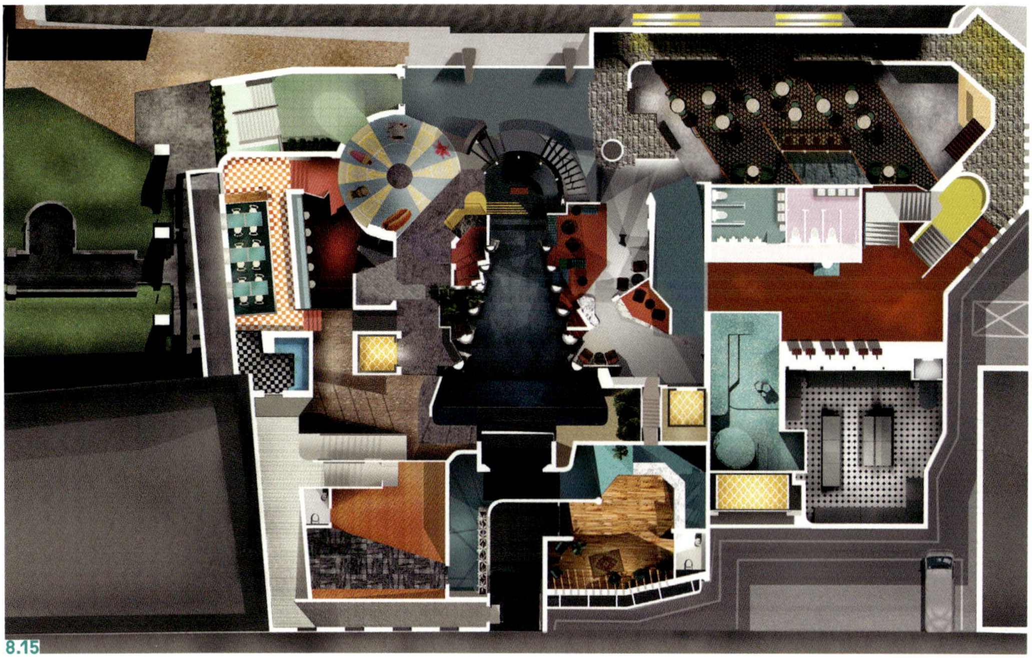

8.15

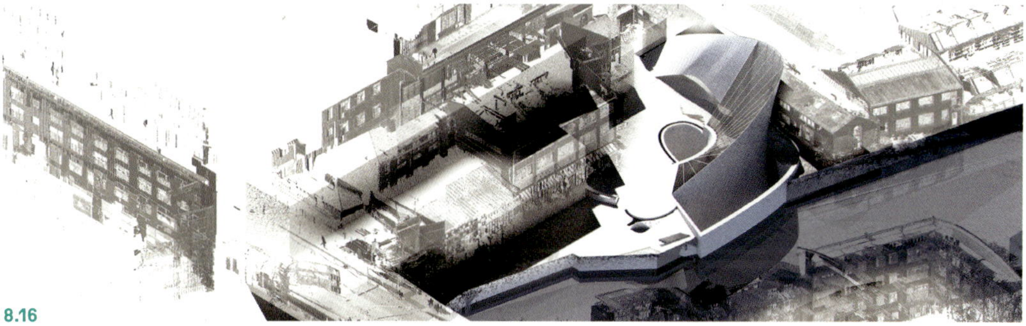

8.16

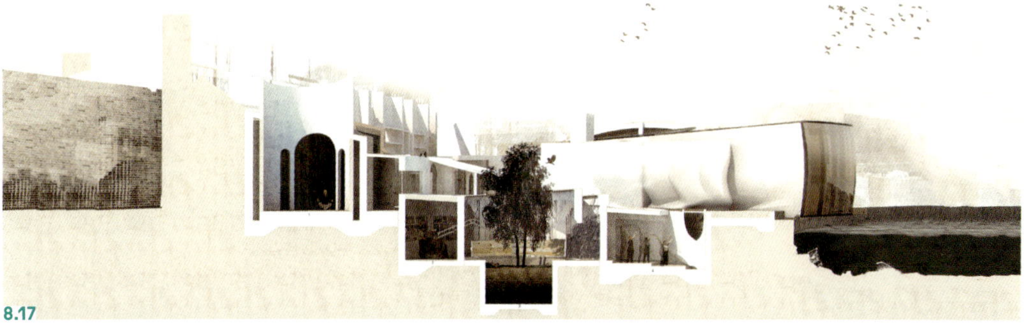

8.17

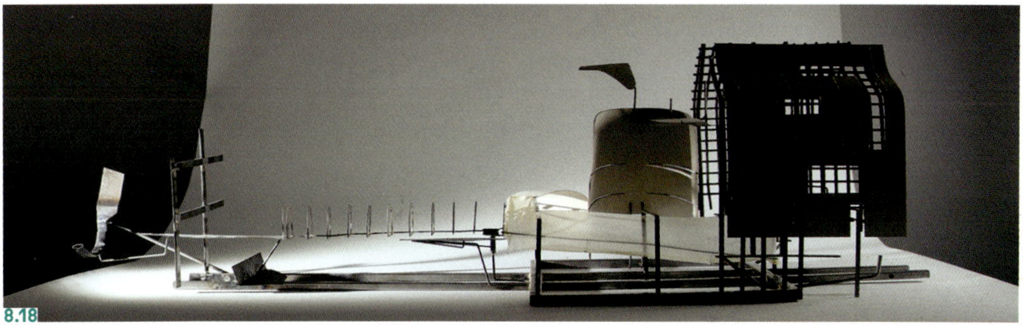

8.18

Figs. 8.19 – 8.21 Charlie Redman Y3, 'Bars of the Unexpected'. Carved out of a narrow slot behind the façade of an industrial lift shaft, the bars are spaces for physical and social prototyping. The high-tech multi-axis articulated stages for dating and tasting sake are developed through in-depth explorations of CNC fabrication and scripted simulation. **Fig. 8.22 Ryan Walsh** Y2, 'Stadium News'. Forensically re-constructing and re-enacting scenes of the news, Stadium News offers a screenless immersive experience and discussion of the week's events. **Fig. 8.23 Krina Christopoulou** Y2, 'Staging Deception'. There is no stage. There is no auditorium. The theatre re-enacts the industrial past of the Regent's Canal with a ground floor of water channels that allow for scenery to float, defining shifting positions of acting and viewing. The sequence between the audience, the actors and the floating scenes creates moments of simultaneous intersecting narratives of distorted chronological and spatial order. **Fig. 8.24 Isaac Nanabeyin Simpson** Y3, 'Discovered Misreadings'. Disobedience becomes a method of exploring architecture, investigating the possibility of creating a space that causes a conversation between a public library and a private studio. The proposal is a vessel that wants to be misinterpreted, that encourages questioning and provokes the discovery of new readings.

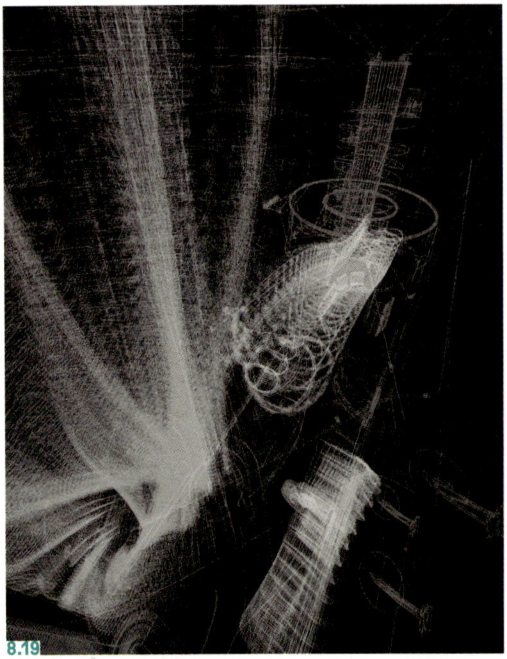
8.19

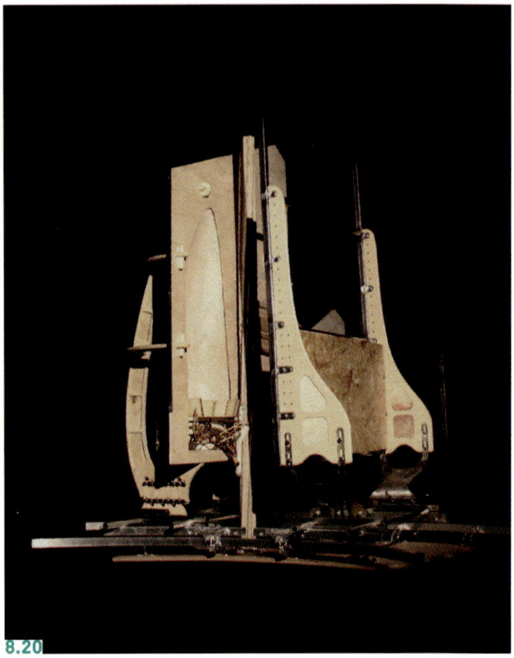
8.20

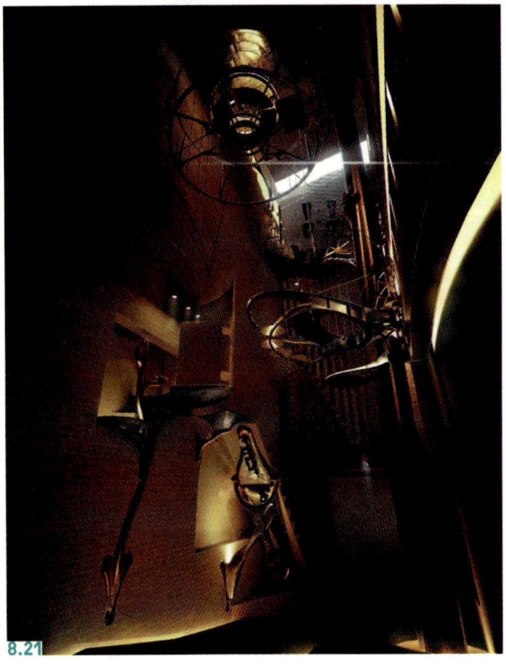
8.21

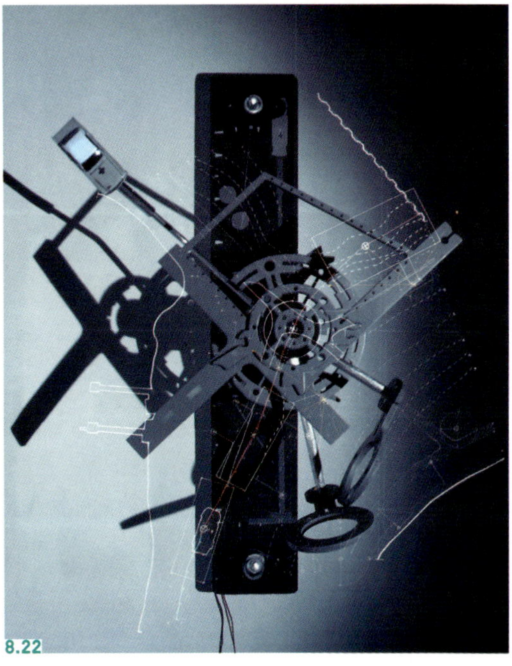
8.22

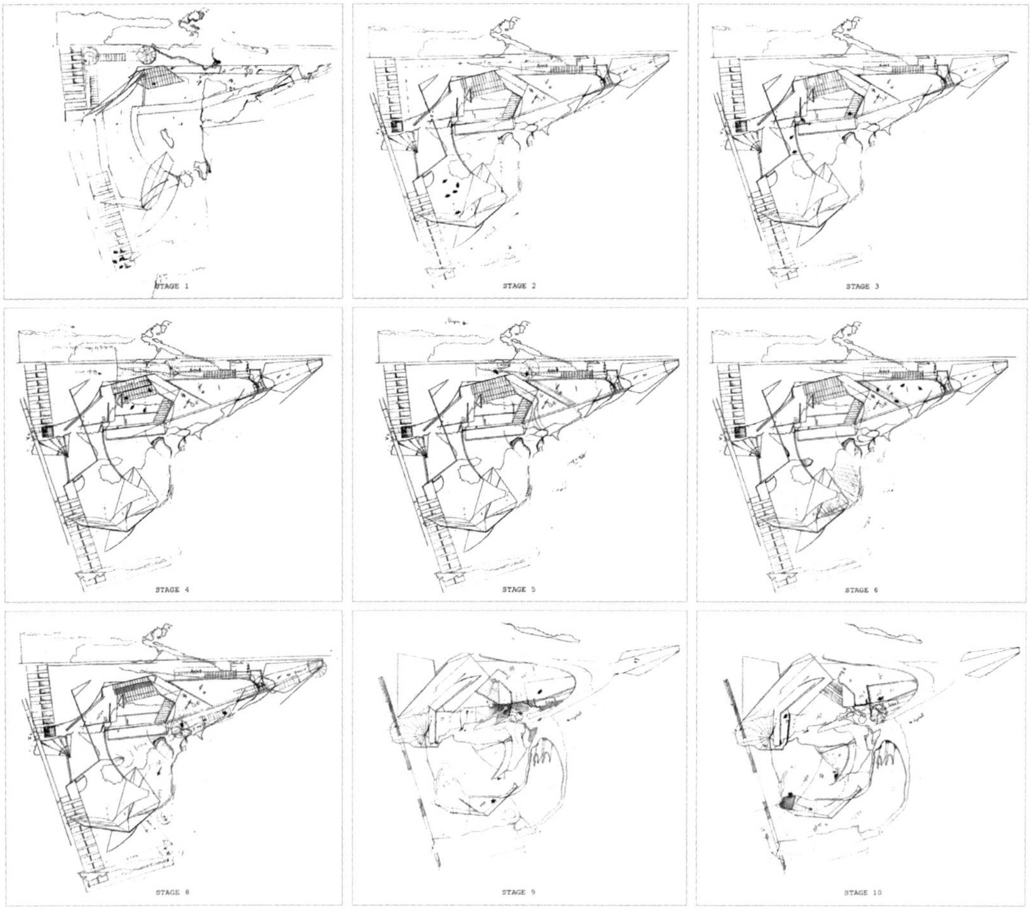
STAGE 1
STAGE 2
STAGE 3
STAGE 4
STAGE 5
STAGE 6
STAGE 8
STAGE 9
STAGE 10

8.23

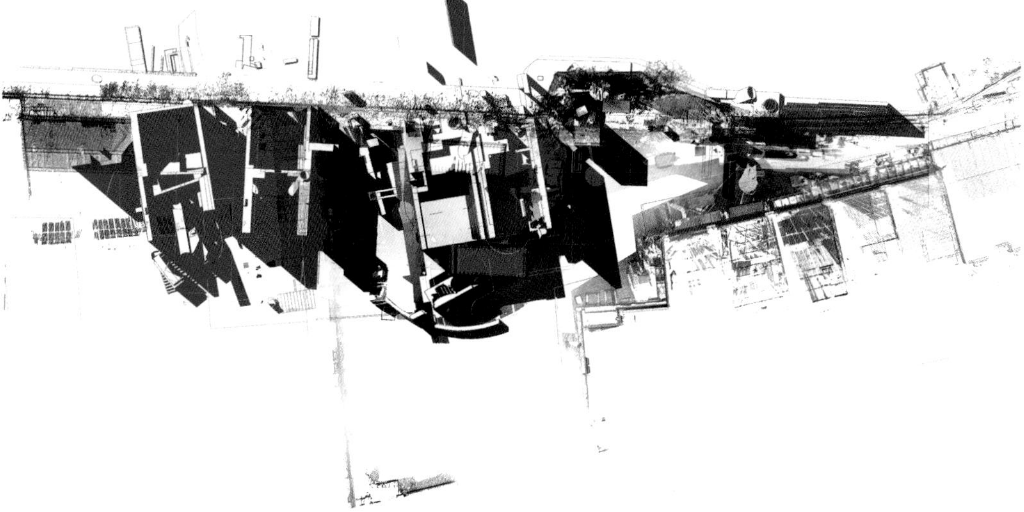

8.24

UG9

Lux::Umbra

Jessica In, Chee-Kit Lai

Year 2
Aya Ataya, Natasha Blows, Wai (Thomas) Chu, Christopher Grennan, Zeng (Glen) Heng, Karina Tang, Connie Tang Koon Cheong, Tze-Chuan (Roger) Tung, Claudia Walton

Year 3
Carrie Coningsby, Alessandro Conning-Rowland, Judy El-Hajjar, Maria Junco, Jaemin Kim, George Proud, Ken Sheppard, Issui Shioura

UG9 continues to work with ongoing collaborator Arup Associates for Year 3 Technical Dissertations. Special thanks to Mick Brundle and James Ward

UG9 also continues an ongoing collaboration with Denis Vlieghe who runs a Physical Computing Workshop as part of Project 1 (Interactive Device)

Special thanks to our critics: Alessandro Ayuso, Scott Batty, Rhys Cannon, Luke Chandresinghe, Nat Chard, Tom Coward, Florian Dussopt, Stephen Gage, Penelope Haralambidou, Jonathan Hill, Carlos Jimenez, Manuel Jimenez, Kyriakos Katsaros, Andre Sampaio Kong, Dionysia Kypraiou, Constance Lau, Tim Lucas, Duncan McLeod, Mads Hulroy Peterson, Donald Shillingburg, Tom Slivans, Giles Smith, Michiko Sumi, Tomas Tvarijonas, Manijeh Verghese, George Wade, Nick Westby

Special thanks for photography workshops by Finbarr Fallon and Jim Stephenson

Please also visit:
Facebook.com/Design.Unit9
Vimeo.com/DesignUnit9

I decided to record "the life of a candle." Late one midsummer night, I threw open the windows, and invited in the night breeze. Lighting a candle, I also stopped open my camera lens. After several hours of wavering in the breeze, the candle burned out. Savouring the dark, I slowly closed the shutter. The candle's life varied on any given night – short intensely burning nights, long constantly glowing nights – each different, yet equally lovely in its afterglow. Hiroshi Sugimoto, 1995

Our investigations this year began with concepts of light and shadow explored via historical, contemporary and speculative technological interpretations. We are curious about the difference in meaning between Western and Eastern interpretations of light and shadow. We continue the threads from last year to explore the following question: in a perpetual overexposed day created by modernity, the Internet and contemporary globalisation, what can these themes of light and shadow offer our architecture in our constantly – allegorically and literally – overlit world?

Lux

The introduction of gas lamps was one of the most important social and political contributions to the Victorian city, creating not just new urban typologies but also new behaviours and a new experience of the city. This transformative nature of light sets the ambition for our preliminary studies into Japan from afar, exploring concepts of light, shadow, materiality, time and technology.

Umbra • Penumbra • Antumbra

The three distinct parts of a shadow set the theme of the main building project of the year. Often used to describe the shadows cast by celestial bodies, they are also used to describe the levels of darkness. Sited in Kyoto, we are interested in how design can influence the lives of many people (real and imagined), how they move and how they live in their environment, the relationships between them and the interaction and inhabitation of these spaces and moments. The role of light and shadow to design the immaterial, the ephemeral-permanent, and an architecture that is beyond the control of the architect are themes central to this year's main project.
——UG9 sees performance as intrinsically linked to the development of technology beyond the discipline of architecture. We are critical of the passive consumption of technology and the lack of criticality in its application to design processes. We continually question the conventions of the production of architecture, pushing the boundaries of making, interactivity and drawing to become an integral part of the design process. We actively promote analogue and digital craftsmanship and time-based media to rigorously test ideas from inception through to final representation.

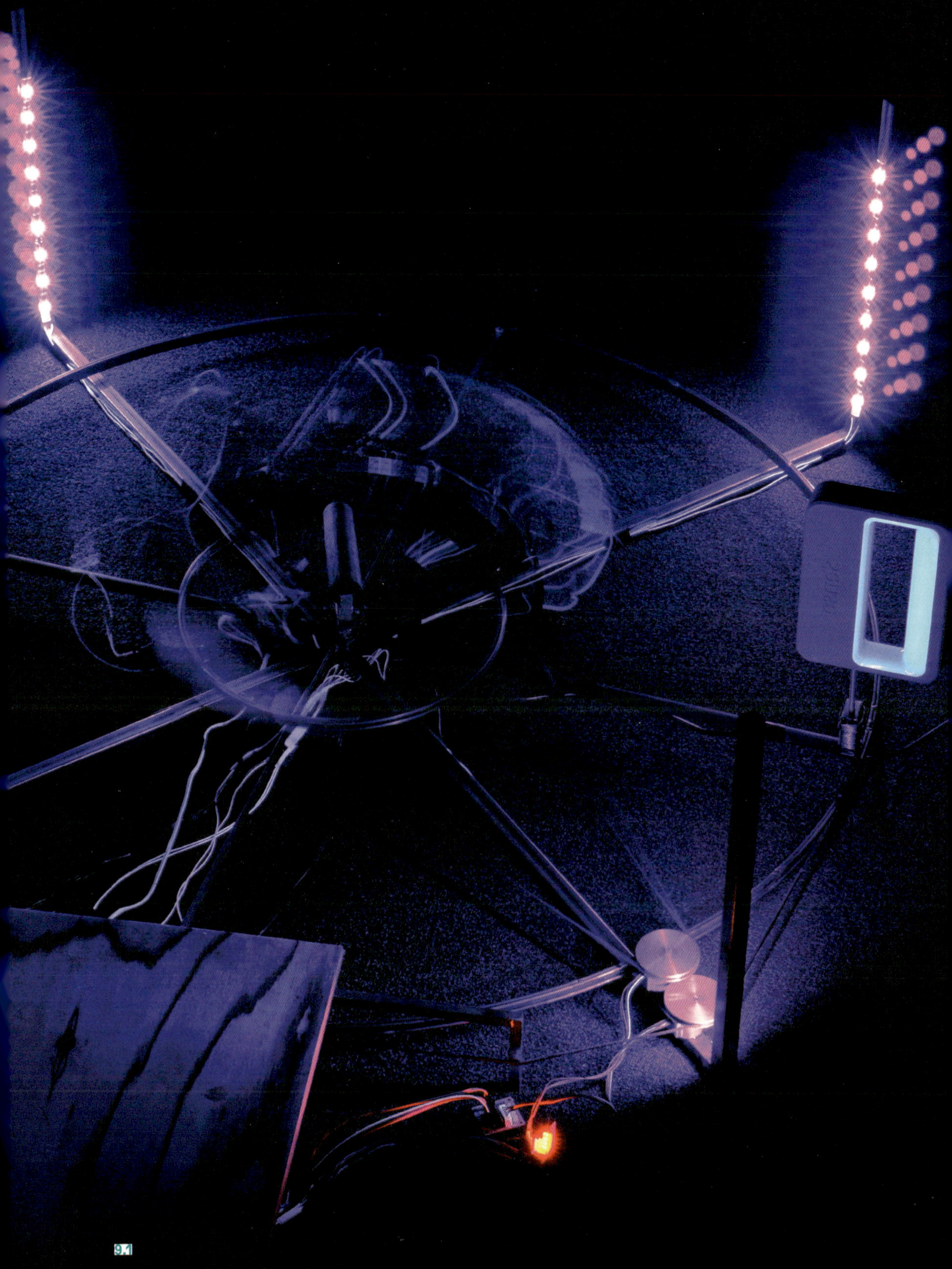

Fig. 9.1 Wai (Thomas) Chu Y2, 'Hidden Beauty', interactive dressing device. Inspired by the hidden boundaries of Yakuza tattoo culture and the Samurai dressing ritual, the device scans the user's arm via a 3D scanner positioned on the outer orbit. The digital contour of the arm is fed into a computer and once processed, a 3D printer pen on a robot arm draws a live 3D tattoo around the user's arm guided by the digital scan.
Fig. 9.2 Tze-Chuan (Roger) Tung Y2, 'Interactive Time Fountain', interactive device. This device is a futuristic time fountain based on the traditional Japanese cistern that tips to measure time through volumes of water. Stroboscopic light and shadow are linked with the viewer's interactions with the fountain, causing the water to seemingly drip at different speeds, both forwards and backwards in time.
Fig. 9.3 Aya Ataya Y2, 'Digital Purification', interactive device. Gestures found in traditional Shinto purification rituals Onusa and Temizuya are reinterpreted into a digital light painting device to create mementos of the experience. Head and hand movements are tracked to recreate active voids in the light surfaces for an exposure of Sugimoto's 'life of the light' that is unique to each personal expression of the ritual.
Figs. 9.4 – 9.7 Issui Shioura Y3, 'Chano-yu Tea Ceremony Lighthouse', interactive drawing, acrylic and acetate layered section with light. The concept of ichi-go ichi-e (a once-in-a-lifetime encounter), a tea ceremony (chanoyu) – is reinterpreted through Gibson's theories of visual perception, affordance and occluding edges of perceived space. The traditional illusional qualities of Roji tea gardens

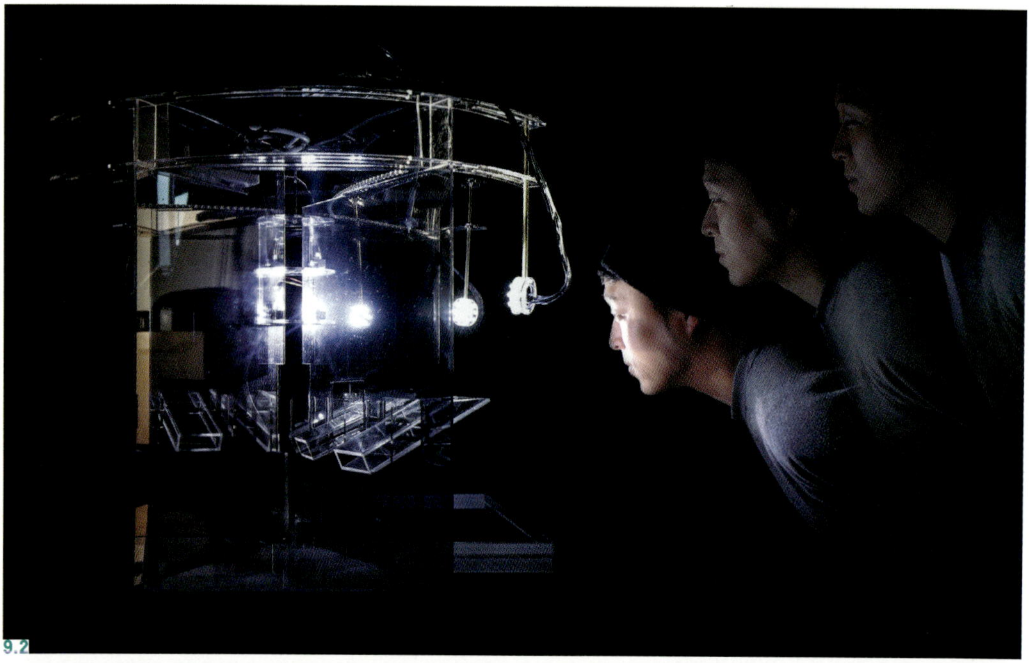

9.2

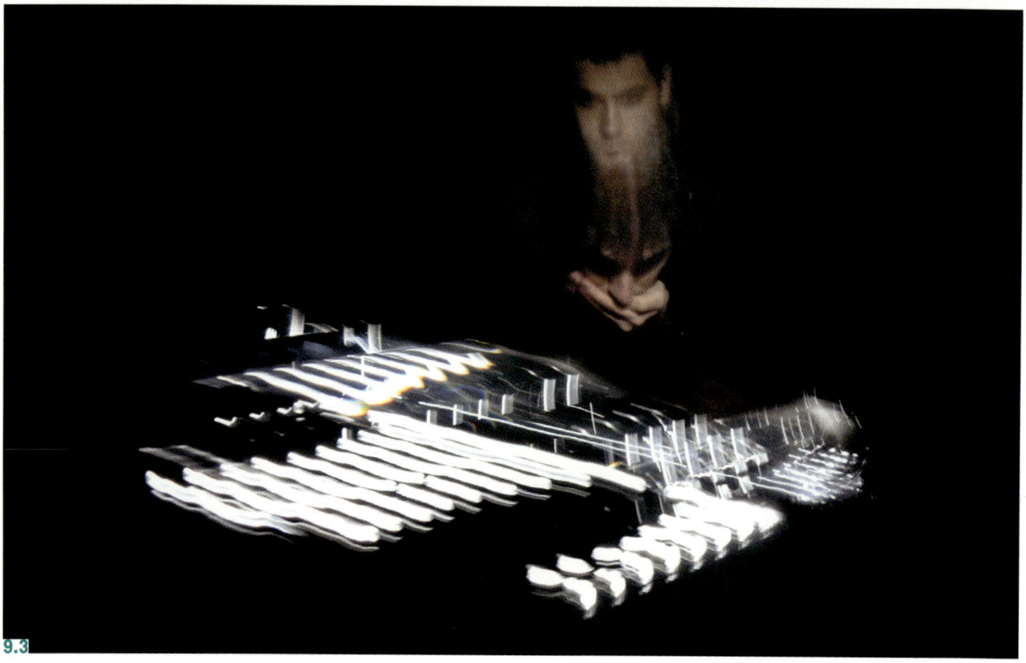

9.3

throughout the seasons is manifested through different journey pathways within the building that are perceptually altered – but not physically elongated – through the precise use of light tube columns and sliding walls. The creation of unique, memorable spatial moments with light induces a separation from reality, to allow for the deep conversations over tea to achieve the core quality and enhanced experience of chano-yu without the strict traditional appearance.

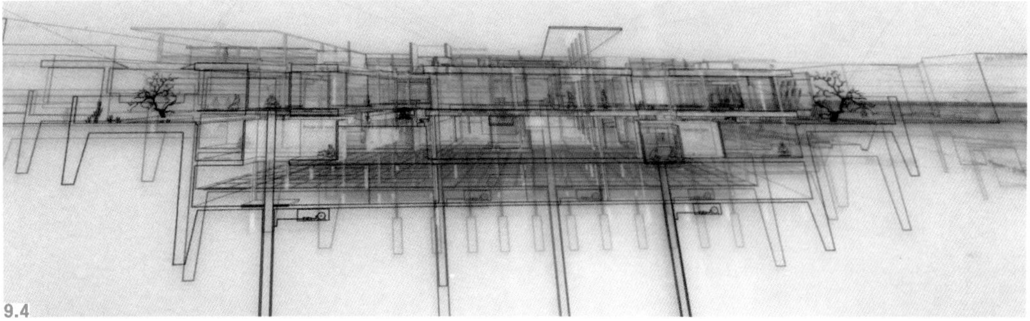

9.4

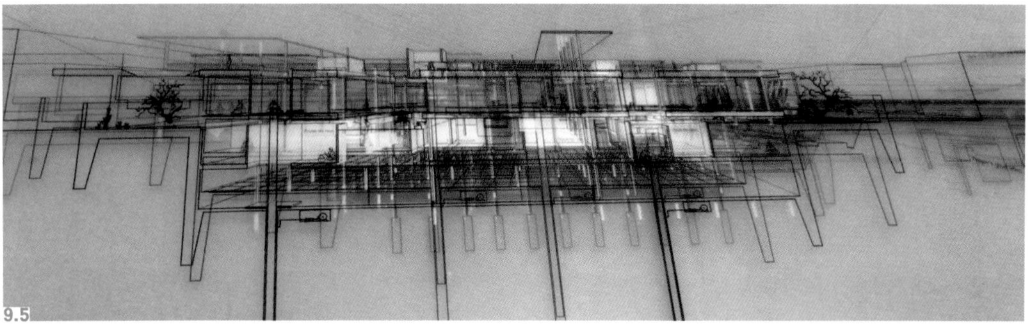

9.5

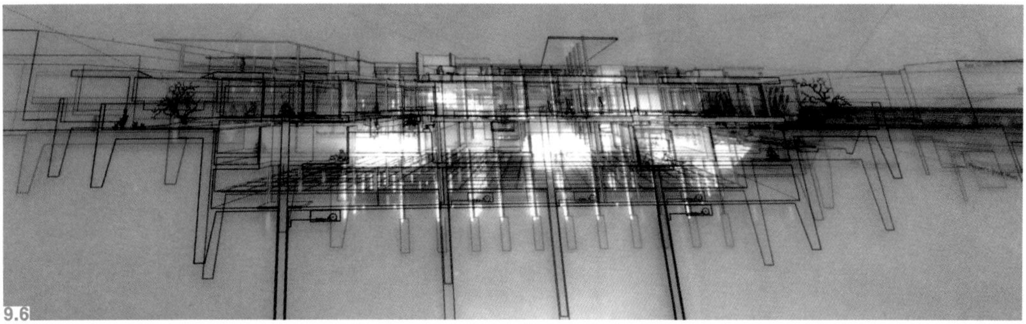

9.6

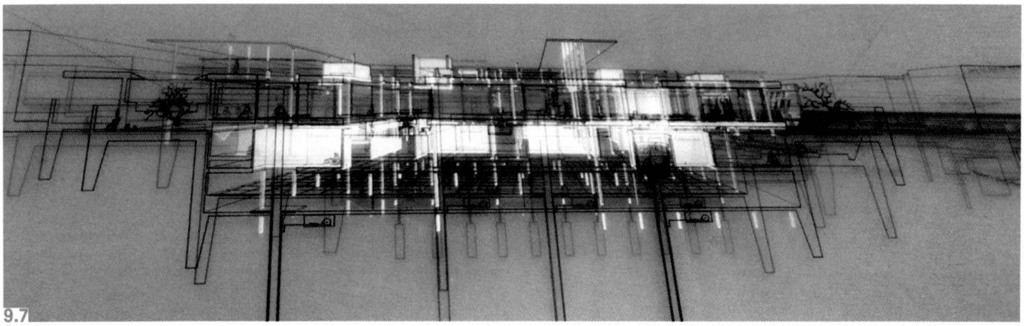

9.7

Fig. 9.8 Zeng (Glen) Heng Y2, 'Kimono Fabric Dye Factory', folded Kimono laser-etched final drawings. The proposal is for a fabric dye factory using natural colouring from recycled food waste collected from the restaurants across Kyoto. The final drawings on calico fabric plays with the conventions of pattern cutting and architectural notations. Through the unfolding, the Kimono orthographic drawings are slowly revealed. **Fig. 9.9 Ken Sheppard** Y3, 'Kyoto 4'33', film still of physical model and audio recording with water. Kyoto 4'33 is a storm surge cistern that acts as an auditorium complex. The infrastructure for storm surge reduces the risk from the monsoon flooding of the neighbouring Kamogawa river, while utilsing the captured water to create a transformative event space for the asynchronous performance of Gagaku music performed during the Jidai Matsuri festival in October. The filling of the structure triggers a transformation from three separate auditoria into one combined auditorium, through a series of floating mechanisms. During the asynchronous performance, sound produced by the three orchestras are reflected into the central cistern to mix and reverberate, depending on the water levels dictated by the region's natural hydrological cycle. **Fig. 9.10 Ken Sheppard** Y3, 'Ceremony', final drawing of installation performance staging. Ceremony explores the concept of Ma – a moment of reflective pause – through a spatial sound and light performance. Three players interpret a Laban-type score on their motion instruments, which is translated into a light and laser projection to visualize the light boundaries created by their performance. As Kiri

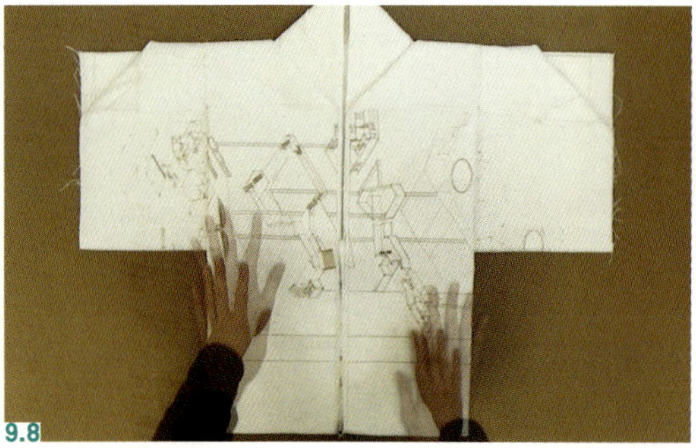

9.8

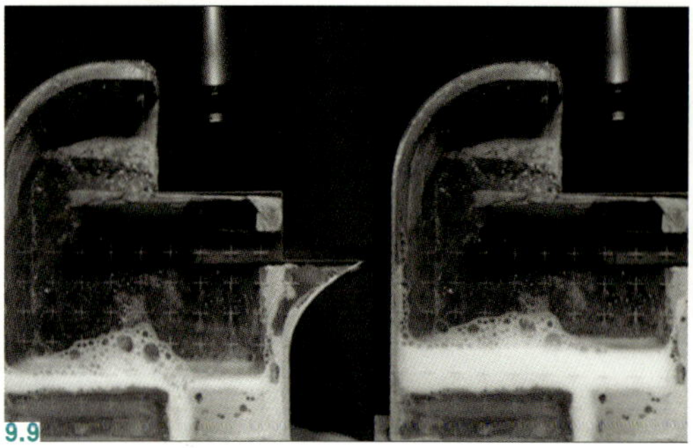

9.9

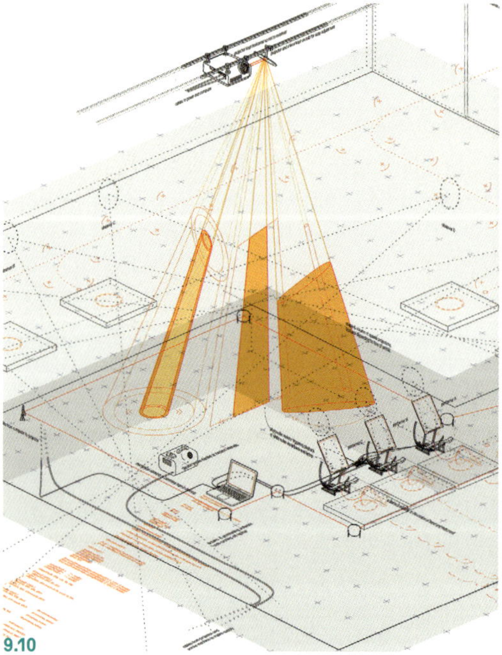

9.10

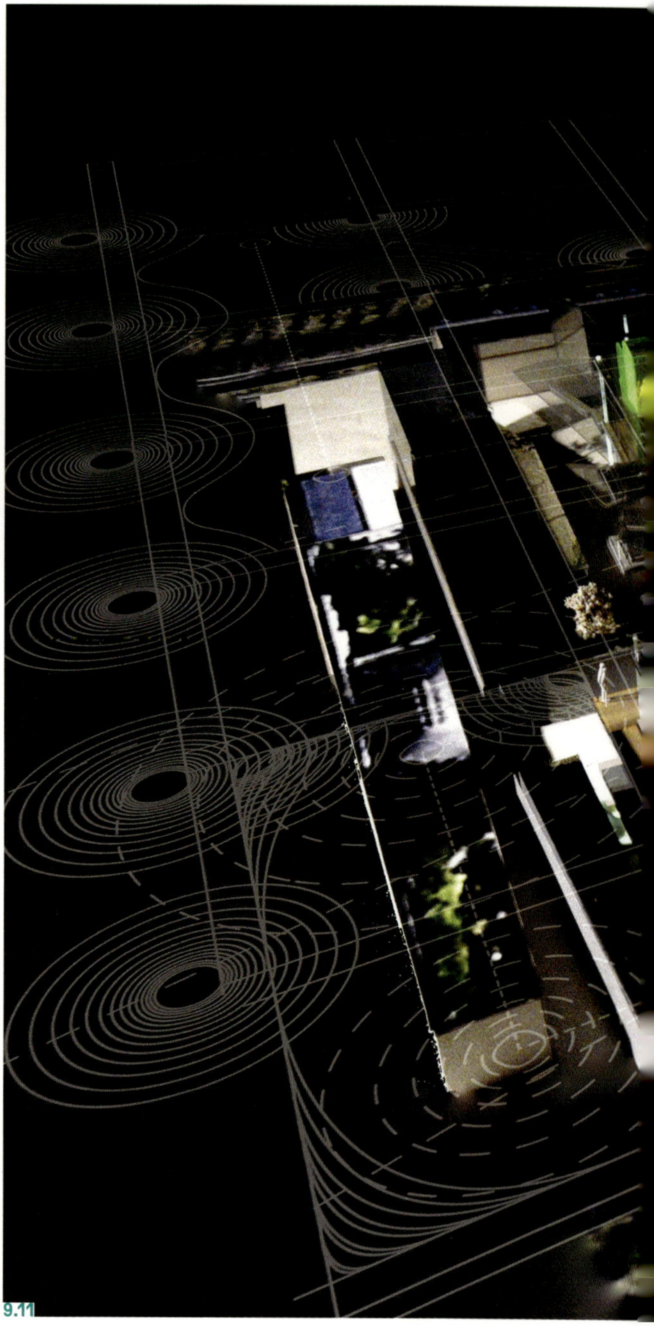

9.11

(or haze) is used as a compositional technique to create visual Ma in traditional Japanese paintings, Ceremony continually redraws Ma through the immaterial medium of projected light volumes, momentarily capturing the ephemeral qualities of the ceremony space. **Fig. 9.11** **Issui Shioura** Y3, 'Chano-yu Tea Ceremony Lighthouse', 1:50 model.

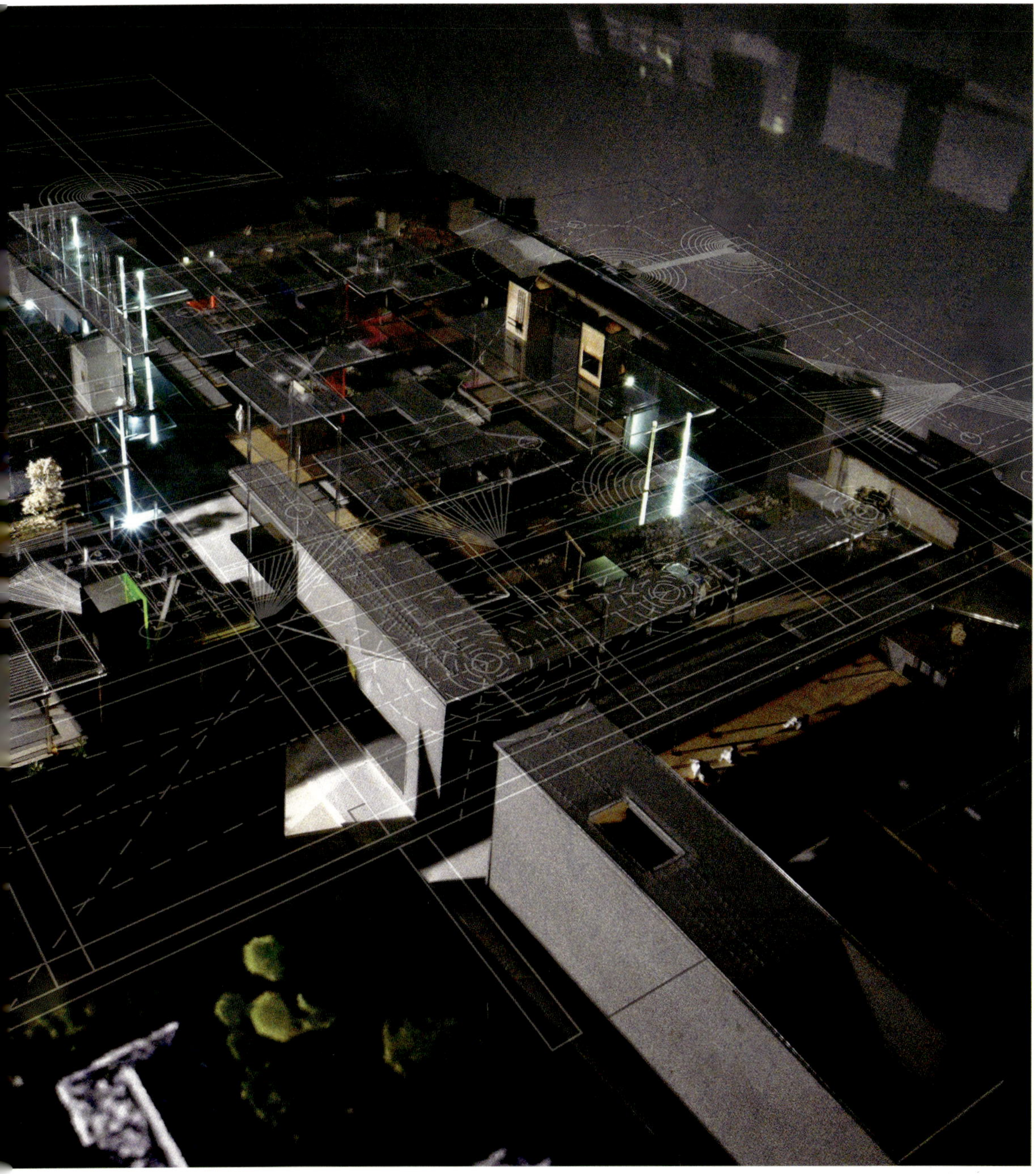

Fig. 9.12 **Alessandro Conning-Rowland** Y3, 'Kyoto Motorcycle City', detail model. The main building sited in central Kyoto and associated infrastructure around the city provides the framework for an annual motorcycle race for the thriving, but locally underappreciated, custom vehicle culture in Japan. The proposal is a symbiotic overlay of architectural artifice against the context of Kyoto's key landmarks. **Fig. 9.13** **George Proud** Y3, 'The Yotsuya Sanchome Bitcoin Bank', augmented sectional drawing. Sited in a residential area within Tokyo, the proposal is for a self-sustaining high-tech community. The bank houses a mine (for bitcoin), which is the primary source of income for the maximum capacity of 70 residents. **Figs. 9.14 – 15** **Alessandro Conning-Rowland** Y3, 'Journey through Shokintei', light-drawing device. The viewer is taken on an immersive collage journey through Shokintei using stylised images (by Walter Gropius, during his visit to the famous teahouse). The device is a series of interconnected Japanese timber screens lined with seemingly black double-printed shoji paper. **Fig. 9.16** **Claudia Walton** Y2, 'Kyoto Hiking Trail', folded trail map drawing. Sited in Arashiyama, the Trail promotes slow tourism, encouraging visitors to reinterpret the landscape in a more personal way, instead of consuming views for their Instagram feeds. Pavilion structures and constructed viewpoints along the trail interact with hikers and with each other. **Fig. 9.17** **Alessandro Conning-Rowland** Y3, 'Kyoto Motorcycle City', unfolded section drawing.

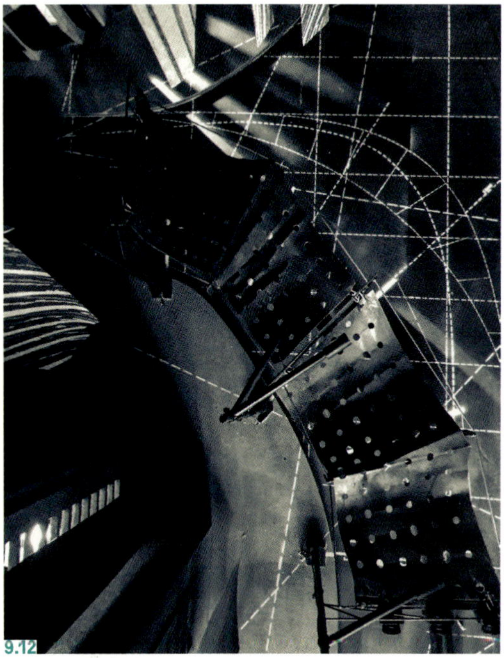
9.12

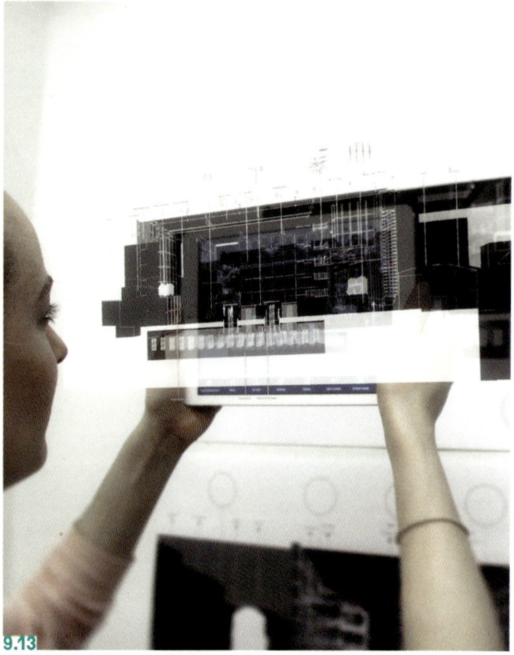
9.13

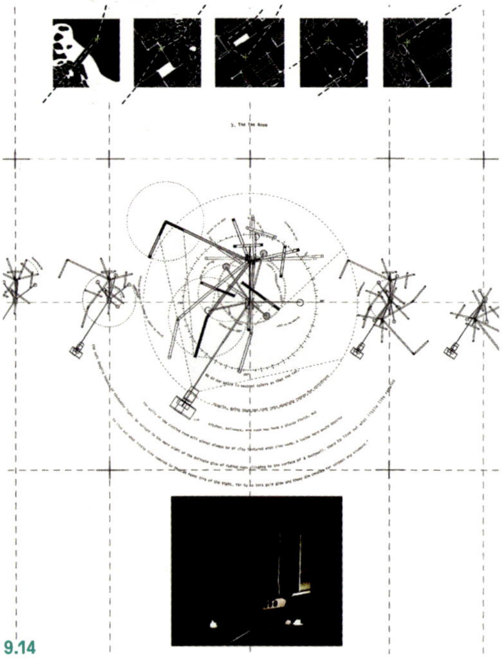
9.14

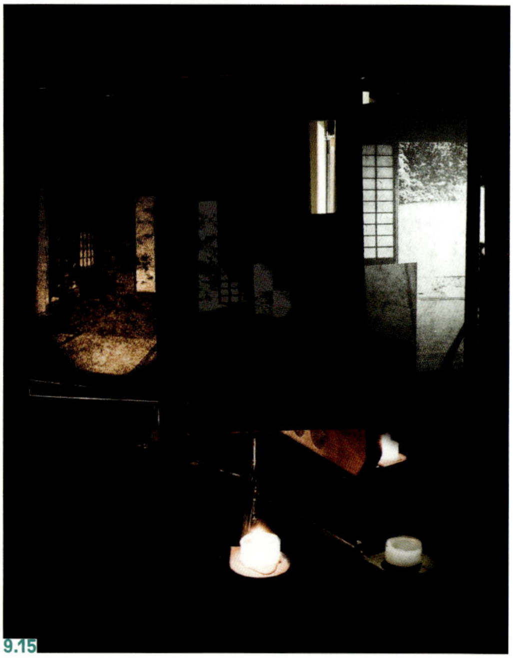
9.15

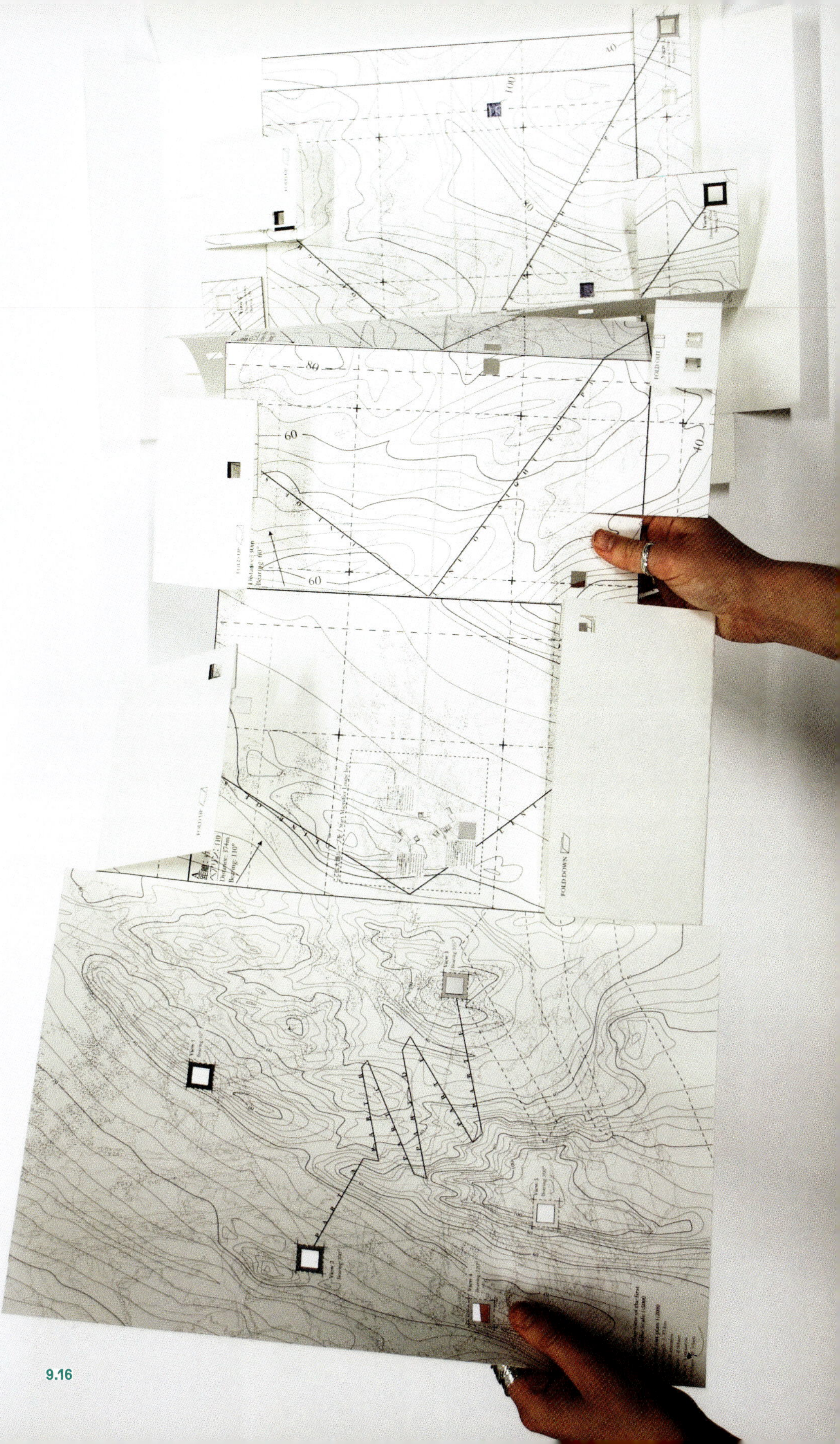

9.16

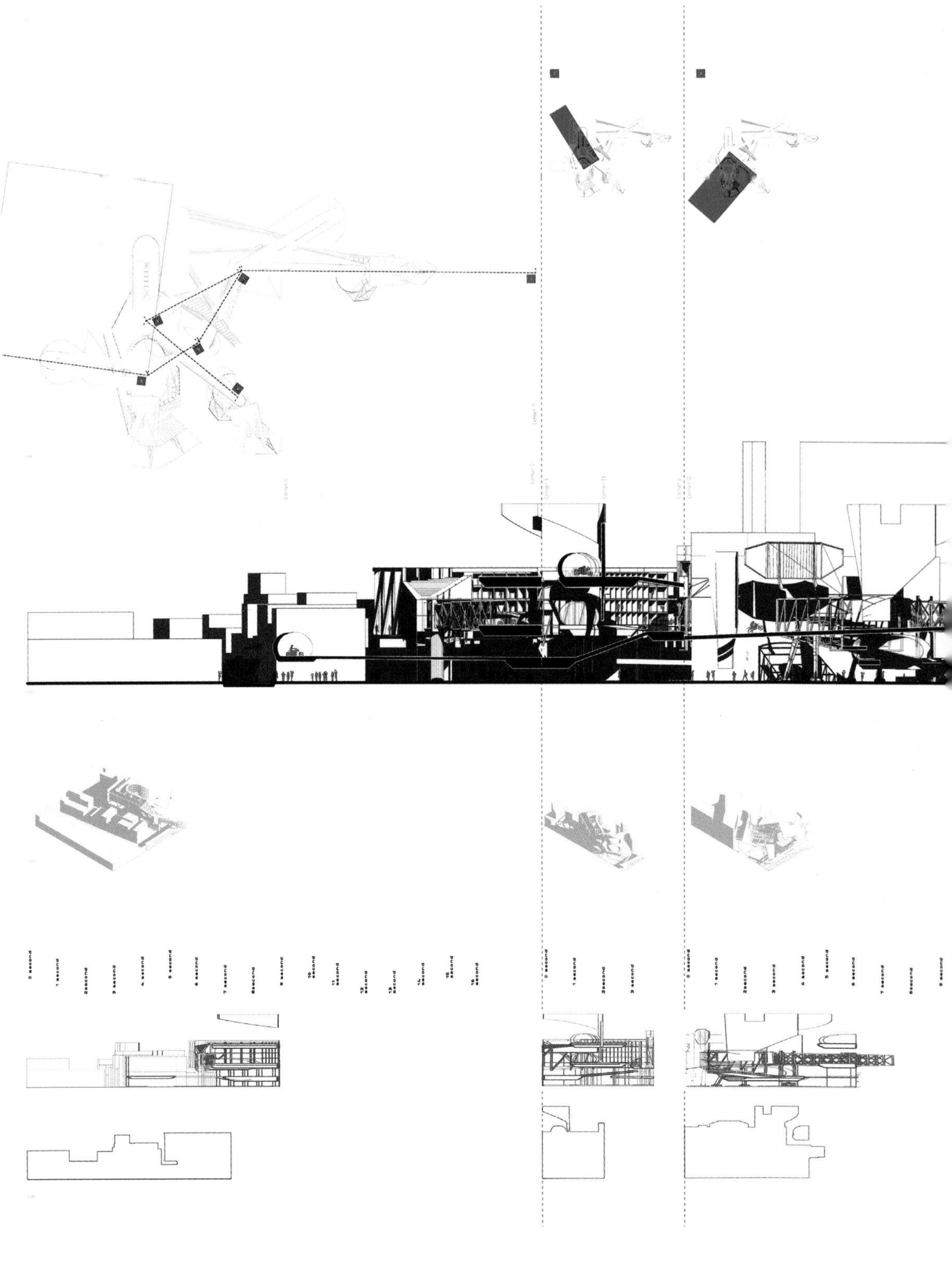

9.17

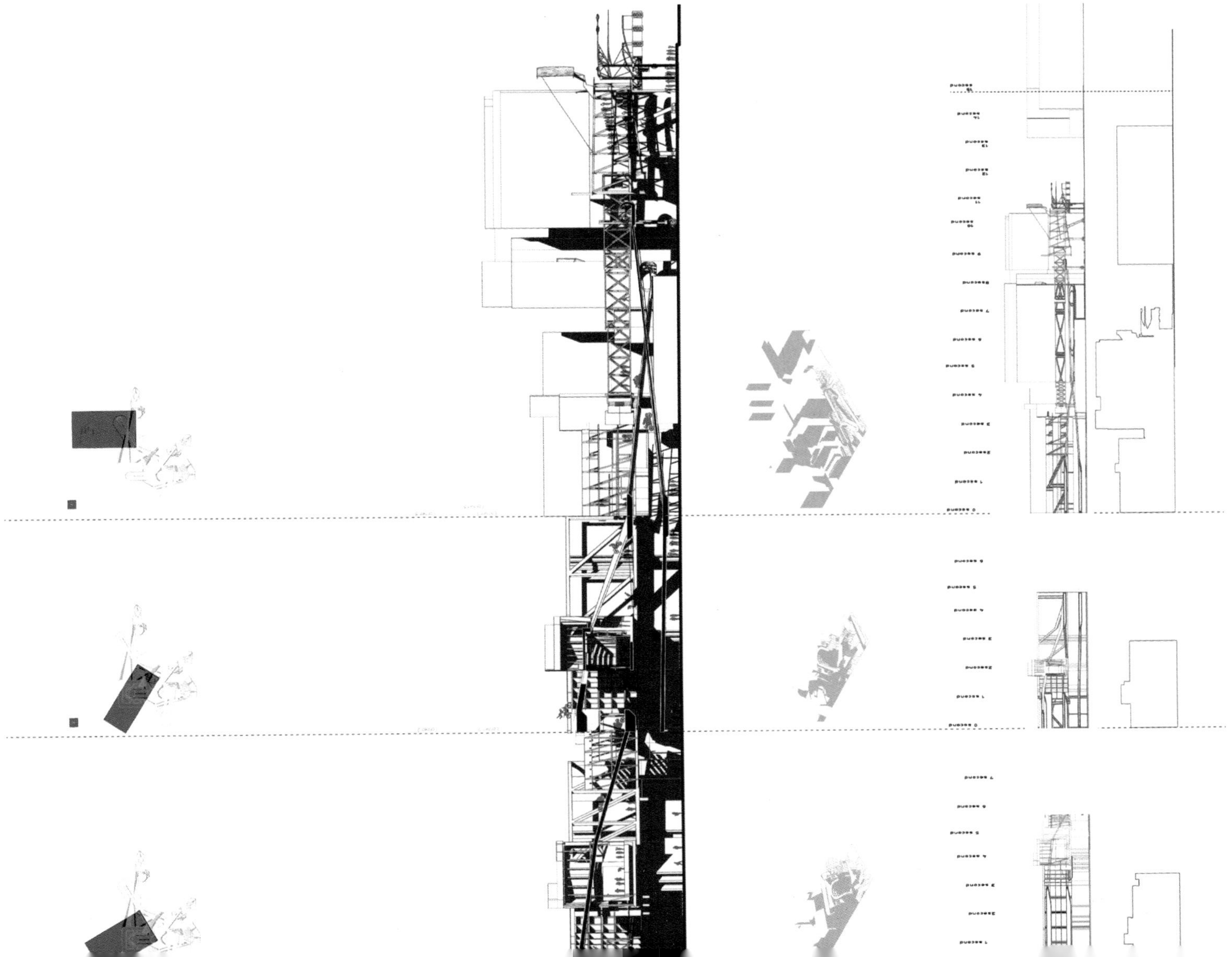

UG10

Intimate Immensity

Tamsin Hanke, Guan Lee

Year 2
Nur (Sabrina) Azman, Sam Grice, Clementine Holden, Carmen Kong, Shi Yin Ling, Elissavet Manou, Gabriel Pavlides, Sam Price, Sam Rix

Year 3
Bingqing (Angelica) Chen, Hoi Man (Christy) Cheung, Romario (Yik Yu) Lai, Dunkaew (Pink) Protpagorn, Sheua Wei (Amanda) Tam, Xinyue (Angel) Yao, Michelle Yiu

Thanks to Joshua Scott (Technical Tutor), Callum Perry (Digital Fabrication) Igor Pantic (Digital Modelling) and Jessie Lee (Ceramic and Glass)

Thanks also to our guest critics: Alice Brownfield, Mollie Claypool, Matthew Butcher, Kate Darby, Holly Galbraith, Colin Herperger, Christine Hawley, Jonathan Hill, Nic Moore, Igor Pantic, Callum Perry, Stuart Piercy, Michael Ramage, Bob Sheil, Victoria Watson, Peter Webb, Ivana Wingham, Paolo Zaide

UG10 is interested both in making things and the environments in which they are made. Students have worked to make and think simultaneously at the scale of the tool and the scale of the landscape, to study the methods and materials from which architecture is produced and how these can be drawn from, and continue to respond to, a place.

——The unit considered the idea of a conserved wilderness, questioning whether continuing to focus upon preserving islands of Holocene ecosystems in this Anthropocene age is anachronistic and counterproductive. Human infrastructure and cultural context are changing as fast as their natural counterparts and allowing them to evolve in parallel is critical to the sustainable future of development. In Hawaii, the accelerated condition of dynamism allowed students to question whether it may be possible to be optimistic about the impact that we can have, by using an understanding of context to propose a positive way to engage with place.

——The unit travelled to the Big Island of Hawaii, a landscape of extreme and constant change. Lava flows perpetually alter and evolve the topography through volcanic activity bubbling just below the surface. Communities must adapt to living on the edge of destruction, and space is compromised by the protection of large pieces of the island for international conservation.

——Students started the year by considering 'on what basis do we begin to build?'. They proposed a vessel based on a research agenda and a material practice that they took from sites around Hawaii in order to propose a new type of architecture that responded to both physical and contextual landscapes of violent change. Methods of construction moved between digital intentions and physical modelling to test the nature of materials alongside the computational generic.

——These ideas were developed through building projects that considered the issue of material use in a place that has to ship all of its construction materials at least half way across the Pacific. Some tried to find a new material language of extraction or harvest, working directly to propose landscapes of timber, and extractive methodologies of volcanic mud and lava rock. Others considered the island's aggressive military history and the ongoing fight for independence after the highly ambiguous annexation to America in 1893. Questions were raised about the economic future and land ownership on an island where, day by day, the sea reclaims territory built on a soft and sandy bedrock of volcanic activity.

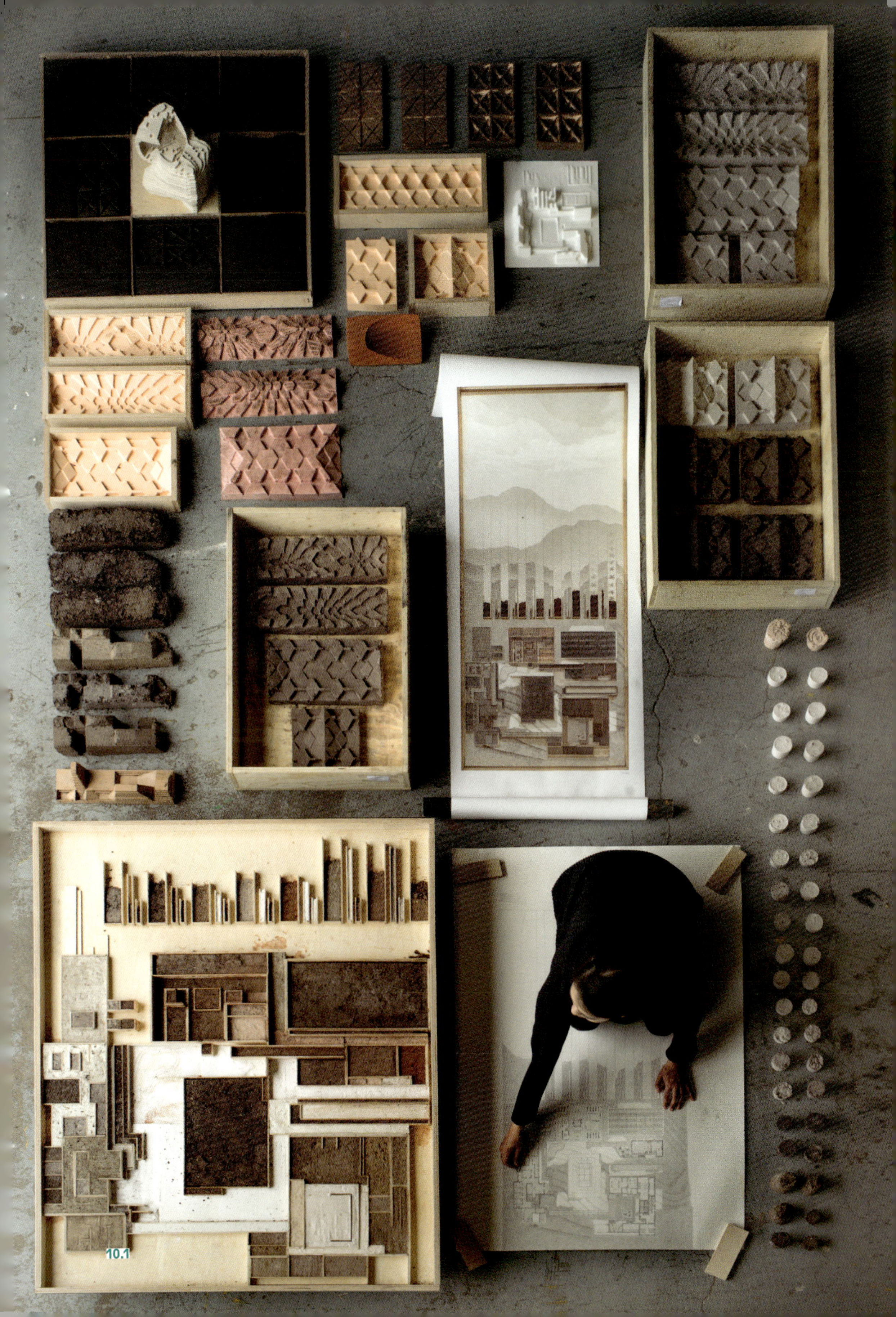

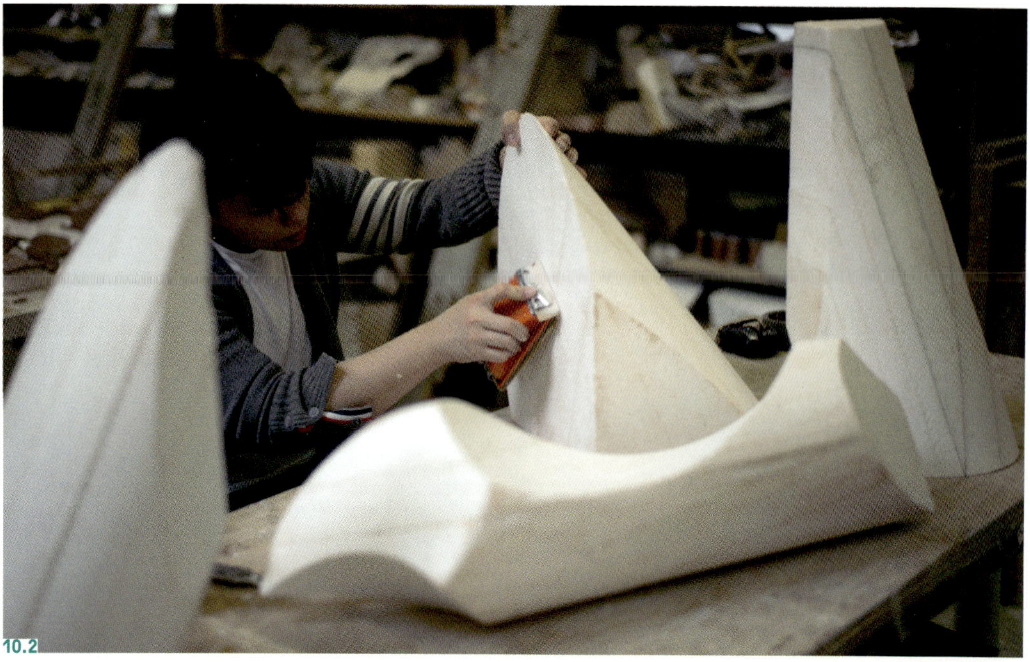
10.2

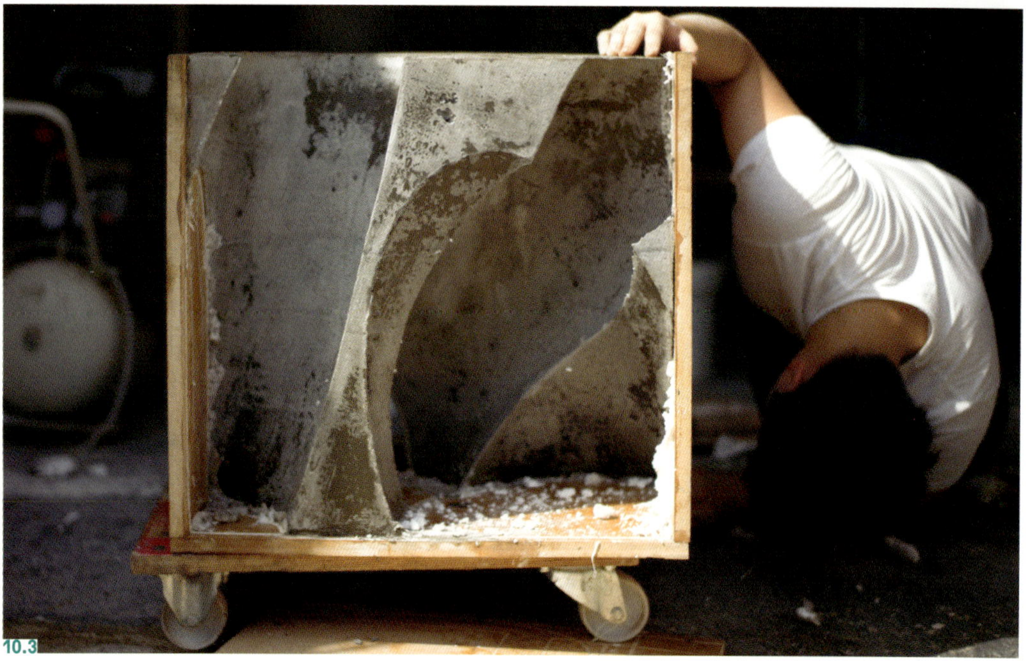
10.3

Fig. 10.1 Michelle Yiu Y3, 'Palette Under The Sun'. Earth buildings at Kakkako waterfront park. Honolulu has a distinct diversity in soil types due to volcanic activity. This offers a palette of materials that could reduce Hawaii's dependency on imported construction material. The mud drawing in this photograph shows the buildings using different construction techniques and soil types from Hawaii to create new textures as landscape and architecture. The building looked to use the distinct qualities of these techniques to propose crossover spaces for a multi-programme educational facility. **Figs. 10.2 – 10.4 Yik Yu (Romario) Lai** Y3, 'Figure Of Voices'. Native Hawaiians have been fighting for their rights since its annexation in the 1890s. Situated in Honolulu, the architecture of carved void/hollowed solid acts as a neutral space for native Hawaiian, all unrepresented nations and people to establish dialogues with the UN. The quality of space is also investigated through 1:1 cast concrete building fragment. The waste mould is made of polystyrene and the cast is made with high strength, low shrinkage flow concrete. The 1:200 final building model is combination of 3D-printed parts and laser cut paper, while the hardwood base is CNC machined.

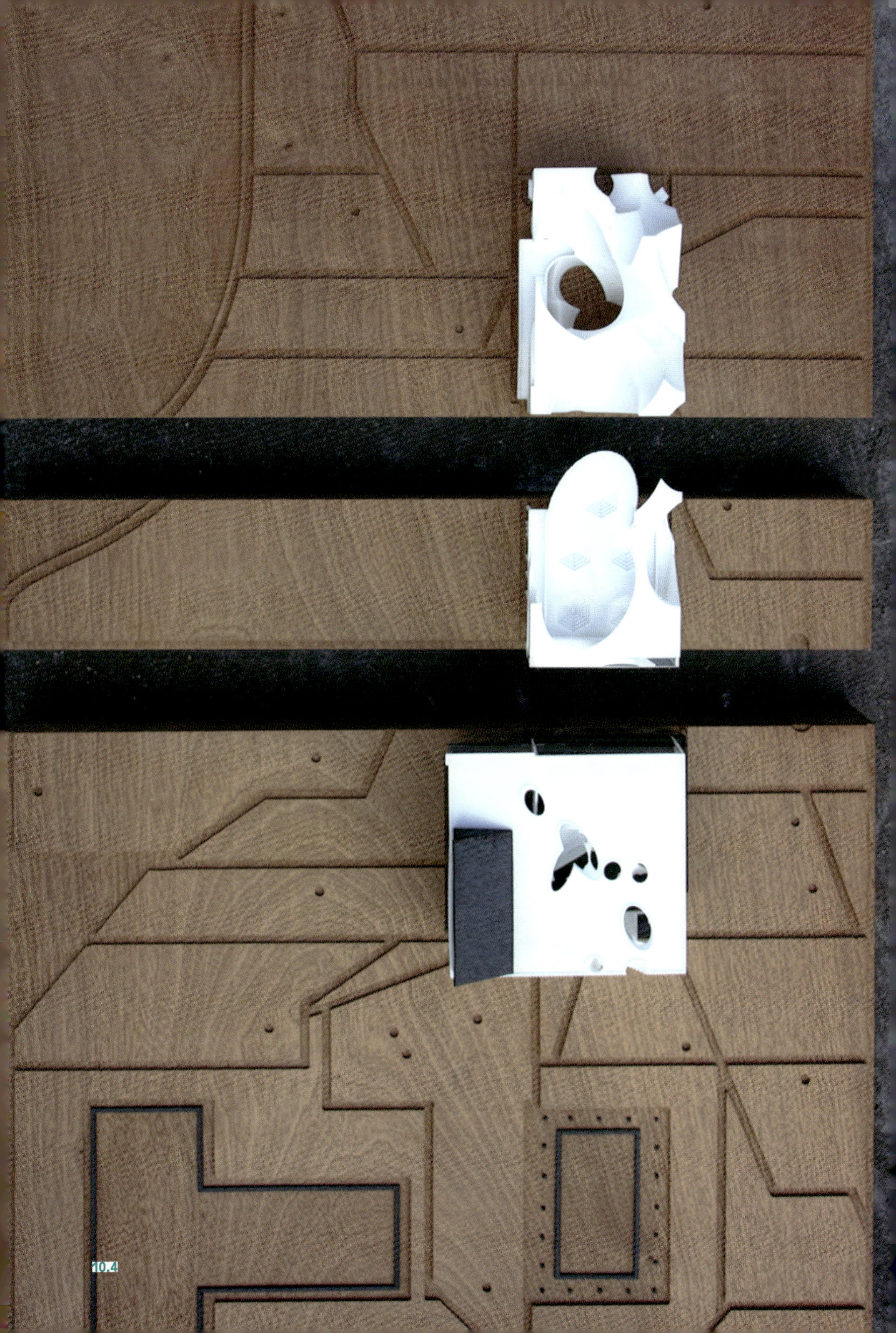

10.4

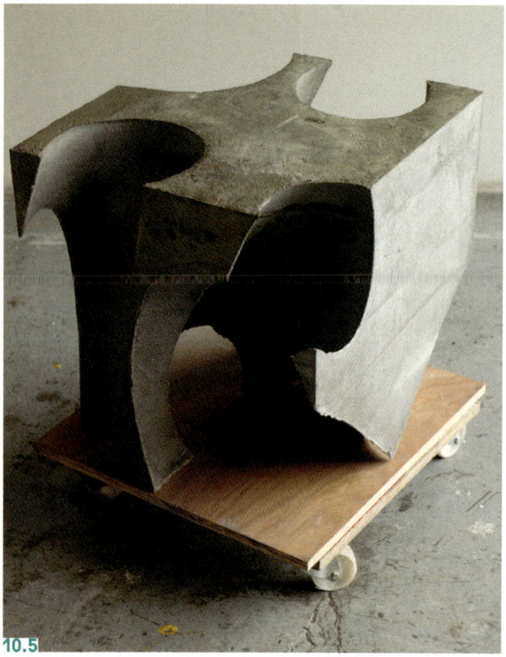

10.5

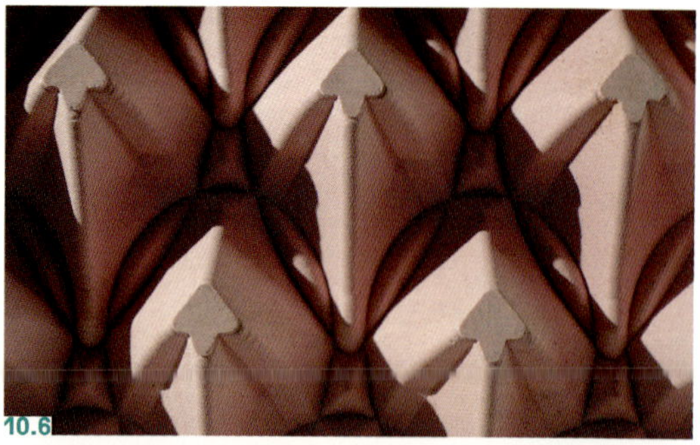

10.6

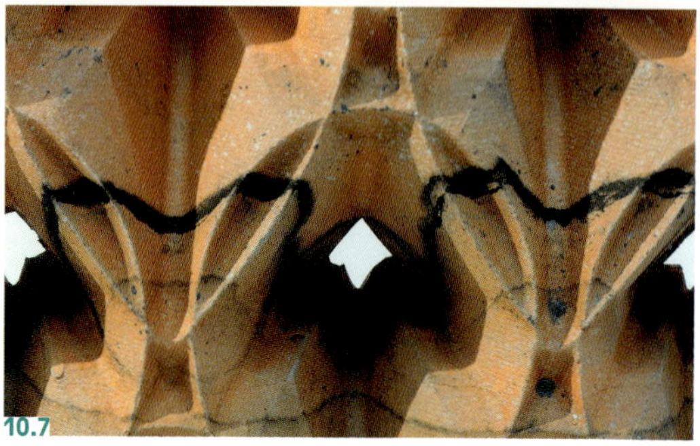

10.7

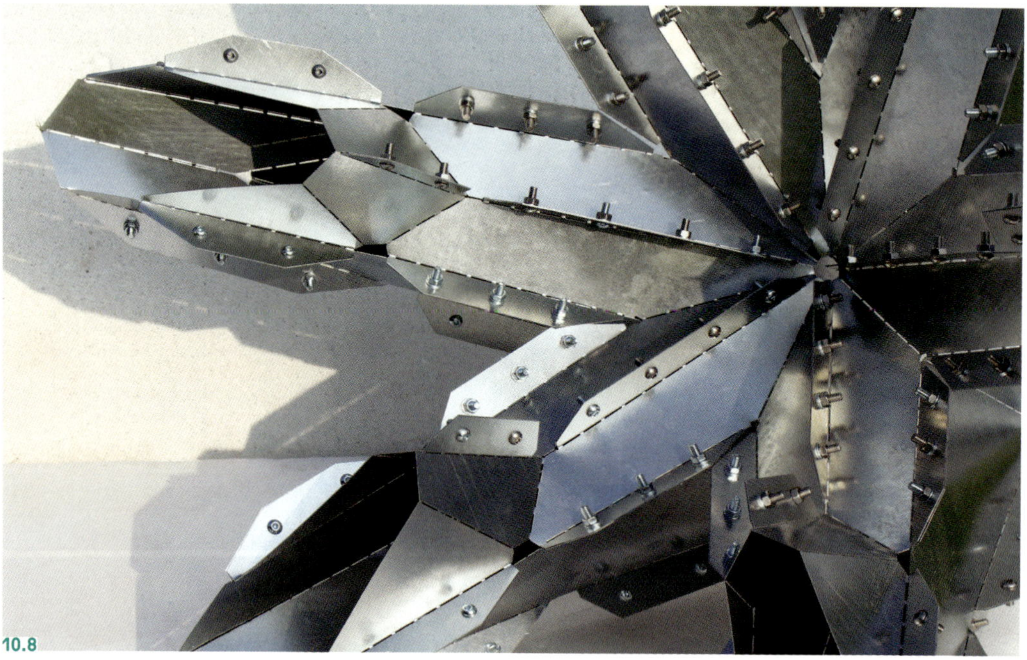

10.8

Fig. 10.5 YikYu (Romario) Lai Y3, 'Figure Of Voices'. Fragment of building proposal cast in concrete. **Figs. 10.6 – 10.7 Shi Yin Ling** Y2, 'The Bill'. A building to host festivities and competitions during the game fishing season. Sited in a poorly maintained but densely occupied harbour, the building tests combinations of materials to register change and ageing. **Fig. 10.8 Sheua Wei (Amanda) Tam** Y3, 'Against The Flow'. Kalapana Community Centre. Sited on the most active lava field on Hawaii's Big Island, the building supports the reclusive community that build their homes in this extreme landscape. Studies tested the thermal capacities of materials to propose a refuge robust enough provide shelter during a future flow. Inspired by Dolosse, this fragment of a column was developed through large-scale CNC punched prototypes at 1:5 and 1:3.

Fig. 10.9 Bingqing (Angelica) Chen Y3, 'Super Spring'. A deep sea water research centre and restaurant in Honolulu. Borrowing from the technology used to pump cold, nutrient-rich deep sea water to power air conditioning in surrounding office blocks, the project looks for alternative uses for this resource. **Fig. 10.10 Carmen Kong** Y2, 'Sunset to Sunrise'. CNC milled pigmented plaster cast with soft brick aggregates.

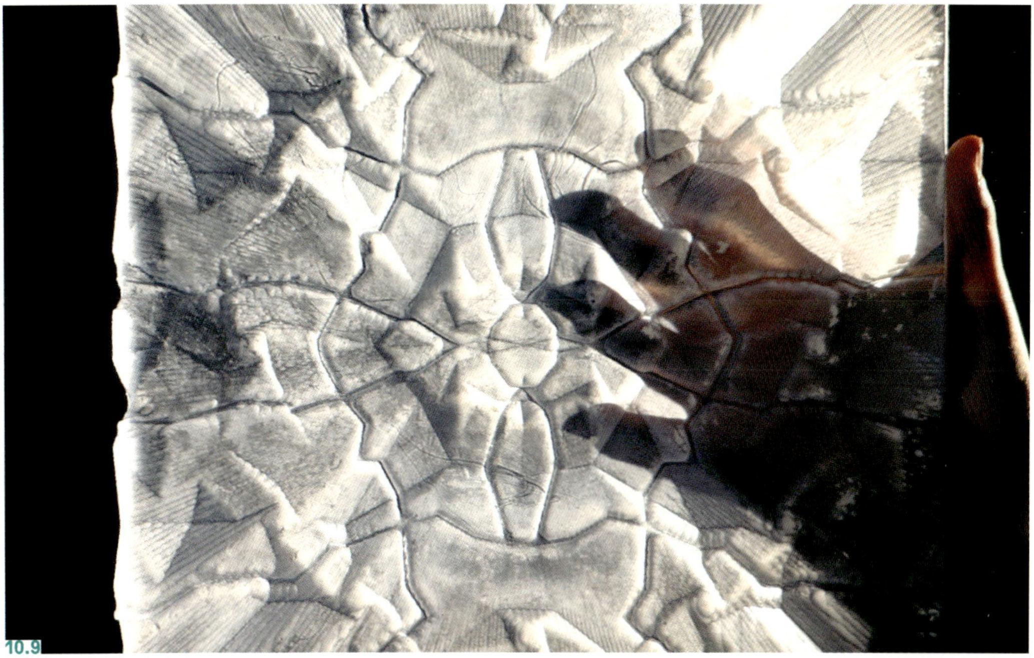
10.9

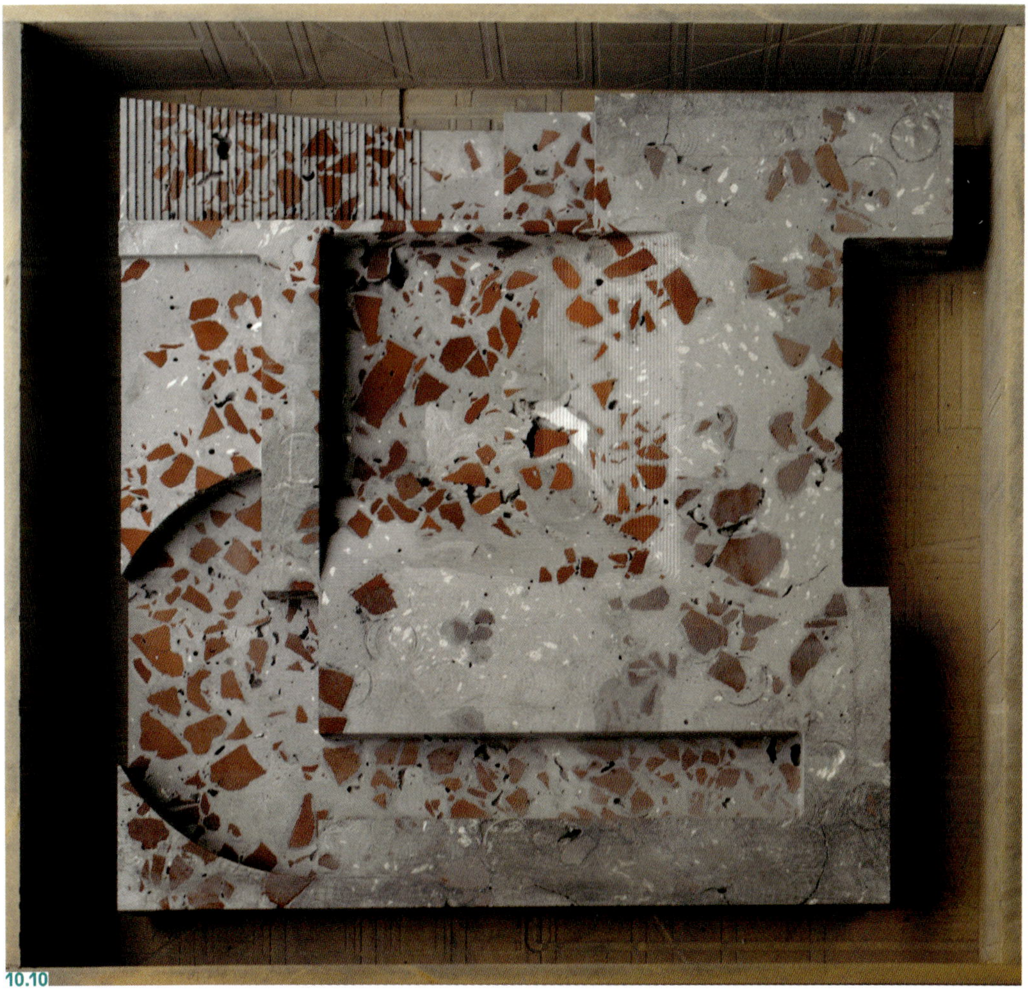
10.10

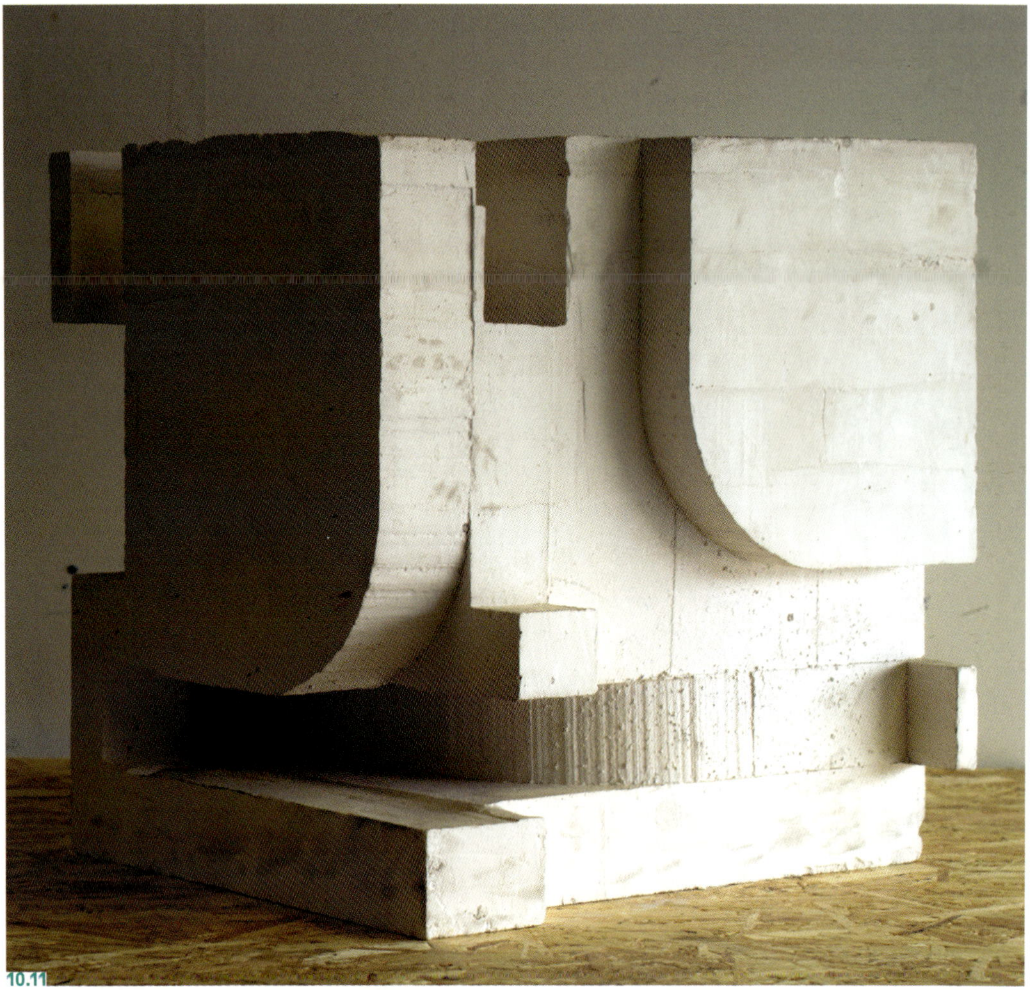
10.11

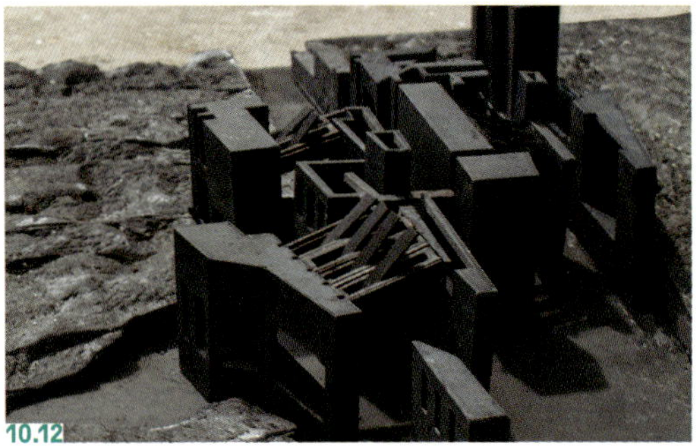
10.12

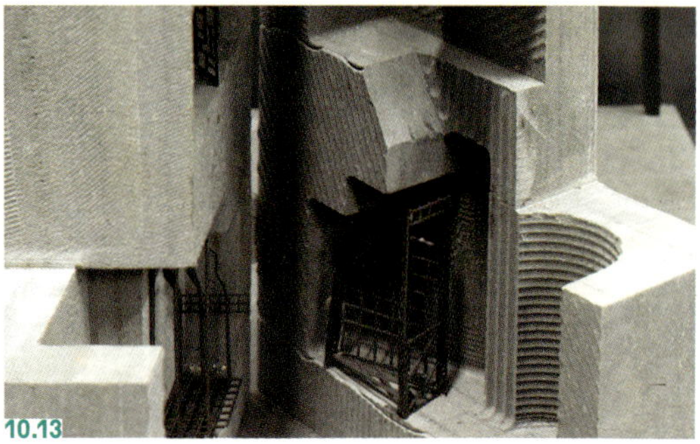
10.13

Fig. 10.11 Carmen Kong Y2, 'Sunset to Sunrise'. A nocturnal building for amateur astronomers sited mid-way up Mauna Kea. The site is charged with conflict between a global scientific community and the significance of the dormant volcano as a culturally sacred place. The design uses channels of moonlight and shifts in ground level to guide users through the architecture in the dark. **Fig. 10.12 Samuel Grice** Y2, 'Wayfinding'. A walker's retreat and rescue centre for explorers lost on the black, scale-less lava fields of Kalapana. The architecture explores stereotomy as a way of using local lava stone as a structural material. Model, showing the proposal as part of a landscape of cut lava, 1:200. **Fig. 10.13 Sam Price** Y2, 'Excavating The Erased'. Considering the additive erasure of Kalapana, as layers of lava repeatedly covers land which is persistently redeveloped. The project looked at excavation as a way of archiving each landscape condition. This 1:100 model uses CNC machining techniques to explore the ground conditions under Kalapana as a site for the architecture. **Fig. 10.14 Hoi Man (Christy) Cheung** Y3, 'Lost And Found'. This 1:20 fragment is a 3D printed sand model. The proposal is a new site for housing a US battleship wreck, USS Utah. The project focuses on the preservation of the shipwreck while facilitating research surrounding the Pearl Harbour attack.

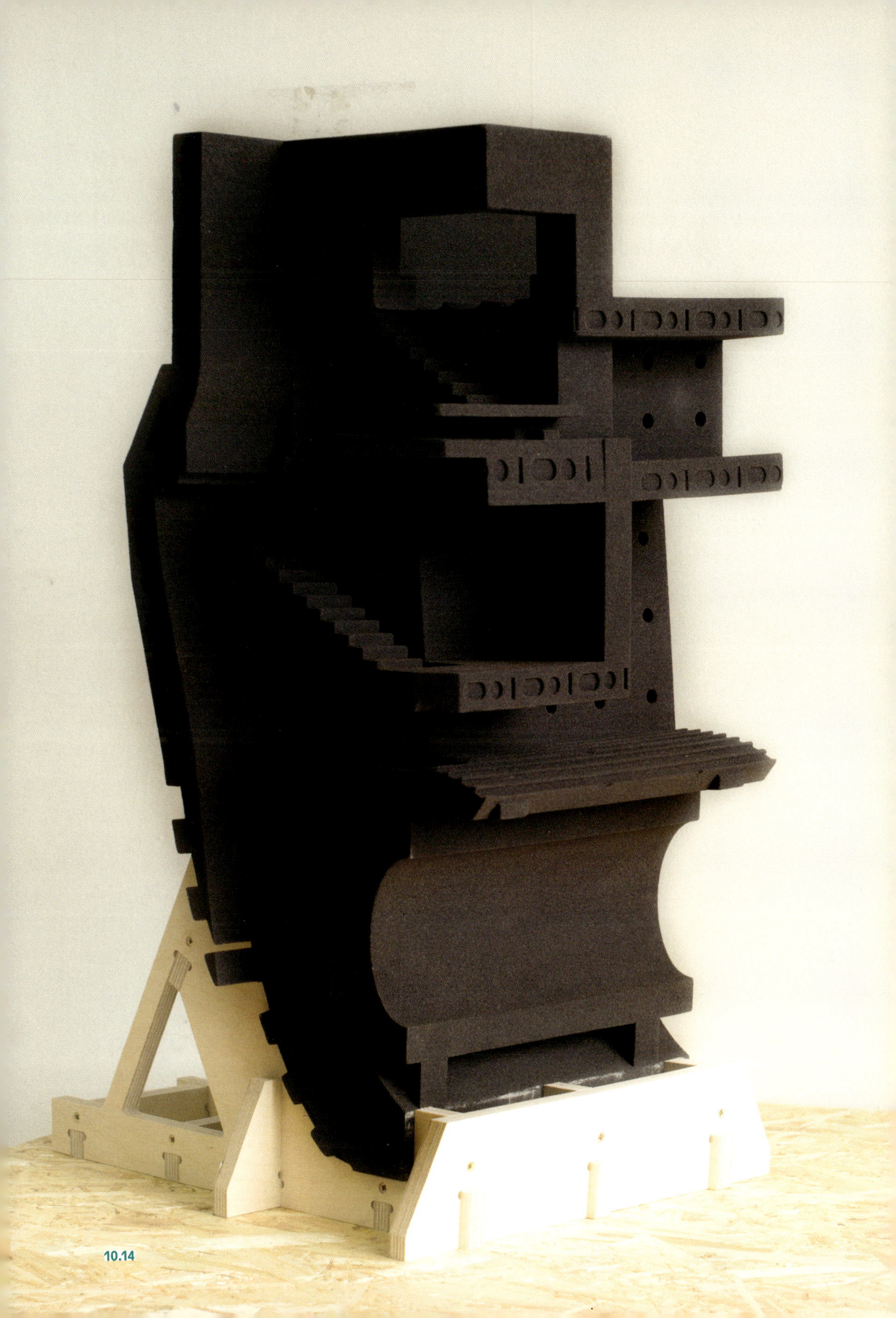

10.14

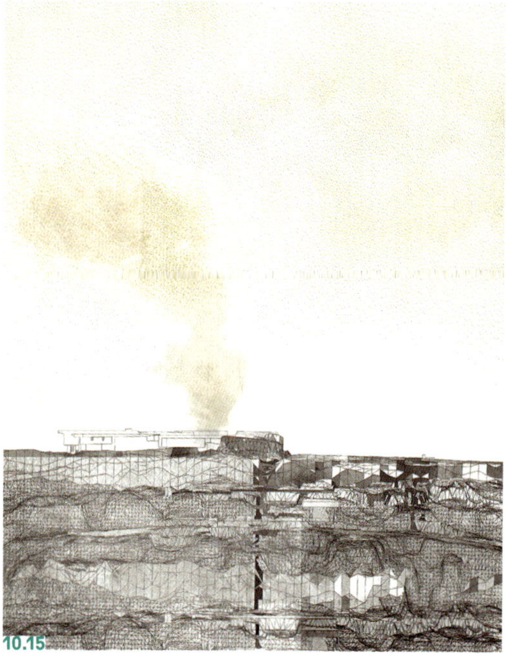

10.15

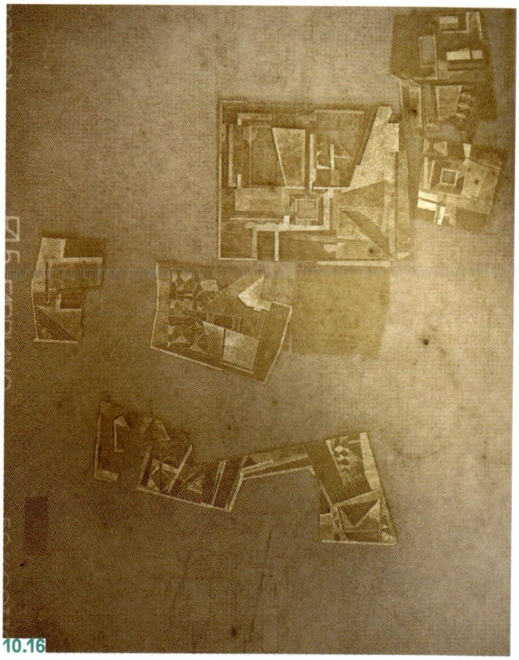

10.16

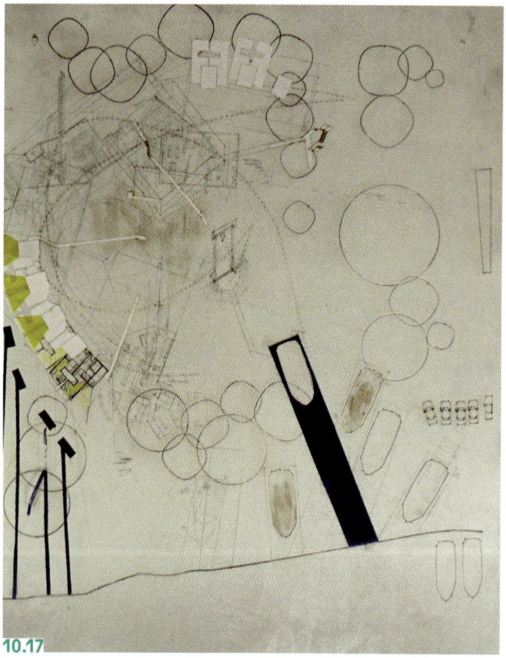

10.17

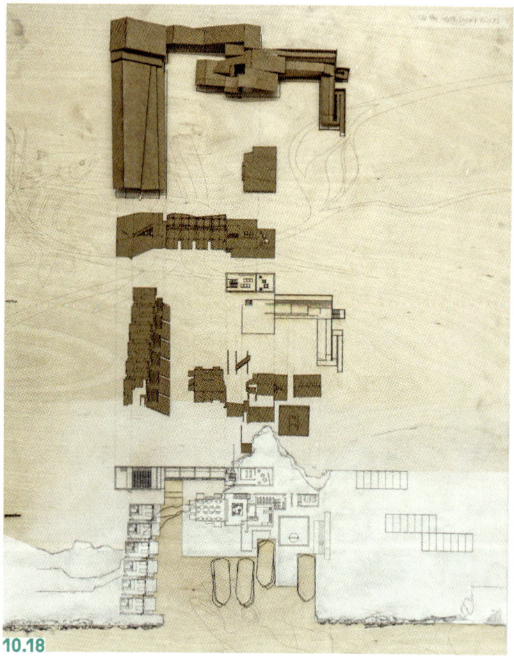

10.18

Figs. 10.15 – 10.16 Elissavet Manou Y3, 'Fishing Temple'. Front elevation and reflected ceiling plan of faceted soffit. This project explores the complex relationship between Hawaiians and their native superstitions through an architecture of shadows and reflection. The roof and landscape are used to catch shadow, redirect wind and funnel light. **Figs. 10.17 – 10.18 Shi Yin Ling** Y2, 'The Bill'. These drawings and paper models together explore different orthographic representations as concepts of architecture itself. **Fig. 10.19 Clementine Holden** Y2, 'Mapping Mahana Bay' This 1:300 paper and clay model is a building and a device for research in oceanographic change. **Fig. 10.20 Nur (Sabrina) Azman** Y2, 'Ahukula'. This project investigates the Hawaiian notion of 'Ahupua', an ancient tradition of land division. Looking for a role that this can play in a contemporary society, the project investigates how self-sufficiency could inform the architecture of a primary school. **Fig. 10.21 Duangkaew (Pink) Protpagorn** Y3, 'A River Runs Through It'. The Hakalau Dance Theatre aims to revive a site historically used for production of sugar. Water becomes part of the building, the roof tiles and the drawing show water channeled to interact with visitors. **Fig. 10.22 Xinyue (Angell) Yao** Y3, 'Timber, Timber'. This collection of buildings serve to educate the public about timber construction using Hawaiian Eucalyptus. Sited in Honolulu Harbour, the project explores the current dependence on construction materials shipped across the Pacific, despite a rich natural resource presence on the island.

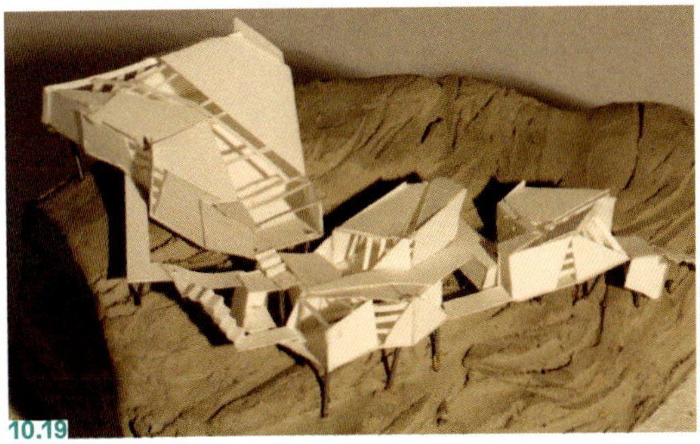
10.19

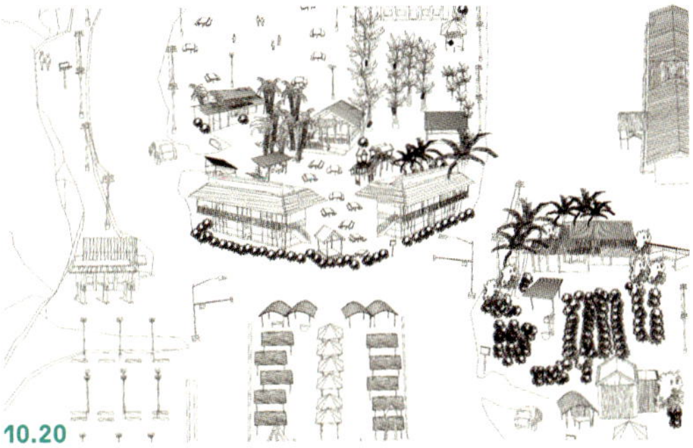
10.20

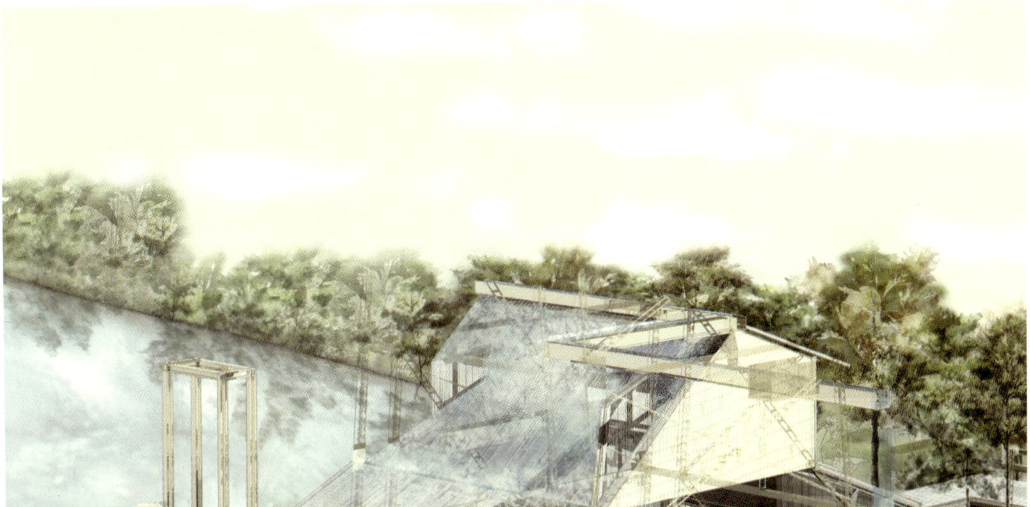
10.21

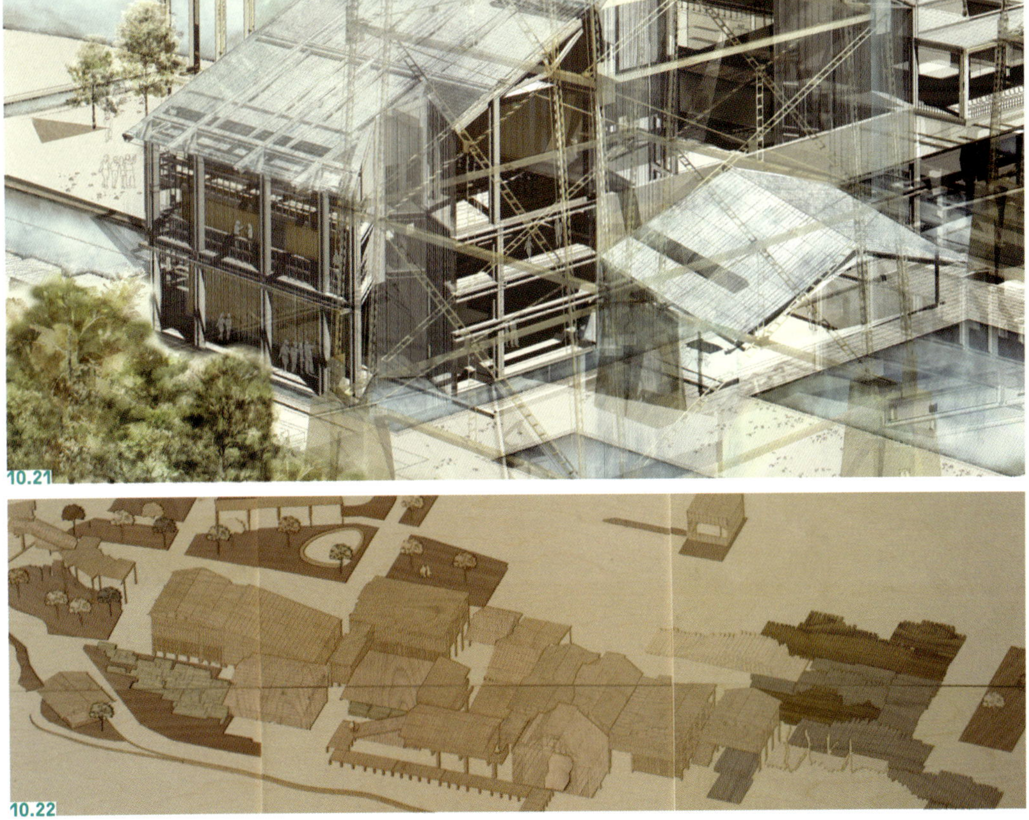
10.22

UG11

Liquid Laboratory

James Hampton, Sofia Krimizi

Year 2
Nour Al Ahmad, Alexandra Cambell, Rupinder Gidar, Nnenna Itanyi, Ziyu (Ivy) Jiang, Harry Johnson, Tung Yi Sardonna Leung, Fola-Sade (Victoria) Oshinusi, Zhi (Zoe) Tam, Ching (Cherie) Wong, Yu (Amy) Wu, Ke Yang

Year 3
Yat (Heidi) Au-Yeung, Ana-Maria Ilusca, Justin Li

We would like to thank our consultants and critics: Chris Carroll and ARUP, Costandis Kizis, Johanna Muszbek, Hseng Tai Ja Reng Lintner, Brendon Carlin, Francesca Hughes, Frederik Petersen, Sara Shafiei, Bob Sheil, Mollie Claypool, Elisabeth Dow, Yota Adilenidou, Delfina Fantini van Ditmar, Stefanos Levidis, Diony Kypraiou, Daniel Rea, Nick Browne, Jessica In, Manolis Stavrakakis, Ifigenia Liangi, Cristiana Chiorino, the Pier Luigi Nervi Project Association and from ETH Zurich: Achilleas Xydis, Sarah Nichols, Guillaume Habert, Nils Havelka

Thank you to our sponsors ARUP

UG11 operates as a material research laboratory, pursuing strategies of making to design new spatial typologies. Through investigation of cast material processes we look for the strange, the banal and the beautiful. We cast concrete. Our process is driven by experimentation on alternative uses of material and our investigation is informed by data collection, measuring and analysis. The material experiments lead us in a constant feedback loop of design stages, physical models, digital aspirations and fabrication techniques.

——We engage with a process that welcomes material mis-use and misbehavior, aspiring to systematise knowledge garnered from failure. We examine the ways technology can push our material beyond established forms and types. By investigating recent concrete fabrication and structural methods, we discover unexpected and productive design processes, potentially defining a new craft; one that can be both morphogenic and typological and will respond to a variety of programmes. Concrete, the protagonist of cast building materials, becomes in the unit the vehicle to disrupt and redefine practices of architectural synthesis. The diversity of scales, design approaches and structural systems applied to our projects has a direct correlation with the protocols of fabrication developed in the beginning of our investigation into the world of cast materials.

——Our field trip adopted the format of a Grand Tour focused on concrete applications, building paradigms and prototypes as well as current material and theoretical research in the field. Starting in Rome, we visited some of the first applications of concrete in the history of architecture and engineering, as well as identifying the sites of operation for UG11 projects in the north part of the city in close proximity with the large-scale Olympic infrastructure, as well as the recent MAXXI Museum. Making our way north to Turin, we visited a series of Pier Luigi Nervi's buildings, the FIAT Factory in Lingotto and the wild rehabilitation of the National Cinema Museum. Our itinerary took us to the Swiss Federal Institute of Technology in Zurich (ETHZ) in order to explore contemporary research on concrete alternatives, dynamic formwork and automated casting. The last stretch of our trip to Switzerland took us to the Rolex Centre by SANAA in Lausanne before spending the night in the monastery of La Tourette, visiting Notre Dame du Haut in Ronchamp and ending in Basel with the Vitra Museum and the Goetheanum, Rudolf Steiner's own design for his school.

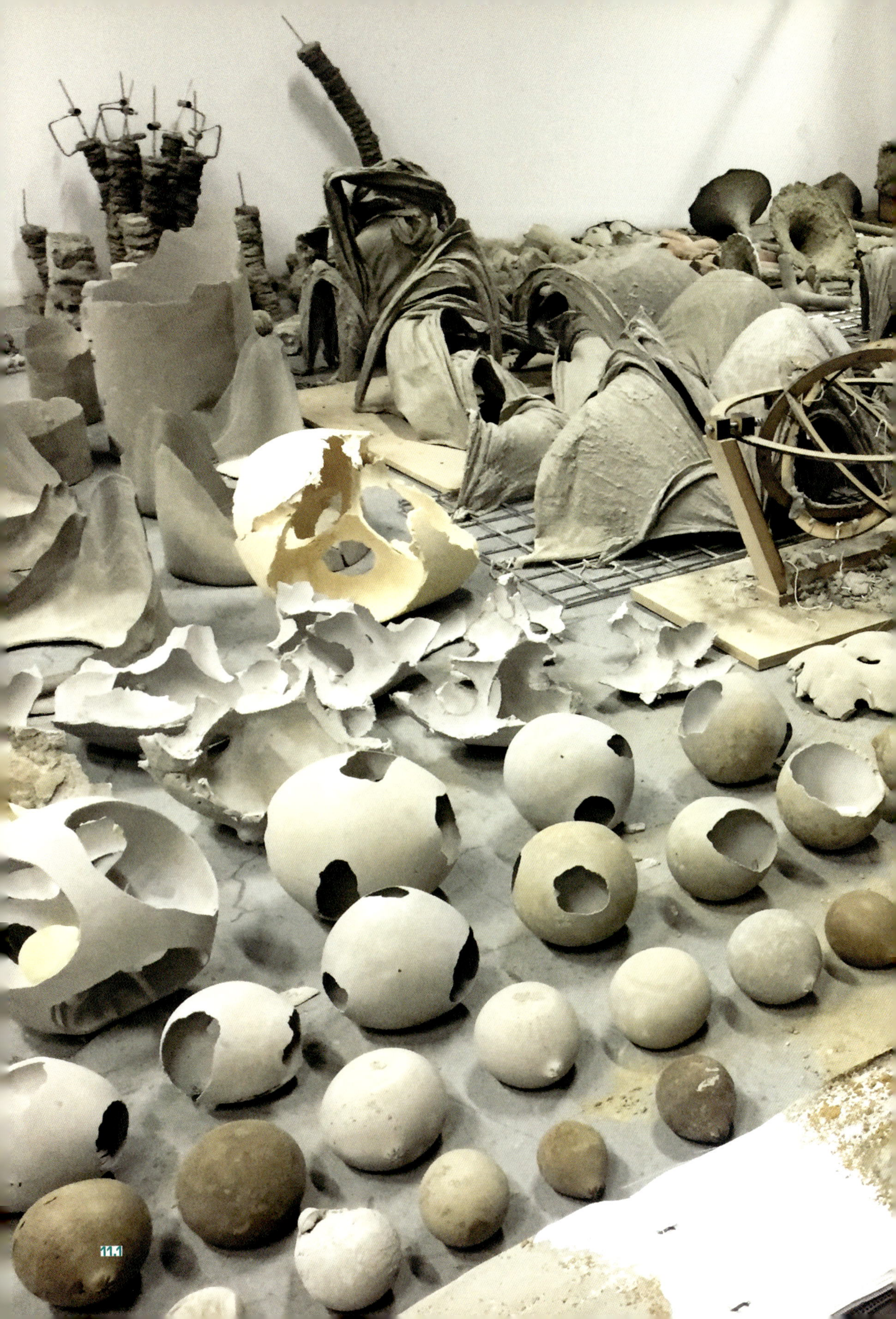
11.1

Fig. 11.1 Group project 'Unit Work Assembly'. Experimentations with unorthodox and misbehaving cast processes aspiring to create new structural and spatial typologies. **Fig. 11.2 Nour Al Ahmad** Y2, 'Human Concrete'. An investigation into the behaviour of human hair-reinforced concrete. Detail of physical model testing density and distribution of hair particles in the concrete mix. **Fig. 11.3 Tung Yi Sardonna Leung** Y2, 'Internally inflatable concrete'. A series of physical experiments testing the relationship between gravity and viscosity on pre-pressurised inflatable moulds. **Fig. 11.4 Ching (Cherie) Wang** Y2, 'Inflatable Lattice'. Hybrid casting device controlling a synchronous flow of air and concrete allowing for multiple chambers of internal complexity to emerge simultaneously. **Fig. 11.5 Ke Yang** Y2, 'Fabric-Formed Concrete Creatures'. An exhaustive investigation in the creation of fabric-formed concrete elements that grow in formal complexity and structural performance. **Alexandra Campbell** Y2, 'Air-Formed Concrete'. An experimentation in dynamic casting through the use of pressurised air flow applied against the direction of casting. **Zhi (Zoe) Tam** Y2, 'Antigravity Casting'. An attempt towards multidirectional concrete casting using a gimbal-enabled device. **Nnenna Itanyi** Y2, 'Stalactite Casting'. The development of a moldless casting method that used the process of dripping to create an inventive structural system.

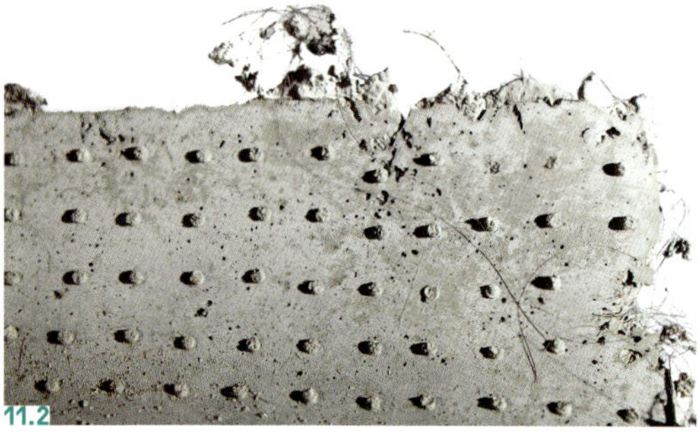

11.2

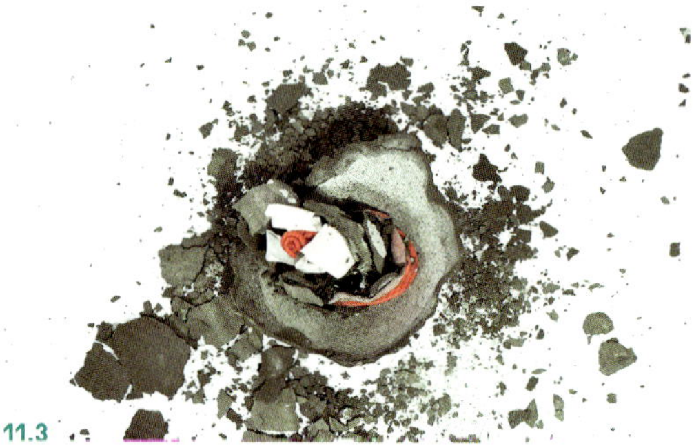

11.3

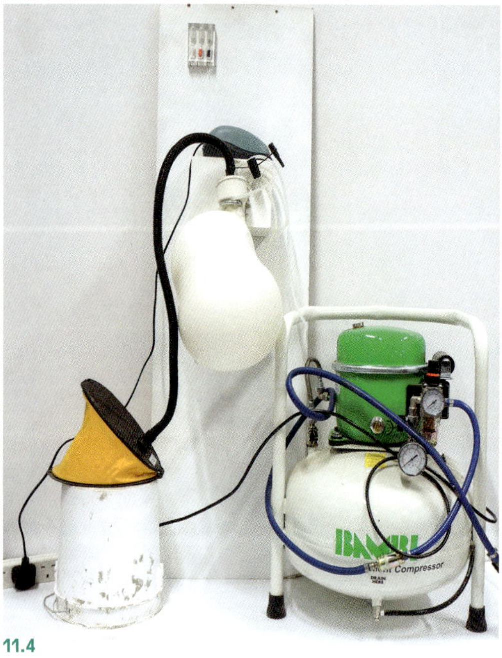

11.4

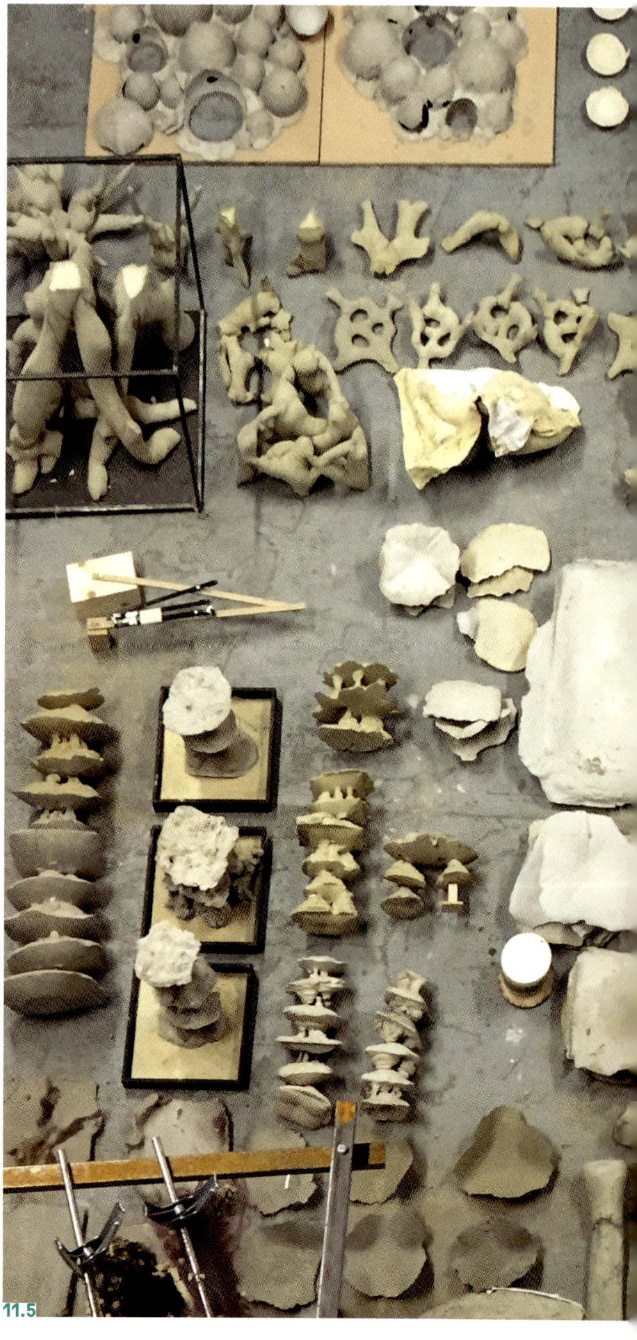

11.5

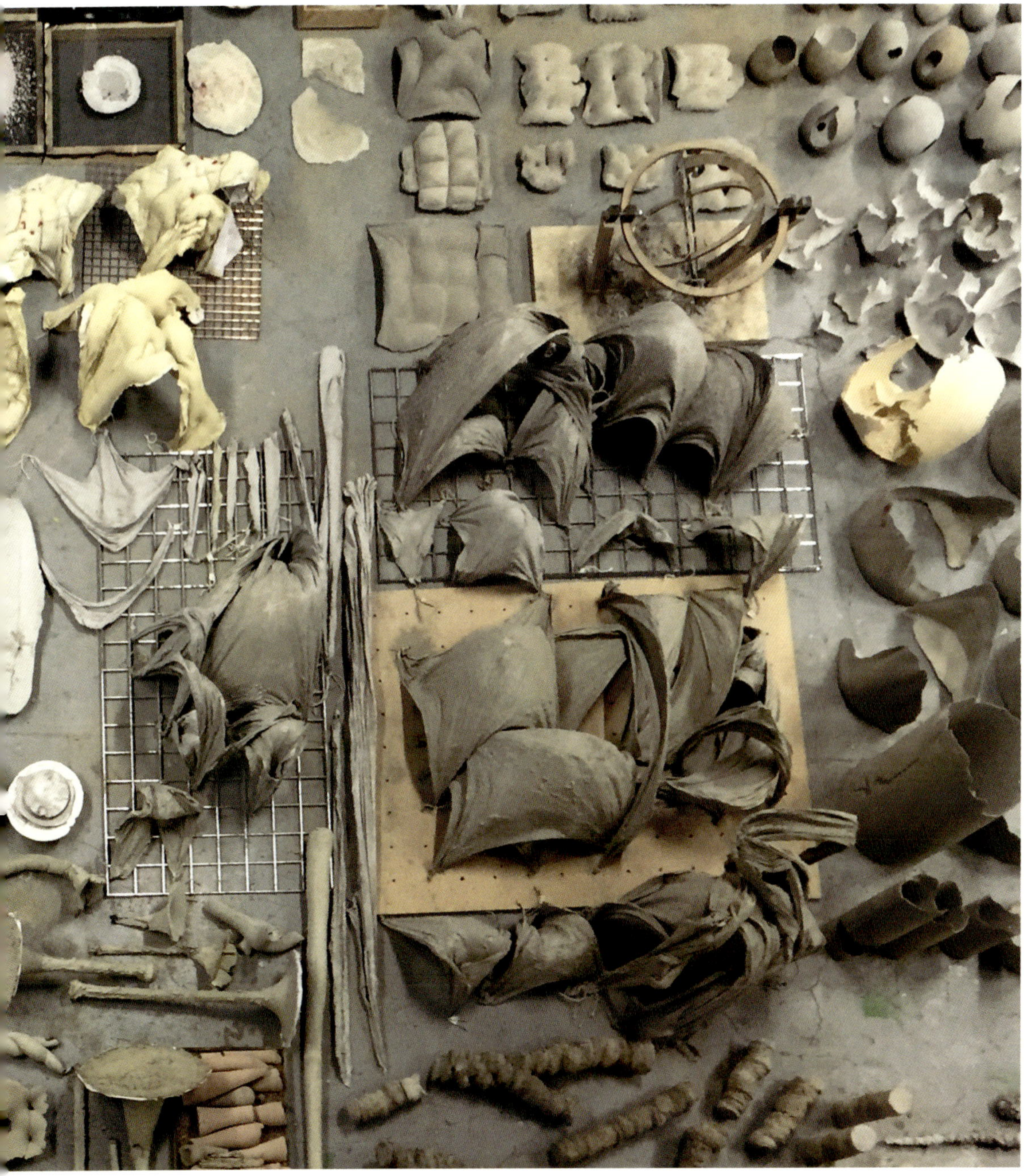

Fig. 11.6 Harry Johnson Y2, 'Concrete-Reinforced Fabric Columns'. An investigation into double reinforcement between fabric and concrete, aspiring to create a system of light vertical elements cast in situ. These photos depict this in full-scale, assisted by Nnenna Itanyi. **Fig. 11.7 Fola-Sade (Victoria) Oshinusi** Y2, 'Photographic Concrete'. An interchange between the protocols of analogue photography development and that of concrete casting. The project developed a methodology for impregnating knitted surfaces with concrete mixes allowing aggregates to define a variety of surface textures. **Fig. 11.8 Rupinder Gidar** Y2, 'Centrifugal Casting'. An investigation into dynamic casting. The project developed a series of casts set in motion under centrifugal forces acting on the concrete mix. Moments of extreme thinness as well as emergent geometries were by-products of the process that informed the work throughout the development. **Fig. 11.9 Yu (Amy) Wu** Y2, 'Gravity-Formed Concrete'. An investigation into using thin concrete shells cast in situ, using fabric as reinforcement. The project developed a combinational method of nesting domes, which allows for a systemic understanding of load bearing.

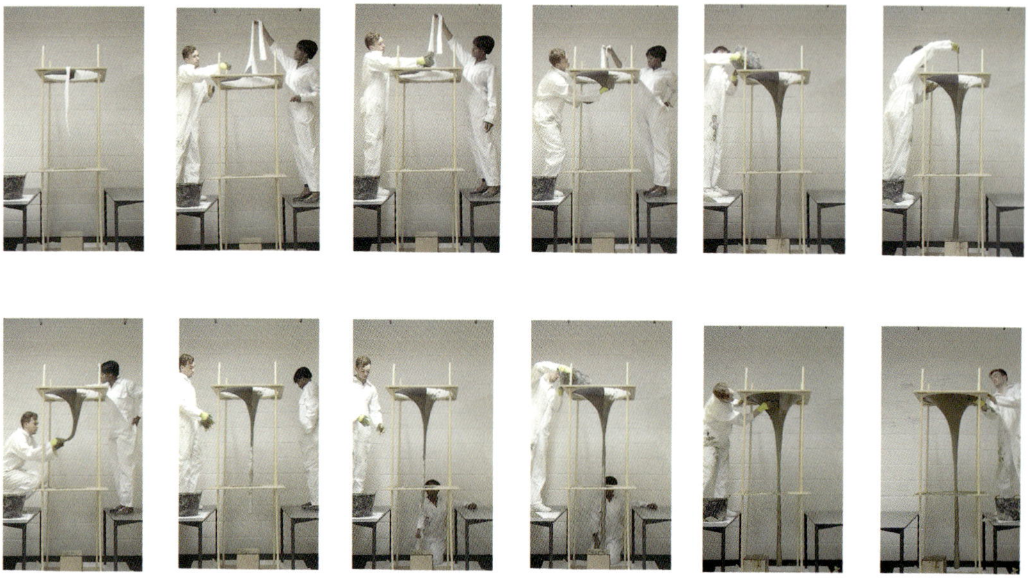

11.6

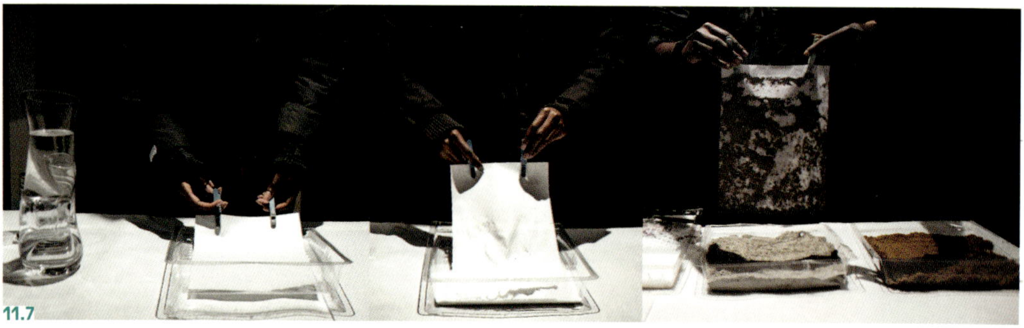

11.7

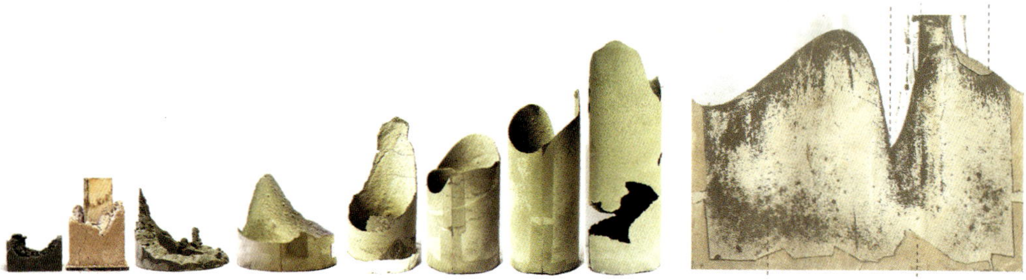

11.8

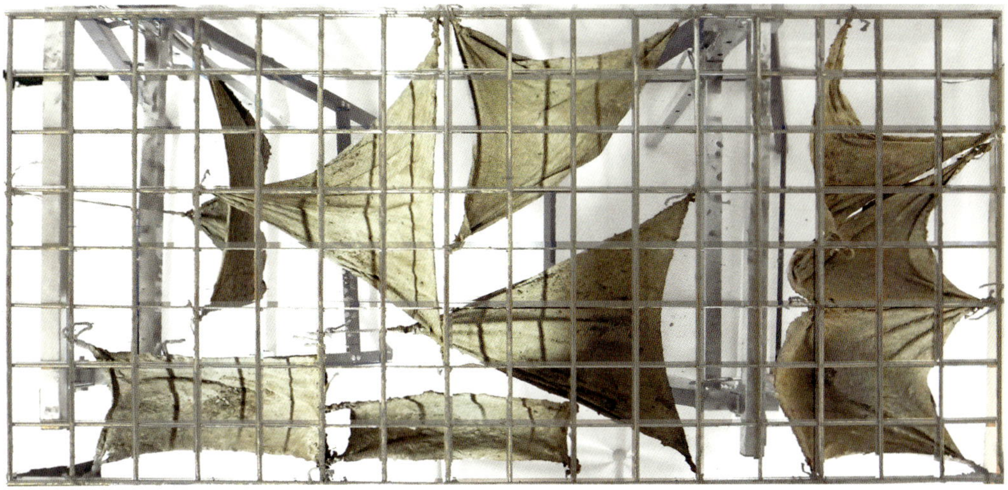

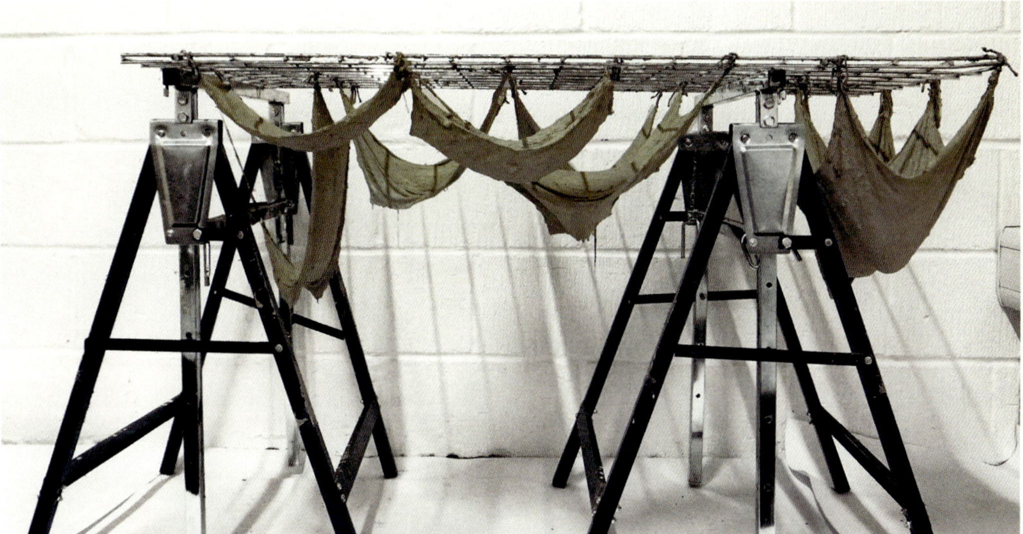

11.9

Figs. 11.10 – 11.11 Harry Johnson Y2, 'Forest as Market'. The project develops a typology for an open air informal market in the sports district of Flamino in Rome through the definition of a breathing concrete epidermis. The system of columns and canopy allows topical control of light and temperature, simulating the spatial conditions identified in a forest field. A reversed ceiling plan describing the variations of ash density in the concrete mixture is applied onto the tensile fabric through the main market space. The project imagines a growth of this urban typology that can occupy different parts of the city at different moments, following particular events and activity. **Figs. 11.12 – 11.14 Justin Li** Y3, 'Slip Film Museum'. The project investigates a system of dynamic concrete slip-printing using the concrete reinforcement bars as paths for printing devices that deposit a constant amount of cast material though their movement. References from a Gothic structural and ornamental repertoire were relevant in the organisation of a continuous interior for the proposal of the museum of cinematic props in Rome. The building developed between two existing storage warehouses that eventually performed as the museum's archival spaces. The notion of 'scalelessness' in the structure is important, since the system has to accommodate props of an extreme size and material diversity. The typology of the museum suggests a non-prescriptive engagement of the visitor with the building, allowing different paths to form amongst the forest of printed columns. Different types of roof tiles control the light conditions below as the museum collection finds itself in flux.

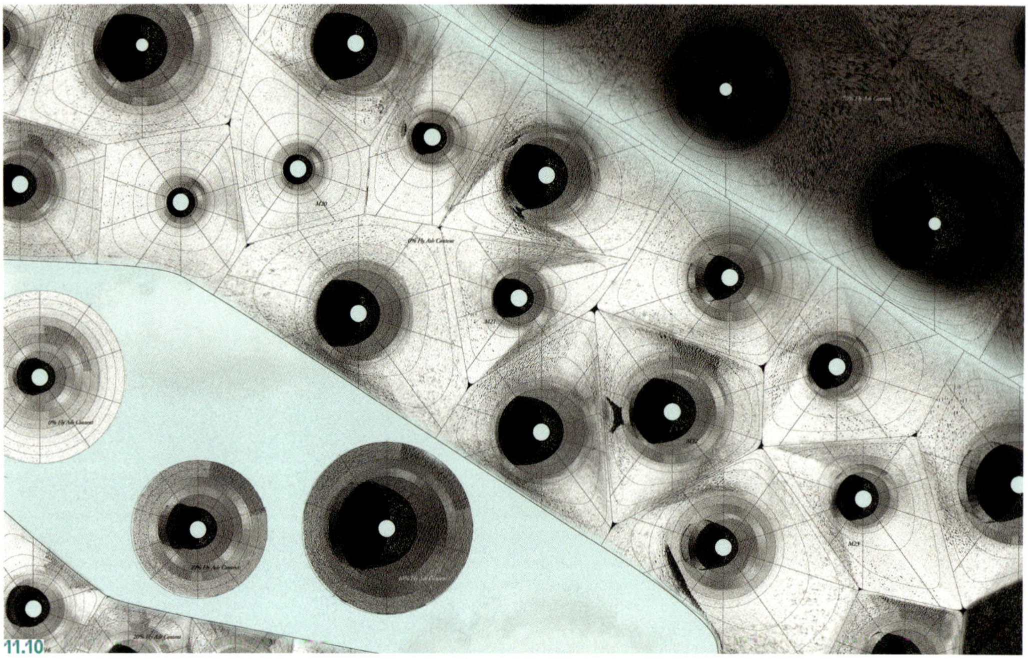

11.10

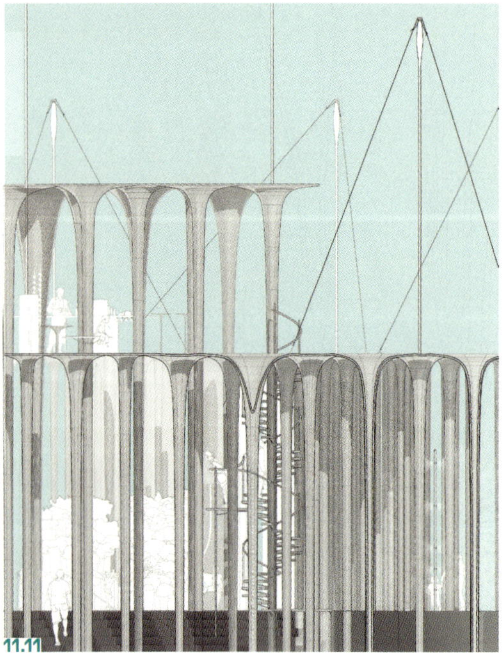

11.11

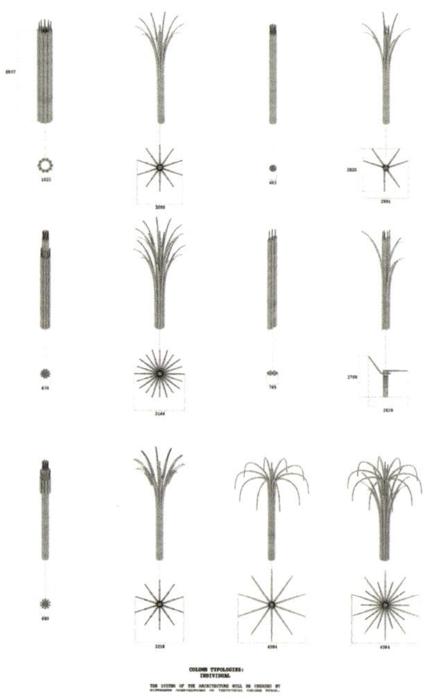

11.12

Figs. 11.15 – 11.16 Rupinder Gidar Y2, 'Centrifugal Healing'. This project continues the investigation of spun concrete. Inhabitable in-situ spun elements aggregate to create an athletic healing hub within the Olympic complex in Rome. The curing time of the centrifugal casts is analogous to the time spent by the patients in each chamber. The interior surfaces provide a register for the motion of the concrete while liquid. A system of joining between casts is developed in the process, allowing for openings and connections to emerge. Typologies of extreme nesting emerge as the pain and pleasure aspects of the programme are placed throughout the field of chambers. The strategy for construction and assembly is differentiated from the analysis of space as inhabited by the healing body.

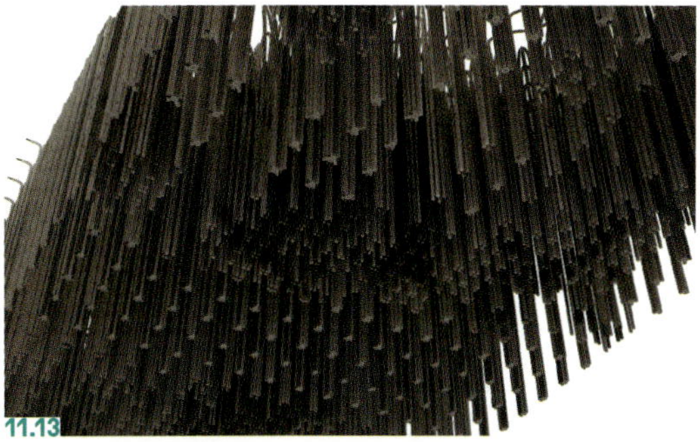

11.13

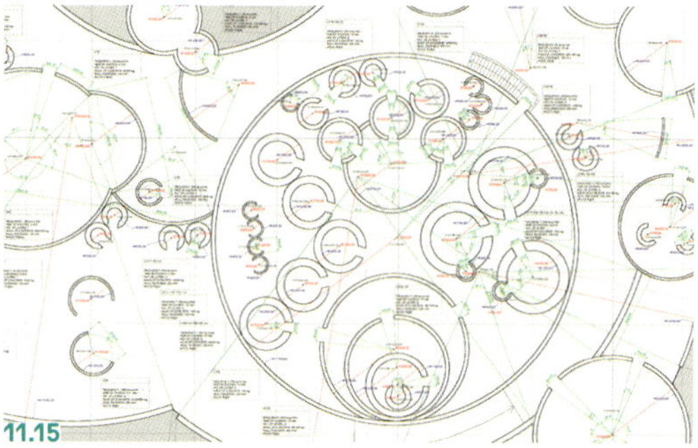

11.15

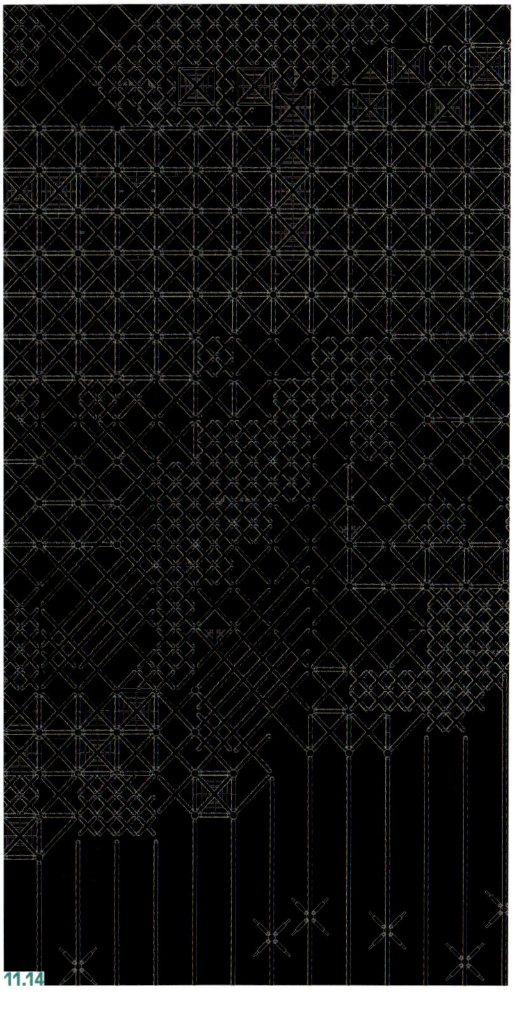

11.14

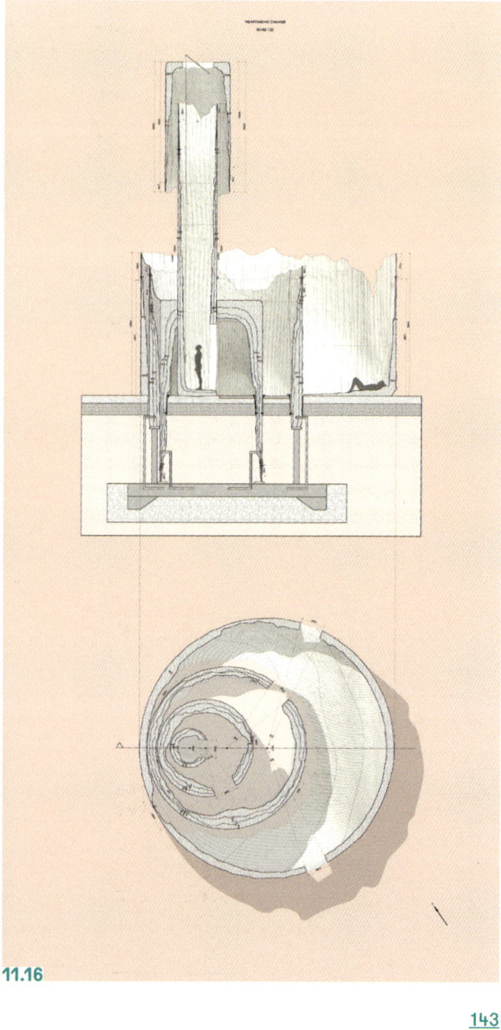

11.16

Figs. 11.17 – Fig. 11.18 Ziyu (Ivy) Jiang Y2, 'Vertical Roman Beach'. The project imagines a vertical urban beach in the district of Flaminio in Rome. The casting method developed by the project directs the vectors of liquid concrete through a series of horizontal elastic filters, while allowing all vertical elements to be formed mouldlessly. Diving platforms and water pools are formed in vertical juxtaposition with each other, allowing the beach program to develop upwards. The totality of the site is considered to be liquid while in the making, creating in this way different depths of swimming and diving water. The thickness of the concrete is inhabited by the secondary programs that expand from the structural core downwards below the level of the water.

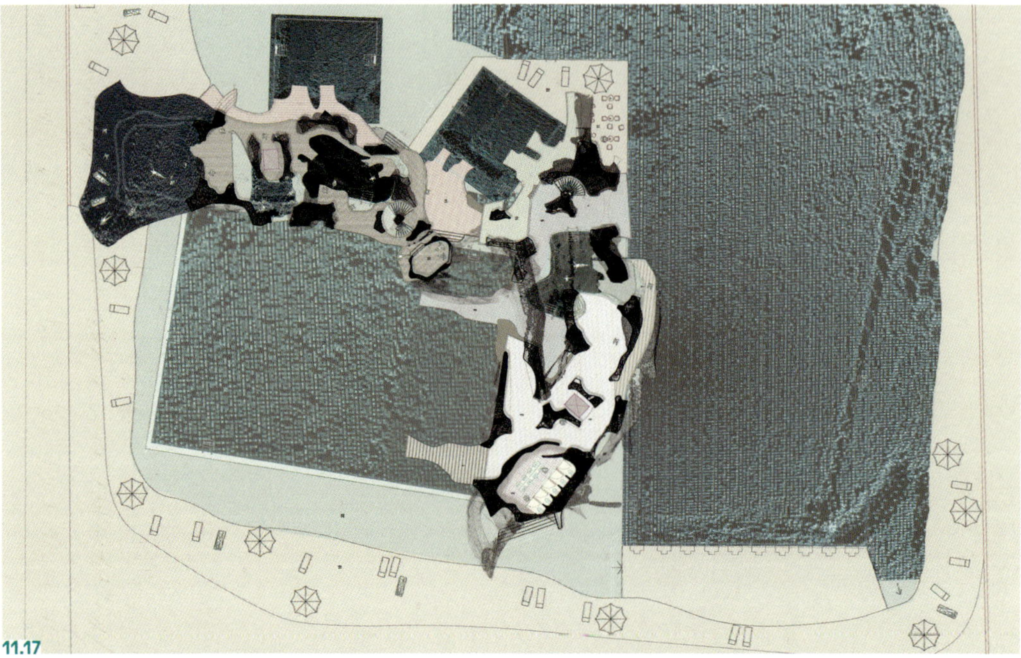

11.17

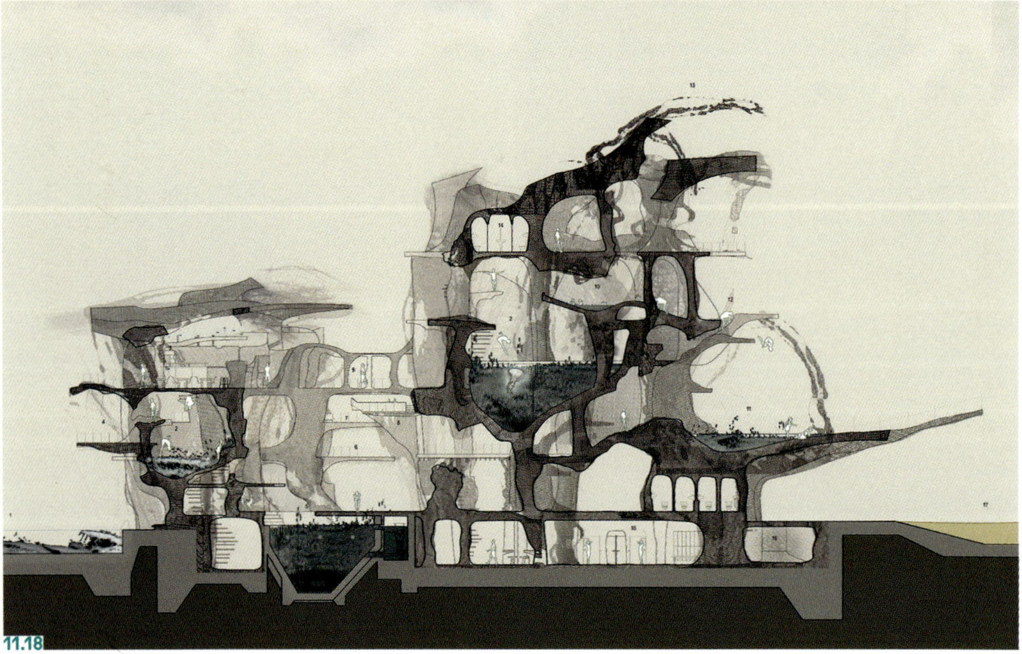

11.18

Figs. 11.19 – Fig. 11.21 Yat (Heidi) Au-Yeung Y3, 'Archive Whispers'. The project investigates the typology of the working archival library focusing on the juxtaposition between the storage of physical manuscripts, digital databases and performance – reading spaces focusing on the genealogy of Roman plays derived from the work of Plautus. A dense and floorless archive hides behind the existing façade of a residential block in the north part of Rome. Through the mass of physical and digital storage, suspended concrete amphitheatres carve through the stacks and operate as hybrids between reading rooms and reenactment spaces for the archived plays. With time, the theatre plots translated into different languages, as Latin morphed into the various Romance languages. With each translation, parts of the plots were lost and rewritten, creating the diversity of theatrical literature and media today. This archive will collect these materials – ranging from the original manuscripts to the digital versions, from the Latin plays to their translations in Romance languages – allowing the history of theatrical literature to be traced. Each level of storage is dedicated to a time period, organised chronologically so that the building is a physical timeline of the development of dramatic text. The collection will continue to grow, and new forms of recording literature will develop in the future. The archive will also continue to excavate downwards, exposing the Roman grounds and writing its history anew.

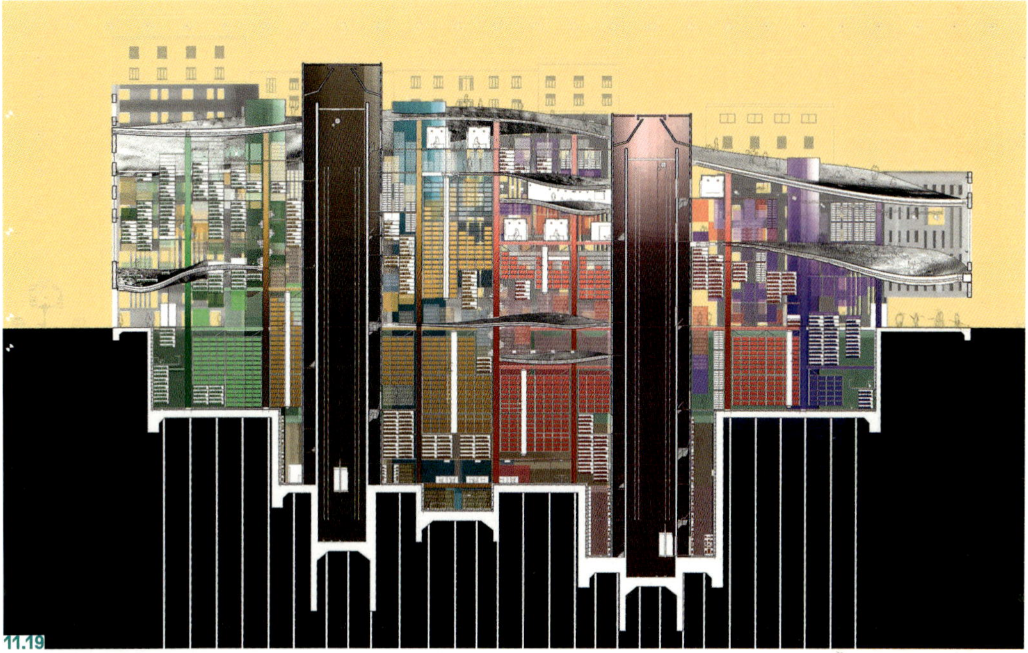
11.19

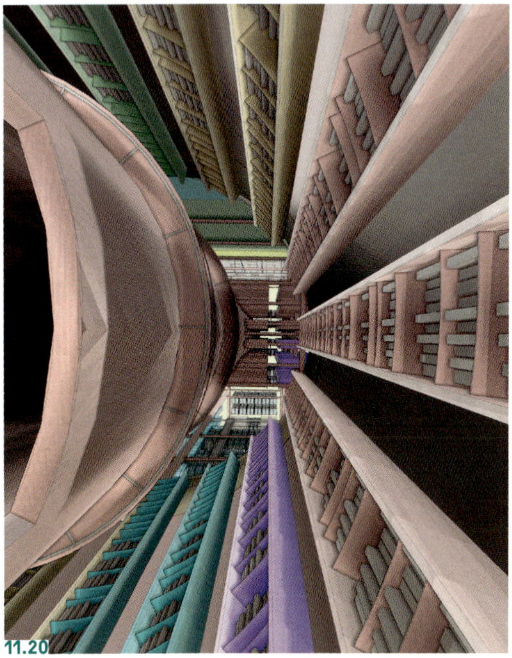
11.20

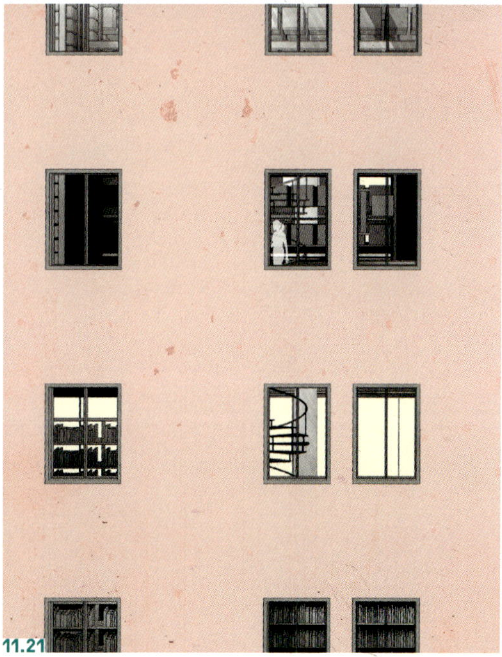
11.21

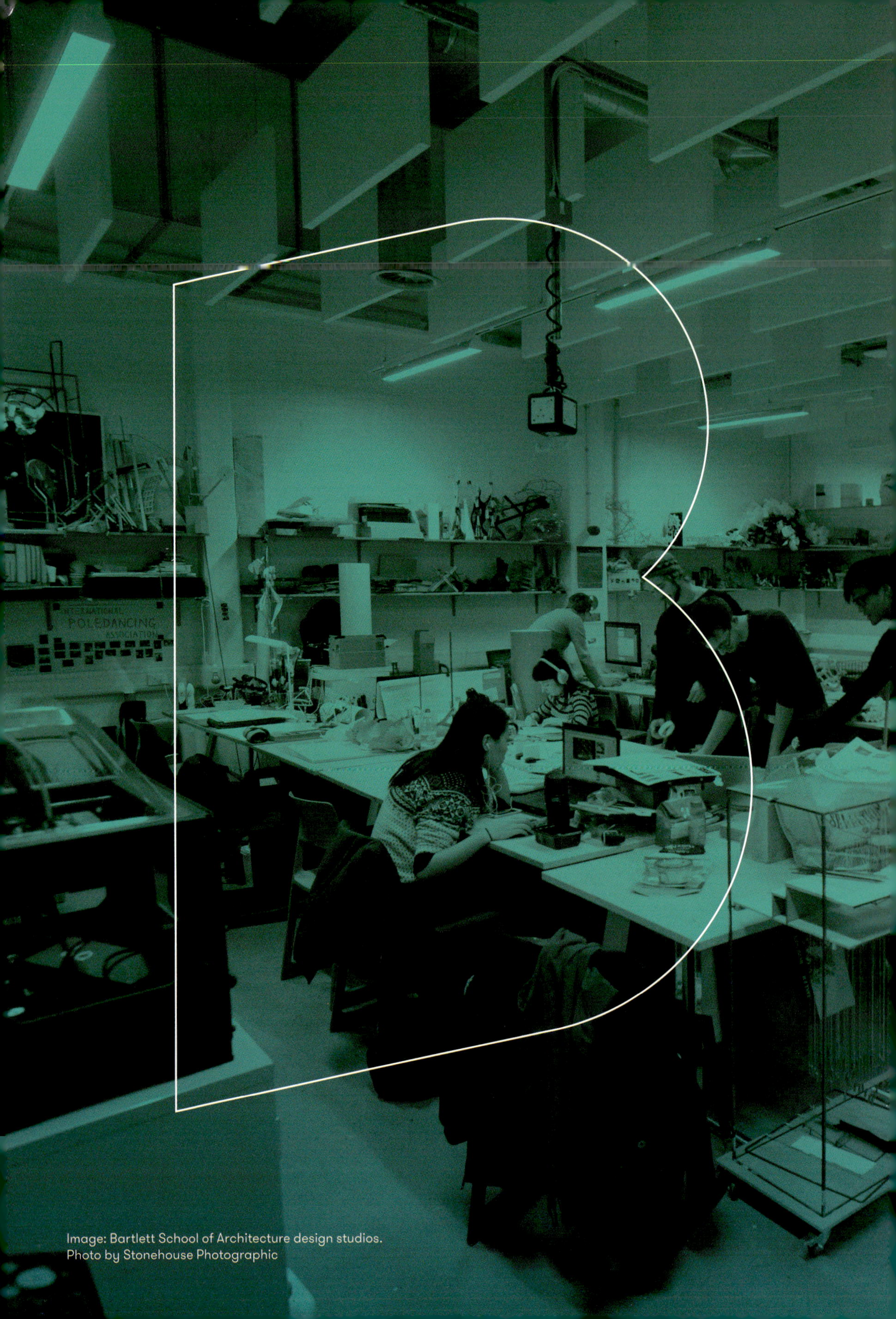

Image: Bartlett School of Architecture design studios.
Photo by Stonehouse Photographic

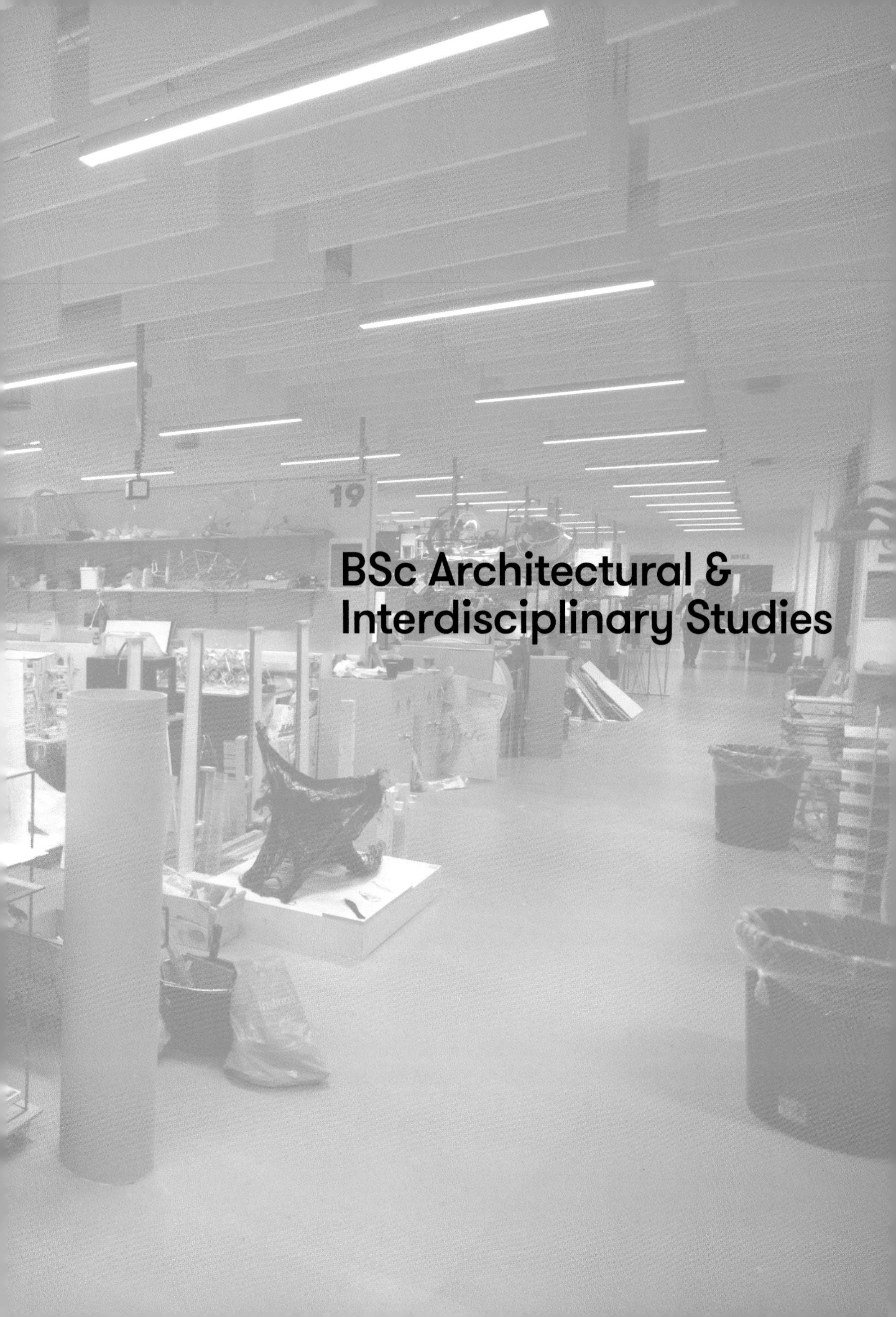

BSc Architectural & Interdisciplinary Studies

BSc Architectural & Interdisciplinary Studies

Programme Director: Elizabeth Dow

Architectural Research & Dissertation
Barbara Penner, Brent Carnell, Nina Völlenbroker

Project X: Design & Creative Practice
Kevin Green, Mara Kanthak, Chee-Kit Lai, Freddy Tuppen, Michelle Young

The Bartlett offers a BSc in Architectural & Interdisciplinary Studies (AIS). Architectural culture has never been exclusively a product certified by architects, but now, more than ever, there are many other people working in related fields – film, media, curation, design and creative practice – who shape debates and ideas around architecture in significant ways. In bringing together architectural research and design and creative practice courses, BSc AIS aims to produce the development of independent-minded graduates who are equipped to participate in these complex debates.

——This unique programme allows students to follow modules within the Bartlett as well as with modules in other UCL departments. It builds on the successful BSc Architectural Studies programme, which ran between 2002-12 and produced over 110 graduates. Graduates have gone on to postgraduate studies and professional careers in a wide variety of fields including: journalism, landscape design, lighting design, international development, fine arts, photography, print-making, arts education and management, events management, urban planning, law, accounting, property valuation, and construction management. They have pursued graduate studies at universities such as the Royal College of Art, Central Saint Martins, Imperial College, London School of Economics and ETH in Zurich as well as at UCL.

——The great strength of the BSc AIS programme is its interdisciplinarity: students are able to tailor their own course of study to suit their particular interests and future postgraduate and career plans. The course suits highly motivated, independent students who are interested in architecture, design, and urban studies, but who also wish to take advantage of electives on offer elsewhere in UCL. Popular choices are Art History, Management, Languages, Economics, Psychology, History, Mathematics, Anthropology, Law, Archaeology, and Geography.

——There are two specially tailored module streams for BSc AIS students within the Bartlett, the first including modules Architectural Research I & II and Dissertation, and the second, our Design and Creative Practice modules, Project X 1, 2 & 3, examples of which are reproduced on the following pages.

The Dissertation

Module Coordinator: Brent Carnell

Reni (Morenike) Onajide

The Yellow Years: Remembering the Revival: Architecture and Women's Liberated Fashion in 1960s Lagos told through my Grandmother's Reflection

With age, I have come to realise that identifying with a nation such as Nigeria on a profound level requires both the acknowledgement of its corruption and strife and also a keen interest in really understanding how it has come to be. This dissertation-*cum*-novel is a reflection of Lagos from 1960-66 told from the standpoint of my Grandmother Kili's recounted experiences. For compositional purposes the storyline is fictional, but the facts and knowledge used to form the story are based on both historically accurate primary and secondary sources. This approach allows me to discover how the country's newly liberated status had a direct impact on the spatial qualities of the architecture in the centre of Lagos, as well as on women's fashion and hair.

——It was two years since the independence of 1960 and Kili could notice the confidence among the people. It was no longer the "newly liberated" atmosphere that she had experienced when she first visited. She had always wanted to visit Independence Square in the central Ikoyi district. At the centre of the square was a water feature with circular designs which water sprouted from. Kili remembers it being perhaps the most modern feature Lagos had produced since its independence. She had arranged to meet up with her friend at the fountain in the late morning. Lara appeared with her hair separated and bound with black wire in circles that looped back on themselves. Kili could not help but admire both spatial works of art: the water feature in front of them and Lara's hair. From the circular designs in the water feature, to Lara's hairstyle, Kili was overwhelmed by the new trends that surrounded her.

——Later that evening at the independence celebration the square had an atmosphere Kili could not explain, but as she looked around she could not help but feel as though it was a hub for feeling at ease. It was clear to her that the square marked Nigeria's freedom. As her feet hit the hard ground in dance, she looked around at all the people that surrounded her. She couldn't tell if it was because they were enjoying the open-air as opposed to being cooped up in a hot hall but the fluidity of the people seemed so free. The water feature was unknowingly circled around as people danced, and it appeared a sense of rhythm had been created by the layout of the square itself. Although the paving that surrounded the feature was square, the people that absorbed it had created a circular rhythm of movement. Nigeria now felt like a stand-alone nation. A nation free to build a square in honour of their own achievements, gather around it and celebrate their freedom.

Thomas Visscher

The Place of Memory in the Internet Age: Communicative, Networked and Evolving Commemoration

The members of my age group constitute the first generation to grow up with the Internet. We now live an existence where the majority have a developed an internet and social media presence. Often our interactions with social networking sites such as Facebook and Twitter seem to exist in their own irreverent media bubble where most online activity consists of the exchange of humour or political stories and videos. However, sometimes profound events from real life pierce through and force us to reassess our assumptions about the presence of virtual spaces.

——For me this happened early last year. When browsing Facebook's never-ending wall of links, I came across a collection of messages for local Islington boy Henry Hicks who had been killed in a scooter accident whilst being followed by a police car on 19 December 2014. His death caused a wide resonance throughout the local generation I grew up in, particularly on social media. This was how I first found out about his passing. I spent a while reading through these messages of love and support which filled his Facebook wall and it struck me as significant that such a place existed where one could be so close to a presence of the deceased that communication through hundreds of comments to that individual could be facilitated. One night in December 2015, I walked past a gathering of around one hundred people outside London's Pentonville Prison. I had stumbled across a vigil and street party for Henry at the site where the accident happened. The area had been turned into a memorial compete with mural and flowers.

——I began to consider what forces anchor memory and emotion to sites such as the Facebook page or the roadside mural. It seems that memory spaces can form around both of these sites due to the significance we give to material traces in the physical world. I am interested in the ways in which certain 'real' places have agency, and the way that social media sites such as Facebook can help maintain a conceptual space where the presence of a deceased individual is still very much felt. My aim is to compare the physical and virtual spaces of memory and to identify the types of remembering that these sites generate. Ultimately I will address how such lingering presences manifest and what the implications are for our understanding of the architecture of the memorial.

——The human urge to commemorate is an incredibly powerful force and can find expression in almost every kind of space, real or imagined. The relation between memory and place is fundamentally important to our understanding of contemporary society and how we conceptualise the experiential world, whilst moving into an ever more digitalised age.

Project X: Design and Creative Practice 1, 2 & 3

Module Coordinators: Kevin Green, Mara Kanthak, Chee-Kit Lai, Freddy Tuppen, Michelle Young

Project X: Design and Creative Practice aims to help students build a creative and reflective practice of their own. It enables them to undertake a mode of working that particularly interests them and through research and iteration develop an independent practice-based project. Students are asked to think of architecture in interdisciplinary ways, explore alternative approaches to design and situate their work within a broader cultural context. A series of key questions confront students at different stages of the year concerning the nature of their practice, the contribution of their work to the broader field of architecture, the originality of their project, and the selection of appropriate media for the ideas pursued.

——Year 1 Project X based their projects on the idea of games. The students have been invited to step out of the ordinary and into: the playground, the realm of the speculative, alternative realities and then into their own games. Design has been defined as a mode of play. Starting off with a ruled-based (architectural) drawing workshop lead by Sayan Skandarajah, with further exploration with physical models, 1:1 devices, experiments and films exploring various forms of making and representation.

——Year 2 Project X students worked on two different projects this year. The first, a three-month interactive group project to create site-specific audio guides for Bloomsbury, London The group endeavor entitled 'Story Telling' explored the city as a museum, or vice versa, through untold histories/narratives blurring between fact and fiction. Jessica In lead a computer and digital sound workshop for our Y2 students, helping each of them develop their technical skills allowing them to create the audio files. The second, entitled 'The Institute of…' was a personal project and each student explored their own unique architectural language that helped define their creative spatial practice.

——Our Year 3 Project X students started the year exploring how specific cultural trends come in and out of fashion, examining and uncovering the patterns in popular culture throughout history. This project encouraged students to research current trends in design, uncover distinct patterns of change in the urban environment and to respond to these patterns by predicting what might come next. The themes and skills explored in term 1 paved the way for students to develop their own briefs that became their projects for term 2, allowing each student to explore their own interests, often bringing in knowledge from modules they take elsewhere in UCL.

——The resulting projects are speculative and diverse, as is the use of differing media, ranging from virtual reality simulations, coding, casting, furniture design, playground design, joinery, film projection, musical composition, photography, community consultation, film documentary, curating and material testing, to name just a few.

Year 1
Lucy Brown, Jasmine Ceccarelli-Dewry, Lier Chen, James Curtis, Luofei Dong, Lillie Hall, Theo Merten-Mancer, Laura Gosney, Sonia Gruenwald, Julia Millang, Vikrim Nagra, Ryuhei Oishi, Ged Ribas-Goody, Grace Simmonds, Signe Swarttou, Jonathan Whitfield

Year 2
Siufan Adey, Iona Farrar-Bell, Rickie Cheuk, Chloe Gould, Sandhya Gulsin, Eloise Maland, Natalie Newsome, Anna Vorsel, Lucy Walmsley

Year 3
Hsiao-Chu (Dormmy) Chen, Misha Deville, Vendella Gambill, Ben Leggett, Anna Minor, Akil Scafe-Smith, Emilie Skaff, Natasha Tennant, Madeleine Valcour, Robyn Vey

Thanks to our consultants and critics: Joey Augustin, Christopher Burman, Alfonso Borragan, Ben Campkin, Elizabeth Dow, Nicholas Feldmeyer, Ben Harriman, Bill Hodgson, Jessica In, Thandi Loewenson, Hugh McEwen, Barbara Penner, Collette Sheddick, Nina Shen Poblete, Sayan Skandarajah, Nick Tyson, Nina Vollenbröker

Fig. X.1 Emilie Skaff Y3, 'Patterns and trends'. This project explores emotive patterns and trends in social media with the 'strip for Jackie' campaign as its starting point. Photograph appropriated from the original #stripforjackie campaign depicting Lebanese Olympic skier Jackie Chamoun.
Fig. X.2 Anna Minor Y3, 'Wire:less'. My wirelessness is grounded in a network of fibre optic cables buried underneath the pavement and snaking along the bottom of the ocean. Every time I make a transaction, take a photo or listen to a tune a part of this subterranean and subaquatic network is activated. A consortium of privately owned corporations and national governments are investing in cables. Today the transoceanic cable network supports 99 percent of all data traffic. As a result, the deepest stratum of the internet is material. It is only in the last hop between the router and my computer that signals are freed from the grid. **Fig. X.3 Maddie Valcour** Y3, 'Lost Spaces'. This project explores a design methodology for making the inaccessible, accessible and the unused, used. Through quick constructed interventions, lost spaces become reactivated.

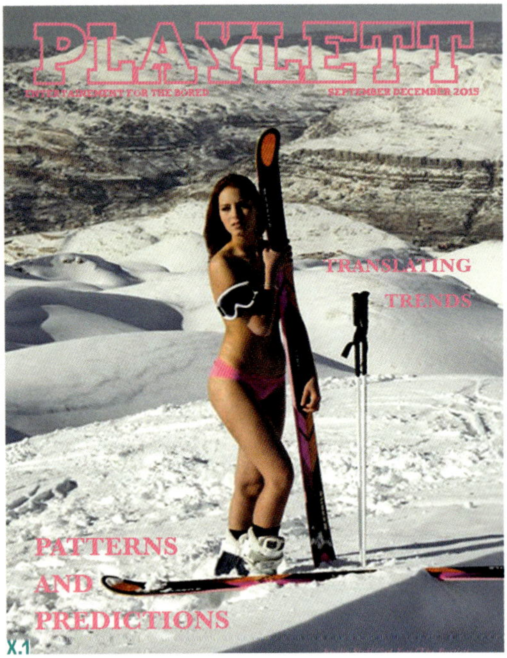

X.1

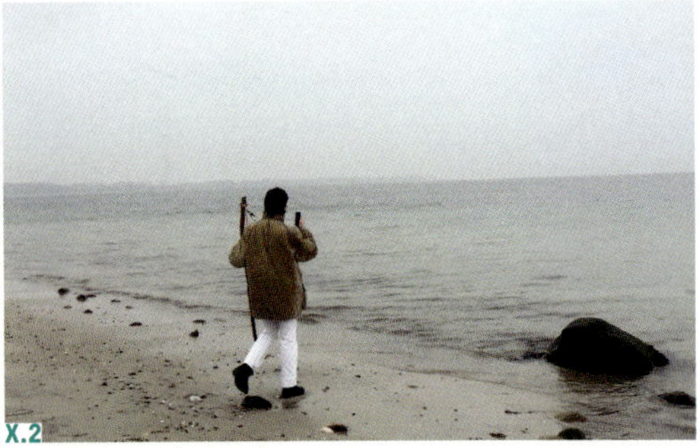

X.2

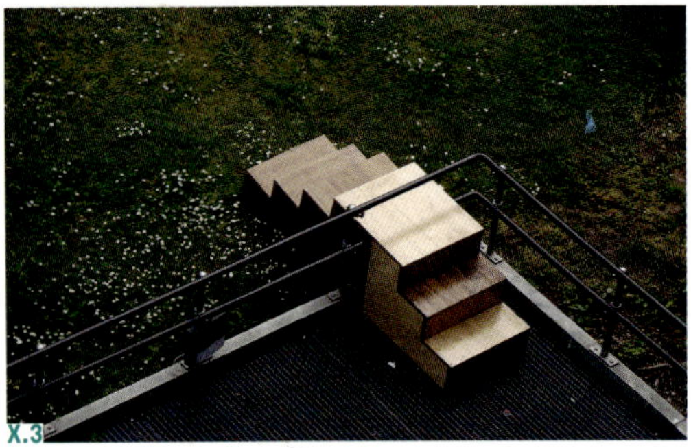

X.3

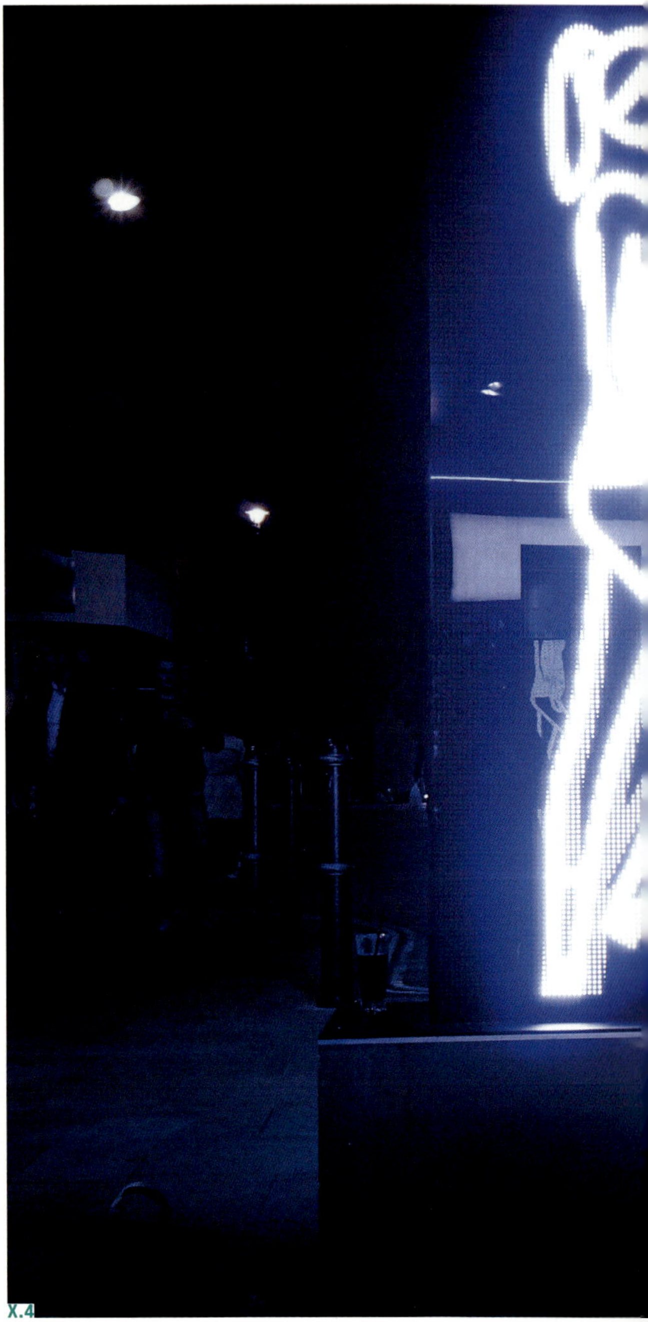

X.4

Fig. X.4 Benjamin Leggett Y3, 'Consciously Numb'. The project explores ways in which the seeing subject in the city is also always seen, examining the consequences of this reflexivity and reflectivity. It asks whether citizens are merging with the city through light-emitting technology, how we are endlessly repeated in the city through mirrored surfaces, and how the cycle of seeing and being seen through surveillance cameras and personal devices has instigated a kind of consciousness under anaesthetic.

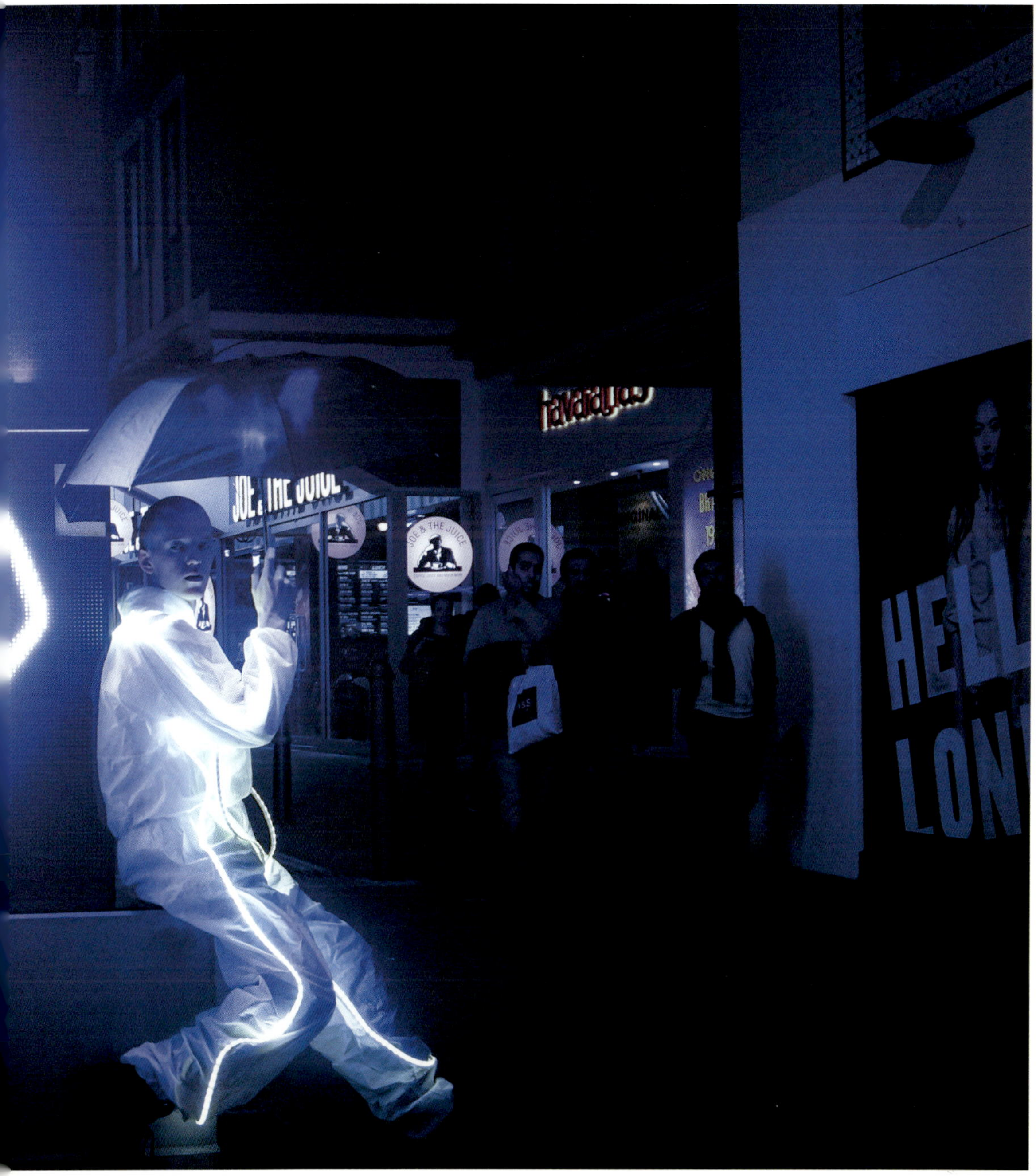

Fig. X.5 Anna Vorsel Y2, 'a.State'. The project looks at authority through the medium of maps, and examines the abstract space that exists between the map and the territory that it is a projection of. **Fig. X.6 & X.8 Eloise Maland** Y2, 'en route'. en route is a collection of voices, illustrating how language and images affect our perception of people. The outcome of the project was a book placed within the British Museum, commenting on the history of Europe and the presence of the colonial narrative in the way we portray, understand and treat refugees. **Fig. X.7 Natalie Newsome** Y2, 'The Vivivaud: an exploration into objects and their relationships with people', film still. The process that lead up to the Vivivaud's creation draws out the idea that objects have a cyclical life; they never die or disappear, but rather, they periodically take on new forms. Furthermore, there are different stages in this lifecycle and an object can move from stage to stage in a spontaneous manner – but it is the fact that this process never ends that makes it cyclical.

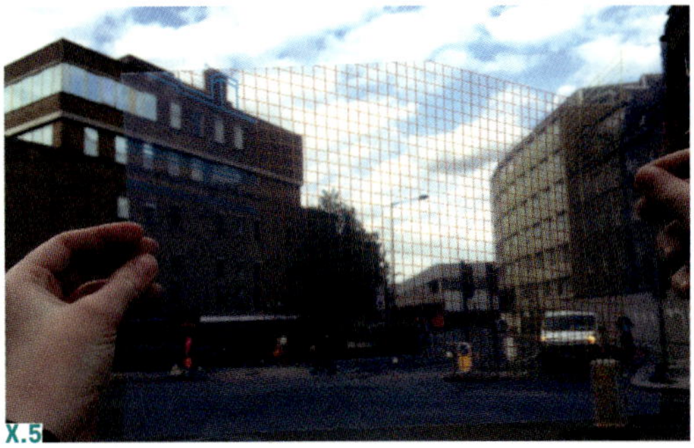

X.5

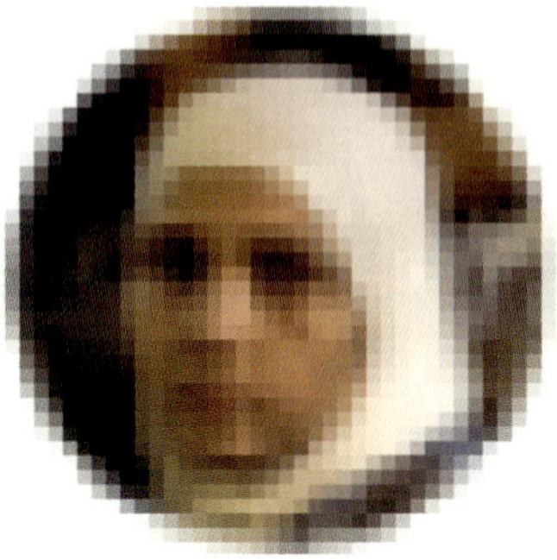

X.6

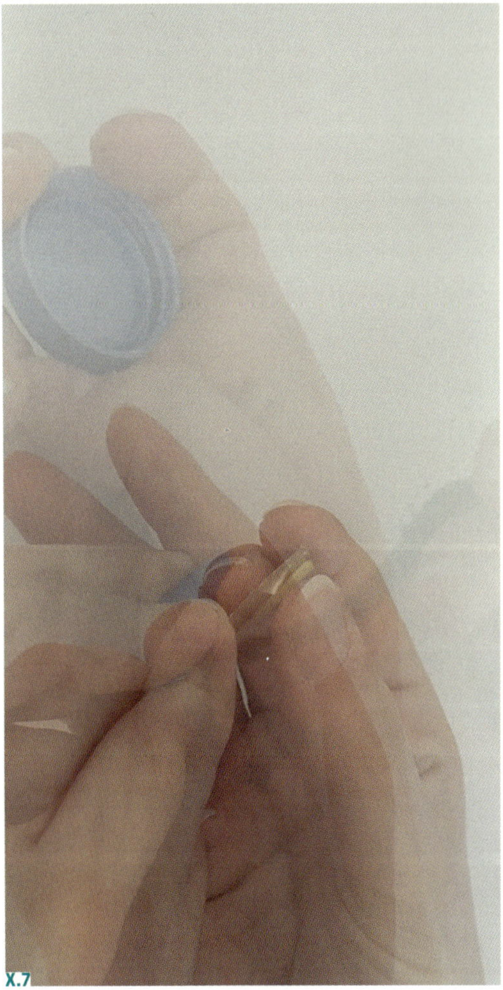

X.7

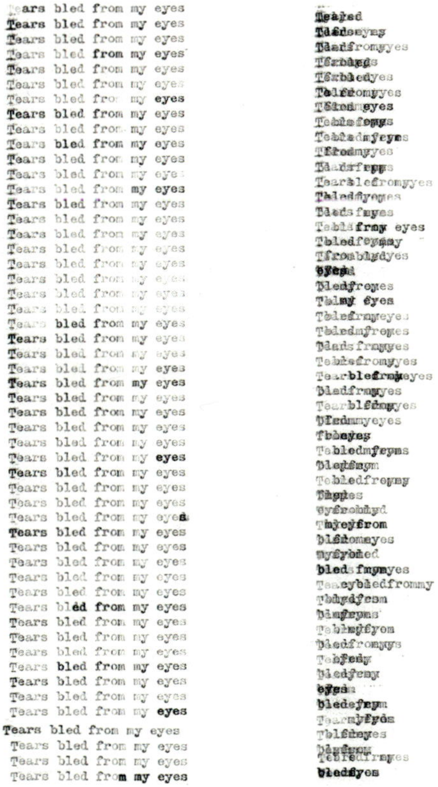

X.8

Figs. X.9 – X.10 Rickie Cheuk Y2, 'PlastiX'. Project PlastiX is about the negative effects of plastics in relation to food. The PlastiX tea ceremony is designed to make one think more about the issue in a novel yet educational way. **Fig. X.11 Lucy Walmsley** Y2, 'The Institute of New Person'. The diary and the video illustrate the power of online social media platforms of capturing and archiving different slices of a person within different times and contexts. These slices, when isolated from the larger online archive and the offline physical person, provide a distorted image and selective impression of the individual. **Fig. X.12 Chloe Gould** Y2, 'The Mystery of the Man Behind World War One'. Accounting the events on and leading up to the 28 June 1914'. An audioguide around the SSEES UCL Library that delves deep in to its Bosnian archives and seeks out the relevant historical references required to build an accurate picture of the events following the 1914 assassination of Gavrilo Princip, the man commonly labelled as the originator of the First World War.

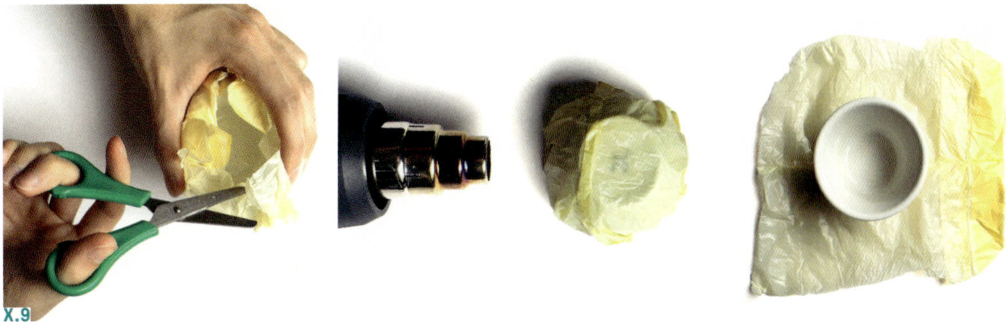

X.9

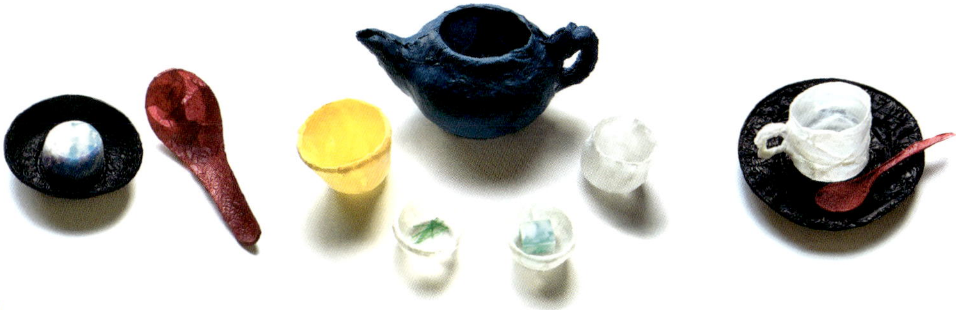

X.10

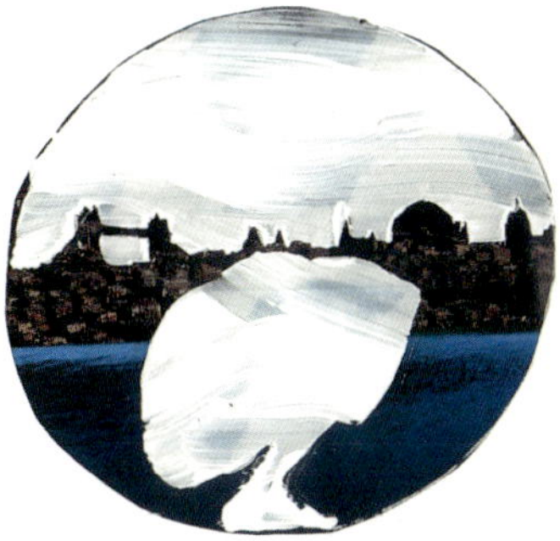

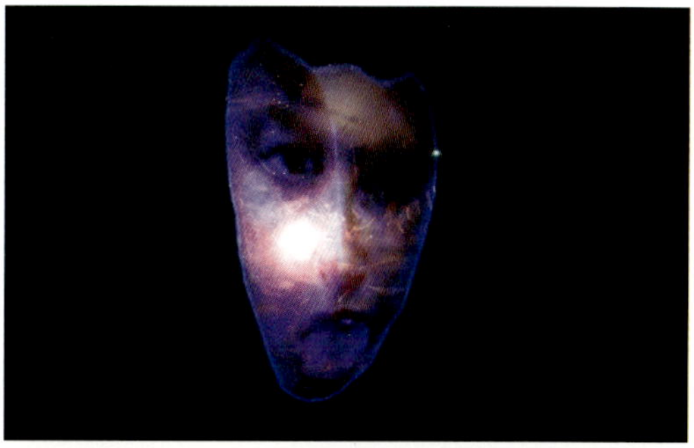

X.11

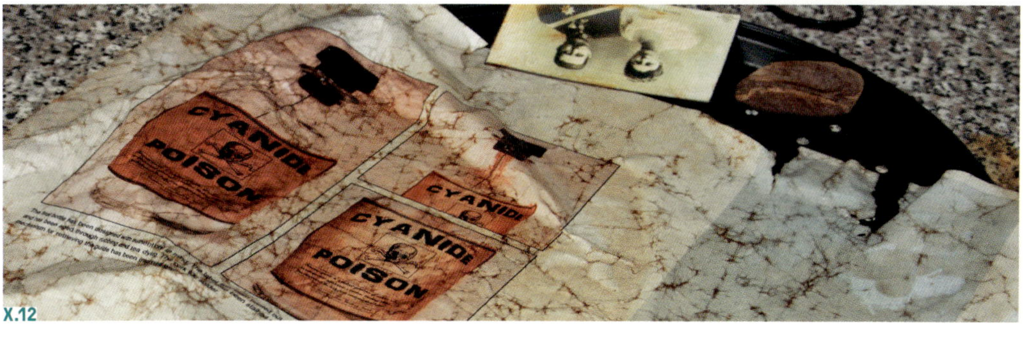

X.12

Fig. X.13 Grace Simmonds Y1, 'Caustic Timepieces'. An investigation into caustic light experiments under an artificial sun. **Fig.X.14 Lucy Brown** Y1, 'Detours for GEOCACHING. Reinterpreting the Natural Environment of the Technological Treasure Hunt'. Instrument No. 2 The unconventional compass. **Fig. X.15 Ryuhei Oishi** Y1, 'Search for Fish'. A house is a platform for a home, where a self is directed both towards a family and towards the 'self'. And thus the distance between self and family, and self and one's 'self' is de-distanced.

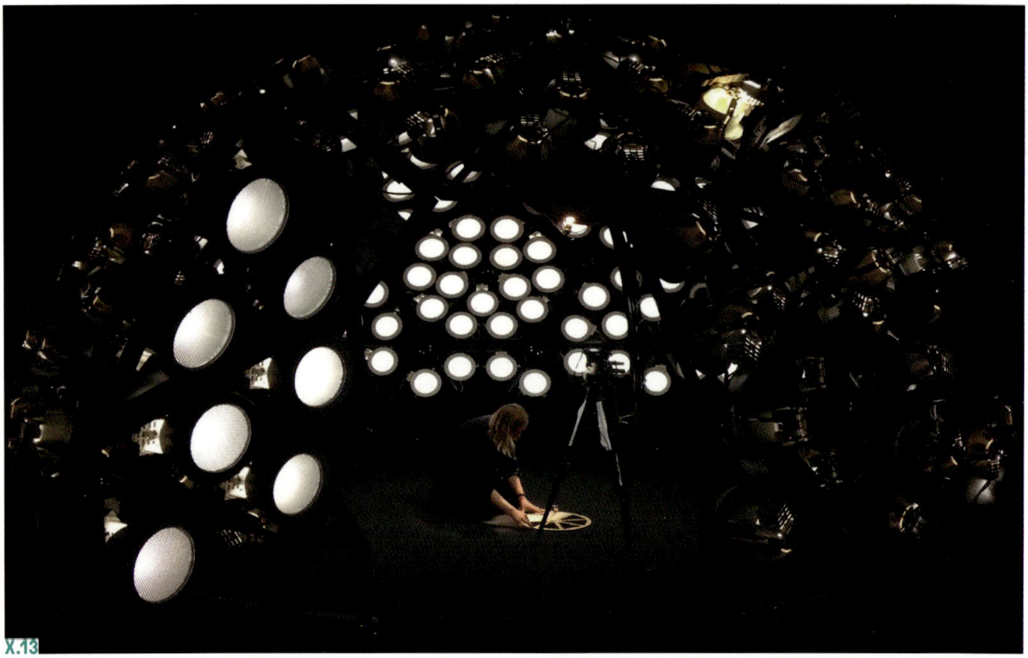

X.13

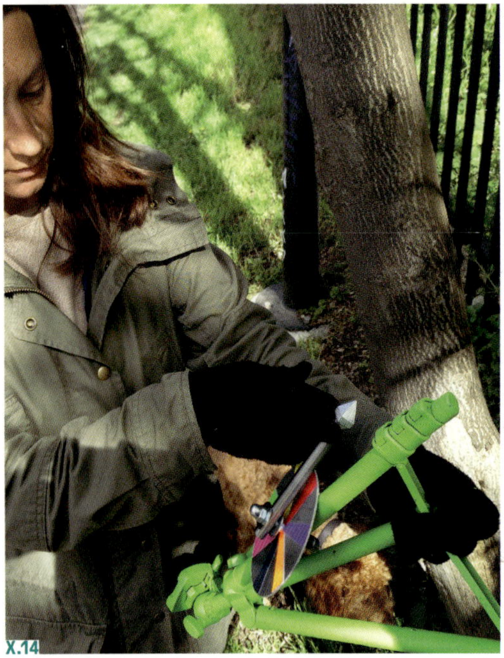

X.14

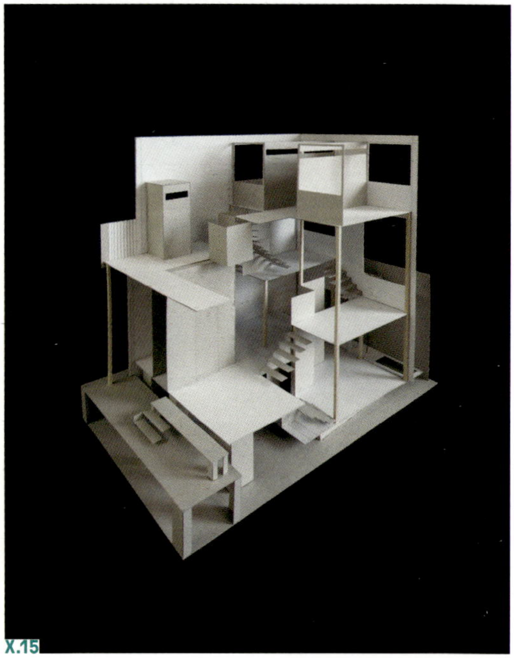

X.15

Fig. X.16 Akil Scafe Smith Y3, 'Trends in Migration'. This project investigates the trends in migration in and out of London and explores their effect on the built environment. **Fig. X.17 Julia Millang** Y1, 'Spacial Improvisitations'. Final site specific composition for a self-build instrument. The project explores the relationship between play and music, notation and interpretation. **Fig. X.18 Ged Ribas-Goody** Y1, 'A Gentle Crash: Self/Space/Perception (Body)'. A tatoo of the implanted metal after breaking the right collarbone. The second destructive act, conclusively, was by the author's own hand. A second crash, between body and body: its permanent vestige, mediated by the metal of the needle, remembers the first. **Fig. X.19 James Curtis** Y1, 'Urban Tennis: Community Sports'. This project is the creation of an adapted tennis match tailored to an urban environment at the canal which allowed the public, whether they were commuters, locals or tourists, to join and play tennis between the water and land. One player stands on a raft, the other on the towpath.

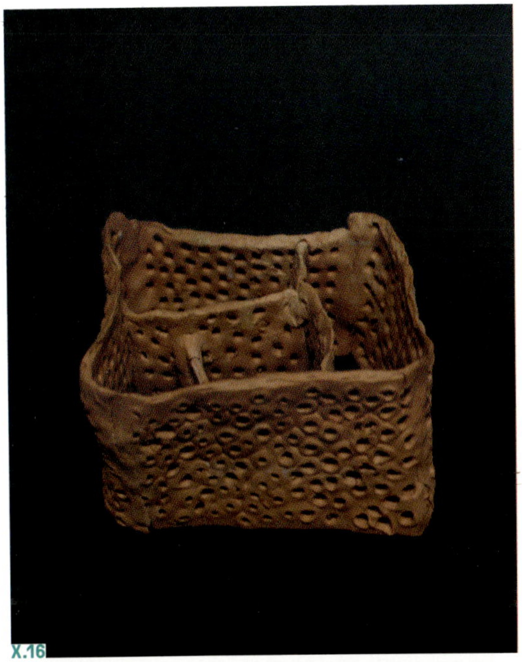
X.16

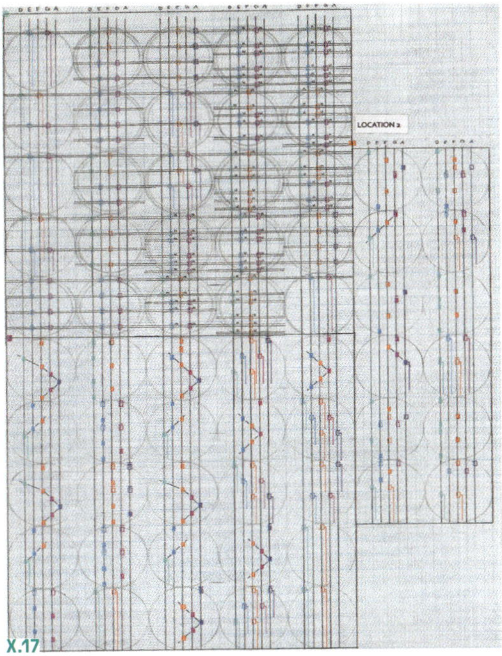

X.17

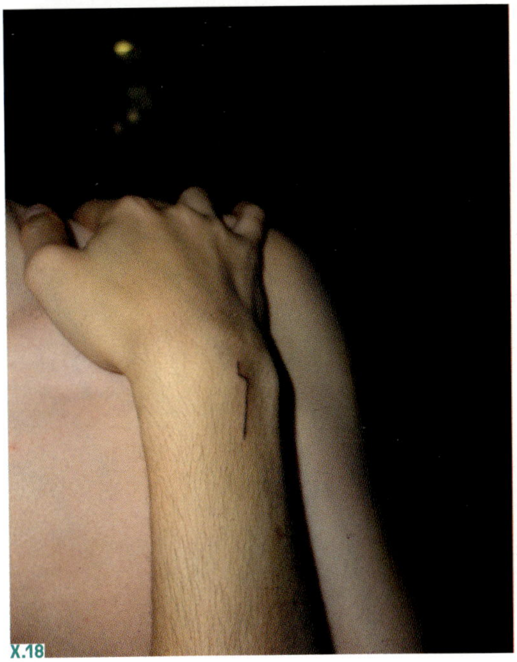
X.18

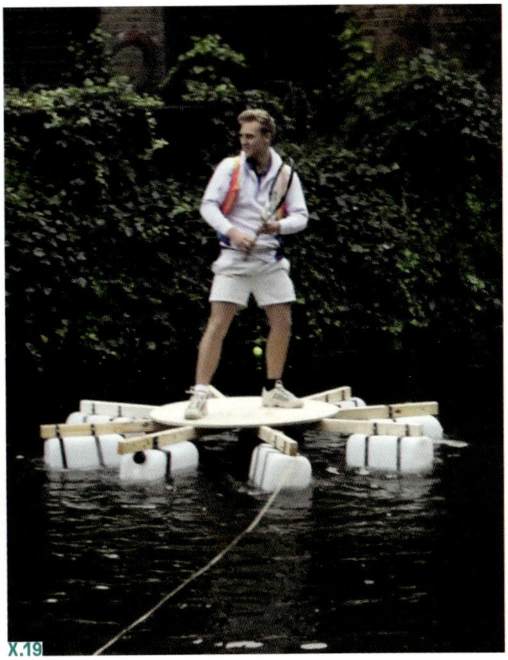
X.19

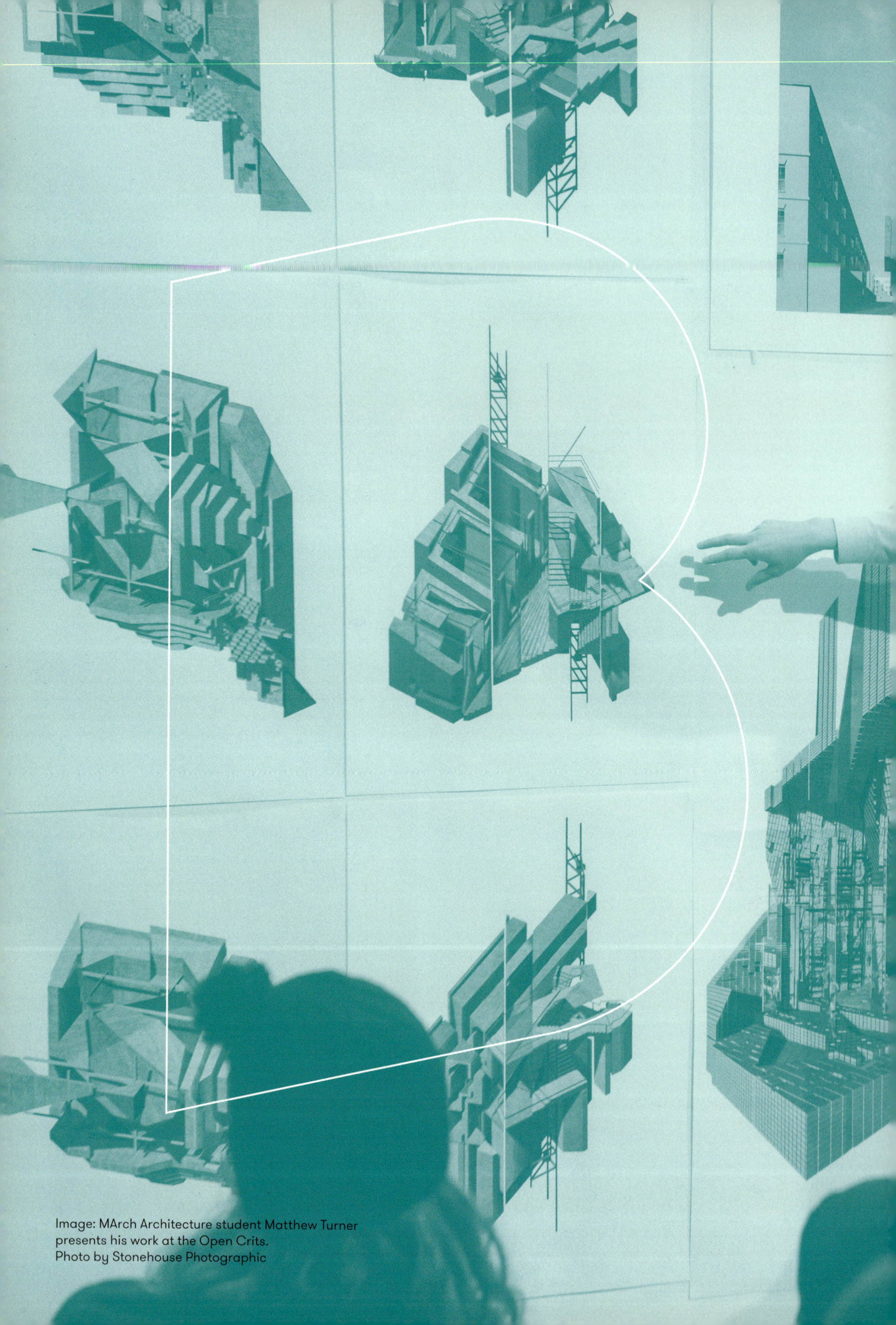

Image: MArch Architecture student Matthew Turner presents his work at the Open Crits.
Photo by Stonehouse Photographic

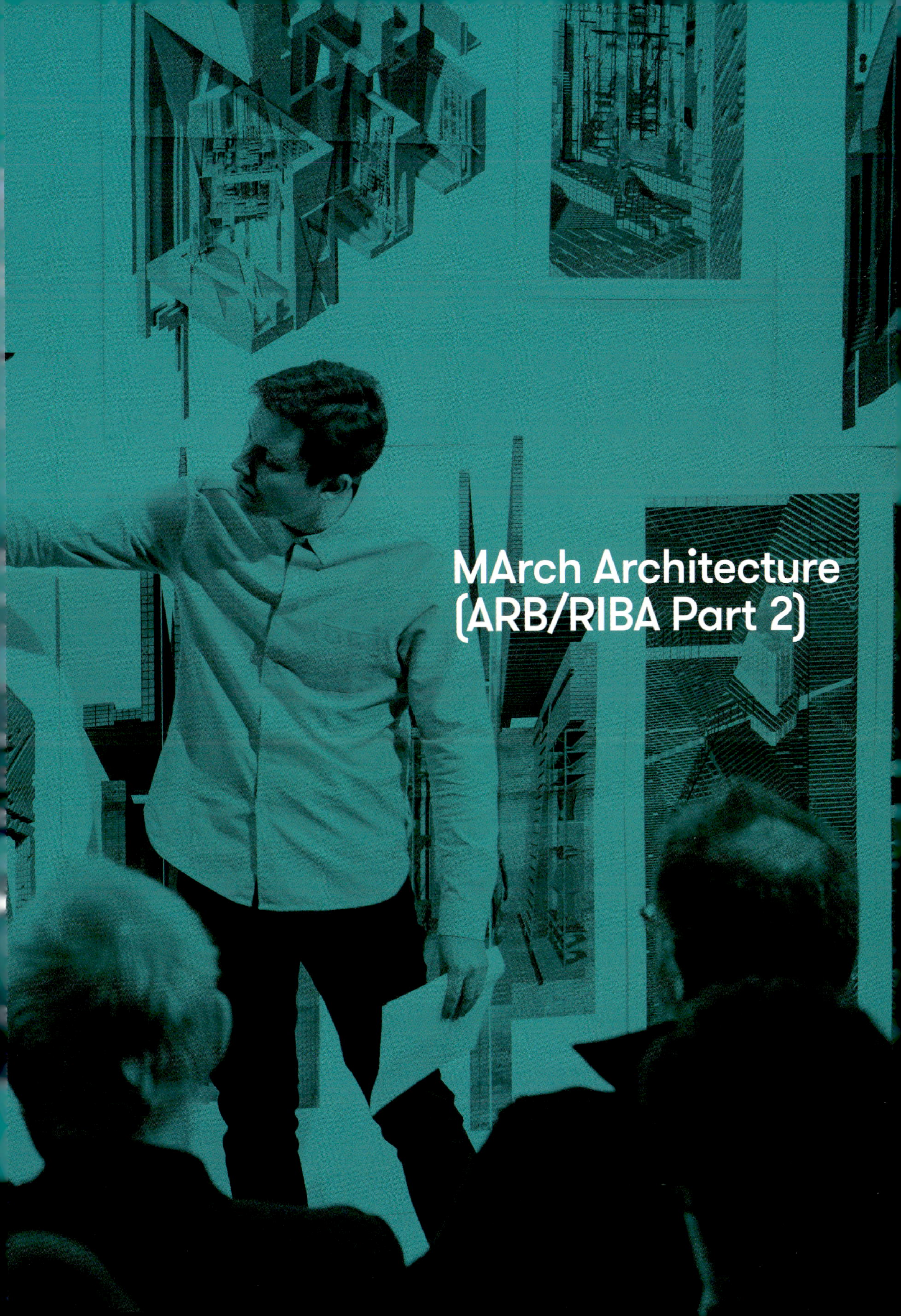

MArch Architecture (ARB/RIBA Part 2)

Unit 10

Poetics of a Resilient City

Bernd Felsinger, CJ Lim

Year 4
Damien Assini, LiJia Bao, Eleanor Downs, Nathan Fairbrother, Isabelle Lam, Kai Hang Liu, Sachi Oberoi, Oskar Olesen, Zhang Wen, Jonathan Wren

Year 5
Chun Ting (Sam) Ki, Ka Man Leung, Michael Quach, James Smith, Eric Wong

Unit 10 would like to thank Simon Dickens for his teaching of the Design Realisation module

What makes a city resilient? Accra, Athens, Bangkok, Barcelona, Chennai, Dallas, Enugu, London, Mandalay, New Orleans, Pittsburgh, Rio de Janeiro, Rome, Singapore, Wellington – a few locations from the long list of the Rockefeller Foundation's '100 Resilient Cities' tasked with this very question. Cities, rich or poor, are particularly vulnerable, and will increasingly be affected by anomalous climate change, natural catastrophe and urban stresses including population migration, high unemployment, inefficient public infrastructure systems, endemic violence or chronic food and water shortages.

——The Rockefeller Foundation's president, Judith Rodin, has defined resilience as "the capacity to bounce back from a crisis, learn from it and achieve revitalization. A community needs awareness, diversity, integration, the capacity for self-regulation and adaptiveness to be resilient." Cities, as organisms, act as indicators of spatial, social and economic trends in a manner arguably far more sensitive than any governance; this can be attributed to the synergy and symbiosis between the urban centre and its inhabitants, quotidian activity and social interaction. A society can only be resilient when the city delivers basic functions to its entire community, in both good times and bad.

——The resilience movement also has important roles to play in both ensuring that current architecture assets and cultural heritage are protected from long-term and acute affects, and in developing revolutionary new spatial programs and systems fit for the challenges of the 21st century. The effects of climate change on the built environment are, for example, not limited to changes of weather, but include the impact on architectural efforts towards changes in behaviour, demographics, population growth and economic environments. Globally, governments are now acknowledging that future environments built on resilient efforts can provide potential multiple co-benefits to cities.

——The Unit's objective is to assess the potential urban transformation opportunities from the resilience movement. Individuals are required to establish an intellectual critical position on 'What makes a city resilient?' and focus on the spatial and phenomenological speculations that emerge when predictive fiction and its poetic function are applied to cities. In PROJECT 1, we will speculate, prioritize and redefine the poetics of urban resilience, focusing on one or a combination of issues around awareness, diversity, integration, self-regulation or adaptiveness. In PROJECT 2, the city will be informed by individual studies to establish core interests and should form the basis of a complex narrative and program. We encourage expressions of personal ideology, scale and working methods in search of visionary and innovative urban architectural proposals.

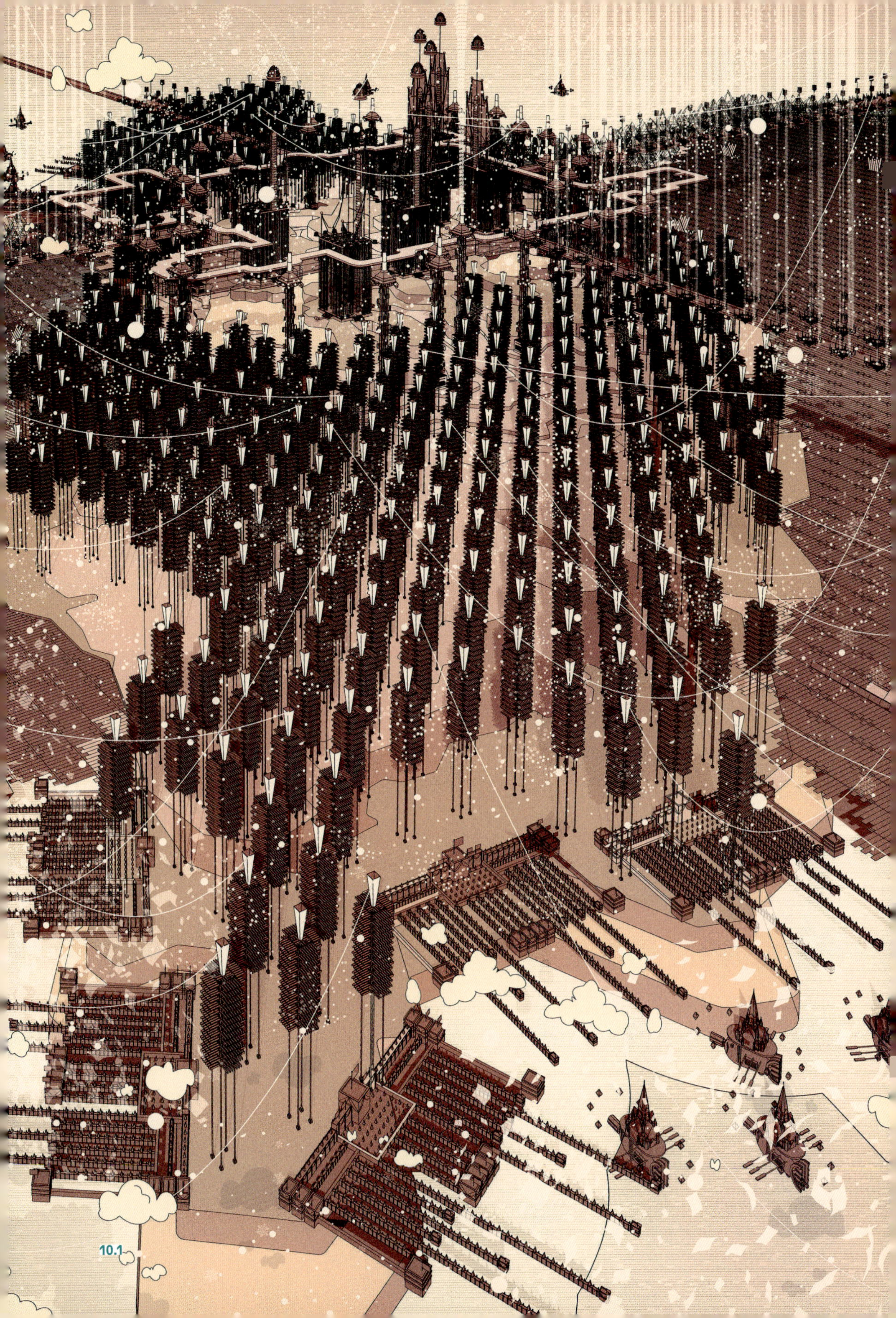
10.1

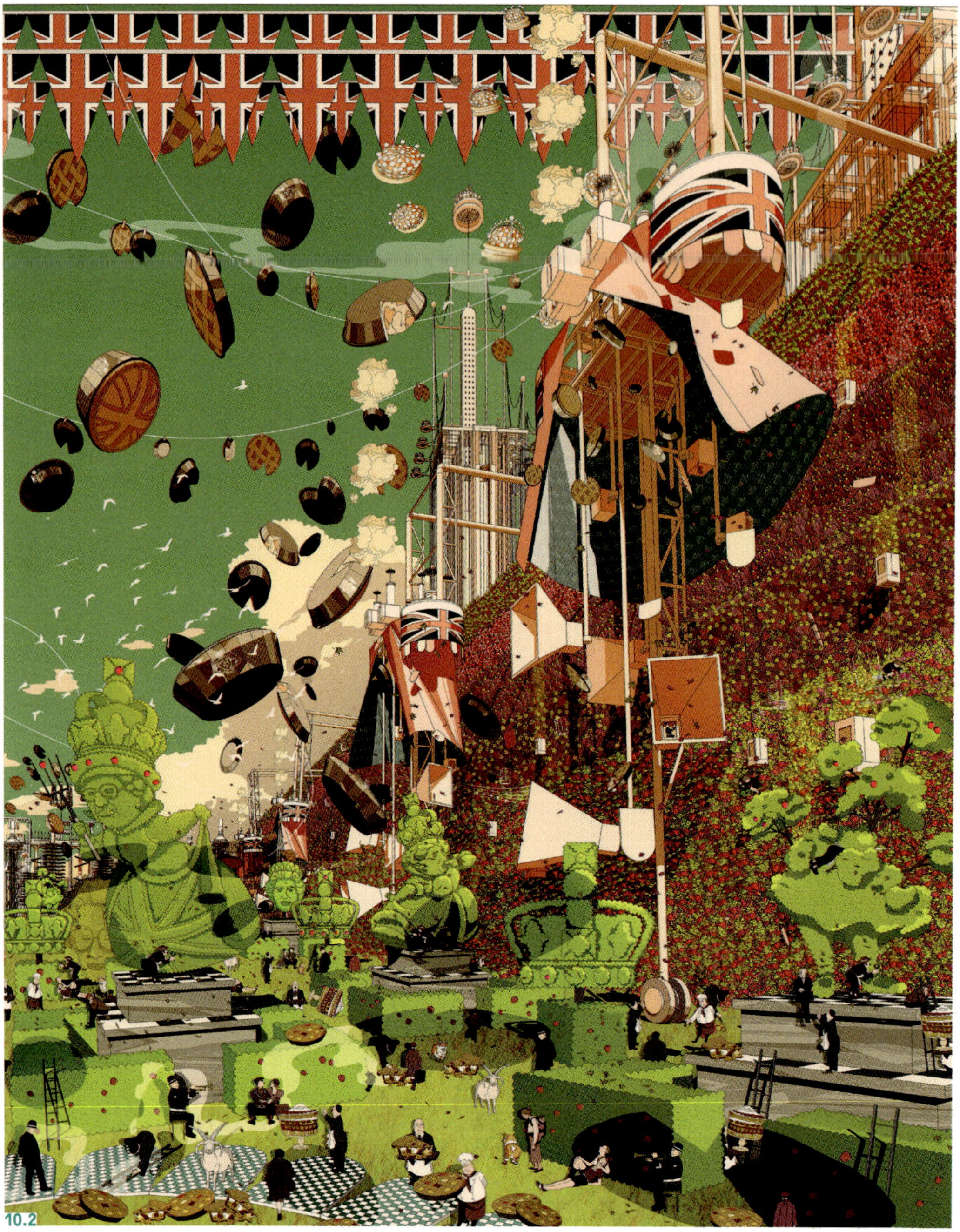

10.2

Figs. 10.1 – 10.3 Eric Wong Y5, 'Cohesion: The Blueprint for a United Kingdom'. Inspired by 'The Blazing World' (1666) by Margaret Cavendish, the new capital city of the UK is the speculative driver and investigative model to cultivate accessibility, green sustainability and compassion. The narrative aims to reunite an arguably broken Britain in the 21st century, providing for the disenfranchised within the UK as well as for increasingly dislocated global communities. While the UK's Parliament performs as the head of foreign policy, the Queen is the champion of national unity. **Fig. 10.4 Ka Man Leung** Y5, 'The Making of Hong Kong: Democracy or Money?'. Through whispers, gossips, and myths, a collection of speculated archaeology of Victoria City reimagines Hong Kong's adaptability to survive through time – from a fishing village to an industrialised town and world financial centre under British Colonialism, to the handover of sovereignty to China. Is the new urbanism driven by concerns of climate change, food and water security, democracy; or by local economic influences at different scales? **Fig. 10.5 James Smith** Y5, 'Midnight in the Garden of Good and Evil'. A response to the Eurozone crisis of 2015 – the economic collapse of Greece and the influx of Syrian refugees – Britain in partnership with Thomas Cook would lease Faliraki off the Greek Government. Brits are encouraged to spend in the new hedonistic holiday resort, while the intervention would offer the refugees a new home, and with it security, retraining and financial independence in the new sovereign land of Rhodes.

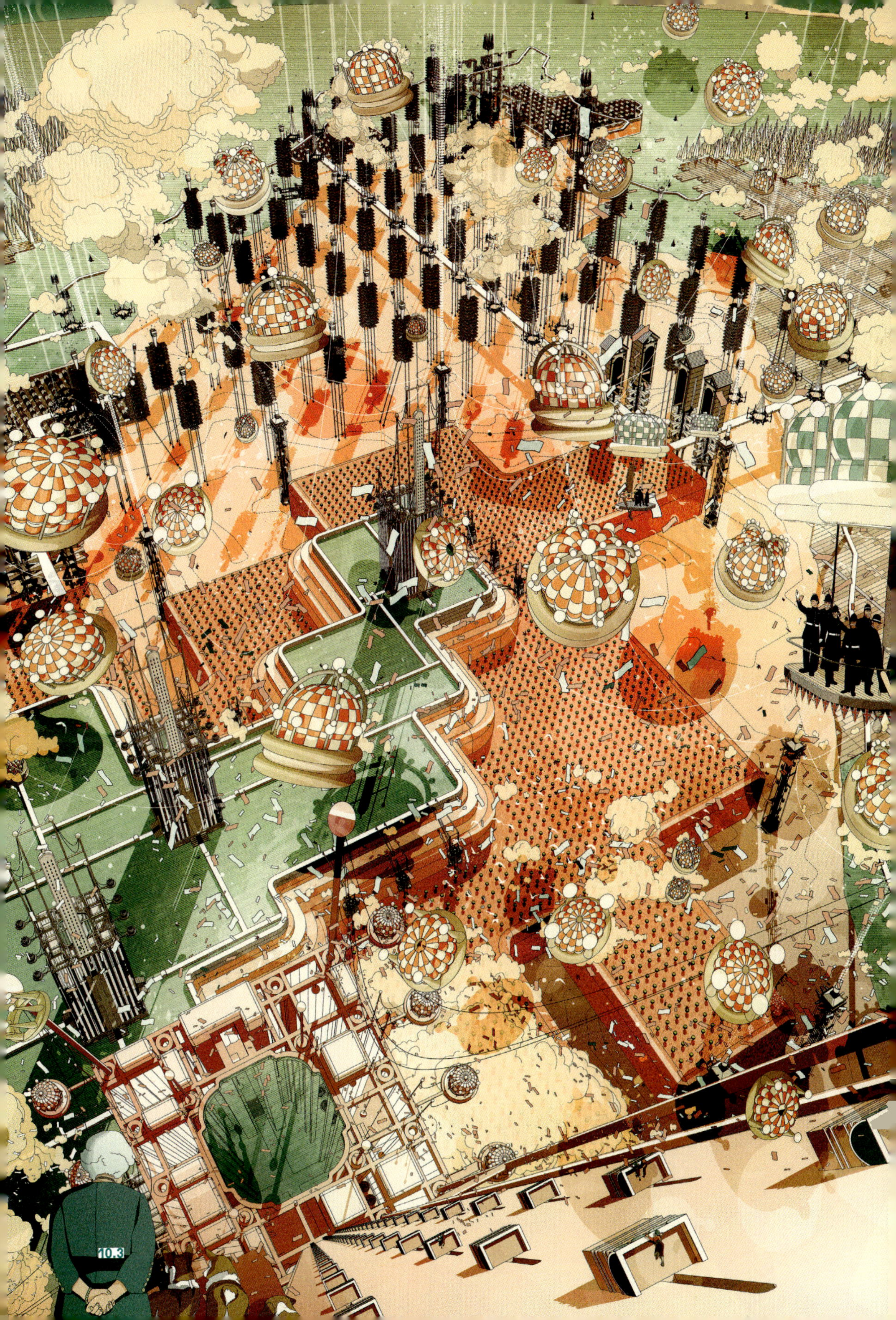
10.3

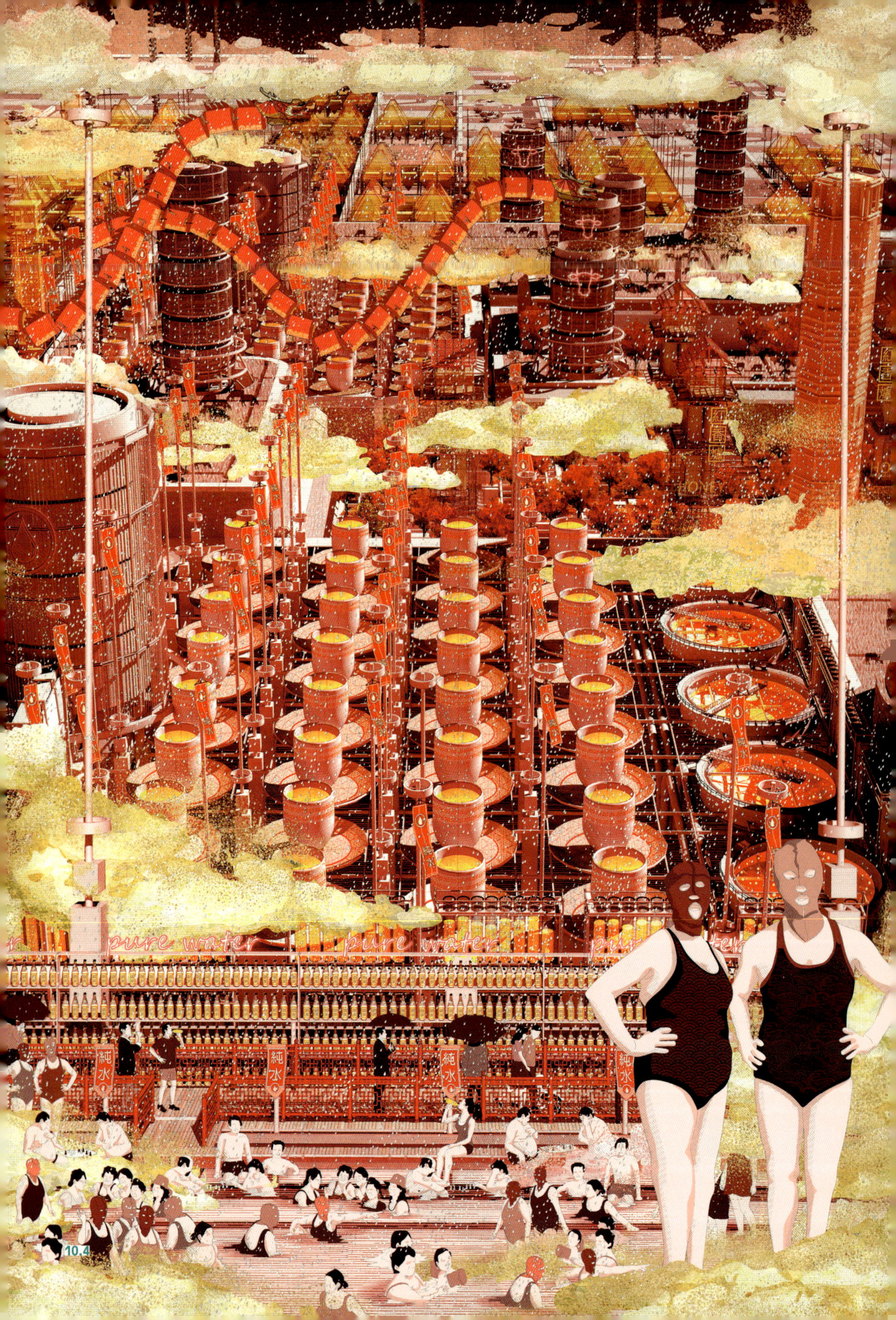
pure water
pure water
純水
純水
純水
10.4

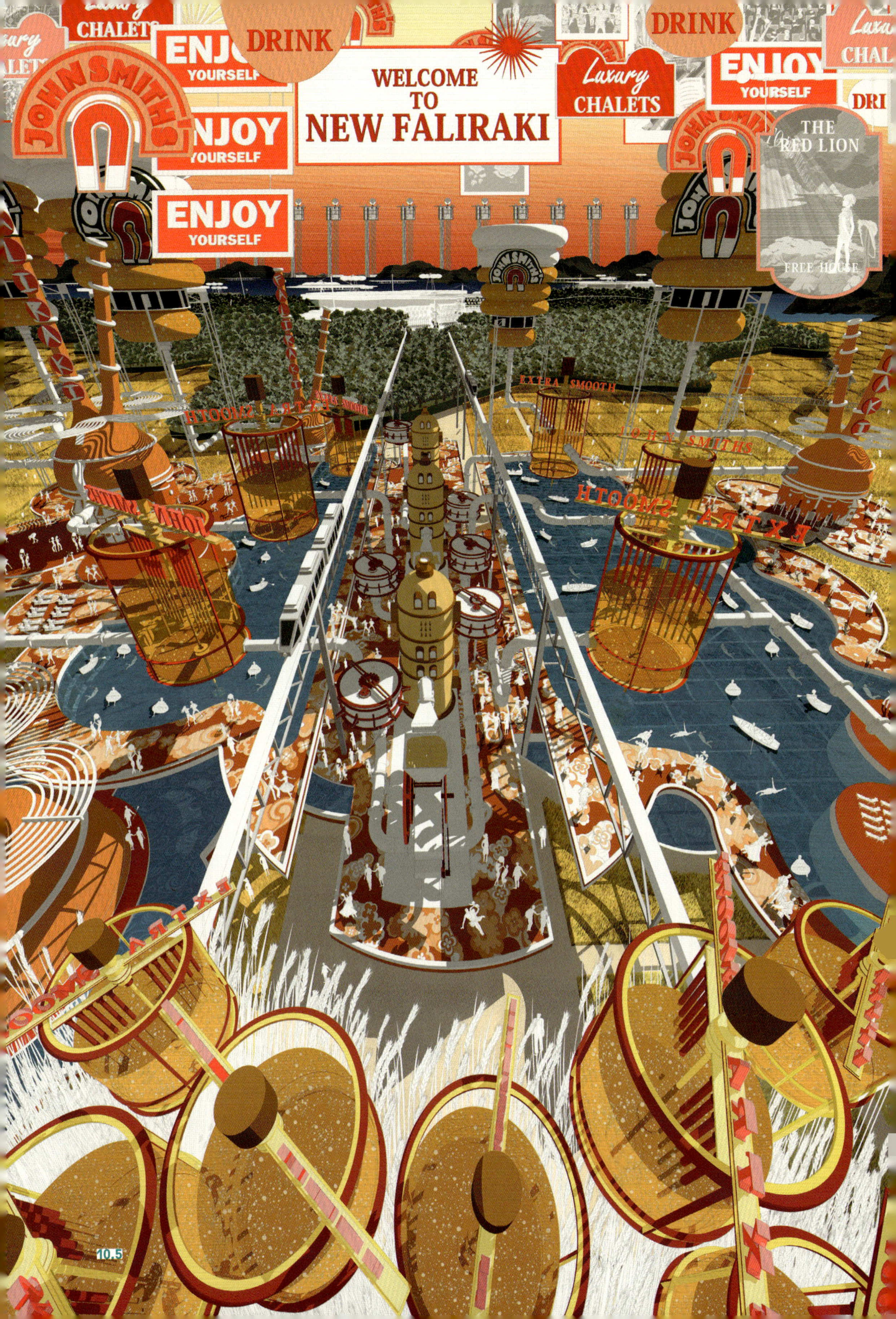
WELCOME
TO
NEW FALIRAKI
DRINK
ENJOY
YOURSELF
Luxury
CHALETS
JOHN SMITH'S
THE
RED LION
FREE HOUSE
EXTRA SMOOTH
JOHN SMITHS

10.5

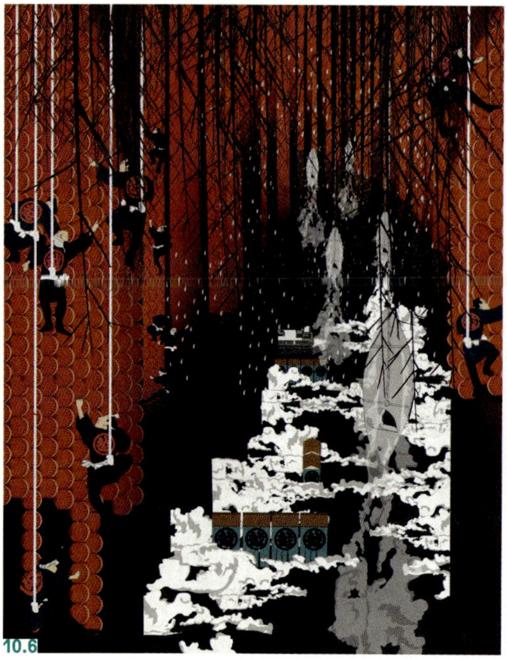

10.6

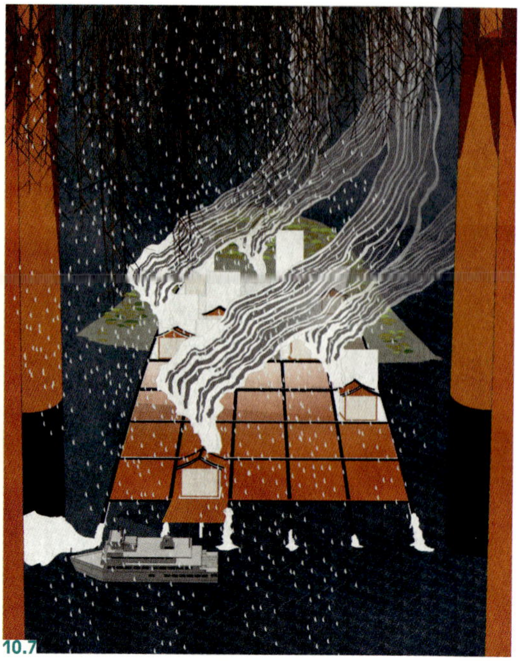

10.7

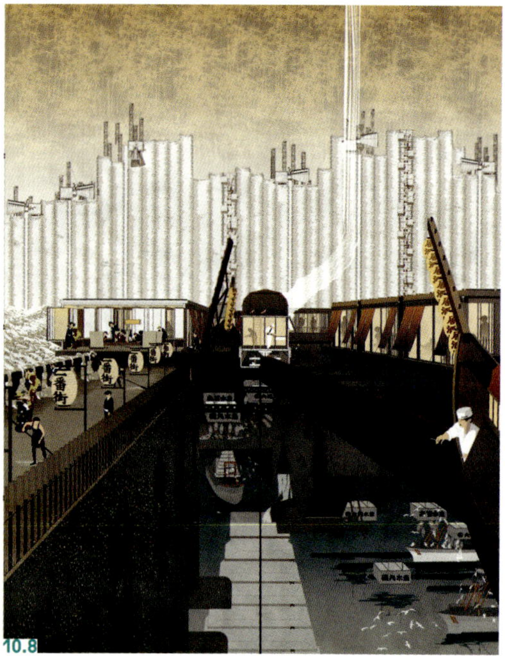

10.8

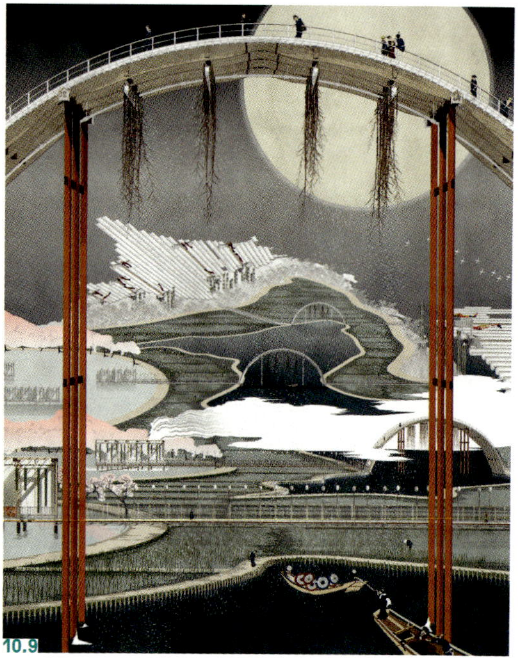

10.9

Figs. 10.6 – 10.10 Chun Ting (Sam) Ki Y5, 'Yen Town: Purity on the Disputed Senkaku Islands'. In mainland China, high pollution and contamination levels caused by industrialisation and capitalism are steering the Chinese elite to search for quality environments and foods of 'purity'. Yen Town is located on Uotsuri-shima (Diaoyu Dao) of Senkaku Islands, the disputed territory between Japan and China. Japan can only retain sovereignty in exchange for clean soil, water, air and pure salt and onsen (hot springs). The Chinese Communist party uses Yen Town as the reward for loyalty whilst promoting communist beliefs. The island would be developed by 5 'honourable' corporations which have long been the favourite brands of the Chinese.

Fig. 10.11 Michael Quach Y5, 'Sapphire City'. A promise, especially promises of a fulfilling life after retirement, is the currency of the intervention. The reimagining of the Emerald City in 'The Wizard of Oz' and an interpretation of Grayson Perry's 'Tunbridge Wells' looks at how the current government and the Conservative party could exploit planning strategies to manipulate the demography into gaining more northern constituencies. The urban development of Morely & Outwood metaphorically forms the critique of social and political aspiration for the elderly, and highlights third age consumerism as a potential way to boost national GDP.

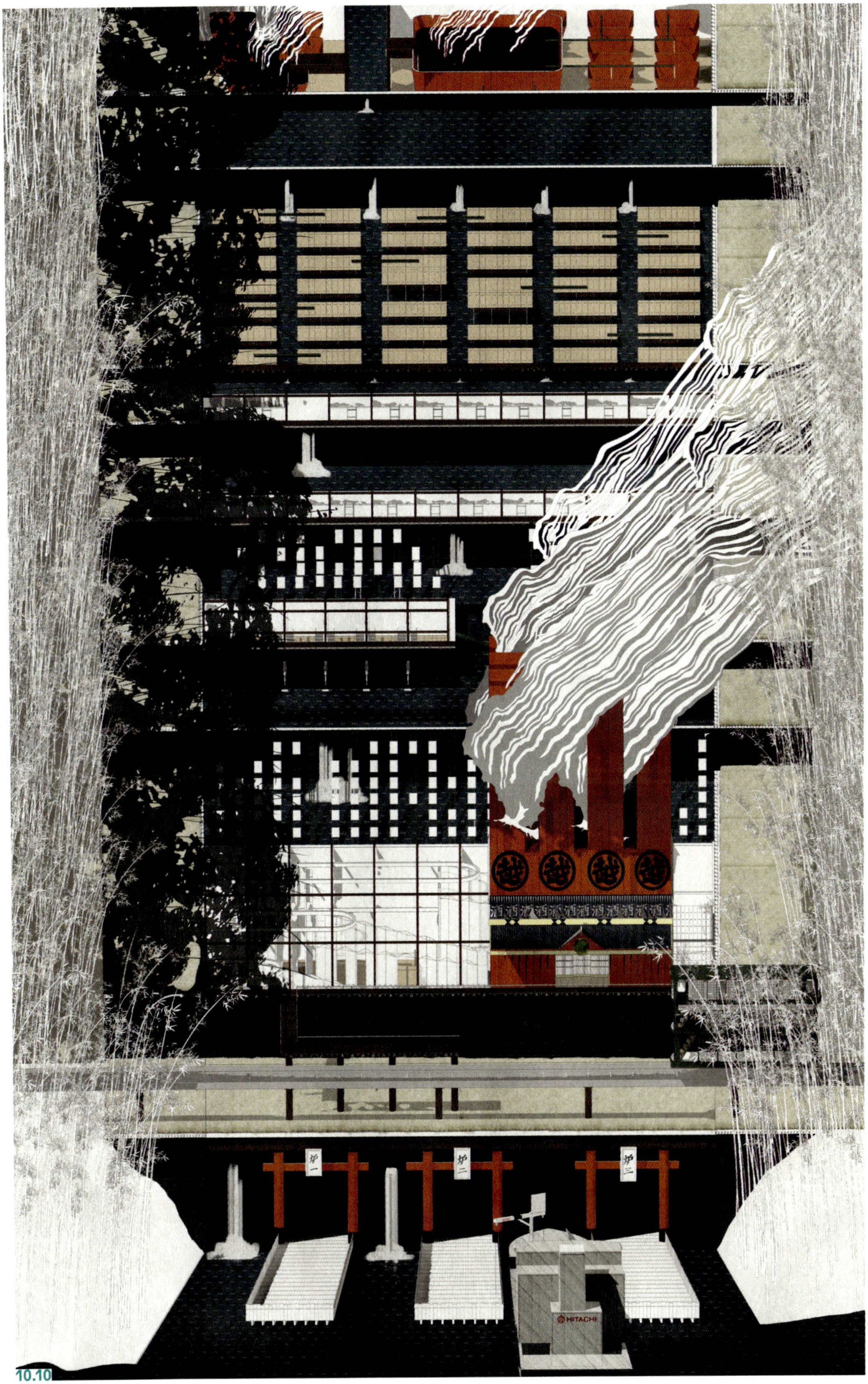

10.10

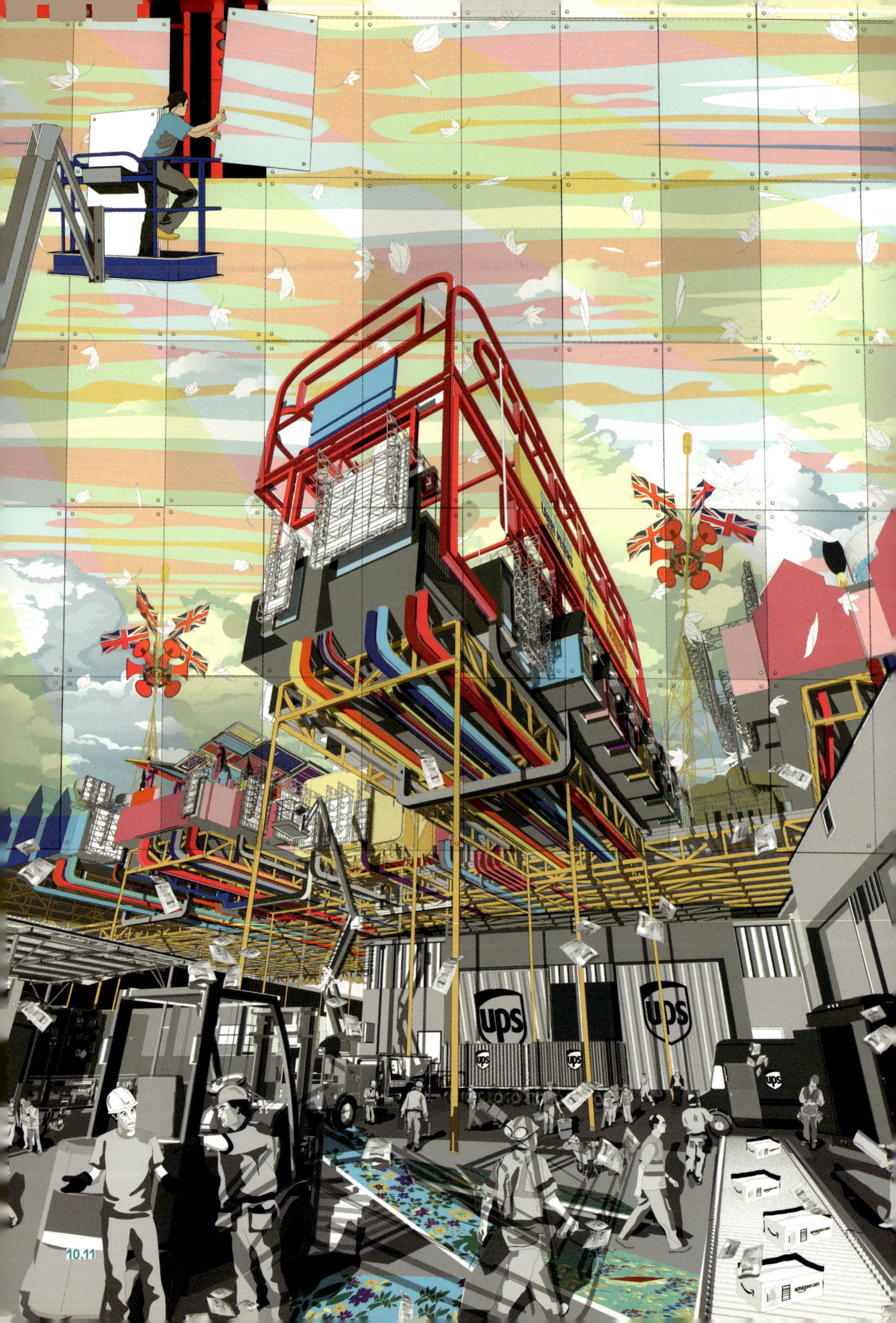
ups
ups
10.11

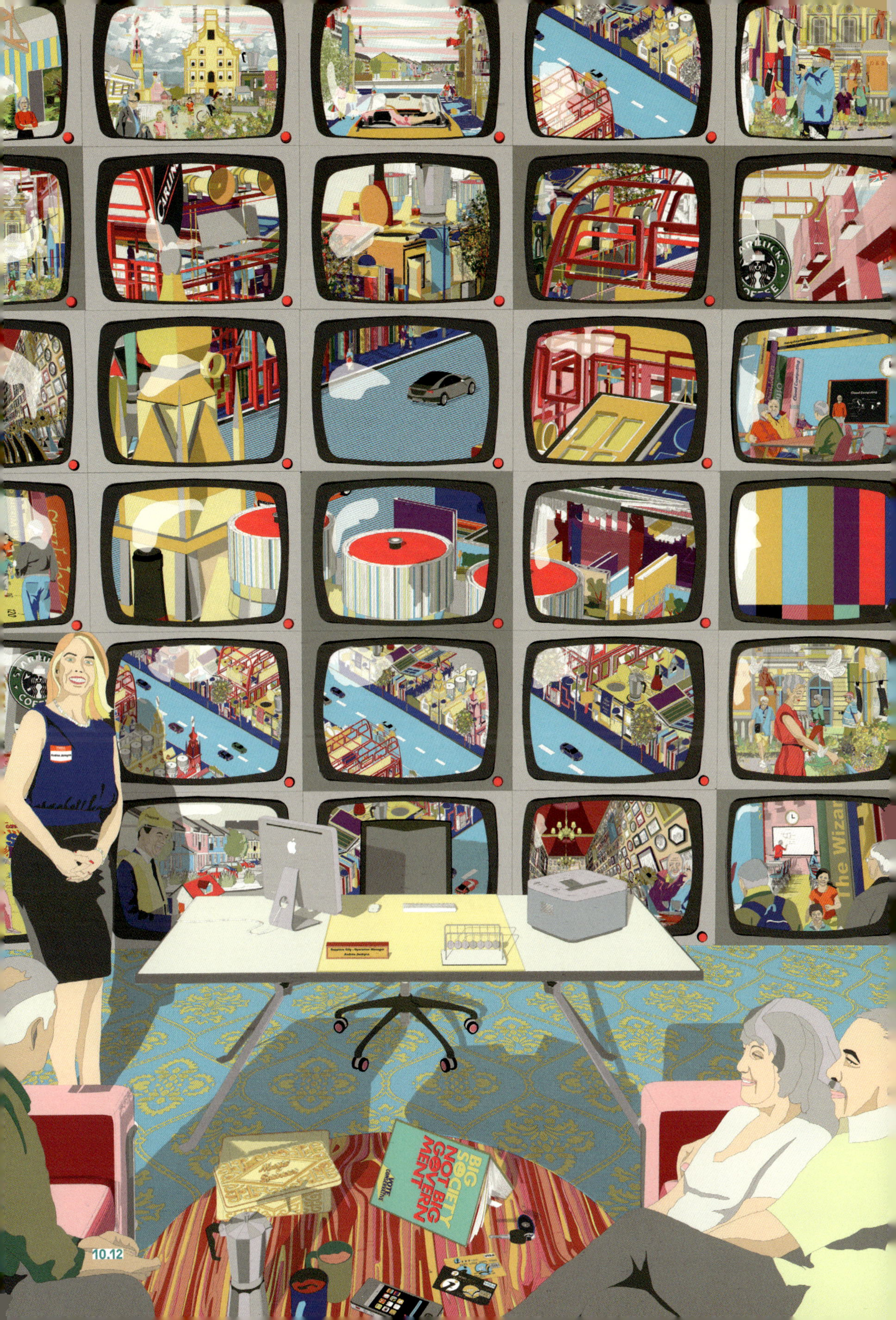
BIG SOCIETY NOT BIG GOVERNMENT
10.12

Unit 11 Incubator

Laura Allen, Mark Smout

Year 4
Alexander Chapman, Christopher Delahunt, Johanna Just, Anthony Ko, Milo de Luca, Vanessa Lafoy, Agostino Nickl, Grace Quah, Ho (Howell) Tsang

Year 5
Felicity Barbur, Robin Farmer, Emma Kitley, Fergus Knox, Adam Lampon, Mohamed (Ali) Qureshi, Fergus Seccombe

Partners: Luke Pearson and Sandra Youkhana

Thanks to Rhys Cannon of Gruff Limited for Design Realisation teaching and Stephen Webster for Structural Consultancy

Critics include: Shumi Bose, Kyle Buchanan, Margaret Bursa, Mel Dodd, Joseph Grima, Dan Hill, Johan Hybschmann, Holly Lewis, Vicky Richardson, Tomas Stokke, Sabine Storp, Finn Williams

Unit 11 is established as a laboratory for research, invention and spatial imagination, pursued through an iterative, inquisitive and imaginative process where modeling is key. We aim to challenge normative architectural conditions through modeling by methods such as replicas, prototypes, science frameworks, operating protocols, and specimens.

——We are interested in developing individual approaches to design, posing real and hypothetical problems that are design-led and fed by research, curiosity and innovation, whereby design is guided by its own productive processes, which are intriguingly varied and dynamic and informed as much by questions as by answers.

——Recently, we have looked at new forms of habitation which draw on the contemporary condition, borrowing and adapting technologies, materials, typologies and conventions from the culture and processes of the city and those of the natural environment. Last year we looked at technological strategies, geographical environments, science facts, science fictions and myths, in conjunction with the extraordinary emerging realties that surround the life of the San Francisco Bay Area.

——This year we revisited these interests in Chicago, where we considered the city in its role as a historical and future incubator of speculative architectural and cultural scenarios. We scrutinized the built, the unbuildable and inbuilt environments of the city. The mechanisms of the inaugural Chicago Biennial and its typical tropes of public art, interaction, installation and pavilion design were contrasted with Chicago's heroic city planning and gargantuan infrastructural schemes.

——Significant sites such as the city's second shoreline, the much-abused Chicago River; the Loop and the 'Forever Open Clear and Free' Lake Michigan shore, were seen in parallel to the speculative physical and cultural constructions of the Expo or Biennal which use architecture as an agent and indicator of political, social and cultural trends and desires. We researched how these contrasting modes of progress incubate new ideas for urban life.

——In Unit 11, students are encouraged to develop their own robust research themes and architectural language, with the ambition that speculative design ideas, informed by research and developed through an iterative design process, seamlessly progress into tantalizing, exquisite and cognizant architectural projects on a multitude of scales.

——Briefs are real (see 'Honey Run' by Felicity Barber, or Emma Kitley's Primary School 'Design/Play' Workshops), hypothetically real (see Fergus Knox's self-propagating timber skyscrapers for Chicago), or exist in a parallel imagined simulacra of the city (see 'Data Scape' by Johanna Just, 'Sim City Sprawl' by Agostino Nickl and 'Chicago Hyperlink' by Chris Delahunt).

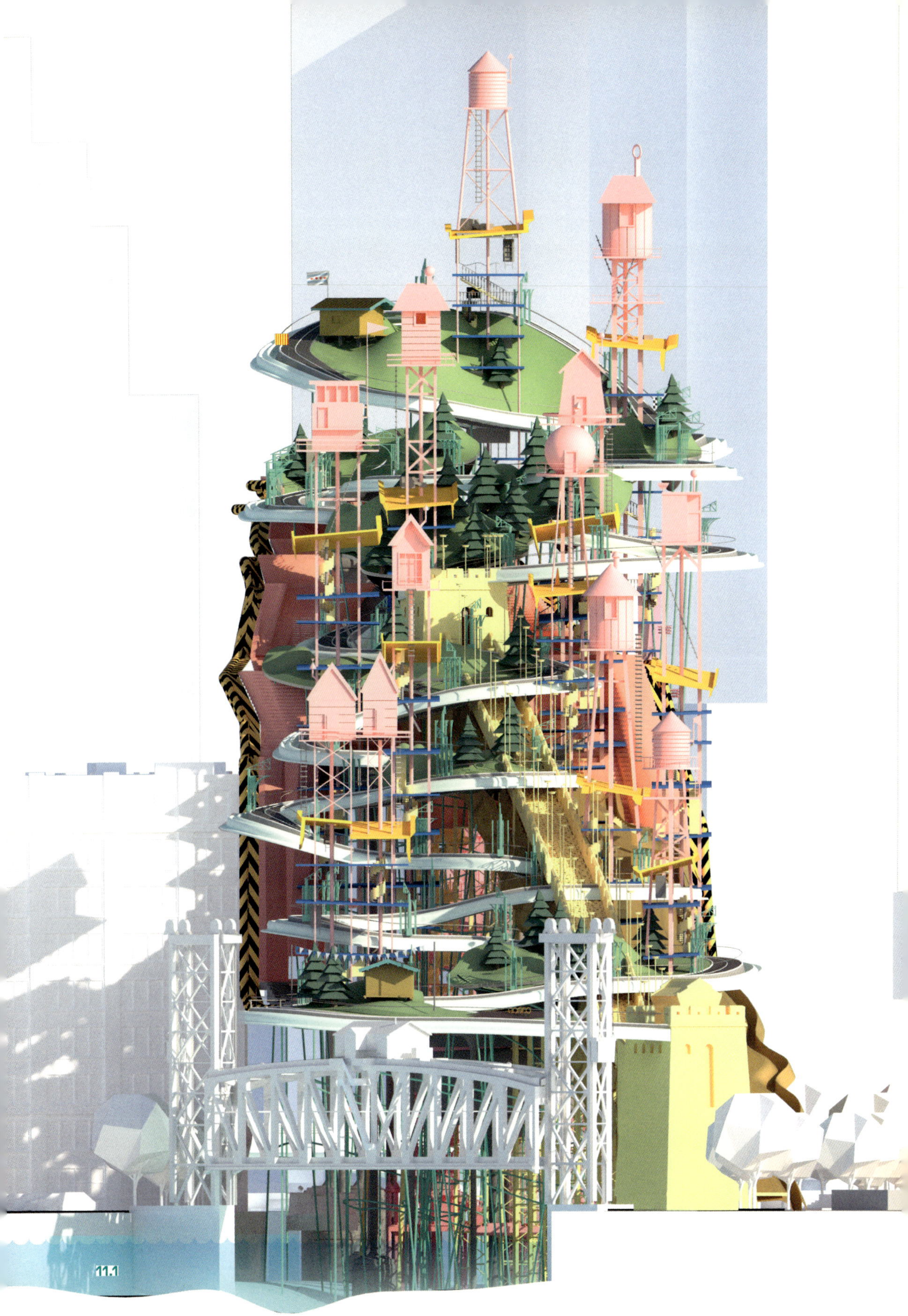

11.1

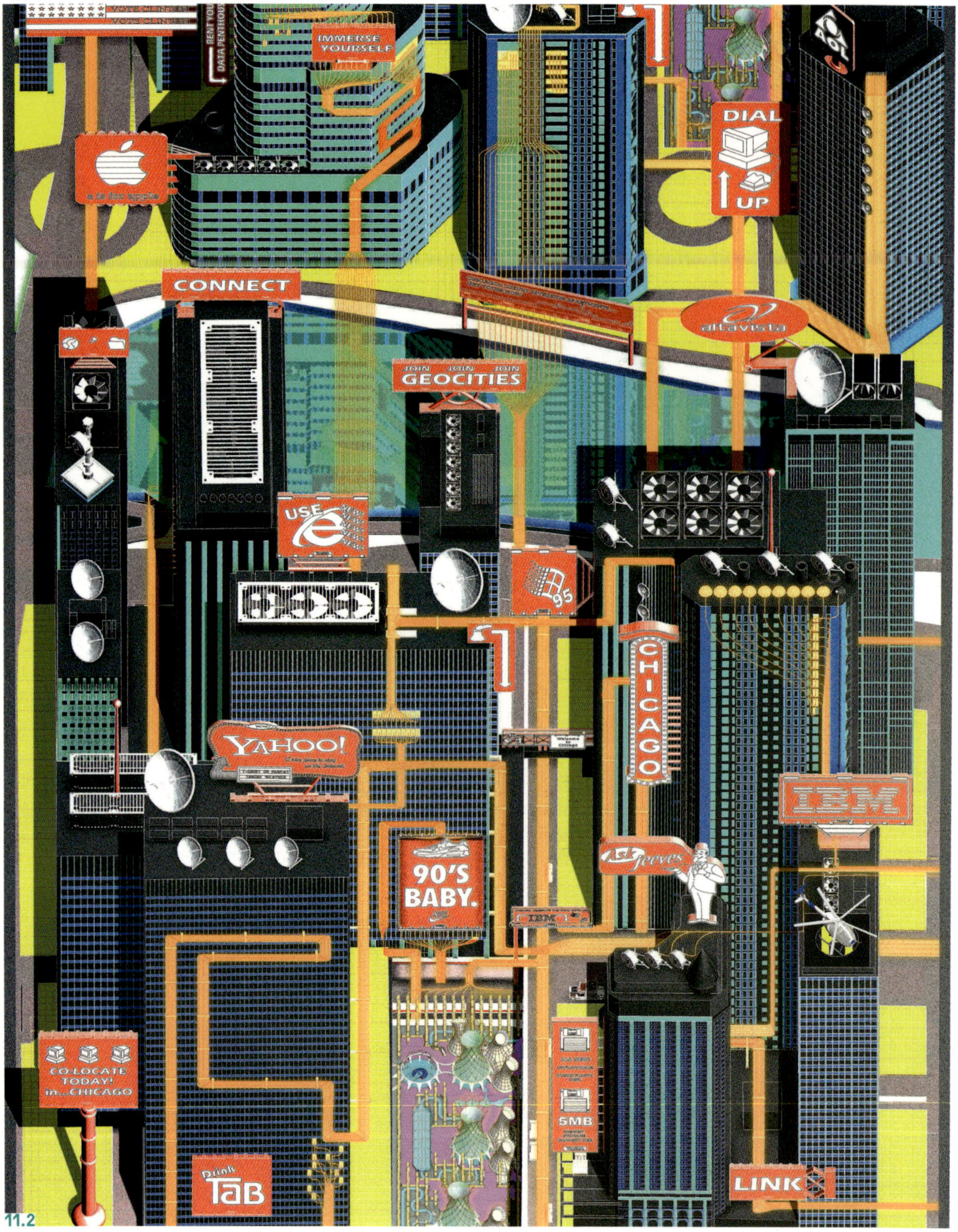

11.2

Fig. 11.1 Felicity Barber Y5, 'Building Image: Mount Chicago'. Building Image is an ethnographical perspective on the architecture of city life, exploring how one simplifies and maps Chicago's urbanism through spatially engaging events. The implementation of a cultural river festival acts to further stimulate city life periodically and in the long-term supports the evolving generational growth of surrounding urban spaces. **Fig. 11.2 Christopher Delahunt** Y4, 'The Chicago Hyperlink', planometric perspective. A citywide masterplan for a visible fibre optic network which aims to assert digital infrastructure into the heart of Chicago. The cables become the central nervous system for the next digital revolution: The Internet of Things. **Fig. 11.3 Vanessa Lafoy** Y4, 'Preservation Chicago HQ'. Salvaged fragments from Chicago's demolished buildings are cast into the walls and debris is placed into gabion baskets to form a public landscape – the new cast spaces like headstones and the rubble, like ashes. As buildings in the city are demolished, more spaces are cast and the HQ grows taller, a constant record of Chicago's lost buildings.

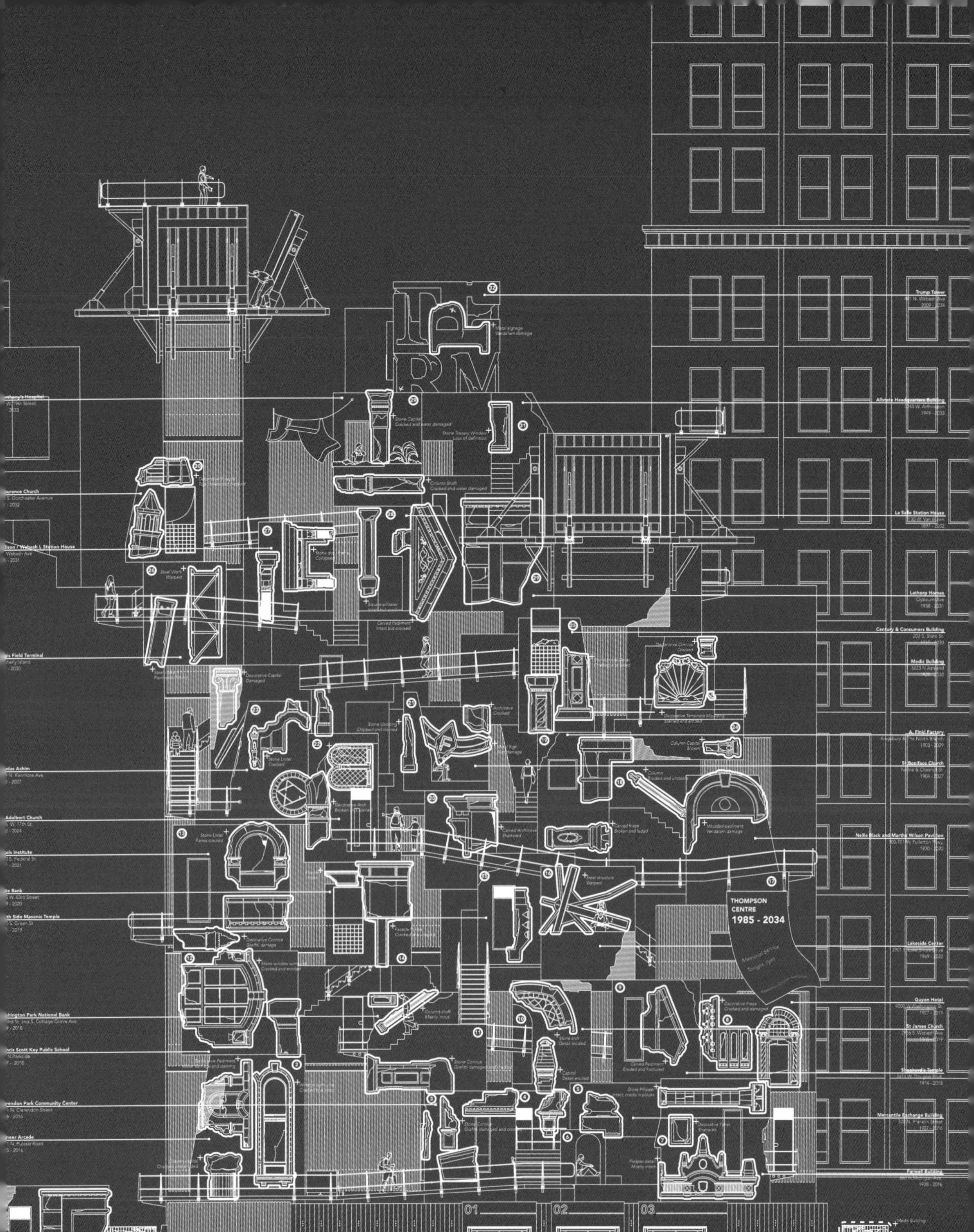
THOMPSON CENTRE
1985 - 2034
Trump Tower
2009 - 2034
Allstate Headquarters Building
1949 - 2033
La Salle Station House
1897 - 2032
Lathorp Homes
Century & Consumers Building
202 S. State St.
Medic Building
A. Finkl Factory
1903 - 2029
St Boniface Church
1904 - 2027
Nellie Black and Martha Wilson Pavilion
1930 - 2022
Lakeside Center
1969 - 2020
Guyon Hotel
1927 - 2019
St James Church
Shepherd's Temple
1914 - 2018
Mercantile Exchange Building
1927 - 2016
Farwell Building
1928 - 2016
01
02
03

11.3

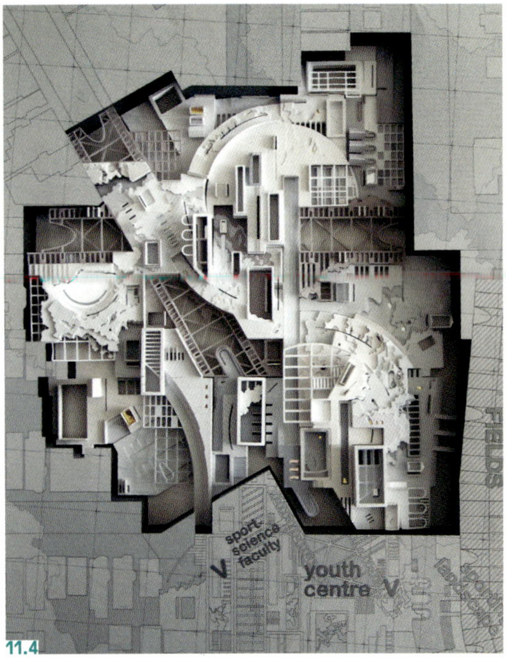

11.4

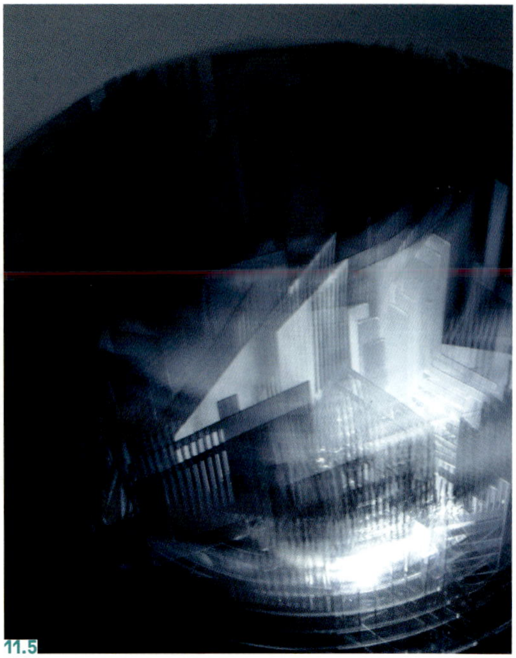

11.5

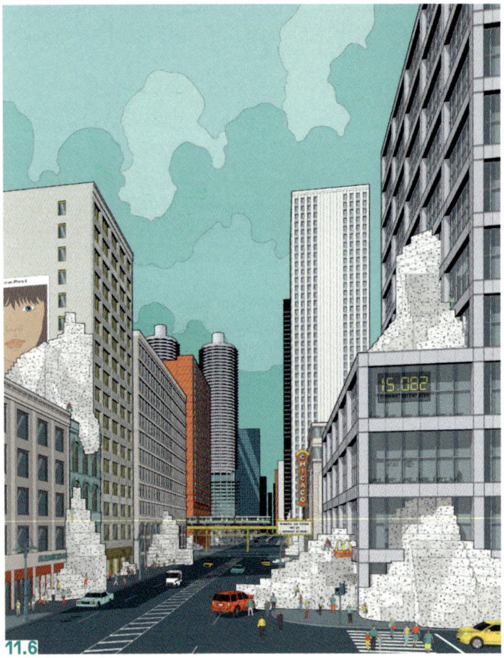

11.6

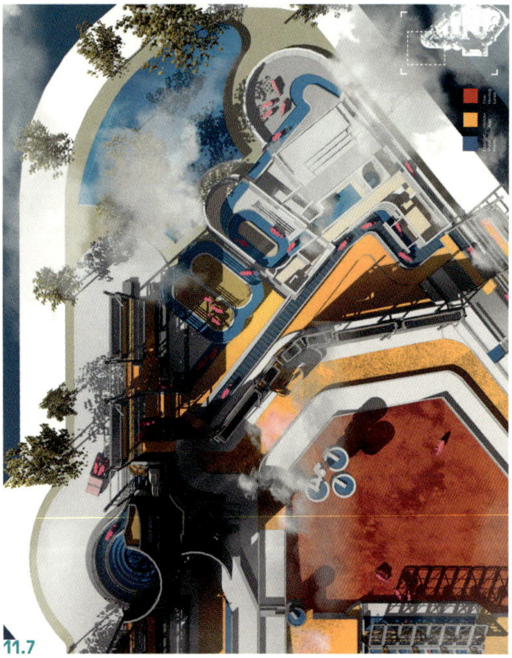

11.7

Fig. 11.4 Robin Farmer Y5, 'An Urban Patchwork'. Proposing an alternative redevelopment surrounding Wrigley Field Stadium, the scheme looks to give permanency to an unstable site through a layered topography of health. **Fig. 11.5 Milo De Luca** Y4, 'Time, Motion and Layers'. The ephemerality of the model's form describes the flexible sequencing and orchestration of space that comprise the project's strategy. The slippage of multiple layers over the course of time articulate new forms and spaces that address the changing conditions within the environment. **Fig. 11.6 Johanna Just** Y4, 'Data Scape'. As WiFi territory increasingly overlays public spaces in the cities, it should be considered as new, virtual urban space, influencing the physical. By materialising the data use in WiFi Hotspots, a new spatial situation emerges: obstructing, bridging and sheltering, the virtual layer is reclaiming its space in the analogue urban realm. **Fig. 11.7 Alexander Chapman** Y4, 'Cowspiracy', The Cowspiracy ranch seeks to question the limits of urban farming in the contexts of Chicago Stockyards, once the meat capital of the world. The scheme addresses both local and citywide emissions of the bovine variety, along with architectural herding mechanisms to retain productivity and herd mentality.

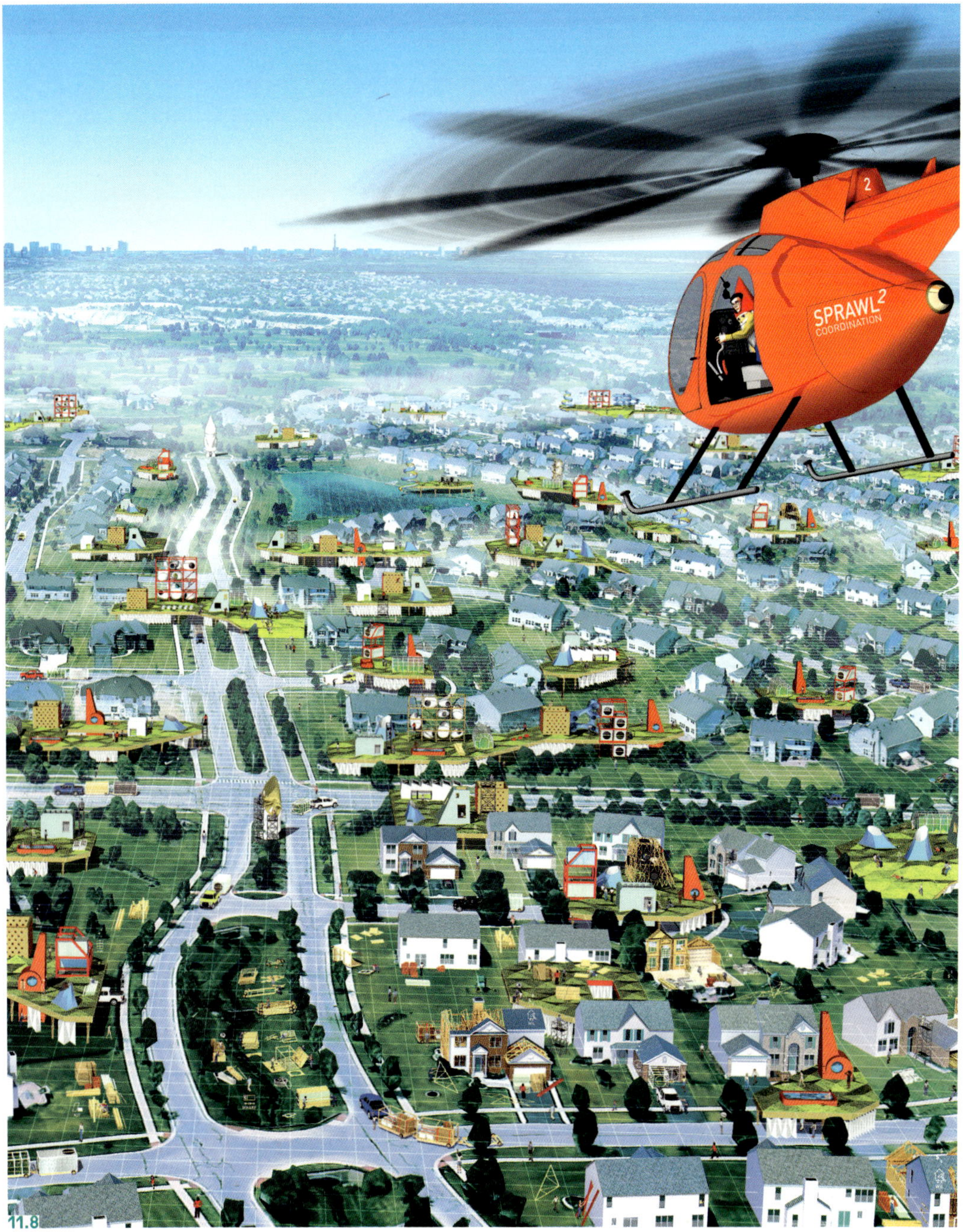

11.8

Fig. 11.8 Agostino Nickl Y4, 'Sprawl 2.0'. Playing against the rules of The Sims, the algorithm of the game is turned into a suburban incubator capable of evaluating lived alternatives. By reimplementing the winning strategies, a DIY manual allows the suburbanites to oversprawl their blank environment with a new suburban layer: one celebrating the common, the shared and the self-built. **Fig. 11.9 Anthony Ko** Y4, 'An Architectural Paradox: Glitched Island'. Paradoxes are encoded within collages as different 'characters'; architectures are extruded from these encoded collages. These are essential historic fragments of Chicago that fall into oblivion during the city's development. Through creating glitches in objects and architectural gestures, paradoxical histories are delineated to resist eradication of evidence and memories of places.

Fig. 11.10 Adam Lampon Y5, 'No Flow City'. Chicago is founded upon heavily contaminated swampland. Climate change and urbanisation place extreme stress on the city sewage system and local environment. My sustainable 'no flow' water management infrastructure integrates within the existing urban grid. Micro-watersheds separate storm water from effluent to enhance the local hydrology and mitigate long-term environmental damage.

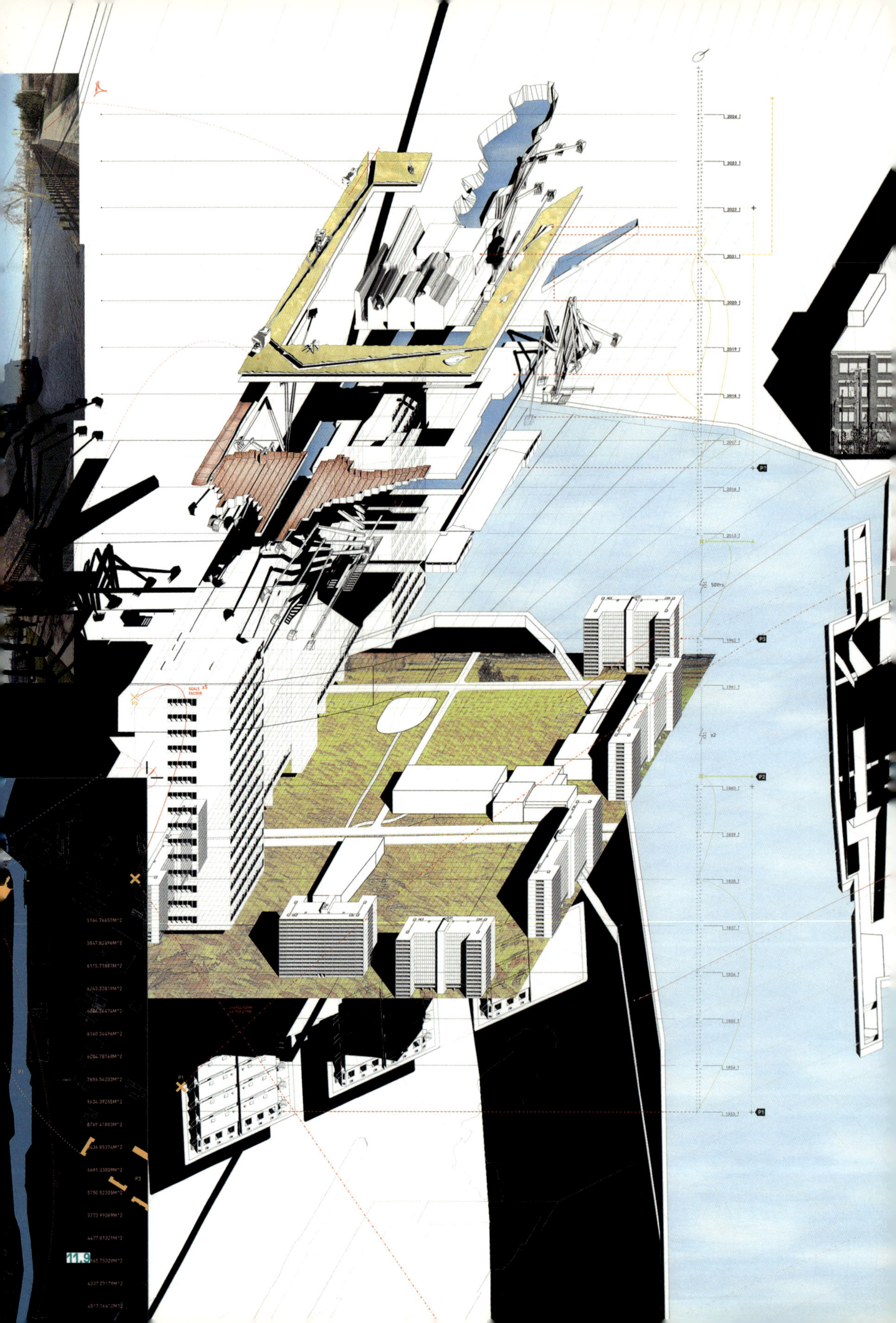

2024
2023
2022
2021
2020
2019
2018
2017
2016
2015
50Yrs
1962
P3
1961
x2
P2
1860
1859
1858
1857
1856
1855
1854
1853
P1
SCALE FACTOR x5
5164.76651M^2
5847.82496M^2
6115.71887M^2
6263.22819M^2
6160.34496M^2
7696.54203M^2
9634.39255M^2
6691.33809M^2
5750.52305M^2
5773.99069M^2
4477.81321M^2
4337.27179M^2
4517.16612M^2
11.9

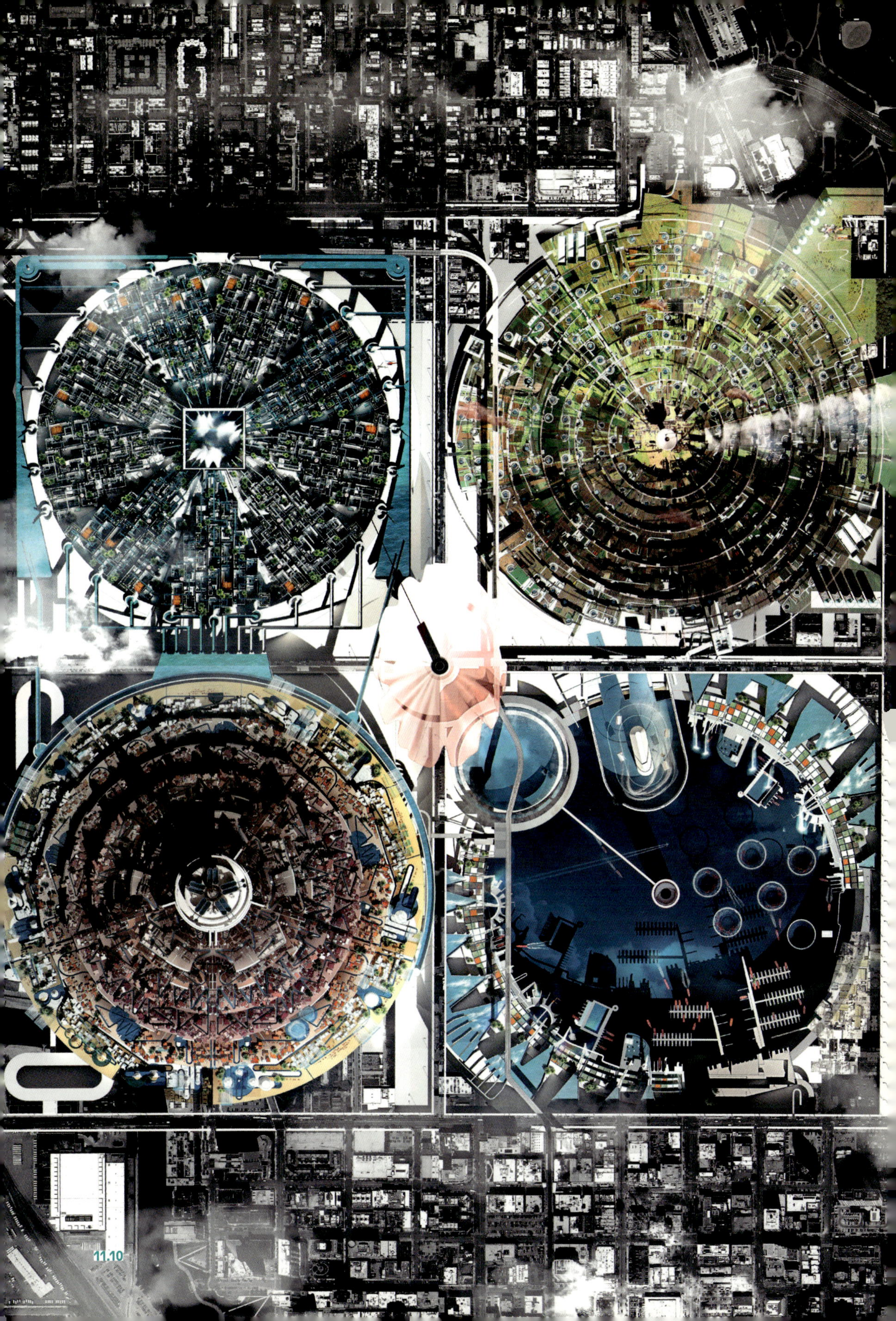
11.10

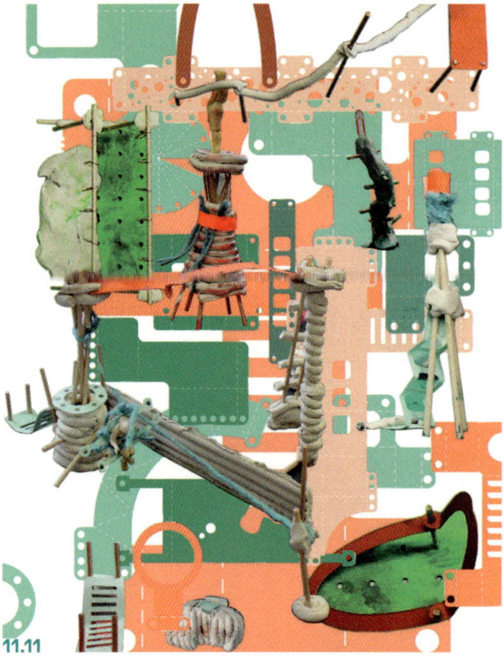
11.11

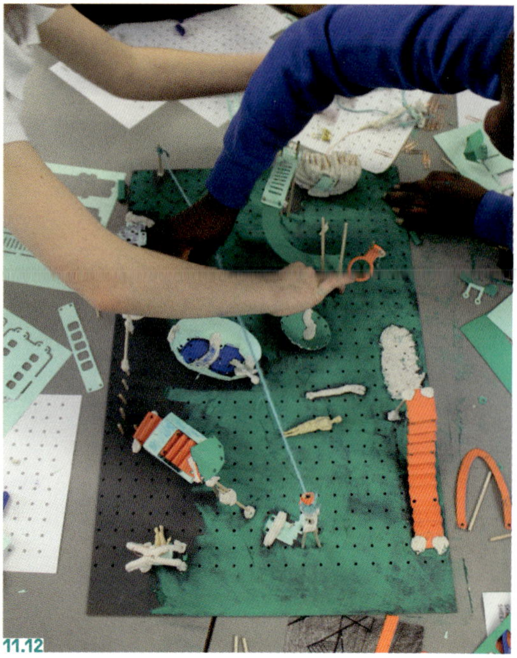
11.12

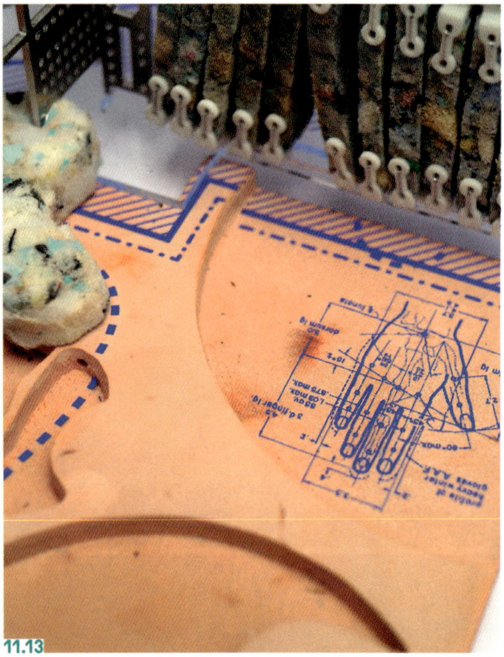
11.13

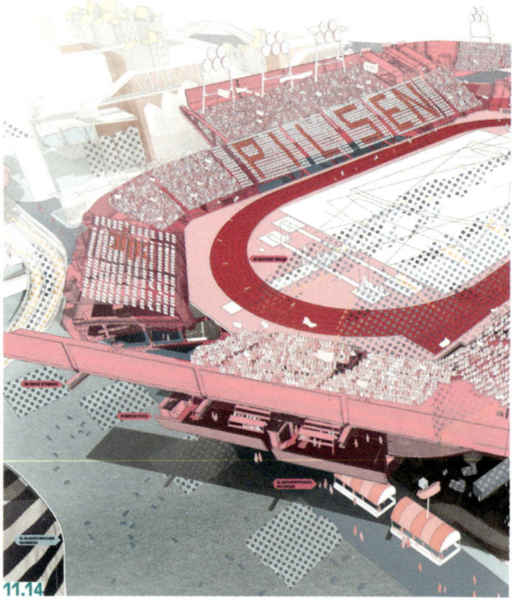

11.14

Figs. 11.11 – 11.13 Emma Kitley Y5, 'Playscapes for Chicago'. Playscapes for Chicago proposes an extended safe passage to school that encourages independent neighbourhood play. The design incorporates a variety of levels and textures, overlooked spaces, water, height, permeable boundaries and an architecture aimed to facilitate the construction, reconstruction and adaptation of their space. The design developed through a series of workshops with a group of Primary School children – using the Flatpack Playscape Kit to design their ideal playspaces. The proposal became a collaborative process using the childrens' ideas and priorities, play theory and material testing. **Fig. 11.14 Fergus Seccombe** Y5, 'Pilsen Olympics'. Learning from the mistakes of Chicago's failed bid for Summer 2016, the Pilsen Olympics are designed with legacy as the priority; providing remediation to the social and environmental problems of Chicago's post-industrial sites. Legacy components are then temporarily misused and altered to form stadiums and accommodation for the Games. **Fig. 11.15 Fergus Knox** Y5, 'A Tall Timber Future'. An investigation into prefabricated timber skyscrapers 'galleons' to be rolled out to the west of Chicago. Prefabricated galleons will challenge existing preconceptions about building with wood. Manufactured within a giant assembly building, its unique branching structure supports modulated accommodation.

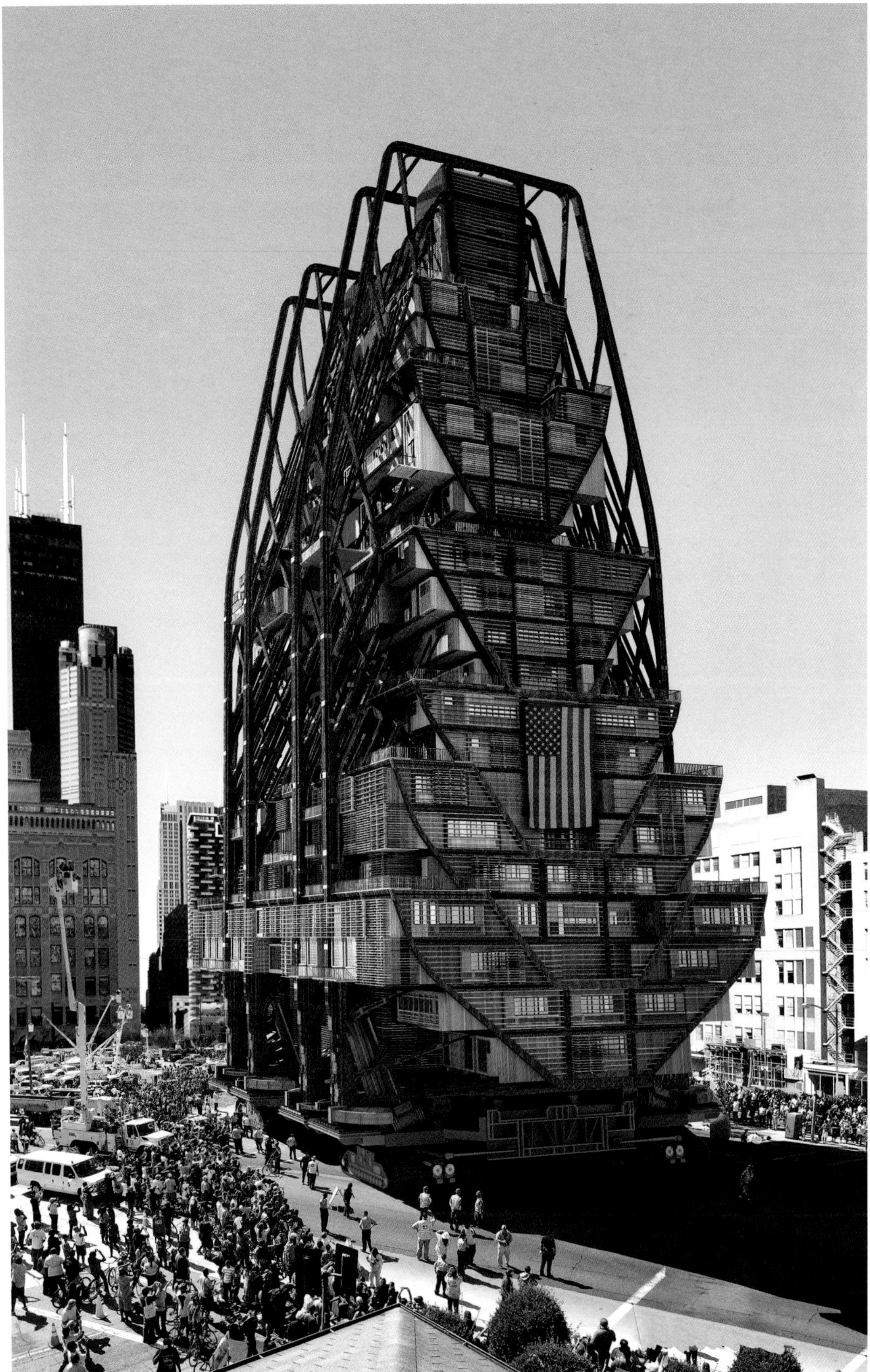
11.15

Unit 12 The Public Private House

Matthew Butcher, Elizabeth Dow, Jonathan Hill

Year 4
Christia Angelidou, Mariya Badeva, Emma De Haan, Mihail Dinu, Simona Fratila, Clare Hawes, Rawan Hussin, Yi Lu, Raphae Memon, Ilaria Rigodanzo, Henry Schofield, Meya Tazi, Ioana Vierita

Year 5
Stephanie Brancatisano, Kacper Chmielewski, Holly Crosbie, Matthew Sawyer, Luke Scott, Zahra Taleifeh, Matthew Turner

Thanks to our Design Realisation tutor James Hampton and structural consultant James Nevin

We would also like to thank our critics: Eva Branscome, Ruth Bernatek, Emma Cheatle, Tom Coward, Edward Denison, Tina Di Carlo, Oliver Domeisen, Murray Fraser, Omar Ghazal, James Hampton, Colin Herperger, Charles Holland, Jan Kattein, Chee Kit Lai, Constance Lau, Ifi Liangi, Jon Lopez, Hugh McEwen, Lesley McFadyen, Hikaru Nissanke, Tom Noonan, Luke Pearson, Mariana Pestana, Rahesh Ram, Peg Rawes, Jane Rendell, Alisdair Russell, Oliver Salway, Tanya Sengupta, Ro Spankie, Eva Sopeoglou, Tijana Stevanovic, Elly Ward, Gabriel Warshafsky, Dan Wilkinson, Alex Zambelli

In Unit 12, we recognise the history within the discipline of architecture – an internal dialogue of evolving ideas, forms and tectonics – and we equally acknowledge the history of architecture's interdependence with social, cultural and political developments. Claiming a degree of artistic autonomy is as necessary to creative speculation as understanding and engaging contemporary conditions. In many eras, the most fruitful innovations have occurred when ideas and forms have migrated from one time and place to another by a process of translation that has been as inventive as the initial conception.

——Critical admiration of the past has often been a creative stimulus in the present. Erwin Panofsky even identifies the start of the Renaissance with the moment when "the whole classical sphere ... became an object of nostalgia". The unnecessary opposition between tradition and innovation was a modernist cliché. But the most celebrated modernists were more subtle in their approach, leading Le Corbusier to compare Platonic forms to cars and Mies Van Der Rohe to state: "I felt that it must be possible to harmonize the old and the new in our civilisation. Each of my buildings was a statement of this idea". Vincent Scully concludes that the architect will "always be dealing with historical problems—with the past and, a function of the past, with the future. So the architect should be regarded as a kind of physical historian". The most creative architects have always looked to the past to imagine a future, studying an earlier architecture not to replicate it but to understand and transform it. Twenty-first century architects need to appreciate the shock of the old as well as the shock of the new.

——A recurring theme states that the house is the origin and archetype of architecture. The home of the home, as we understand it today, is seventeenth-century Netherlands, when domestic architecture became private and familial. In subsequent centuries, the segregation of functions within the home mirrored the segregation of functions within the city. Challenging this isolation, Louis Kahn recalled the Renaissance analogy of a house and a city to characterise the house as the smallest social institution, concluding that, "every building is a house, regardless of whether it is a Senate, or whether it is just a house." Our project this year is the design of a house-institution for an international organisation or society in London, which as a place to live and work has a public and a private life.

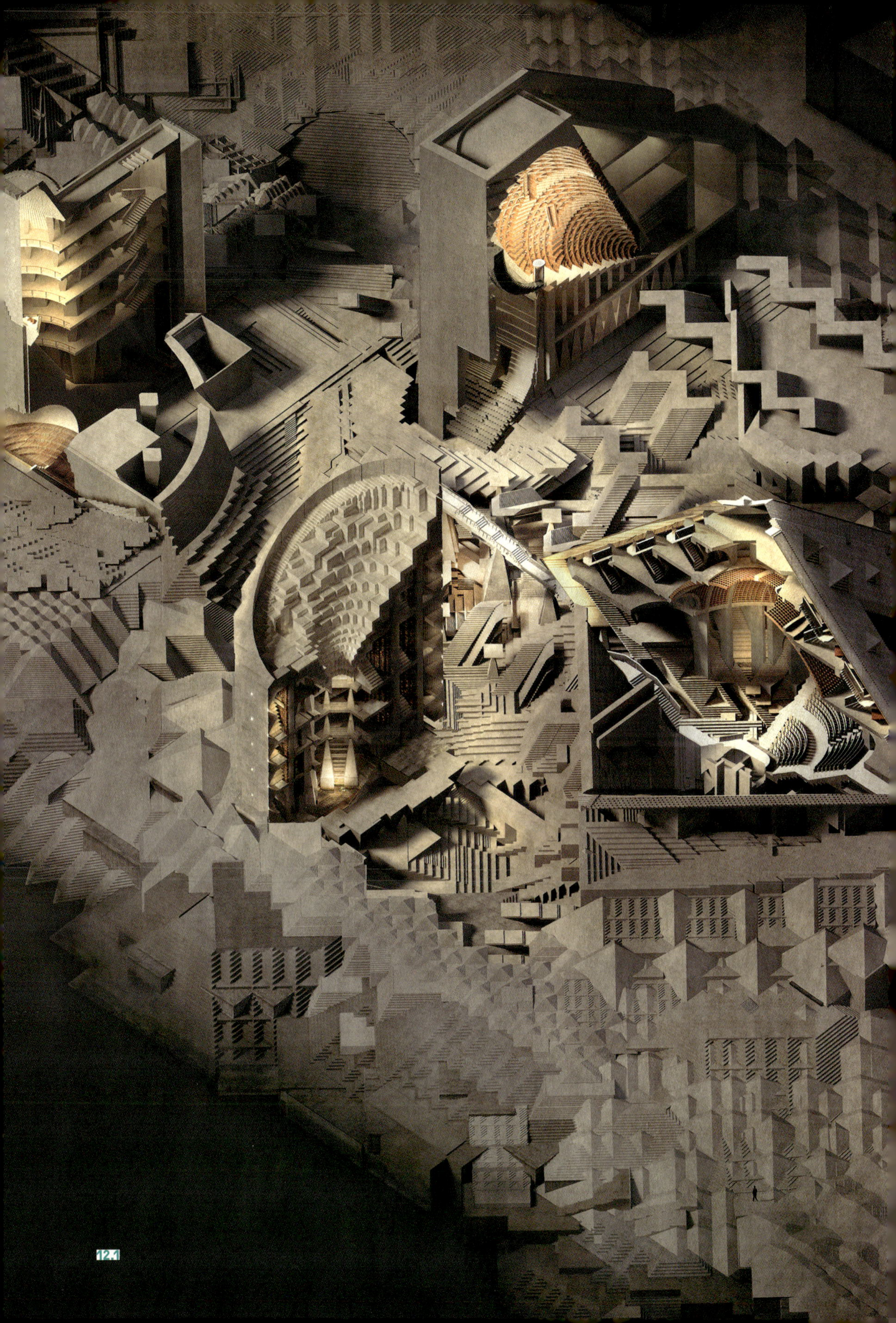

12.1

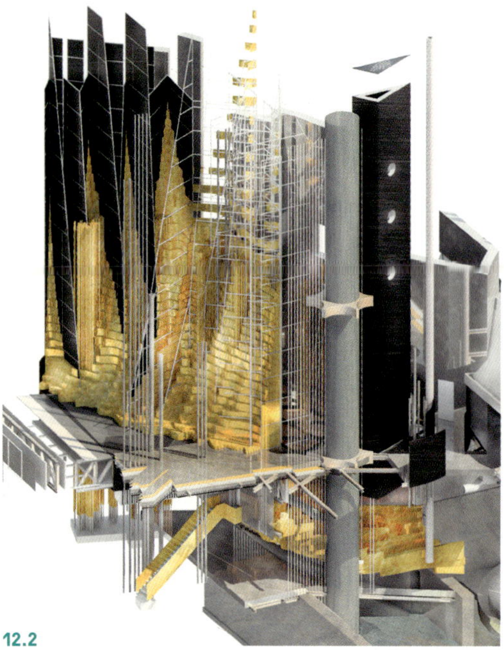

12.2

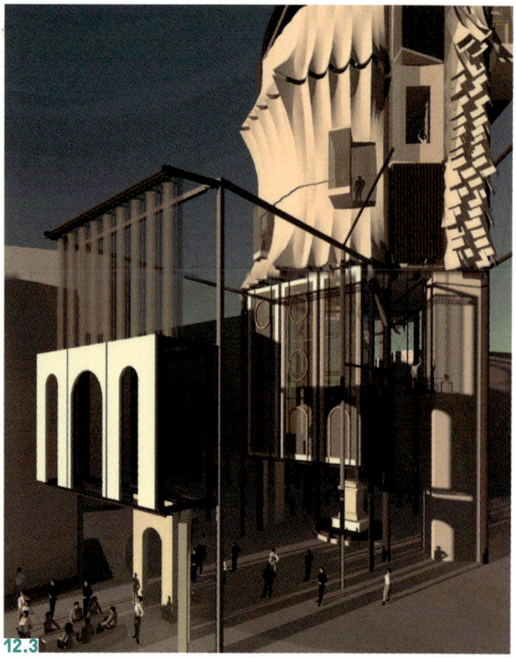

12.3

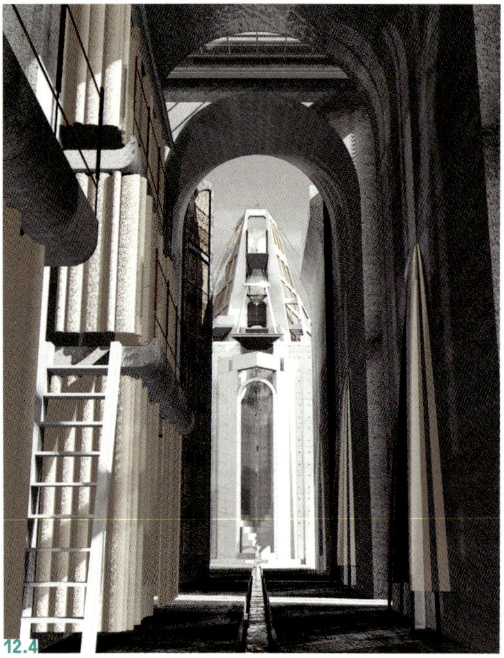

12.4

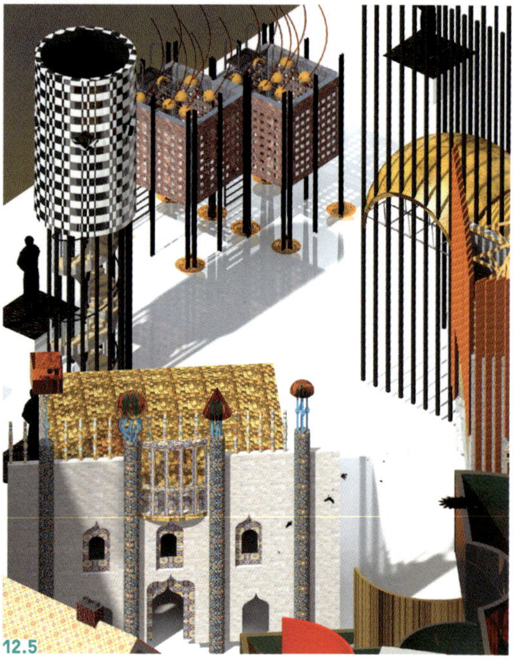

12.5

Fig. 12.1 Kacper Chmielewski Y5, 'Humanistic Typology'. The project investigates a relationship between elements of ecclesiastical architecture and the fulfilment of the psychological needs of humanity, with special attention to religious interpretation of light. Questioning the notion of Divine Light, the project proposes its replacement for secular society – Humanistic Light – relating translucency of digitally milled marble to the works of Johannes Vermeer, and humanist values. **Fig. 12.2 Christia Angelidou** Y4, 'The Future of Humanity Institute'. The project unfolds as a narrative, which takes part in a world that is in chaos politically, socially and environmentally. The spaces witness contradictory events and programmatic impossibilities: surgeons, philosophers and astrophysicists all congregate until new hypotheses appear. The collage technique is evident in the juxtaposition of materials and the fragmentary conditions hint of an architectural language of assemblage. **Fig. 12.3 Raphae Memon** Y4, 'The Theatre of Tectonic Veils'. As a tower of theatre, the building hides and reveals the backstage nature of everyday performance on the streets of Seven Dials. By night a scenography emerges to transform the area into a working stage-set. Veils become tectonic and spatial as actor/spectator boundaries are broken, and the public space performs within a new narrative. **Fig. 12.4 Yi Lu** Y4, 'Confucius Institute'. Located on Wood Wharf, a former dockland close to Canary Wharf, the institute acts as a temporal retreat allowing people to slow down the pace. The architecture is interpreted in phenomenological dimensions, directed towards spatial

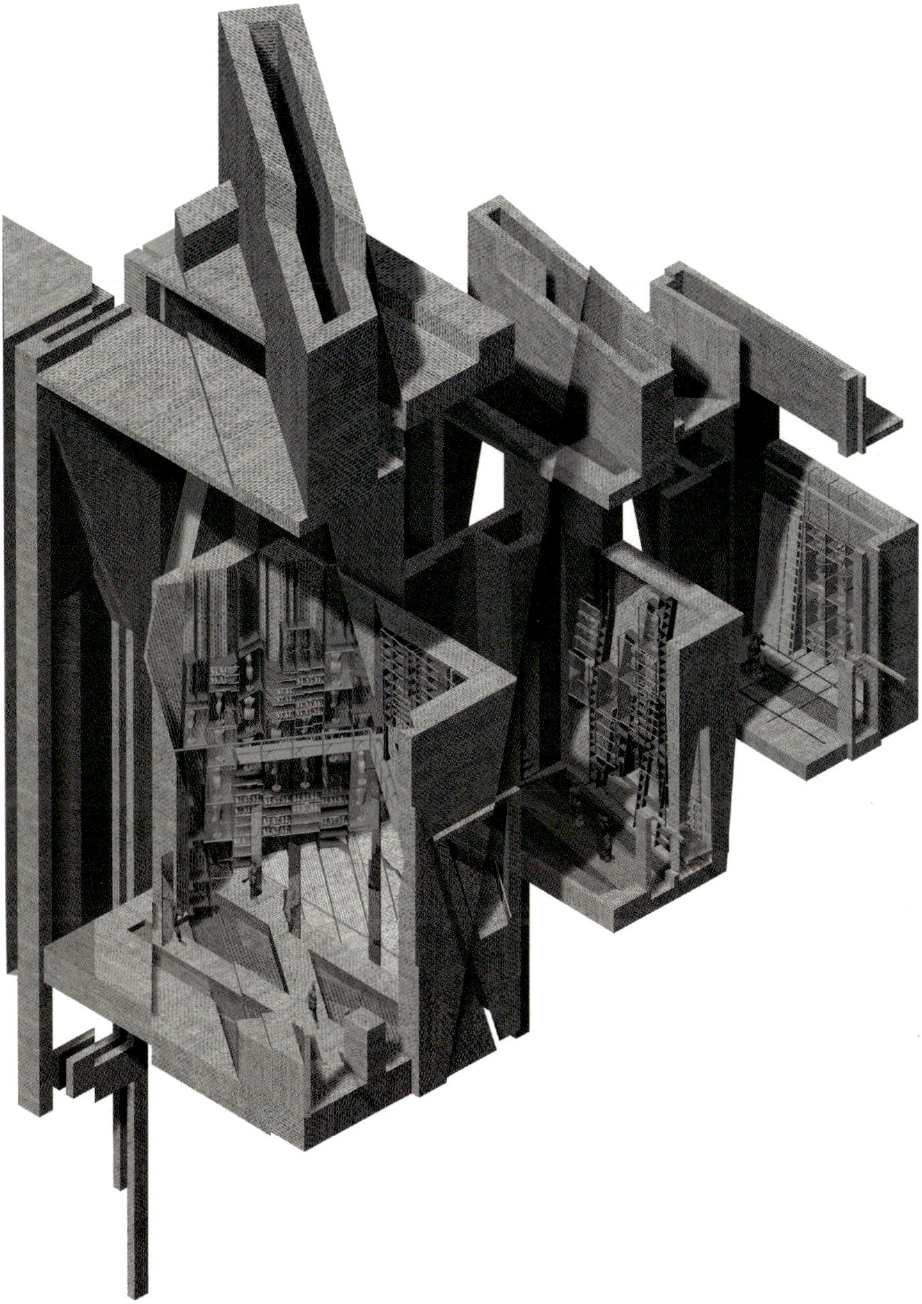

12.6

sequence, light, and material, which formulates users' multi-sensory experience and ultimately leads to one's spiritual cultivation – the core thinking in Confucian philosophy. **Fig. 12.5 Mariya Badeva** Y4, 'The UNPO Public Private House'. Remembering that autonomy refers to notions of separation, opposition, confrontation and critical distance, and defined by certain new typologies, the project proposes a house-institution for the Unrepresented Nations and Peoples Organisation – UNPO. The project highlights the creative tension between the claim to autonomy and the social and political realities of the present. **Fig. 12.6 Matthew Turner** Y5, 'The New London Law Court' questions the traditional solidity of the language of the law court, in which the architecture is often one of stability and reassurance in opposition to the ambiguity of right and wrong. It is located at the confluence of The River Fleet and The Thames, a hinterland between the power of The City and Westminster. The location was once known as Alsatia, a sanctuary that was immune to the powers flanking it. Thus, the building inhabits a fluctuating intersection of both the political and environmental.

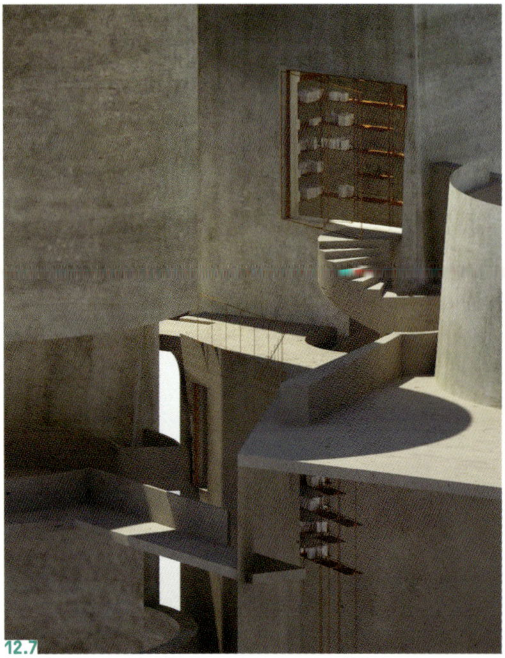
12.7

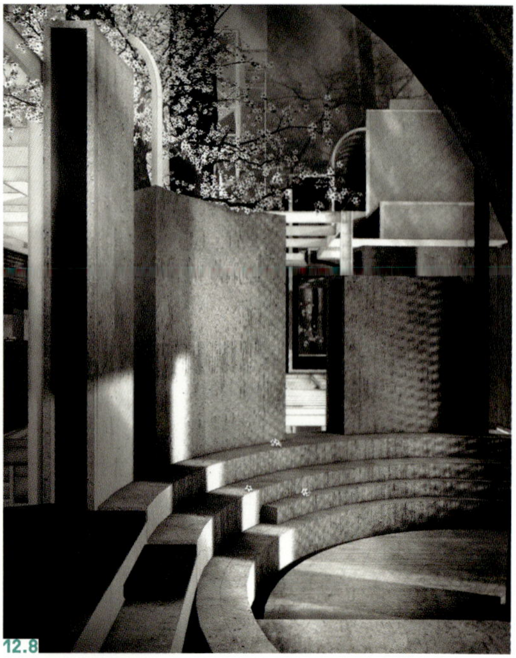
12.8

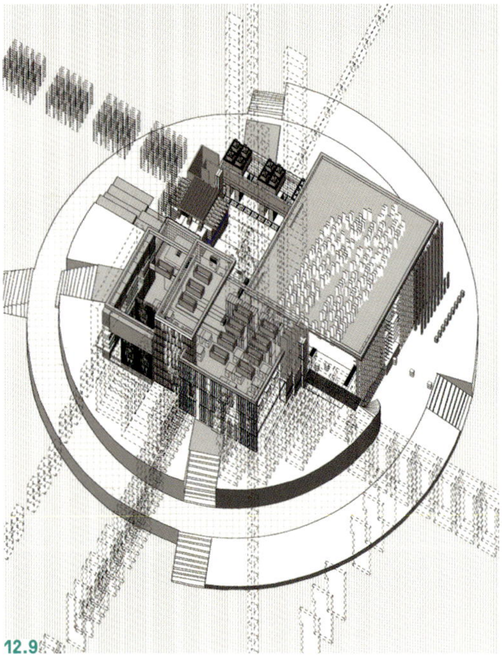
12.9

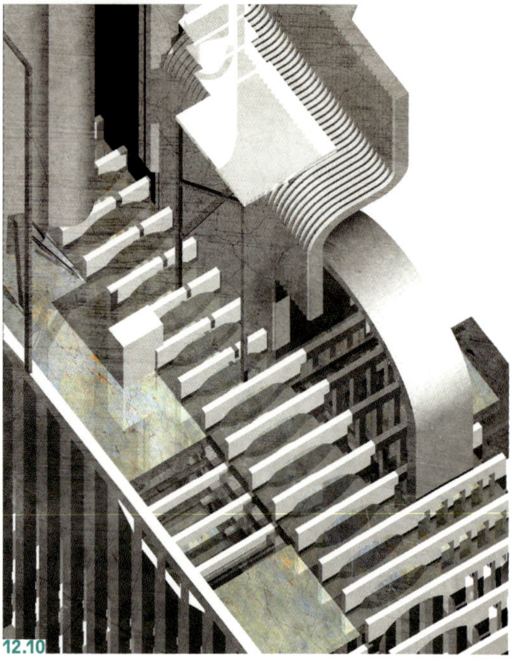
12.10

Fig. 12.7 Ioana Vierita Y4, 'A House for Natural Philosophers'. The proposal explores the possibility of a fully permeable research institution. As a reflection of the empiricist way of learning, based on intuitive thought and personal understanding, the experience of the building resides in the perception of ephemeral moments, playing on the idea of distorted memories and unfamiliarity of space that once seemed familiar. **Fig. 12.8 Rawan Hussin** Y4, 'The International Climate Change Register'. The isolated structure seals itself in an ancient woodland, and explores the relationship between the natural and artificial. The institute will contribute towards the Intergovernmental Panel on Climate Change to review and assess the most recent scientific information produced on site. **Fig. 12.9 Emma De Haan** Y4, 'The Compulsive Creator's Drawing Centre'. Within every creative process, there is a compulsive obsession with production. A pattern of creation – a compulsion to draw. The building explores the explainable and the inexplicable, conscious and subconscious, intended and accidental. Examining how users may interrupt a desired system creating an exquisite corpse, grafting owner and un-ownership. **Fig. 12.10 Mihail Dinu** Y4, 'Royal Commission for Perpetual Peace'. Negotiations involve intense dialogue between two or more parties. In the proposal delegates assess the viability, stability and risk of their strategies with every exchange. The design reflects on these human practices and negotiates timescales, skills and the human component into a unified space, radiating architecture.

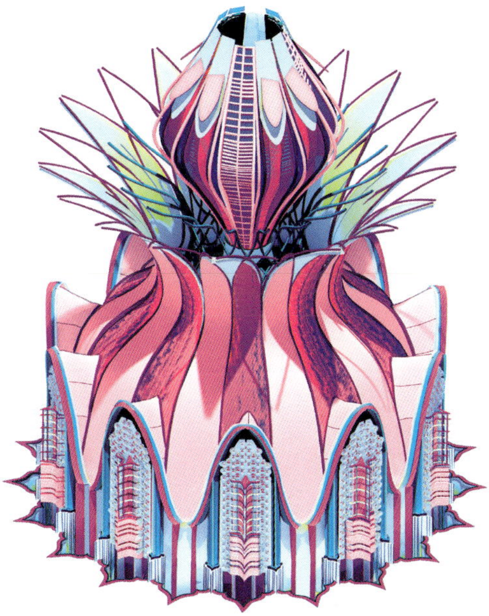

12.11

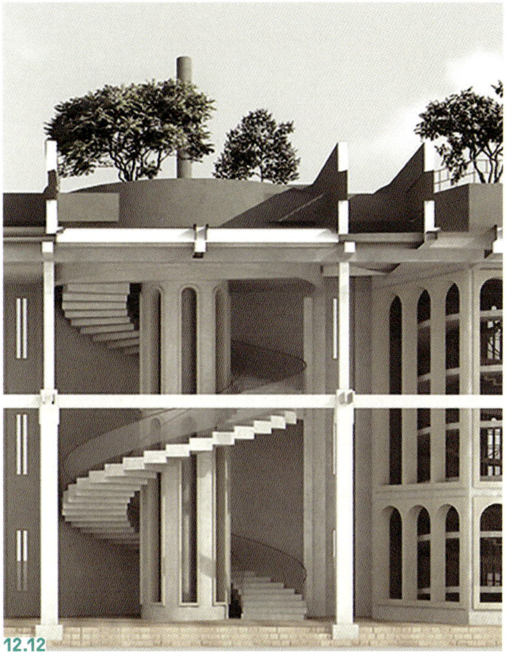

12.12

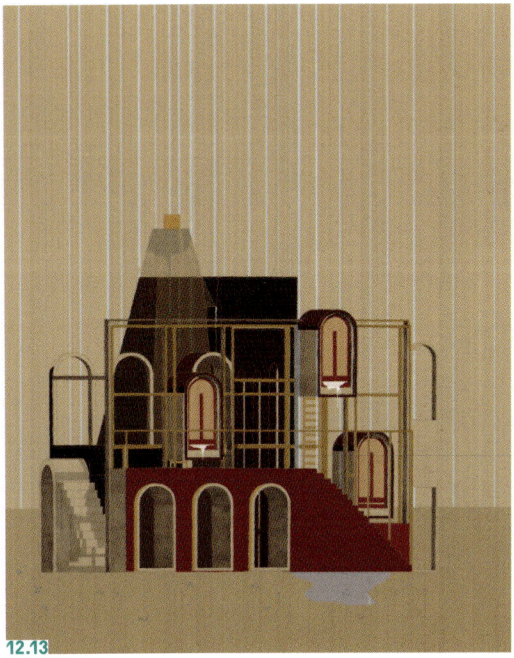

12.13

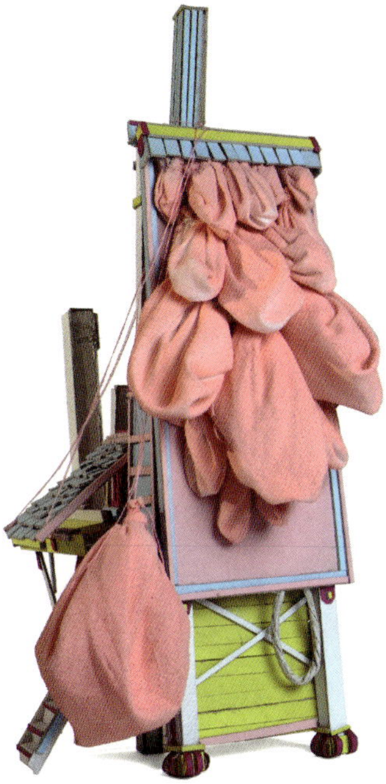

12.14

Fig. 12.11 Henry Schofield Y4, 'Exuberance Architecture'. A language derived from analysing the dichotomy between religion/hedonism. The project references versions of the temple of worship and the garden of paradise that it depicts. Exotic fruits, lavish colours and voluptuous bodies are three key typologies recognised throughout the temple that have been applied to the design of a Soho Love Hotel and City of London Police Station. **Fig. 12.12 Simona Fratila** Y4, 'Deptford School of Etiquette'. The proposal comes as a reaction to current economic investments by looking at different forms of capital. It follows Pierre Bourdieu's interpretation of mannerism as a form of cultural and embodied capital. Architecturally, the project analyses the concept of stairs, reinterpreting them symbolically as a form of social ascension.

Fig. 12.13 Meya Tazi Y4, 'Nascere: The House of the Stewards of the Orchard' escapes the inception of humanity as a geological force, modifying man's behaviour with its non-human creation. In a forced intimacy and coexistence, human labour redeems the contaminated land of Silvertown for the life of a new orchard – a territory where man-made does not resist the autonomy of nature. **Fig. 12.14 Clare Hawes** Y4, 'Tower Hamlets Civic Centre'. The project proposes a new civic centre for the communities of Tower Hamlets. Visitors are encouraged to donate materials at the wedding and memorial ceremonies, offering visitors a sense of ownership. The building is an architecture of celebration: celebrating life, death, community and place.

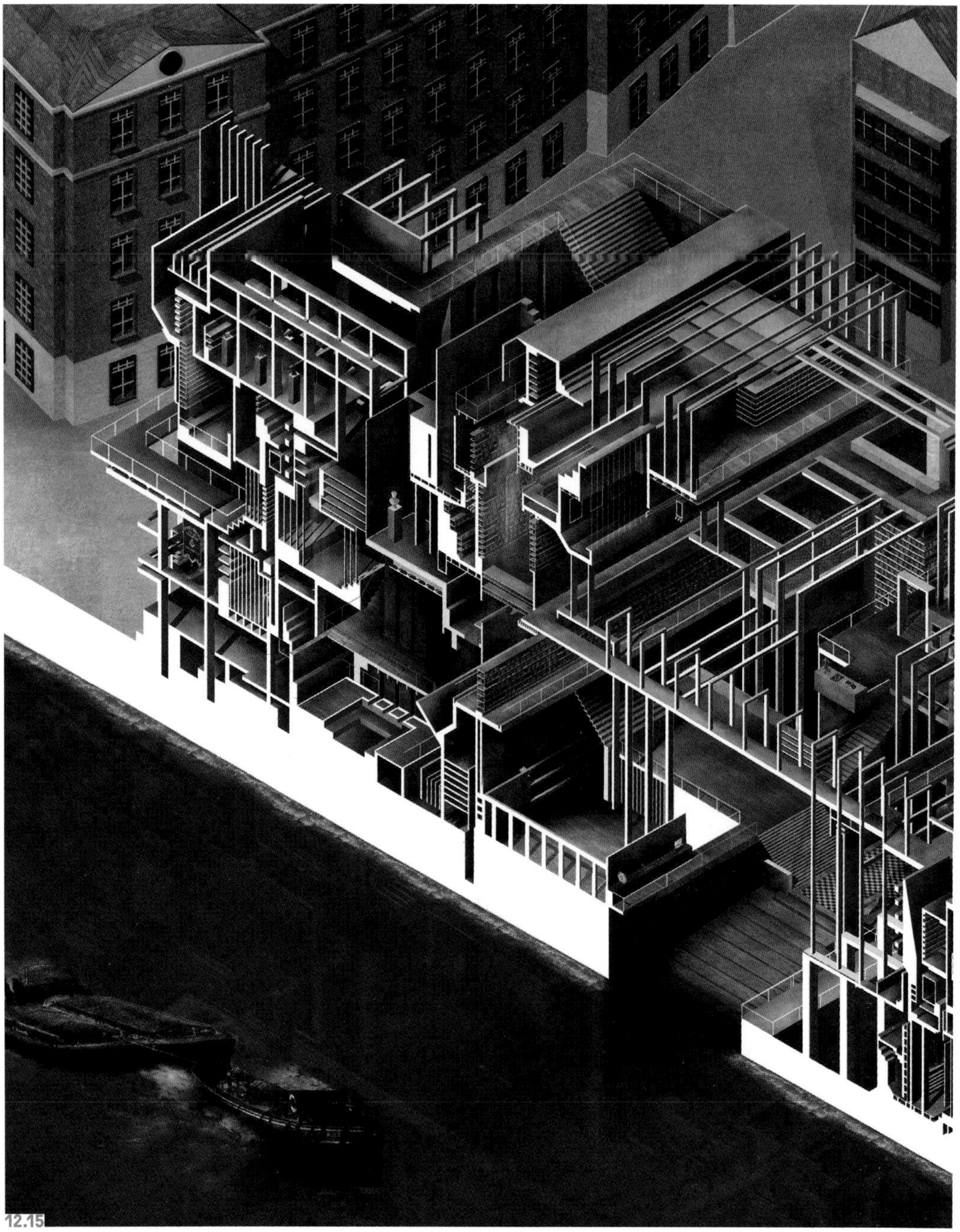

12.15

Fig. 12.15 **Matthew Sawyer** Y5, 'The Masonic Temple'. The proposal metaphorically utilises the Freemasons' infamous relationship with public and private spaces to critique the increasingly urgent issue of undemocratic land ownership in London. The architectural typology is crafted around the notion of transparency, as its revealing cross-sectional façade exposes the Temple's daily work both to its surroundings and within its context. The architecture directly responds to the critique by providing moments of openness, contrasted against the historic Masonic privacy. This ultimately causes its visitors to question their ability to experience the architecture in its entirety.

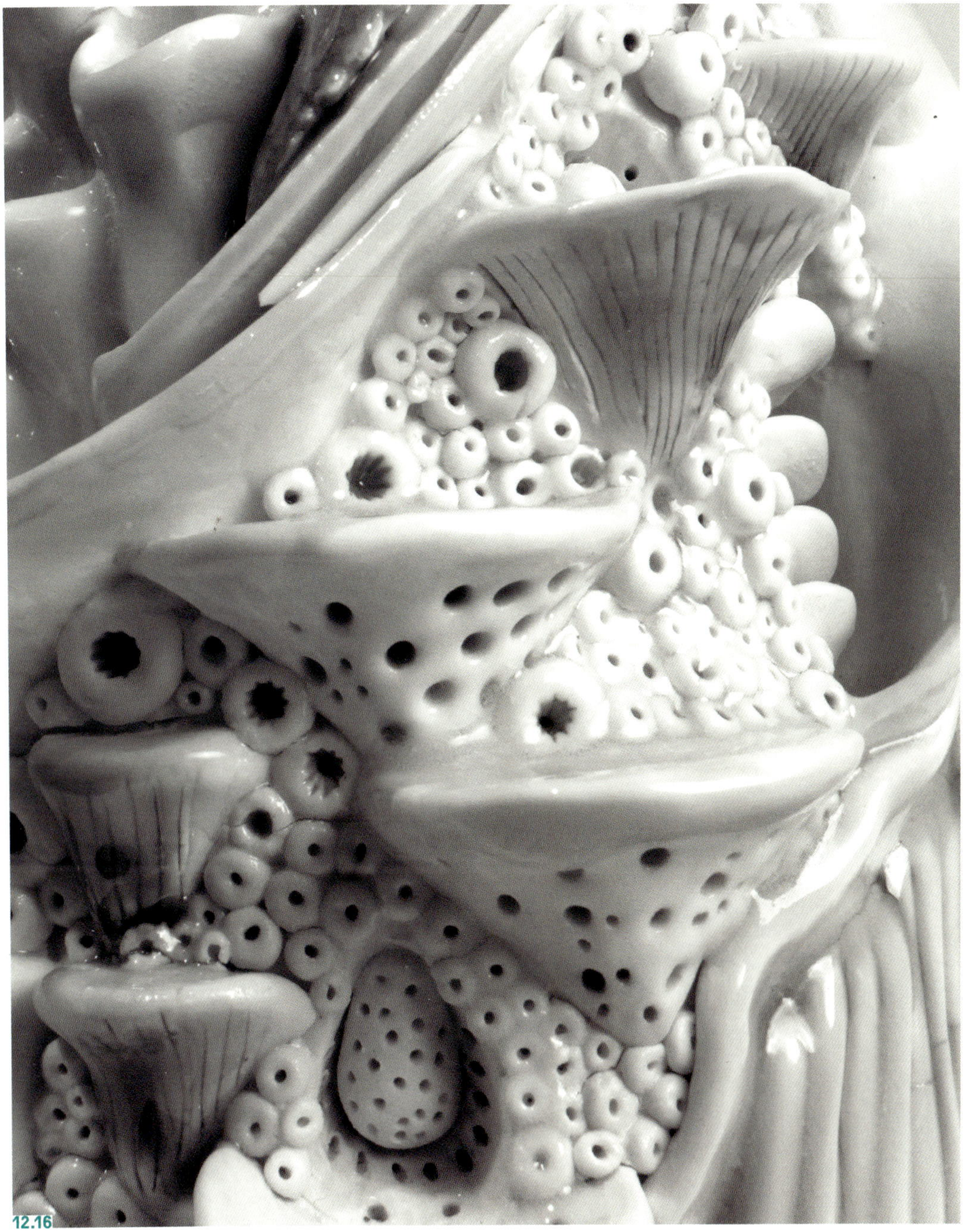

12.16

Fig. 12.16 Holly Crosbie Y5, 'Gallions Reach'. A hydrological landscape that aims to decontaminate a toxic urban site. The proposal divides the site into smaller test sites, each on a ten-year cycle of stabilising the contamination and providing a safe and usable public space. The language of the architecture has evolved through the manipulation of water and as a continuation of the landscape. The buildings are formed of nested layers; the outer layer provides a protective shell that is softened by the weather, while in contrast; the inner habitable layers are highly glazed, cleaned and polished. The internal spaces provide varying degrees of environmental comfort with no definitive threshold between interior and exterior.

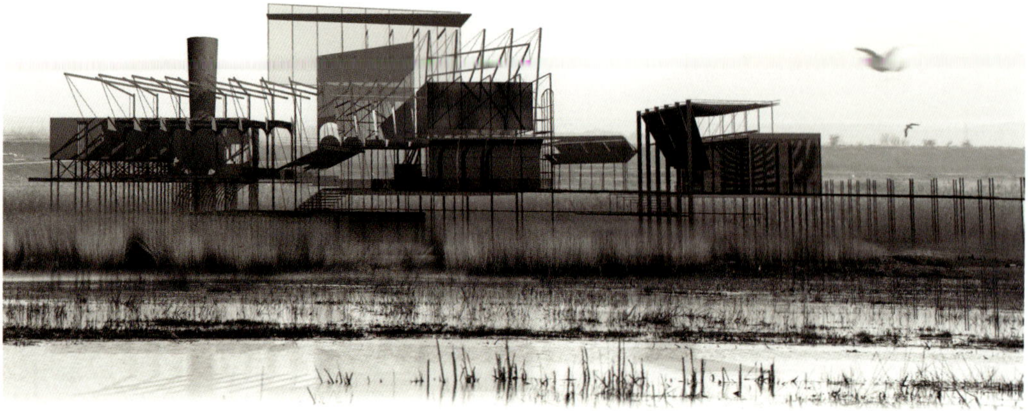

12.17

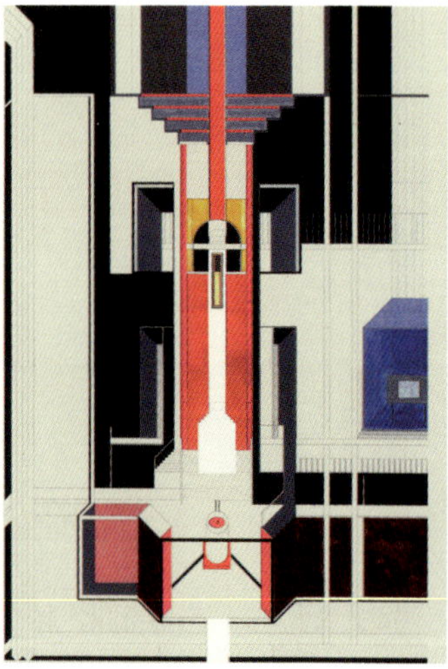

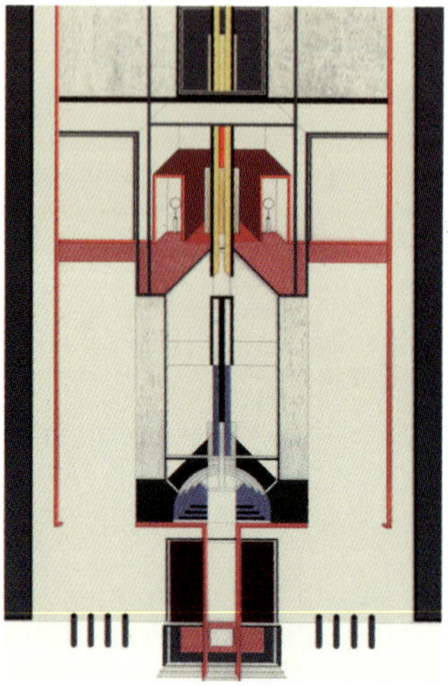

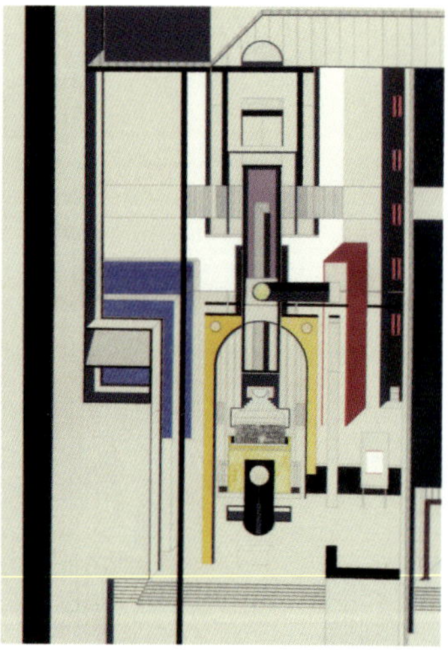

12.18

Fig. 12.17 Stephanie Brancatisano Y5, 'The Global House of Mayors' proposes an alternative mode of democratic urban governance which resonates in the dual global/local condition of our urbanised world. Sited at Rainham Marshes in the Thames Estuary, the House is in constant exchange with nature, seeking to inform the decision-making processes of the mayors. **Fig. 12.18 Zahra Taleifeh** Y5, 'The Registry – Birth, Marriage, Death'. A model building for the devotion of objects, identity and sexuality as opposed to social hierarchy, wealth and power. The project speculates a Registry Office as a place that re-emphasises the ceremonial aspects of registration rather than the administrative processes, a monument to the public and a site of 'public intimacy'.

Fig. 12.19 Luke Scott Y5, 'Law and the Natural Order'. The proposal recognises the Law as a distinctly human practice; its associations being with the civilised and structured society. In order to isolate and enhance the platonic nature of this practice, it is embedded within an expressly organic, non-human condition, as the hard lines and choreographed occupation of the Court meets the sporadic life of the forest.

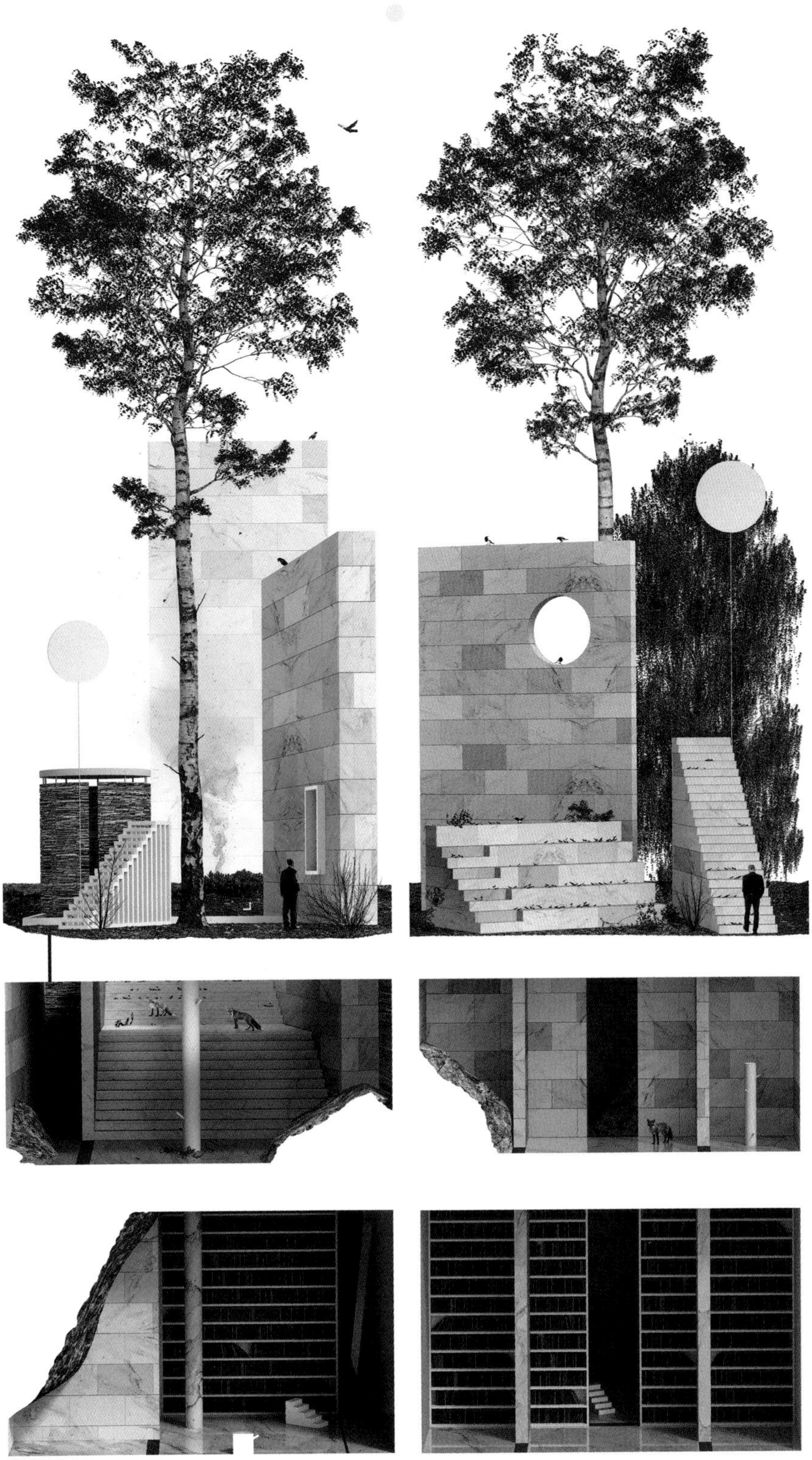

12.19

Unit 15

States of Entanglement – Sensational Rio!

Aleksandrina Rizova, Stefan Rutzinger, Kristina Schinegger

Year 4
Thomas Bush, Qidan Chen, Qiuling Guan, Juwhan Han, Yue Ma, Elena-Cristina Militaru, Helen Siu, Bethany Penman, Dionysios Toumazis, Ching Yiu Wong

Year 5
Che-Hung Chien, Yulia Gilbert, Ruxandra Maria Gruioniu

Consultants: Kyriakos Anatolitis (Atelier Ten), David Edwards (Herzog and de Meuron), Paul Officer (Design ID)

Critics: Isaïe Bloch (UCL), David Campos, Sam Clark (PLP Architecture), Christina Dahdaleh (UCL), Oliver Domeisen (UCL), David Edwards (Herzog and de Meuron), Gianmaria Givanni (Studio Givanni), Pravin Ghosh, Jack Newton (RSHP), Paul Officer (Design ID), Ricardo de Ostos (UCL), Gilles Retsin (UCL), Javier Ruiz (UCL), Johannes Schafelner (Zaha Hadid Architects)

This year, students' projects were situated in Rio de Janeiro, a spectacular metropolis in a stunning natural setting. Rio is an amalgam shaped by cultural and economic extremes, such as the polarity of prevalent Catholicism and the intense physicality of samba and the carnival; the separation between extremely wealthy and impoverished groups; and the antipodes of dense urbanization and the tropical beauty of Rio's National Park, to name but a few.

——Rio is also a fascinating mixture of cultures and ethnicities. It appears as a fragmented archipelago with segregated city parts on both sides of the spectrum – indigent favelas on the one hand and fortified buildings for the rich on the other. At first glance, Rio's extremes tend to provoke shock and fascination. However, what turns it into a sensational and optimistic metropolis is its energetic public life and space, most tangible along its accessible beaches, which are populated by a large mix of different social groups.

——The dynamics that transformed Rio into a modern metropolis can still be seen in its abundance of stunning modernist masterpieces. Modernist architecture aims at harmonizing opposites (such as human and natural habitats, city and landscape, and buildings and infrastructures) whilst allowing them to retain their autonomous elements.

——Postmodernity favours overlapping of styles and the collage, thereby celebrating complexity and contradiction. At the turn of the century, digital architecture became interested in hybridization and seamlessness. Rio was our testing ground to develop contemporary strategies towards dealing with contradiction and fissures within the city. The notion of entanglement became our instrument to observe and analyse public space and the performative aspects of its related typologies. Students explored extreme conditions, natural and artificial landscapes and fringes of social interfaces in order to propose new multi-programmatic buildings and spaces.

——The year commenced with a short project in order to define an individual spatial interpretation of the year's topic. After the field trip, students chose individual sites and developed a building project in Rio. Unit 15 students are asked to explore innovative fabrication techniques, dynamic digital prototypes and material intelligence. Students develop a broad range of digital and analogue making skills informed by adaptive environmental and natural systems. Our experiments drift between analogue and digital – the hand and the computer – thus creating a state of hybrid entanglement.

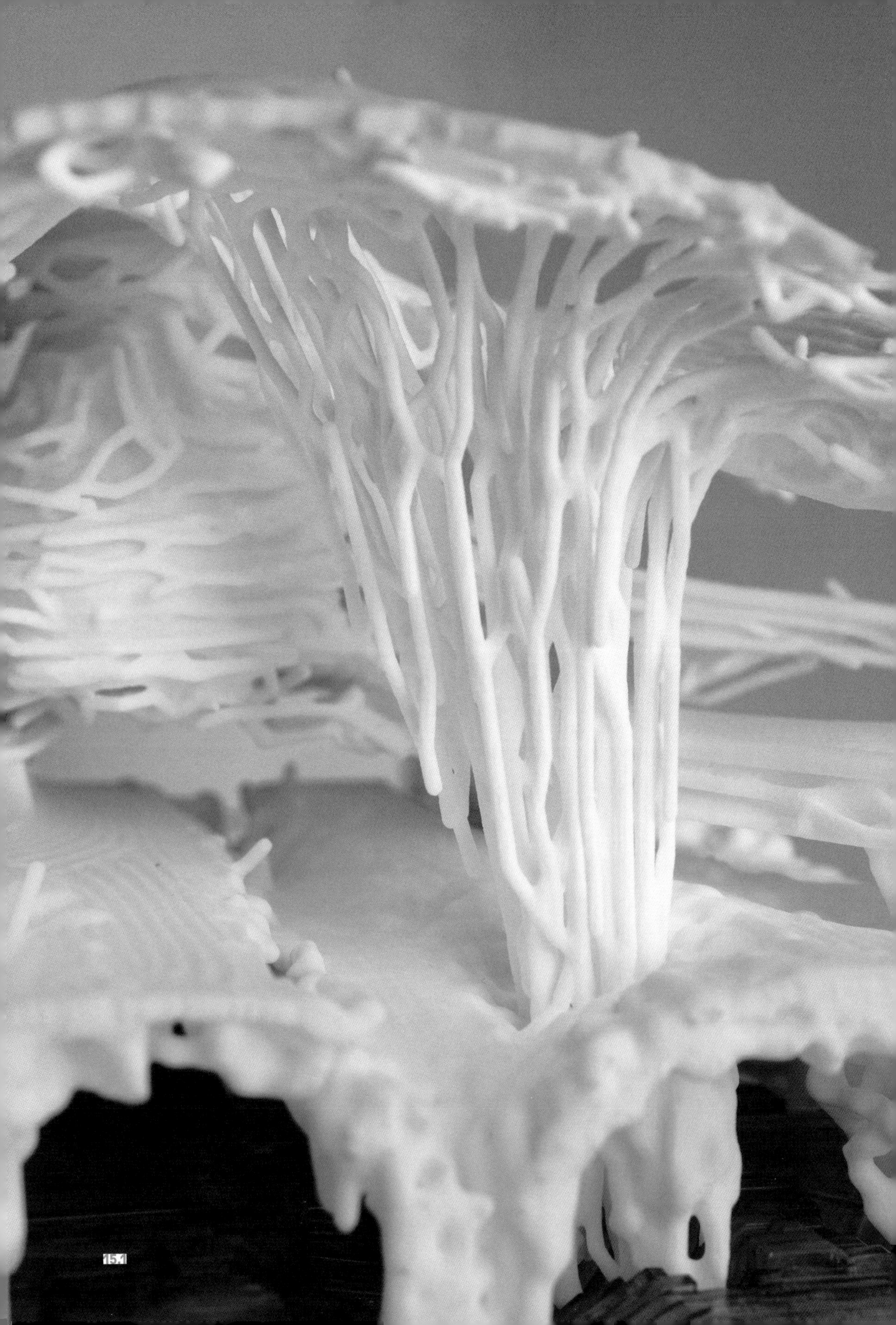

15.1

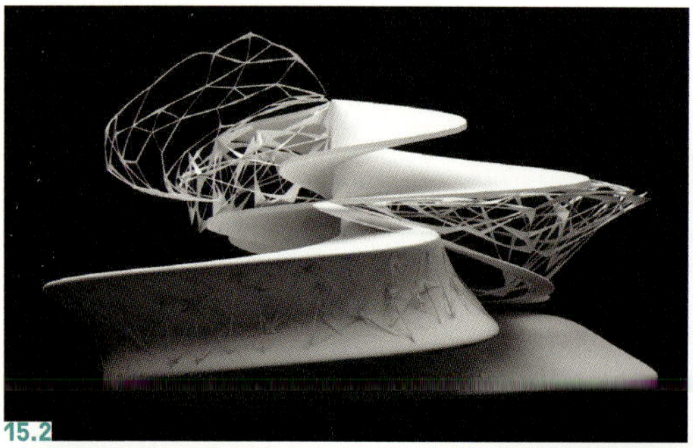
15.2

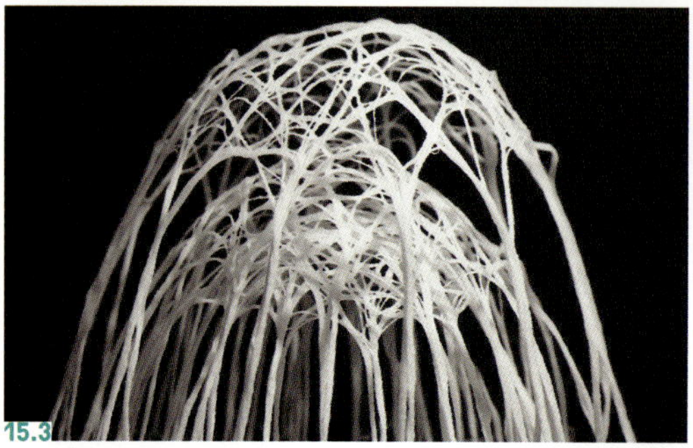
15.3

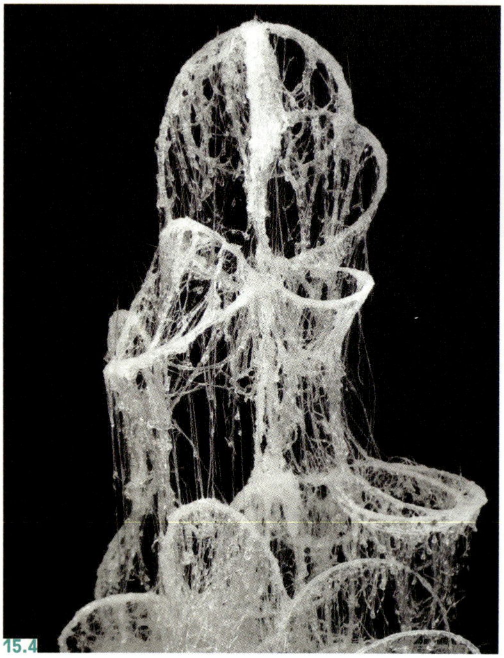
15.4

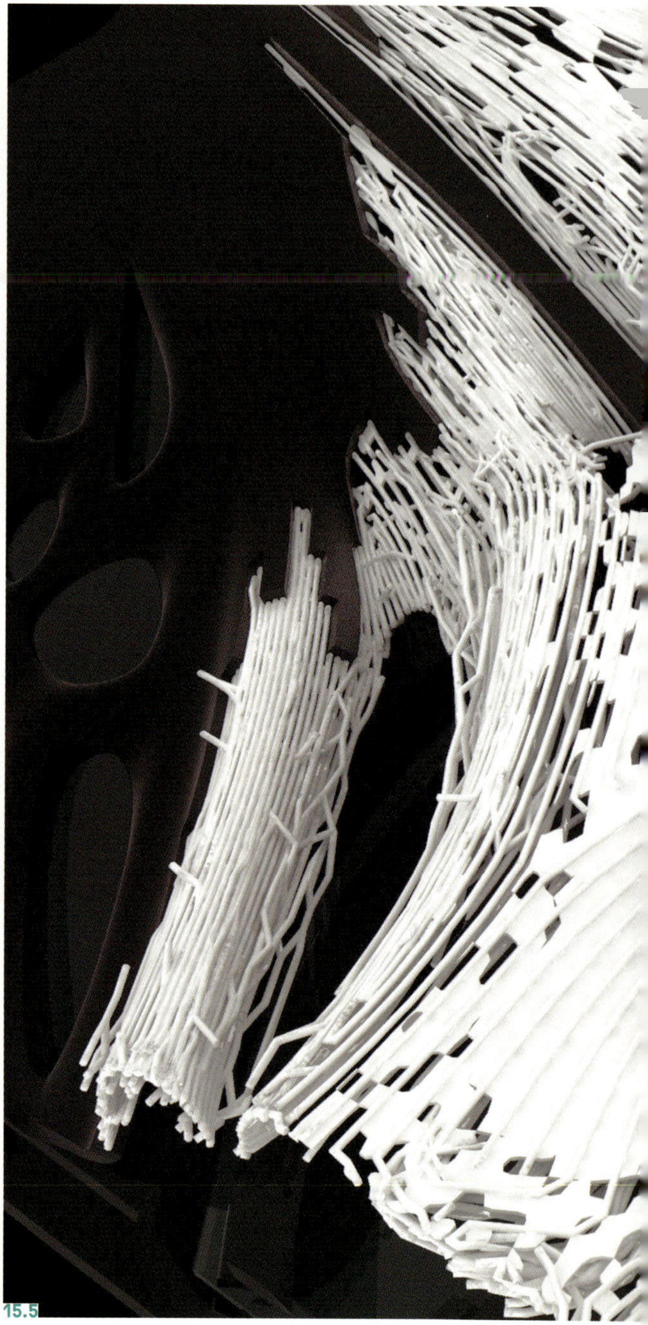
15.5

Fig. 15.1 Che-Hung Chien Y5, 'Permeable Fibrosity'. The notion of permeable fibrosity derives from the generation principles of living organisms where their intricate pattern formations evolve through interaction with external force conditions. Taking this as a starting point, the project aims at translating these fibrous patterns into a performative structural system with inherent spatial qualities and furthermore explores a permeable boundary between land and water in the port region of Rio de Janeiro. **Fig. 15.2 Ching Yiu Wong** Y4, 'Entanglement: Domino House'. Early ink drop experiments challenge the typical typologies of vertical and horizontal elements and inform a new domino house where floors and walls are treated as a continuous surface merging and wrapping around to create interconnected spaces. The definition between floors is blurred, establishing a smooth transition between circulation, surface and space. Through digital analysis, surfaces are developed as structural shells with a delicate array of openings. **Fig. 15.3 Qidan Chen** Y4, 'Self-organised Formation: Urban Environment Centre & Swimming Pools'. Located in Rio's historical city centre, near Praça XV de Novembro and the ferry station, the building aims to provide a public place for visitors and present environmental issues such as the Amazon forest deforestation and seawater pollution in Brazil. The structural design is based on a self-organisation strategy explored though physical models and digital simulation. **Fig. 15.4 Cristina Militaru** Y4, 'Hybrid Entanglement: Material Experiment'. The project investigates the relationships within a fluid material as a self-organising

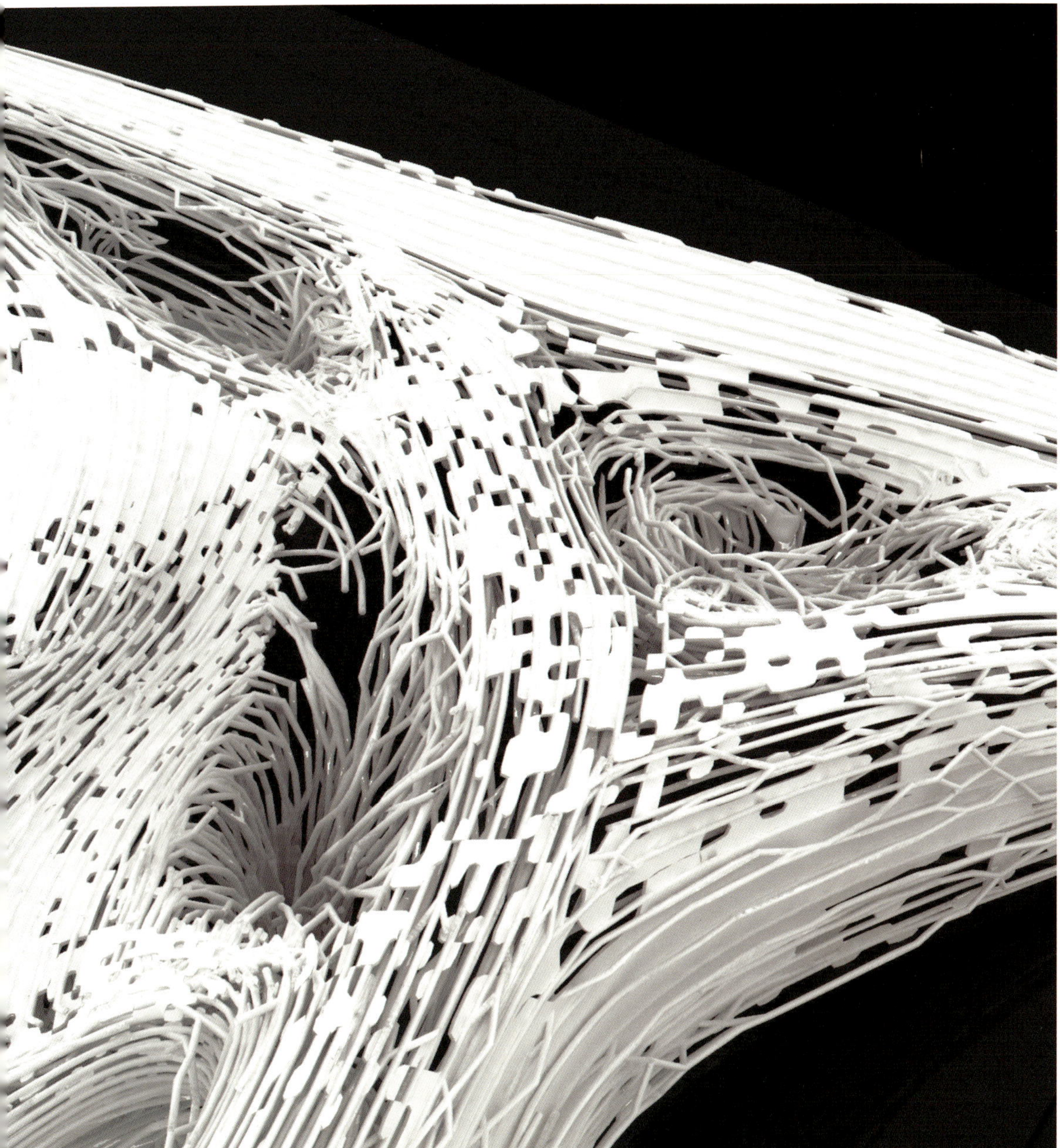

medium and movement. The material's natural performance informs the resulting system, in which the substance begins to entangle, creating its own structural strategy.
Fig. 15.5 Che-Hung Chien Y5, 'Rio Domestic Ferry Terminal'. The proposed domestic ferry terminal creates a dynamic interface between the old industrial port area and a new public-scape. The fibrous formations create a permeable water landscape which acts as an obstacle when organising and separating arrival and departure circulation. The building comprises an undulated ground plane that floods locally in relation to the tide, thus establishing moments of pause and route diversion within the busy terminal. The roof evolves into floors and columns made up of multiple components which can be reconfigured to allow flexible use and easy future repair.

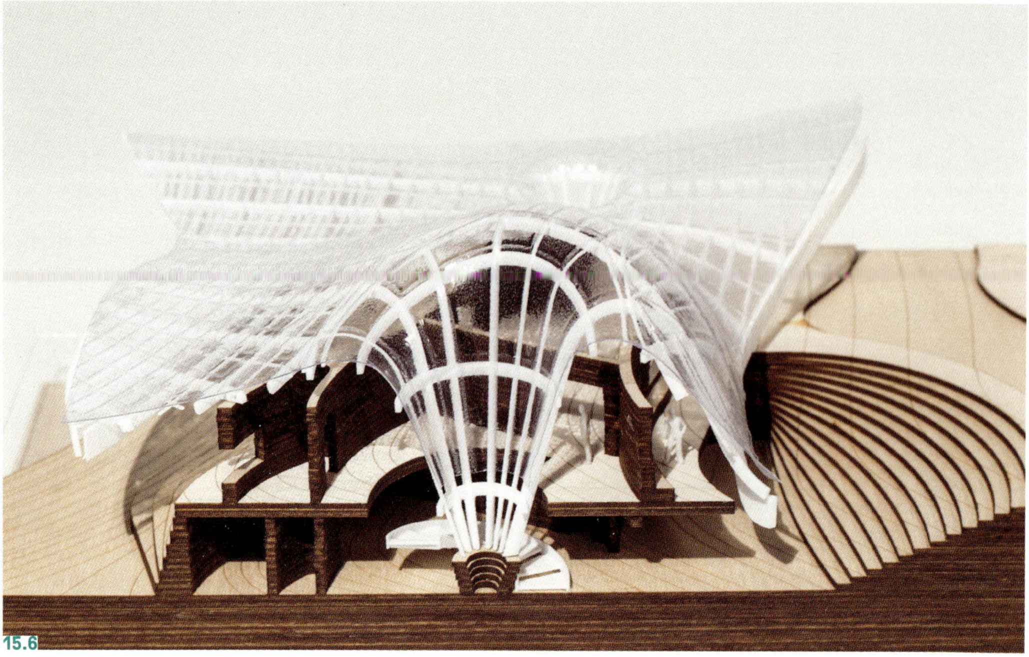

15.6

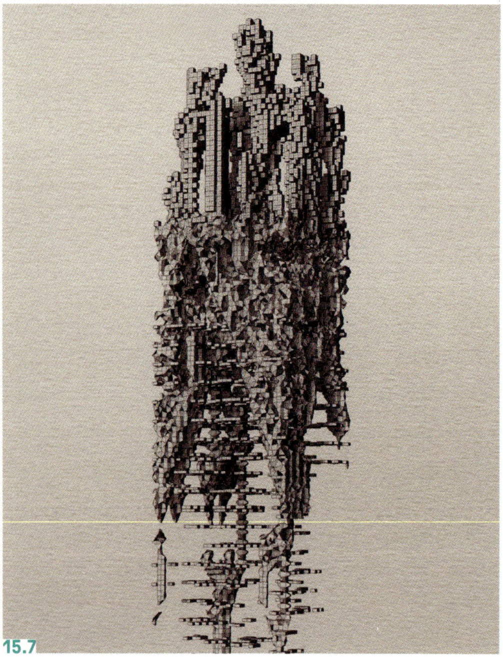

15.7

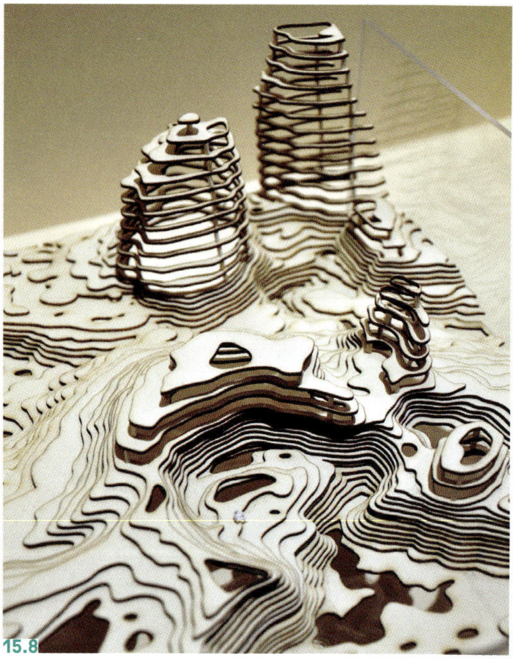

15.8

Fig. 15.6 Bethany Penman Y4, 'The Kinaesthetic Marina – Guanabara Cable Park and Watersports Centre'. Situated along the coast of Rio de Janeiro, in an area currently closed off to the public, the project provides direct access to the water through a national competition swimming pool, training pool, children's water-play area, kayaking training pool and a national-level 600m wakeboarding cable park. The structure consists of a sweeping canopy, formed using computational tools, that aims to temper the environment for the spectators below. The canopy penetrates the lower ground floor changing rooms, allowing natural light to flood these semi-basement areas. The building opens up the coast, addresses pressing environmental concerns and provides Rio with its first cable wakeboarding and water-skiing facility. **Fig. 15.7 Yue Ma** Y4, 'The Diminishing Pavilion'. Early studies in crystallisation led to an interest in the distinctive morphology of particle aggregation at different material states, later applied on an architectural scale. The vertical cachaca distillery showroom in Rio de Janeiro consists of porous brick walls designed to provide views in and out, and also to condition the building. **Fig. 15.8 Qiuling Guan** Y4, 'Rio Samba Club'. The project is inspired by explorations in fluids material behaviour which are later translated digitally through simulations and physical models. The proposal features a continuous layered landscape which grows vertically to form the building façade louvres, stairs and balconies. The Samba Club provides an open space for dancing, and living space for the artists, whilst also creating a new public plaza.

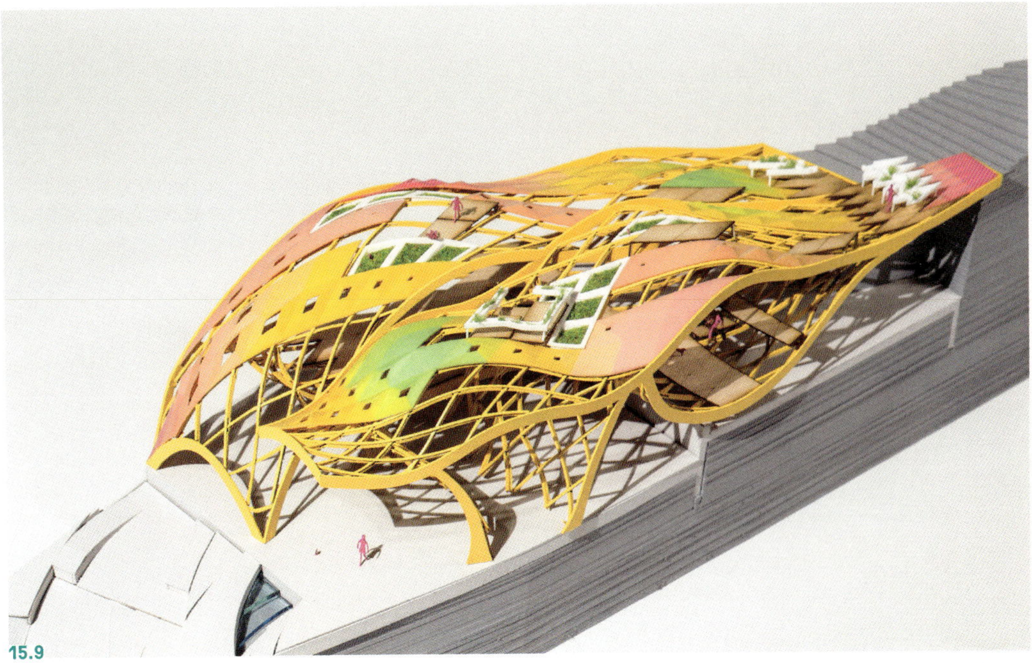

15.9

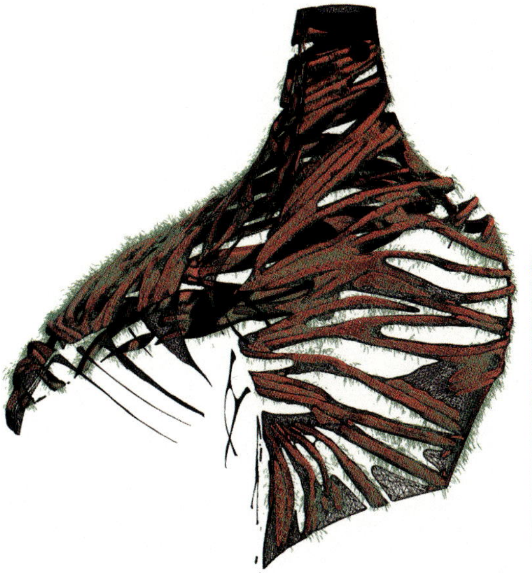

15.10

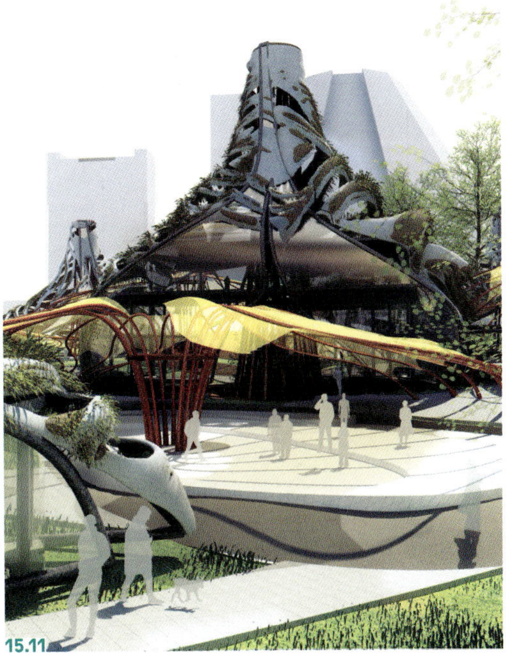

15.11

Fig. 15.9 Helen Siu Y4, 'Inhabited Roof: Community Market & Feijoada House'. Located between Rio's regeneration harbour area and an old favela, the project provides a much-needed communal space to bridge the two polarised communities. Inspired by initial studies on knitted patterns and structures, timber strips interweave to form a delicate roof structure which connects to the landscape. The roof structure forms suspended markets hovering above the hill. Individual roof cells respond to different programmatic requirements and environmental conditions and accommodate skylights for natural lighting, grass pods for passive cooling, and hydroponic vessels for Feijoada ingredients.

Figs. 15.10 – 15.11 Yulia Gilbert Y5, 'Rio De Janeiro Civic Hall'. The new civic hall provides a meeting point for a representative from each of the 150 neighbourhoods in the city. The project establishes an inhabited landscape where the public and the city's administrators can meet and exchange views in a secure debating environment in order to solve problems and build relationships. The building consists of self-contained internal spaces for meetings and debates and informal external courtyards and landscaped areas that connect to the existing cathedral nearby. Initial research into sculpted concrete skin led to articulation of the building façades allowing for vegetation to occur over time, providing shading and cooling.

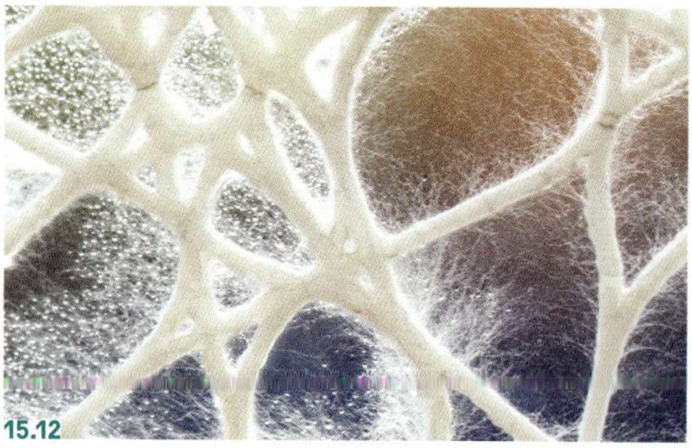

15.12

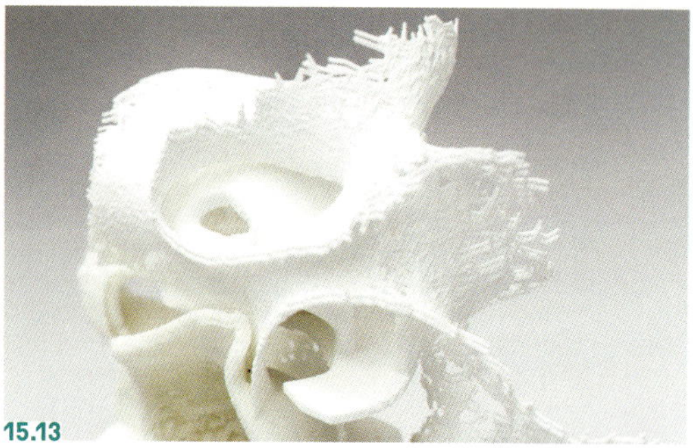

15.13

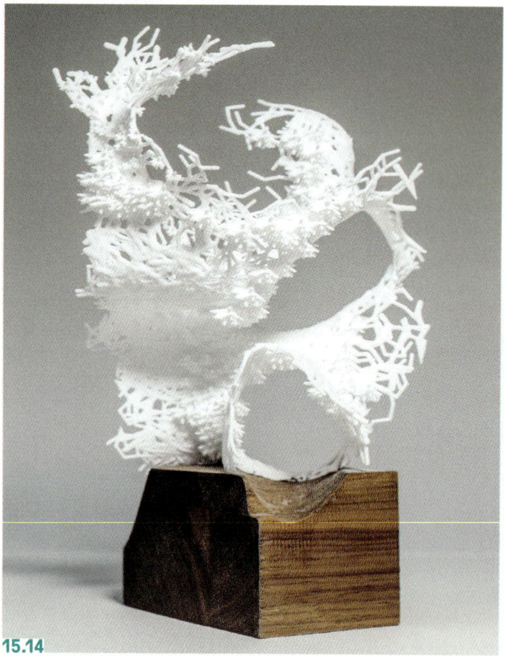

15.14

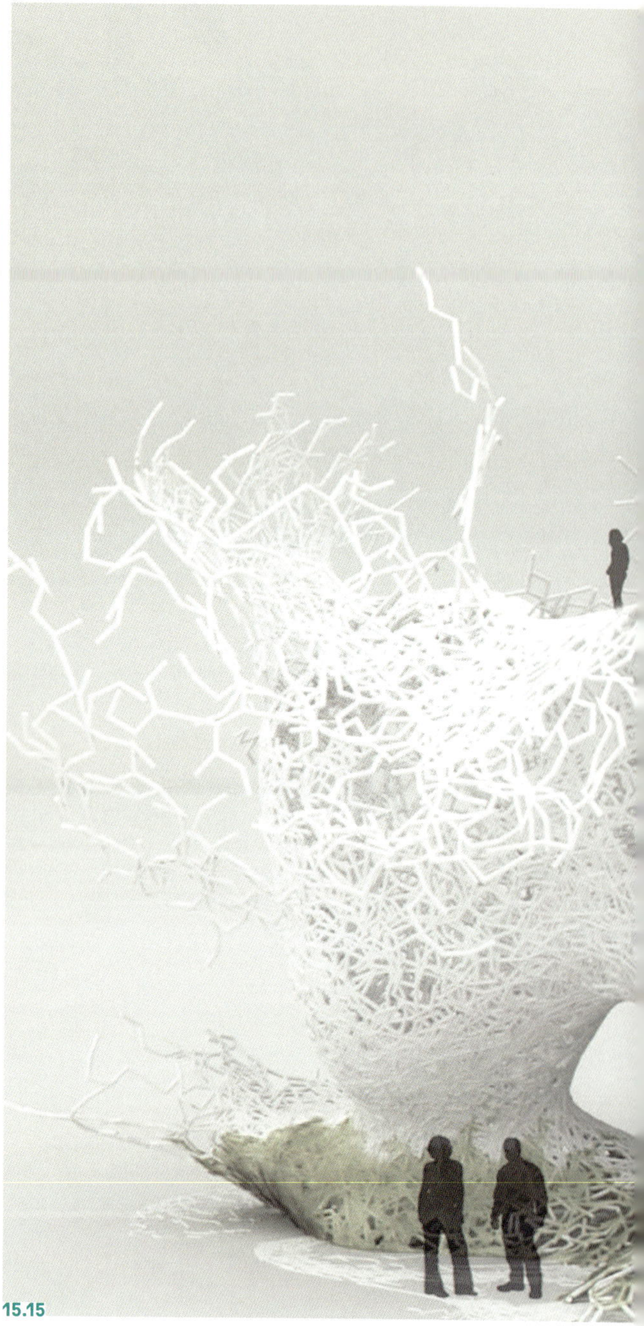

15.15

Figs. 15.12 – 15.15 **Ruxandra Maria Gruioniu** Y5, 'Growing Entangled Morphologies: Mycelium Therapeutic Hub', Rio de Janeiro, Brazil. The project proposes a new typology for an architectural social hub that is able to metabolise similar to living organisms, being inclusive of notions of shape changing, self-organisation, adaptation and resilience. The design comes as a powerful statement of the 'wellness' benefits resulting from employing living systems within the creation of architectural space. It emphasises that a 'living building' does not only benefit us from a technical point of view but also as a medium for enhancing the 'wellness' of our lifestyle through the employment of natural, living beauty. Initial landscape interventions are developed as a flexible public space, which in time is populated with complex scaffolds designed to trigger mycelium growth. The scaffolds are programmed to present a different array of density gradients and materiality for controlling and guiding the desired growth and its life-cycle alternation. The result is a dynamic building system that evolves and performs in accordance with environmental conditions such as light and humidity as well as human inhabitation.

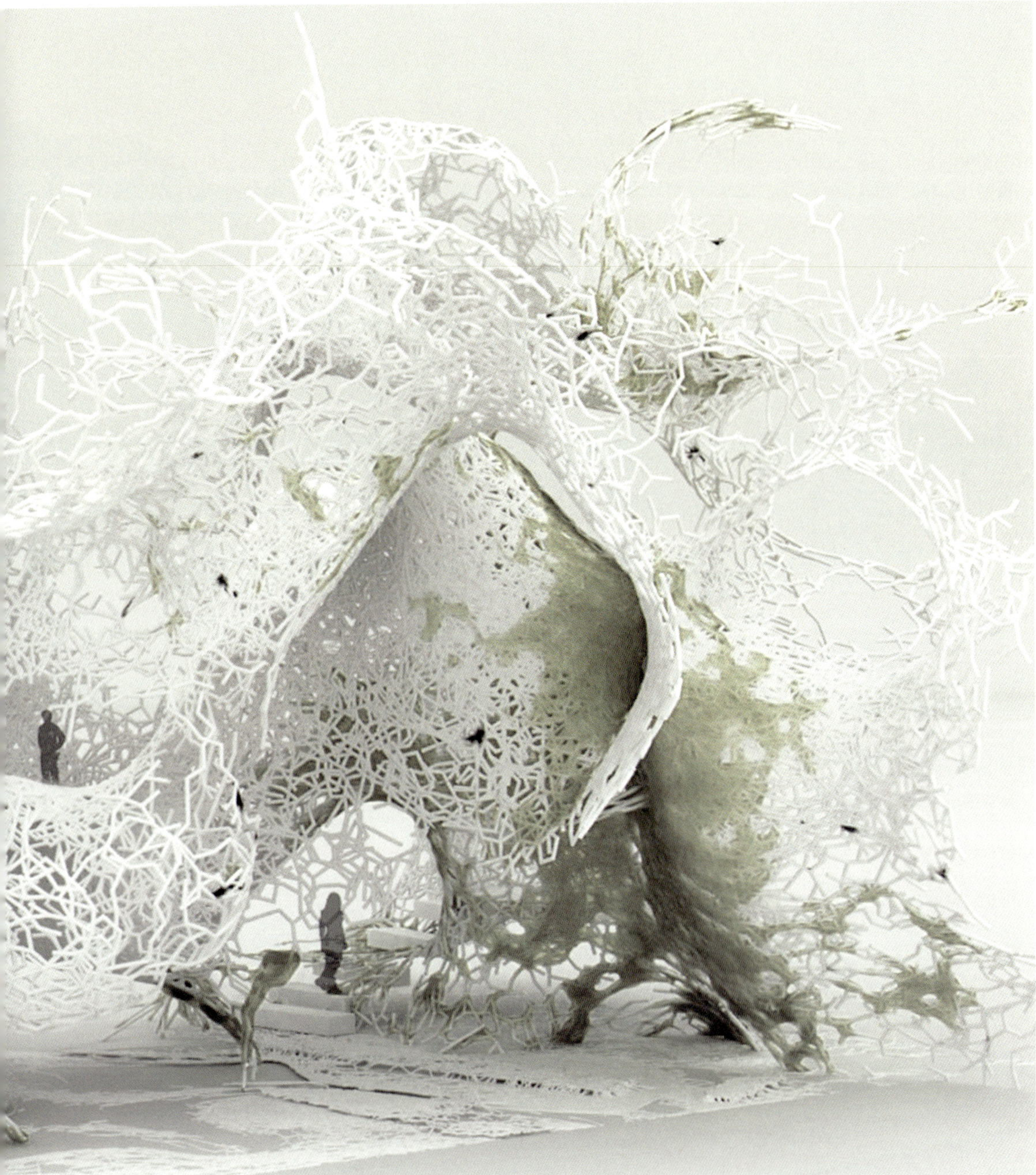

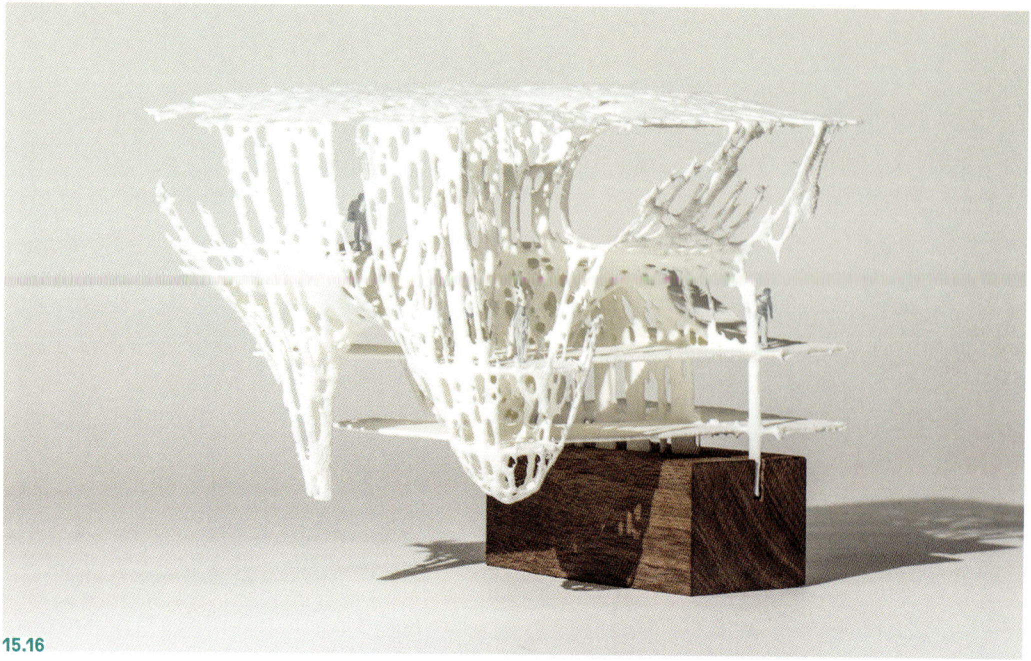

15.16

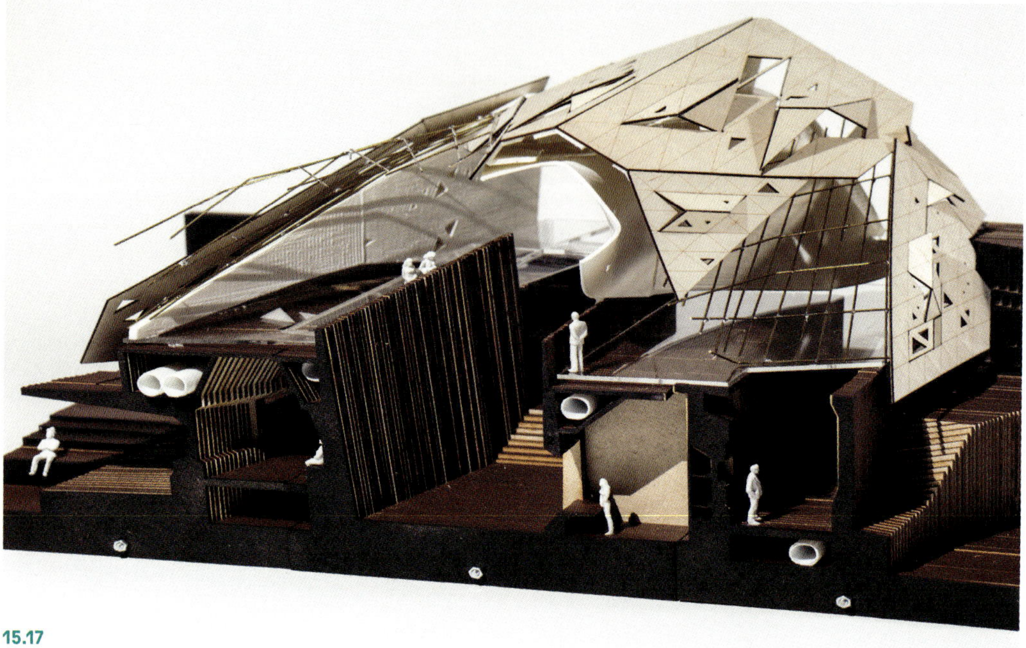

15.17

Fig. 15.16 Dionysis Toumazis Y4, 'Spatial Strands: Centro de Capoeira'. Located in the industrial part of Rio de Janeiro between the oldest port of Rio and the oldest favela, the Centro de Capoeira hosts capoeira and music classes, the biggest Afro-Latino exhibition space in Rio and a new public plaza in the area. The building's design is inspired by an initial material experiment which was later digitally simulated. The combination of structural, environmental and programme solutions creates unique spatial and lighting qualities.
Fig. 15.17 Juwhan Han Y4, 'Pochèism Re-defined: Cartographical Artists Hub', Rio de Janeiro, Brazil. The project is inspired by early wax and water entanglement studies where a series of poche spaces were discovered. By carving and subtracting from the existing site topography, hidden spaces are revealed and used as seating and exhibition areas in the museum while the roof in contrast is extremely lightweight and porous. **Fig. 15.18 Thomas Bush** Y4, 'The Performing Station – Samba Theatre and Cable Car Station'. The project builds upon a widely used transport strategy in Rio de Janeiro – the cable car. The building negotiates the extreme topography whilst signifying the cultural significance of samba and the carnival to the city and the favelas. The cable car station connects two large cultural institutions: the Samba School and the Samba Drome, whilst also passing through the heart the Morro Da Providencia (Rio's oldest favela). The open air theatre is a dynamic element that performs alongside the station and the samba dancers, changing the spatial and shading conditions throughout the day.

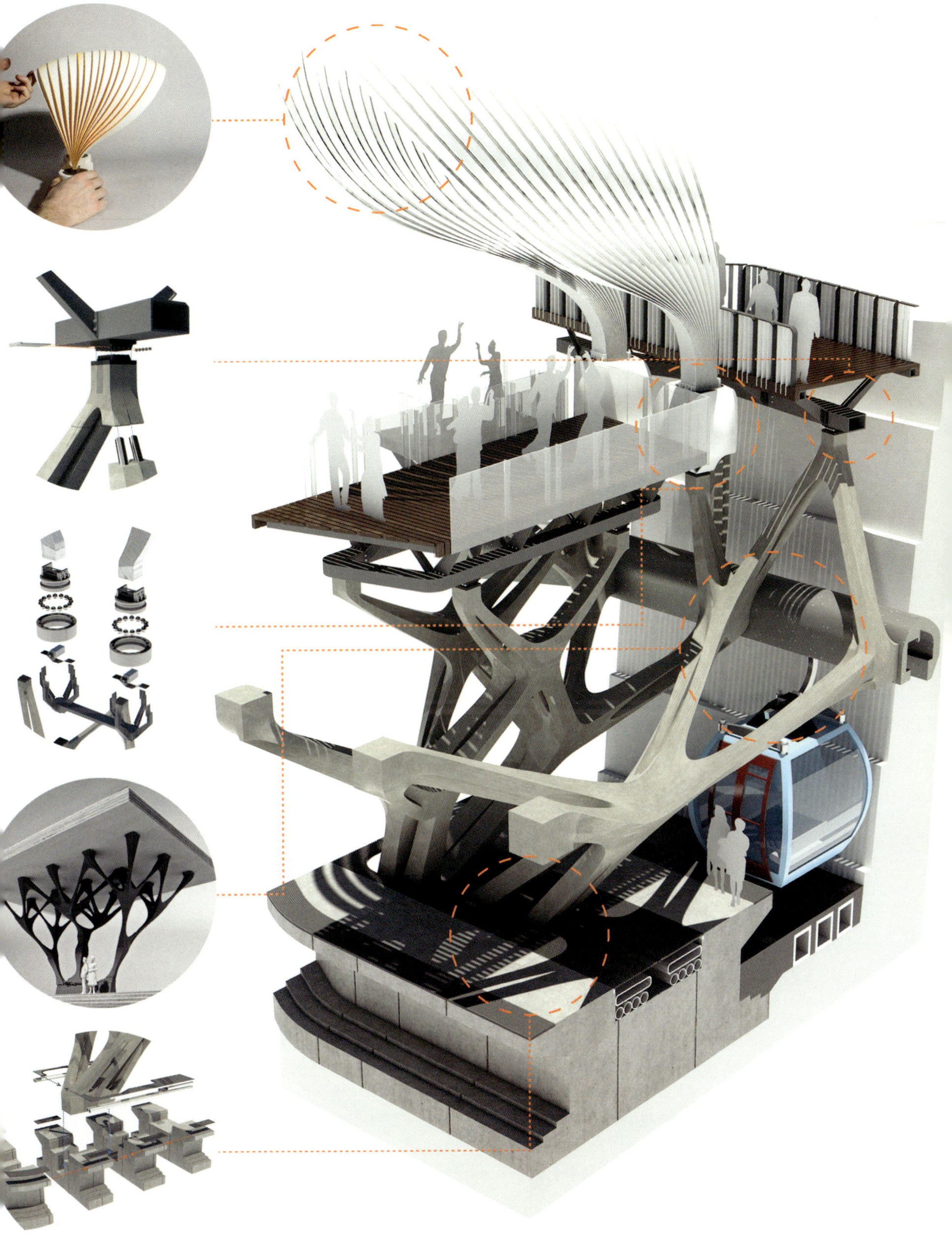

15.18

Unit 16

Supernatural

Johan Berglund, Dirk Krolikowski, Josep Miàs

Year 4
Supichaya Chaisiriroj, Eleanor Figuiredo, Joshua Honeysett, Amani Radeef, Cassidy Reid, Simran Sidhu, Alexia Souvaliotis, Ozan Tokzas Blauel, Yin To Tsang, Anthony Williams

Year 5
Robin Ashurst, Richard Breen, Ashley Fridd, Chelsea Hodkinson, Elzbieta Kaleta, Janice Lau, Katherine Prudence, Louise Schmidt, Amy Wong

Many thanks to Mario Pirwitz, Falko Schmitt, Will Jefferies, Jan Guell, Francis Roper, Tosan Popo, Marc Subirana, Carles Sala, Tupac Martir, Chiara Montgomerie, Xavier Ferres, Damjan Iliev, Julia Backhaus

In Unit 16, we have developed a close symbiosis between academic research and architectural practice. Our way of working is close to how projects are developed in our practices, with constant testing and "reflecting through action" in order to challenge the limits of architecture. Our work is centered around the production of buildings, landscapes and spaces, with a clear understanding of and interest in their relationships with the city. We see architecture as an act of realisation; of making real that which was only previously a brief thought, a vague concept or a utopian dream. Through this act we have the power to transform the world around us, and with that, the responsibility to make sure we leave something positive behind. This year, the unit went to Panama City, a complex city in rapid transformation. Our proposals are situated in and around the city and the Panama Canal Zone.

——In Panama, nature is always present. The cities and man-made environments constantly battle the invasive force of nature. Over millennia, man has sought to tame nature, harness and control it. This has caused a long-standing conflict between the natural and the urban, where the search for everything bigger, faster and better has led to the precarious situation we find ourselves in today.

——Panama epitomises this extremely fragile equilibrium between nature and architecture; one which can unravel in specific geographic scenarios. The two forces, one ancient and unexpected and the other based in knowledge and strategy, set up a dialogue from two radical positions. As a result, life in Panama is expressed in extreme form, where the physical world emerges as a stage for confrontation. The power of nature imposes rhythms and effects on our environment, while architecture too often reacts in a violent way. Panama today is a clear example of this: a place defined by beautiful woods, rainforests and the ocean, in amidst commercial skyscrapers that jut out from the earth's surface and the (in)famous canal, which appears as a scar on the skin of the planet.

——At the same time, man's search for development and evolution has given rise to incredible inventions, events and places. The unit strongly believes in progress and a constant search for the new and unseen. We therefore set out to find a balance between both forces, a middle way that allows for the possibility of a compatible, complementary co-existence between both realities.

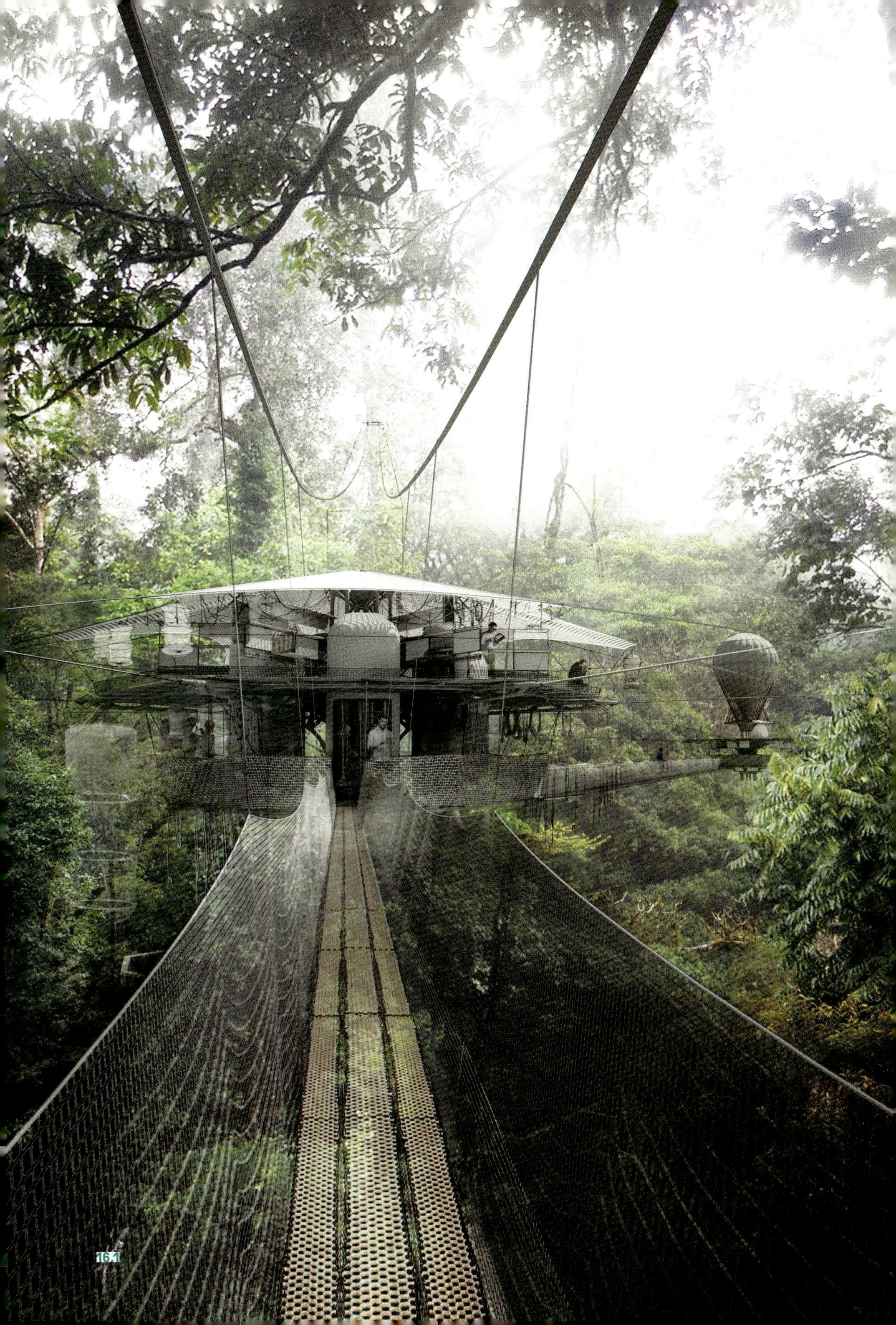
16.1

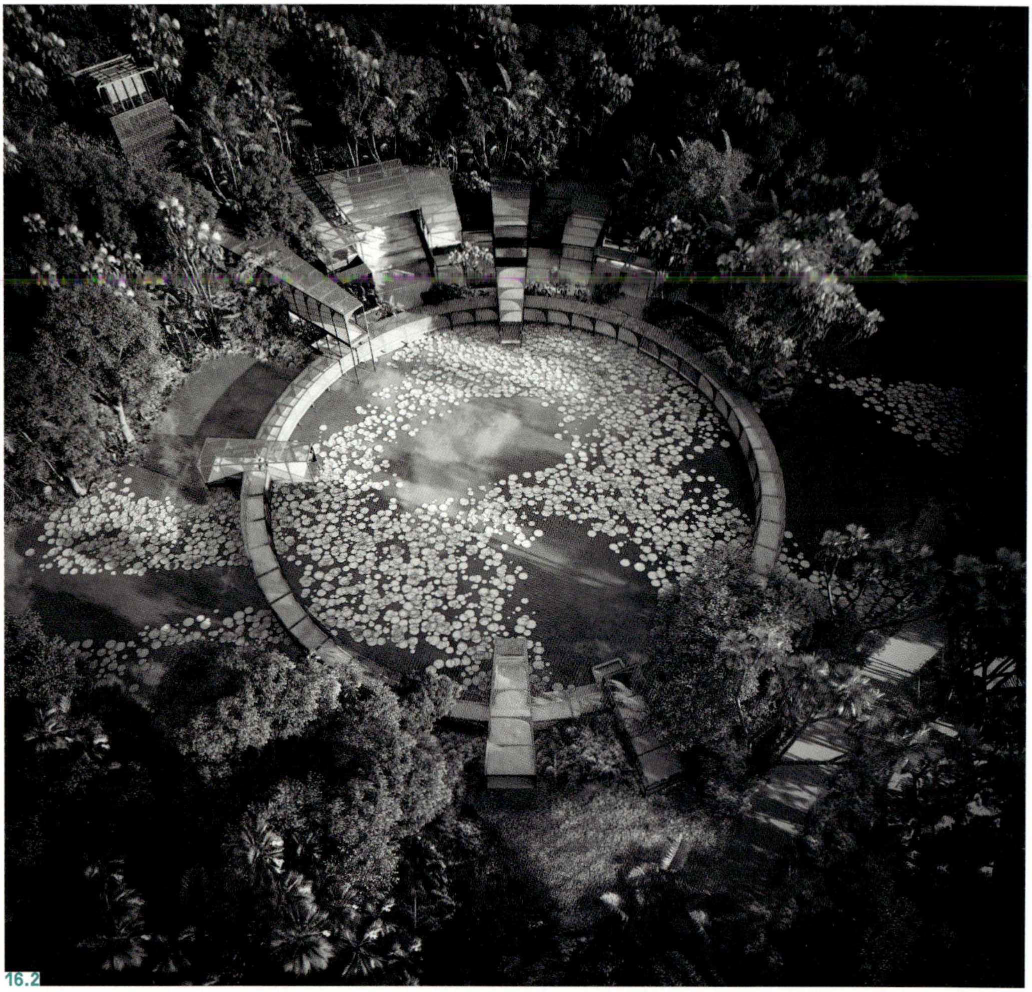

16.2

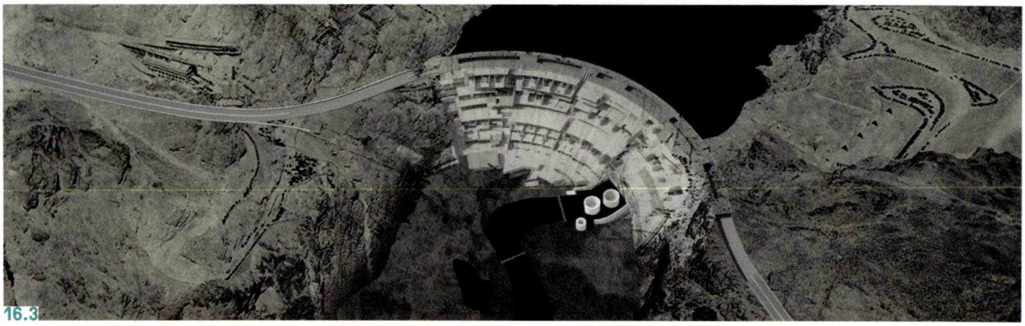

16.3

Fig. 16.1 Ashley Fridd Y5, 'The Last Biotic Frontier - Exploration Vessels for the Rainforest Canopy'. Walkway Approach to Vessel Type A, providing canopy-level research facilities for the Smithsonian Foundation. **Fig. 16.2 Louise Schmidt** Y5, 'Frame of Mind', overview of Educational Visitors' Centre. **Fig. 16.3 Chelsea Hodkinson** Y5, 'Inhabited Community Dam', overview render. **Fig. 16.4 Joshua Honeysett** Y4, 'Ship Dis-assembly Facility'. Sectional isometric, cutting through the facility, housed in the locks at Miraflores. **Fig. 16.5 Ashley Fridd** Y5, 'The Last Biotic Frontier - Exploration Vessels for the Rainforest Canopy'. Collection of ultra-lightweight structural components for the research vessels.

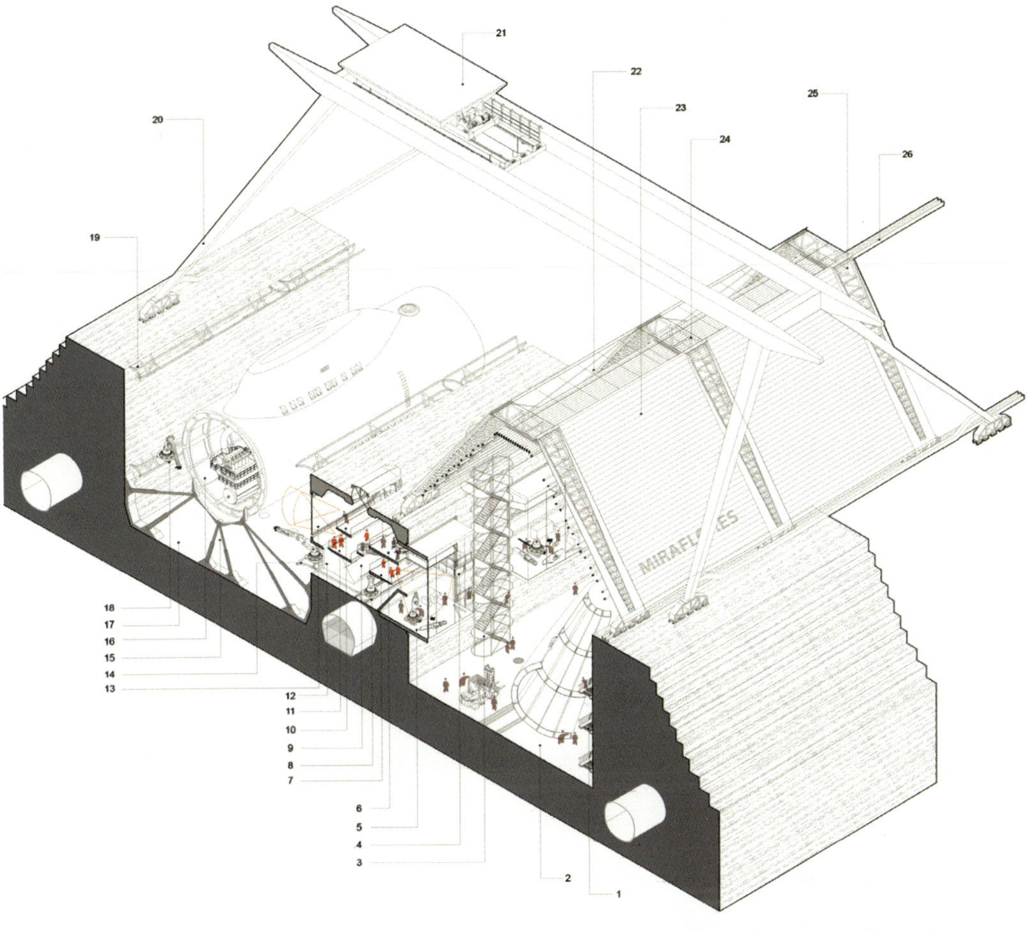

16.4

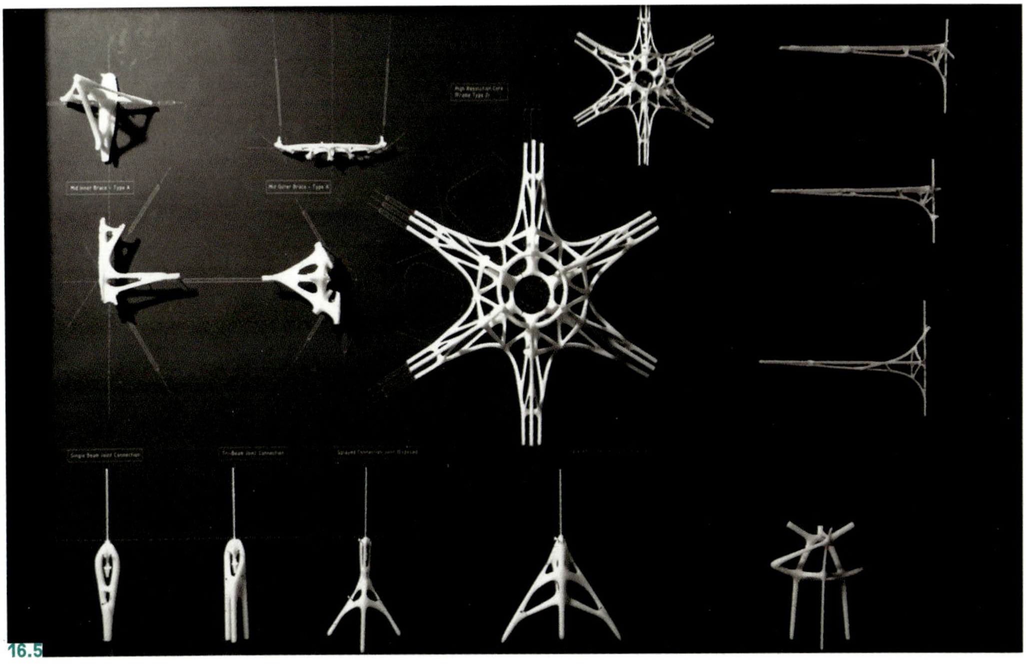

16.5

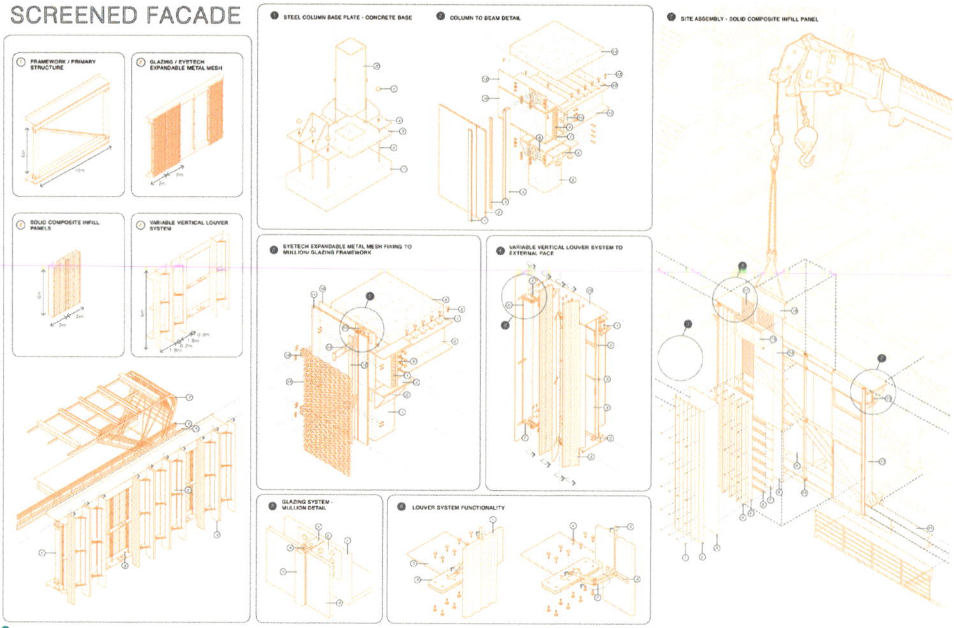

16.6

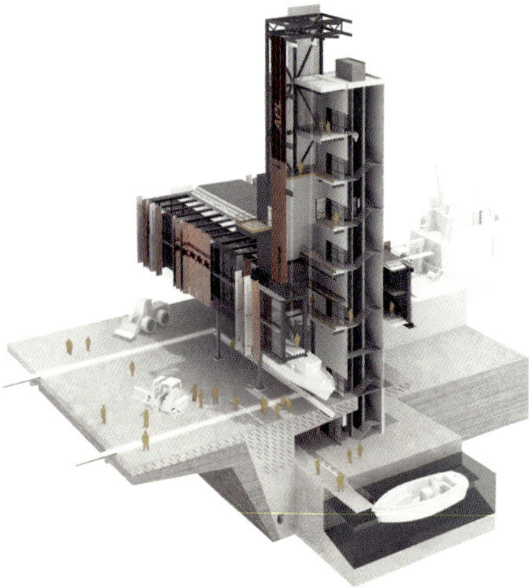

16.7

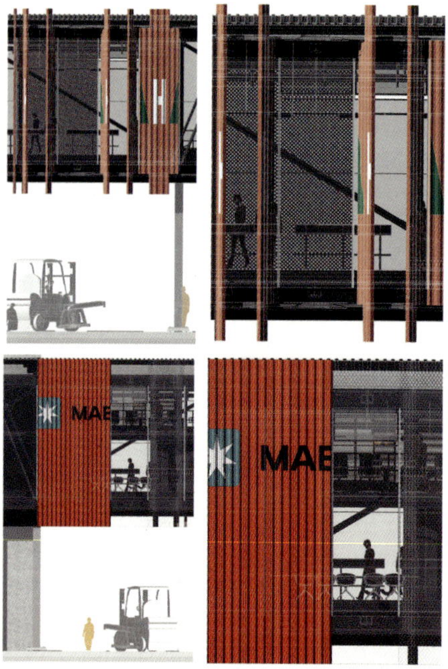

16.8

Figs. 16.6 – 16.8 Amani Radeef, Y4, 'Balboa Public Dry Docks'. Detailed façade connections study, sectional perspective through exhibition tower, façade study. **Fig. 16.9 Richard Breen** Y5, 'Biorock Growth Facility', Central Laboratory and Fabrication Shed.

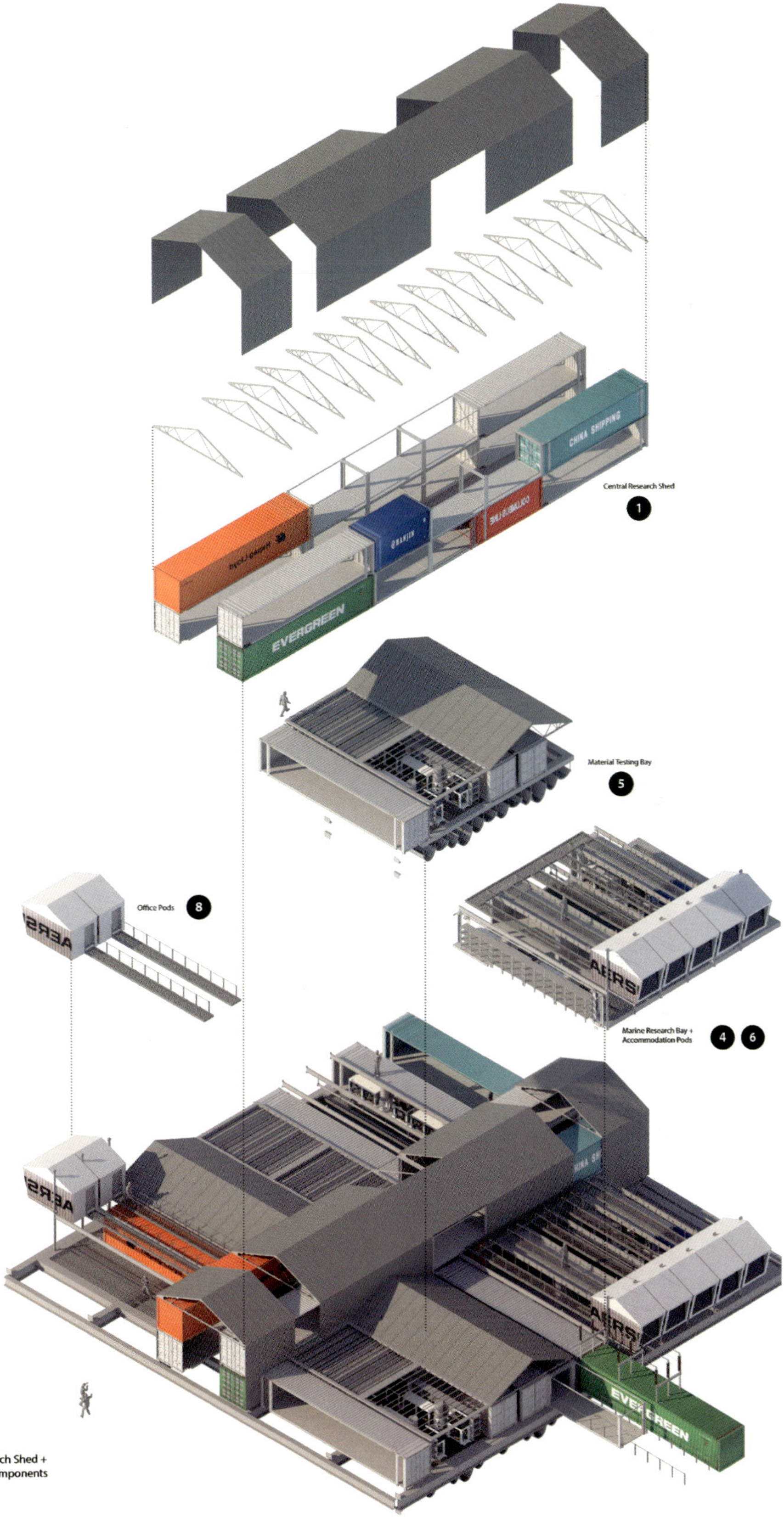

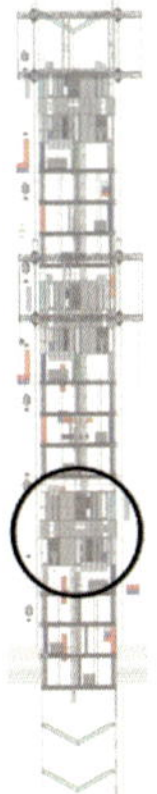

+ Central Research Shed + Associated Components

16.9

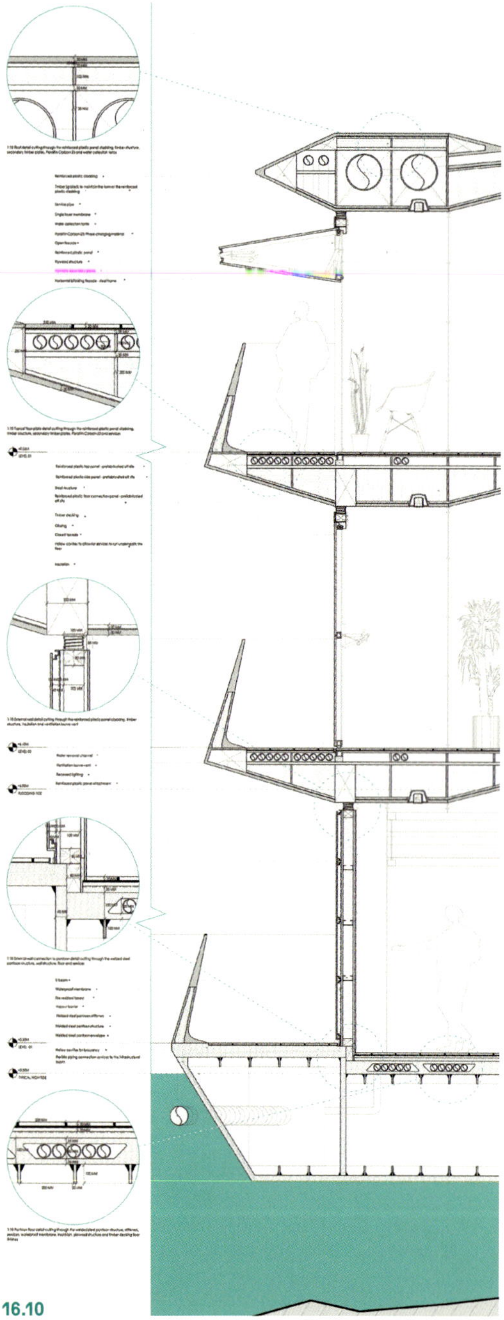

16.10

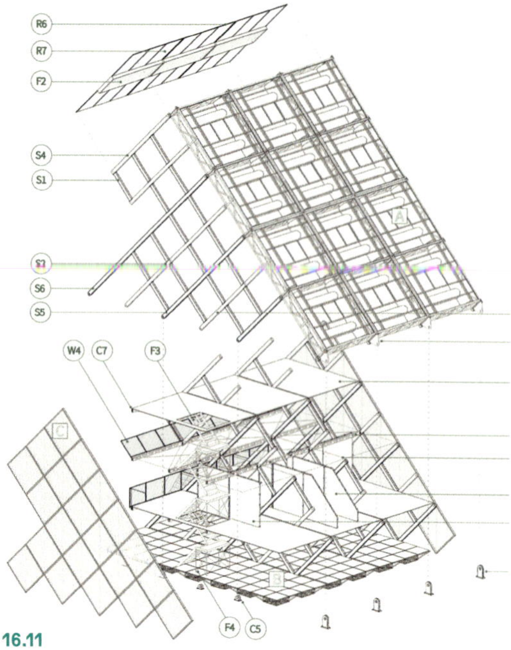

16.11

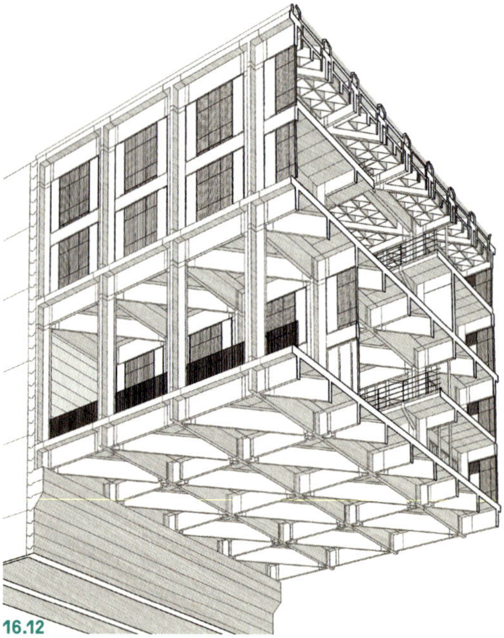

16.12

Fig. 16.10 Cassidy Reid Y4, 'Mixed Use Development'. Final 1:20 Section through floating residential element. **Fig. 16.11 Supichaya Chaisiriroj** Y4, 'Chagres Basecamp'. Detailed structural elements. **Fig. 16.12 Anthony Williams** Y4, 'Naval Architecture School Panama'. Detailed isometric view.

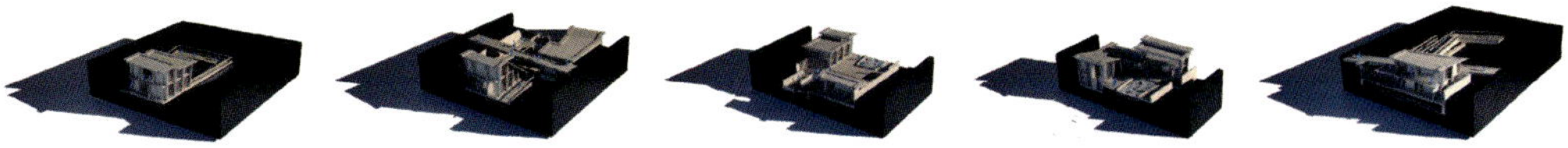

16.13

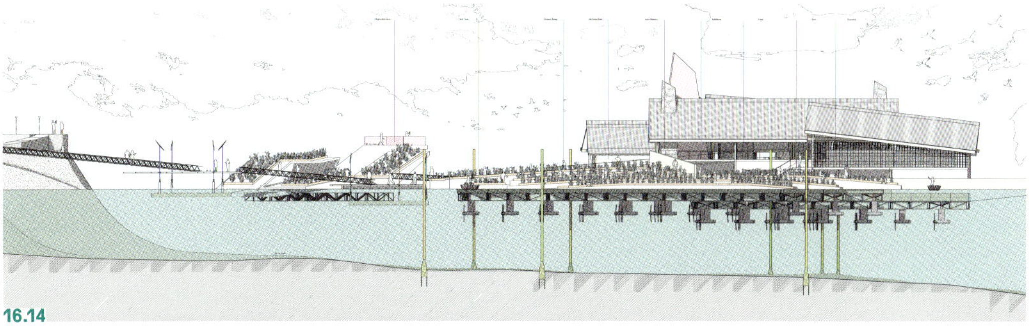

16.14

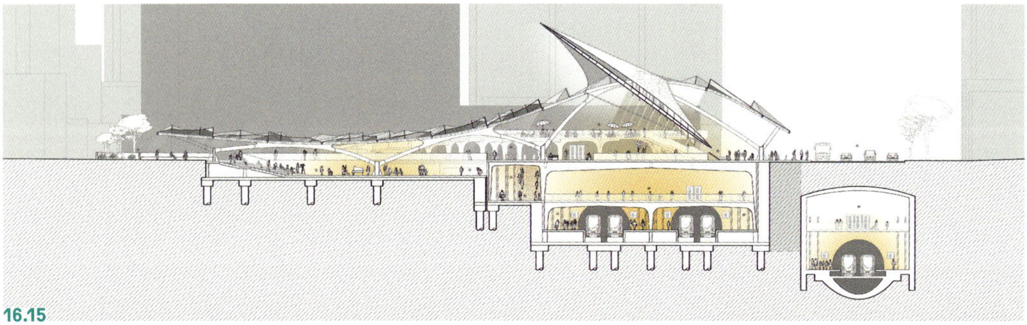

16.15

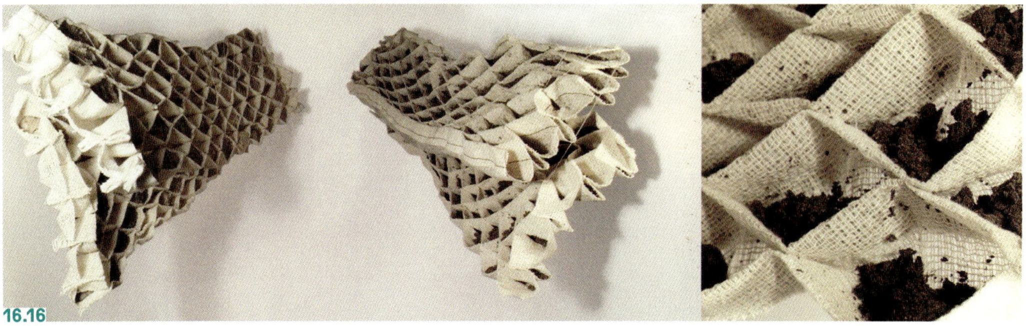

16.16

Fig. 16.13 Eleanor Figueiredo Y4, 'Hydro-Remediation Platform'. Final Models. **Fig. 16.14 Yin To Tsang** Y4, 'Floating Pharmaceutical Centre and Gardens'. Elevation. **Fig. 16.15 Elsbieta Kaleta** Y5, 'tropoFABric ARCHITECTURE – Iglesia del Carmen Train Station & Public Square, Panama City'. Short section. **Fig. 16.16 Ozan Toksoz Blauel** Y4, 'Museum of Excavated Earth'. Geocell retention installation.

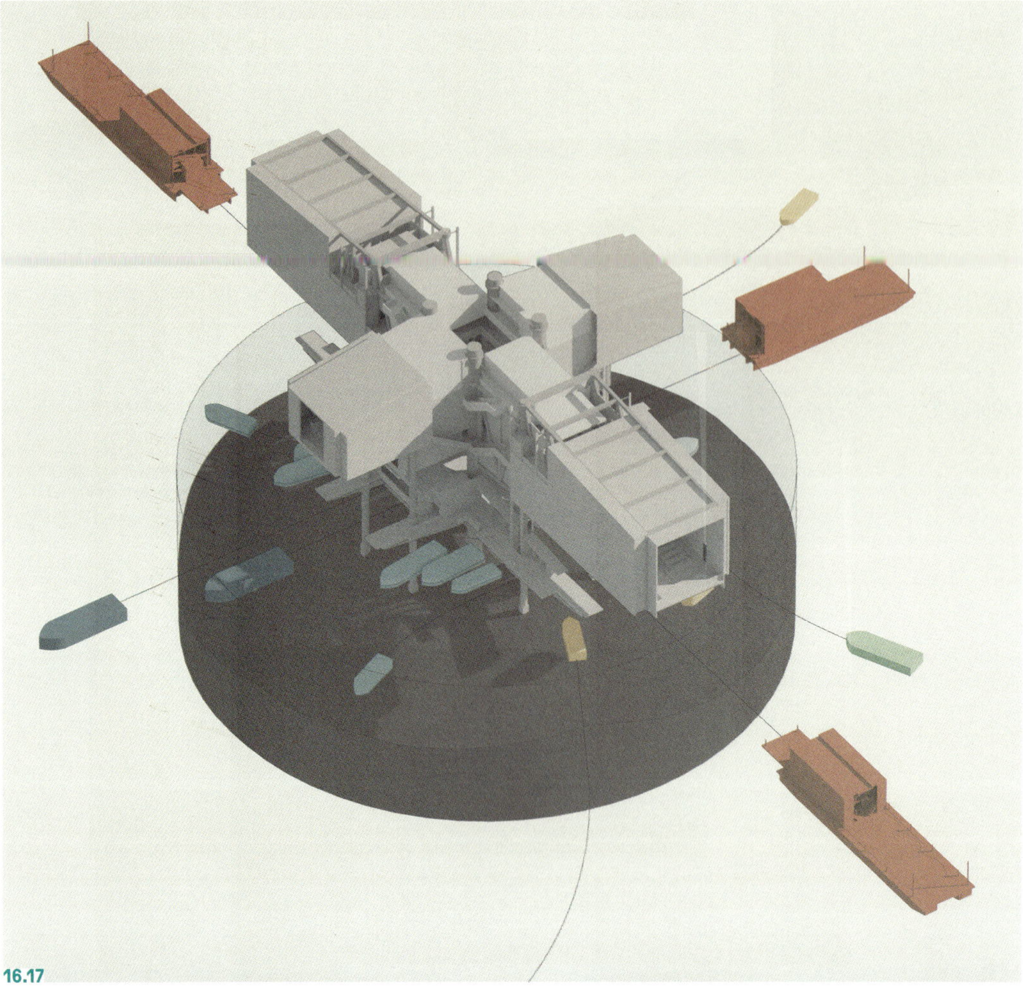

16.17

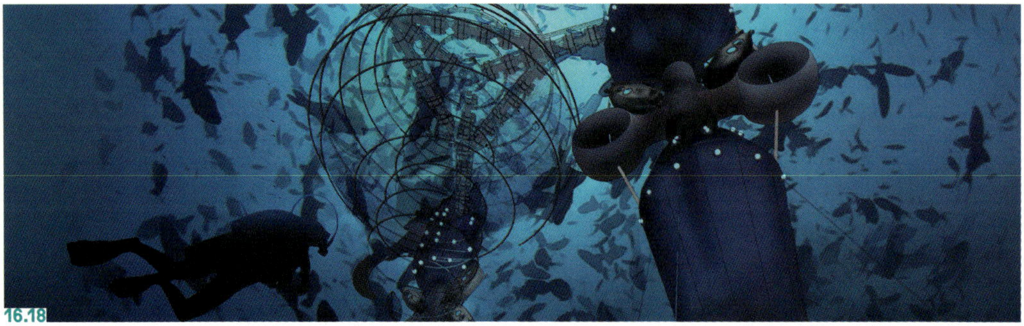

16.18

Fig. 16.17 Robin Ashurst Y5, 'Gatun Lake Community Lighthouse'. Static and floating elements. **Fig. 16.18 Simran Sidhu** Y4, 'Submerged Smithsonian'. Perspective collage view. A diver's view of looking up towards the surface of the sea and the submerged marine research facility in Panama Bay, a facility adopting weighting and buoyancy strategies to inhabit the underwater environment.

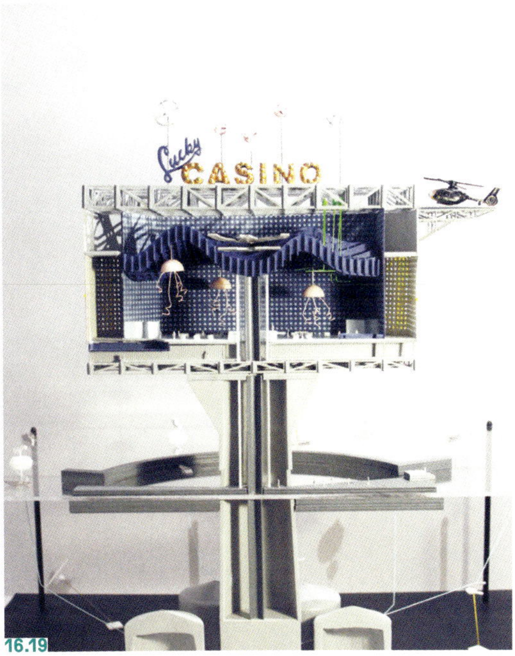

16.19

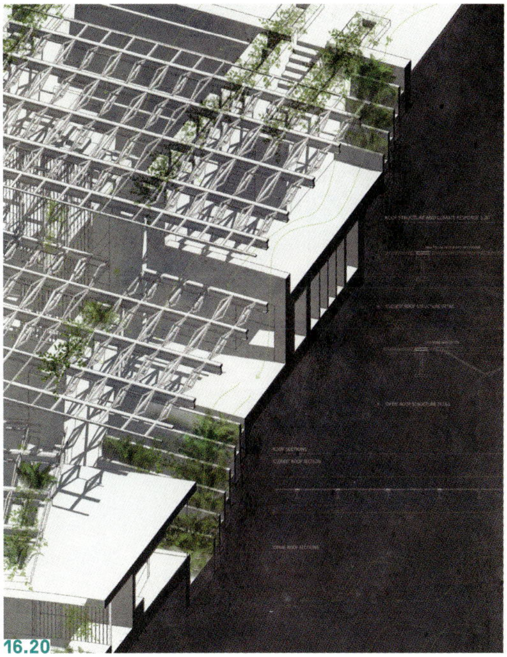

16.20

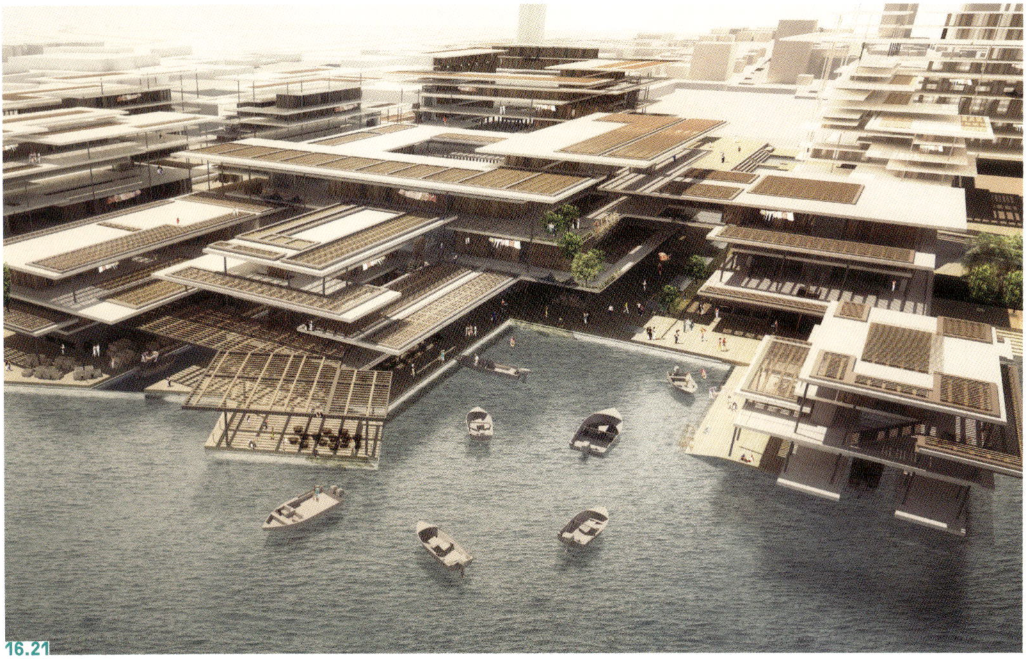

16.21

Fig. 16.19 **Alexia Souvaliotis** Y4, 'Off-Shore Casino'. Sectional model. **Fig. 16.20** **Katherine Prudence** Y5, 'Botanical Gardens of Cerro Ancon'. Responsive roof strategy and sectional diagram. **Fig. 16.21** **Janice Lau** Y5, 'Regenerating Boca La Caja'. Overview render of the fisherman's wharf.

Unit 17

Taking Time

Níall McLaughlin, Michiko Sumi

Year 4
Malina Dabrowska, Ashley Hinchcliffe, Carl Inder, Vasilis Marcou Ilchuk, Oscar Plastow, Henry Svendsen, Christie Yeung

Year 5
Paloma Rua-Figueroa, Cherry Beaumont, Lok Kan Chau, Joanne Chen, Tahmineh Hooshyar Emami, Minghui Ke, Tony Lees, Agata Murasko, Charlie Page, Shirley Tsang, Chenhan Wang

For making our year so stimulating, special thanks to:

Fieldtrip: Kaji-Kinran textile; Mie Prefectural Government; Jetro; Ise Shrine; Takenaka Corporation; Osaka Institute of Technology; Naohisa Kama, Hiroki Kuratani and Shuzo Sumi for generous support.

Critics: Julia Backhaus, Hannah Corlett, Murray Fraser, Jonathan Hill, Takehiko Iseki, Rick Joy, David Kohn, Yeoryia Manolopolou, Jack Newton, James O'Leary, Sheila O'Donnell, Frosso Pimenides, Bob Sheil, Peter Stutchbury, Simon Tonks, Mike Tonkin and John Tuomey

Design Realisation tutors: James Daykin and Lee Halligain with Structural Engineer Tim Lucas from Price & Myers

Year 4 project: Peter Scully, Nick Westby and William Victor Camilleri from B-made, and Bill Hodgson

Sponsorship: Bartlett School, Autumn Down, Bespoke Homes, Insley & Nash, Joseph Waller Fabrication, Pennine Stone and Sasakawa Foundation

Thirteen hundred years ago, two buildings appeared at the opposite ends of the great Eurasian landmass. One is MacDara Chapel on an island in Galway in the west of Ireland, and the other is Ise Shrine in a forest in Japan. Two buildings conceived in entirely disconnected cultures, they show remarkable similarities. The forms and meanings endure as the buildings decay and are rebuilt. Time itself is a significant aspect of their architecture. Both are versions of previous buildings that existed on the site and borrow forms from their now-lost ancestors. But, the buildings also differ significantly from each other: the Christian chapel is built to endure for millennia on its blasted site. Once a timber structure, it is now rebuilt in stone to last until the end of time. The Shinto Shrine achieves permanence by being rebuilt in perfect replica on an adjacent empty lot, taken apart every twenty years.

——This year, Unit 17 took the theme of time as its subject and explored it through Landscape, Construction and Dream. Making charged constructions in significant landscapes took us into the boundary between the knowable world and the world of the unsayable.

——On our field trip to Japan, we had a tour of the Ise Shrine by the architect in charge of its reconstruction, visited the Kaji-Kinran textile factory in Kyoto and the restoration site of Kofukuji Temple in Nara. We learned skills in joinery workshops from the best woodworkers. Some students made individual research field trips to the snow landscapes of Shirakawa Go, contemporary Naoshima Island and Tokyo.

——All students spent the first term designing a ghost building to stand beside the tiny stone chapel in Ireland. It was a freely imagined projection of its lost wooden ancestor. We selected and combined ideas to a singular form. Year 4 spent the rest of the year working solely towards the design and construction of the ghost building on the opposite shore of the MacDara Island. To execute this construction, the students not only developed their design skills but managed cost and programme, applied for planning, detailed, procured and built the project at the same time. The building will be celebrated on 16 July when many visit for the annual pilgrimage day of St. MacDara.

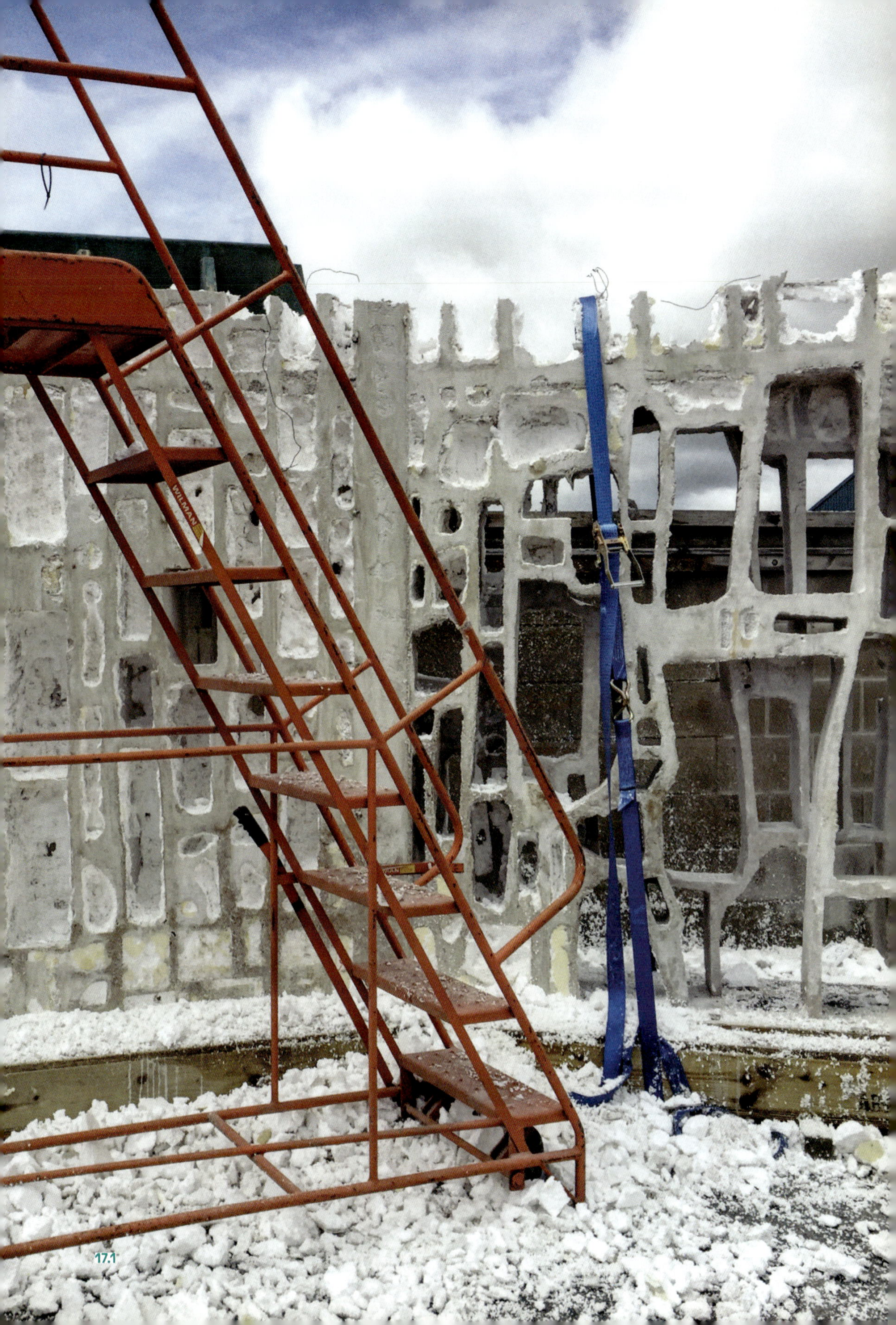

17.1

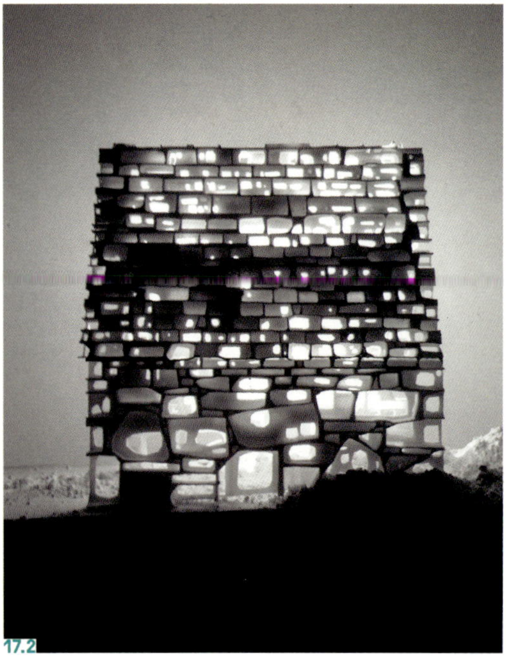
17.2

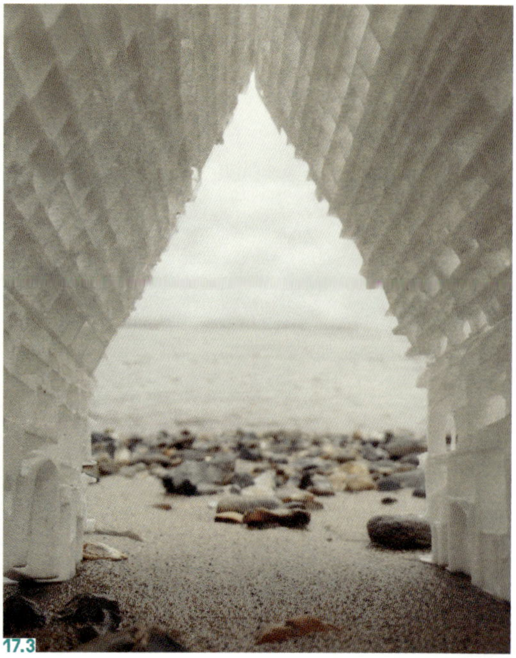
17.3

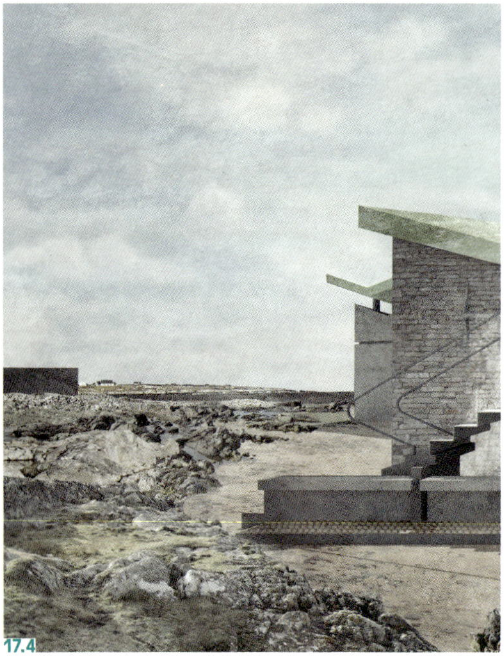
17.4

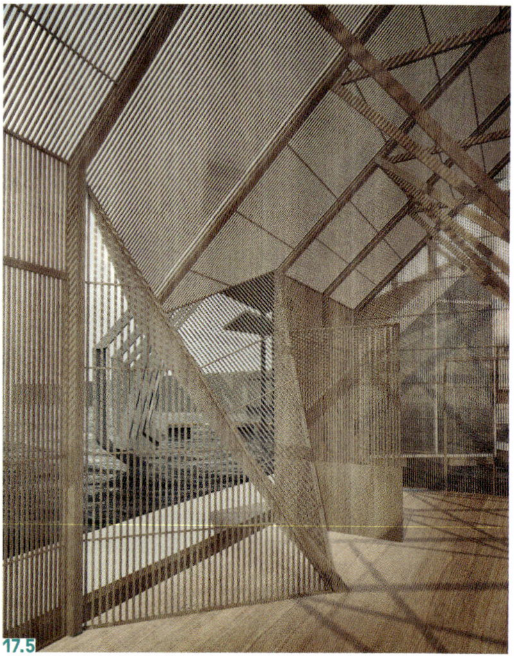
17.5

Fig. 17.1 Group Project, Y4, 'Ghost Chapel'. 1:1 GRC cast piece of external fabric. The concept originated from the natural phenomenon of magnetic forces created by the red granite on MacDara Island. The design reflects compression and attraction by eliminating the stones of the original chapel and constructing its negative. **Figs. 17.2 – 17.3 Cherry Beaumont** Y5, 'Structural Negative'. The Ghost Chapel is a structural negative of St. MacDara's chapel – solidifying the gaps of the drystone construction whilst letting light fill the space where the stones should be. The tides and cows interact with the building on a daily basis, slowly dissolving the saltlick construction, leaving behind a skeletal negative of the chapel on the Atlantic coast. **Figs. 17.4 – 17.5 Paloma Rua-Figueroa** Y5, 'The Harbour Carved into Stone: Algae and Fish Market'. A contemporary fishing harbour and market facility has been created to accommodate local fishermen and the harvest, processing and sale of their products. The architecture responds to the function of spaces, ranging from a heavy presence deeply embedded within the coastal rocks of Connemara, to light, deployable floating spaces. **Fig. 17.6 Joanne Chen** Y5, 'Reimagined Factory'. The project raises a critique on the contemporary view of work as compensatory toil rather than self-fulfillment and pleasure. The factory moves away from operations of conformity by manufacturing bespoke home furnishings and decorations in Hammersmith in an attempt to re-engage craftsmanship with contemporary technologies. Each production space is tailored to bespoke stages of the production process.

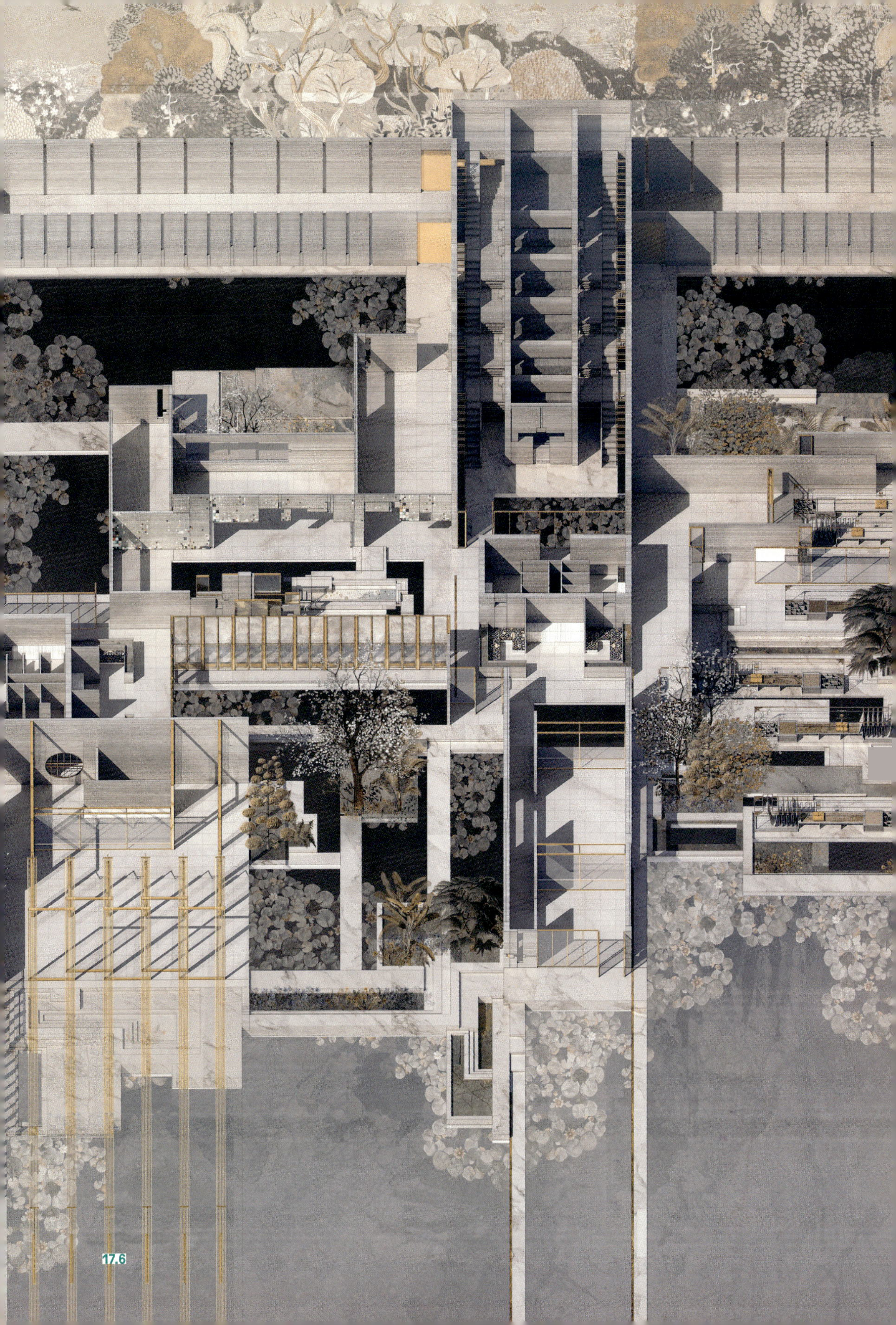

17.6

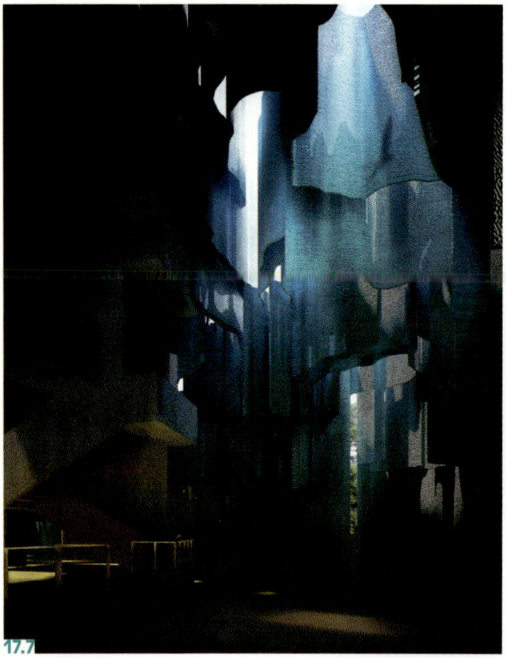
17.7

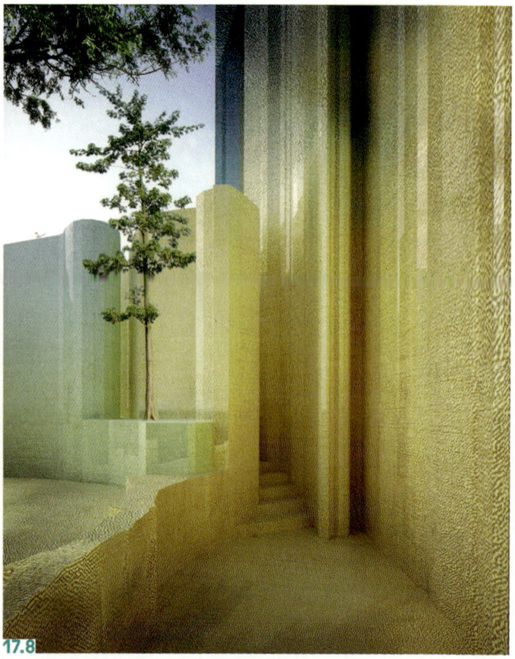
17.8

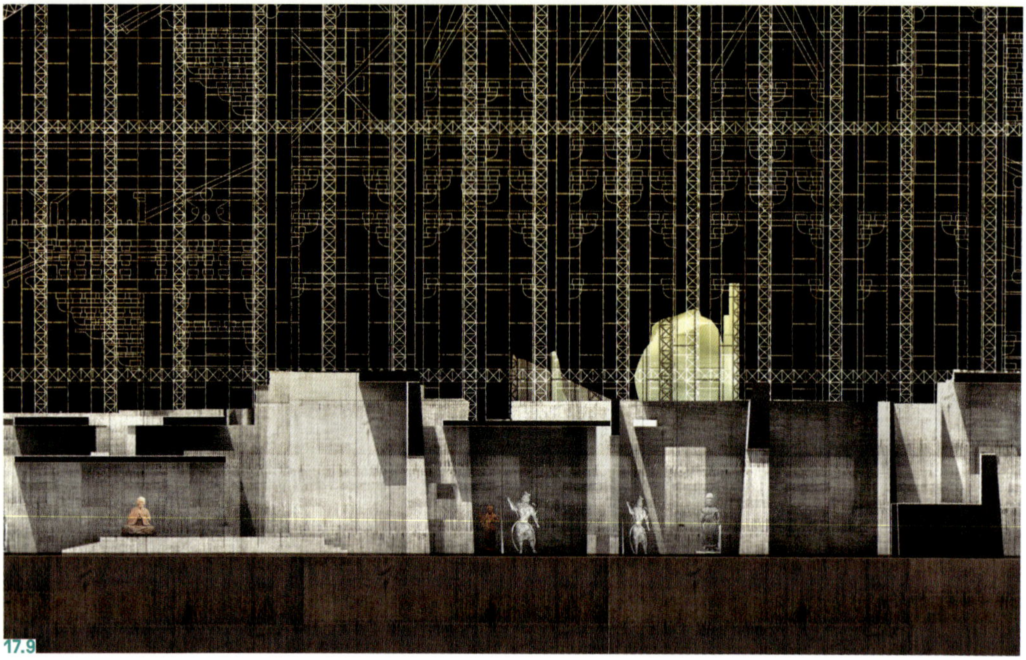
17.9

Figs. 17.7 – 17.8 Chenhan Wang Y5, 'Morecambe Bay Memorial Landscape'. This project explores the relationship between building and nature in the representation of landscape in Chinese paintings. The scheme combines a radio station with birdwatching facilities. The radio station broadcasts to migrants working in the bay in Chinese and is available across the UK, whilst providing a physical point of refuge. Within the gardens, there are several birdwatching hide-outs that allow visitors to view the migrant bird population of the bay. **Fig. 17.9 Charlotte Page** Y5, 'Between Impermanence'. Daibutsu-den in Nara, 751AD, has been reconstructed several times and is exemplary of Japanese heritage, reflecting the cultural and social processes of Japan. Everything is in a state of flux. The intervention is understood as an audience that frames moments in time during the temple's ruination, reconstruction and afterlife. The scenery shifts as the building weathers, the copper Kegon sect vestment allows for visitors, every 'occasion' of impermanence is perceived. **Fig. 17.10 Tahmineh Hooshyar Emami** Y5, 'The Jungle School for Displaced Alice'. The unlikely story of Alice being a refugee in Wonderland is transposed onto the site of the Jungle Refugee Camp in Calais in France as an attempt to create a site-specific typology of a formal/informal educational facility for unaccompanied minors. The school is a conglomeration of found materials and furniture, a collage world of accidentalism and fragmentation which create moments of peace amidst the surrounding chaos.

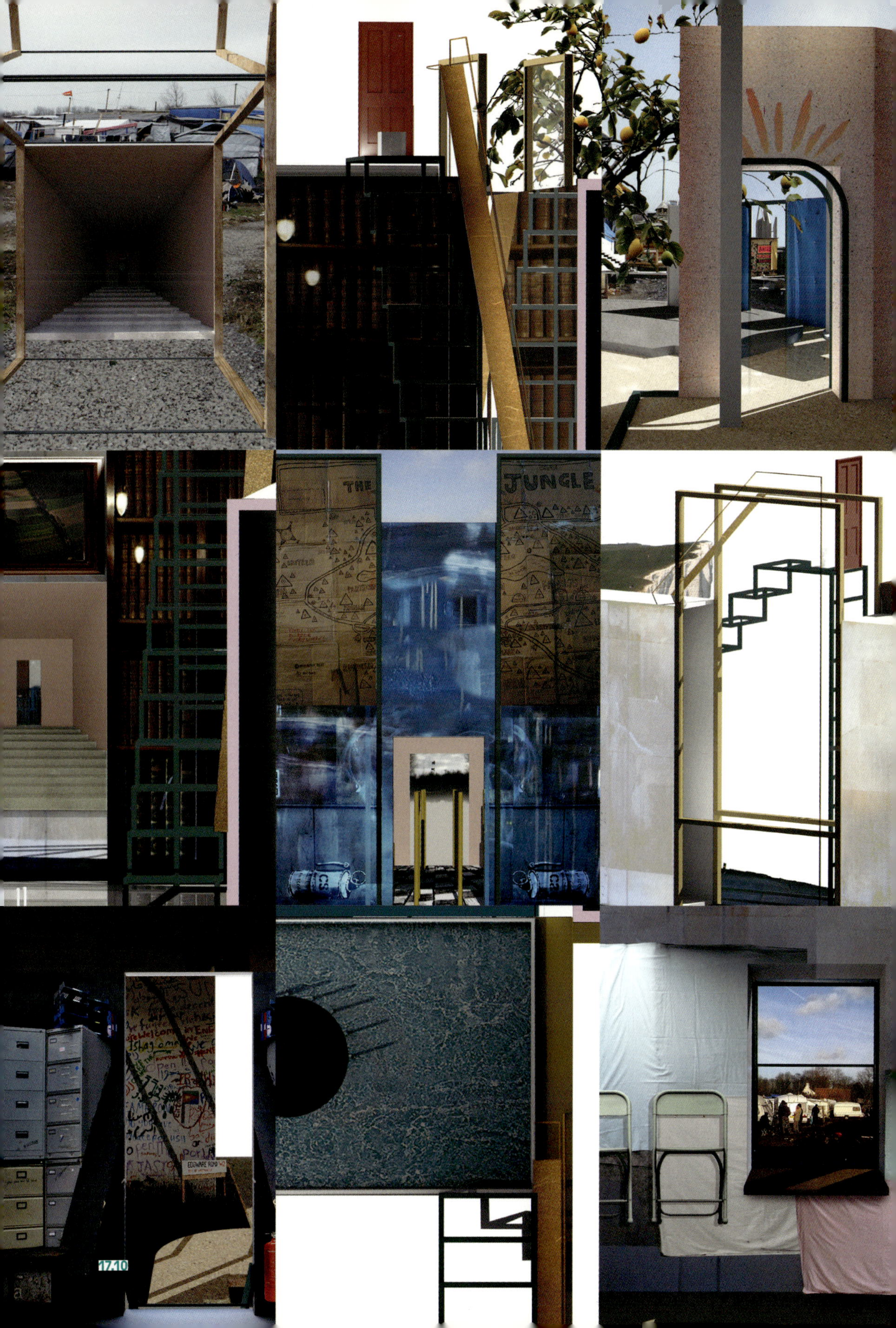
THE
JUNGLE
1710

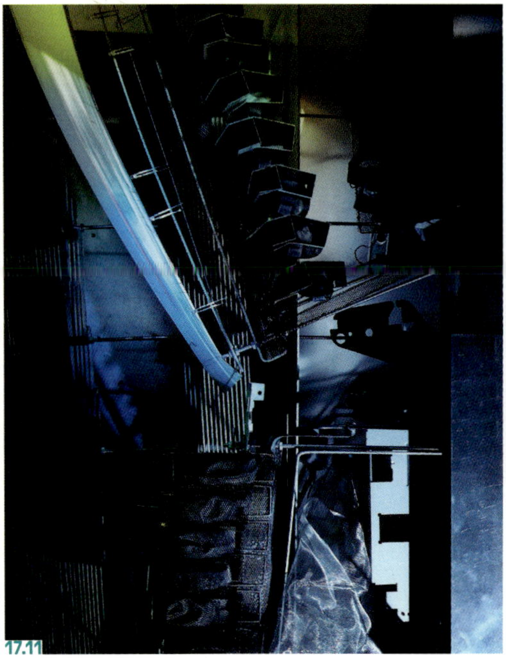
17.11

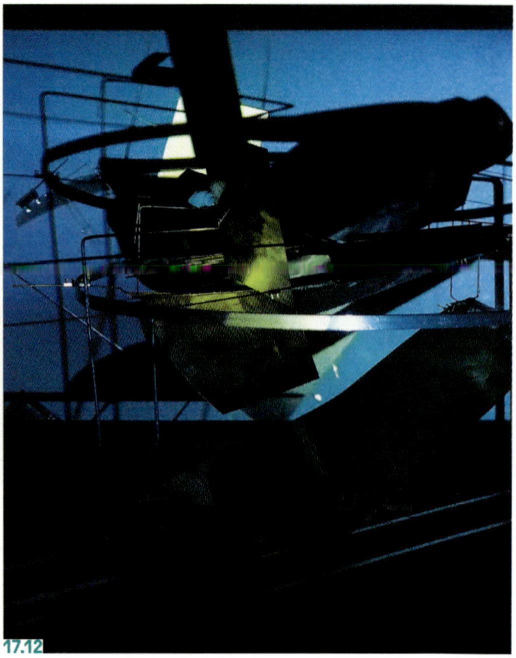
17.12

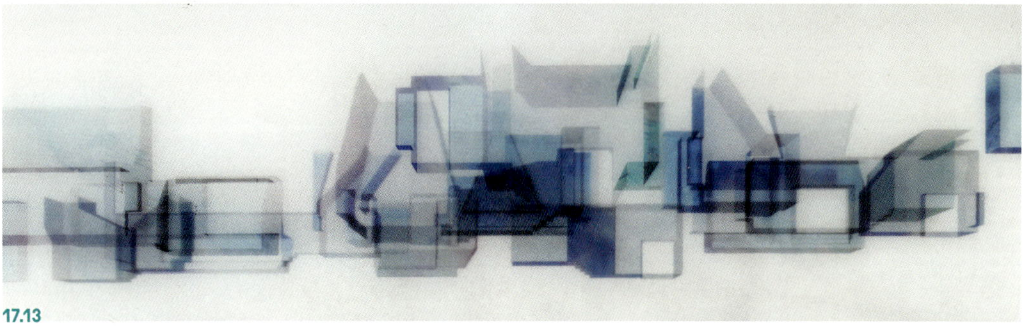
17.13

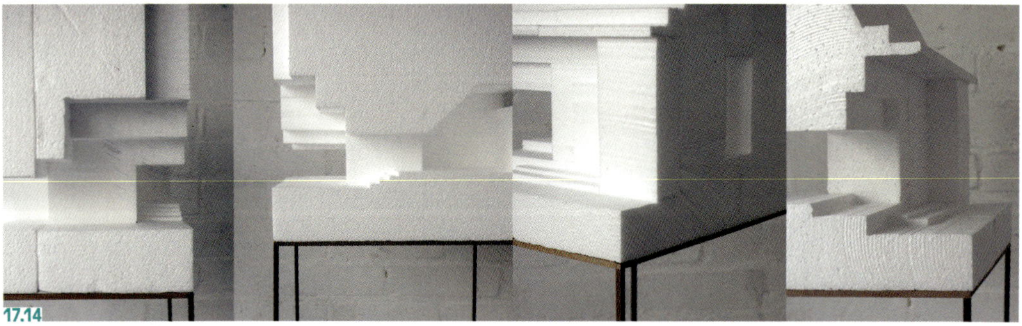
17.14

Figs. 17.11 – 17.12 Agata Murasko Y5, 'Reception Hall for Mr Midnight of Tokyo' is a building for an indistinguishable, exhausted and expressionless modern 'hero' of Tokyo – a Salaryman. The building sits in a void of Shinjuku Station and is a liminal space between real and surreal, awake and oneiric and diurnal and nocturnal worlds. **Figs. 17.13 – 17.14 Tony Lees** Y5, 'Hostel along the old Tokaido', Hakone, Japan. Time and the elements refine the clay and timber of the forest, until the inhabited building site is transformed through flame. Visitors embark on a collective understanding of how to exist within. The hostel in Hakone is a moment in time; beyond that it represents a kind of cultural remembrance through marks of its own creation that were in turn inspired by Japanese crafts and aesthetic principles, reimagined in new ways.

Fig. 17.15 Lok Kan Chau Y5, 'Lantau Commune: Das Lied von der Erde'. Cosmos, gravity, mountain, sunset, labour, cotton tree, climate change, bitter melon, sweet potato, storm, ruin, funeral. This is a song of the Earth, a translation of Erh Li's Transcendental Taoism into architecture. Sited in front of the legally protected but currently threatened landscape reserve on Lantau Island in Hong Kong, it is a place of farming, organising workshops, storing books, providing food and accommodation for long distance hikers. An educational institution, a belief carrier, a horizontal building in a vertical city.

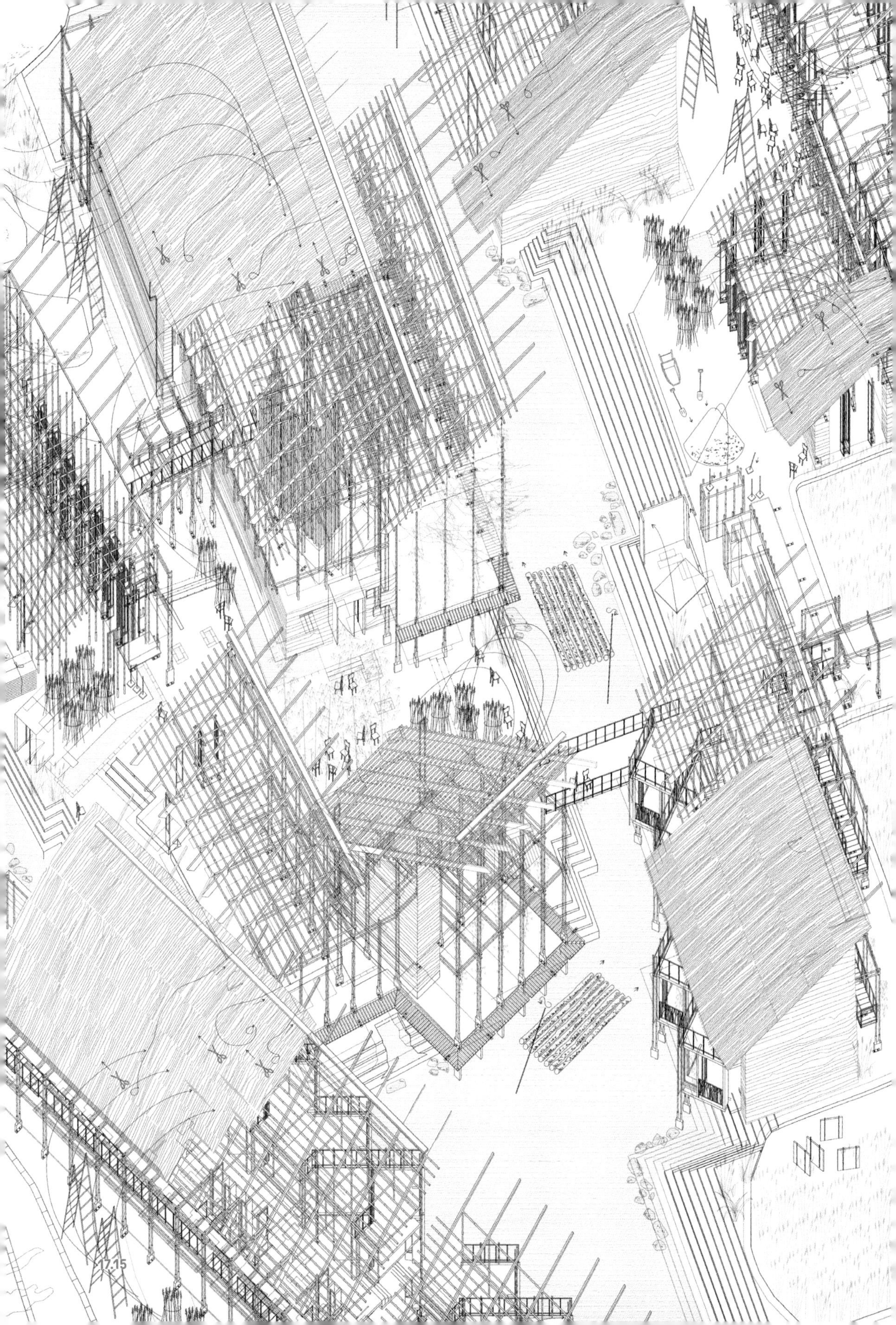

17.15

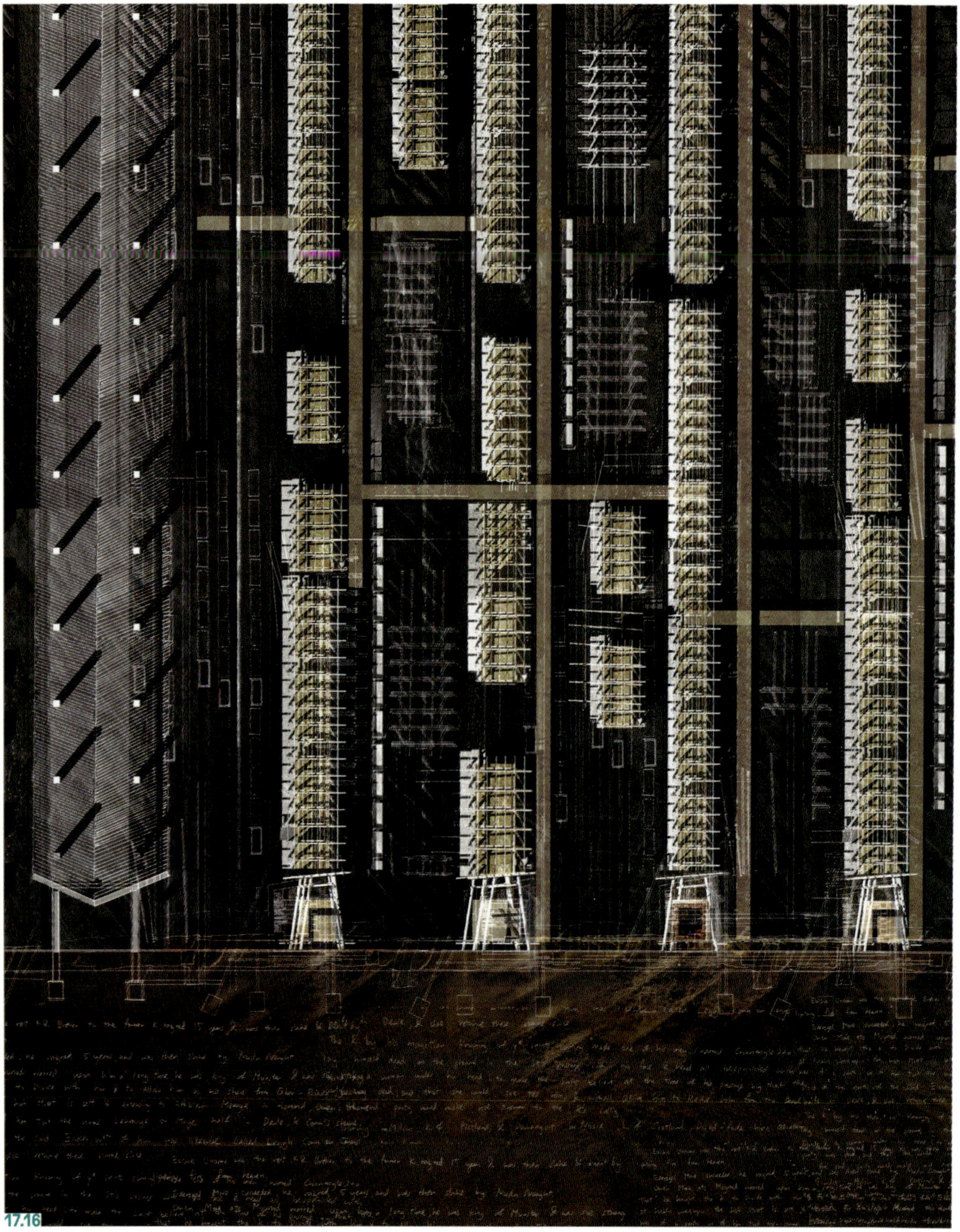

17.16

Fig. 17.16 **Shirley Tsang** Y5, 'The Diocese Archive of the Church of Ireland'. Peat bog, peat briquette, bog trains, a lightweight timber structure and brass are used to create an archive for the Diocese. The Church archive complex is composed of a public frontage, concealing the Archive Headquarters, Reading rooms, physical and digital archives beyond, all standing in a garden with interweaving walkways. The archives store items after they are received from the church whereas additional structures hold the historical letter records. The project focuses on reminding hidden histories which should not be forgotten. Besides its powerful presence for the community, the Church Archive also preserves the bog lands from extinction. **Fig. 17.17** **Minghui Ke** Y5, 'Open-air Kabuki Theatre, Shirakawago, Japan'. The project proposes an open-air Kabuki theatre for winter performances in Shirakawago. This traditional Japanese performance art is facing a challenge in regenerating itself from dereliction. The historical development of the performance itself is closely related to and shaped by the evolution of the architectural form of the Kabuki theatres. Hence, the proposal aims to connect these traditional forms with the surrounding natural landscape, creating a series of 'performance moments' to regenerate the ancient performative art. The movement and melting of the snow in time influences the atmosphere of the performance and becomes an indispensable element in understanding this new type of Kabuki.

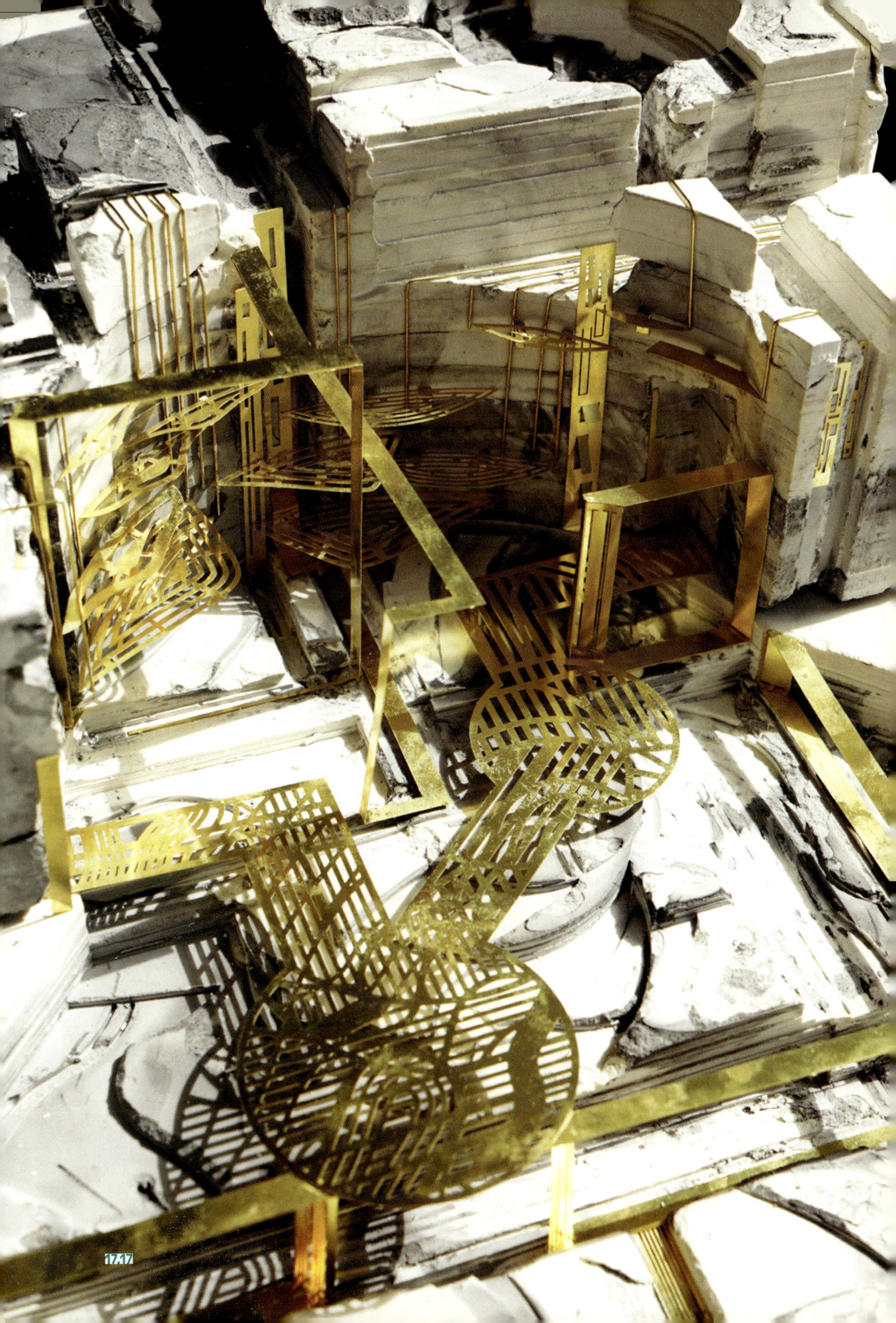

17.17

Unit 18 Portraits of Nature

Isaïe Bloch, Ricardo de Ostos

Year 4
Arti Braude, Maisie Chan, Anjie Gu, Man Jia, Aleksandra Kravchenko, Matteo Mauro, Nicholas Stamford, Risa Tadauchi, Samuel Whiting

Year 5
Anthony Awanis, Shu Ran, Thomas Reeves, James Tang, Man Tai (Adrian) Yiu

With thanks to our consultants and critics Julia Backhaus, Christina Dahdaleh, Christine Hawley, Michelle Hudson, Nannette Jackowski, Manuel Jimenez Garcia, Jakub Klaska, Abel Maciel, Yael Reisner, Javier Ruiz, Stefan Rutzinger, Kristina Shinegger, David Tajchman, Athanasios Varnavas

Beyond a critical point within a finite space, freedom diminishes as numbers increase. This is as true of humans in the finite space of the planetary ecosystem as it is of gas molecules in a sealed flask. The human question is not how many can possibly survive within the system, but what kind of existence is possible for those who do survive. Frank Herbert, Dune

Instead of asking what nature is, Unit 18 investigated the politics of thinking about nature in the context of Brazil, in order to test digital architectures of cultural expression and sensorial surprises. Unit 18, or Generational Phantoms, is interested in researching how architecture translates and expresses culture with a focus on digital media and practices of making. Students operate between reading, writing, digital modelling and fabricating and are encouraged to create critical arguments via architectural form and ornamentation. In this year's brief, whilst studying radical ecological agendas from ecofeminism to eco-marxism, Portraits of Nature found opportunities and contradictions within which architecture could operate.

——In Brazil, the Unit travelled to the state of Rio de Janeiro and found cities, neighbourhoods, natural reserves and institutions working on the edge of man/nature relationships. Working between shaping landscapes and building massing studies, projects addressed thresholds of a changing cityscape due to mega sport events and rapid urban development.

——Risa Tadauchi created a Fatigue Rehabilitation Centre in Flamengo Park, inspired by Roberto Burle Marx's landscape design in combination with the recent Olympic Games. Her design mixed objects and landscape concepts, bringing surrealism and color exposure to translate not only body fatigue symptoms but also urban fatigue to sporting events. Investigating the edge of city and rainforest, Nic Stamford proposes a complex set of elevated experiential buildings, in order to explore the threshold between the urban and the natural fabric of Rio de Janeiro. Tree buildings of different heights explored an earth-like materiality between top and bottom vistas, enabling a time-base adaptation with the fauna and flora on the site. At the edge of a favela, Anthony Awanis explores a syncretic culture that proposes an architecture of lines versus volumes for an Afro-Brazilian religion. Similarly, Adrian Yiu based his investigation into Brazilian anthropophagy on designing a economical and expressive way to quarry in a urban set.

——Between physical and digital, natural and urban, thinking and making, Generational Phantoms explored architectures based on individual thinking and critical expression.

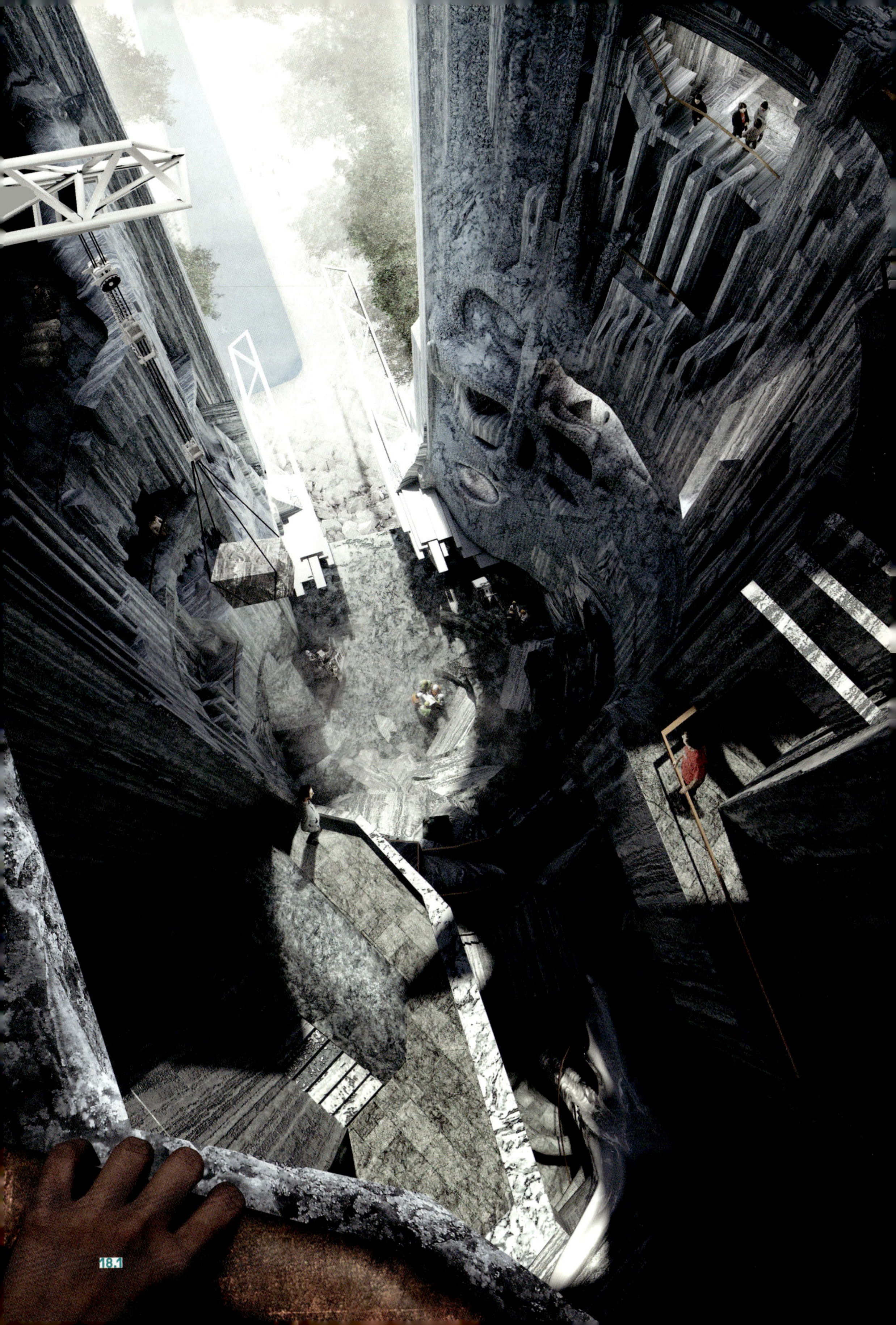

18.1

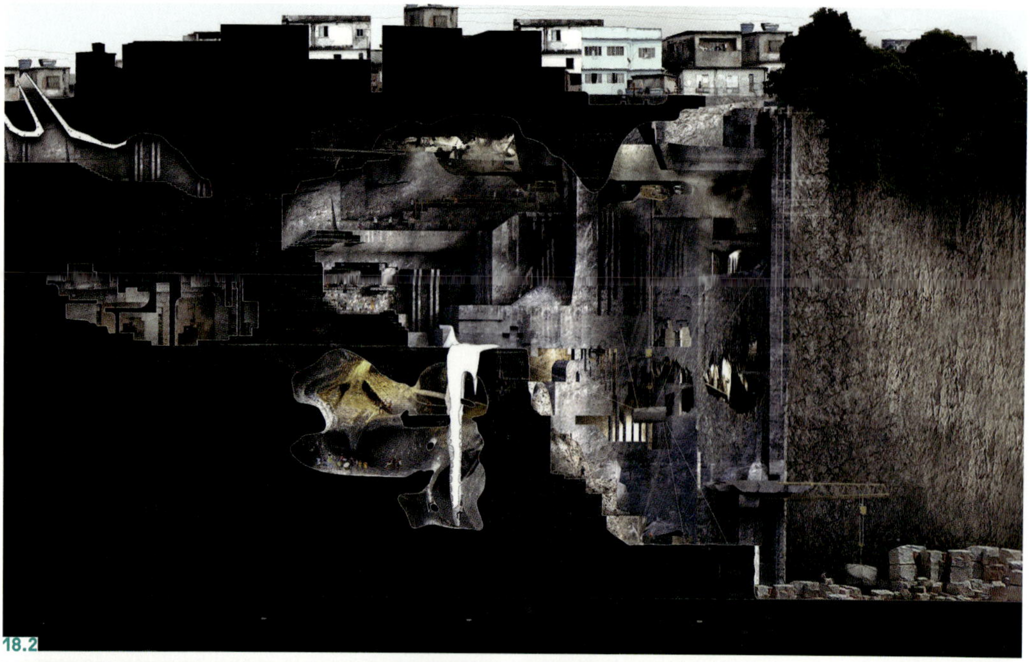

18.2

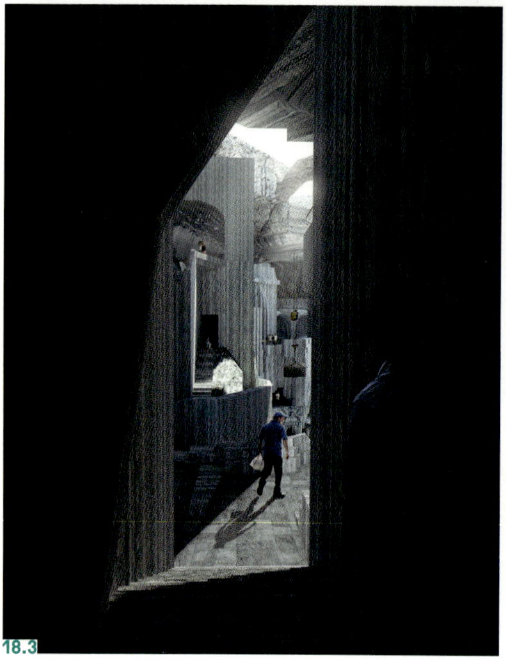

18.3

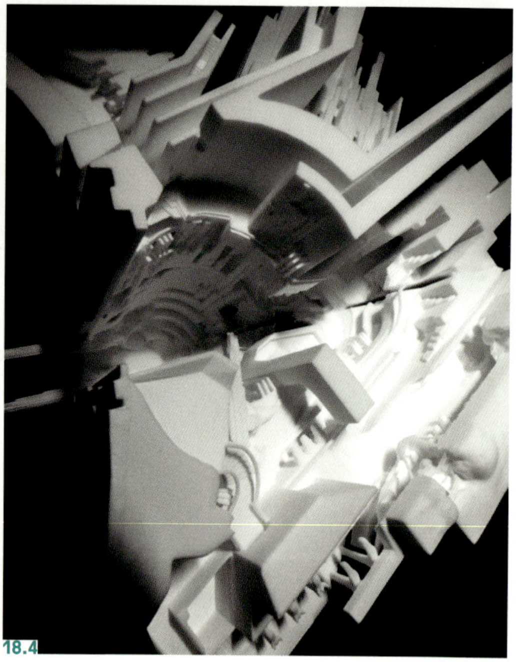

18.4

Fig. 18.1 Man Tai (Adrian) Yiu Y5, 'Anthropophagic Territory'. View from quarry interior looking down on newly carved spaces and the city of Rio de Janeiro. The scheme aims to create an economically independent zone to provide social opportunities for the community by reestablishing the quarry. All profit will fund the social programme and provide further excavation for civic spaces through quarrying. **Fig. 18.2 Man Tai (Adrian) Yiu** Y5, 'Anthropophagic Territory'. Section through 'Morro da Providencia' and quarry. Inspired by ideas of Anthropophagy the project blends infrastructure and social economy to create a variety of spaces. Capturing the relationship between time and social reality, the quarry adopts a state of constant physical expansion, and its relevance to the community it serves grows in tandem. Eventually splitting the cliff open, the internal lived experience of the people is exposed. **Fig. 18.3 Man Tai (Adrian) Yiu** Y5, 'Anthropophagic Territory'. View from a passage portal looking towards community hall. The project seeks to reunite the people with their environment, through spatial and sensational experiences. Spaces are designed to evoke emotional expressions. Their functionality is set out and then adapted by the users allowing for contingency. **Fig. 18.4 Man Tai (Adrian) Yiu** Y5, 'Anthropophagic Territory'. Model showing the core quarry and extending social spaces. Different quarrying methods are used to create various spatial and tactile qualities.

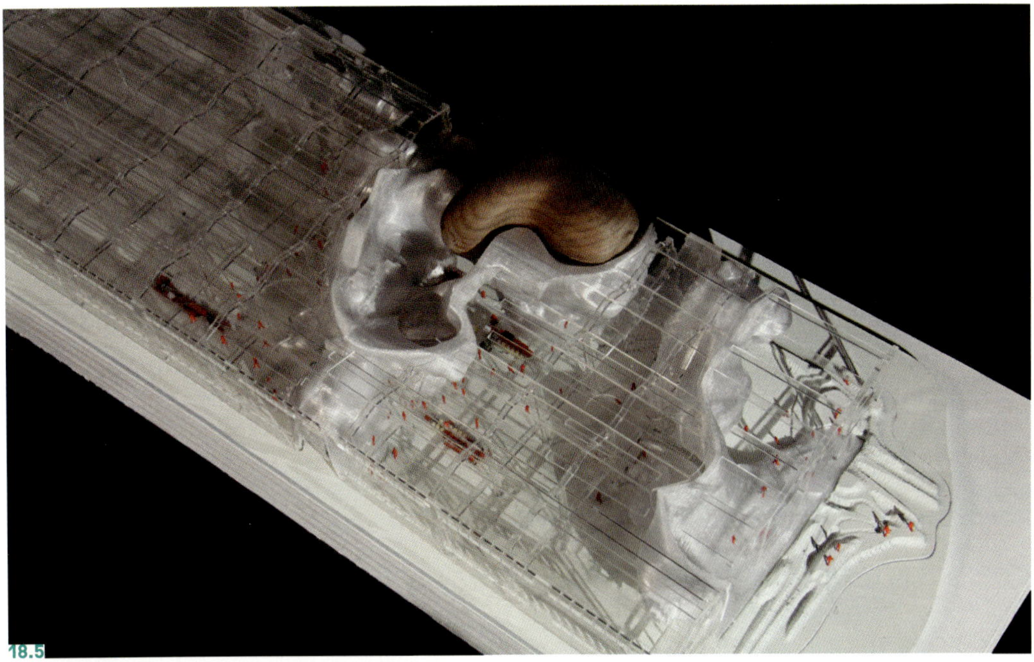

18.5

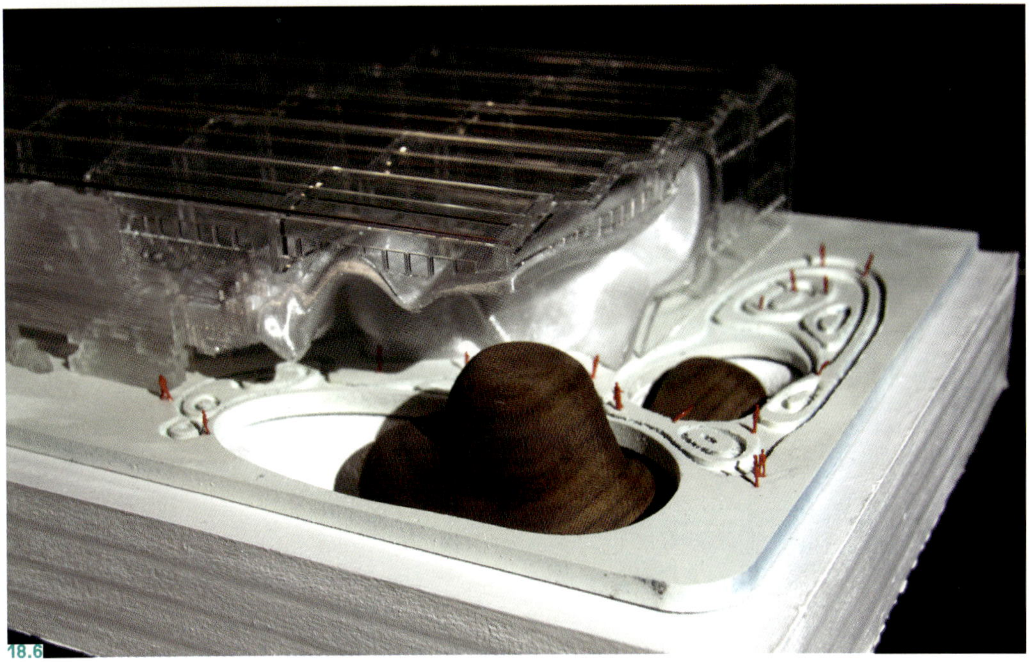

18.6

Fig. 18.5 **James Tang** Y5, 'The Protest Art Installation'. Physical model showing design appropriation of existing warehouse where artists and the public interact and discuss the future of Rio de Janeiro city developments. **Fig. 18.6** **James Tang** Y5, 'The Protest Art Installation'. Physical model showing different geometrical appropriations.

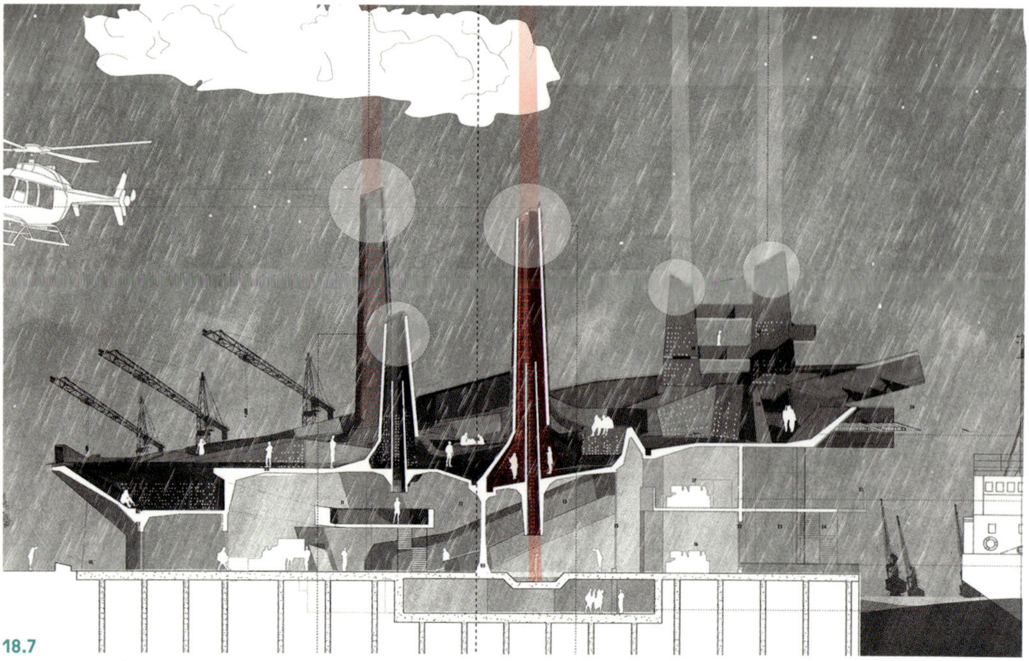

18.7

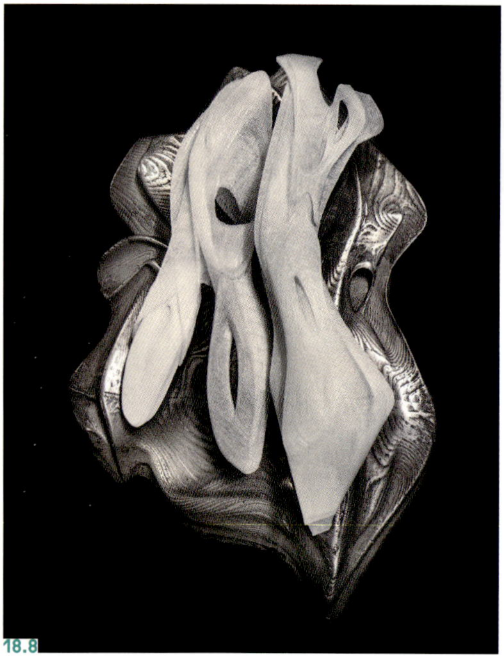

18.8

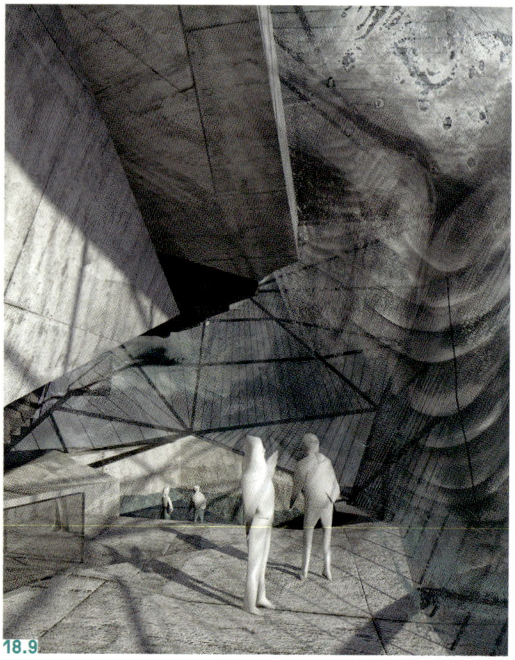

18.9

Fig. 18.7 Sam Whiting Y4, 'Better Safe than Sorry – A Survivalist's Echo Chamber', cross-section. The project aims to translate information processes into an architectural media device in order to educate and prepare residents of Rio de Janeiro in regards to flooding and landslide risks within the area. **Fig. 18.8 Matteo Mauro** Y4, 'Sand Culture'. Landscape massing model studies. Located in Copacabana beach, the project proposes a permanent, creative, research platform testing new ideas about sand and hosting temporary educational and recreational events. **Fig. 18.9 Aleksandra Kravchenko** Y4, 'Quilomba 2020'. Interior render with semi-opaque recycled plastic façade. The project proposes a centre for former Brazilian maids, where they can train in using a variety of arts and crafts techniques to recycle waste and debris collected from on-site in Marina da Gloria along Rio's polluted Guanabara Bay. **Fig. 18.10 Risa Tadauchi** Y4, 'Flamengo Park Fatigue Rehabilitation Centre'. The project explores the constant exposure of Rio to mega sports events, creating a humorous fatigue centre to welcome exhausted marathon runners and citizens alike. **Fig. 18.11 Risa Tadauchi** Y4, 'Flamengo Park Fatigue Rehabilitation Centre'. Landscape study inspired by Burle Marx's exuberant colours and design. **Fig. 18.12 Anjie Gu** Y4, 'Culture Centre for Maracanã Village'. Derived from the social events of a group of urban Indians and the government, the project aims to address the constant conflict between urban development and native culture. Render showing an interpretation of the idea of boundary in indigenous culture.

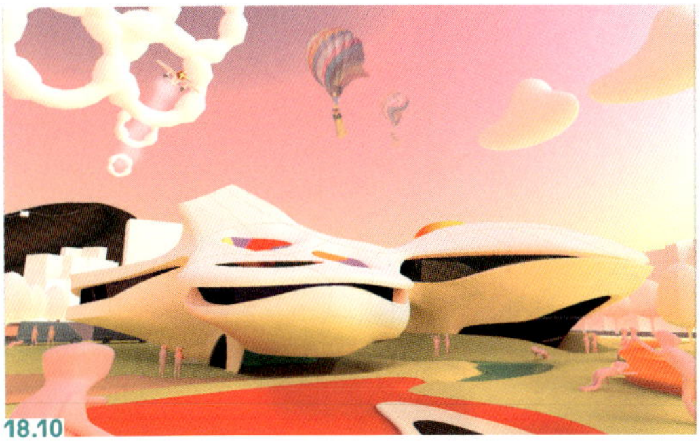
18.10

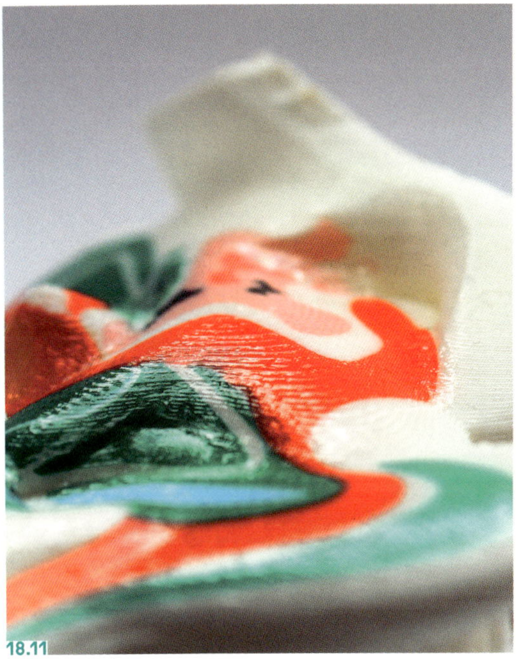
18.11

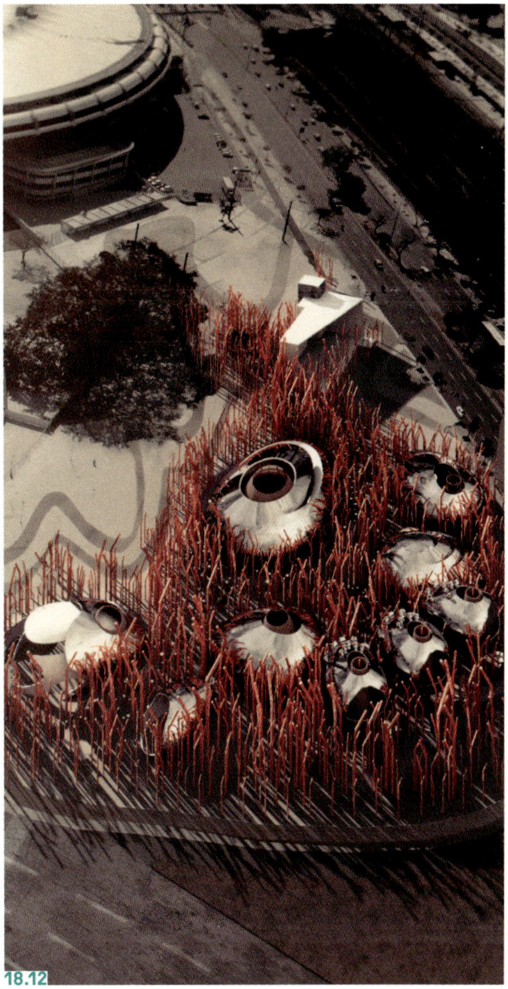
18.12

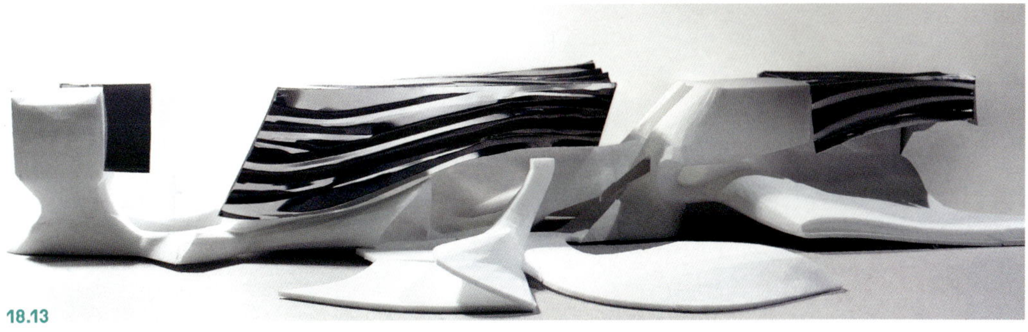
18.13

Fig. 18.13 Maisie Chan Y4, 'The Ugly Truth'. Model investigation for elevated artists' workshop, landscape plaza and tram rail passage.

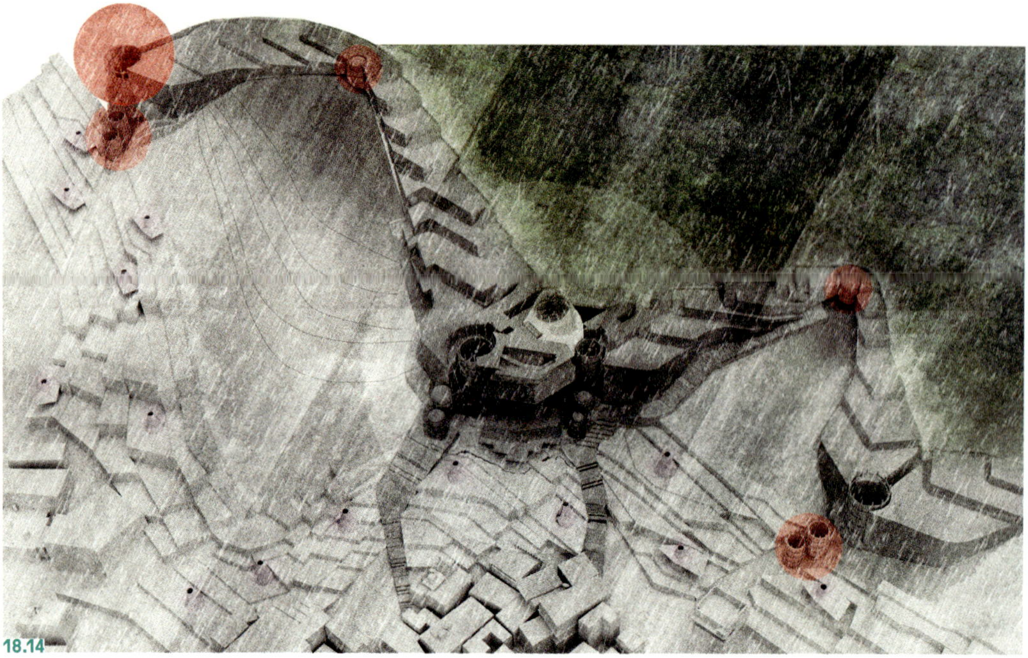

18.14

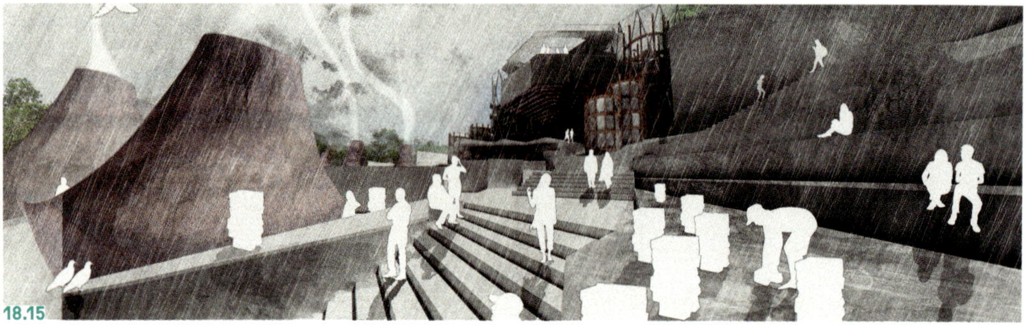

18.15

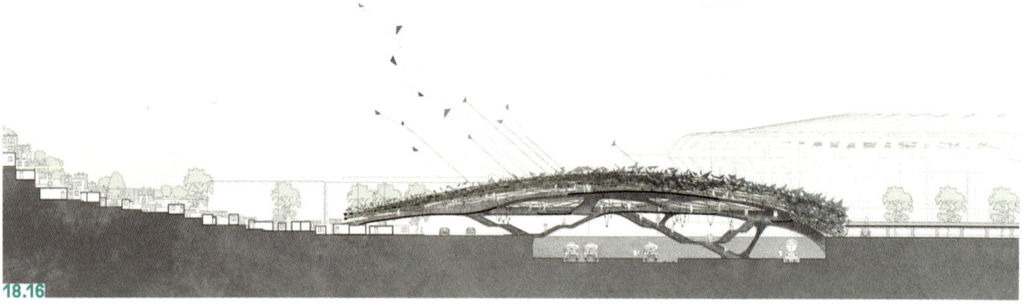

18.16

Figs. 18.14– Fig. 18.15 Thomas Reeves Y5, 'Rocinha Mudslide Barrier'. Between infrastructure and architecture, the project articulates a mud barrier in Rocinha, Rio de Janeiro with civic and working spaces. The design has a relationship with nature as the barrier protects the favela residents from the threat of mudslides and creates a boundary between the favela and the forest further up the mountain. **Fig. 18.16 Ran Shu** Y5, 'Free Market'. A bridge, a market, and a new connection between two distinct neighborhoods set the project strategy as both economical and social. Inspired by kiting, the design merges both heavy and light components.

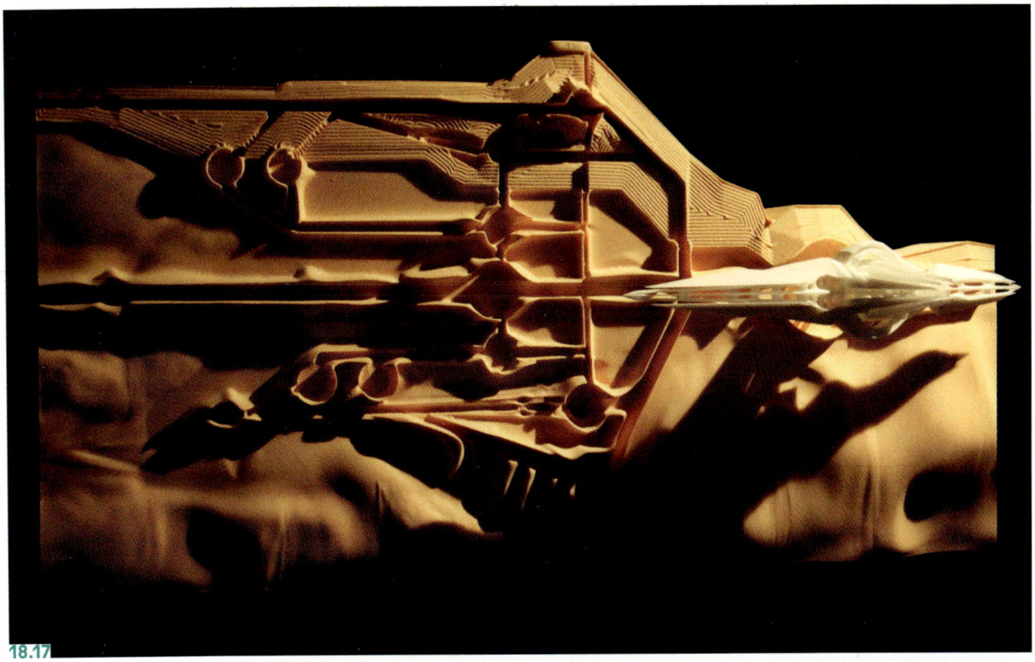

18.17

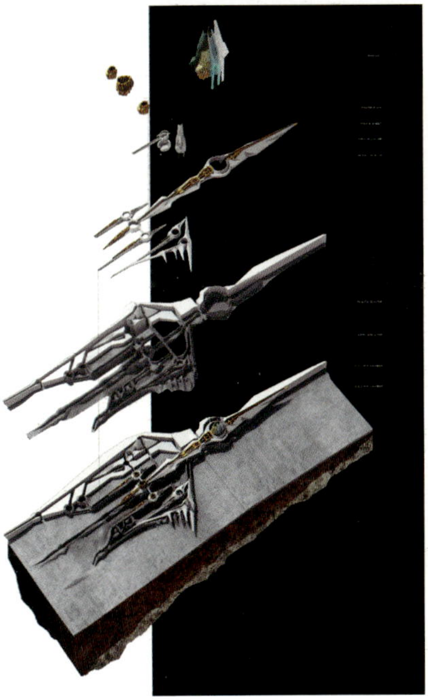

18.18

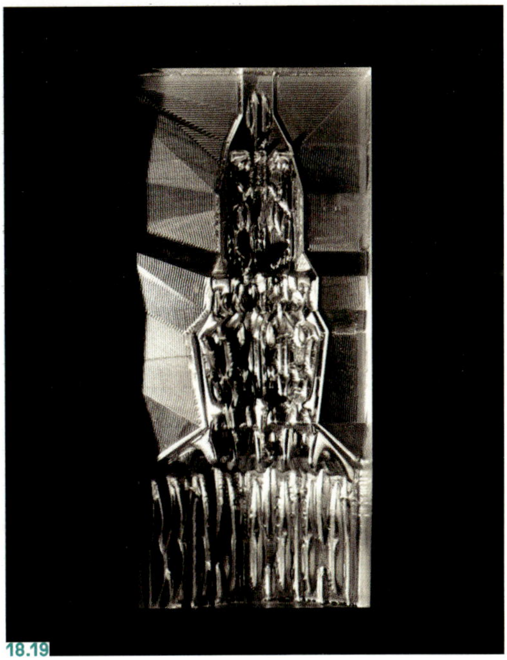

18.19

Fig. 18.17 Anthony Awanis Y5, 'The Exile Temple'. CNC model exploring path marking on landscape. **Fig. 18.18 Anthony Awanis** Y5, 'The Exile Temple'. Set within the context of Rio de Janeiro, the project explicitly aims to formulate a new typology of the Candomble temple, an Afro-Brazilian religion practiced by the Quilombo people, who are descendants of slave workers. **Fig. 18.19 Anthony Awanis** Y5, 'The Exile Temple'. Aluminum milled model of main Candomble temple with striations and contours.

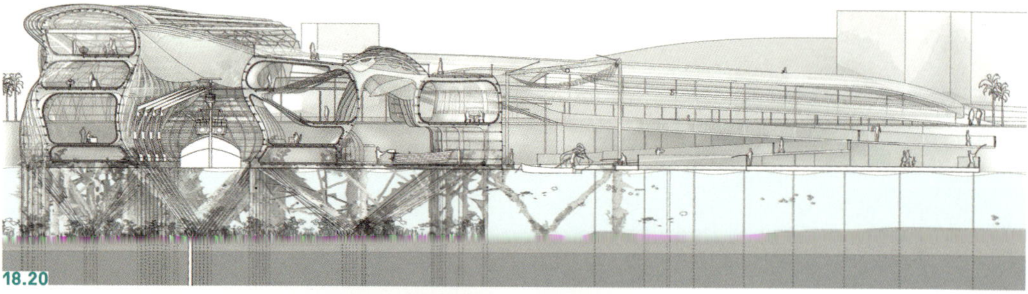

18.20

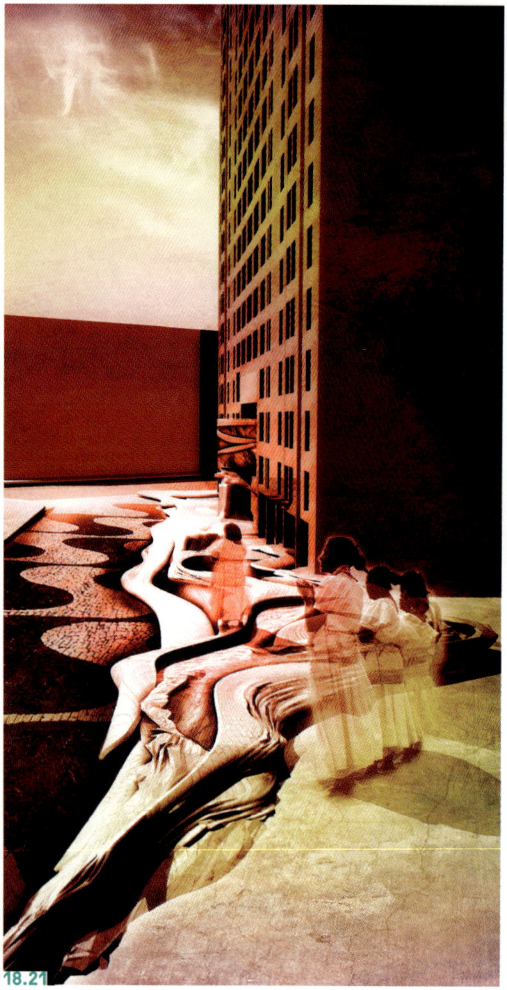

18.21

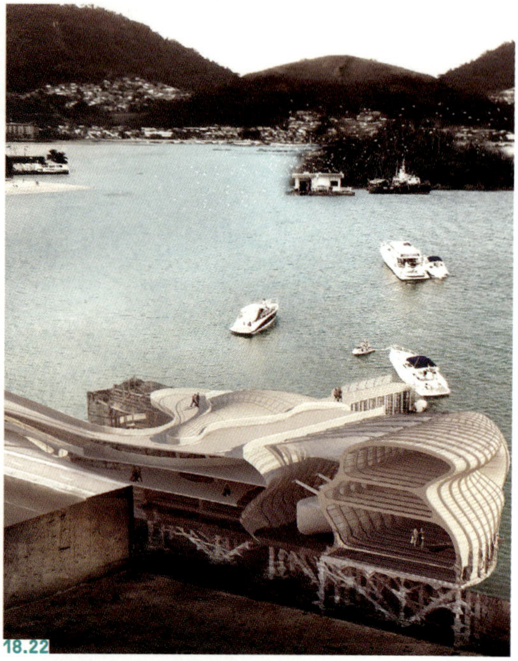

18.22

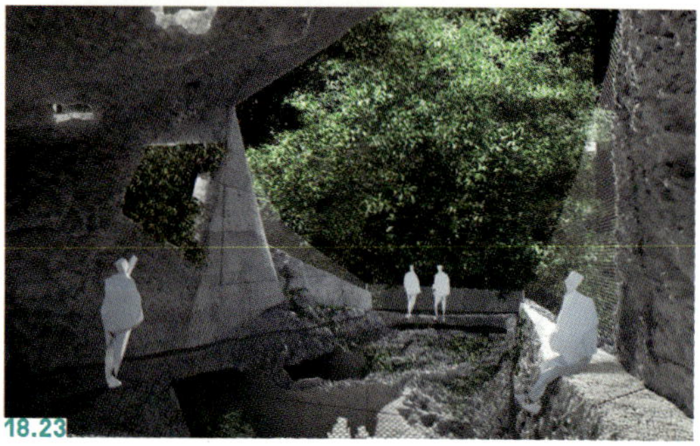

18.23

Fig. 18.20 Man Jia Y4, 'Reconstitute Ambiguous Nature/Culture-Artisanal Fishery Workshop', cross-section. The project speculates on the tension, interaction and possible common development of the waning traditional small-scale fishery culture and the rising ecological tourism in Angra under the state's environmental conservation policy. **Fig. 18.21 Arti Braude** Y4, 'The People's Market'. A textured market landscape seeps through an abandoned building at the site of the Historic Port at two levels, acting as a socio-spatial bridge between the Port's Afro-Brazilian 'Povo de Santo' community and Olympic development. The building houses a food and trinket market, event space, and advocacy centre for the residents of the town. **Fig. 18.22 Man Jia** Y4, 'Reconstitute Ambiguous Nature/Culture-Artisanal Fishery Workshop'. This section render emphasises the project as a public insertion aiming to shape a more diverse image of the city. **Fig. 18.23 Nic Stamford** Y4, 'Urban Rainforest Power Plant'. Sub-Canopy Observation Station. The project looks at the boundary between the city and the rainforest, proposing an architecture which explores material, context and cohabitation proximity while providing a platform for varying degrees of interaction.

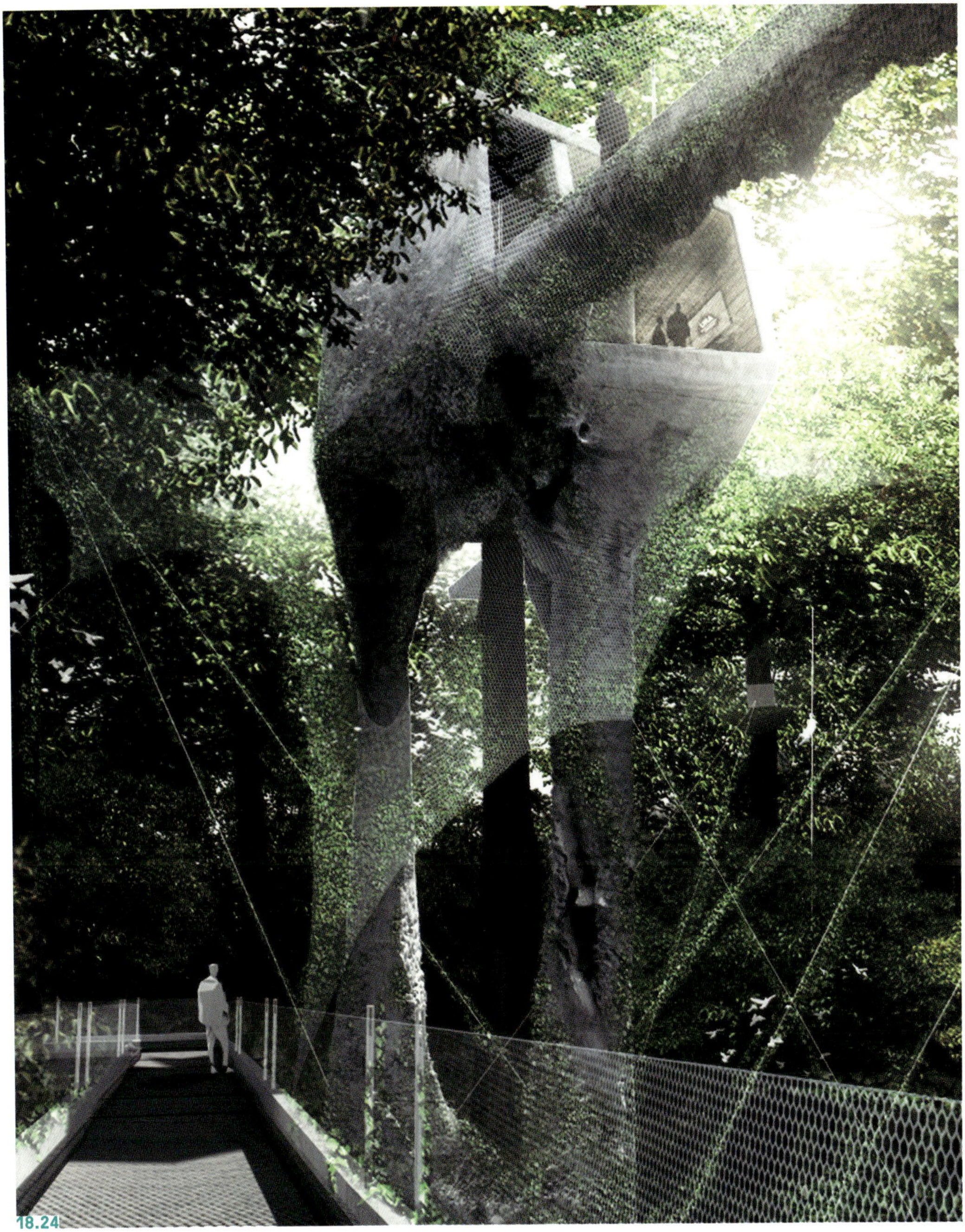

18.24

Fig. 18.24 Nic Stamford Y4, 'Urban Rainforest Power Plant'. Emergent Observation Station. The split buildings make use of the existing rainforest structures, being suspended from the primary trees so as make as little permanent ground impact as possible, while providing unique vantage points within the many different layers of the forest.

Unit 19

The Laboratory of Mereology

Mollie Claypool, Manuel Jimenez Garcia, Gilles Retsin

Year 4
Tzoulia Baltsavia, Jaspal Channa, Zuzana Sojkova, Gintare Stonkute, Ivo Tedbury, Joshua Toh, Kuba Tomaszczyk, Oscar Walheim, Xin Zhan

Year 5
Elliot Mayer, Sukriye Robinson, Julian Sivaro

Many thanks to our supporting tutors: Vidal Fernandez (Rogers Stirk Harbour + Partners), Design Realisation Tutor Christian Dercks (Arup), Structural Consultant

And many thanks to our invaluable critics: Isaïe Bloch, Brendon Carlin, Tomasso Franzoloni, Evan Greenberg, Kostas Grigoriadis, Sofia Krimizi, Hseng Linter, Javier Ruiz, Harald Trapp, Tomas Tvarijonas, Manijeh Verghese

Thanks to our sponsor ABC Printing

Set in Argentina, particularly in the metropolitan area of Buenos Aires, this year, Unit 19 proposed novel housing models based on a new understanding of serialisation and discreteness, enabling an increased automation of architecture while exploring new territories for design.

——The unit work questioned the prevailing paradigm for computation in the past two decades, one that understood architecture as a continuously evolving organic body, growing and adapting under external forces. Rather than borrowing models from nature, the students investigated an architectural ontology based on sharpening the tension between architecture and its parts.

——This year's research explored fabrication techniques that are fundamentally digital, rather than analog, discrete rather than continuous, and increasingly fast and assemblage-based. Discrete, or 'digital' fabrication processes are based on a small number of different parts connecting with only a limited number of connection possibilities. The design possibilities (spatial, typological, tectonic, material) – or the way elements can combine and aggregate – is defined by the geometry of the element itself. Given the framework of discrete fabrication, where the geometry and definition of a part generates the whole, *mereology* (the theory of parthood relations, of the relations of part to whole and the relations of part to part within a whole) became an important concept for the work.

——We looked into establishing novel types of methods for design and fabrication based on low-cost, simple, quick and reversible methods of assembly into highly-detailed, heterogeneous and structurally sound architectures. Increased computational capabilities are able to push the initially modernist understanding of architecture as an assemblage of prefabricated, discrete elements into an unexpected new domain of previously unachievable detail, materiality, structure and aesthetics.

——By questioning and designing the system of production behind their building block, students developed provocative social and political scenarios intrinsic to their design projects. These scenarios range from exploring a fully automated society without work (Julian Sivaro, Year 5), to collectively-owned self-assembling robotic exoskeletons which enabled continuously adapting buildings (Ivo Tedbury, Year 4). Other projects question the impact of the digital on the way we handle data, create instruction and think about authorship and originality (Elliot Mayer, Year 5 and Oscar Walheim, Year 4). Projects also took on board questions of analogue craft and digital materiality in mass production, designing prototypical systems for manufacturing (Sukriye Robinson, Year 5 and Jaspal Channa, Year 4), amongst others.

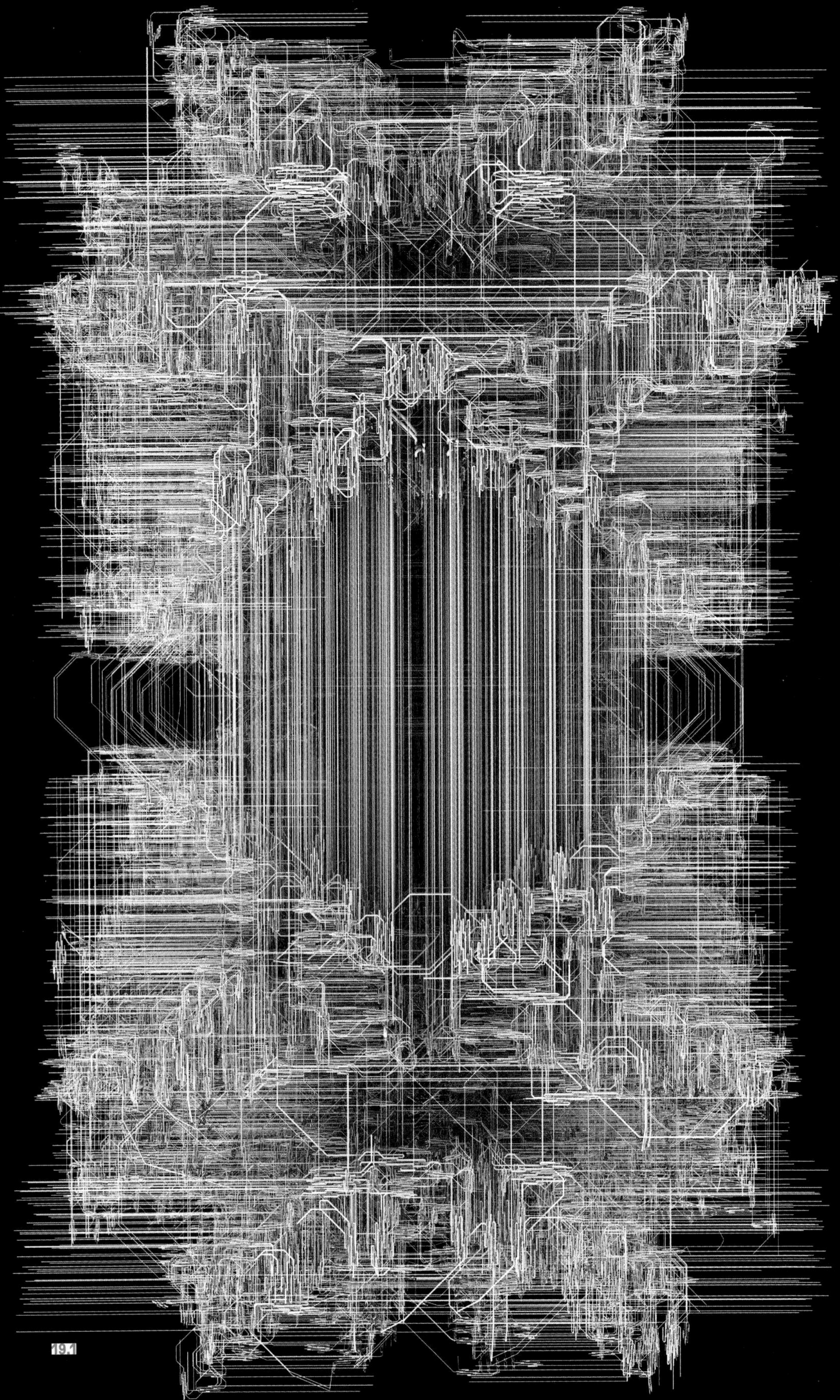
19.1

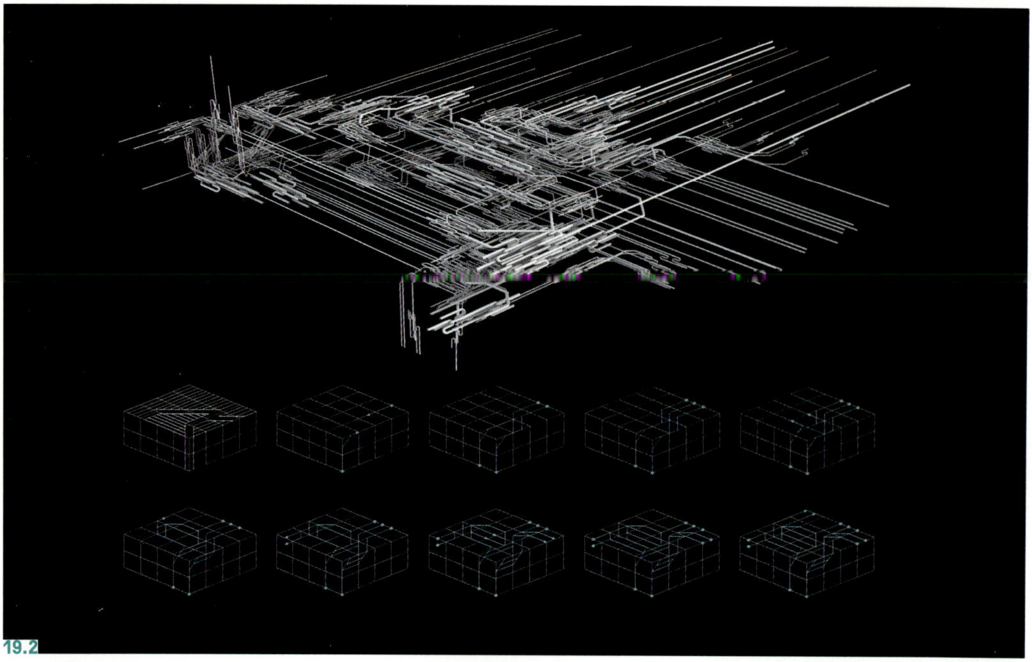
19.2

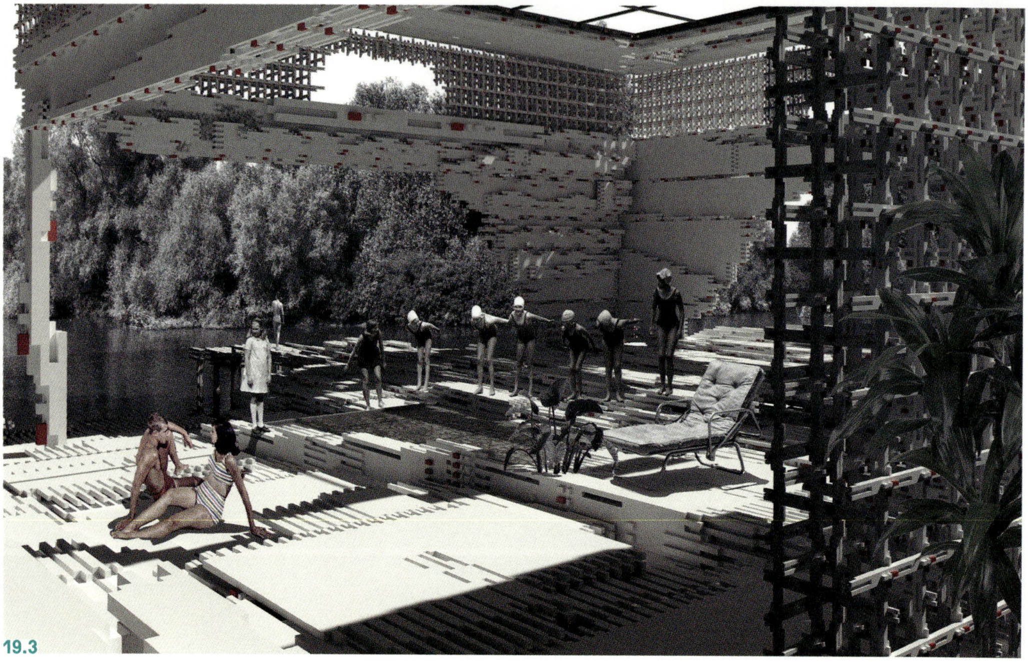
19.3

Figs. 19.1 – 19.2 Elliot Mayer Y5, 'Vectonics'. The project developes mechanisms that extract fundamental attributes of built space, deriving the creation of new digital forms through an indexical organisation of discrete parts that simulate these attributes. The development of a radical tectonic and programmatic assemblage is built upon the computational folding and sequential interlocking of standardised bent metal pipe geometries. These generated interlocking aggregations are fundamentally dictated by overarching generic laws of interaction prescribed by both the designed manner of the brick-to-brick connection and the repetitive sequence embedded in the collective formations. Advanced concepts of generative part-to-whole relationships explore the subversive concept of digitising the interpretation of space through the reproduction of a series of distinct architectural typologies identified within the urban grid plan of Buenos Aires. This discourse devolves the architectural engagement with spatial design by empowering the relevance of automated digital manufacturing in an age where the limitations of urban architectural production are confined to given programmes of space. This radical building logic is constructed in the order of: typological precedent (existing building), classification (identification of spatial hierarchies), extraction (record of representative data), assimilation of features (reinterpretation), and reinvention of architectural form.
Fig. 19.3 Julian Sivaro Y5, 'Post-Work City'. This project imagines a future in which most jobs have been automated, in which the conflict between labour and capital has been

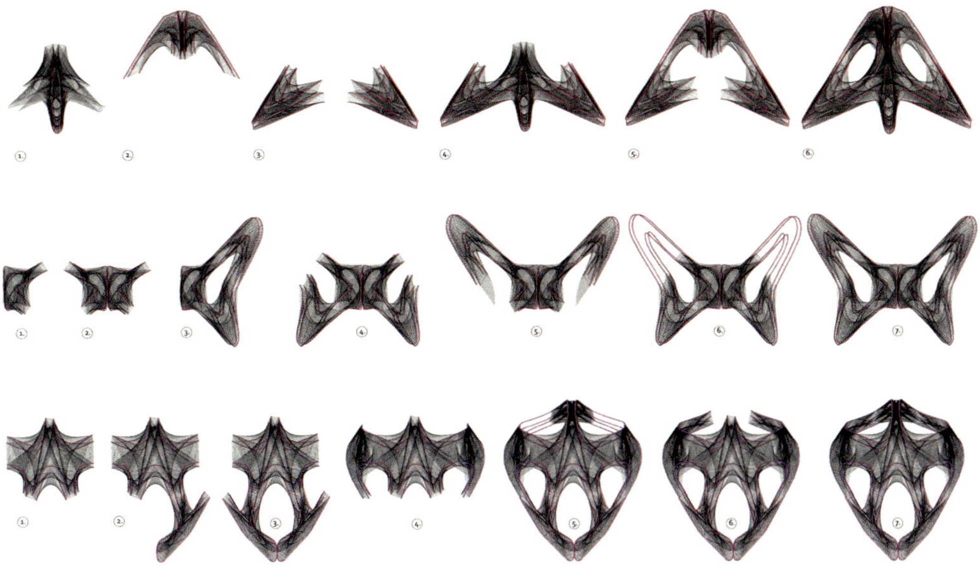

19.4

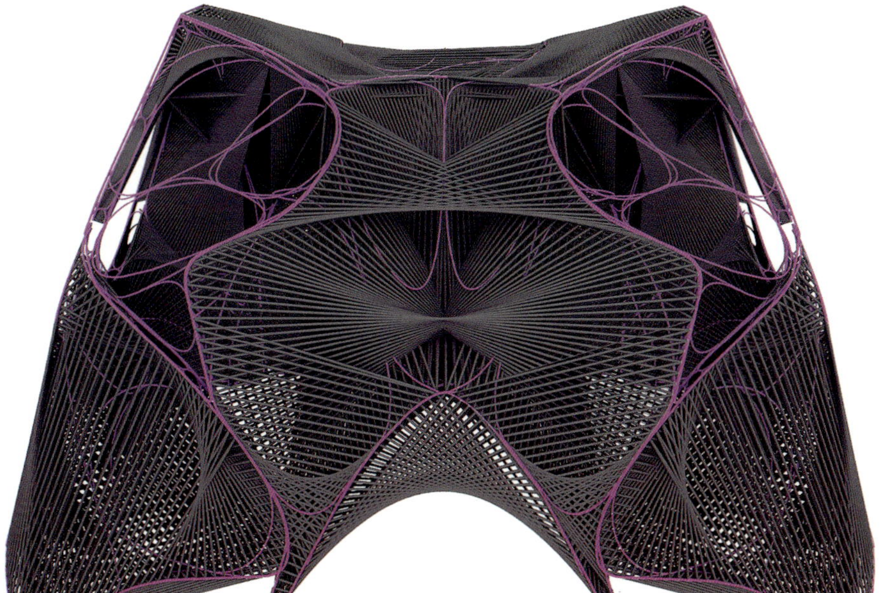

19.5

resolved through public ownership of automata. The writings and drawings try to imagine the infrastructure of full automation and the spaces of full unemployment, placing them in the Delta del Paraná, north of Buenos Aires. Digital materials are not only the means to successfully automate the construction process, but the symbol and working parts of a shared housing program in constant flux. This program prefigures a post-familial and form of living, predicated on sharing domestic labour and enjoying each others' company. **Figs. 19.4 – 19.5 Sukriye Robinson** Y5, 'Fiberoo'. The project is an innovative production system for both discrete and continuous architecture. Through rigorous testing, a new bamboo fibre composite was designed. Using bamboo on each of its scales creates a holistic approach to materials – utilising a low-cost, highly renewable natural material. Addressing part-to-part and part-to-whole relationships, individual robotically fabricated elements come together to create an innovative architectural solution. The system can respond to any site conditions and parameters through the capability of total customisation. The bamboo composite opens the door for bamboo to become a standardised construction element – something the construction industry currently struggles with for such a variable natural material. Structural analysis is used to inform the robot of material distribution. The system gives the freedom for customisation as well as standardisation through a universal kit of parts or bespoke elements.

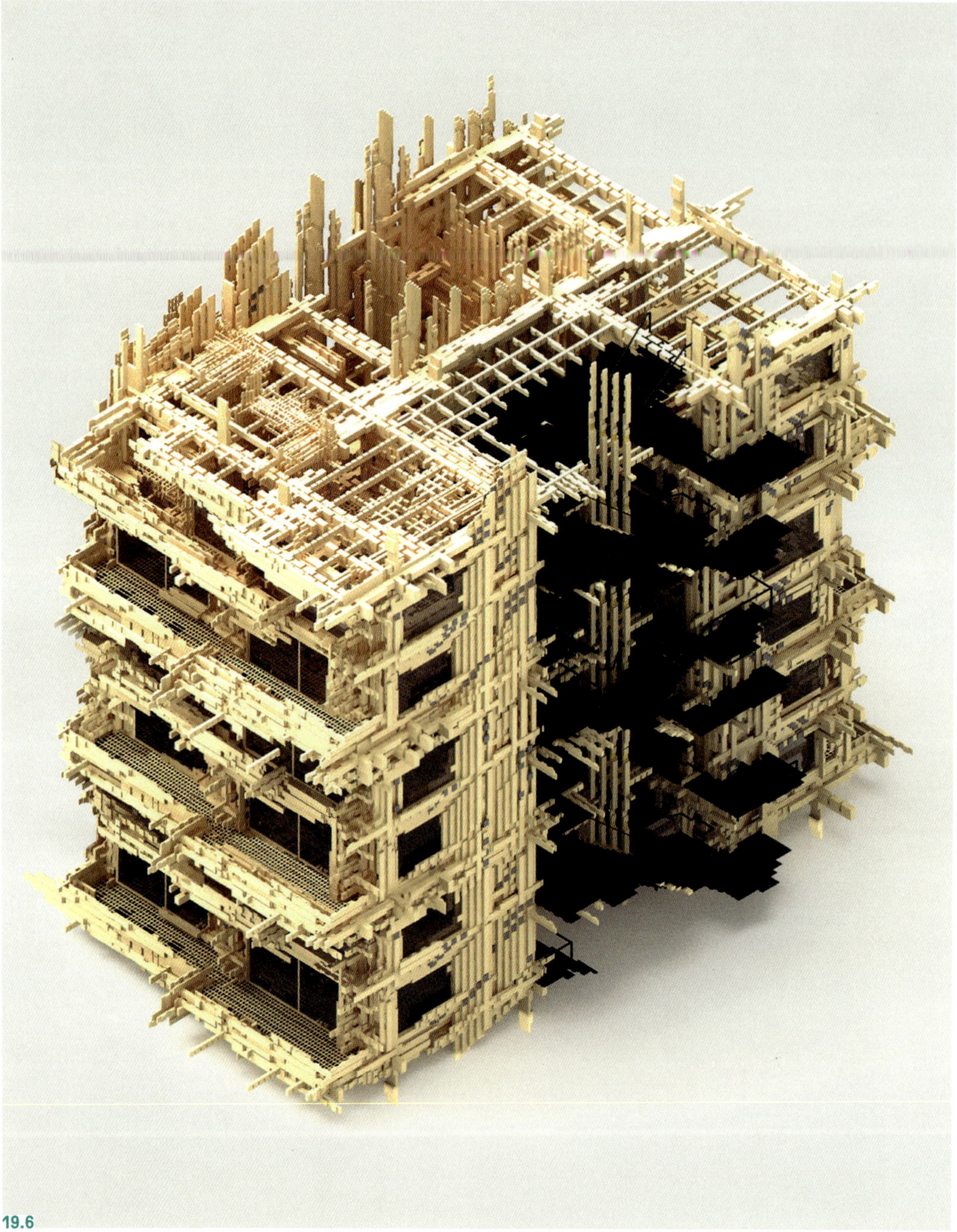

19.6

Fig. 19.6 **Tzoulia Baltsavia** Y4, 'RWG'. The mereological brick system questions the predominant modernist architecture of discrete elements, as we know them today. Instead, it proposes a breakdown of these elements into individual components that come together to form a continuous building environment where spatial boundaries are blurred. The building proposal breaks away with the 'functionalist' living environment of the Maison Domino, while dealing with a range of brick aggregations that are non-deterministic. The system is conceived to be easily assembled and disassembled, dealing with concepts of spatial adaptability and material recycling. Working with discrete building components allows for cost-effective solutions in fabrication and rapid construction processes in a competitive and automated market of tomorrow. **Fig. 19.7** **Joshua Toh** Y4, '[FA]BRIC'. The aim of this research is to explore the architectural possibilities of a stuctural 3D woven fabric, a concept that facilitates the realisation of seamlessly integrated multiple surfaces, allowing for a complexity of geometry and surface that is otherwise difficult to realise. Design research into the possibility of designing a non-standard architecture of pure seamless surface was conducted, and a deployable system of lightweight housing proposed. **Fig. 19.8** **Xin Zhan** Y4, 'Artist Hub and Gallery'. Taking mereology as the main subject of research and experimentation, the structures of this architecture are constructed from reinvented 'brick'. It could be manufactured from weathering steel (COR-TEN) or other bendable sheet

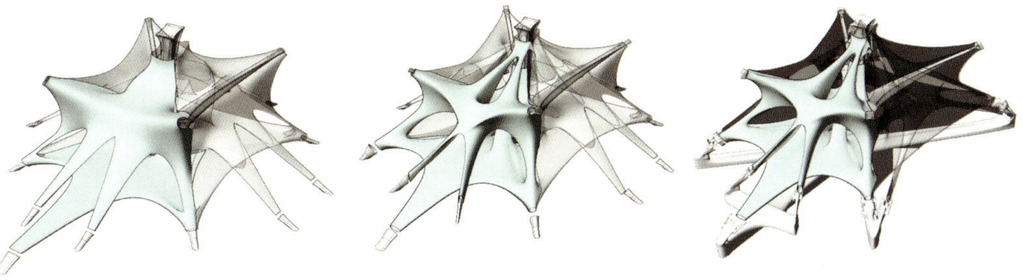

19.7

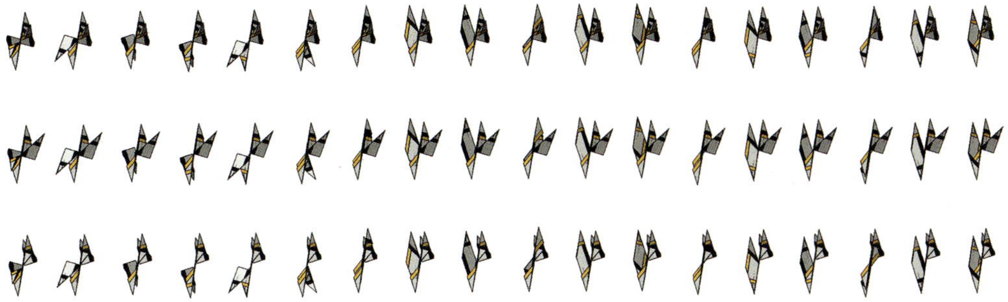

19.8

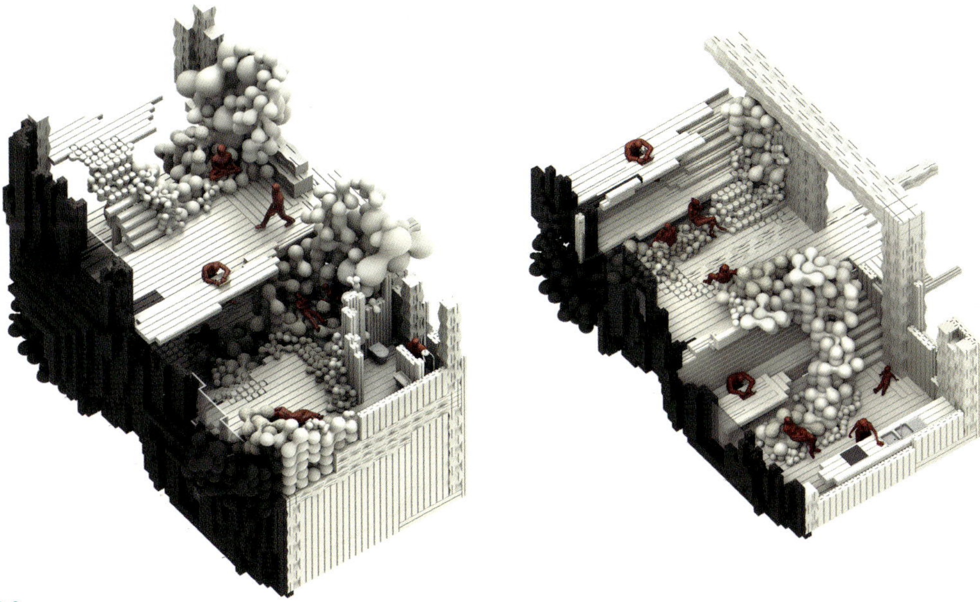

19.9

material using a special programmed robotic machine. The method of on-site manufacturing process could speed up the process of construction. The architecture fragments of facade, roof, wall and floor consist of same elements, and the definition of each fragment therefore could be redefined and reconsidered. The project is therefore an experimental project of applying a mereological brick system to a prototypical site.
Fig. 19.9 Gintare Stonkute Y4, 'v0xel'. The project proposes a rethink of a brick, its function and its relationships to other details of the building. v0xel investigates how a universal piece can be used to form parts of a building, whilst improving speed of construction and assembly as well as financial benefit. The project investigates the requirements and constraints of Buenos Aires, revealing how the aggregation of parts can meet social needs and, unlike its modular predecessors, still provide architectural expression. The project developed a universal brick based on a voxel system, which can be articulated into two different versions (sharp or blobby), displaying adaptation possibilities for buildings of other functions. The relationship of these articulations blurs boundaries between structural and building elements, and inside and outside, providing transition between open and private spaces and an opportunity for residents to shape spaces.

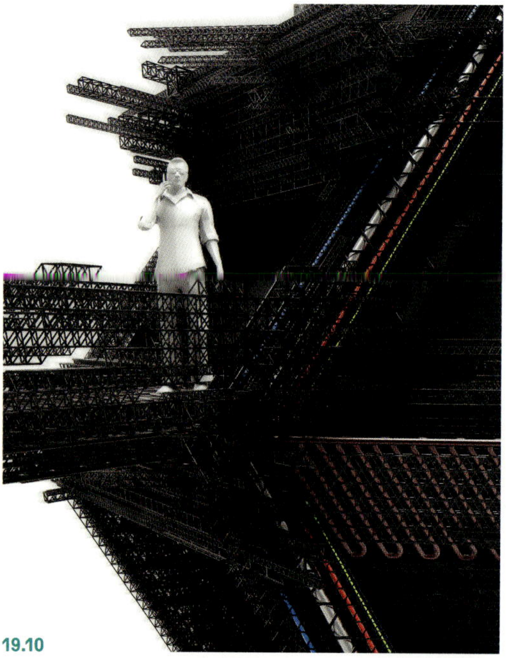

19.10

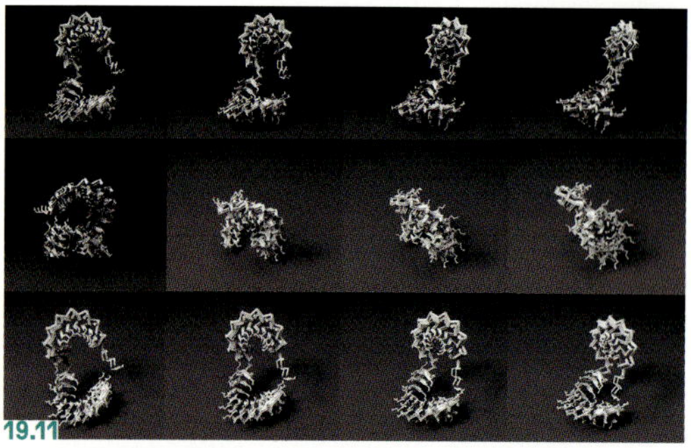

19.11

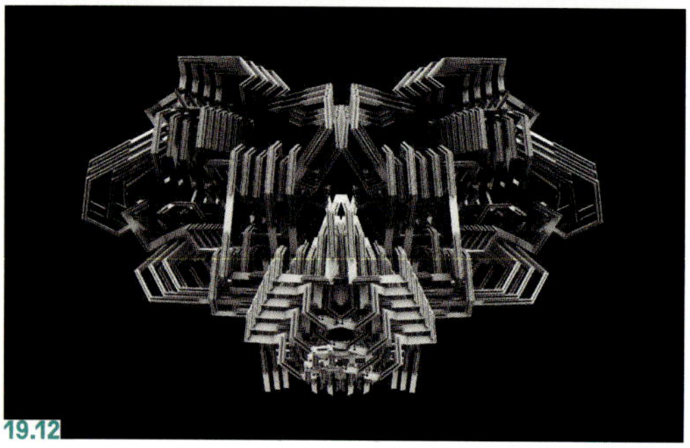

19.12

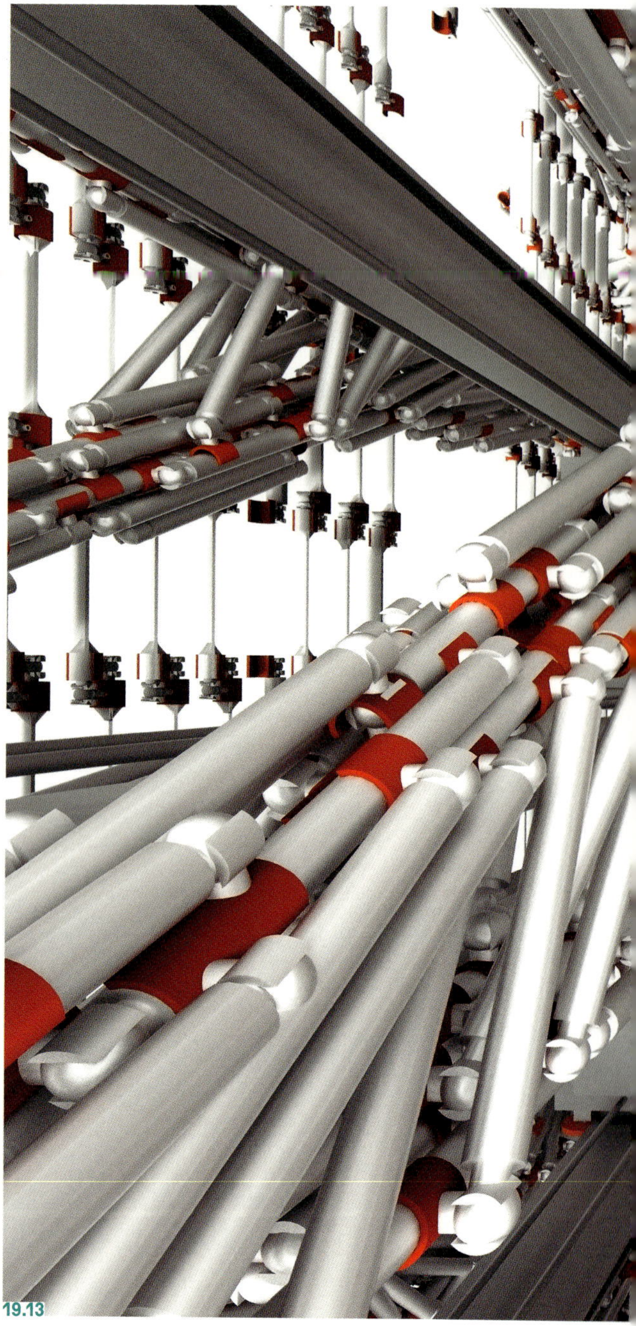

19.13

Fig. 19.10 Jakub Tomaszczyzk Y4, 'Uni-Truss'. The Uni-Truss system is a reinterpretation of a traditional truss structure. Conventionally, steel trusses are designed for worst case loads. However, the Uni-Truss system's biggest scale components are designed for medium loads which, if needed, can be reinforced with smaller-scale components to provide more strength. This increases the structure's performance and reduces material use, which is an important parameter when responding to the housing crisis in Buenos Aries. The system is also able to integrate insulation and services, making the construction process easier with all the layers of the building contained in one system. A series of rules are implemented to inform the construction process. For instance, plastic welding as a connection method and the action of cutting are forbidden – these allow irregular forms to appear naturally without formally designing them. This can be understood through Mario Carpo's 'sensual experience of design without thinking' where, in the case of this system, the main restriction is a limited set of components that, as a natural consequence, regulates the aesthetics of the generated architecture. The Uni-Truss system addresses the Zero Waste policy in the Buenos Aires Plan. Architecture is created out of recycled plastic bottles and turned into Uni-Truss components. Assuming a 40-year lifespan, this system is then recycled along with existing raw plastic waste and turned into new components. **Figs. 19.11 – 19.12 Zuzana Sojkova** Y4, 'Landscape for Habitation'. The project explores conditions of habitation through a design of a discrete building element.

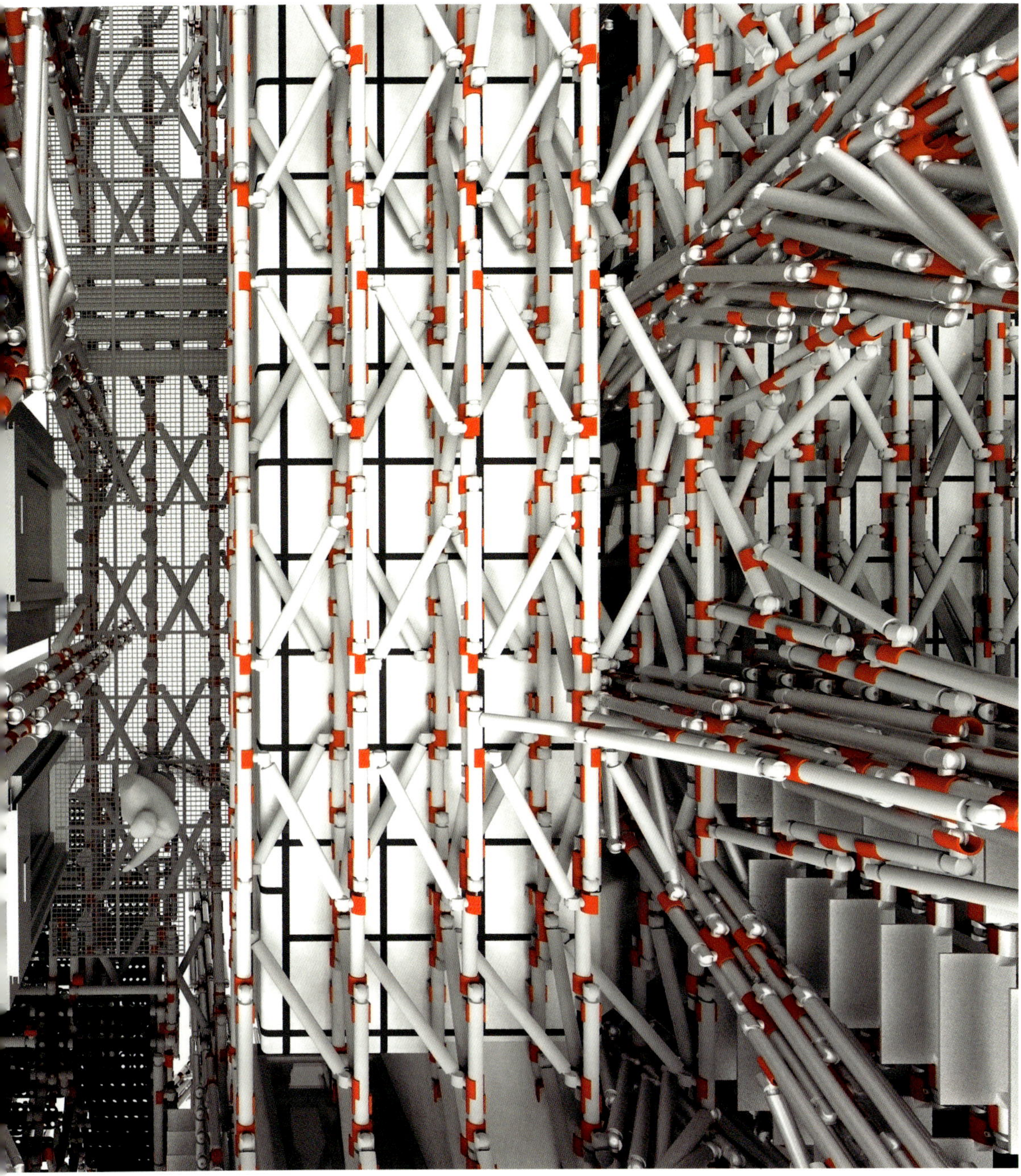

Through a bottom-up approach to the project, the bricks and their connection system are developed at the beginning and subsequently multiplied and aggregated. The priority is to create a building system that rethinks traditional construction methods rather than a single building that responds to a particular site. When moving to the architectural scale, the project attempts to integrate mechanical and electrical services into the accessible hollow brick cores by connecting them into continuous channels. This approach creates a dynamic environment – a landscape for habitation that influences how people move through the space. **Fig. 19.13** **Ivo Tedbury** Y4, 'Dynamic Construction Tower'. Operating within the context of the Buenos Aires housing crisis, which affects 500,000 people, the project proposes the radical separation of the 'home' from the 'building' it resides within. The 'building' is composed of a discrete system of self-assembling 'Dynamic Construction Particles' (DCPs) which provide structure, circulation and environmental control (making use of exo-muscular robots to give the particles individual self-locomotion). The 'home' is composed of a separate discrete system of floor, ceiling and wall elements which can be arranged according to the occupant's needs. The occupant only owns the enclosure elements, hugely reducing the financial cost of the home, and can purchase more or sell them over time according to their specific demands, while the DCPs rearrange the surrounding building to support these changes.

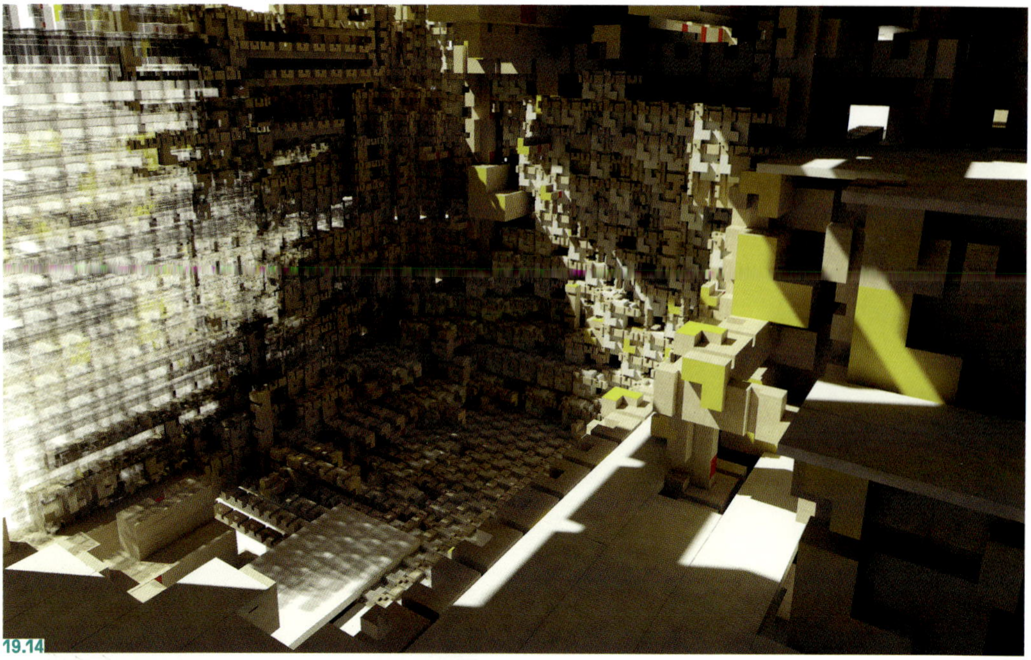

19.14

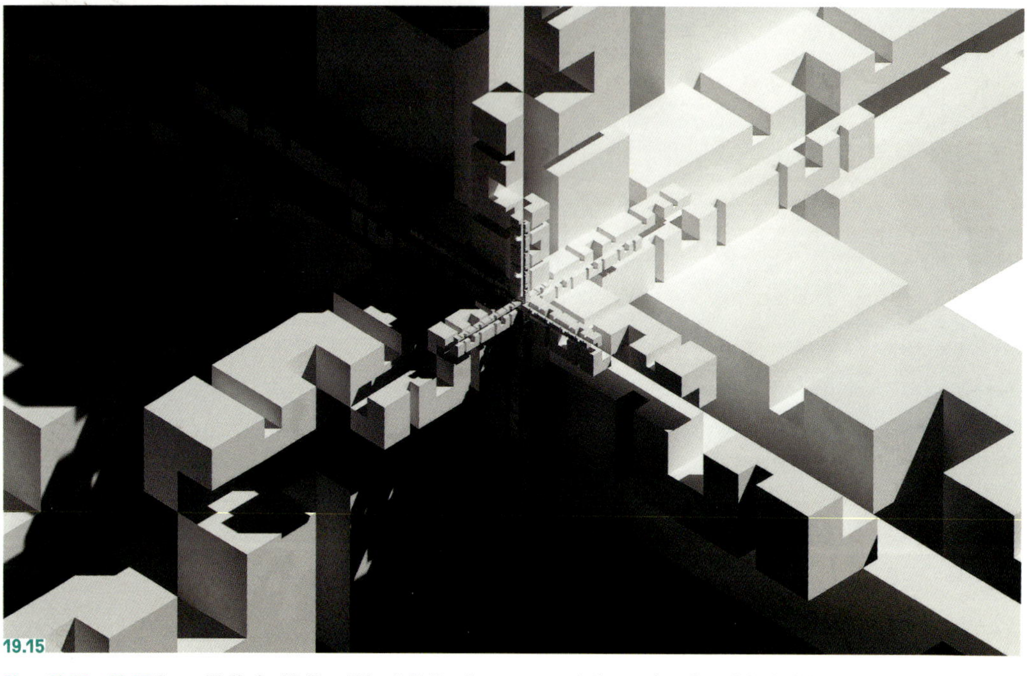

19.15

Figs. 19.14 – 19.15 Oscar Walheim Y4, 'Rood i Geel'. Taking the 'Cartesian Joint' employed in Gerrit Rietveld's Rood Blauwe Stoel as a starting point, this project investigates a new form of 'universal brick' that connects in three axes – a serially repeated discrete building element that can create new architectural tectonics. This discretisation of architectural construction questions both the modernist model prevalent in contemporary architecture and the more recent notion of continuous construction that accompanies advances in 3D printing. Ultimately, this leads to new methods of describing and translating architectural information itself. The investigation uses three studies to guide the research; the re-interpretation of a 1920s Modernist apartment plan, a contemporary building proposal located in Buenos Aires and a speculative exploration of the building system's potential.
Fig. 19.16 Jaspal Channa Y4, 'States of Permanence'. This developed from an initial investigation into an elongated timeframe of construction; overlapping with the idea that dwelling can occur concurrently within this. The backdrop of a speculative pilgrimage route leading up Argentina's vast Pampus provided a scenario for the system to aggregate into a series of nomadic sanctuaries scattered along this route for pilgrims and travellers to dwell in. It uses the process of manufacturing through a series of machines and moulds to enable localised, continual manufacturing, whilst incorporating knowledge from historical nomadic traditions of Latin America. The project's aim is to create a unique, yet familiar, language explored within individual, bespoke architecture.

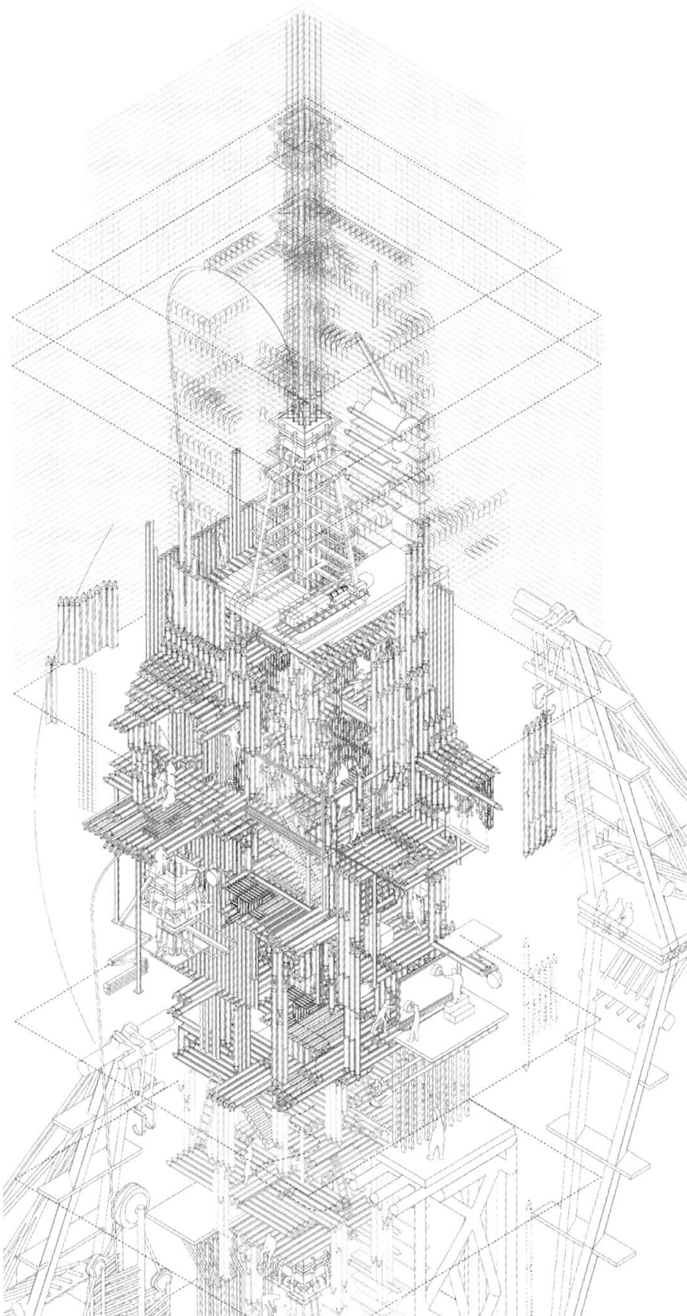

19.16

Unit 20

Convoluted Geometries, Hybrid Programmes, Intertwined Spaces

Marjan Colletti, Marcos Cruz

Year 4
George Bolwell, Mon Han, Patrick Mawson, Matthew Pratt, Jessica Wang, Man Wong

Year 5
Daniel Coley, Chris Falla, Andreas Körner, Panagiota Kotsovinou, James Mills, Firas Saad, Jia Saw, Wai Wong, Selina Yau, Vincent Yeung

Thank you to our consultants and critics Moyez Alwani, Richard Beckett, Isaïe Bloch, Andy Bow, Andrew Haworth, Susanne Hofmann, Damjan Iliev, Hina Lad, Malca Mizrahi, Justin Nicholls, Michael Pelken, Laura Petruso, Yael Reisner, Javier Ruiz, Robert Stuart-Smith, Lena Vasileva, María Eugenia Villafañe, Seda Zirek

Thank you to our partners Grünhelme.de

Students in Year 5 focused on Istanbul, Turkey, one of the world's greatest urban hubs; a convergence of East and West located across two continents. The buzzing urban, historic, religious, political and entrepreneurial background of the city created the framework for projects that aimed at the urban contextualisation of public institutions where global and local needs are juxtaposed and confronted. Istanbul emerged from the cultural torrents of civilization. Today, in a time of extreme religious and political confrontations between the Western and Islamic worlds, and one of migrations and crises, the city has gained once more a pivotal importance with regards to the world's future stability.

——Students in Year 4 focused on Kigali, Rwanda. Scarred by the 1994 genocide and civil war, Rwanda is nicknamed the Land of Eternal Spring. With a small population that is expected to triple by 2040, Kigali, the capital city, is becoming the economic and cultural hub of central Africa. Our projects revolved around the brief of the world's second Chrislamic Church-Mosque where hi-tech (computer-aided, digitally skilled, innovative) design proposals were translated into low-tech (affordable, easily and locally assembled, basic materials) building strategies, aimed to be realised and built in Kigali. The brief was developed in collaboration with the humanitarian association Grünhelme, Germany and in partnership with several other academic institutions that were also involved in charity projects in Africa.

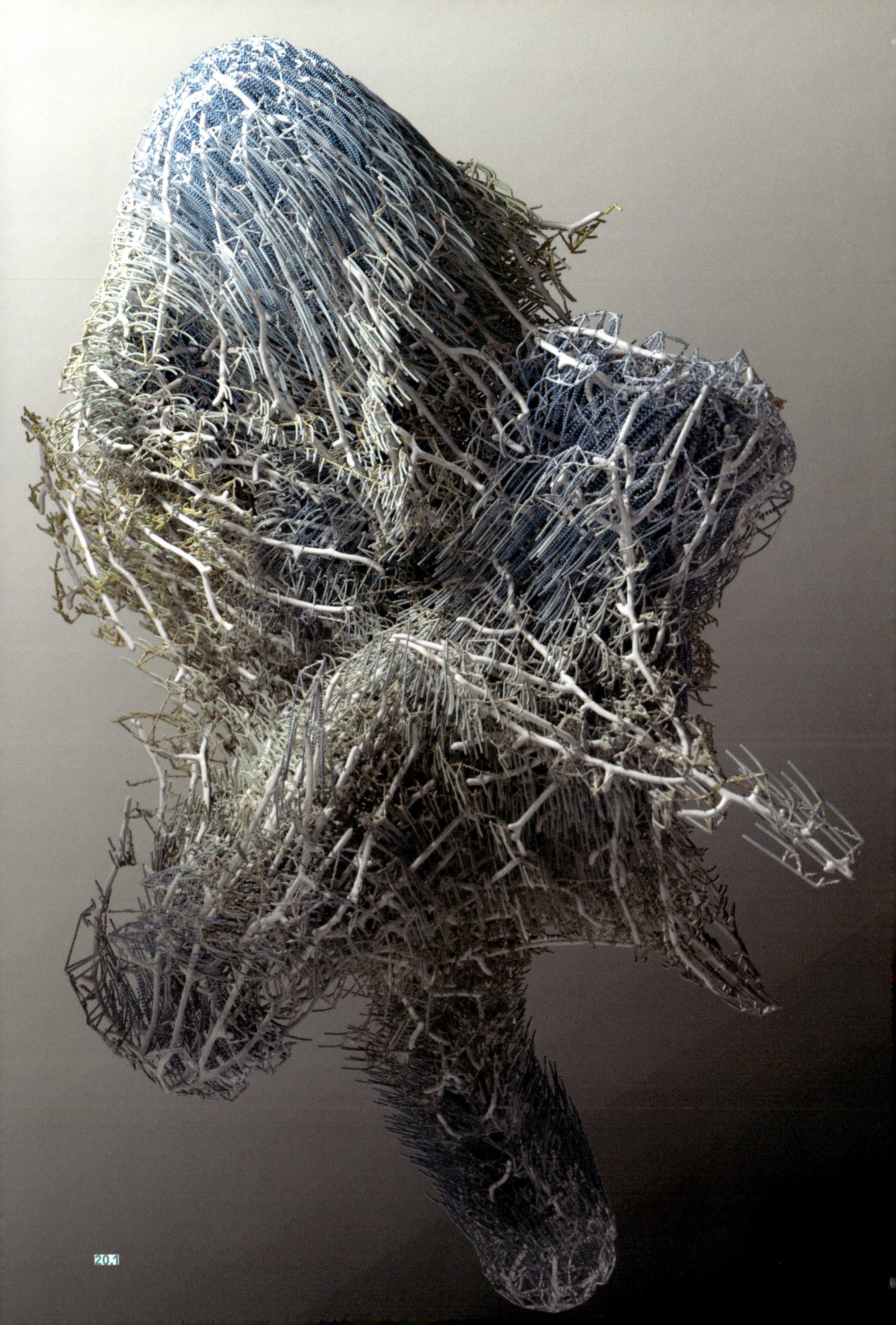

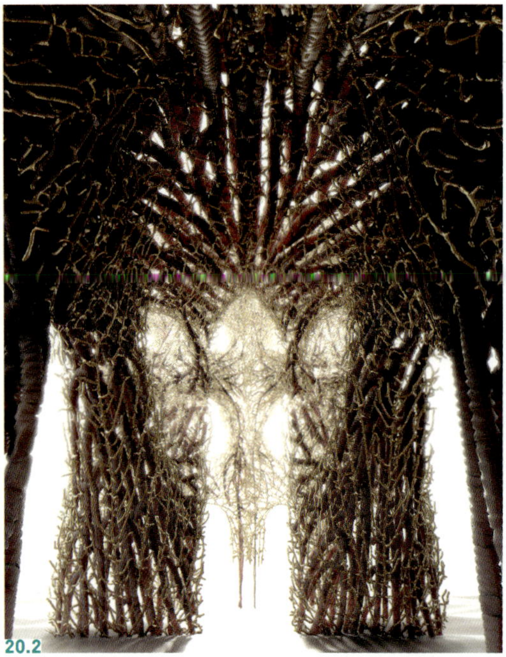

20.2

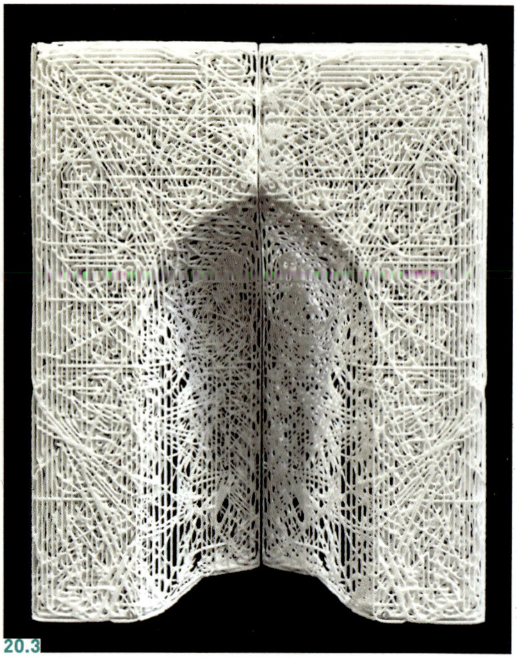

20.3

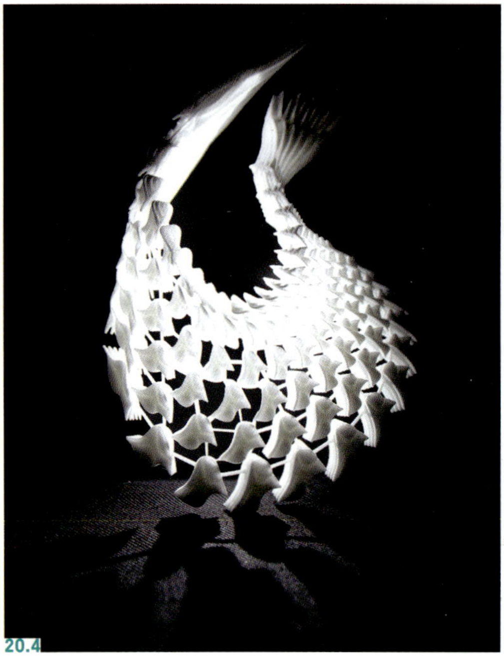

20.4

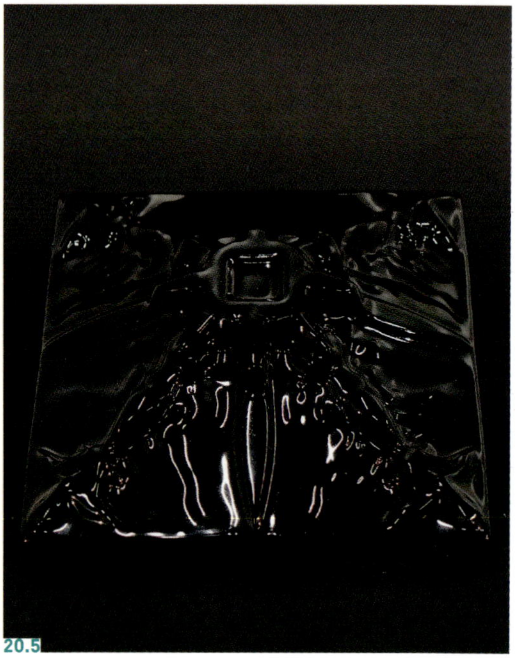

20.5

Figs. 20.1 – 20.2 Chris Falla Y5, 'Digital Genotype'. No longer a concept of the natural, genetic hyperspace emerges as an authentic dimension of digital virtuality. This machinic domain is governed by relational possibilities; whereby computation and biology converge within logical frameworks of time-initiated algorithmic genomes, generating non-Euclidean evolutionary data morphologies of encapsulated information. **Fig. 20.3 Man Chung (Tom) Wong** Y4, 'Crystal Lattices'. The Mihrab (Islamic prayer corner) structure is designed using particle systems that mimic organic crystal lattice growth to achieve a fragile and ephemeral structure that generates different light conditions. **Fig. 20.4 Jessica Wang** Y4, 'Spatial Illusion'. The project is a compilation of modular, dynamic and light experiments in search of the optimum semi-permeable form. **Fig. 20.5 Firas Saad** Y5, 'Sinuous Tile'. Exploring the potential to create a three-dimensional tile with a skin-like, convex, concave morphology. The final component design of a glazed ceramic tile with a highly complex surface topology invokes suggestions of a material awakening.

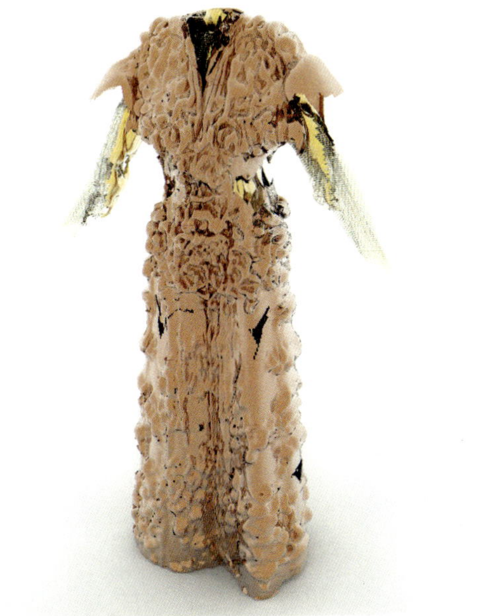

20.6

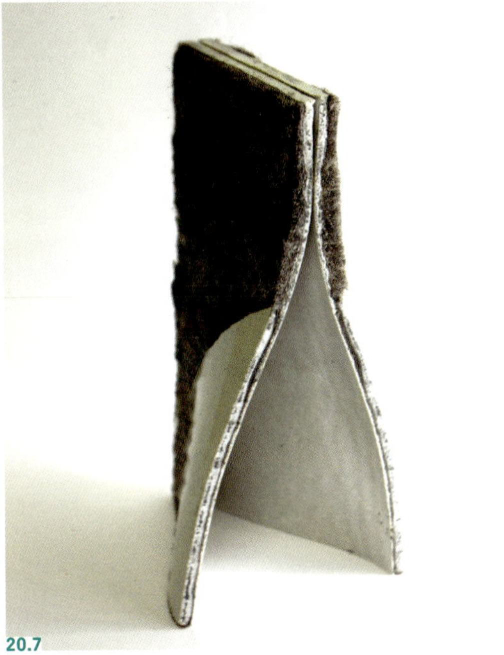

20.7

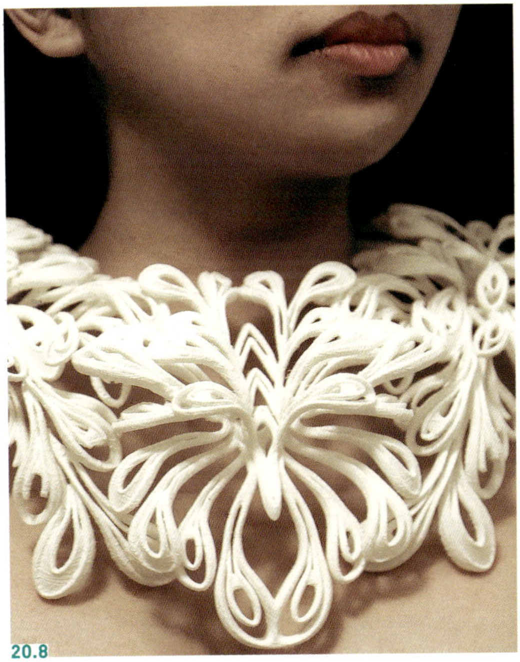

20.8

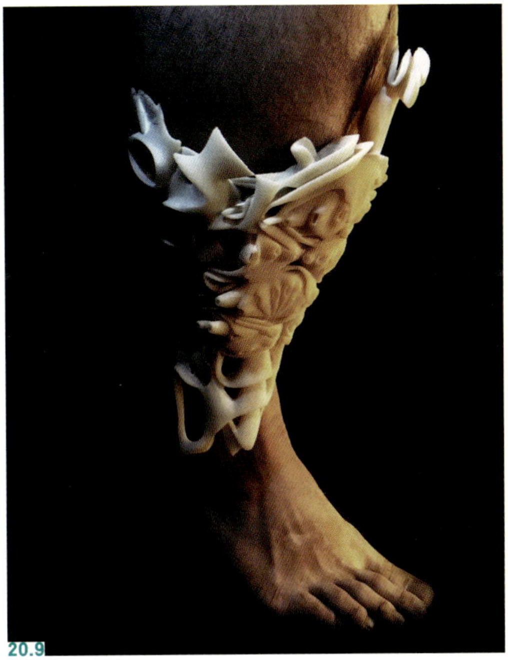

20.9

Figs. 20.6 – 20.7 Wai Yin (Vivian) Wong Y5, 'Dress' - 'Felt-crete'. Study of Istanbul fashion inspired by the traditional Bindalli Entari design of the Ottoman period. The new pattern of the dress is created by digitally inverting and inflating the pattern of the Bindalli dress using sculpting software. 'Felt-crete' is a material investigation of felt composite to be applied to the building industry. The natural wool felt bonds naturally with cement/jesmonite to create a hybrid material for the building façade or interior wall. No additional gluing solution is needed to secure the two materials. Felt creates a natural acoustic, thermal waterproof barrier and the concrete provides structural support. **Fig. 20.8 Selina Yau** Y5, 'Florid Beauty'. A 3D printed neckpiece exploring the materialisation of the blooming petaloid through the ornamental forms of the petal and the stem. **Fig. 20.9 Daniel Coley** Y5, 'Of Corpo. Reality'. Using the study of a recovery space for stroke victims, the project explores the notion of an architecture which derives as a prosthetic augmentation of the inhabitant body.

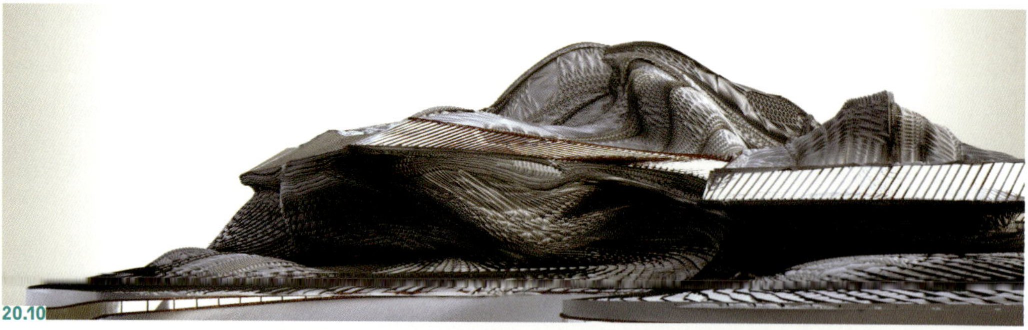

20.10

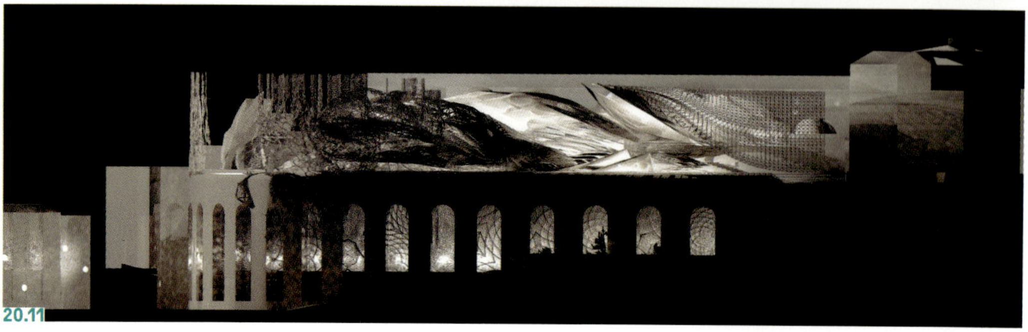

20.11

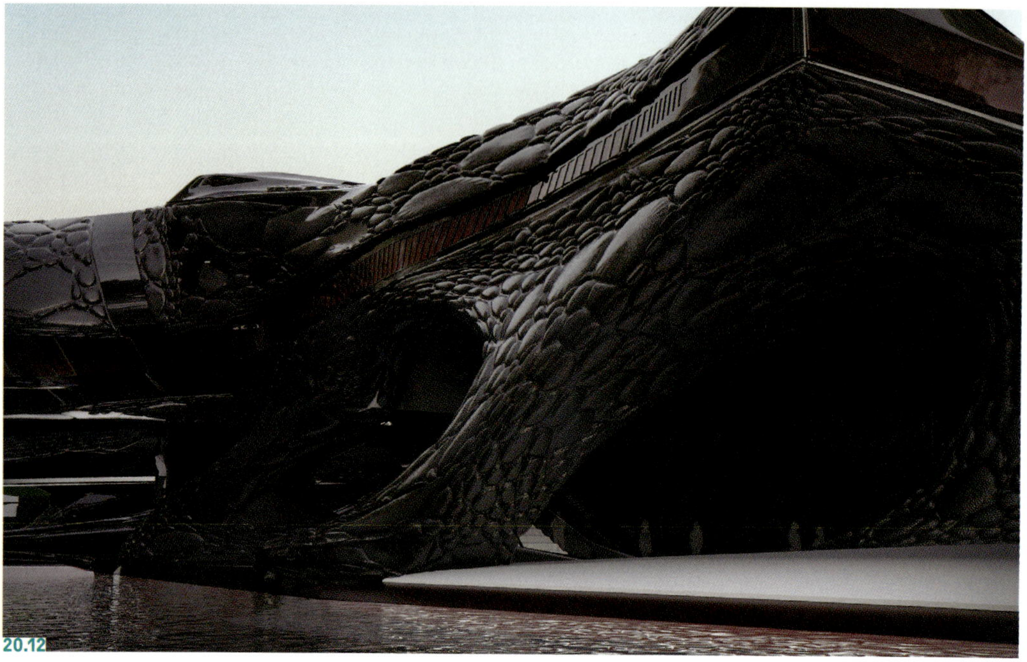

20.12

Fig. 20.10 Jia Jian Saw Y5, 'The Equestrian Guild of Istanbul'. Informed by human and equine form, the speculative redesign of the Equestrian Guild introduces varied layering to integrate soft materials which mimic the ornamental leather patternisation of saddles. **Fig. 20.11 James Mills** Y5, 'Imaginary Archive'. The project investigates principles and methodologies of Sufism. It is developed through a sequential progression from the vegetal to the abstract, from the real to the ideal, or the circle to the square, by seven valleys. Each valley reflects its description in the famous Sufi story by Farid Attar, the 'Conference of the Birds', a figurative story that describes the Sufi path. **Fig. 20.12 Firas Saad** Y5, 'Istanbul Institute for Gastronomy'. The philosophical idea of 'Numen' and its application to architecture employs animalistic attributes, reintroducing ideas of aliveness and formal dexterity, usually absent from contemporary digital design protocols. **Fig. 20.13 Panagiota Kotsovinou** Y5, 'Istanbul's Branching Arcades.' The project explores the potential applications of L-Systems and evolutionary growth processes in architectural design. Algorithms supplement the design of structures based entirely on identical or self-similar components, enabling modular repetition to coexist with variation and dynamic transitions in scale, density and tectonic weight.

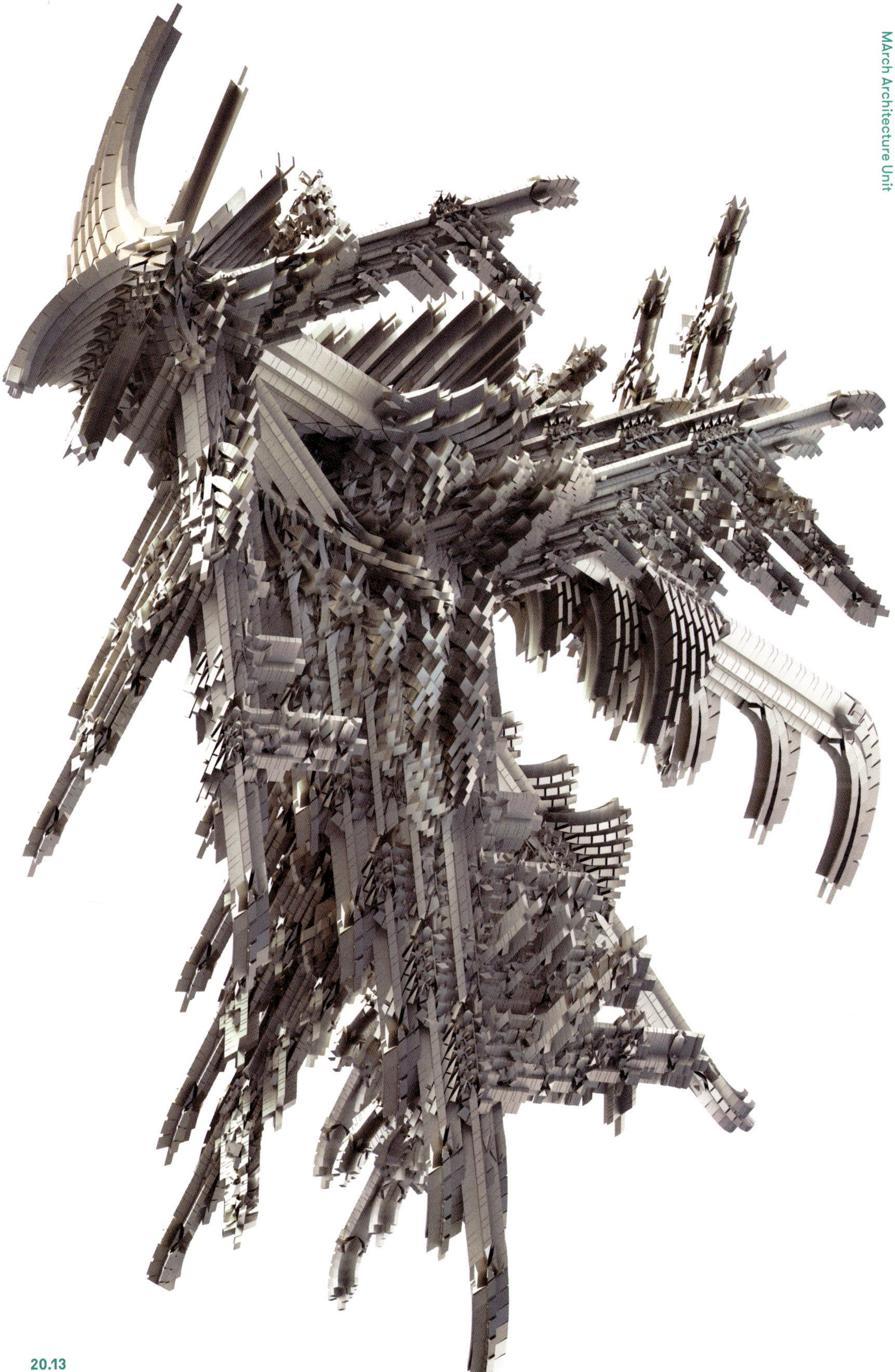

20.13

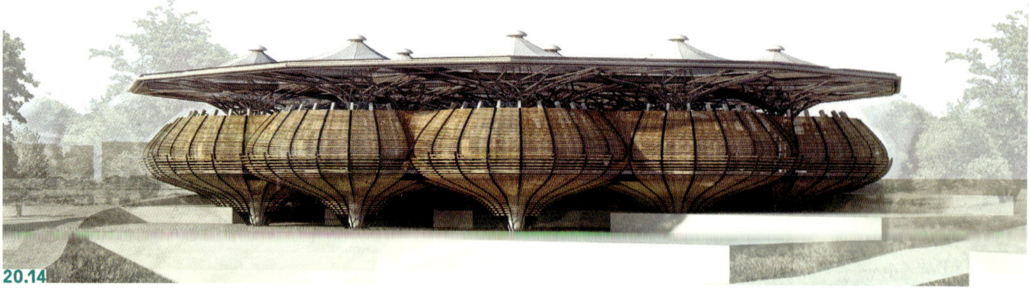

20.14

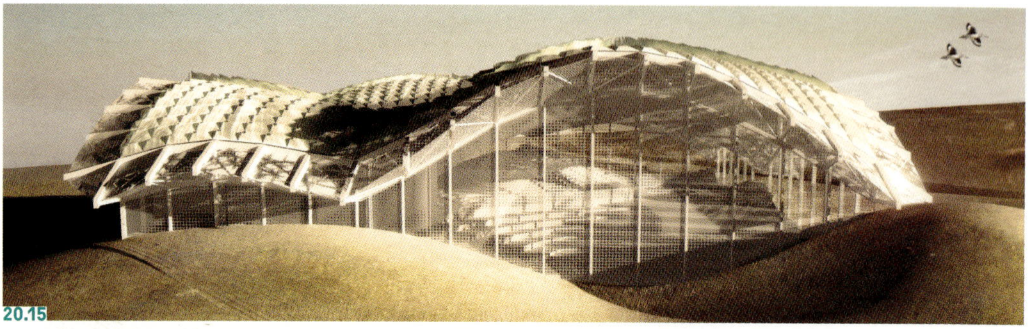

20.15

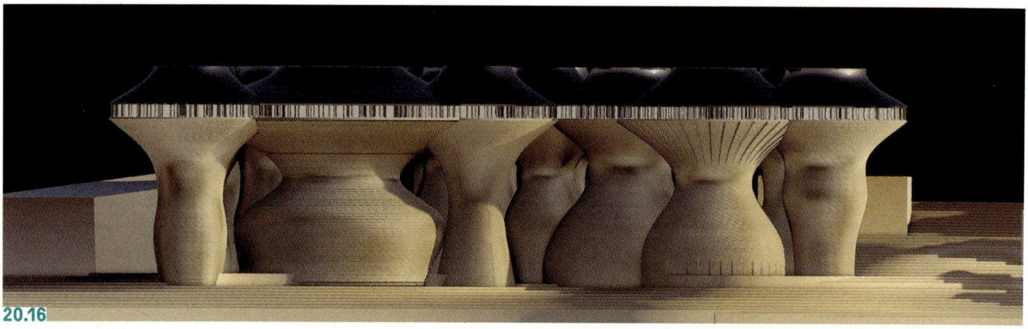

20.16

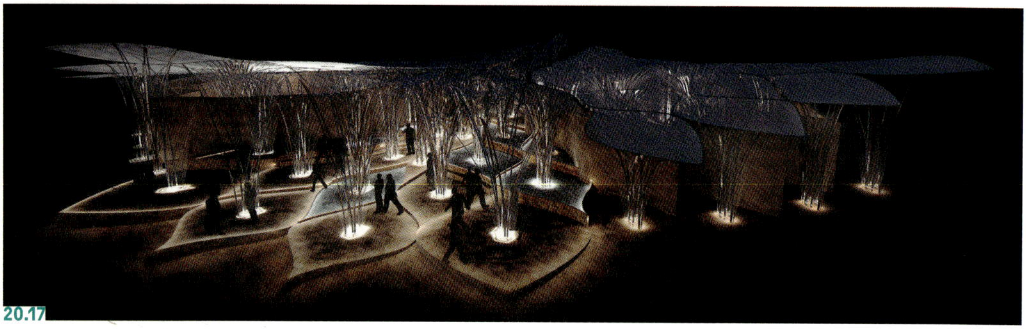

20.17

Fig. 20.14 Mon Thi Han Y4, 'A Breathing Piece of Architectural Ecology'. A layered façade system creates a volumetric, porous array of modular bays, which are applied in the context of a Church-Mosque in Kigali. **Fig. 20.15 Man Ching (Tom) Wong** Y4, 'Undulating Urban Landscape'. The Kigali Church-Mosque uses an undulating interior surface aligning with an urban open landscape to generate various spatial conditions to respond to diverse religious and communal activities. **Fig. 20.16 George Bolwell** Y4, ' Lofted Clay Vessels'. Volumes rise to form a shading canopy. Enclosed spaces accommodate Christian worship whilst sheltered interstitial areas provide a flexible Mosque plan. Roof lights are designed to allow varying levels of light according to the religious significance of a given space. **Fig. 20.17 Matthew Pratt** Y4, 'Geometry and Resolution of Fibrous Systems.' Religious relationships between floor and sky are expressed as a heavy stepping contoured landscape, providing a platform for thin elastic structures and a light and an ethereal roof. **Figs. 20.18 – 20.20 Andreas Körner** Y5, 'Environmental Ecoysis - Urban Forum Istanbul'. The forum houses a library, an underground archive, a datacentre and an open campus, including a palm house. The excess heat of the datacentre heats the rest of the program in winter by utilising the predominant natural wind directions onsite for distribution. Performative layers control the indoor and outdoor climate zones.

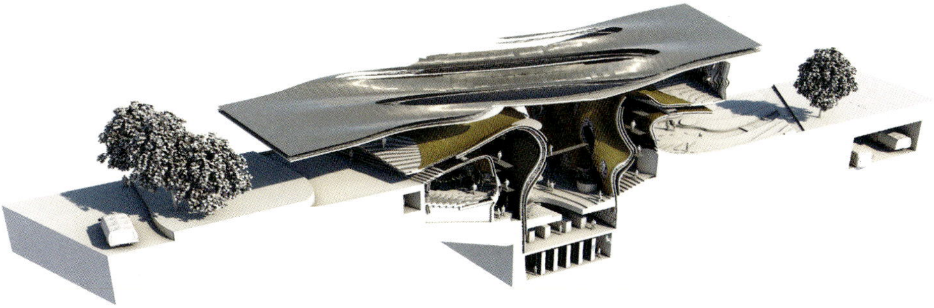

20.18

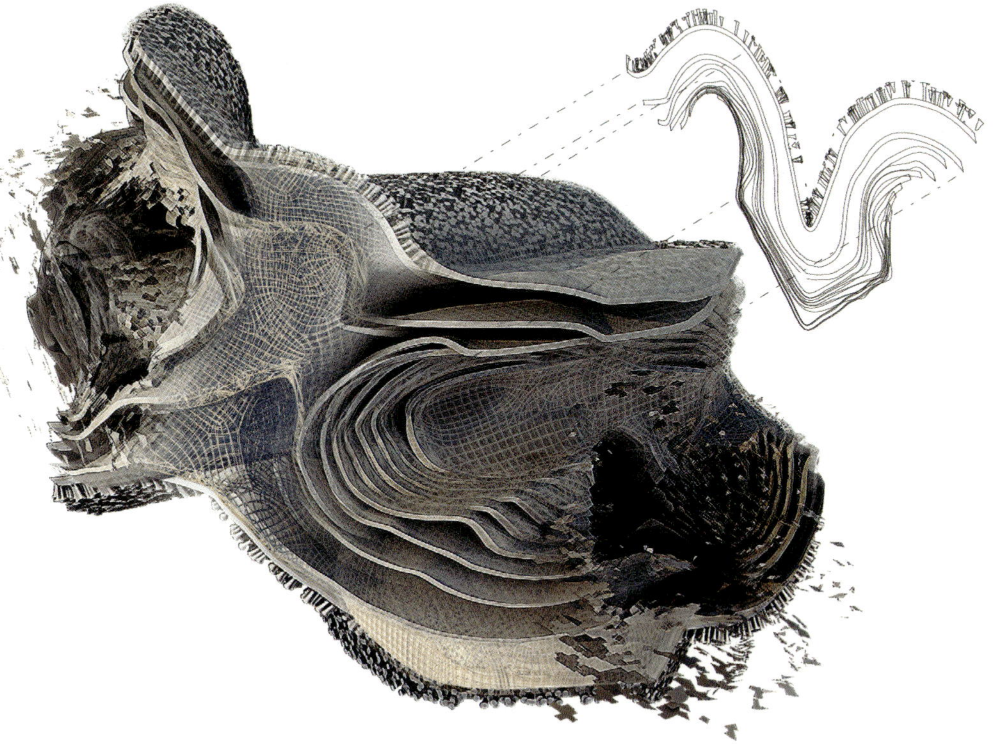

20.19

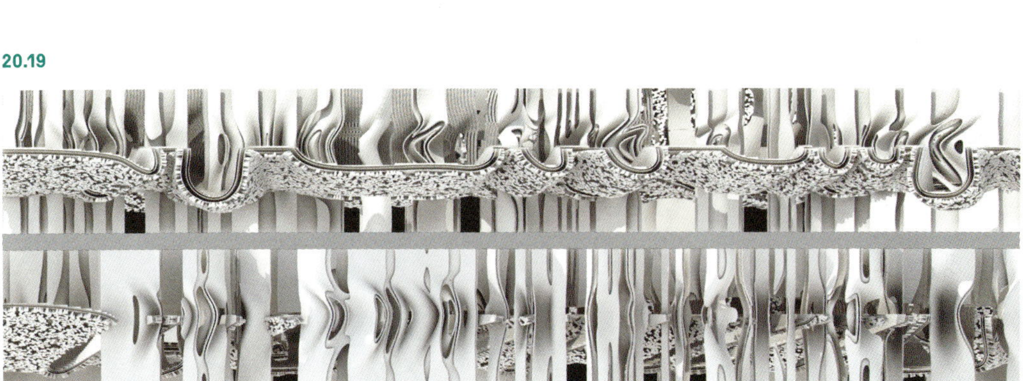

20.20

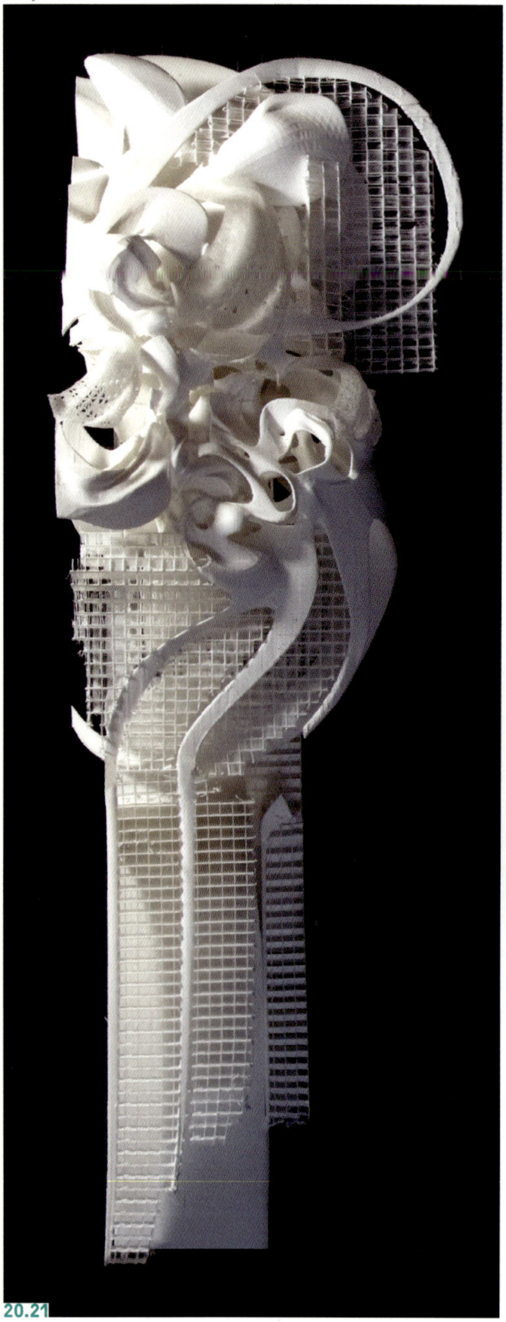

20.21

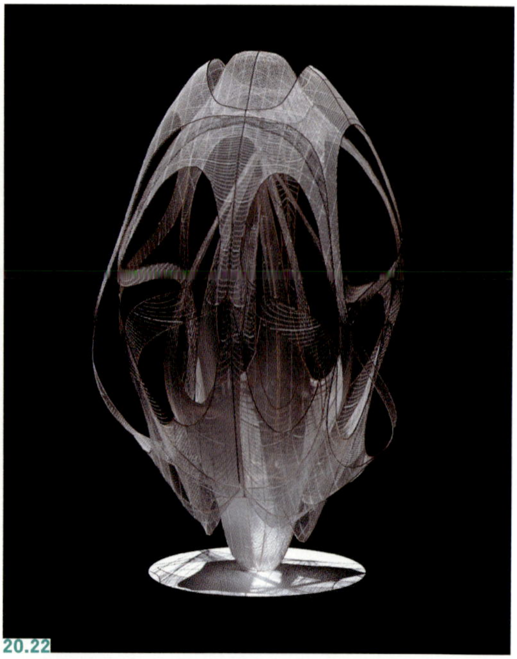

20.22

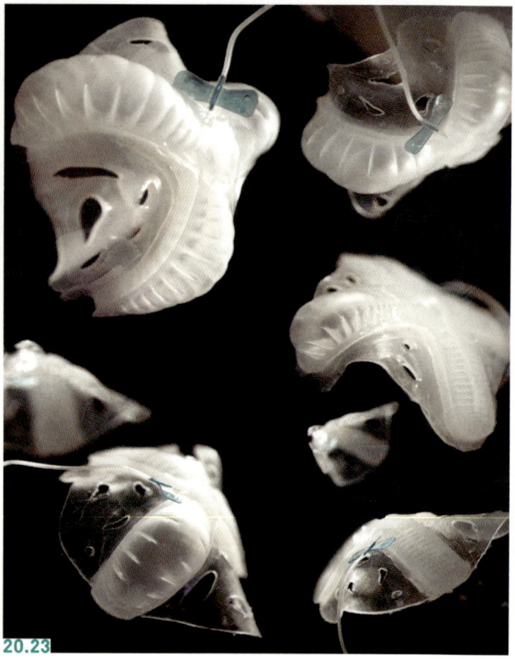

20.23

Fig. 20.21 Selina Yau Y5, 'Florid Beauty'. Based on scientific and artistic abstraction of nature, this project explores the post-digitalisation of florid intelligence through the ornament and Alois Riegl's 'Kunstwollen' as a creative will to drive the aesthetic condition of hybrid variance and beauty within the transfigurative classification of the contemporary flower. **Fig. 20.22 Patrick Mawson** Y4, 'The Blending of Architectural Entities'. The project brings forth a covert architecture of framed viewing moments by multilayered geometrical repetition, material voids and optically dynamic structural elements to reveal order amongst otherwise perceived chaos. **Fig. 20.23 Vincent Yeung** Y5, 'A Breathing Piece of Architectural Ecology'. Exploring the softness in nature through silicone. Understanding the hardness of this particular type of synthetic plastic allows the soft robot to perform a similar motion and body language to jellyfish. **Fig. 20.24 Daniel Coley** Y5, 'Of Corpo.Reality'. Therapeutic processes are embedded into the design proposal which interact with the body during recovery, working as both a multiple-user prosthetic and a healing tool. Rather than the recovery space being a room filled with standalone tools, this research develops a synergic form of the machine/room/body mutant. The case study of the room becomes a malleable module within the wider context of a rehabilitation clinic on site in Istanbul. The definition of the medical prosthetic is intersected with the prevalent guidelines and provisions that shape recovery rooms; where user and room are hybridised for different operational purposes.

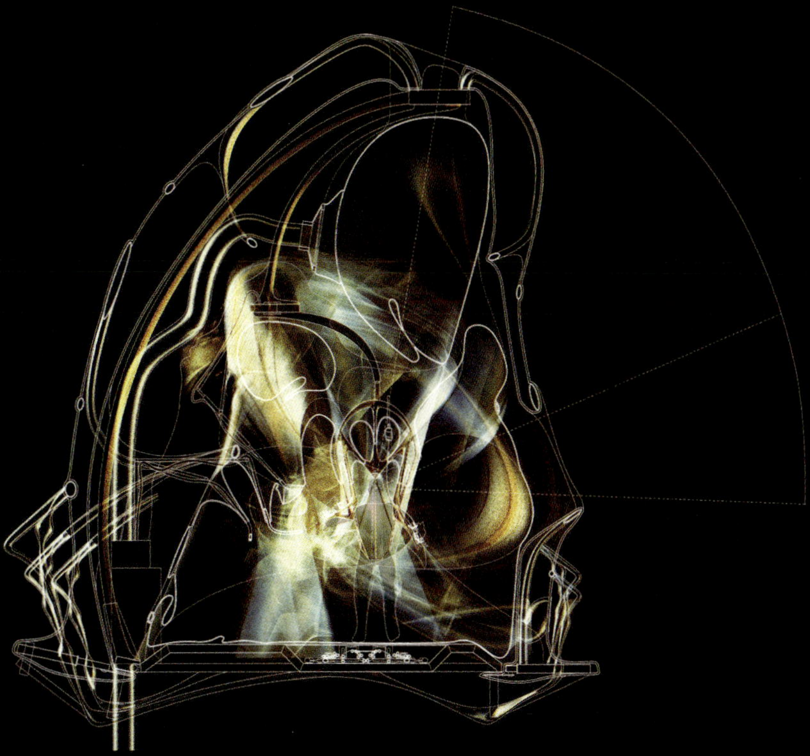

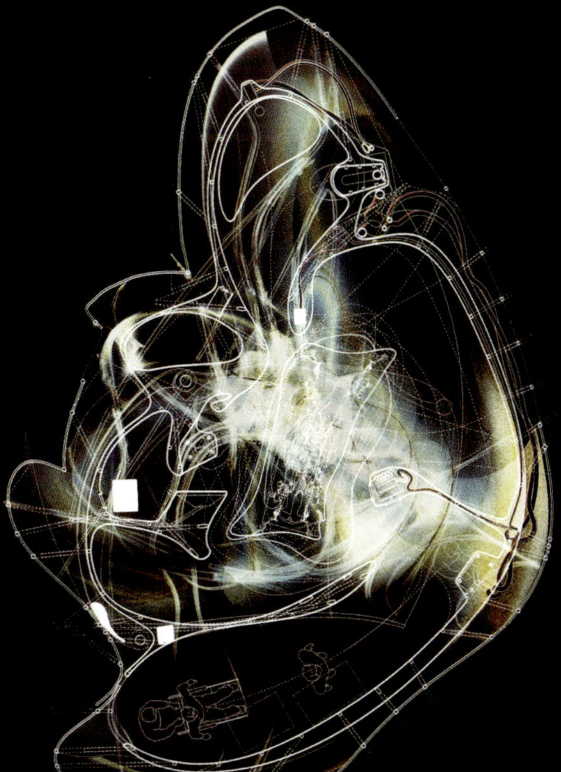

20.24

Unit 21

import/export

Abigail Ashton, Andrew Porter, Tom Holberton

Year 4
Paddi Benson, Jonathan Davis, Matthew Mitchell, Tom Savage, Katherine Scott, Sally Taylor, Yiren (Aviva) Wang, Camilla Wright

Year 5
Maria Filippou, Layal Merhi, Yolanda Leung, Sophie Richards, Samson Simberg, Tomohiro Sugeta, Angeline Wee, Sarish Younis

Thanks to Structural Engineer Brian Eckersley at EOC; and critics Prof Christine Hawley, Prof Stephen Gage, Dr Rachel Cruise, Sayan Skandarajah, Paul Legon, Ned Scott, Jasmin Sohi, Johan Hybschman, Mags Bursa, Tony Smart, Isaie Bloch, Francesca Hughes.

Thanks to our sponsors PDP London Architects – www.pdplondon.com

Marseille is France's second city by population. What it lacks in terms of the grand formality of the capital it more than makes up for with its cosmopolitan and colourful complexity, defined primarily by the Mediterranean port condition. Whilst this historical condition has produced a rich social, political and cultural territory there is also now a legacy of poverty, unemployment, social division and crime.

——Whilst the social, political and topographical condition of the city as an ongoing framework of exchange was of interest to the unit, we also continued with our project to explore the context of the city in terms of its invisible meta-data and how this, when treated as raw material, can be deployed as a source of invention and speculation for a new architecture. Urban space is increasingly defined by the infrastructures of communications, information and social interaction through new media. However, as these contemporary technologies develop at a rapid pace, the traditional paradigms of physical space become increasingly disconnected and irrelevant. The unit continued to explore how this disconnection can be addressed and new hybrids of hard and soft architecture can be invented and emerge.

——The unit considered how such metaphysical data systems can be a creative opportunity for interpretation and inventiveness that might in turn create, and participate in, the cultural and experiential life of the city. Further to which, the slippages, quirks and misinterpretations through translation of such information systems provided an equally rich source for new digital constructs and material outcomes.

——The students were asked to identify a system of information or data set and consider how they might deploy this within a design process or strategy. Different strategies were employed, information was derived from sound, temperature, humidity and other environmental origins. Some were based on societal information, human behaviours, communications and new media data sources. Political, economic and legal frameworks were also sources of data utilized. The unit formulated methods and techniques that developed the mechanics of how this data could be translated across software platforms.

——The unit is interested in the manifestation of such hybrids of immaterial and physical space into outcomes that are resolutely framed as design propositions; a new morphology of data-driven architecture.

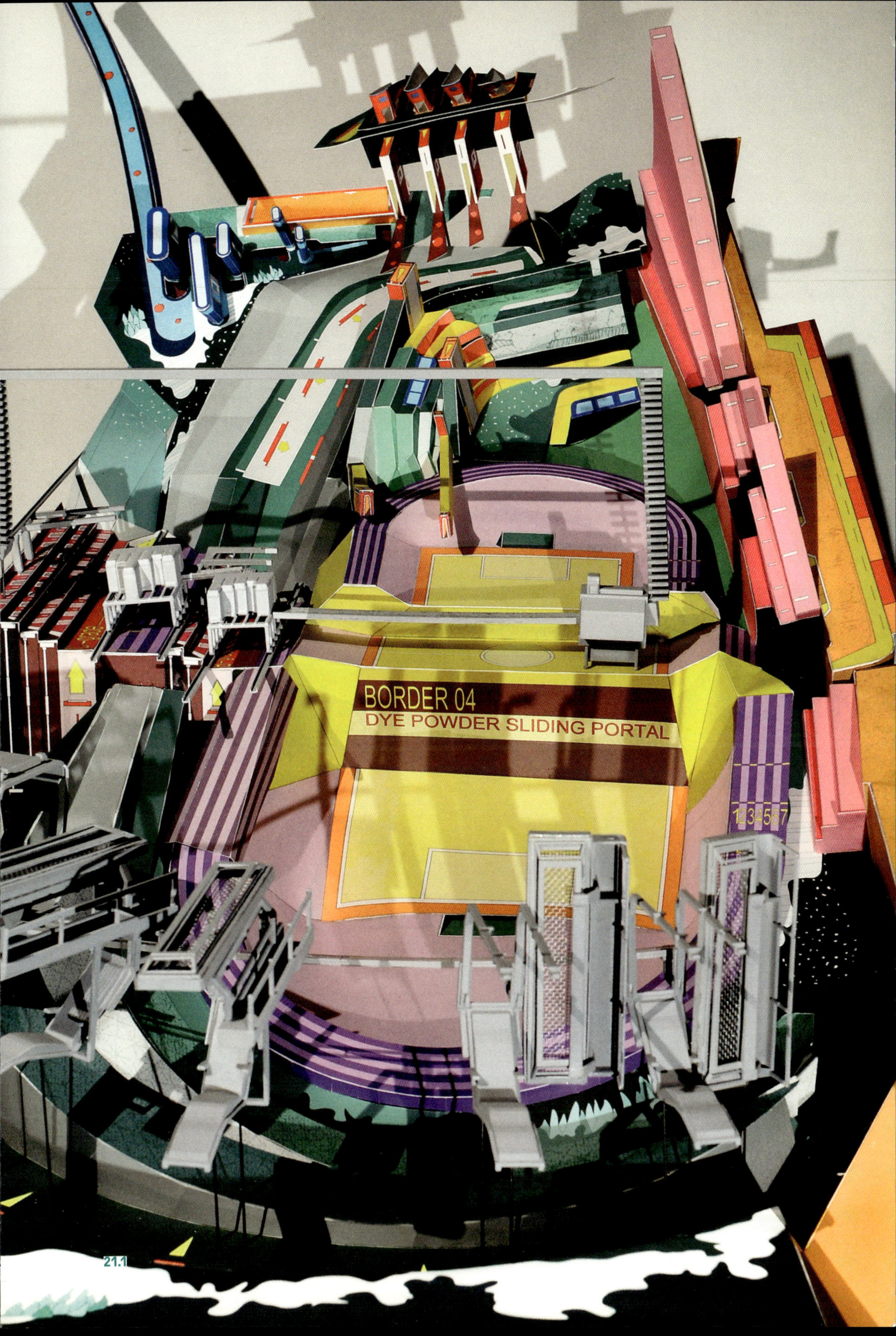

21.1

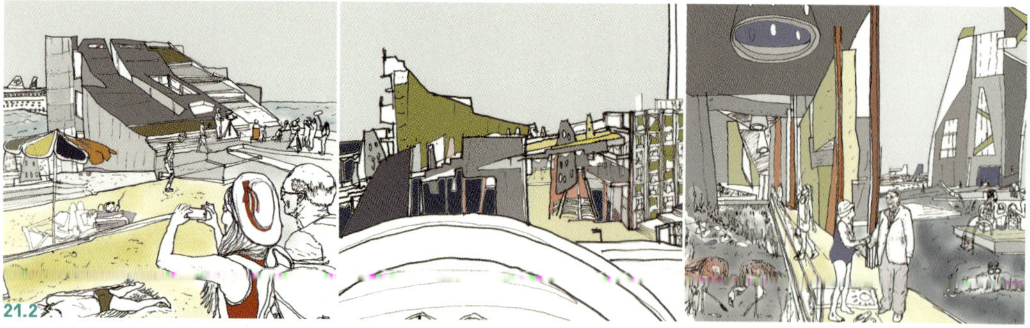

21.2

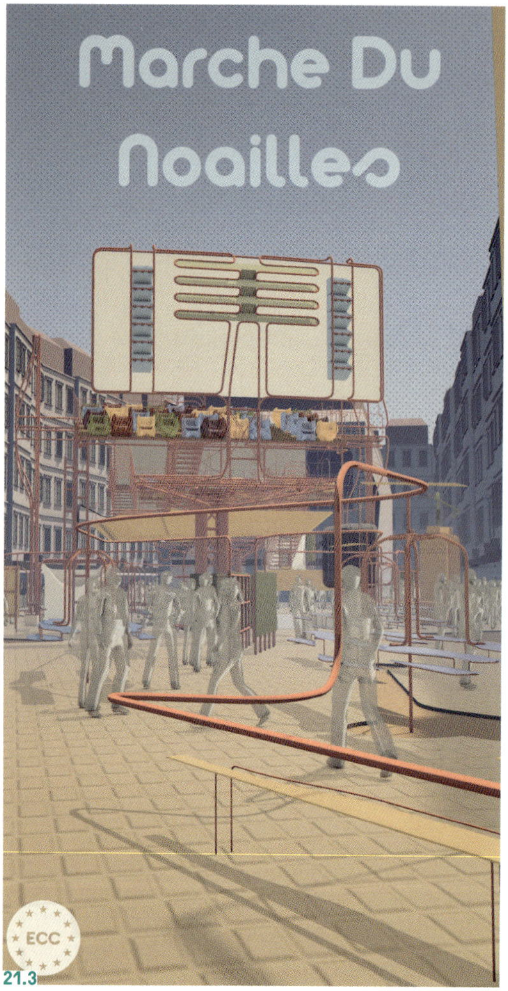

21.3

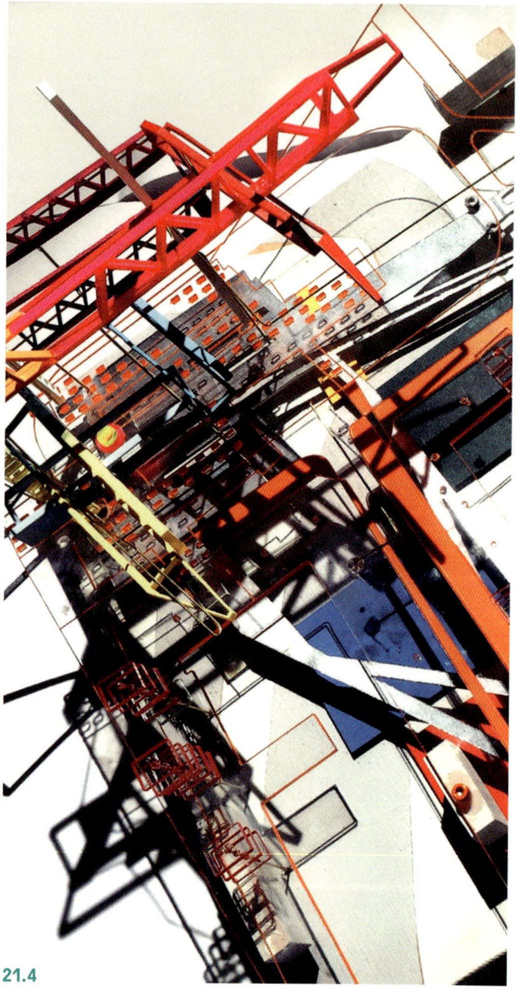

21.4

Fig. 21.1 Yolanda Leung Y5, 'Promo-granate'. Promo-granate is a pomegranate production line and urban park located in Marseille. The project seeks to change the image of Marseille as a drug city and assist the pomegranate trade the same way it did the opium trade in the French Connection in the 70s. In the design project, the nature of different boundaries is associated with different elements of the urban park. **Fig. 21.2 Katherine Scott** Y4, 'Metropole Aix-Marseille-Provence: A New Political Centre for a New Territory'. With the formation of a new territory, binding Marseille to its neighbouring Provençal towns, this scheme proposes a new civic role for this region's new political hub. Combining the workplace with leisure, a beach acts as a democratic tool to re-involve the citizens into the act of politics. Narratives investigated the way different people will participate in the scheme and how this can lead to unexpected encounters and exchanges. **Fig. 21.3 Tom Savage** Y4, 'L'Immaginaire Collectif De Marseille'. Using French cinema as a tool for investigation, the proposal explores a new marketplace against the backdrop of a central and unofficial district which typifies the perception of the city it is located in. Cinema is used to explore the long-established French love affair with film as a means of self-expression. By distilling and dissecting these films, the proposal recombines their raw data as a set of new cinematically inspired structures, with the aim of creating an enhanced identity for Marseille that can help to foster an appreciation of the unique qualities of the city in its residents.

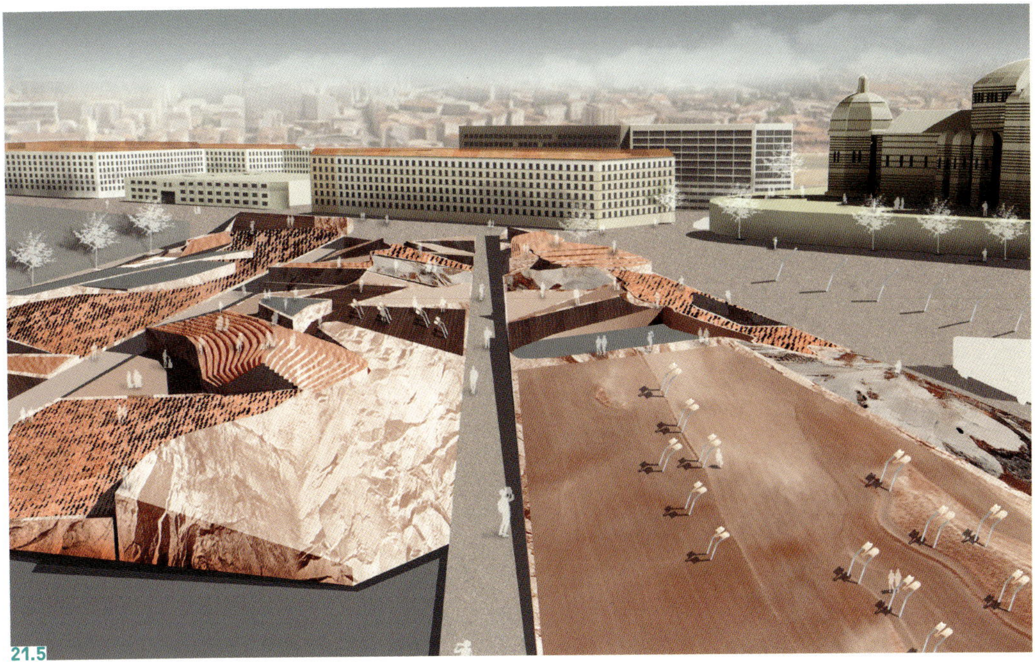

21.5

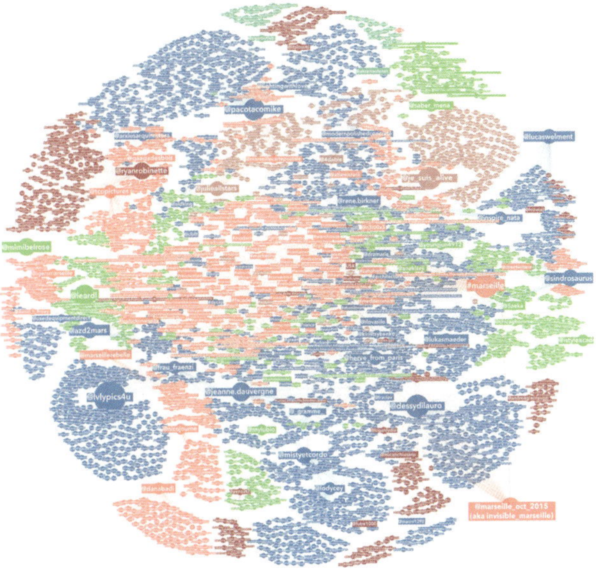

21.6

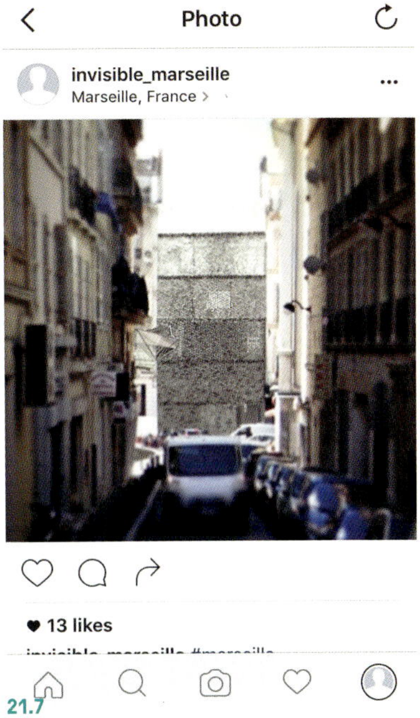

21.7

Fig. 21.4 Yiren (Aviva) Wang Y4, 'Calibreur de La Joliette'. The project tests out possibilities of city calibration at a local scale. By defining the Unité d'habitation as an 'ideal' modular piece of city, the project is based on comparing the proportion of spaces with different functions at various neighbourhoods and that in Unité d'habitation. As a project commissioned by the Euroméditerranée, Calibreur de La Joliette will not only benefit the local community but also turn Place de la Joliette together with Les Terrasses du Port Shopping Centre into Marseille's new cultural centre. **Fig. 21.5 Marianna Filippou** Y5, 'Marseille Cruise Landscape'. A proposal for a cruise boat terminal in the form of a landscape as an extension of the city of Marseille. The design is based on the circulation routes of cruise passengers entering and leaving the site. Its main feature is a field of terracotta tiles layering the glazed roof of the proposed structure in order to control direct sunlight. Its materiality directly refers to Marseille's image as a tiled roofscape and responds to the specific climate of a Mediterranean port city. **Figs. 21.6 – 21.7 Tomohiro Sugeta** Y5, 'Translating Collective Portraits of City to Urban Interventions: Imaginary Marseille on Instagram'. Can data from social networks be manifested as physical structure in the city? The focus of the project is to explore the possibilities in designing urban interventions by translating data obtained from Instagram in Marseille. This bottom-up approach informed principles and site strategy, while the project attempts to reinvent civil space through a top-down analysis of sixteen years of minutes at city council.

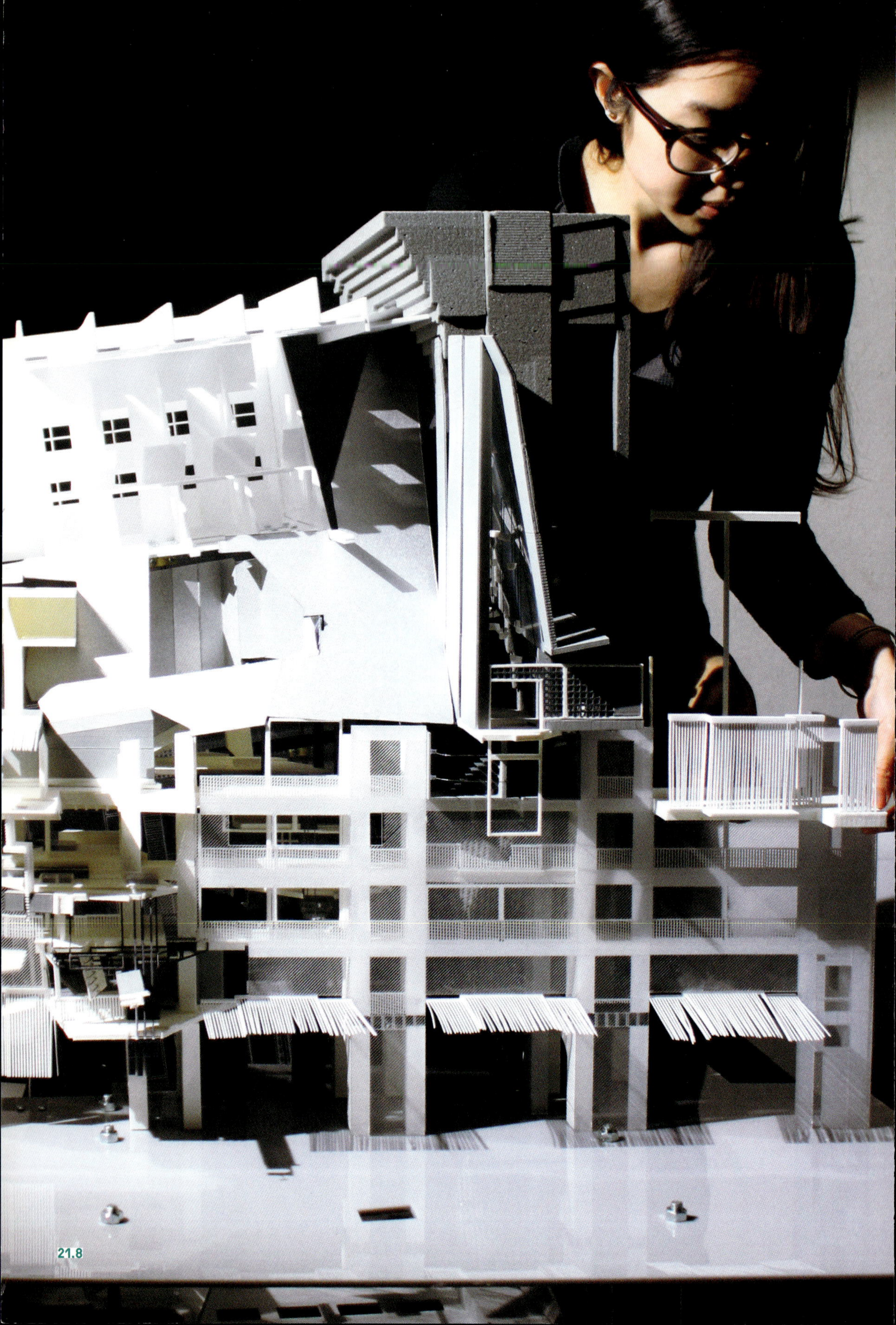

21.8

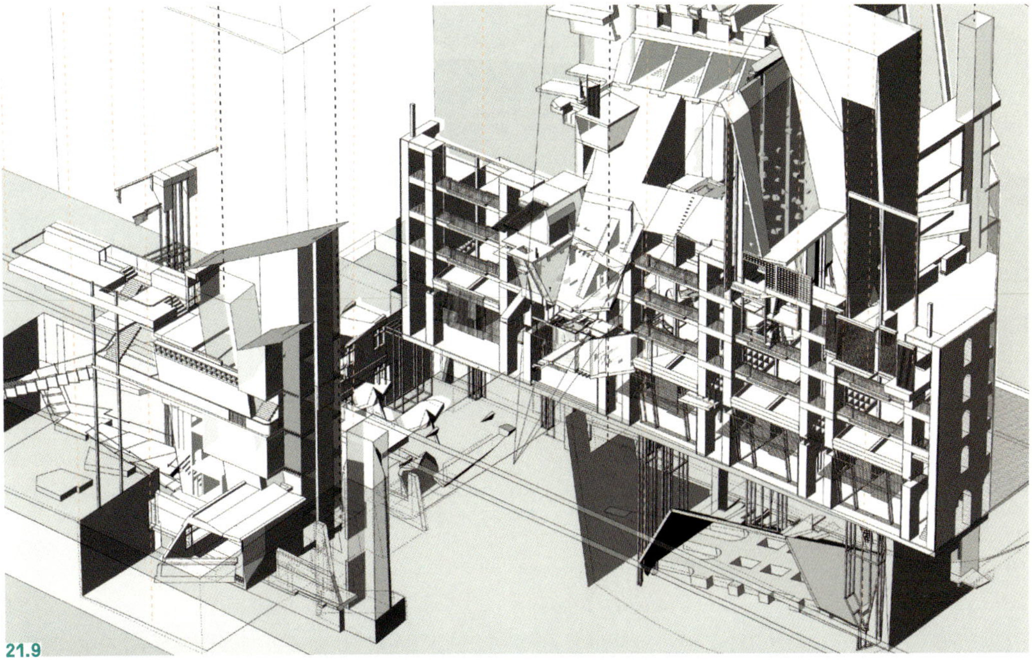

21.9

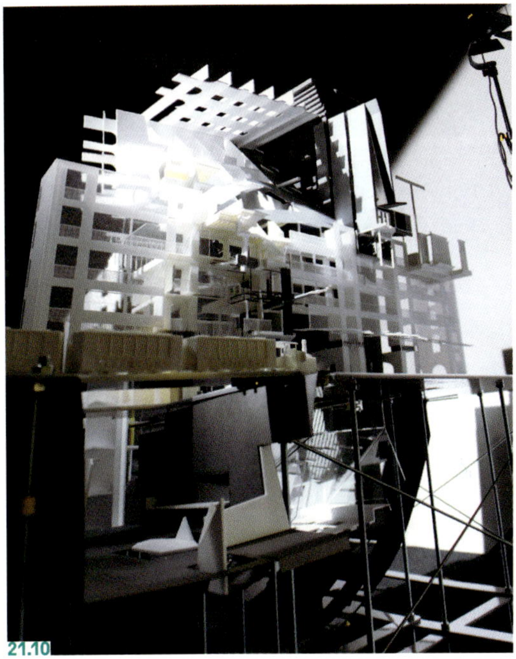

21.10

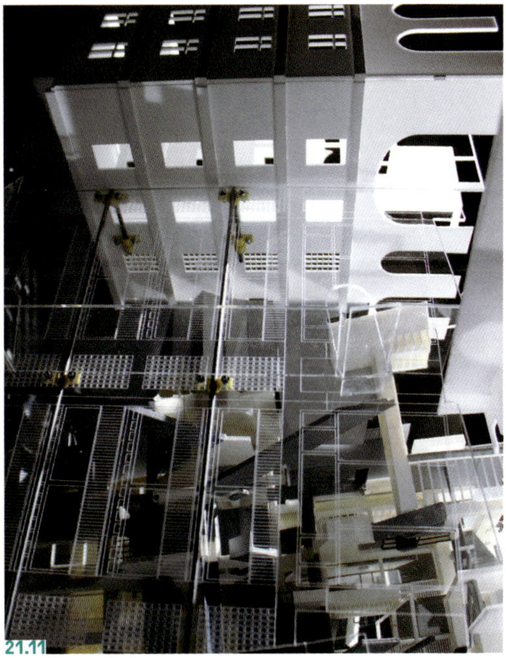

21.11

Figs. 21.8 – 21.11 Angeline Wee Y5, 'Un Immeuble Meuble / A Movable Immovable'. Conservation principles, fundamentally based on changing 'cultural values', are integrated into written urban planning policy, then translated into built form. This project explores the quirks and possibilities of applying such fixed regulations to material heritage at varying scales, celebrating subjective interpretation of legislation in the name of conservation. Modifying buildings along Marseille's iconic Vieux Port, it draws from the existing Code du Patrimoine, observations of preservation in the city and other methods of memorial, using algorithmic modelling to create a rules-based design system, representing non-negotiable and, at times, nonsensical application of certain heritage-based planning policies.

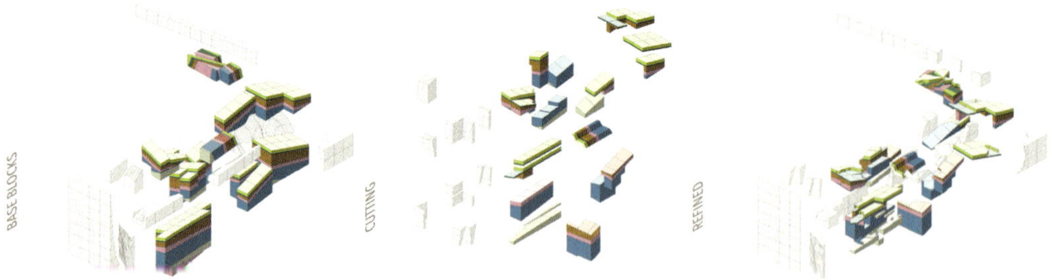

21.12

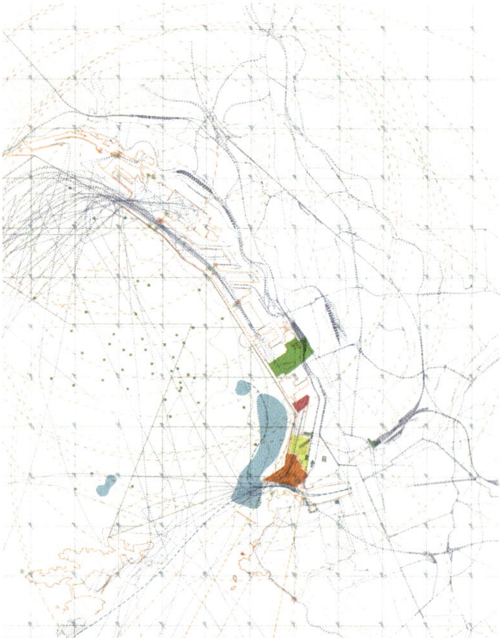

21.13

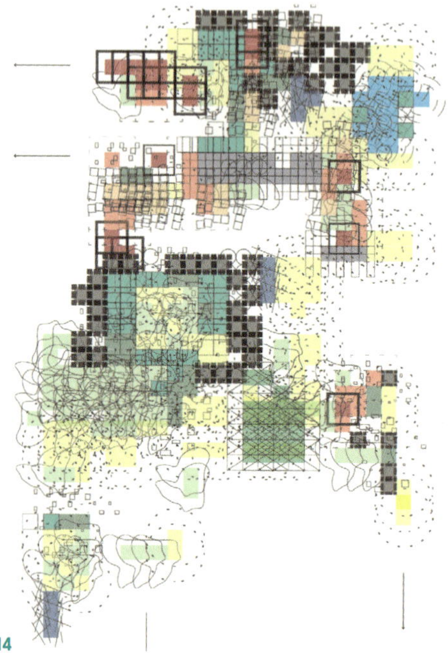

21.14

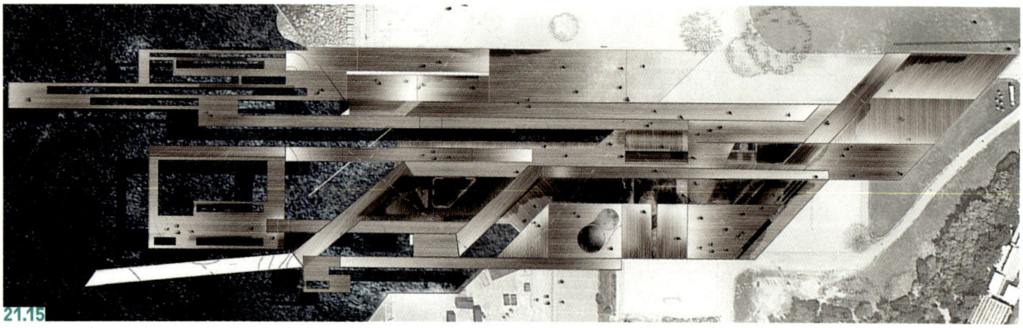

21.15

Fig. 21.12 Camilla Wright Y4, 'Limestone Museum'. The Museum is a testament to Marseilles' relationship with its adjacent limestone outcrop. Being intrinsic to time, layers within the stone are parallel to the narrative of limestone in the construction of Marseille and the formation of the Limestone Creeks. The prized nature of the stone led to an archaeological approach to quarrying, such that the limestone and its spectrum of data became the object of excavation. **Fig. 21.13 Sally Taylor** Y4, 'Marseille Fos: Reuniting the City with the Sea'. Marseille's Fos Port has large amounts of traffic arriving and departing on a daily basis; tankers, cargo and passenger cruise vessels. Through mapping these boats, hidden and temporal lines of the courses taken are exposed, documenting a very local and unique series of movements. The city's waterfront is obstructed by barriers resulting in little interaction with the Mediterranean Sea. **Fig. 21.14 Jonathan Davis** Y4, 'A new organisational strategy of the Mediterranean'. The Project - an alliance of port cities independent of national identity creating 'networked urbanism'. This is formed by connection and vector rather than division and territory, and develops a new spatiality through utilising the grid-like structures of the Marseilles quayside. **Fig. 21.15 Layal Merhi** Y5, 'Prado Tranquille'. Investigating questions of culture, identity, and temporality, this project is an insertion on the edge of the Mediterranean. The intervention leverages Marseille's diverse culture and urban history, referencing the Prado and the 'bowl' as the site in question, a program also key to the south of Marseille.

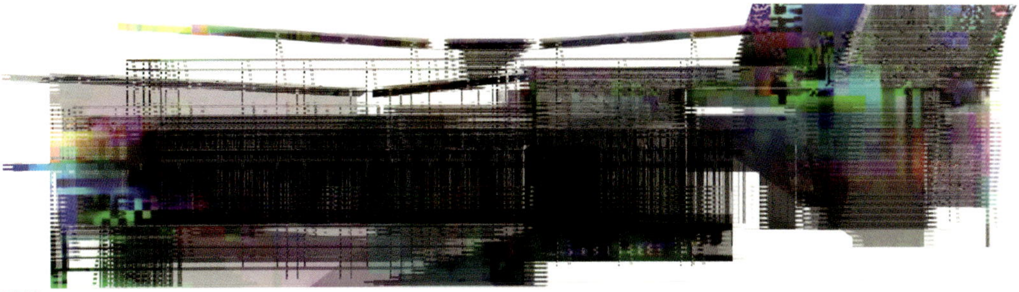

21.16

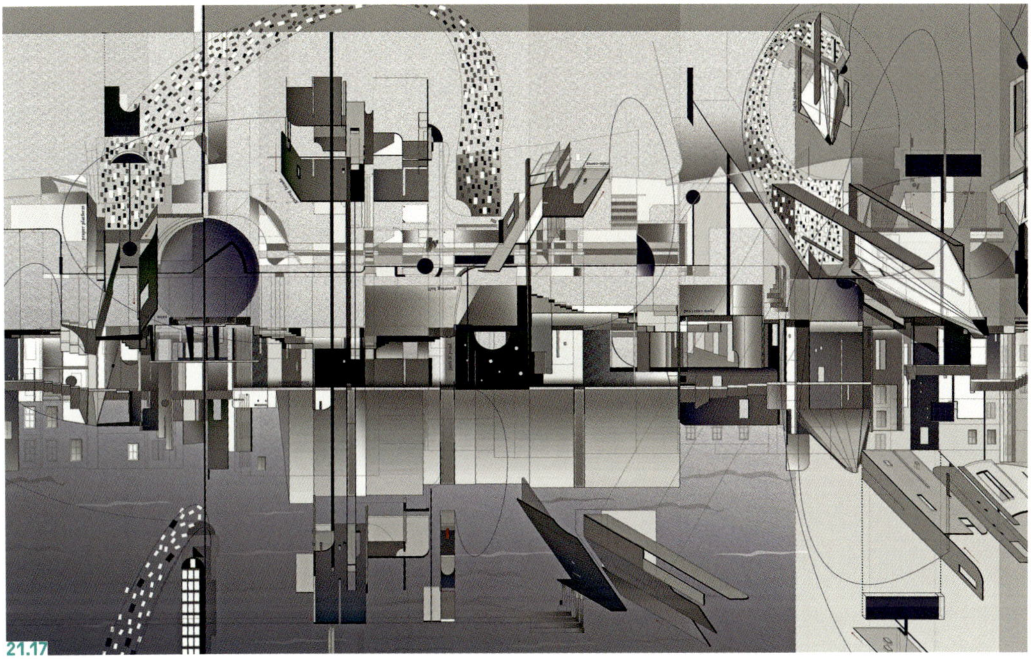

21.17

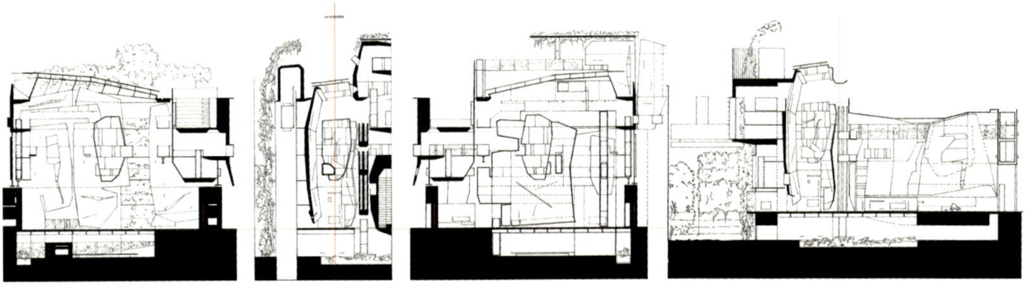

21.18

Fig. 21.16 Samson Simberg Y5, 'Marseille Music and Cultural Centre'. Marseille has seen a wave of surveillance cameras being installed across the city with some 1,800 cameras currently in place. Located along a series of unmonitored routes cut hidden 'corridors' (a series of unseen, routes cut through the urban fabric of the city, unmonitored by the CCTV network), the Marseille Music and Cultural Centre seeks to re-associate Marseille's 'unwanted' with their city, facilitating the city's alienated musical and artistic heritage whilst responding to the ambiguous and often unresolved qualities of CCTV. **Fig. 21.17 Sarish Younis** Y5, 'Rue Des Mosquée'. The spilling of devotees upon the street is a recurring circumstance of overcrowded cellar mosques. The project, situated in the belly of the city, echoes this controversy by reconstructing a typical street into one of prostration. This recreates the communal conditions between the cultures in an open public platform, conjoining the sacred and secular programmatic acts, as well as extending the dialogue of the known traditional house of prostration. **Fig. 21.18 Paddi Benson** Y4, 'Éclat[S] Du Mythe'. The compound identity of Marseille is an inextricable interweaving of myth, reality, seen and unseen – a modernist construct: the industrial revolution, the continuous flux of migration, its colonial past, and the turbulence caused by inequality have all contributed to the creation of a unique image of the 'phocaean city'. Each of these temporal imprints inherits a modernism that was never finished or achieved, which collectively illustrate the cultural entanglement of past and present Marseille.

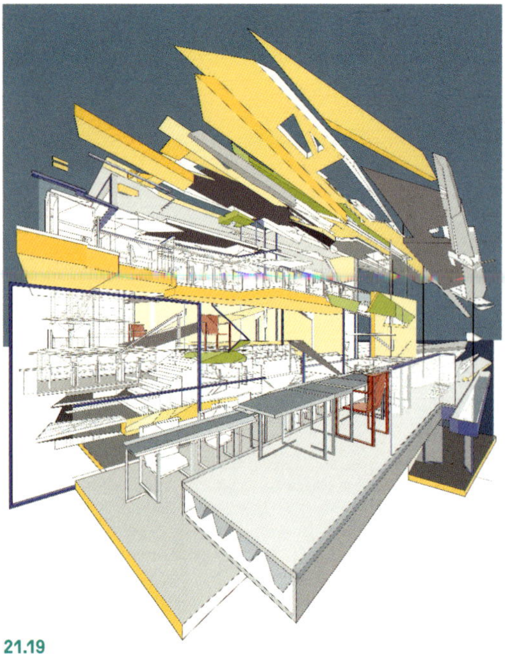

21.19

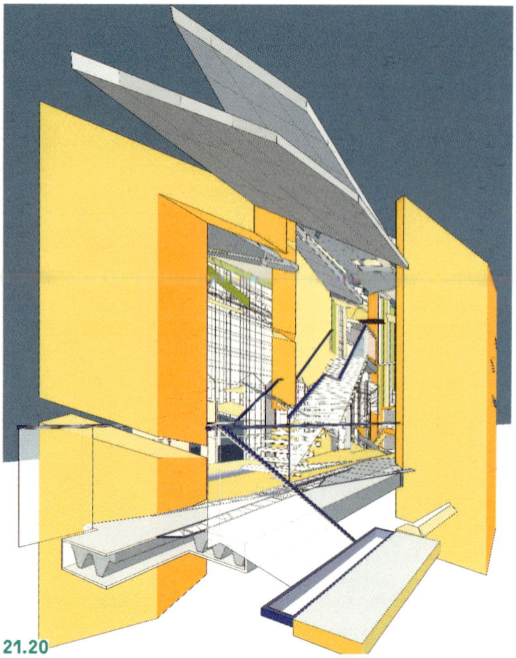

21.20

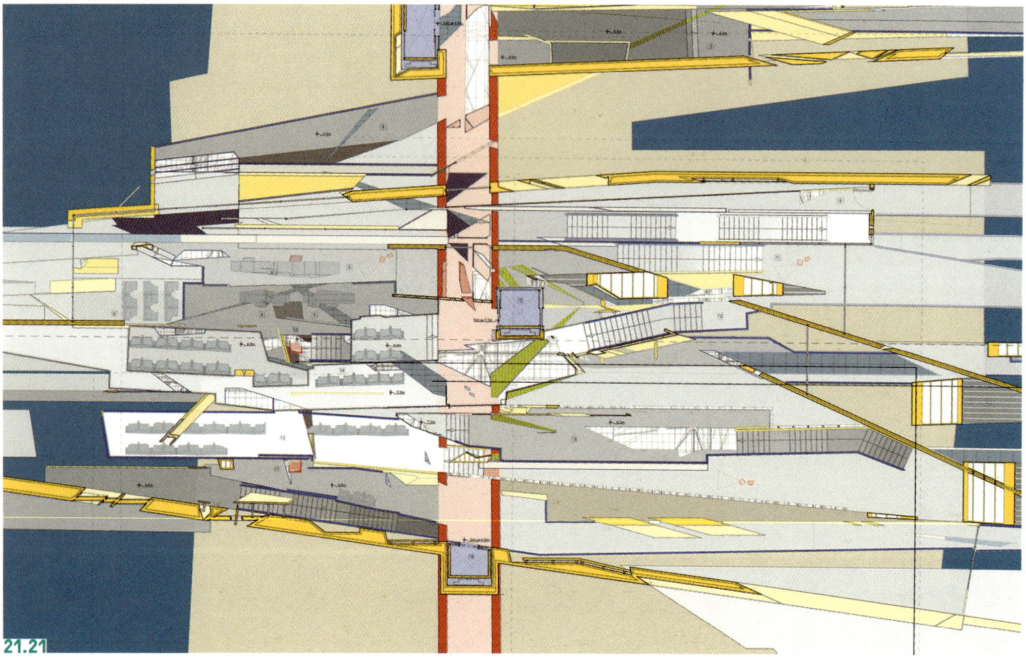

21.21

Figs. 21.19 – 21.22 Sophie Richards Y5, 'The French Connection_Marseille and the Physical Internet'. The project proposes a new legal quarter for the city of Marseille. Using the Hague as a precedent for an international system of law, the International Court of Internet Justice proposed here is a global law court, which would review cases from all continents, using a new system of specialised internet law. The project operates at two scales. At the scale of the city, the project proposes a network of interventions, which fit into the existing fabric of Marseille. The project also works at the scale of a courthouse, considered as a 3D network of time, interaction, separation and process.

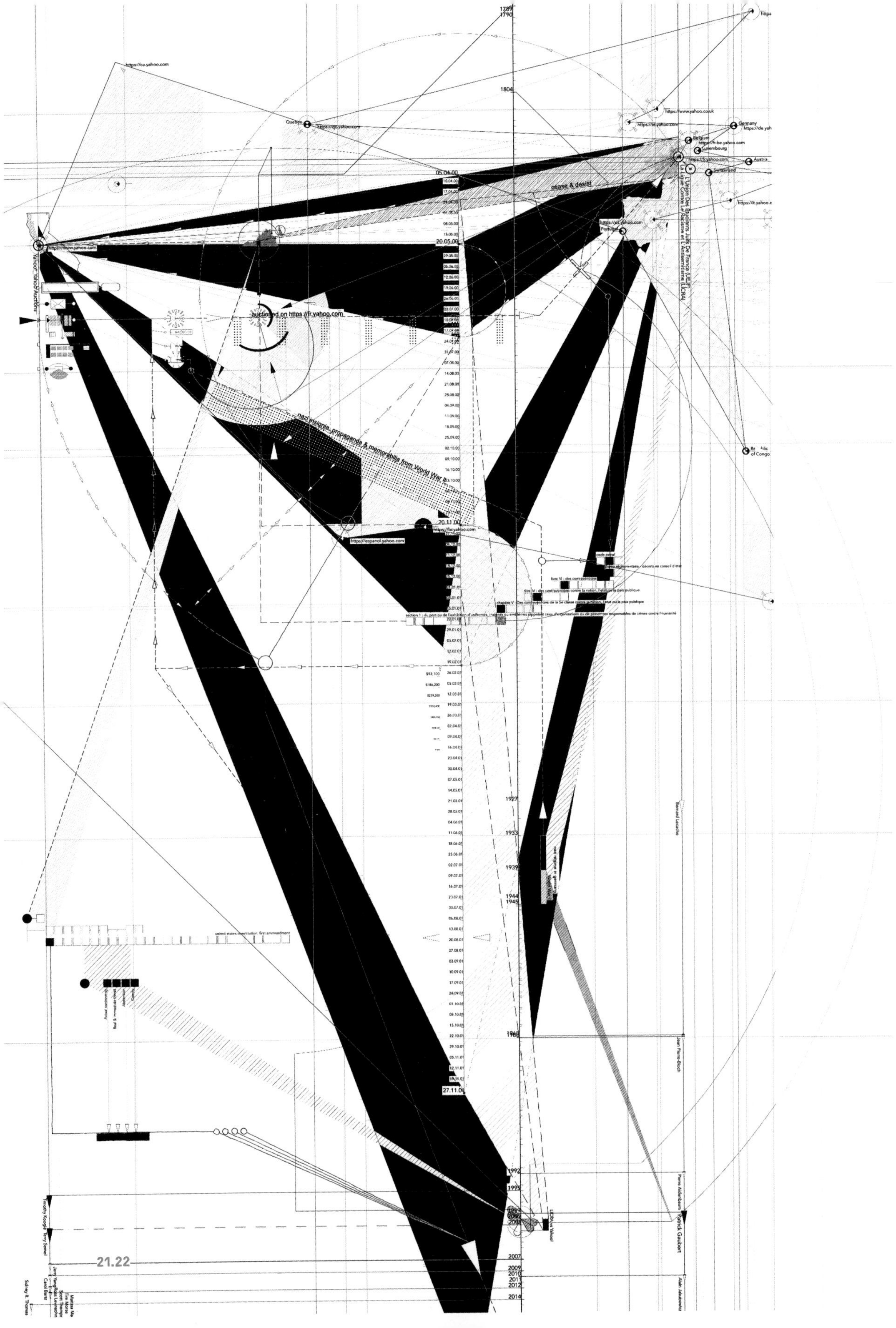

https://ca.yahoo.com
Quebec
https://qc.yahoo.com
https://www.yahoo.co.uk
https://ie.yahoo.com
Germany
Belgium
https://fr-be.yahoo.com
Luxembourg
https://fr.yahoo.com
Austria
Switzerland
https://it.yahoo.com
https://es.yahoo.com
Portugal
https://www.yahoo.com
Yahoo!, Yahoo! Auctions
cease & desist
L'Union Des Etudiants Juifs De France (UEJF)
La Ligue Contre Le Racisme et L'Antisémitisme (LICRA)
auctioned on https://fr.yahoo.com
nazi insignia, propaganda & memorabilia from World War II
https://espanol.yahoo.com
https://br.yahoo.com
of Congo
code penal
titre IV : des contraventions contre la nation, l'etat ou la paix publique
1789
1790
1804
1927
1933
1939
1944
1945
1968
1992
1995
2007
2009
2010
2011
2012
2014
05.04.00
20.05.00
20.11.00
27.11.00
united states constitution, first ammendment
Bernard Lecache
Jean Pierre-Bloch
Pierre Aidenbaum
Patrick Gaubert
Alain Jakubowicz
LICRA vs Yahoo!
Timothy Koogle
Terry Semel
Sidney R. Thomas
21.22

Unit 22

Women And Architecture

From the Egalitarian Fight to the Female Brand Strategy – a Great Chance to Change Architectural Meanings

Izaskun Chinchilla Moreno, Carlos Jiménez Cenamor

Year 4
Georgina Halabi, Hei Tung (Whitney) Wong, Huma Mohyuddin, Yuen (Elaine) Tsang, Jack Sargent, Laura Young

Year 5
Ana Alonso Albarrarín, Ruben Everett, Max Friedlander, Hao Han, Lily Papadopoulos, Oliver Partington, Li Wang, Shuo Yang, Timmy Yoon and Nawanwaj Yudhanahas.

We would like to thank the B-made team for their valuable support to all Bartlett students! We are grateful to Fani Kostourou, Athina Lazaridou, Covadonga Gutierrez Busto, Adriana Cabello, Gonçalo Lopes, Pedro Gil, Frederik Petersen, Jan Kattein, Bruce Irvin, Barbara Penner, Sophia Psarra, Blanche Cameron, Diego Delas, Marco Godoy, Yael Reisner, Christine Hawley, Chee-Kit Lai, Javier Lezaun, Eva Alvarez, Oscar Brito, Anna Mill, Joanne Preston, Clarissa Yee, Claire Taggart, Lulu Le Li, Ronald Cheape and Nerea Calvillo for bringing all their passion and knowledge to the Unit crits and workshops, and to Victoria Bateman for her marvelous teaching support and coordination of our Ho Chi Minh City workshop

We would also like to express our enormous gratitude to the whole of the Bartlett Office – nothing could be achieved without you. What a team!

Thank you to sponsors Luis Vidal + Architects and Ho Chi Minh City University of Architecture

In his 1920s manifesto 'Five Points of Architecture', Le Corbusier proposed an architectural vision for the twentieth century. When we look at its five points, it is clear that they are all related to technology. Le Corbusier advised architects to support their buildings with pilotis; to design open plan; to show that the façade is independent of the structure; to design horizontal windows; and to design flat roofs that included gardens. Even this idea of including a garden was intended as a celebration of technology, given that the cityscape had recently become visible from planes.
——This year, we asked our students to design spaces in which the female mindset was fully applied and empowered. From this, we extracted five points:

1. Allow your inhabitants to hold their babies while they work. Many students mixed uses on the same plot and construction, allowing personal and professional life to overlap.
2. Encourage your users to bake bread, just like their Grandma did. A significant number of our projects suggest that happiness can be easily achieved through time-honoured activities such as cultivating roses, reading or drawing. This proposes a sort of critical disengagement: you don't need to change your car every five years or update the colour of your sofa according to a magazine; there are ways to balance life that do not have such a direct link with consumption.
3. But also enable them to search for bread recipes on their tablet. Many of our projects found that the internet and digital networking were the best allies for successfully empowering the female brand.
4. Treat your users' bodies well – allow them to be naked, sad, tired or happy, but comfortable. Temperatures, textures, sound and subjectivity were part of most of our exercises that centred on user experience; these are important and should not be overlooked.
5. Push the space to allow full development of users' lifestyles. In a world where people make a living filming their daily activities on YouTube, architecture can promote the strategic development of customized lifestyles, allowing people to build relationships or make money through the buildings that they own, rent or use.

The difference between our five points and Le Corbusier's is obvious: our goal is to empower people, rather than empowering industry. We can now ask our readers – are female architects more focused on improving inhabitants' lives, while their male colleagues are focused on pushing the boundaries of technological solutions? If this is the case, the idea of an egalitarian struggle doesn't quite make sense. Female architects should not be fighting for the same identity as their male counterparts; they should instead develop their own. This, simultaneously, will improve what architecture is – and can be – for everyone.

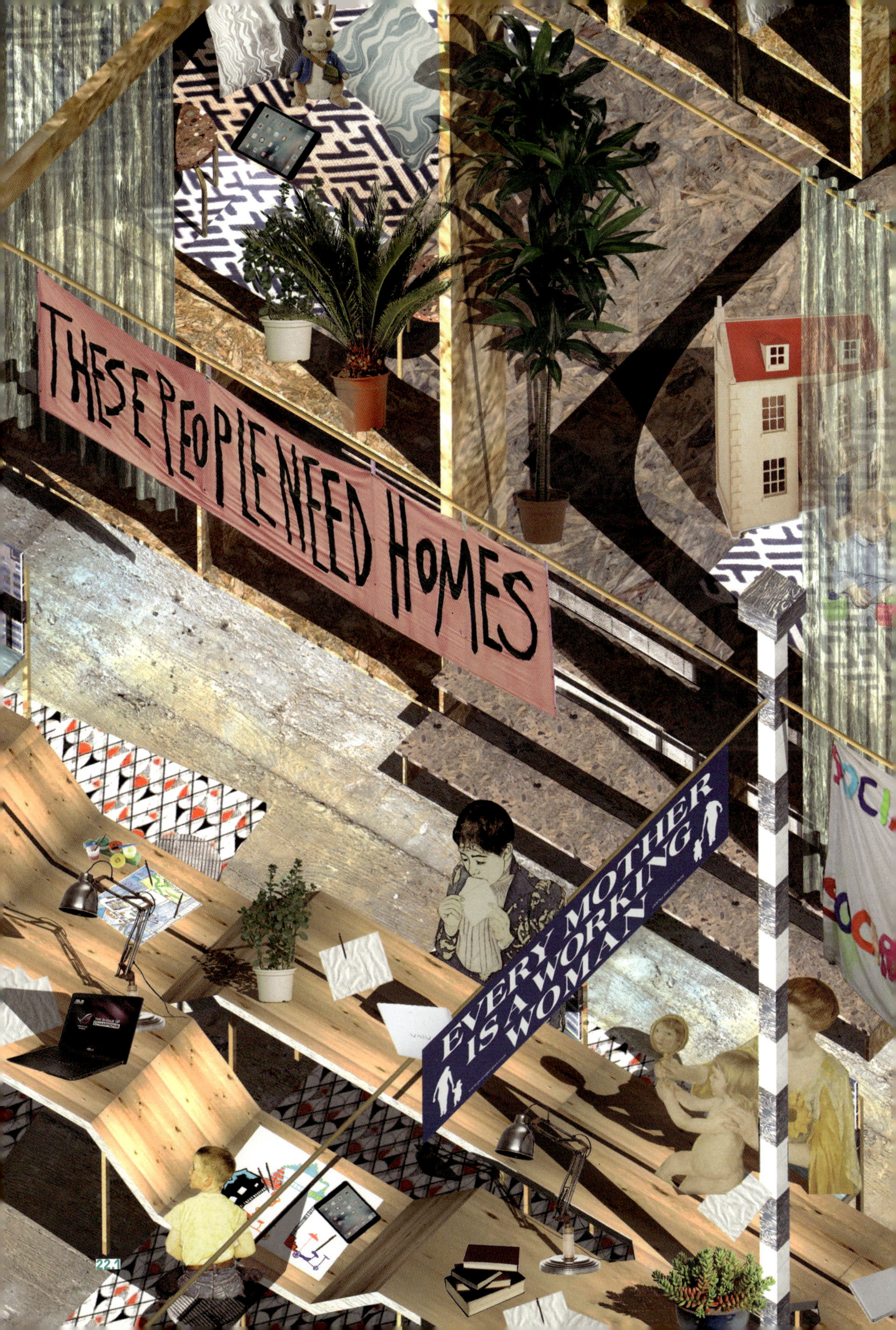

22.1

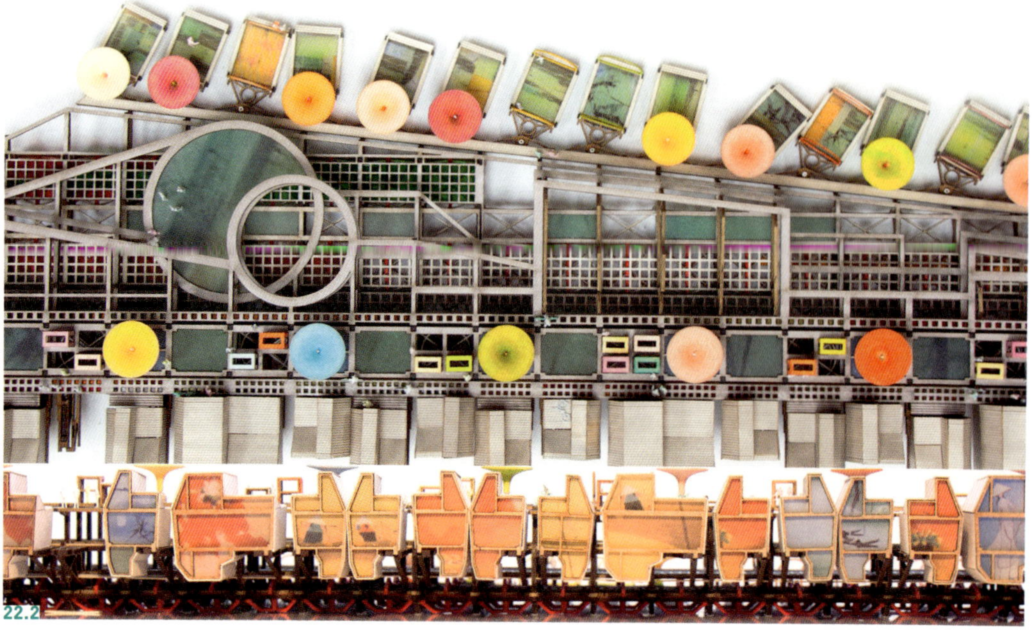

22.2

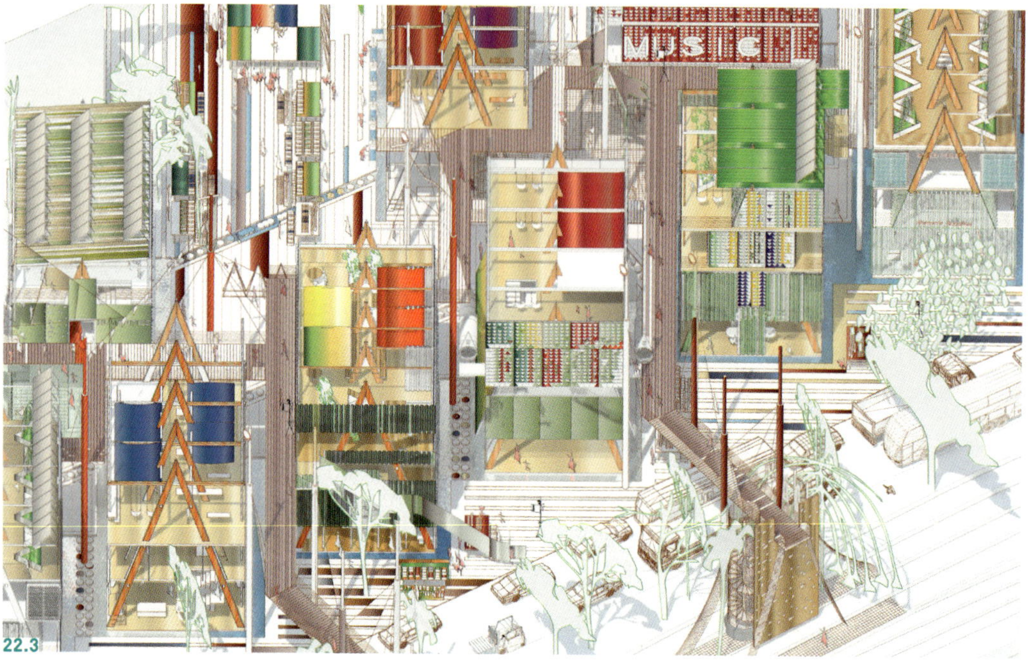

22.3

Fig. 22.1 Oliver Partington Y5, 'The Newham Cooperative'. The project looks to employ female-led principles of urbanism to develop a large, disused site in Newham. Through the celebration of the collective, the new framework for housing concentrates on establishing new typologies for shared housing, work spaces and childcare. The method of housing delivery also looks to empower the residents by creating a structure where households take an equal stake in the land, allowing the groups to develop their own piece of city. **Fig. 22.2 Max Friedlander** Y5, 'Women's Community Bridge Saigon'. Traditional Vietnamese craft as a tool for social change is explored through the lens of the female user. The bridge forms a link between two contrasting communities, facilitating the urban cohesion of the city. It seeks to empower women through challenging the existing domestic realities and allowing them to formalise an identity beyond the home. Workshops, parks, childcare and other functions are woven together into a playful landscape that reflects local cultural traditions and encourages dynamic engagement with the building. **Fig. 22.3 Jack Sargent** Y4, 'Durbar Dharmasala School, Kathmandu, Nepal'. Via a series of interventions that work independently and alongside one another, this proposes a timeline of works that develop from small interventions tapping into broadcast networks through to purpose built communication, internet and structural systems. The responses combine programmes that empower women by facilitating and maximising their public exposure, breaking down the gender barriers and roles within Nepali society.

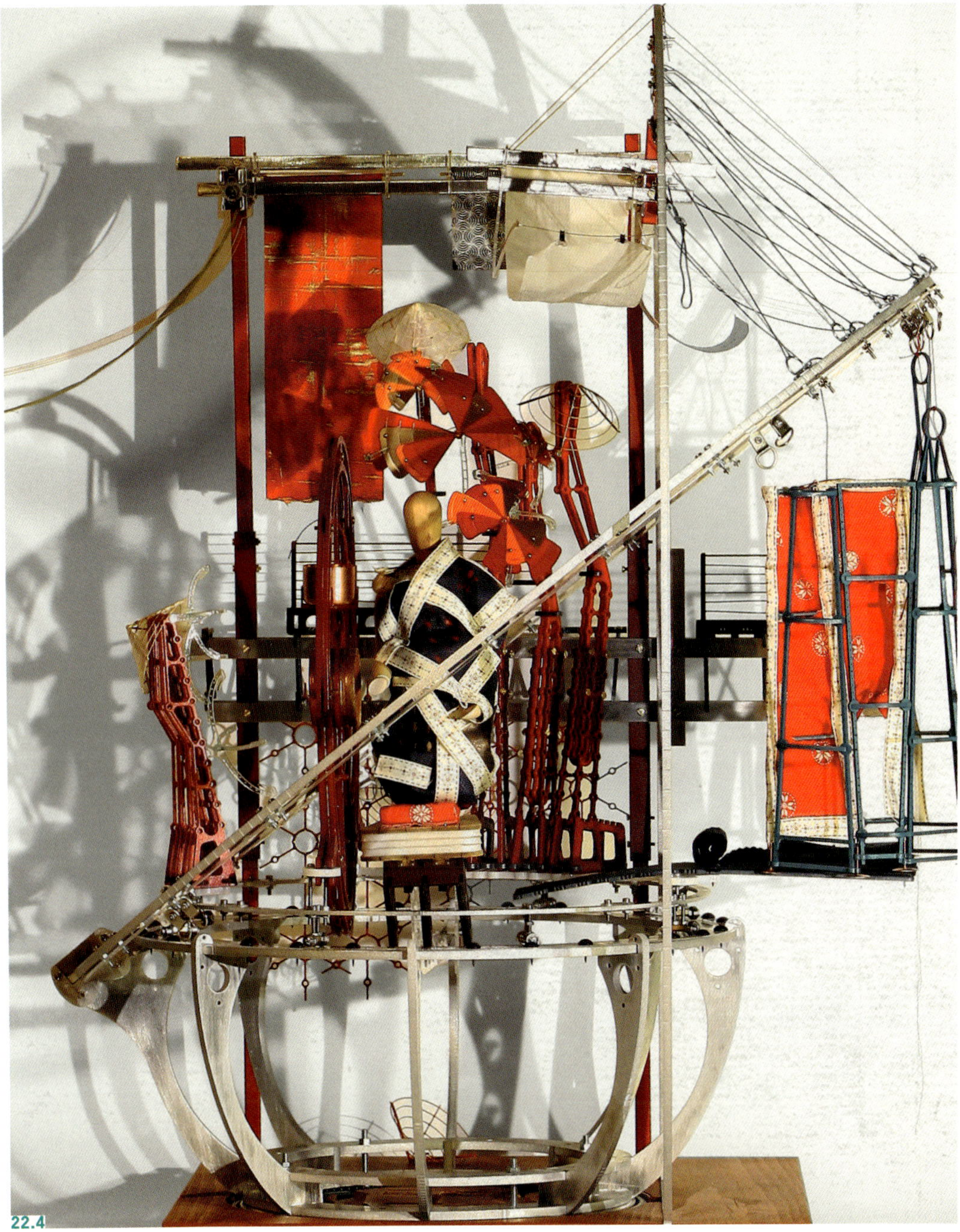

22.4

The floating nature of the structure passively circumvents the issue of seismic activity in the region and lyrically embeds a sanitary operation within its programme. **Fig. 22.4 Shuo Yang** Y5, 'Woman, Buddhism & Capital'. The project is a speculative proposal of a socially engaged Canary Wharf. It discovers how a new type of Buddhist built environment might apply female-centric principles in order to regenerate a socially engaged community within Canary Wharf. The challenge to the existing economic system is to integrate these new cultural and social forms of capital, creating new spatial networks within this revitalised context. The armillary sphere uncovers a new Buddhist archetype for Bhikkhuni activities.

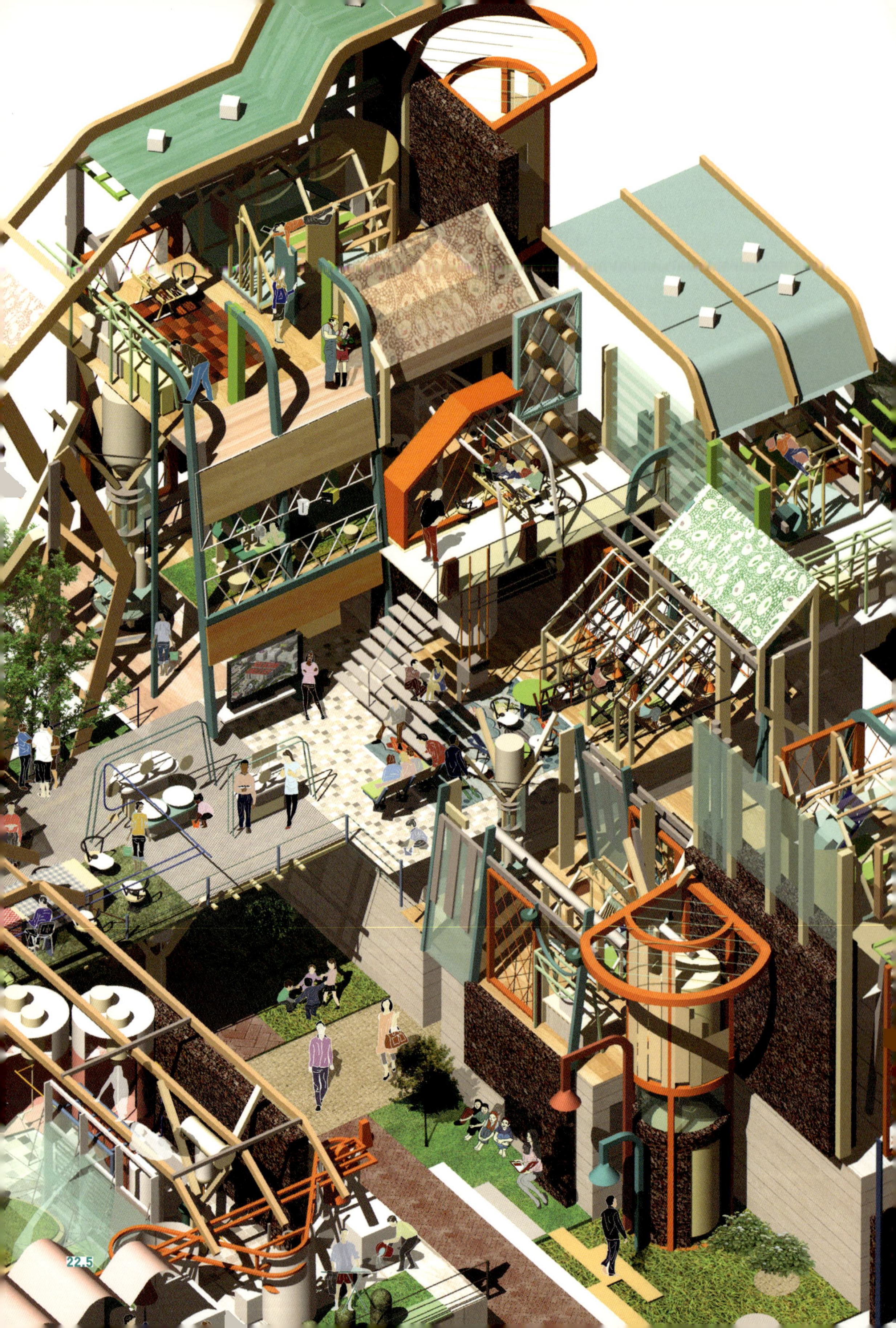
22.5

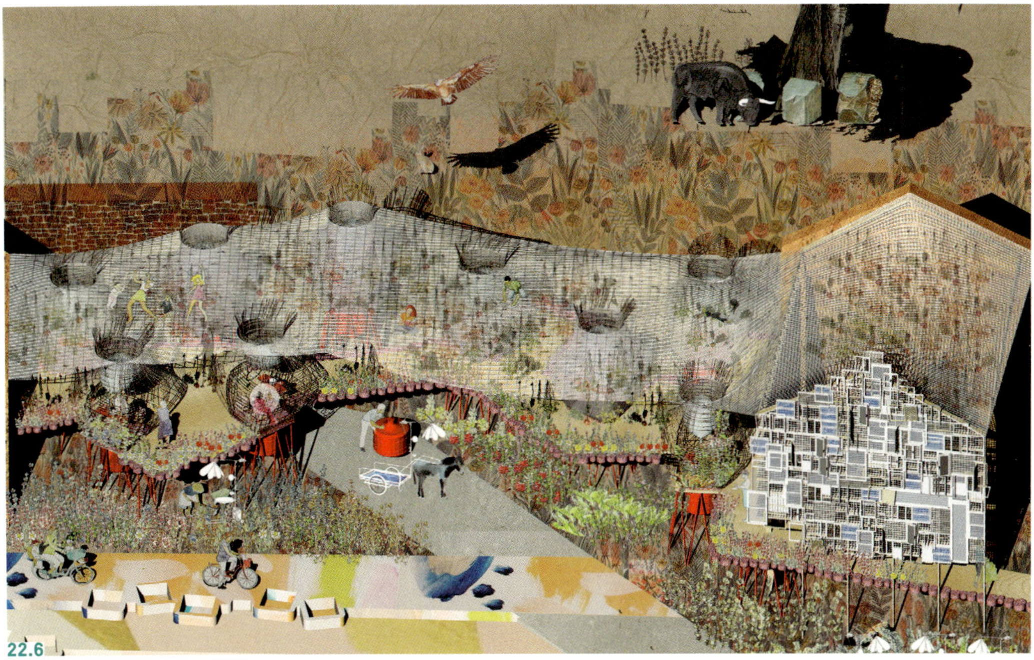

22.6

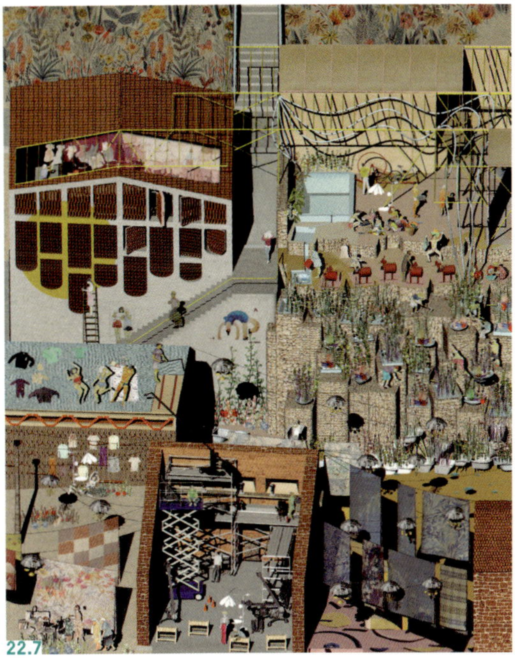

22.7

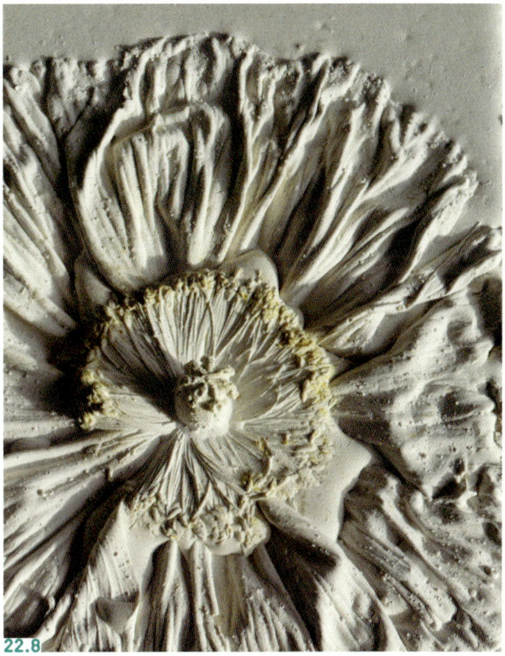

22.8

Fig. 22.5 Hao Han Y5, 'The Matriarchal Energy Industry'. A masterplan investigating the physical infrastructure of a 'female' form of environmental engagement. Through a study of matriarchal principles and the clean tech industry, a series of typologies and energy agents are developed to be deployed around the city of Santa Clara, California. Action-based engagements and curated routine disruptions are put forward to produce a new form of sustainable lifestyle. **Figs. 22.6 – 22.7 Ana Alonso Albarracín** Y5, 'Sweet Conciliation'. Through YouTube, a group of Spanish housewives have created a network of support and influence about housekeeping, a job they are both proud of and brilliant at. The project interprets them as 21st century material feminists. A reality series to be featured on YouTube's new subscription service is proposed. This enterprise aims to pump new life into rural Spain, filled with abandoned villages. The design is informed by the housewives' YouTube videos, and applies their tips to urban and architectural scales. **Fig. 22.8 Rubén Everett** Y5, 'In The Big City'. A closer look at London revealed a lack of commemoration for women in the city. This project reacts to this by creating a feminist microcosm within the big city. Inspired by five female figureheads, the project explores an urban landscape that aims to invigorate, enrich and rejuvenate Silvertown, through the exploration of a new community built to commemorate the work of these extraordinary women.

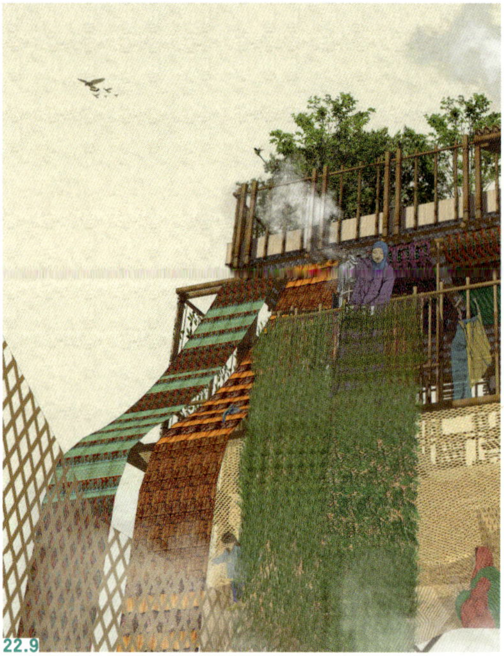

22.9

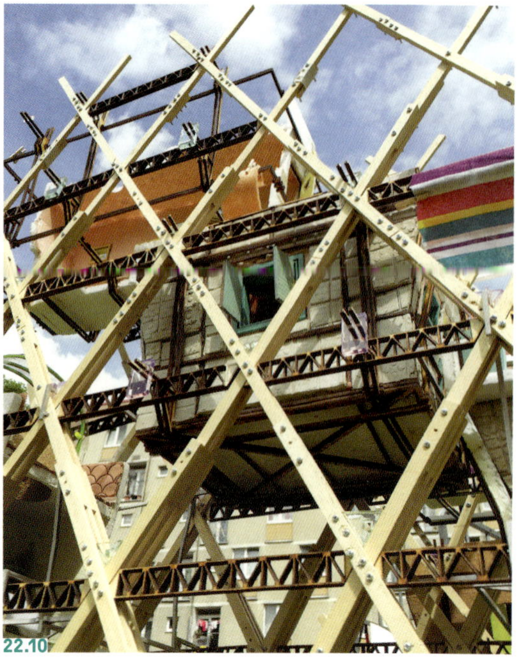

22.10

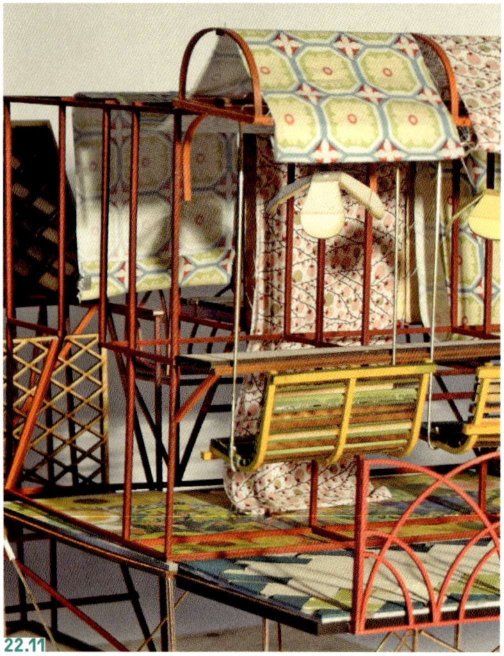

22.11

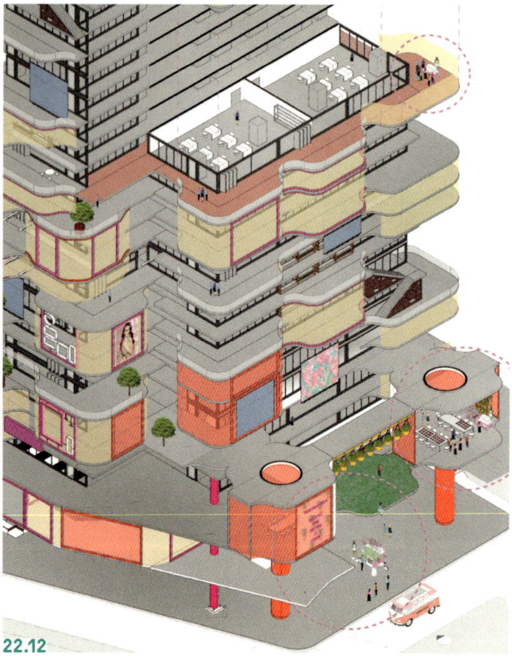

22.12

Fig. 22.9 Huma Mohyuddin Y4, 'Learning Centre for Herbal Medicine and Building Construction'. It is common for women in rural Pakistan to be denied an education or the chance to pursue work. This proposal empowers women by allowing them to gain knowledge of herbal medicine, local construction methods and business skills, to help provide alternative means of health and income, as well as empowering other rural women through sharing their knowledge. **Fig. 22.10 Georgina Halabi** Y4, 'The Lysistrata House and Forest Garden'. In response to the 'New Homeless,' the programme is a self-build shelter and edible landscape for a community of women in Athens, called Lysistrata. However, parallel to the misfortune that has hit the city, comes the opportunity for development – a rise in urban farming in the form of allotments and community gardens. The project proposes common facilities and one-room housing typologies that accommodate vegetable gardens, walls, terraces, and of course, women. **Fig. 22.11 Nawanwaj Yudhanahas** Y5, 'The Co-Op LAB of the Island of Widows Koh Kret, Thailand'. The project proposes four scales of interventions to raise awareness in everyday science and participation in environmental conservation. The typologies, located across the island, range from scale S: tool kits, M: mobile laboratories, L: field restaurants (pictured) and XL: the Co-Op Market. Each typology aims to empower the women, from their health, knowledge, and independence, to joining forces as a community. Architectural language is a hybrid between existing agricultural infrastructures and local architecture. **Fig. 22.12 Hei Tung (Whitney) Wong** Y4,

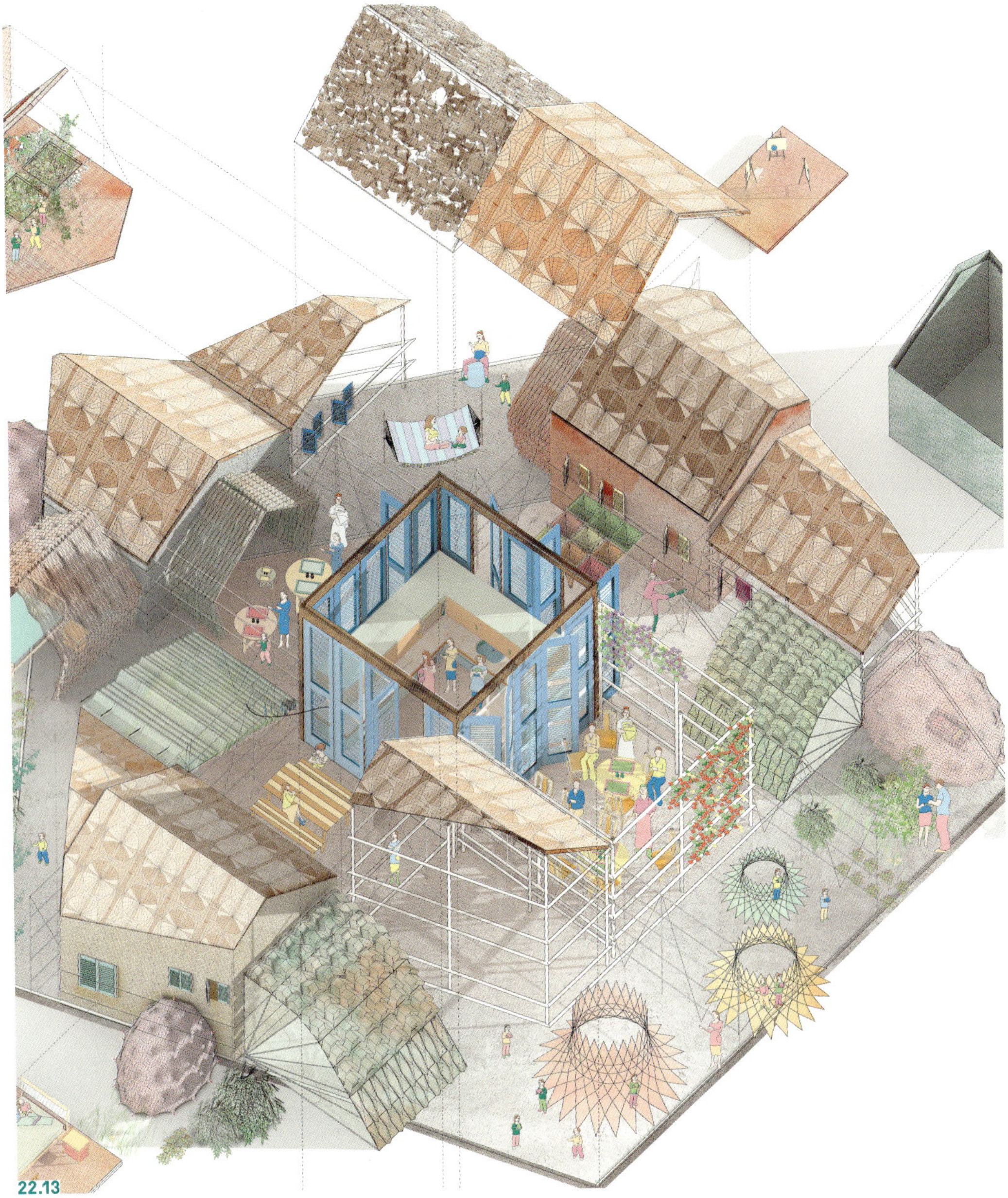

22.13

'The Maids' Cooperative'. The scheme empowers domestic workers by restructuring the domestic service industry into a cooperative. In place of live-in domestic helpers, the domestic service industry is restructured into a professional business where users regenerate and improve skills, utilising their knowledge through economic and social interaction. Using the façade of the building, the cooperative manifests the empowerment of these women and creates a celebration between culture, nature and the strength of women, by exposing the production and organisation onto its external envelope. **Fig. 22.13 Lily Papadopoulos** Y5, 'A Life-Giving Catalyst'. The Greek islands face a lack of maternity facilities, forcing women to travel to the mainland to give birth. This project's aim is to alleviate this situation, creating everyday environments which recall past childbirth events as communal and celebratory, in contrast to today's preconceived role of the pregnant body as a patient. Expanding family houses, start-up agro-businesses and doctors offering services in exchange for hospitality, allows for the rebirth of depopulating villages, which potentially dissolves hierarchies and transforms power relations.

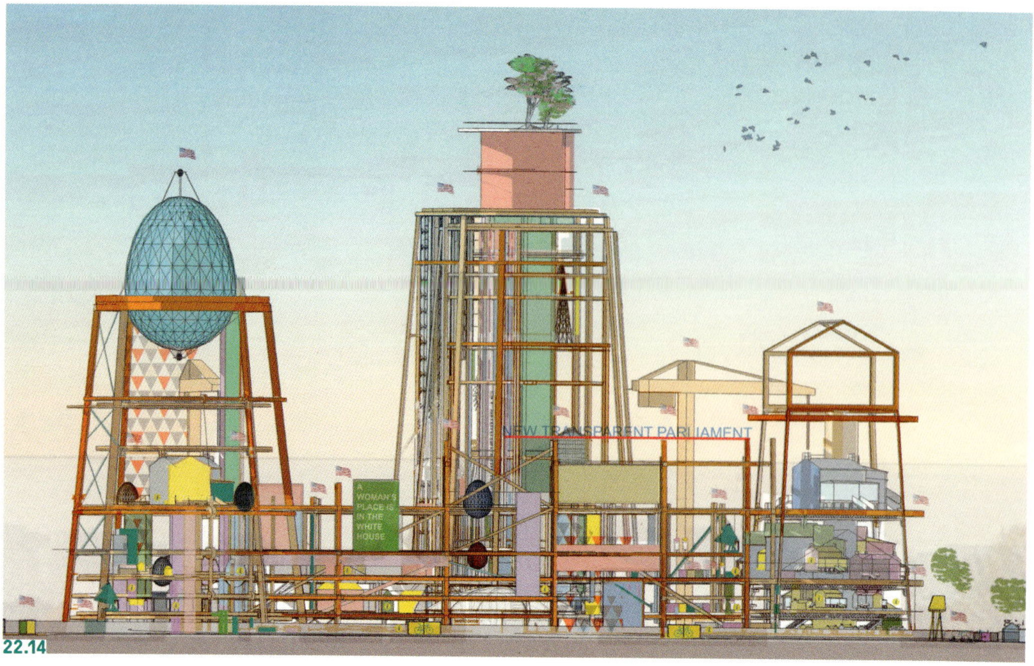

22.14

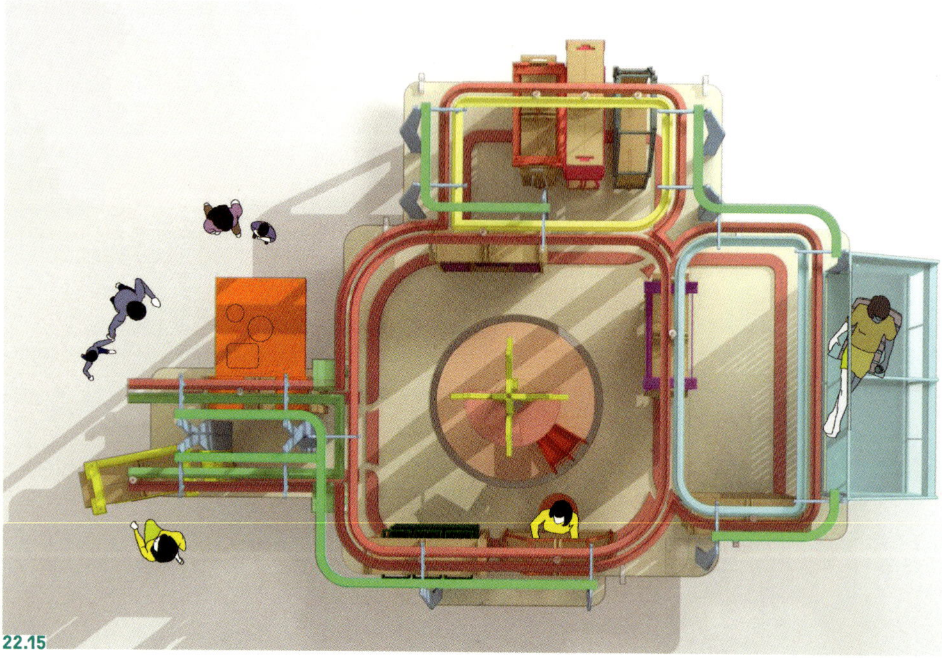

22.15

Fig. 22.14 Laura Young Y4, 'House For Hillary [The New Transparent Parliament], Washington DC 2016'. Following Hillary Clinton's elected presidency in 2016, her new parliamentary framework proposes a democratic forum of continued construction, both physical and digital, engaging the public with an equal and evolving politics accessible to all Americans. Originating from The White House Pavilions Project, the house will test architectural manifestations of Hillary's key policies: domestic space, work space and climate. The scheme will grow into the surrounding National Mall, activating the key public space through political exchange and broadcast. **Fig. 22.15 Yuen (Elaine) Tsang** Y4, 'Makers' Market Community Project'. The project is used as the testing ground to reassert the programmatic relevancy of co-workspace, residence and market as a place of collaborative enterprise led by online DIY communities favouring women. 'Compartmentalising' their lives into multiple cabinets encourages the fluid society to find the highest common factor of what could be reused and what is unique to each person to be shared to maintain near zero marginal cost through an online platform and offline physical world. **Fig. 22.16 Li Wang** Y5, 'The Gentlewomen's House.' The project explores how weather recomposes the architectural environment, from the path to interior space through sensory perceptions. Where the sense of direction can be emphasised by silence and noise, physical boundaries can be soft. Spaces are defined by textures of the materiality, so that architecture is more intimate and sensitive to all users.

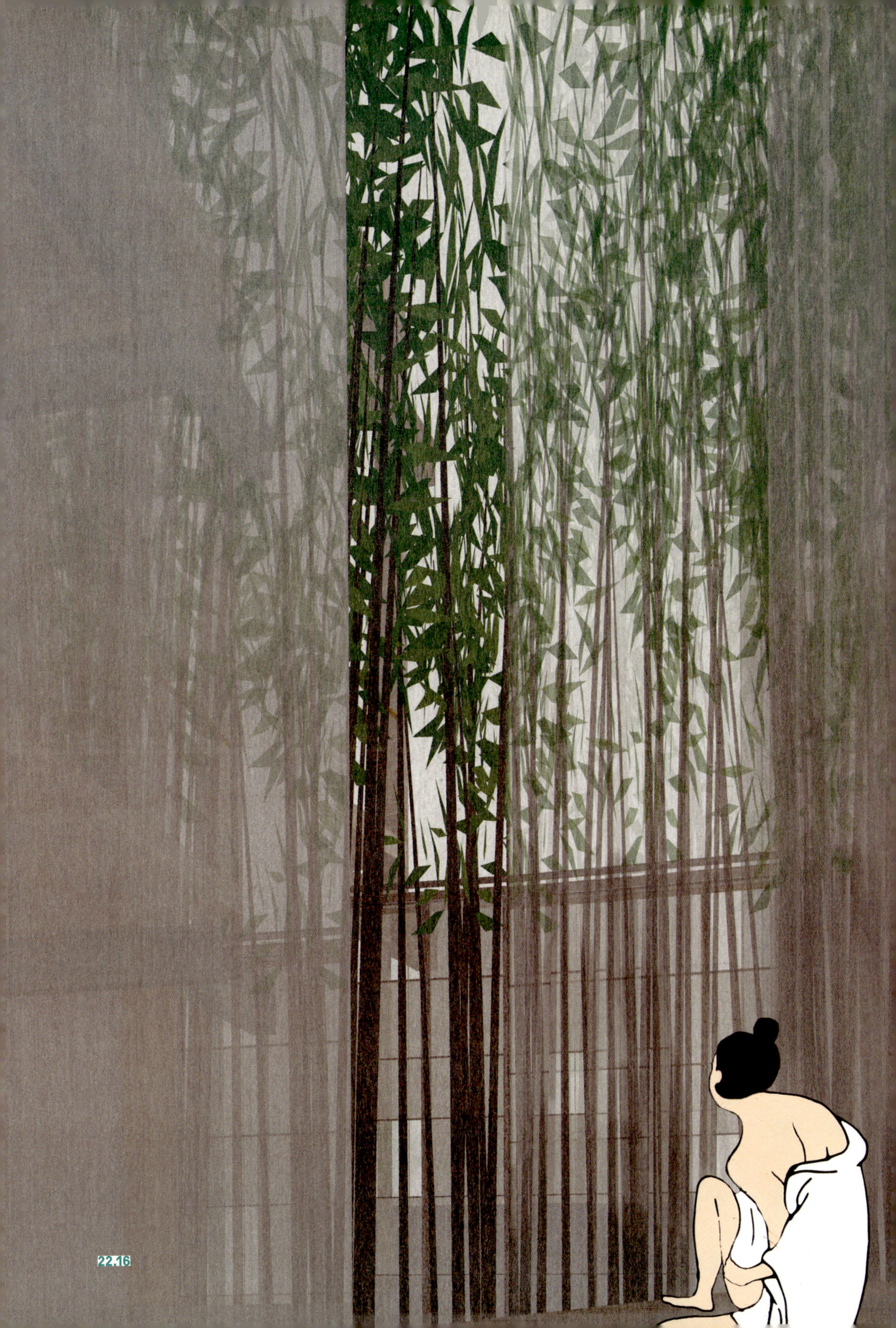

22.16

Unit 23 Constructing Pleasures

Nat Chard, Colin Herperger

Year 4
Dean Hedman, Jiatong (Karen) Hu, Andrea Matta, Kirsty McMullan, Ian Ng, Thomas Parker, Daniel van der Poll, Peter West

Year 5
Michael Arnett, Amy Begg, Joshua Broomer, Rania Francis, Muhammad Hussan Jubri, Flavie Caroukis, Wynne Leung, Luke Lupton

Design Realisation tutor: Ralph Gunson Parker

Thanks to consultants and critics James Craig, Bastian Glaessner, Tamsin Hanke, Perry Kulper, Shaun Murray, Jerry Tate, Emmanuel Vercruysse, and Simon Withers

Thanks to our sponsors RIAA Barker Gilette Solicitors

A background concern in the unit is the relationship between ideas and techniques; both in the way ideas can be embodied in materials and processes and in how thinking through materials and processes (in making and drawing) can tease out ideas. To help find some precision in such methods, we looked at the work of a number of anthropologists who instead of locating artefacts within established epistemologies have been constructing epistemologies directly from the artefact. The question we have been looking at is how to construct architecture in such a way that those who come across or occupy it might be seduced to have the same relationship with the building that these anthropologists have with the artefacts they study. Is it possible to construct an architecture where those who engage with it construct cosmologies that emanate from the architecture's apparent logic?

——To support our studies into these questions we ran two parallel projects; an invented object and a piece of architecture. The aim was to set up an ongoing dialogue between the research object, through which ideas within the architecture could be tried out as a (small) reality, and the architecture. In a number of cases this led to objects that in some way predicted the architecture, often as practical and conceptual tools to draw – and draw out – the ideas.

——We wished to avoid prescribing objects or architecture primarily through practicalities and instead wanted to look at broader senses of purpose, hence the title 'Constructing Pleasures'. We were looking for motivations that might in modest ways infect a larger cultural realm than the piece being designed.

——We started the year with visits to the Pitt Rivers Museum to imagine our own realities out of its artefacts and Rousham Park to study how the internal program infects the surrounding world. We also visited a range of intensely personal buildings in northern Italy where immense care had been invested in building their ideas as fulsomely as possible.

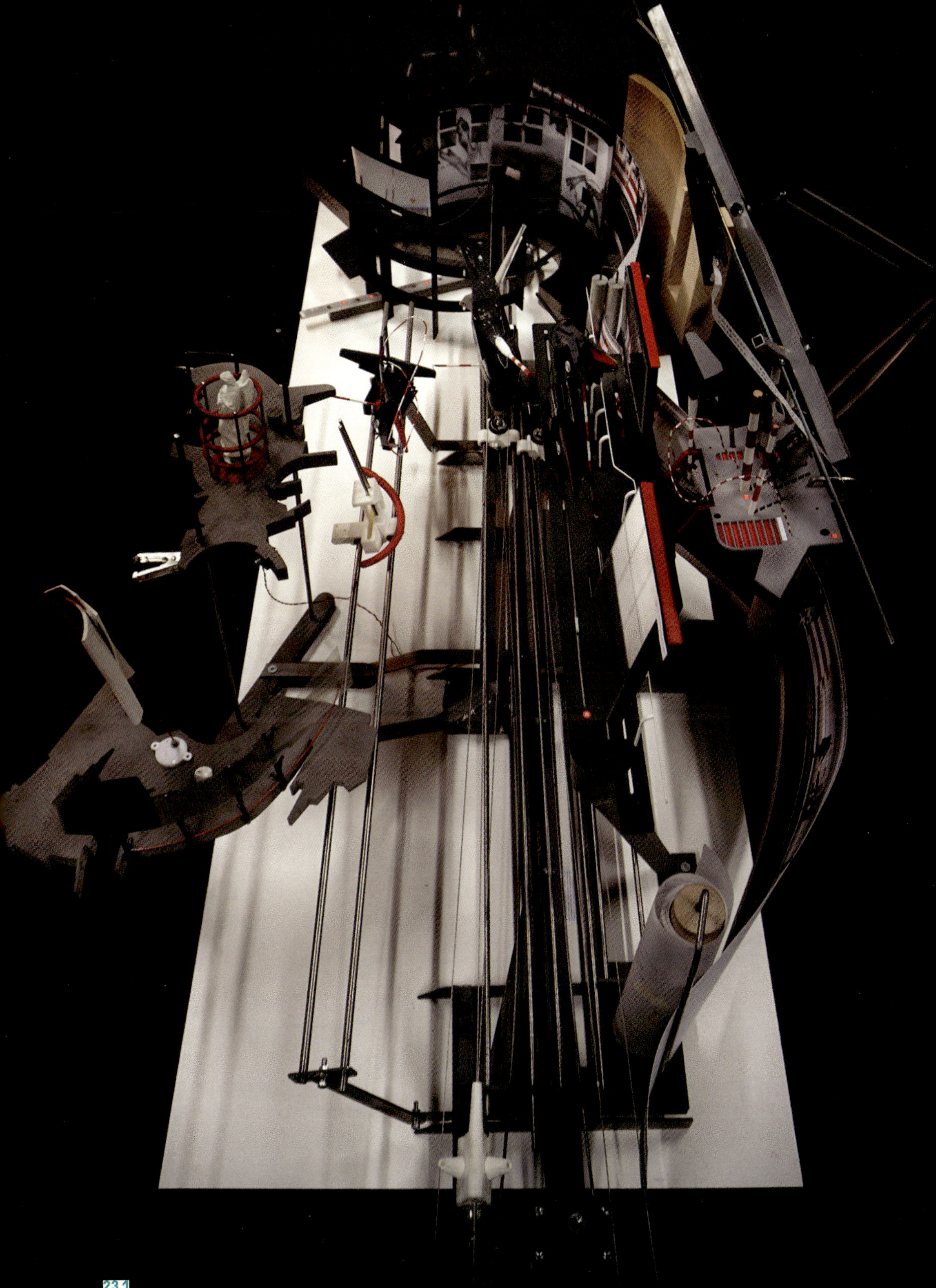

23.1

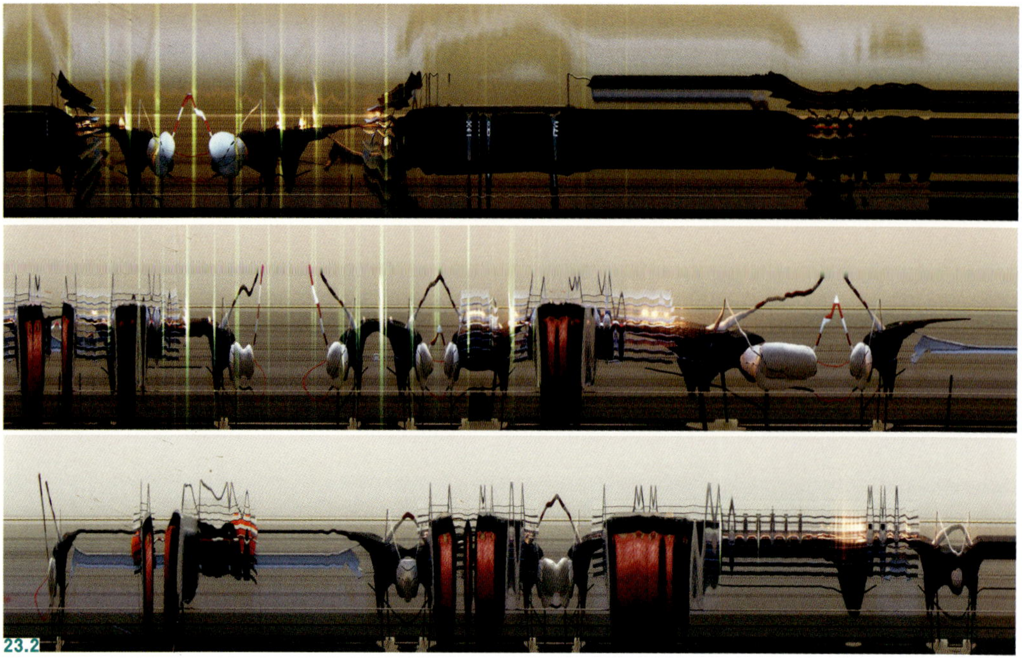

23.2

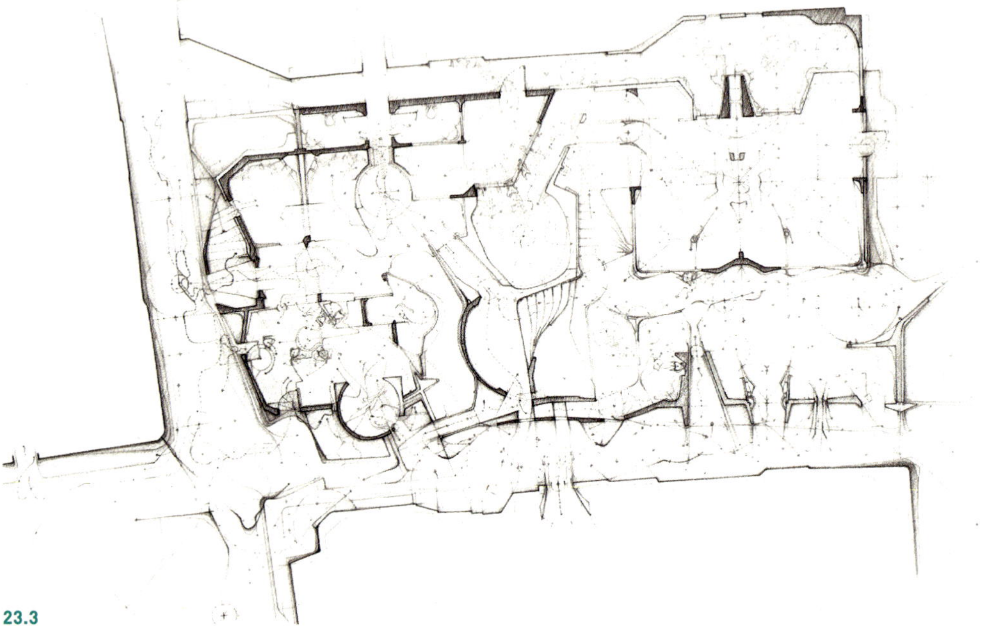

23.3

Figs. 23.1 – 23.2 Luke Lupton Y5, 'Occupying The Unknown'. Architectural spectrometers reveal unknown worlds, locked behind ostensible exteriors. They are theatres of exploration, in which scenarios are choreographed to expose and interrogate instances of particularity, caught in an amalgamation of environment, body and context. The devices capture the tangible triangulation of pure duration – an epi-genius-loci that divulges physical substance on which to design. The horseracing track emerged, holding subtle layers of programmatic encryption beneath its surface. **Fig. 23.3 Flavie Caroukis** Y5, 'The Orchestrated Café'. A choreographic architecture which explores the dynamic nature of improvisation in order to provoke its audience in an intuitive and inquisitive manner. Indulging in the sensation of kinesis, the architecture is inspired by the world of performance, with its choreography expressing the multiple possibilities of movement within an ordinary setting of a café. The space seeks to unexpectedly provide its occupants with an extraordinary sense of reality.

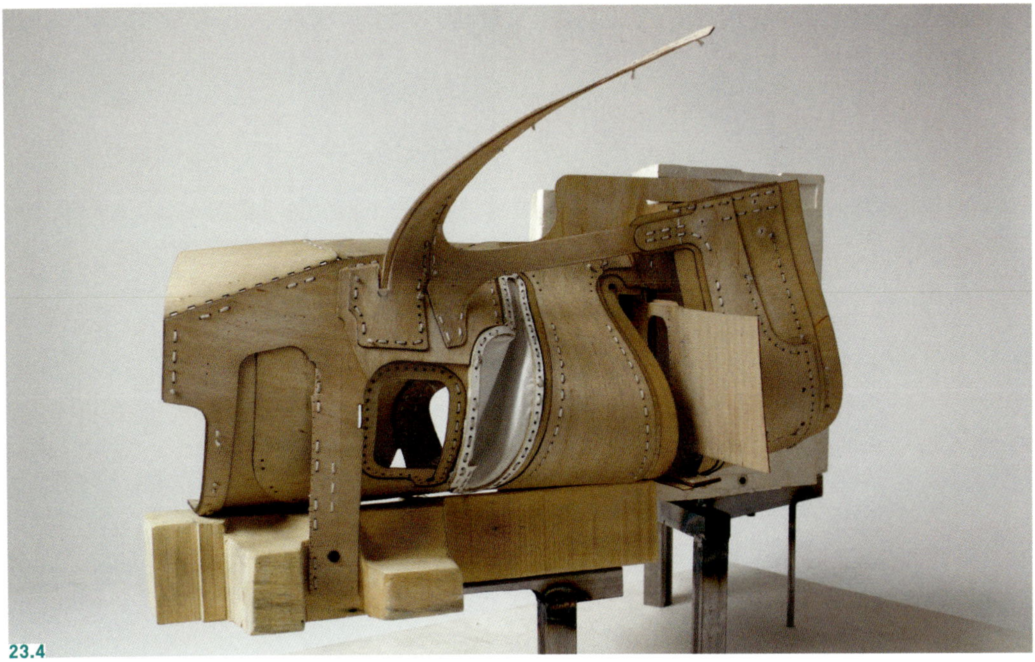
23.4

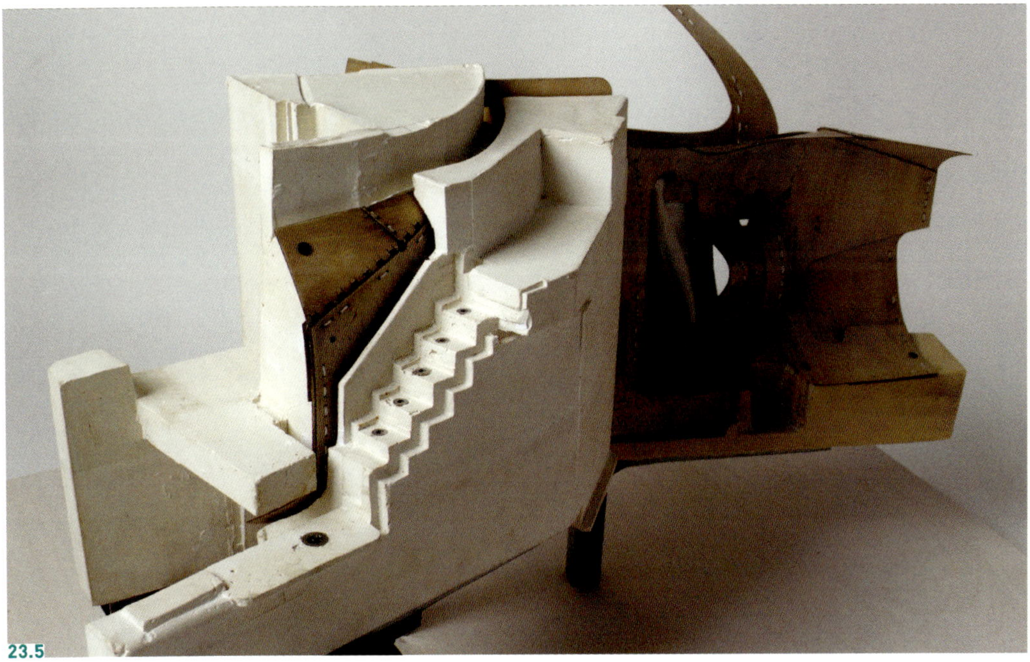
23.5

Figs. 23.4 – 23.5 Amy Begg Y5, 'The Tailored House of Nesso Pier'. In-between states and subtle shifts form a domestic territory of discovery and exploration. The house delights in the possibility of precise tailoring and unexpected fit whilst also acknowledging the pleasures that ambiguity and uncertainty can offer. The act of dwelling and inhabitation becomes unique. Specific experiences orientate our understanding of space but remain open to the potential for alternative possibilities.

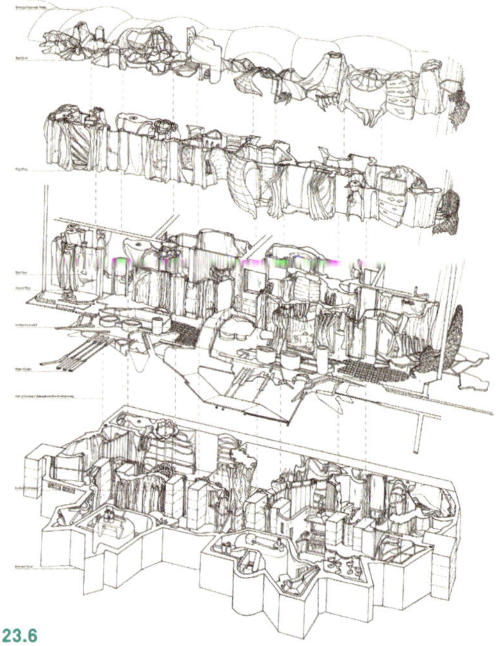

23.6

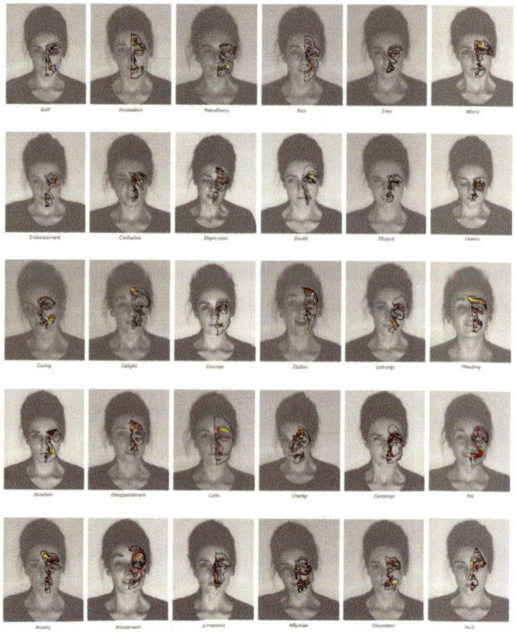

23.7

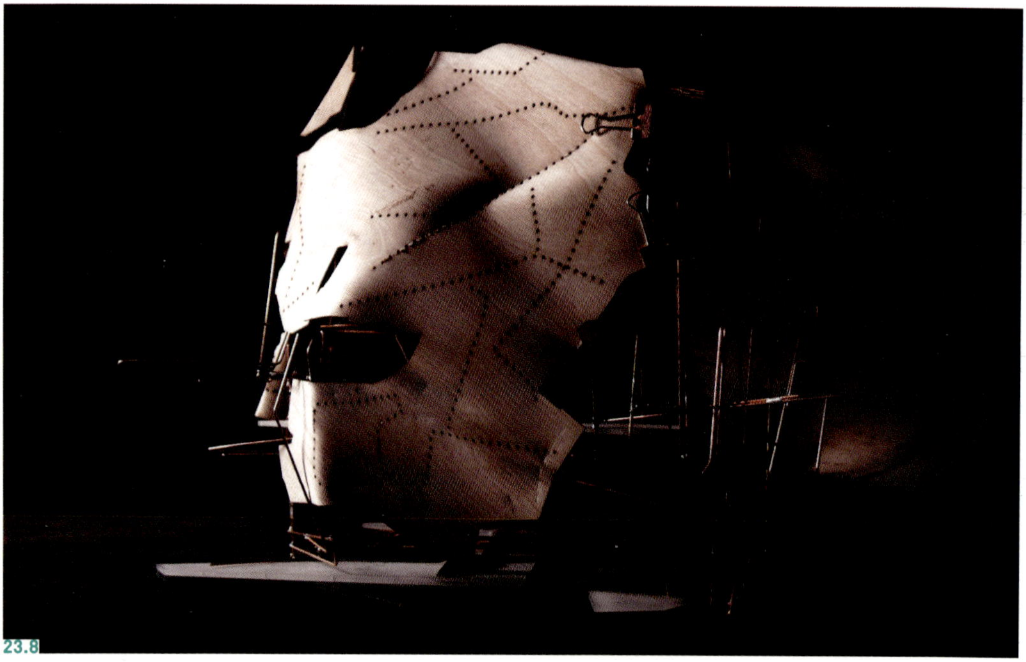

23.8

Figs. 23.6 – 23.7 Kirsty McMullan Y4, 'If These Walls Could Talk'. Investigating how architecture could be as expressive as its occupants. What if instead of humans learning to settle for the buildings they occupy, the buildings could learn to be more like humans? This posits an architecture that does not always co-operate, but would always be active in the conversation. **Fig. 23.8 Joshua Broomer** Y5, 'The Scenographic Edge'. This project is the creation of a cinematic playhouse, constructing a series of moments that combine the actors, the audience, the new, the existing and the outside world. The edges created reveal and contain these different 'actors' to become implicated in the show; between reality and a fabricated scene. **Fig. 23.9 Mohammed Syafiq B Hassan Jubri** Y5, 'Towards an Ambidexterity in Architecture'. Anna (instrument) drawing building plan. The project questions the unfamiliar aberrations of the left hand in drawing ambidextrous twin symmetrical spaces; based on Roger Sperry's split-brain experiments, the value of ambidexterity in architectural drawing and spatial thinking. Drawing instruments are invented as a tools of discussion, teasing out the unfamiliar conventions of the 'left hand'. The resultant architecture, a bicurriculum primary school, embodies the dual cognitive process of the brain, constantly encouraging alternative ways of learning.

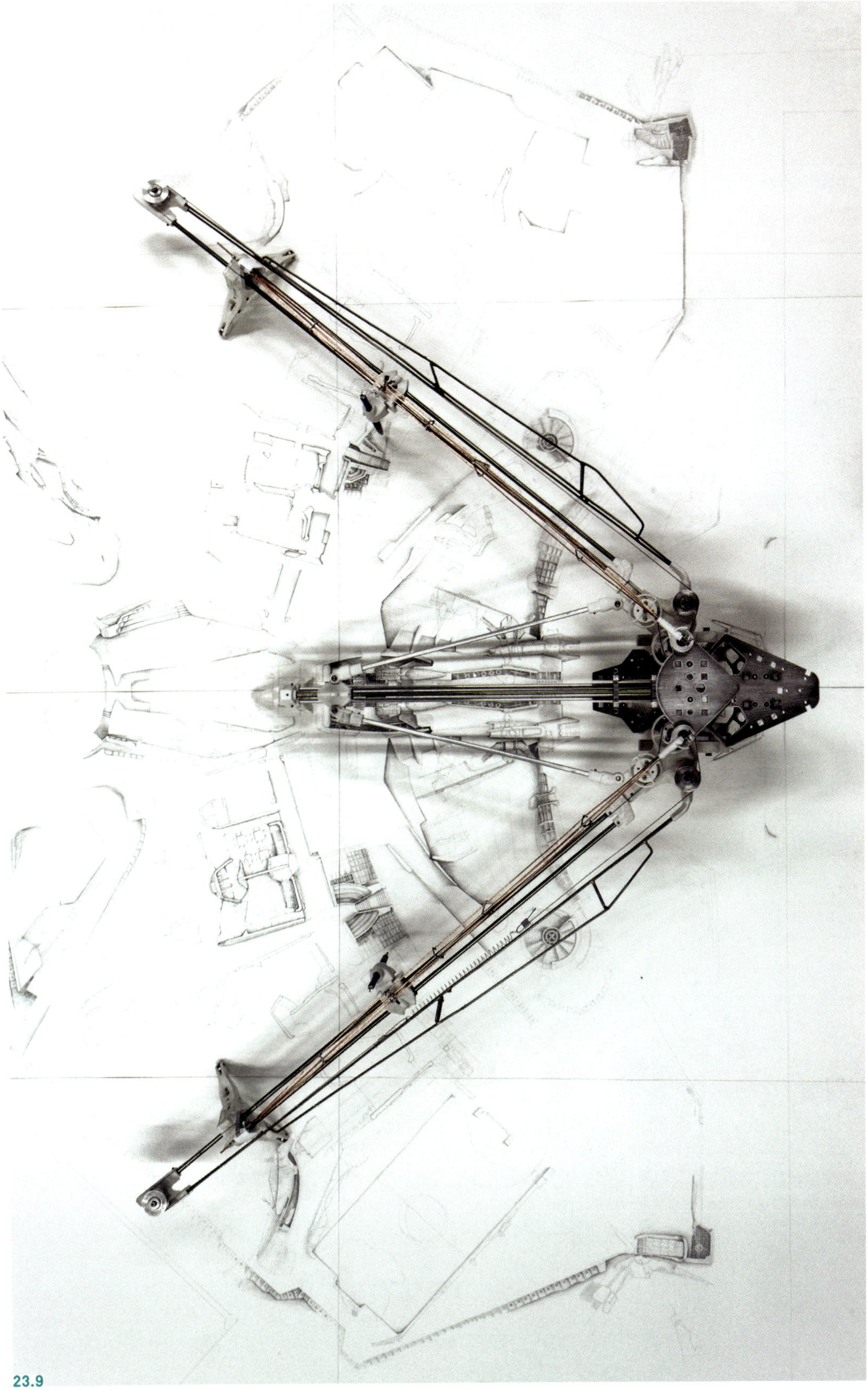

23.9

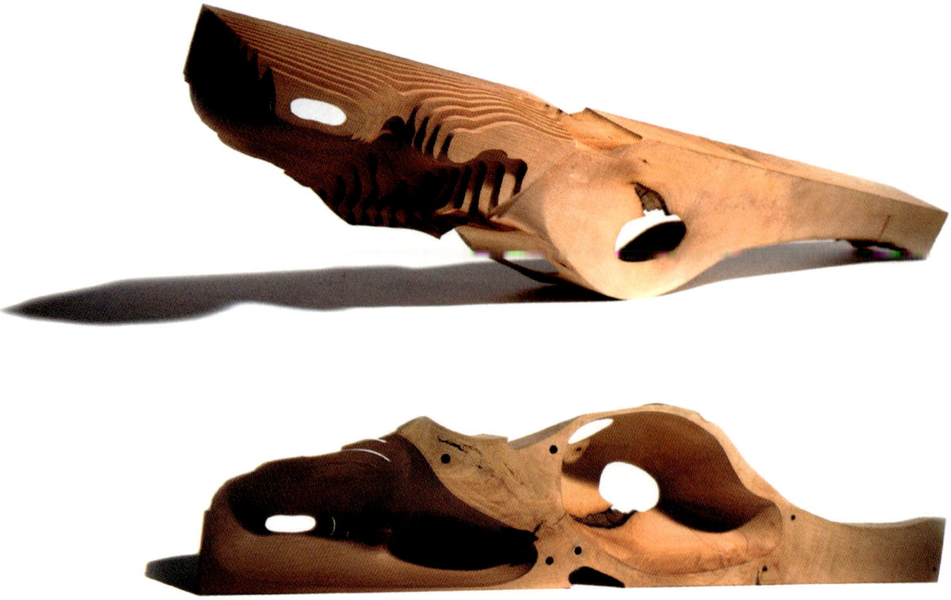

23.10

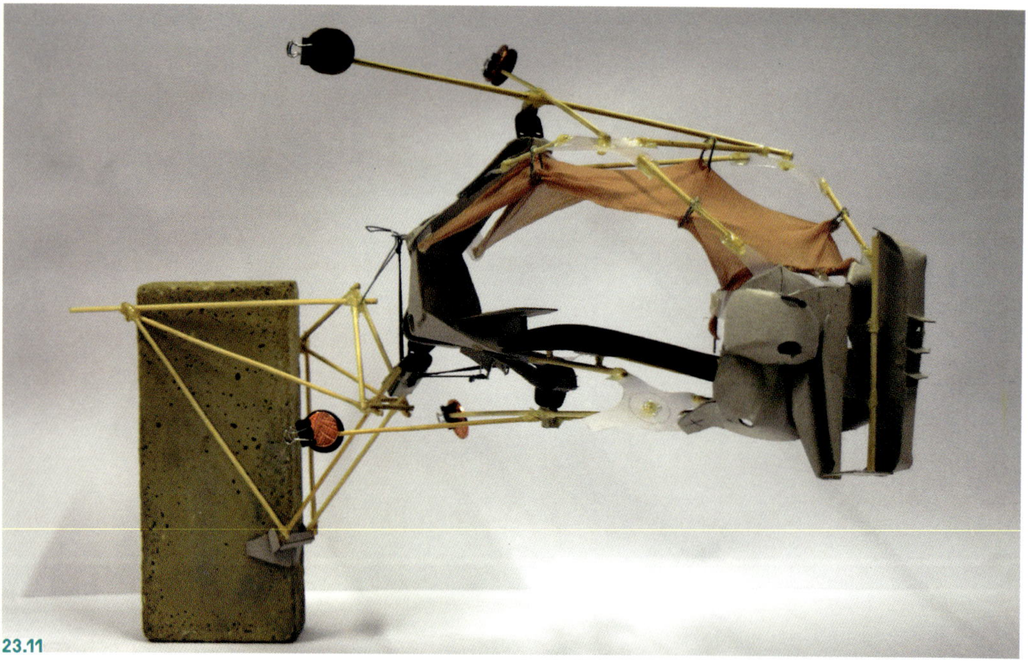

23.11

Fig. 23.10 **Michael Arnett** Y5, 'The Florentine Clinic'. The role of the object in architectural design is investigated through making, exploring how the logic of the object can infect and inhabit other spaces with its character. **Fig. 23.11** **Peter West** Y4, 'Occupy Cavallerizza'. Situated in an illegally occupied building in Turin, an architectural balancing act implicates the body of the occupant in worlds beyond itself. **Fig. 23.12** **Dean Hedman** Y4, 'The Arboreal Archive & Research Lab'. Interested in our understanding of material space, the archive uses anisotropic gestures of wood as the primary design input. Through exposing hidden clusters of information in assembled spaces, the architecture is a deliberate attempt to construct internal didactic environments.

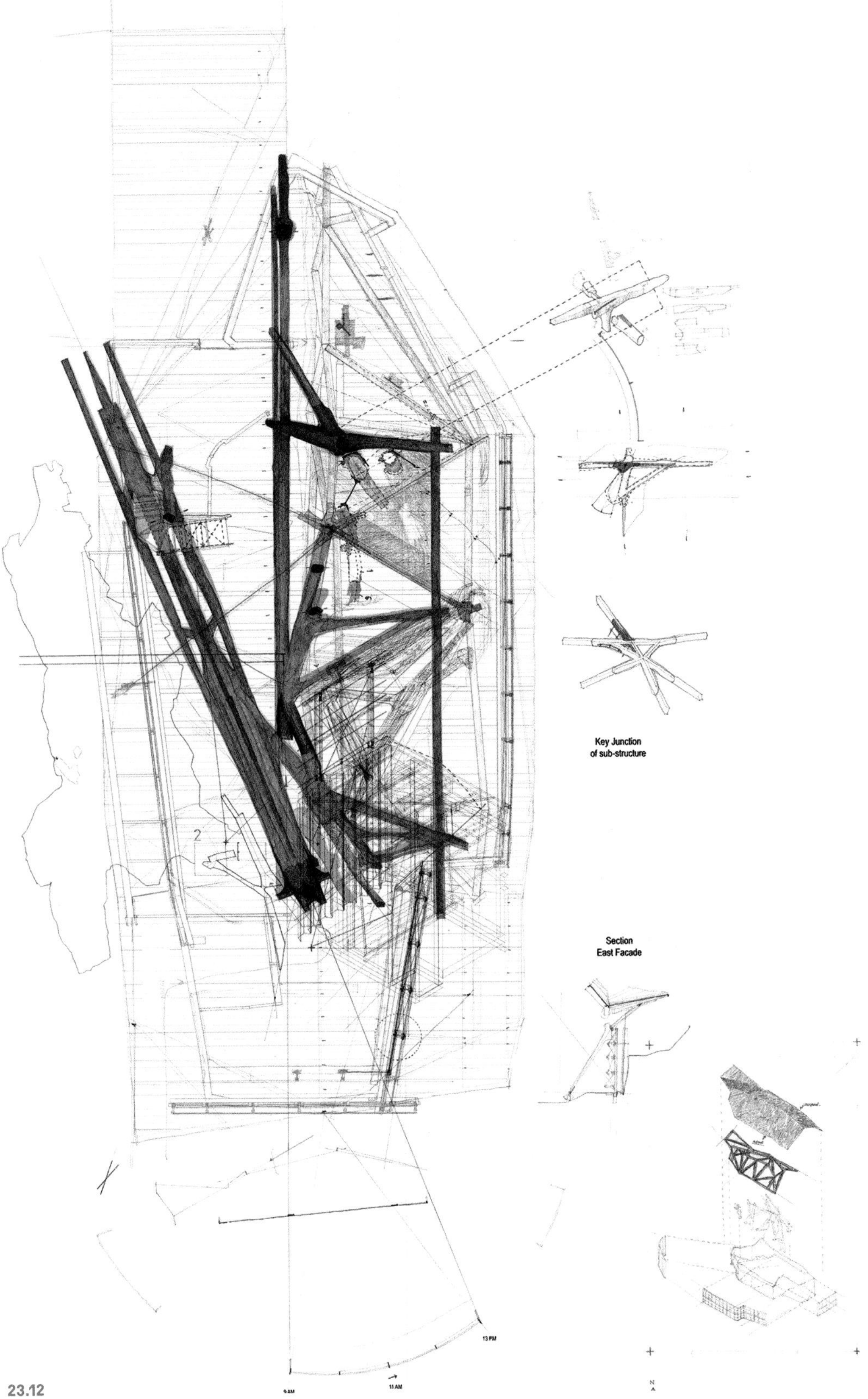
Key Junction
of sub-structure
Section
East Facade
13 PM
11 AM
9 AM
N

23.12

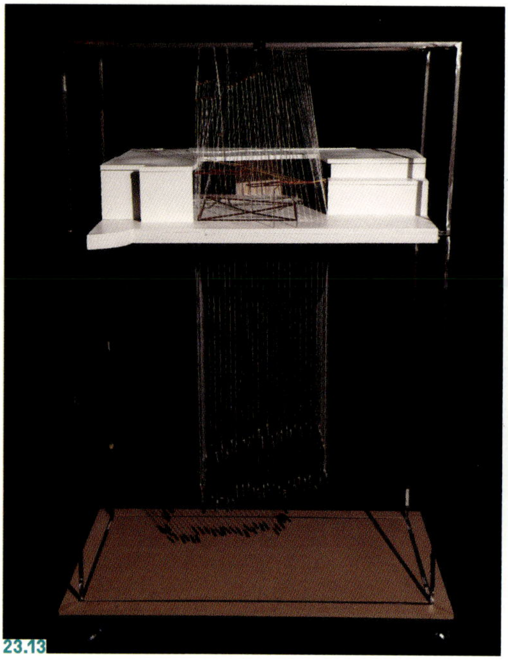

23.13

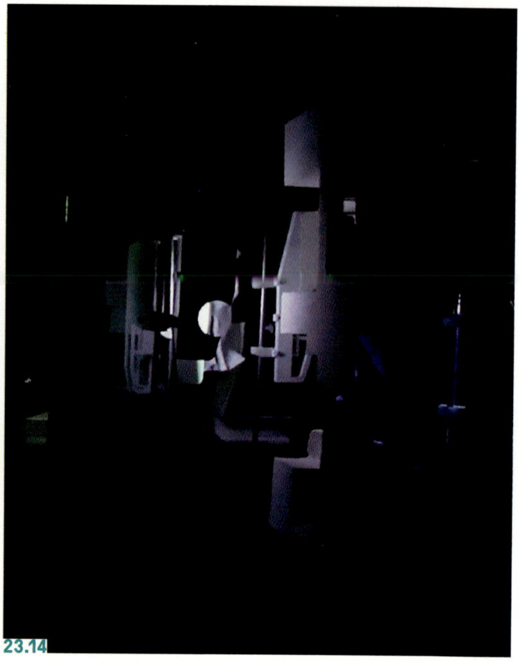

23.14

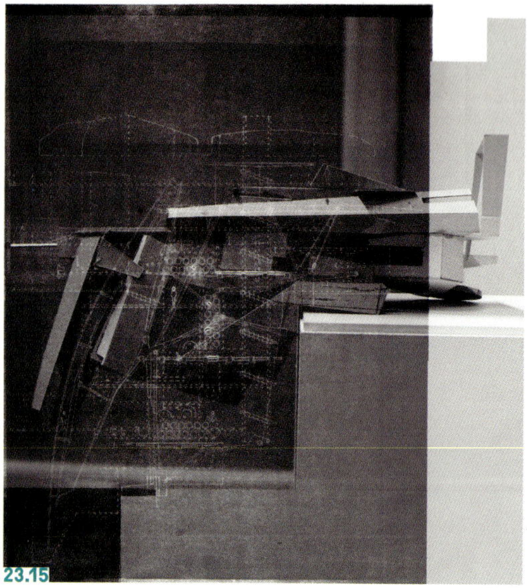

23.15

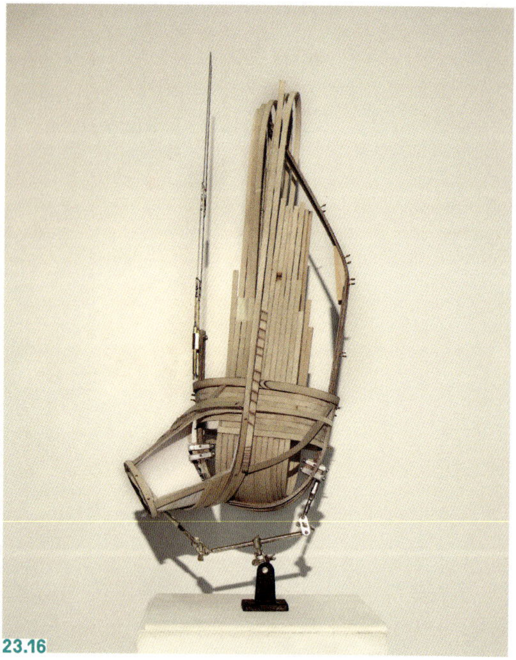

23.16

Fig. 23.13 Jiatong Hu Y4, 'The Murazzi Dance School'. This project explores the potential and possibility of mapping unknown relationships between geometries and different territories. The design focuses on the negotiation between public and private spaces and the transitions in between, with an emphasis on weaving a public route through private or semi-private entities. **Fig. 23.14 Thomas Parker** Y4, 'Chasing Phantoms'. Phantom schisms and spectral jitters – these are occurrences that may only appear for a fleeting moment across an indefinite time. The architecture explores notions of a world caught on the periphery of our momentary perception, captured in a series of interventions grounded in fact, yet deliberately fictitious. **Fig. 23.15 Dan van der Poll** Y4, 'The Poetry of Decay'. An investigation into the initial states of erasure, their intrinsic relationship with architecture and the construction process, and the creation of new archaeologies. Aggregated states of flux take the form of a responsive architecture, which tells the story of its history, purpose and function. **Fig. 23.16 Andrea Matta** Y4, 'The Boat Museum'. Exploring conservation and craftsmanship in the investigation of manufacturing techniques involved in local handicrafts. The study appreciates the skills and tacit knowledge embedded in a series of wooden boat constructions.

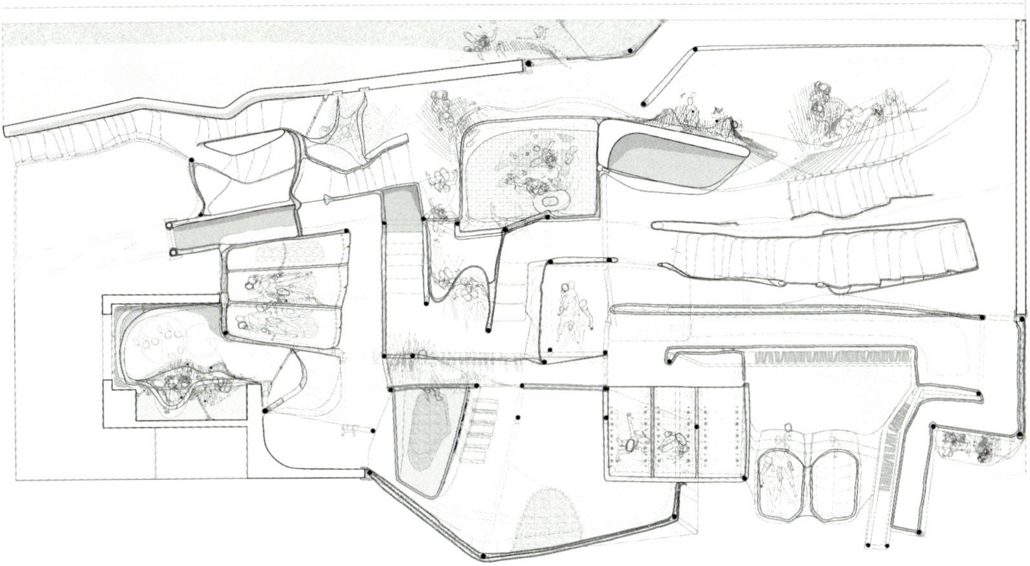

23.17

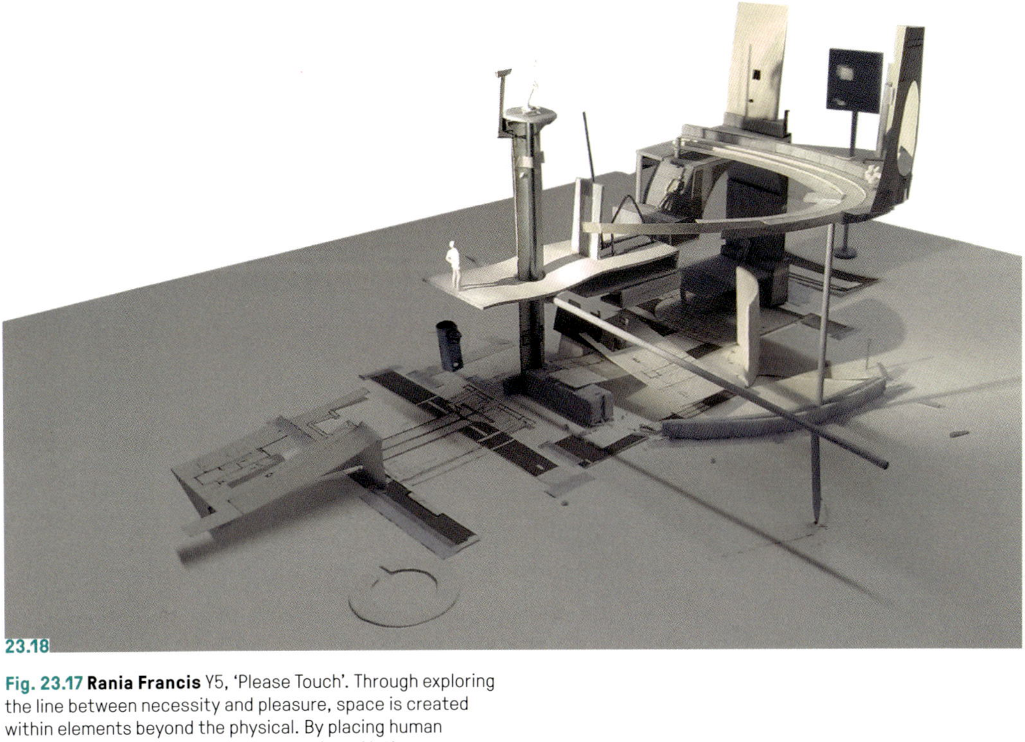

23.18

Fig. 23.17 Rania Francis Y5, 'Please Touch'. Through exploring the line between necessity and pleasure, space is created within elements beyond the physical. By placing human interaction at the forefront in the creation of intimacy, the architectural surface transgresses boundaries.
Fig. 23.18 Wynne Leung Y5, 'Theatre of the Everyday'. Our minds and behavioural reactions are sometimes augmented or encouraged by the existence of momentarily mundane spatial / time voids. Personal desires are encouraged to be incrementally explored, creating momentary acts of guilty pleasure.

Unit 24 Against the Flow

Penelope Haralambidou, Simon Kennedy, Michael Tite

Year 4
Sabina Berariu, Thomas Brown, Clare Dallimore, Matthew Lucraft, Martyna Marciniak, Gergana Popova, Nick Shackleton, Jasper Stevens

Year 5
Haesung Choi, Nichola Czyz, Finbarr Fallon, Stefana Gradinariu, Azizul Hoque Mariya Krasteva, Stefanos Levidis, Ting-Jui (Brook) Lin, Ziyi (Bill) Liu, Antonio Zhivkov

Workshops: Factory Fifteen, Tomas Millar, Kevin Pollard, ScanLAB Projects

Special thanks to: Kairo Baden-Powell, Alastair Browning, Ben Shetterline, Emir Tigrel, Angeliki Vasileiou

Critics: Ollie Alsop, Anna Ulrikke Andersen, Alessandro Ayuso, Paul Bavister, Matthew Butcher, Luke Chandresinghe, Peter Cook, James Craig, Hal Currey, Kate Davies, Elizabeth Dow, Max Dewdney, Marcela Araguez Escobar, Murray Fraser, Ruairi Glynn, Colin Herperger, Jonathan Hill, Alex Holloway, Kelvin Ip, Platon Issaias, Jan Kattein, Chee-Kit Lai, Ifi Liangi, Keiichi Matsuda, Sam Storr McGill, Tim Norman, James O'Leary, Manuel Toledo Otaegui, Luke Pearson, Dan Scoulding, Renée Searle, Catrina Stewart, Henri Williams

Unit 24 employs film, video, animation, drawing and modelling techniques to generate architectural propositions, harnessing the potential of time-based media in the production of space.

——We nurture freethinkers who investigate ideas and techniques in collaboration with other like-minded experts. This year, after securing funding for workshops and new equipment, students benefitted from our expanded network of associated specialists, architects, animators, virtual reality tinkerers, filmmakers and musicians in a series of bespoke master classes.

——This year's theme focused on shifting notions of the 'local' and the 'global', reading both not as spaces, but as flows. The world has imploded. Instantaneous information flow rules all – the new 'digital local' makes the Global Village into the Google Earth. Location is irrelevant... or is it? Local news. Local weather. The local pub. Local architects. What do we mean when we talk about the local? Is it a place? Is it part of the psyche? Can its value be measured? Who can be a local? Can technology ever be local? And what about architecture?

——Challenging the forces of universalising technological progress, we invited students to find a 'critical regionalism' for the information age, interrogating globally available open-source technologies in search of the particular and the local. We questioned the tendency to retreat into the home-grown, the tribal and the regional and asked whether the local simply inflects the global condition or whether it can be a driver for change.

——The Thames, then. Our local river. A shimmering causeway flowing to the centre of the universe, or the disgusting urinal of a washed-up, morally bankrupt city? Defining the Thames in the singular is facile. At once staggeringly ugly and magnificently sublime, its length spans innumerable conditions: cupping the sweetbreads of international corporate investment but also cultivating new ecosystems. It has witnessed the emergence and growth of London and will outlive it.

——In November, we travelled to and dispersed ourselves throughout Japan; walking the river route against the flow from Osaka to Kyoto; exploring backstreets in Tokyo; visiting Hiroshima; sailing to Naoshima, hoping to learn from what Arata Isozaki termed 'Japan-ness': a local architecture that can harness the forces of globalisation.

——Year 4 students proposed filmic architectures that utilised the estuarine zones in and around the Thames, searching for an alternative future of the local, while Year 5 students developed their own personal agendas locally and globally.

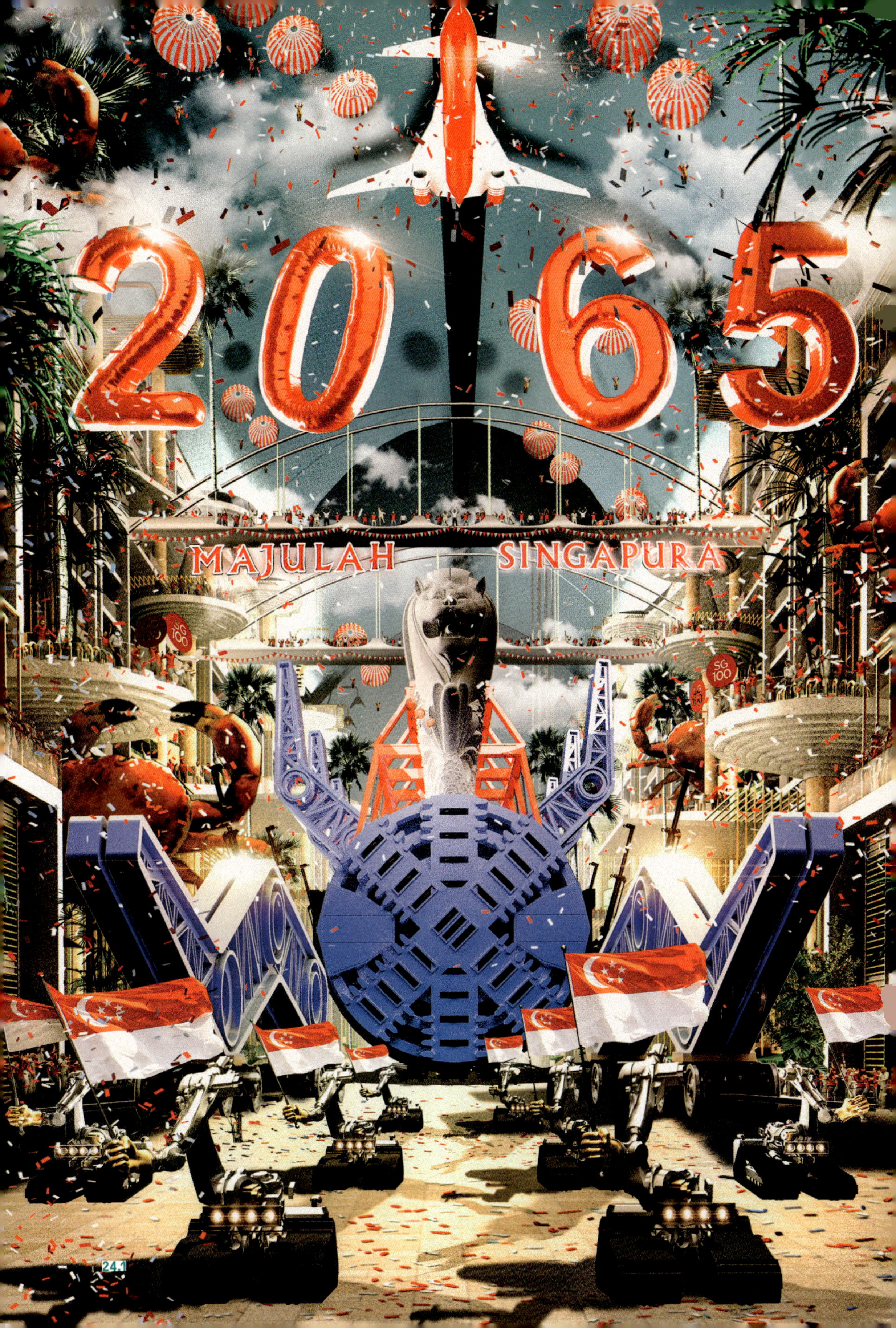

24.1

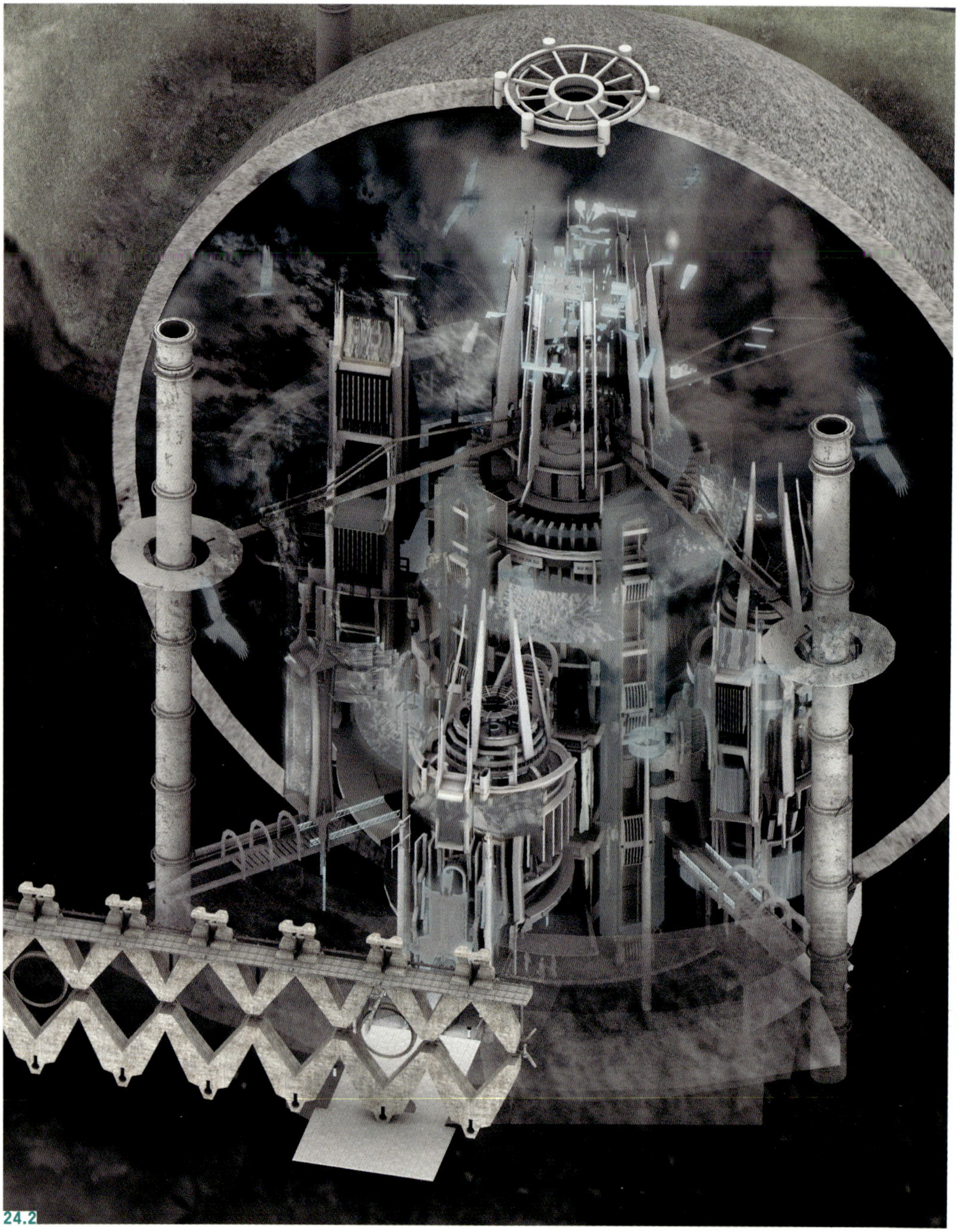

24.2

Fig. 24.1 Finbarr Fallon Y5, 'SG100'. Fin imagines a future subterranean expansion of Singapore, where inflatable structures breathe naturally cooled cave air, supported by modular super-frame structures. The film portrays the 2065 centennial of independence celebrations, when the traditional military parade is reconfigured to a choreographed march of robotic construction technology. This 'Metropolis'-inspired vision is a Technicolor polemic that challenges the ethics of large-scale infrastructural projects and their dark consequences, such as the exploitation of foreign workers.
Fig. 24.2 Haesung Choi Y5, 'Holographic Theatre'. In science fiction cinema, the hologram has become ubiquitous shorthand for the futuristic and the intangible. Located on an old battery in Tokyo Bay, Hae explores the theatrical qualities of this 'mythical hologram' and overlays it onto a physical structure to propose a hybrid inhabitable and tectonic holographic experience. Seen as a fabric that can shroud and conceal, Hae's hologram can also reveal a visceral 'brighter real'.
Fig. 24.3 Azizul Hoque Y5, 'Whalemart'. Aziz's re-imagining of Tokyo as a city of hyper-convenience plunges us headlong into the shemozzle of an artificially intelligent drone service industry that swarms above and around us, eager to cater to our every need. Acting like an urban reef, the city hosts an aquatic caste system of robotic crustaceans; from delivery shrimps to whale-like storage zeppelins, rubbish collecting crabs and mobile sushi kiosks. In this pumped-up anime-inspired city, the rules of transaction have been re-written and the bass has permanently been turned up to ten.

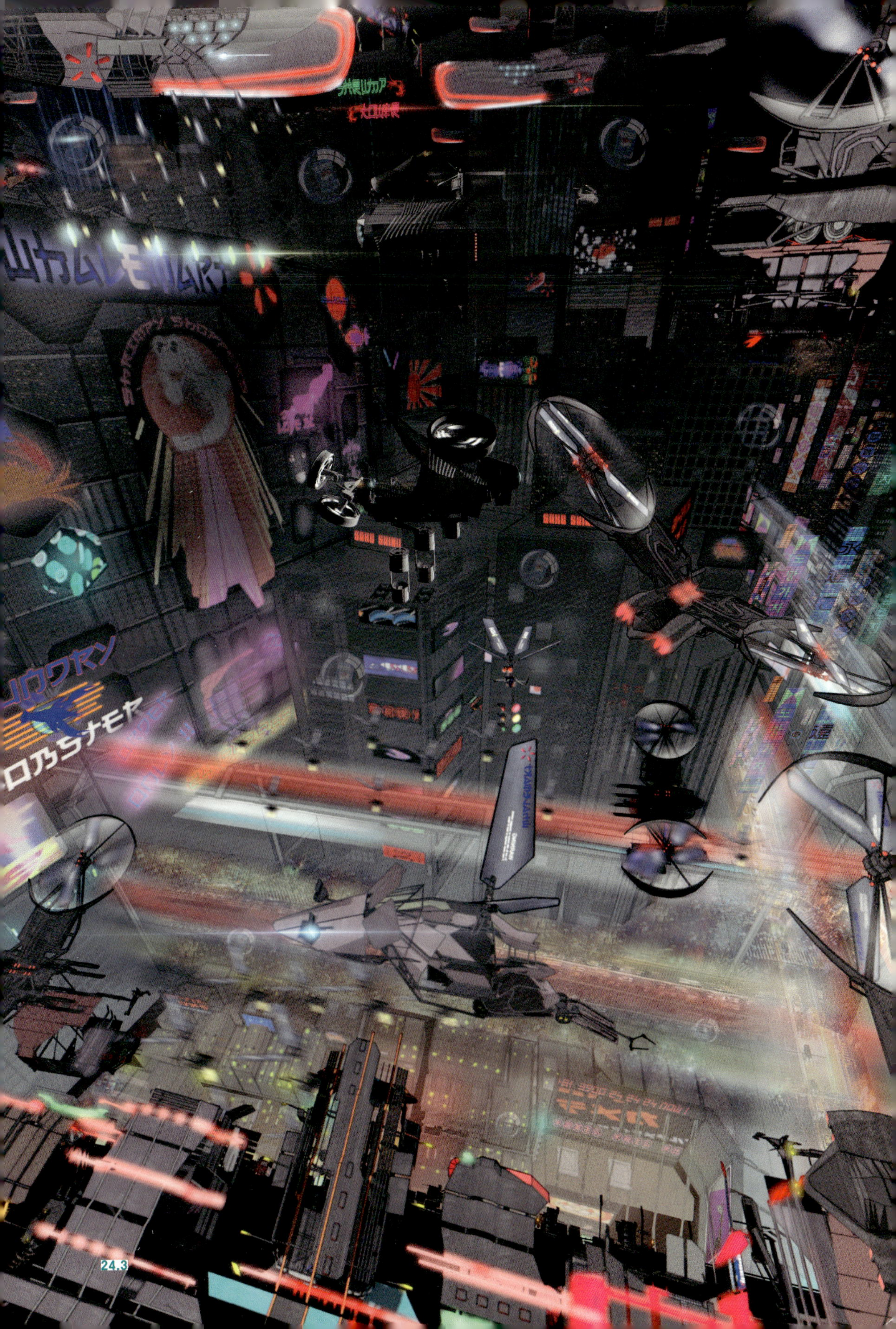

24.3

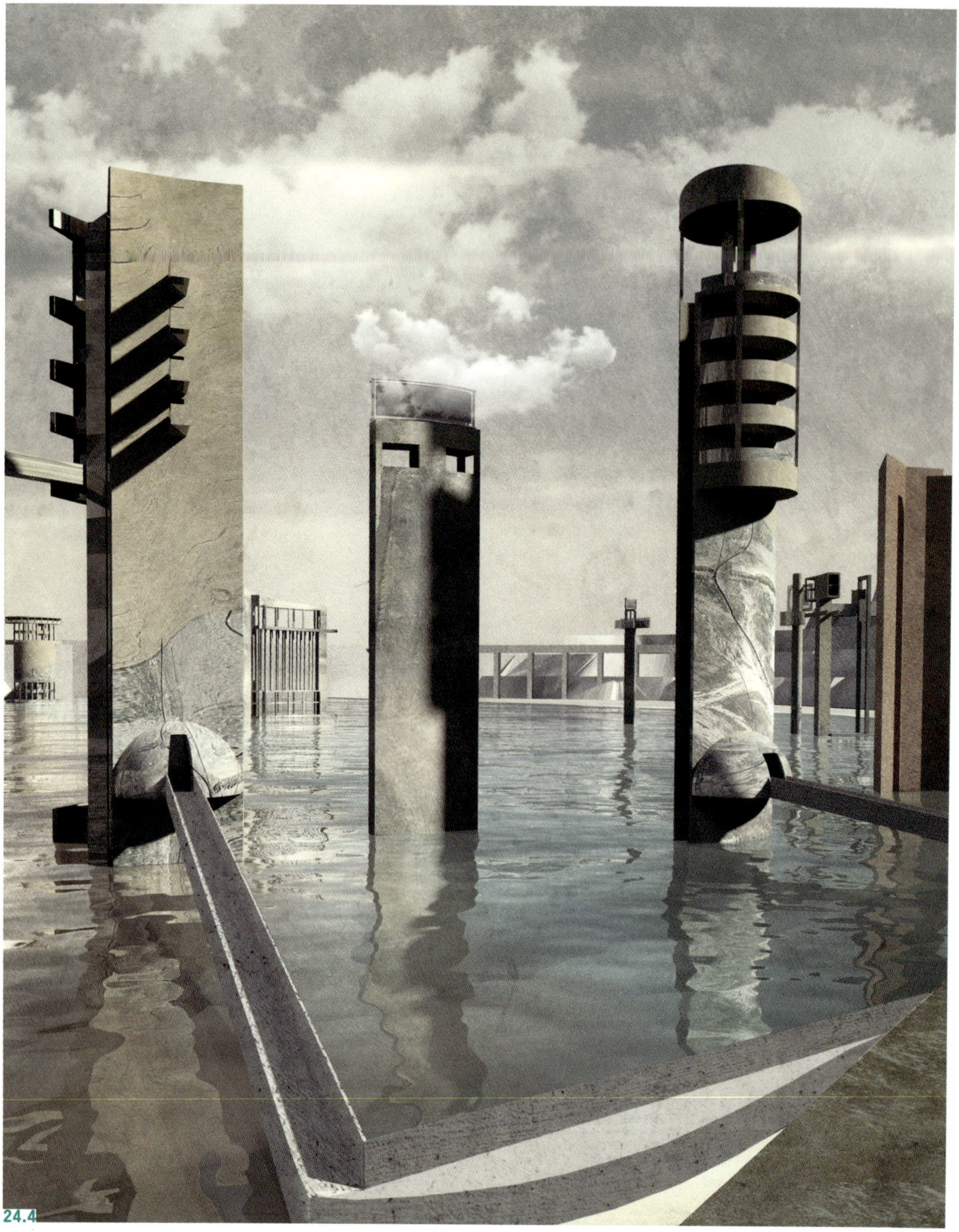

24.4

Fig. 24.4 Stefana Gradinariu Y5, 'The Fourth Nature'. The project deploys a 'critical realist' reading of mutant landscapes resulting from long-term and large-scale mining activities in the Apuseni Western Mountains of Romania. Three host sites in the area are key locations: the Rosia Montana gold mining community; the Roșia Poieni copper quarry and the Sesei Valley sludge bed. Stefana's Hydrological Institute aims to heal the damaged, contaminated land and protect it from future exploitation. A series of tower-like structures scatter the quarry bed, echoing the haunting imagery of the flooded dwellings of the valley and acting as a warning flare to future generations. The project seeks to atone for the natural, cultural and historical vandalism played out in the region, by giving voice to the traumatised landscape.

Fig. 24.5 Nichola Czyz Y5, 'The Long Now Foundation'. Named after the institute established by Stewart Brand and Brian Eno, Nico's project is guided by an interest in instilling long-term thinking. It is the result of a pilgrimage route along the River Thames from the sea to the source, during which a brick is made from the river's clay. Once fired, and on the ninth day of walking, the brick is placed at the source as the seed of a temple projected to grow over the next 10,000 years. Rules derived from the structure of bismuth crystals guide the placement of the bricks and the labyrinthine architecture that emerges over time is the result of the pilgrims' interpretation, forming a 'ruin in reverse'. The project is situated between land art and essay film, questioning the role of time in architecture, as well as the role of the architect as author.

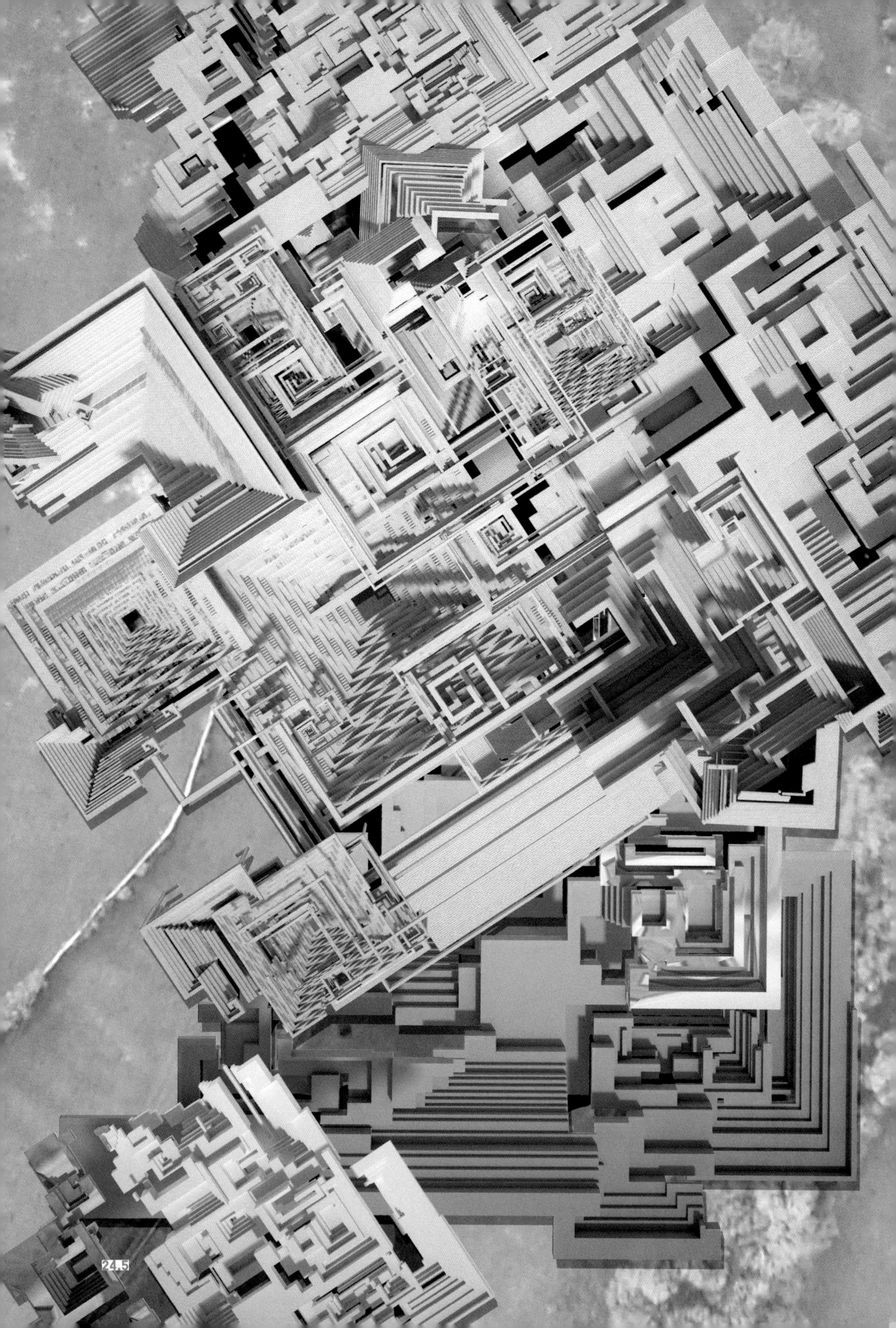
24.5

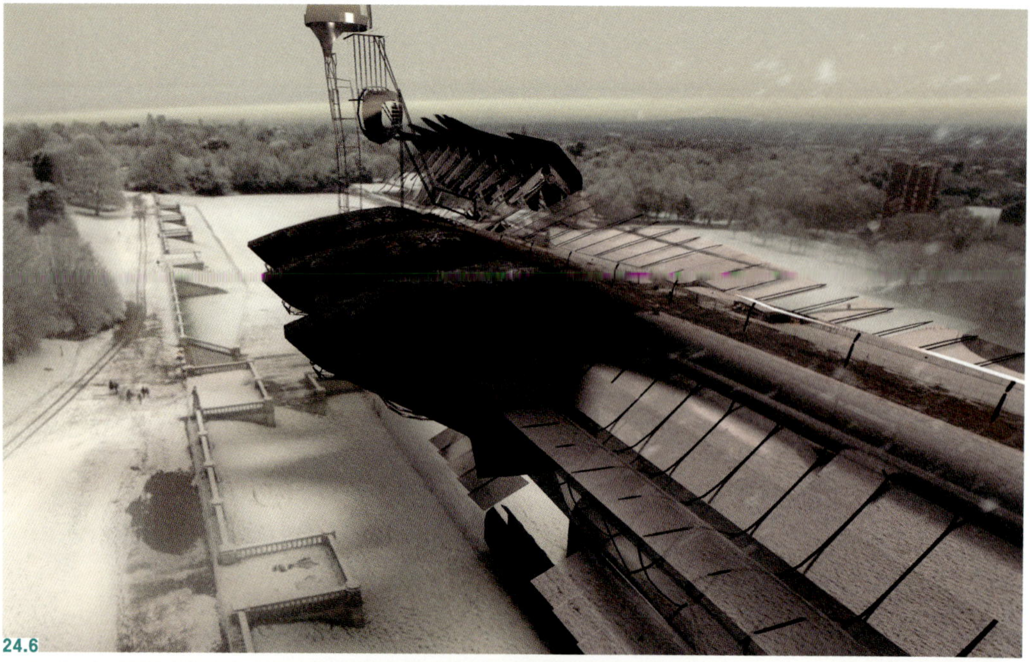

24.6

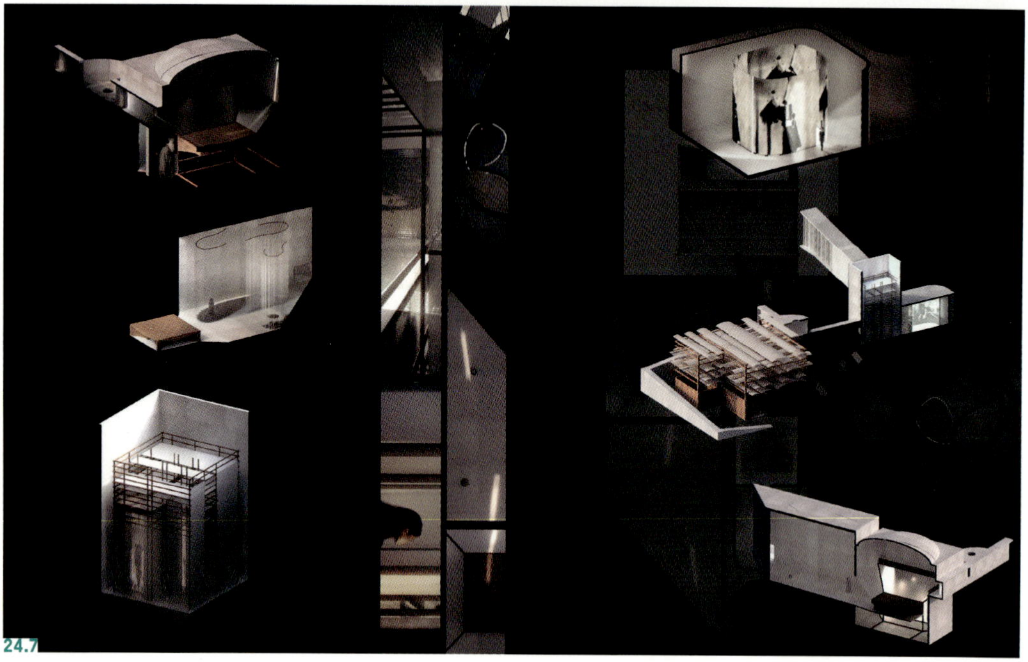

24.7

Fig. 24.6 Antonio Zhivkov Y5, 'Palace of Motion'. Acting as a futuristic reincarnation of the original Crystal Palace, this project explores the possibilities of interaction between the human body and new technologies. The building is designed as a constantly changing entity; a dancing partner to human movement. Through an iterative process of motion capture and modelling, bodies and the corresponding building elements become gradually abstracted until the boundaries between the different joints and limbs vanish, creating a spectacular architecture that feels alive. **Fig. 24.7 Mariya Krasteva** Y5, 'Reading between the Shadows: Mukaejima Film Island'. An exploration of the themes of identity, architecture and light through a study of early Japanese cinema. This posits a new typology, an immersive film museum inspired by the legends of the 'Golden Age': Tanizaki, Ozu and Mizoguchi. Through the manipulation of daylight and projected light, aspects of three key films become embedded within the architecture. The building carries material and intangible traces of Japanese history, perpetually played out in time. **24.8 Stefanos Levidis** Y5, 'Embassy of the Displaced'. Established between London, Athens and Lesvos in December 2015, this is a design-based collective that operates both in-the-field and remotely, providing spontaneous responses to the refugee crisis. The 'Embassy' serves as a design-for-survival laboratory, a visual archive of the refugees' journey and an institution on the side of the displaced, aiming to symbolically frame the plight of displacement through scanning technology and architectural design; ultimately suggesting a land for the landless.

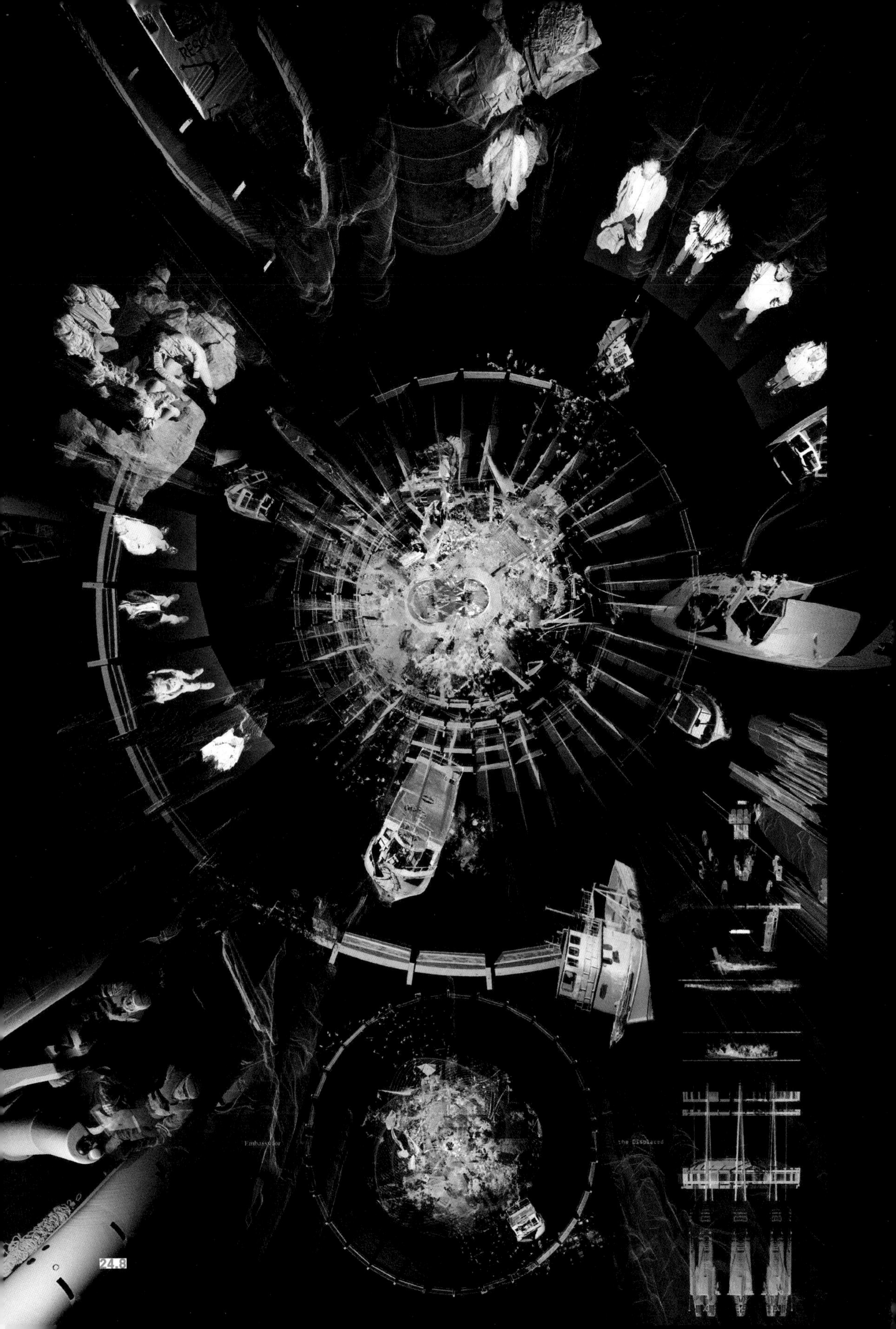

24.8

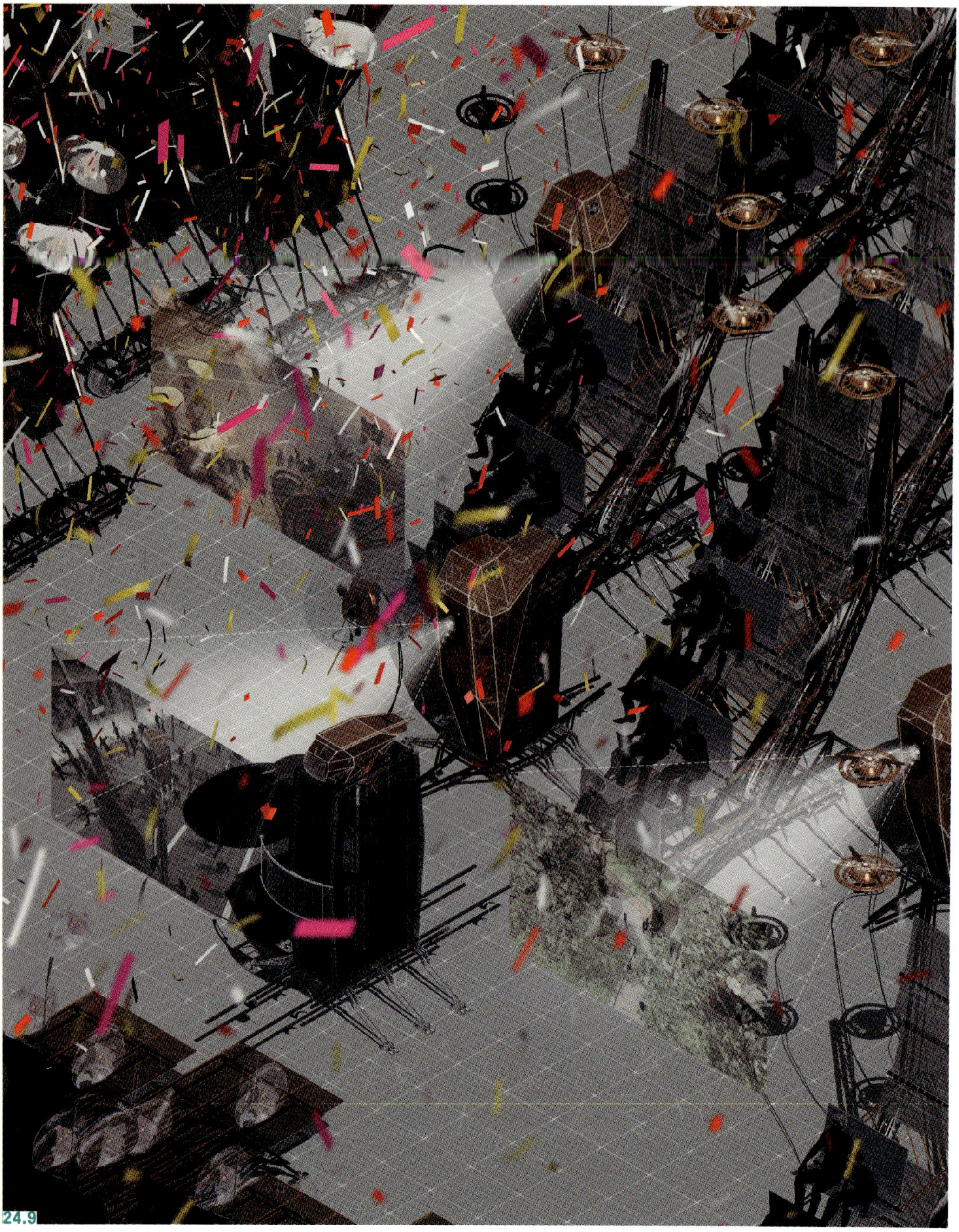

24.9

Fig. 24.9 Ziyi (Bill) Liu Y5, 'Osaka Expo 2020: Mikoshis of Surveillance and Spectacle'. Based on traditional Japanese concepts of public space, the project proposes a new typology for the world exposition through the reconstruction of the processional and temporary qualities of the Japanese Matsuri (festival). Conceived as an extension of Arata Isozaki's rebellion against the government's top-down control, this project serves as a commentary on the act of surveillance both as a covert strategy used during Expo'70 and as a novelty of increasing fascination within contemporary society.
Fig. 24.10 Ting-Jui (Brook) Lin Y5, 'An Anatomical Embassy'. This project is conceived as a refurbishment of the current home for the Embassy of Japan in Piccadilly, imagining its temporary relocation to the north edge of the adjacent Green Park. The procedural, operational and diplomatic organs of the embassy become ceremonially eviscerated from the Victorian body and spill out into the park, like scattered 'seeds', which grow into small pavilion-like interventions. These vessels become re-inserted into the original building after a period of open use within the park: the two identities and two sets of vocabularies – architecture and garden design – eventually grafting and budding together. This 'dual' embassy (that of Green Park and that of 101-104 Piccadilly), embodies Venturi's ideas of 'duality', 'fragments', 'individuals', and 'the whole' and becomes a carefully considered diplomatic architecture of formality, inflection and negotiation.

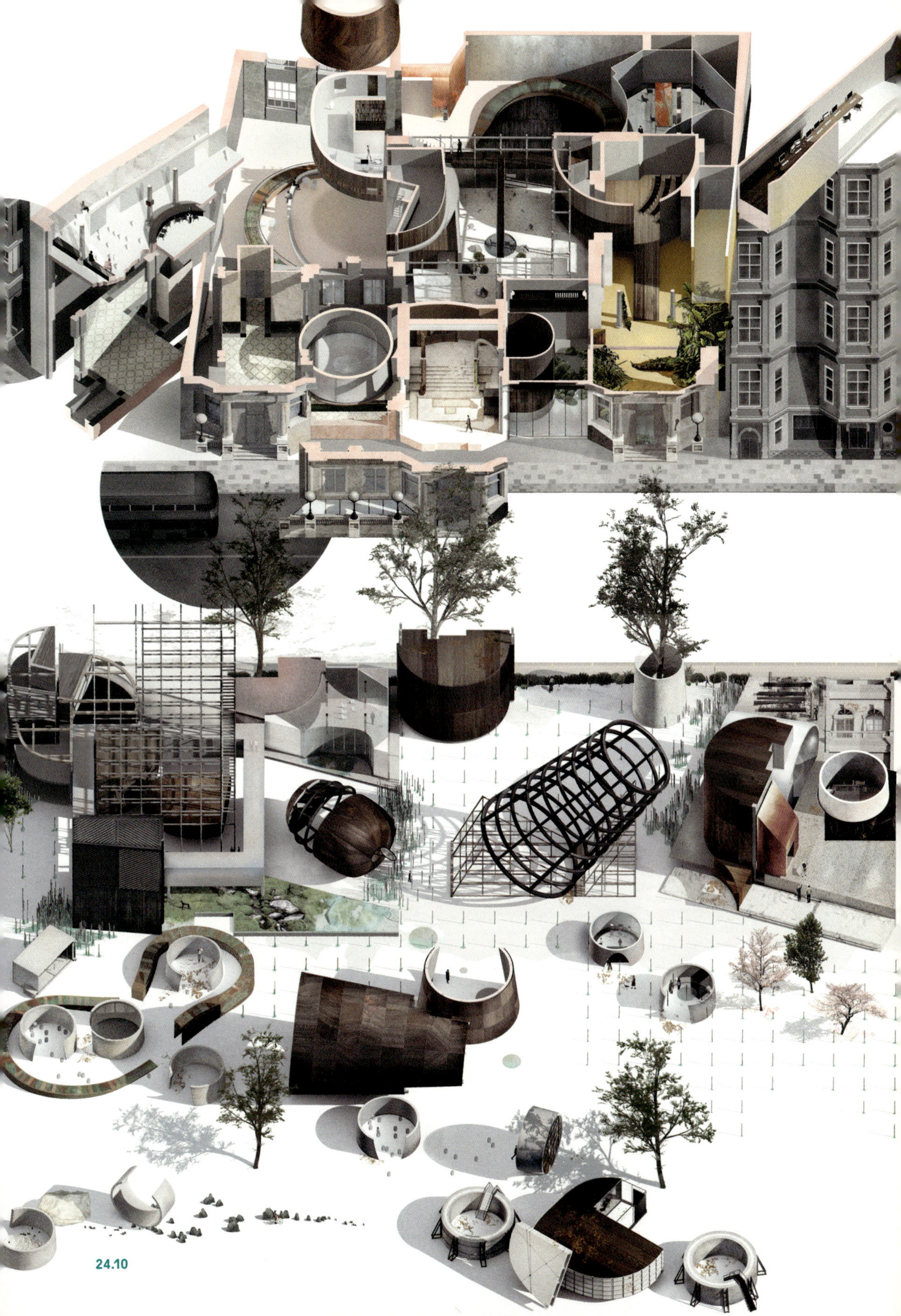

24.10

Year 4

Design Realisation

James O'Leary, Dirk Krolikowski

Thank you to our DR Lecturers: Daniel Bosia (AKT II), Damian Eley (ARUP Structures), Jan Guell (RSH+P), Xavier de Kastelier (Foster + Partners), Sara Klomps (Zaha Hadid Architects), Dirk Krolikowski (The Bartlett, UCL), Tim Lucas (Price & Myers / The Bartlett, UCL), Ho-Yin Ng (AL_A), James O'Leary (The Bartlett, UCL), Joanna Pencakowski (RSH+P), Mario Pirwitz (JSWD Cologne), Hareth Pochee (Max Fordham), Simon Ruppert (Bollinger + Grohmann), James Thonger (ARUP Structures)

We are grateful to our DR Practice Tutors: Rhys Cannon (Gruff Ltd.)

Simon Dickens (Youmeheshe), Vidal Fernandez (RSH+P), Pedro Gil (Studio Gil Architects), Lee Halligan & James Daykin (Blee Halligan Architects), James Hampton (Periscope), Tom Holberton (Rick Mather Architects), Dirk Krolikowski (The Bartlett, UCL), Justin Nicholls (Fathom Architects), Ralph Parker (Price & Myers), Aleksandrina Rizova, Stefan Rutzinger & Kristina Schinegger (SOMA Architecture), Michael Tite (Michael Tite Architecture Ltd), Anna Woodeson (LTS Architects)

Thanks to all the Structural Consultants that have worked with individual students to realise their projects, and to Max Fordham, Environmental Consultants to all design units

Image: Unit 17 Ghost Chapel Project, Connemara, Ireland

The Design Realisation (DR) course provides the opportunity for all Year 4 Masters students to consider how buildings are designed, constructed and delivered. Students are asked to reflect upon their relationship to technology, the environment and the profession, via an iterative critical examination of the major building design project taught within the context of individual design units in Year 4. They are simultaneously supported by an extensive lecture series, seminars and cross-unit crits. The course forms a bridge between the worlds of academia and practice, engaging with many internationally renowned design practices and consultancies. A dedicated practice-based architect, structural engineer and environmental engineer support each design unit, working individually with students to develop their work throughout the programme.

——This year we have seen excellent work in DR, making it exceptionally difficult to select the winner of the DR Innovation award, kindly sponsored by Saint-Gobain. The prize is shared between five students, whose response to DR has been genuinely innovative. This year's Saint-Gobain Innovation Award goes to: Jonathan Davies, Unit 21; Joshua Honeysett, Unit 16; Matthew Lucraft, Unit 24; Agostino Nickl, Unit 11 and Amani Radeef, Unit 16.

——Jonathan Davies' work outlines a new form of urbanism along the Mediterranean. It is conceptually rich whilst drilling down to incredible levels of detail, right down to the legislative. Joshua Honeysett's proposal emerges from keen contextual observations in Panama. He creates an architecture that reforms the way the redundant ship technology of the Panama locks is used, creating a space suspended between technological adventure and fiction. Matthew Lucraft's work is conceptually driven, with a thorough understanding of the local context of Dagenham and cooperative housing. An elegant system-driven solution is proposed that modifies Japanese construction principles to construct a new English vernacular architecture.

——Agostino Nickl's project is a detailed deconstruction of the American suburban housing model, where standards are questioned and new possibilities arise. This delightfully witty project is executed with skill and precision, down to the level of 1:1 details and prototypes. Amani Radeef's work is a thorough investigation into the tectonics of a new visitor centre near Panama City, amplified by the use of digital prototyping. The project investigates several areas of innovative technology in the arena of marine and submersible architectures and propels them into compelling new architectural configurations.

——As well as these projects, we must make a special mention of the work of Unit 17 this year. Working as a group, they have designed and constructed a small chapel in Connemara on the west coast of Ireland. Through this process they have raised project funding, secured partners, talked to local media, worked through various iterations and built their proposal without compromise. Well done to all for an outstanding effort that has stretched the parameters of the possible in DR.

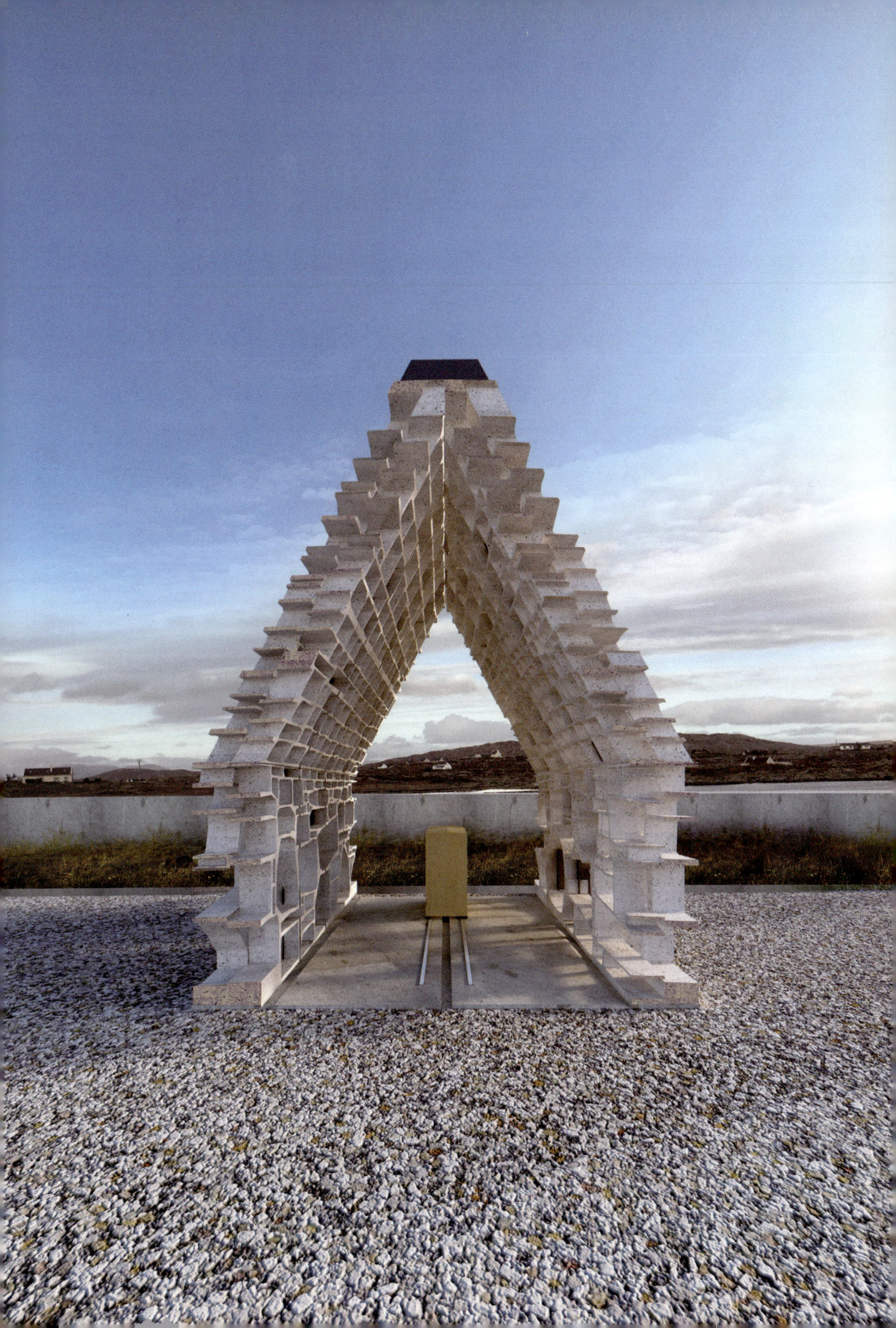

Year 4

Advanced Architectural Studies

Module Coordinator: Tania Sengupta

Seminars
Flexible Bodies, Flexible Selves
Tijana Stevanovic
Hidden Histories and Multiple Modernities
Edward Denison
U-topographics: Utopic Journeys into Postmodern Culture
Robin Wilson
How Change Happens: Architecture and Politics of Place
Daisy Froud
Gothic Designs, Gothic Desires
Jeffrey Miller
Senses and the City
Jacob Paskins
Between the Neurological and the Ecological
Jon Goodbun
Type: Culture, Meaning, Practice, Politics
Tania Sengupta
Architecture, Art & the City
Eva Branscome
Ornament: Barbaric Splendour or Architectural Sophistication?
Oliver Domeisen
Architecture and the Image of Decay
Paul Dobraszczyk

The Advanced Architectural Studies module, in the first year of the two-year professional Masters programme, focuses on architectural histories and theories. It is a space in which we reflect on architecture within a broader critical, intellectual and contextual field, simultaneously producing and being produced by it. Here, we try and locate architecture's linkages to other disciplinary and knowledge fields, from the scientific and technological to the social sciences and the humanities. We straddle empirical observation and theory, design and history; the iconic and the everyday.

——The course bears a number of possibilities – as a critical approach to augment design, as a parallel domain to test out design approaches and as a discrete or autonomous domain of architectural engagement. It focuses on three key types of academic development: first, that of a reflective, critical and analytical approach; the second, of research instinct and investigative methods; and the third, of skills of synthesis, writing and articulation. The module also acts as foundational ground for the Masters thesis that the students do in the final year of the MArch programme.

——The course consists of a set of lectures followed by the core of the module, which is a set of six tutor-led seminars on a diverse range of themes. These straddle geographically the architectural histories of various global contexts, and thematically issues such as buildings, urbanism, typology, ecology, politics, technology, production, public participation, urban regeneration, phenomenology, historiography and representation (see column). The lectures are on the architectural, urban and spatial histories of sequential moments of the nineteenth and twentieth centuries, but rendered through the individual conceptual and methodological frameworks of each of the seminar tutors. At the end, based on their learning from the lectures and seminars, the students formulate a critical enquiry around a topic of their choice and produce a 4,000 word essay.

Opposite left: Concept Art for Alien by H. R. Giger (Giger, 1979)
Opposite right: Fragments from A House for Essex and Nuestra Senora del Pilar

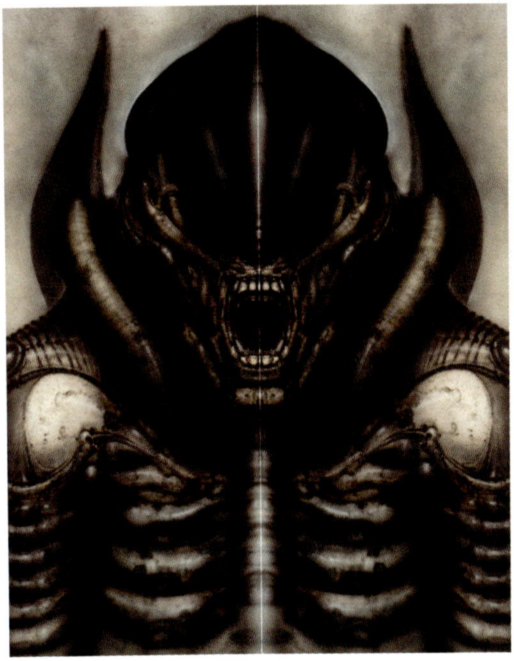

Joshua Toh
Alien Rococo – Beauty and the Beast
Supervisor/ Tutor: Oliver Domeisen

Hans Rudi Giger's creations for Ridley Scott's 1979 film *Alien* are a standout artistic achievement of the 20th century. Comparing Giger with Hieronymous Bosch and Salvador Dali, Timothy Leary describes them as 'blessed Alienists' who 'keep the human race in moist touch with our… primordial… past'. Despite its curious quality and 'potent horror', Giger's work is 'uniquely gripping' and crucially, 'elegantly baroque', as James R. Cowan evocatively proposed (Giger, 1979).

——This essay probes this relationship, comparing Giger's set designs for Scott's *Alien* to the Bavarian Rococo, which was less burdened than Italian baroque by 'pathos and rhetoric' and embodied "… works of art as occasions for an enjoyment that is its own justification," (Harries, 1983). The study analyses examples of Bavarian Rococo to understand their sources of beauty. Subsequently, by identifying similar elements in Giger's Alien, it extracts the underlying principles of decorative art there. It then tests the author's hypothesis that Giger's work treads a fine line between coherence with and subversion of these principles, generating a unique brand of monstrosity rooted principally in the aesthetic and which perhaps explains the simultaneous responses of delight and horror that Giger's Alien elicits.

Kirsty McMullan
Architecture and the Notion of 'Value'
Supervisor/Tutor: Tania Sengupta

In both *A House for Essex* by FAT and Grayson Perry and the self-built cathedral *Nuestra Senora del Pilar* by the Spanish monk Justo Gallego Martinez, the architecture is a vehicle for engagement between the authors and an imaginal figure. One is a polished 'narrative' monument to a fictitious character within a legitimate construction industry, whilst the other is an ongoing, DIY, unsanctioned accumulation of materials and processes dedicated to a religious deity. Although poles apart, they share an unusually mythical, self-generated brief and tirelessly construct a place of 'value'. However, their critical receptions differ greatly, raising questions about norms of architectural validation within contemporary society.

——This essay looks at how these two buildings configure author-idol relationships, engage an audience and exploit or critique normative architectural values driven by dominant powers. It argues that these projects enable an expansive imagination of architecture including under-exploited DIY technologies, non-expert authorship, vernacular materials and everyday fragments. Crucially, perhaps one of the most potent ideas these projects explore is process versus result – architecture as social rehearsal – bestowing new value to 'paper projects', temporary buildings and the imaginary as serious play.

Year 5 Thesis

Edward Denison, Robin Wilson, Oliver Wilton

The Thesis enables Year 5 students to research, develop and define the basis for their work, addressing architecture and relevant related disciplines such as the visual arts, humanities, cultural theory, anthropology, computation, physical or social sciences, engineering, manufacturing, environmental design and urbanism.

——Students undertake the work in depth, supported by specialist tutors who are individually allocated to students based on their stated areas of interest, in consultation with their design unit tutors. The result is a study of 9,000 words or equivalent that documents relevant research activities and outcomes and typically includes one or more propositional elements that may include the development of an argument or hypothesis, the development of a design strategy, or the development and testing of a series of design components in relation to a specific line of inquiry or interest.

——The Thesis is an inventive, critical and directed research activity that augments the work students undertake in design studio. The symbiotic relationship between thesis and design varies from being evident and explicit to being situated more broadly in a wider sphere of intellectual interest.

——Work from the module has won the RIBA President's Medals Dissertation Prize and we anticipate that a number of theses from this year's academic cohort will be developed into external publications.

Thesis Tutors

Hector Altamirano, Alessandro Ayuso, Andy Barnett, Matthew Barnett Howland, Jan Birksted, Brent Carnell, Simon Carter, Emma Cheatle, Ed Clark, Amica Dall, Meredith Davey, Edward Denison, Paul Dobraszczyk, Oliver Domeisen, Murray Fraser, Daisy Froud, Stephen Gage, Emily Gee, Stelios Giamarelos, Gary Grant, Jane Hall, Sean Hanna, Platon Issaias, Jan Kattein, Zoe Laughlin, Guan Lee, Stephen Lorimer, Luke Lowings, Tim Lucas, Abel Maciel, Anna Mavrogianni, Jeffrey Miller, Euan Mills, Harry Parr, Luke Pearson, Sofie Pelsmakers, Hareth Pochee, Rokia Raslan, Jane Rendell, David Rudlin, Peter Scully, Tania Sengupta, Bob Sheil, Neil Spiller, Nina Vollenbröker, Tim Waterman, Robin Wilson, Oliver Wilton and Simon Withers.

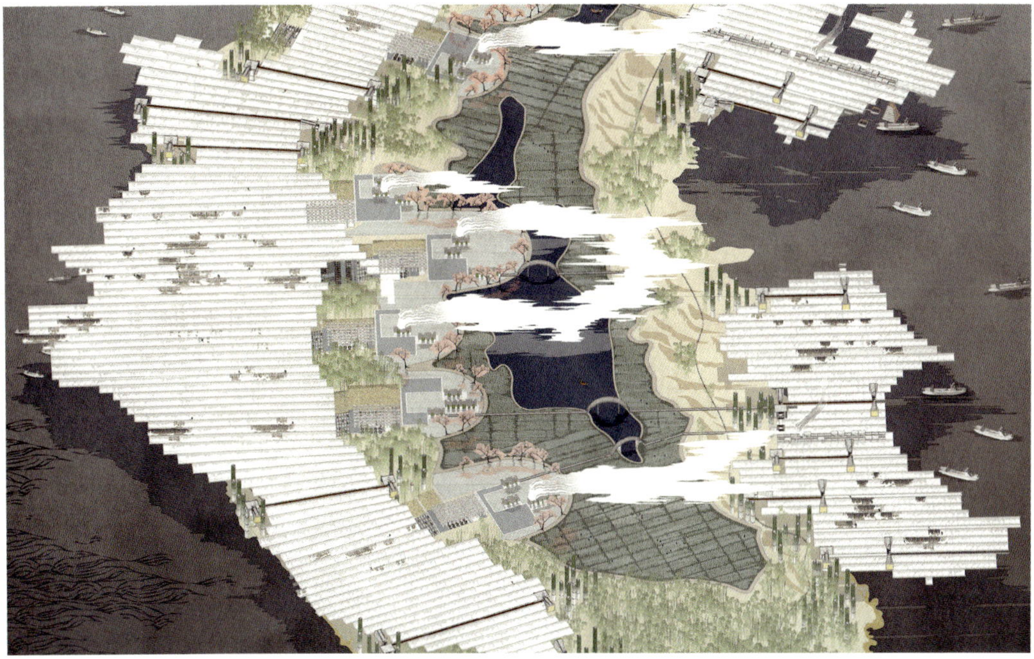

Chun Ting (Sam) Ki

The Contested City: Contested Urban Space from Pan-Asian Perspective

Thesis Tutor: Dr. Edward Denison

This study entails an architectural reading of Contested Space in an Asian context during the pivotal period of Asian modernisation from the mid-eighteenth to the early-twentieth century.

——Cultural interactions between western and Asian countries became increasingly vigorous and complicated during this period. The expansion of western powers in the east upset the equilibrium among Asian countries and heralded the age of modernity. Concomitantly, contested space appeared in manifold forms under this unstable international framework: trading zones, foreign settlements, treaty ports, concessions and colonies. Alternative cultures and powers co-existed inside these territories. Urban space became a theatre for competition between nations. This study analyses the spatial characteristics of these contested territories through five exemplary case studies from the period of Japanese national isolation to the outbreak of the Asia-Pacific War.

——This investigation is inspired by a 1996 Japanese film, 'Swallowtail Butterfly'. The five case studies interrogate the notion of contested space through three themes provoked by the film: contested urban form, contested regime and contested identity.

——The first thematic investigation explores the spatial formation and theoretical foundation of contested space through the case studies of urban sectors in Nagasaki and Pusan in the period before Asian modernity. The second thematic study focuses on the contested regimes and political systems that emerged in Kulangsu (China) and Taipei (Taiwan) during the period of colonial and quasi-colonial expansion. The two sites staged the contest between opposing regimes that in both cases found expression in the architecture and urban form.

——Building on the experiences of the first two studies, the third explores the idea of contested identity. The spatial characteristics of contested space will be examined through an analysis of the capital city of the Japanese puppet-state of Manchukuo: Hsinking. The collective identity, distinct from either Japanese or Chinese, demonstrates how a third identity of contested space was constructed.

——Through a critical analysis of the spatial reading of contested urban form, regime and identity, this study aims to shed new light on the notion "contested space" in the comparatively overlooked non-western context, revealing insights into national, regional and global relations whose importance and meaning for architecture and urbanism is not merely confined to history, but continues in the twenty-first century.

Image: Portrait of a contemporary contested city situated in the disputed territory, Uotsuri-shima, between Japan and China in the East China Sea, informed by the historical research of contested space in Asia.

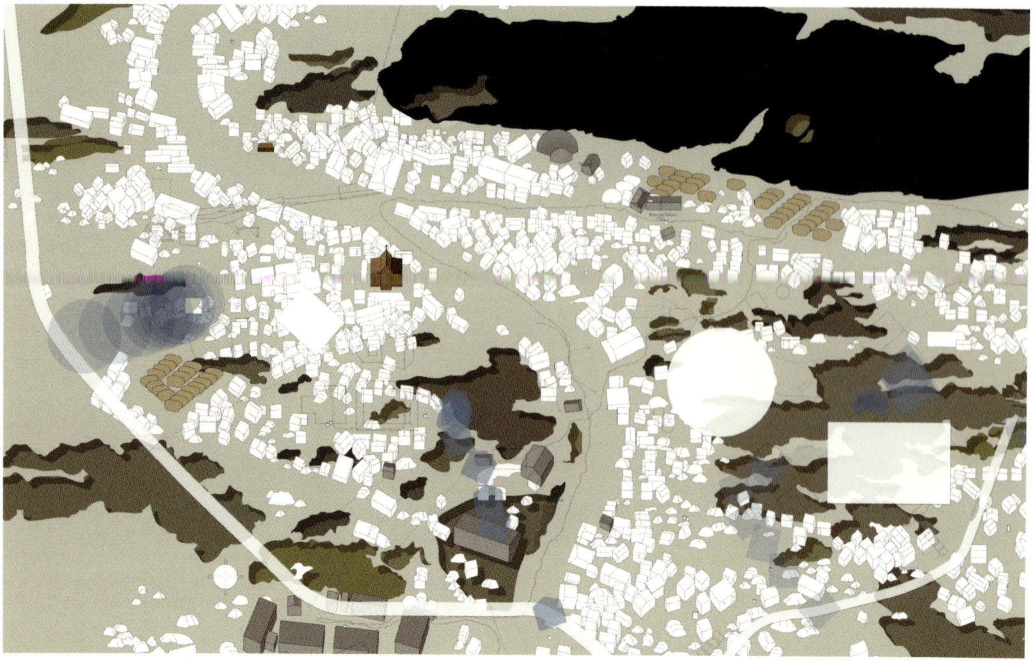

Tahmineh Hooshyar Emami

EXPLORING IN-BETWEENness: Spaces of Contradiction in Refuge

Thesis Tutor: Emma Cheatle

In light of the current political turmoil in the Middle East and due to the consequential increase in mass migration, a new breed of cities and spaces is emerging which blurs the boundaries between temporariness and permanence. The thesis investigates the spatial implications of refuge in the context of enforced mobility on the European route to safety. Within this new urban subspecies, named 'the in-between city', which becomes the place of contradiction, traditional spatial conceptions no longer apply. Architectural necessities, such as doors, walls and rooms, which are traditional markers of domesticity, borne out of our desire to set ourselves territorial boundaries, become invadable barriers.

——Critical and creative writing and storytelling are used as tools to explore these notions in the Jungle refugee camp, located near the port of Calais, focusing on its liminality and its transitory geopolitical and demographic position. The camp is a test-bed to investigate the architectural objects which stand in for large-scale notions of checkpoints, borders and countries. For instance, the bed encapsulates the idea of reciprocal effect between body and space, whereas the door is the embodiment of the idea of passing from one state to the other. The house beyond the door, with its four walls, encloses the space of domesticity, materializing its borders and symbolizing territories of the country, whilst the corridor epitomises passage and transition and stands for the sequence of countries along the refugee trail.

——'Alice's Adventures in Wonderland and Through the Looking-Glass' has been chosen as a political allegory in fiction that underpins and structures a critical analysis of the spatial politics of refuge in three books. The investigation into Carroll's dream-spaces targets fundamental questions surrounding concepts of spatial memory and perception. It is a starting point for the author to analyse how our bodies are defined, shaped and influenced by space, in this context. Alice becomes the vehicle that allows us to look through the lens of a single child and investigate the particularities of immigration from a specific perspective. She is redefined as part child, part author and concurrently, the voice of every refugee the author has interacted with during her site visit. The subject is borne out of an amalgamation of factual and imagined realities, reflected in storytelling and journal writings.

Image: Mapping the physical construct of the Jungle refugee camp as seen during the site visit in January 2016.

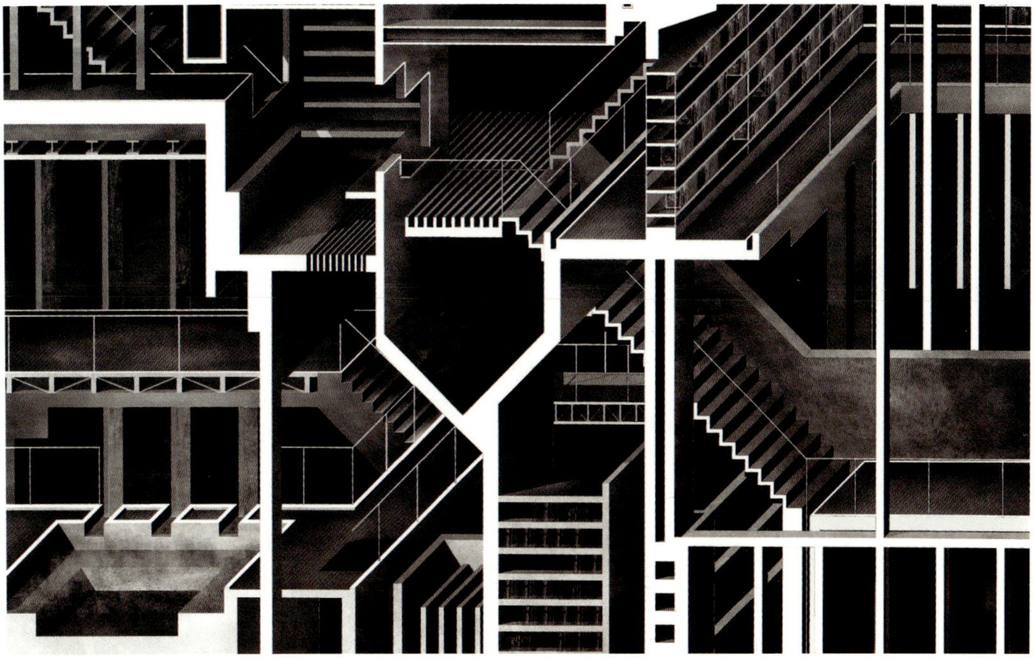

Matthew Sawyer

A New Perspective: Piranesi and the Fantastical Capriccio

Thesis Tutor: Luke Pearson

Capriccio. ca|pric|cio. A painting or other work of art representing a fantasy or a mixture of real and imaginary features[1]

——The capriccio defines the exact point where fantasy collides with the realism of architecture. This quasi-realism nurtures a fantastical space for total creativity that has enabled the capriccio to inspire architects for centuries. In the seventeenth century, it was employed as a tool for architects to dream metaphysically and idealistically within the possible and impossible limitations of architecture. Despite its undeniable historic importance, today it is an almost entirely forgotten form of architectural representation. This is possibly a result of the technological revolution that is shifting the culture of the architectural drawing into a period of graphical standardisation, which is counter to the capriccio's surprising difference.

——This thesis is a historic investigation into the architectural capriccio through a study of Giovanni Battista Piranesi's highly influential 'Le Carceri' prison series. Today, Piranesi's fantastical prison scenes have become a cornerstone of speculative architectural drawing, yet currently little work has considered why it is his most capricious series, nor how caprice manifests itself. By examining his etchings the paper attempts to propose its own 'three rules' that form the foundations for producing a convincing capriccio. The dissection specifically focuses on Piranesi's use of baroque composition, paradoxical perspectives and believable tectonics to outline his intentions of blurring the boundaries between the real and imaginary in an attempt to produce a fantastical world.

——Research is strengthened by utilising first-hand investigations into enlightenment era drawing methods and interviews with relevant artists, in an attempt to not only examine Piranesi's construction of the capriccio, but to also outline where his inspirations were founded. Finally, the paper attempts to contextualise the capriccio by using the 'three rules' to consider whether it still exists within our shifting technological sphere. By analysing modern cinematography, architectural drawings and artwork, the exploration demonstrates the limitations to technological advancement and thus its restrictions on the capricious speculative drawing. Through this historical dissection the paper outlines the importance of continuing the lineage of the capriccio, and evaluates whether it is still possible to produce a capricious drawing within our increasingly technological context.

1. Oxford English Dictionary. (date unknown) 'Capriccio', http://www.oxforddictionaries.com/definition/english/capriccio (accessed 23 November 2015).

Image: A fantastical library by the author, utilising the baroque compositional techniques of Giovanni Piranesi and a unique oblique anamorphic perspective.

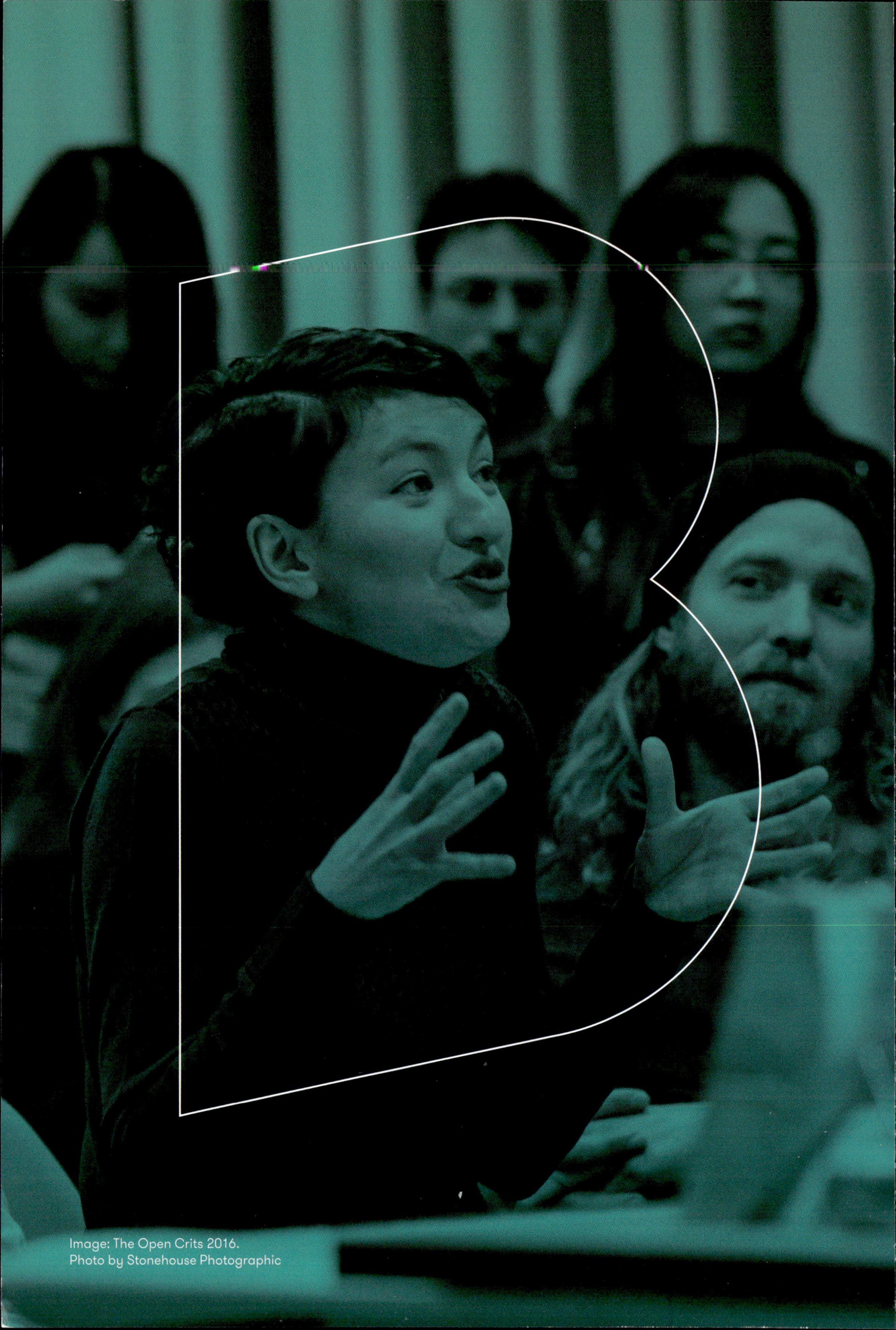

Image: The Open Crits 2016.
Photo by Stonehouse Photographic

MArch Architectural Design (B-Pro)

Programme Director: Alisa Andrasek

Labs

Wonderlab
Alisa Andrasek

BiotA Lab
Richard Beckett and
Professor Marcos Cruz

Interactive Architecture Lab
Ruairi Glynn

Report Coordinator
Professor Stephen Gage

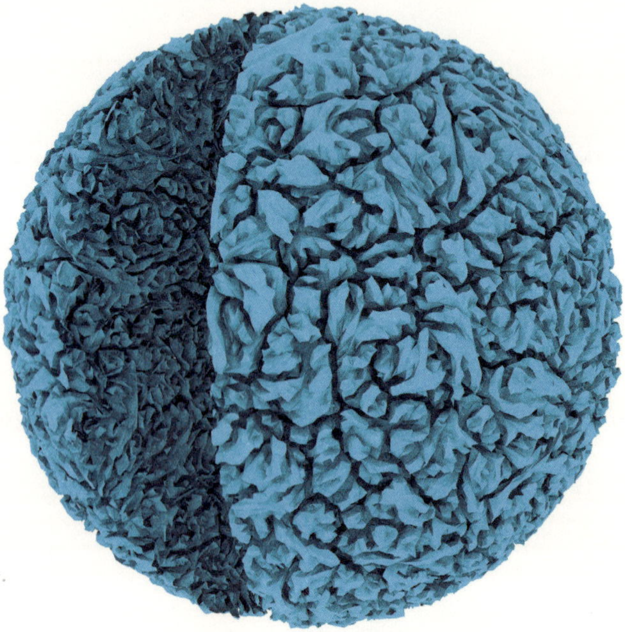

Image: MArch AD, Wonderlab, RC1, White Rabbit 'Alien Resolution'

The Masters programme in Architectural Design (AD) is a 12-month full-time post-professional course, leading to a Masters of Architecture (MArch) degree. It is part of B-Pro, the umbrella structure for post-professional Masters programmes at The Bartlett School of Architecture, directed by Professor Frédéric Migayrou. Composed of an international body of experts and students, it is designed to deliver diverse yet focused strands of speculative research, emphasising the key role computation plays within complex design synthesis.

——With access to B-made, one of the most advanced fabrication workshops in Europe, AD students are introduced to highly advanced coding, fabrication and robotic skills, aimed at computational and technological fluency. Simultaneously, students are exposed to larger theoretical underpinnings specifically tailored to their enquiries. Students are part of a vibrant urban and professional community, in one of the most exciting cities in the world, enriching the process of learning and opportunities for networking.

——The course is organised into three Labs, offering students the chance to choose a distinct field of enquiry. The latest approaches to robotics and AI, CNC fabrication, 3D printing, supercomputing, simulation, generative design, interactivity, advanced algorithms, extensive material prototyping and links to material science are all explored.

MArch Urban Design (B-Pro)

Programme Director: Mark Smout

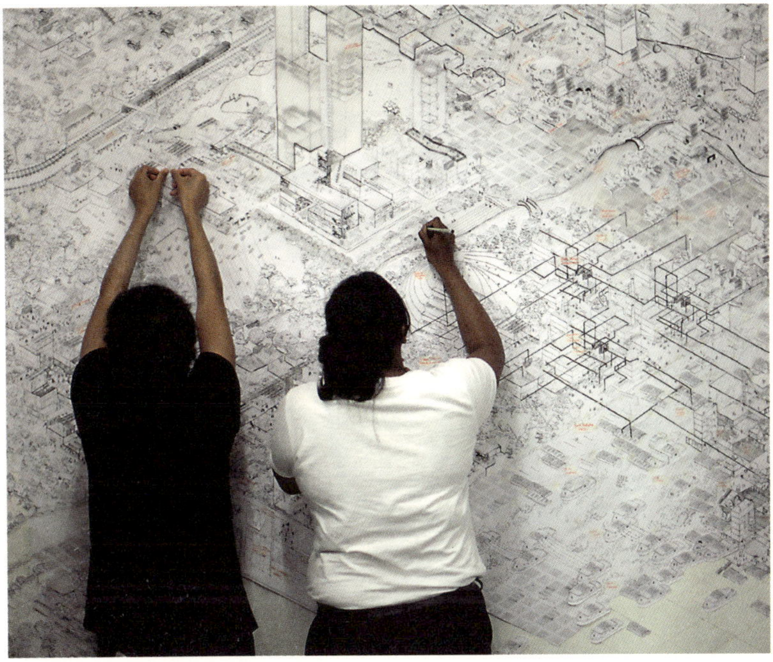

The MArch Urban Design (UD) is a 12-month studio-based programme that brings together a new generation of designers and thinkers from across the world. It is established to provide a rich and challenging environment for long-term research into the challenges of global urbanisation and the creative potential of speculative design. It is part of B-Pro, the umbrella structure for post-professional Masters programmes at The Bartlett School of Architecture, directed by Professor Frédéric Migayrou.

——Urban design is a particular form of enquiry into the nature of the city, its form and function. It seeks to understand the city as a place of human coexistence and to devise strategies and projects to guide its future development and evolution. Throughout the UD course, students are encouraged to innovate and explore new ideas in design and theory. They are introduced to design skills and techniques, critical enquiry and related technologies. They use this experience to shape polemic interventions, and through the design portfolio and thesis, develop speculative projects on a variety of scales. Students are encouraged to explore and understand their host city, London, whilst in residence, a city that arguably is one of the richest and most diverse in the world.

Research Clusters

RC11
Sabine Storp, Patrick Weber

RC12
Usman Haque, Adam Greenfield

RC14
Roberto Botazzi, Kostas Grigoriadis

RC16 / Urban Morphogenesis Lab
Claudia Pasquero, Maj Plemenitas

RC18
Enriqueta Llabres, Zachary Fluker

Sir Banister Fletcher Visiting Professors
Dan Hill, Joseph Grima

Image: 'The Incomplete City' A week-long design workshop taught by the Sir Banister Fletcher Visiting Professors for 2016, Dan Hill and Joseph Grima, with Marco Ferrari

MA Architectural History

Programme Director: Dr Peg Rawes

Teaching Staff
Professor Iain Borden, Dr Ben Campkin, Professor Mario Carpo, Dr Edward Denison, Professor Murray Fraser, Dr Barbara Penner, Professor Jane Rendell, Dr Tania Sengupta, Amy Thomas, Nina Vollenbröker, Dr Robin Wilson, Stamatis Zografos

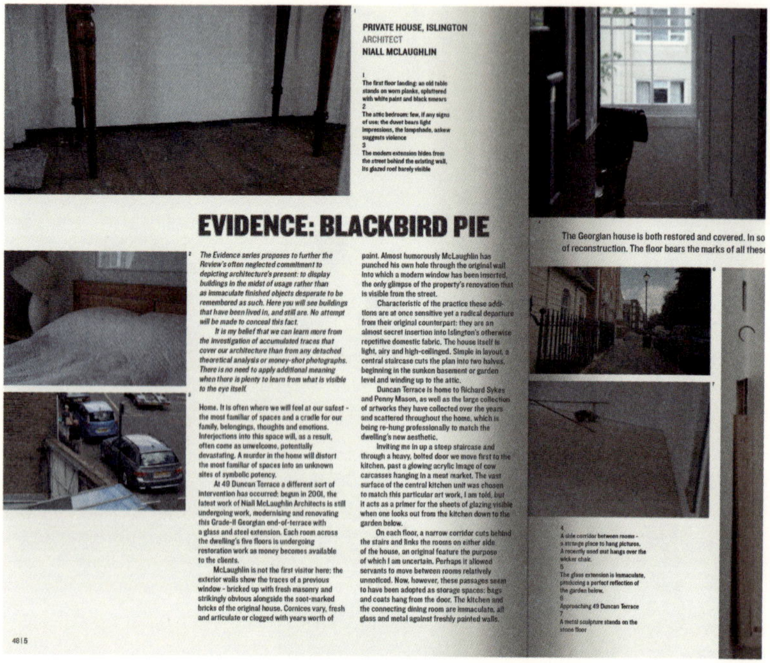

PRIVATE HOUSE, ISLINGTON
ARCHITECT
NIALL MCLAUGHLIN

1
The first floor landing: an old table stands on worn planks, splattered with white paint and black smears
2
The attic bedroom: few, if any signs of use; the duvet bears light impressions, the lampshade, askew suggests violence
3
The modern extension hides from the street behind the existing wall, its glazed roof barely visible

EVIDENCE: BLACKBIRD PIE

The Evidence series proposes to further the Review's often neglected commitment to depicting architecture's present: to display buildings in the midst of usage rather than as immaculate finished objects desperate to be remembered as such. Here you will see buildings that have been lived in, and still are. No attempt will be made to conceal this fact.

It is my belief that we can learn more from the investigation of accumulated traces that cover our architecture than from any detached theoretical analysis or money-shot photographs. There is no need to apply additional meaning when there is plenty to learn from what is visible to the eye itself.

Home. It is often where we will feel at our safest - the most familiar of spaces and a cradle for our family, belongings, thoughts and emotions. Interjections into this space will, as a result, often come as unwelcome, potentially devastating. A murder in the home will distort the most familiar of spaces into an unknown sites of symbolic potency.

At 49 Duncan Terrace a different sort of intervention has occurred: begun in 2001, the latest work of Niall McLaughlin Architects is still undergoing work, modernising and renovating this Grade-II Georgian end-of-terrace with a glass and steel extension. Each room across the dwelling's five floors is undergoing restoration work as money becomes available to the clients.

McLaughlin is not the first visitor here: the exterior walls show the traces of a previous window - bricked up with fresh masonry and strikingly obvious alongside the soot-marked bricks of the original house. Cornices vary, fresh and articulate or clogged with years worth of paint. Almost humorously McLaughlin has punched his own hole through the original wall into which a modern window has been inserted, the only glimpse of the property's renovation that is visible from the street.

Characteristic of the practice these additions are at once sensitive yet a radical departure from their original counterpart: they are an almost secret insertion into Islington's otherwise repetitive domestic fabric. The house itself is light, airy and high-ceilinged. Simple in layout, a central staircase cuts the plan into two halves, beginning in the sunken basement or garden level and winding up to the attic.

Duncan Terrace is home to Richard Sykes and Penny Mason, as well as the large collection of artworks they have collected over the years and scattered throughout the home, which is being re-hung professionally to match the dwelling's new aesthetic.

Inviting me in up a steep staircase and through a heavy, bolted door we move first to the kitchen, past a glowing acrylic image of cow carcasses hanging in a meat market. The vast surface of the central kitchen unit was chosen to match this particular art work, I am told, but it acts as a primer for the sheets of glazing visible when one looks out from the kitchen down to the garden below.

On each floor, a narrow corridor cuts behind the stairs and links the rooms on either side of the house, an original feature the purpose of which I am uncertain. Perhaps it allowed servants to move between rooms relatively unnoticed. Now, however, these passages seem to have been adopted as storage spaces: bags and coats hang from the door. The kitchen and the connecting dining room are immaculate, all glass and metal against freshly painted walls.

The Georgian house is both restored and covered. In so
of reconstruction. The floor bears the marks of all these

4
A side corridor between rooms - a strange place to hang pictures. A recently used mat hangs over the wicker chair.
5
The glass extension is immaculate, producing a perfect reflection of the garden below.
6
Approaching 49 Duncan Terrace
7
A metal sculpture stands on the stone floor

48 | 5

Architecture consists not only of buildings and projects, but also of the life that takes place within them, and the ideas and discussions that they give rise to. The MA Architectural History actively explores what history can do for architecture: students develop skills for interrogating, extending or reframing the discipline and its phenomena, often by situating architecture within broader debates about culture, history and politics.

——These 'situated histories' show us the active roles that architectural history has today: how it can transform and innovate our understandings of the built environment; how it can change our modes of engagement with cities and buildings; how different materialisations of history have different powers and effects; how modes of verbal and visual expression can produce changes in audiences. Frequently, the work brings in ideas from different fields to re-situate architecture both within the discipline and beyond; for example, in relation to: ecological, feminist, digital or post-colonial theory; film, conceptual art or literary criticism practices; urban ethnography or activist politics. Each final project is an experiment in which a specific architectural phenomenon is examined in the light of a particular theory or set of ideas, to see how our view of it might change – or, alternatively, how a theory needs to be refreshed.

——In October 2015 the programme's new Situating Architecture Symposium published this work: **http://situatingarchitecture.tumblr.com**

Image: Jon Astbury 'A Record Of The Unsettling Present: The Forensic Criticism of N. Ratsby in *The Architectural Review* (1996 – 2006)'

MA Architecture & Historic Urban Environments

Programme Director: Professor Murray Fraser

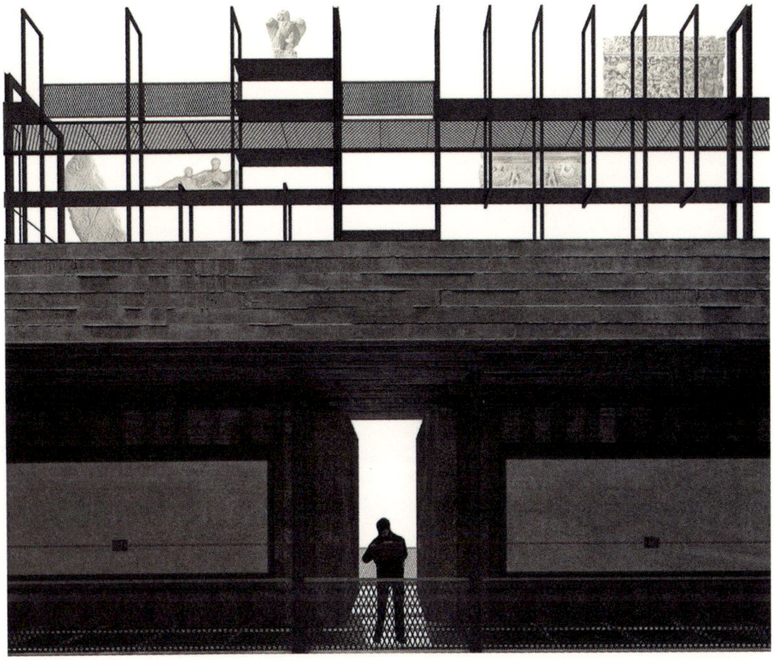

Teaching staff
Dr Eva Branscome, Dr Edward Denison, Nasser Golzari, Peter Guillery, Helen Jones, Dr Aileen Reid, Harriet Richardson, Mark Rist, Professor Andrew Saint, Dr Yara Sharif, Philip Temple, Colin Thom

The MA Architecture & Historic Urban Environments pioneers the development of a more diverse and creative approach to the reinterpretation and re-use of historical environments in cities around the world, for example, through imaginative architectural designs and urban strategies, whilst factoring in issues of cultural heritage.

——This 12-month programme is exceptional in linking the core research challenge of innovative design with in-depth processes of urban surveying, recording, mapping and analysis. As such, the programme has a strong international component, viewing cities around the world as fascinating locations for investigations into architectural and historic urban environments, with London being the prime example.

——The programme is delivered through a combination of lectures, seminars, practical workshops, fieldwork visits, and individual and group tutorials. Assessment is through project critique reviews, project portfolios, coursework essays, individual and group presentations, a dissertation/major project and a viva examination with an external examiner. Core modules include: Design Practice for Historic Environments; Design Research Methods for Historic Environments; Issues in Historic Urban Environments; Surveying and Recording of Cities; and Urban Redevelopment for Historic Environments.

Karl Karam + Niki Tsirimpi, 'Data Mining at the Thames'. A new pier built into the River Thames provides facilities for scientists and mudlarks keen to retrieve artifacts from the river, one of the largest archaeological sites in the world

MRes Architecture & Digital Theory

Programme Directors: Professor Mario Carpo, Professor Frédéric Migayrou

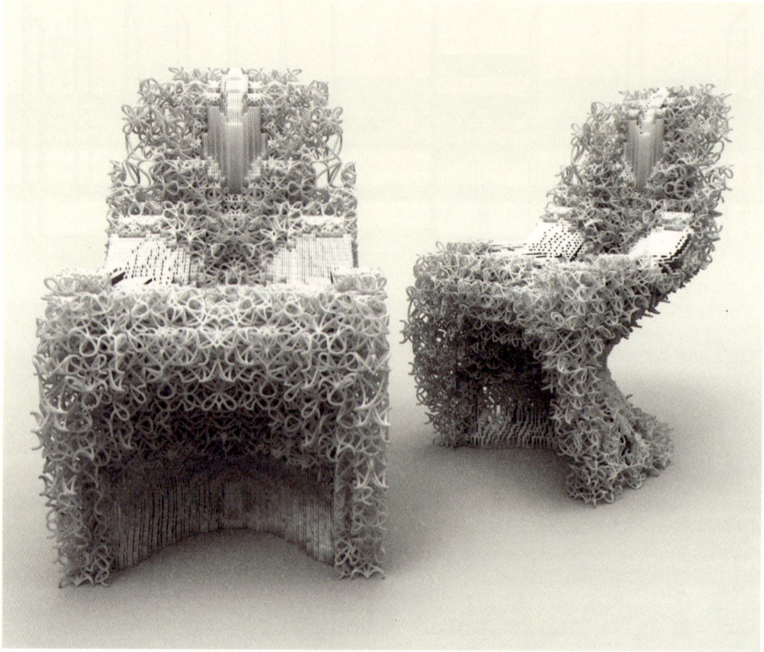

Led by Professors Frédéric Migayrou and Mario Carpo, the Masters by Research (MRes) Architecture & Digital Theory is dedicated to the theory, history and criticism of digital design and digital fabrication. This intensive 12-month programme provides a grounding in research for students who have either trained in the design professions, or have a background in digital technology or the digital humanities, and wish to further their understanding of digital innovation. In its inaugural years, the programme will focus on the challenge of complexity in computational design, and on its aesthetic, technological, economic and epistemological implications.

——Research topics currently under consideration include: agent-based conception; the new sciences of simulation, optimisation and form-finding; the transdisciplinary scalability of computational models; robotics and the engineering and modelisation of new materials and of variable property materials; the history of digital notations and the demise of notational processes in the current data-driven computational environment.

——Digital design and digital conception will also be considered from epistemological and historical perspectives, from cybernetics through to the most innovative experiments in various disciplines. This critical dimension, emerging from an exhaustive archaeology of these discourses, will be related to socio-political contexts at an international level, in order to redefine the mutations, status and efficiency of design in the digital world.

Image: MArch AD, Wonderlab, RC1, White Rabbit 'Alien Resolution'

MSc/MRes Architectural Computation

Programme Director: Dr Sean Hanna

Teaching Staff
Ava Fatah, Ruairi Glynn, Dr Christopher Leung, Dr Sam Griffiths, Dr Martin Zaltz-Austwick

Module Tutors
Angelos Chronis, Martha Tsigkari

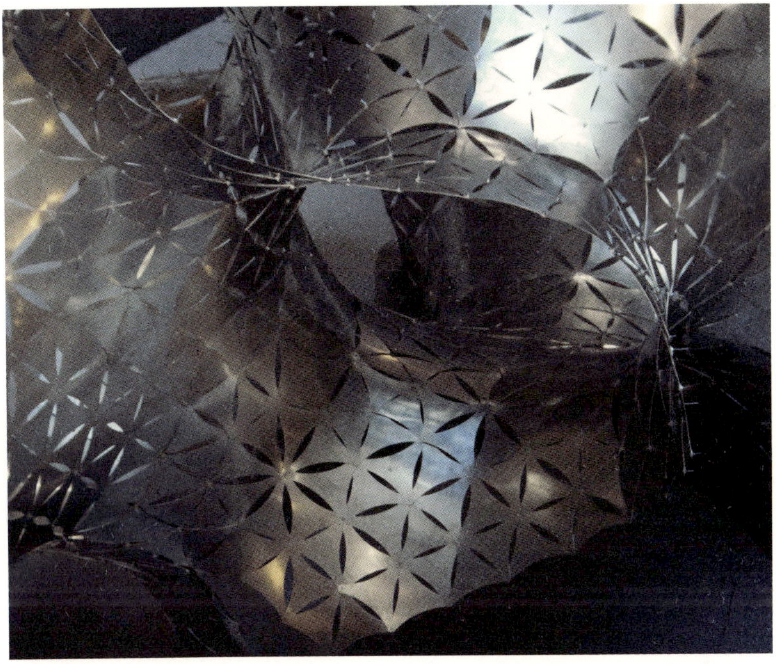

Renamed from Adaptive Architecture and Computing and relaunched for 2016-17, The Bartlett's Architectural Computation (MSc/MRes AC) programmes engage and advance the main technologies by which tomorrow's architecture will be designed and constructed. From parametric design and Computer Aided Design (CAD) to automated manufacturing, to 'big data' analytics, computation is increasingly important as a tool in our built environment. Our courses are designed to provide students with a depth of understanding to exploit computation fully in the context of world-leading design, research and industry. However, we also see computation as a technology that drives fundamental shifts in industry and society, and, more radically, as one that also alters the way we produce and think.

To this end, the learning of technical knowledge, such as computer coding, plays a stronger role than in many comparable courses, not only as a skill, but as a framework for thought. This technical knowledge is supported by a broad theoretical understanding of algorithms and philosophies of artificial intelligence and related domains. Students apply this knowledge in active design or scientific research projects that frequently make contributions to the field that are recognised internationally. Thesis work may take the form of exhibitions in venues, such as the Royal Academy of Arts, London; and the Centre Georges Pompidou, Paris; open source software for design or CADCAM; and internationally peer-reviewed publications.

Image: Vlad Tenu, 'Minimal Complexity', 2009, MSc Adaptive Architecture and Computation

MSc/MRes Spatial Design: Architecture & Cities

Programme Directors: Dr Kayvan Karimi, Dr Sophia Psarra

Teaching Staff
Kinda Al-Sayed, Dr Sam Griffiths, Dr Kayvan Karimi, Professor Alan Penn, Dr Sophia Psarra, Dr Kerstin Sailer, Professor Laura Vaughan

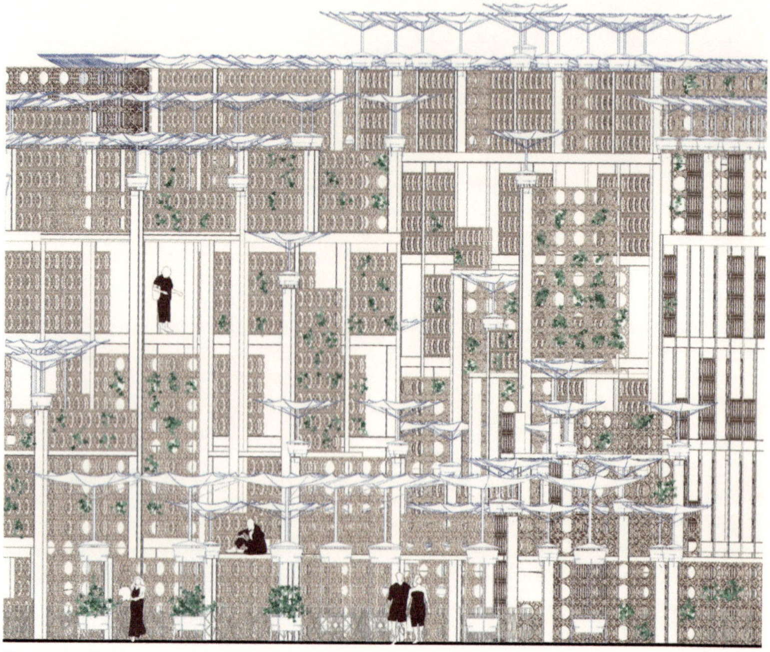

The MSc/MRes Spatial Design: Architecture & Cities (MSc SDAC) centres on furthering students' understanding of architecture and urban design as instruments in the development of contemporary society. The programme offers them a self-directed route of study, concentrating on research skills, enabling them either to take their existing architecture and urban design experience to a higher level, or set them up for a PhD. Using the theoretical and analytical framework of space syntax, the programme involves the study of architecture from individual buildings to small-scale urban design through to planning entire cities.

Students develop in-depth theoretical and practical knowledge of the built environment and its functions considered as spatial, physical and human systems, and acquire a high level of skill in research and analysis of the built environment and its functions, in support of better, more humane design. Both programmes provide them with a stimulating course focused on the research and analysis of buildings and cities as patterns of space inhabited by individuals, communities and organisations. Instead of confining architecture to the role of designing iconic buildings – and the city to economic development and policy – the course takes a combined theoretical and analytical approach to architecture, urban design and planning, in the service of constructing a better-built environment for society and an improved public realm.

Nazila Maghzian, 'Rising Rocinha: de-marginalizing the informal through socio-economic solidarities'. 2015-16 E-merging Design Research (EDR) Module

Pg Dip in Professional Practice & Management in Architecture (ARB/RIBA Part 3)

Susan Ware

The Professional Studies team aims to educate and equip a generation of architects to practice in an increasingly diverse and challenging environment. We do this by providing teaching and learning which encourages students to develop the skills beyond those required at threshold level by the basic professional criteria through reflection, appraisal, critical enquiry and research. We ask students to explore the role of the architect in the changing global construction industry in order to examine the effect of politics and economics on the design and procurement of the built environment in future practice. In addition, we encourage students to explore an entrepreneurial approach to using their practice and business management skills in an increasingly competitive professional environment.

——The programme provides the students with the skills, knowledge, ability, judgment and integrity to be competent to practice and register as an architect through ARB and obtain Chartered Membership of the RIBA. The RIBA and ARB professional criteria are used as a basis to establish evidence of candidates' fitness to practice, and threshold of competence (in terms of knowledge and ability) and professionalism (in terms of conduct and responsibility). However, the demanding programme aims to extend the students' learning well beyond the minimum required for professional registration. The school draws extensively from longstanding connections with practice and the construction industry to deliver teaching and learning at the forefront of current practice.

——The flexible modular programme can be taken over 12, 18 or 24 months and is delivered through a comprehensive series of 55 lectures given by experts both from practice and from within the Faculty. The structure allows for a diversity of delivery and assessment methods replicating real-life scenarios, roles and responsibilities from practice. A module coordinator, who is either a member of the Professional Studies team or an expert from practice, leads the teaching in each of the six modules. Students taking the final Module 6, the case study based module, are supported by a team of tutors for a series of one-to-one tutorials.

——In addition, the professional studies team provide a Year Out Programme and range of CPD short courses and other practice/ registration-orientated courses.

MPhil/PhD Architectural Design

Programme Director: Professor Jonathan Hill
Programme Coordinator: Dr Penelope Haralambidou

Leading to a PhD in Architecture, the MPhil/PhD Architectural Design programme allows especially able and reflective designers to undertake research within The Bartlett School of Architecture's speculative and experimental ethos. The first to be established in the UK, The Bartlett MPhil/PhD Architectural Design is internationally recognised as one of the most influential doctoral programmes dedicated to architectural design.

——The programme draws on the strengths of design teaching and doctoral research at The Bartlett, encouraging the development of architectural research through the interaction of drawing and writing. An architectural design doctoral thesis has two interrelated elements of equal importance—a project and a text—that share a research theme and a productive relationship. The project may be drawn, filmed, built, or use whatever media is appropriate.

——UCL's multi-disciplinary environment offers a stimulating and varied research culture that connects research by architectural design to developments in other disciplines, such as anthropology, art, digital media, engineering, geography and medicine. The PhD Architectural Design programme is intended for graduates of architecture and other disciplines who wish to pursue research by architectural design. 55 students from over 20 countries are currently enrolled.

——The Bartlett School of Architecture's two PhD programmes organise a number of annual events for doctoral students. PhD Research Projects, an exhibition and conference with presentations by current practice-based PhD students in The Bartlett Faculty of the Built Environment and the Royal Academy of Music, is held in Term 2. Invited critics in 2016 were Dr Pier Vittorio Aureli, Architectural Association; Dr Sarah Callis, Royal Academy of Music; Professor Murray Fraser, The Bartlett School of Architecture; Dr Hélène Frichot, KTH Royal Institute of Technology, Stockholm; and Professor Neil Heyde, Royal Academy of Music. Throughout the year, *PhD Research Conversations* seminars are an opportunity for doctoral candidates to present work in progress.

Current Students

Yota Adilenidou, Bihter Almac, Luisa Silva Alpalhão, Nicola Antaki, Nerea Elorduy Amoros, Anna Andersen, Jaime Bartolome Yllera, Paul Bavister, Richard Beckett, Katy Beinart, Giulio Brugnaro, Matthew Butcher, Armando Caroca Fernandez, Niccolo Casas, Ines Dantas Ribeiro Bernardes, Bernadette Devilat, Killian Doherty, Daniyal Farhani, Judit Ferencz, Pavlos Fereos, Susan Fitzgerald, Ruairi Glynn, Isabel Gutierrez Sanchez, Colin Herperger, Bill Hodgson, Sander Holsgens, Popi Iacovou, Christiana Ioannou, Nahed Jawad, Dionysia Kypraiou, Hina Lad, Felipe Lanuza Rilling, Tea Lim, Thandiwe Loewenson, Jane Madsen, Samar Maqusi, Matthew McDonald, Phuong-Tram Nguyen, Oliver Palmer, Christos Papastergiou, Luke Pearson, Mariana Pestana, Arthur Prior, Felix Robbins, David Roberts, Natalia Romik, Merijn Royaards, Wiltrud Simbürger, Eva Sopeoglou, Camila Sotomayor, Ro Spankie, Theo Spyropoulos, Dimitrie Stefanescu, Theodoros Themistokleous, Quynh Vantu, Cindy Walters, Dan Wilkinson, Henri Williams, Seda Zirek, Fiona Zisch

Graduating Students

Joanne Bristol, Pablo Gil, Polly Gould, Alex Zambelli

Current Supervisors

Alisa Andrasek, Professor Peter Bishop, Dr Camillo Boano, Professor Iain Borden, Professor Victor Buchli, Professor Mario Carpo, Dr Ben Campkin, Professor Nat Chard, Dr Marjan Colletti, Professor Sir Peter Cook, Professor Marcos Cruz, Dr Edward Denison, Professor Murray Fraser, Professor Stephen Gage, Prof Jeremy Gilbert, Dr François Guesnet, Dr Sean Hanna, Dr Penelope Haralambidou, Professor Christine Hawley, Professor Jonathan Hill, Dr Kayvan Karimi, Dr Jan Kattein, Dr Adrian Lahoud, Dr Chris Leung, Dr Jerome Lewis, Dr Yeoryia Manolopoulou, Prof Mark Miodownik, Dr Caroline Newton, Prof Raf Orlowski, Professor Sebastien Ourselin, Jayne Parker, Professor Alan Penn, Dr Barbara Penner, Dr Sophia Psarra, Dr Peg Rawes, Professor Jane Rendell, Professor Bob Sheil, Mark Smout, Professor Philip Steadman, Dr Hugo Spiers, Professor Neil Spiller, Professor Michael Stewart, Professor Philip Tabor, Dr Claire Thomson

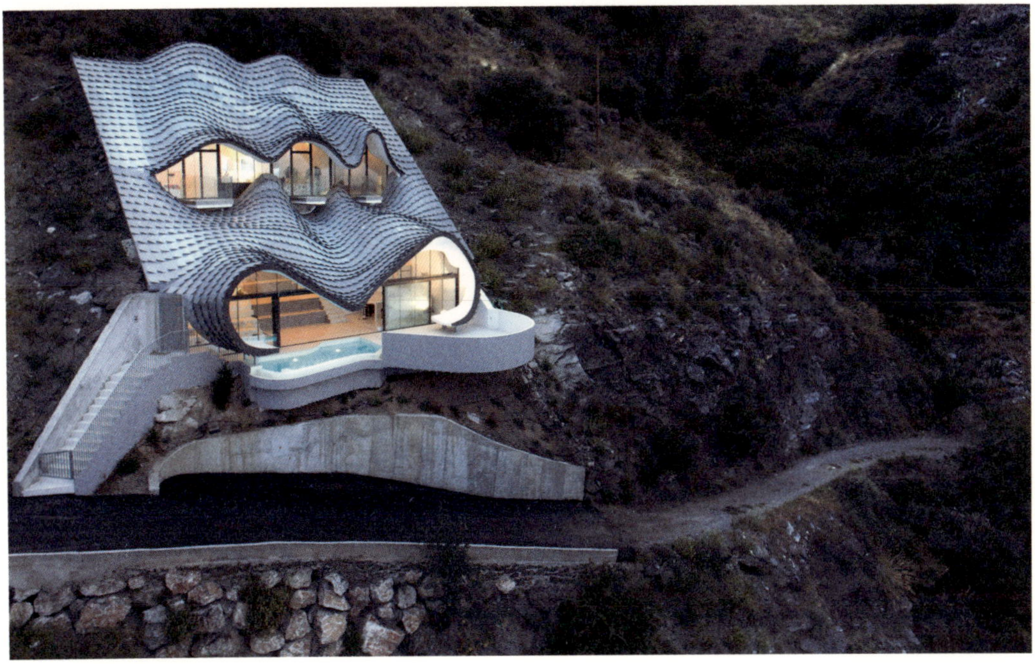

Graduating Students

Dr Joanne Bristol
Interspecies Spaces: écriture féline
Principal Supervisor: Professor Jane Rendell
Secondary Supervisor: Dr Peg Rawes

Dr Pablo Gil
Numen Architecture. An Architecture Influenced by the Numinous Attributes of Animals
Principal Supervisor: Professor Stephen Gage
Secondary Supervisor: Professor Marcos Cruz

Dr Polly Gould
No More Elsewhere: Antarctica through the Archive of the Edward Wilson (1872-1912) Watercolours
Principal Supervisor: Professor Jane Rendell
Secondary Supervisor: Professor Victor Buchli

Dr Alex Zambelli
Scandalous Artefacts: Visual and Analogical Practice between Architecture and Archaeology
Principal Supervisor: Professor Jane Rendell
Secondary Supervisor: Professor Victor Buchli

Image: Dr Pablo Gil, 'Numen Architecture. An Architecture Influenced by the Numinous Attributes of Animals.' House on Cliff, front view. Photograph by Jesús Granada

MPhil/PhD Architectural History & Theory

Programme Director: Dr Barbara Penner
Programme Coordinator: Dr Penelope Haralambidou

Current Students
Wesley Aelbrecht, Tilo Amhoff, Sabina Andron, Vasileios Aronidis, Gregorio Astengo, Pinar Aykac, Tal Bar, Ruth Bernatek, Rakan Budeiri, Chin-Wei Chang, Mollie Claypool, Sevcan Ercan, Marcela Araguez Escobar, Pol Esteve, Stylianos Giamarelos, Nadia Gobova, Irene Kelly, Jeong Hye Kim, Claudio Leoni, Kieran Mahon, Carlo Menon, Megan O'Shea, Dragan Pavlovic, Soledad Perez Martinez, Matthew Poulter, Regner Ramos, Sophie Read, Sarah Riviere, Ryan Ross, Ozayr Saloojee, Huda Tayob, Claire Tunnacliffe, Freya Wigzell

Graduating Students
Kate Jorden, Torsten Lange, Amy Thomas, Danielle Willkens

The Bartlett School of Architecture's MPhil/PhD Architectural History & Theory programme allows students to conduct an exhaustive piece of research into an area of their own selection and definition. Great importance is placed on the originality of information uncovered, the creativity of the interpretations made, and the rigour of the methodological procedures adopted.

——Approximately 25-30 students from around the world are enrolled at any one time for MPhil/PhD research in this field. The range of research topics undertaken is broad, but most explore the history and theory of architecture and cities from c. 1800 to the present day, with an emphasis on the critical reading of these subjects from cultural, political and experiential viewpoints.

——The MPhil/PhD Architectural History & Theory programme draws on the expertise and experience of the Bartlett School of Architecture's team of architectural historians and theorists, who are recognised internationally for their contributions to the field. The programme itself is very dynamic with an active series of talks, seminars, and conferences which students are expected to attend. In keeping with UCL's multi-disciplinary ethos, connections between architectural research and other fields are encouraged, and there are active collaborations with the Departments of Anthropology, Fine Art and Geography, and UCL Urban Lab.

Current Supervisors
Dr Jan Birksted, Professor Peter Bishop, Dr Camillo Boano, Professor Iain Borden, Dr Victor Buchli, Professor Mario Carpo, Dr Ben Campkin, Dr Edward Denison, Professor Adrian Forty, Professor Murray Fraser, Professor Jonathan Hill, Professor Timothy Mathews, Dr Barbara Penner, Dr Sophia Psarra, Dr Peg Rawes, Professor Jane Rendell, Dr Stephanie Schwartz, Dr Tania Sengupta

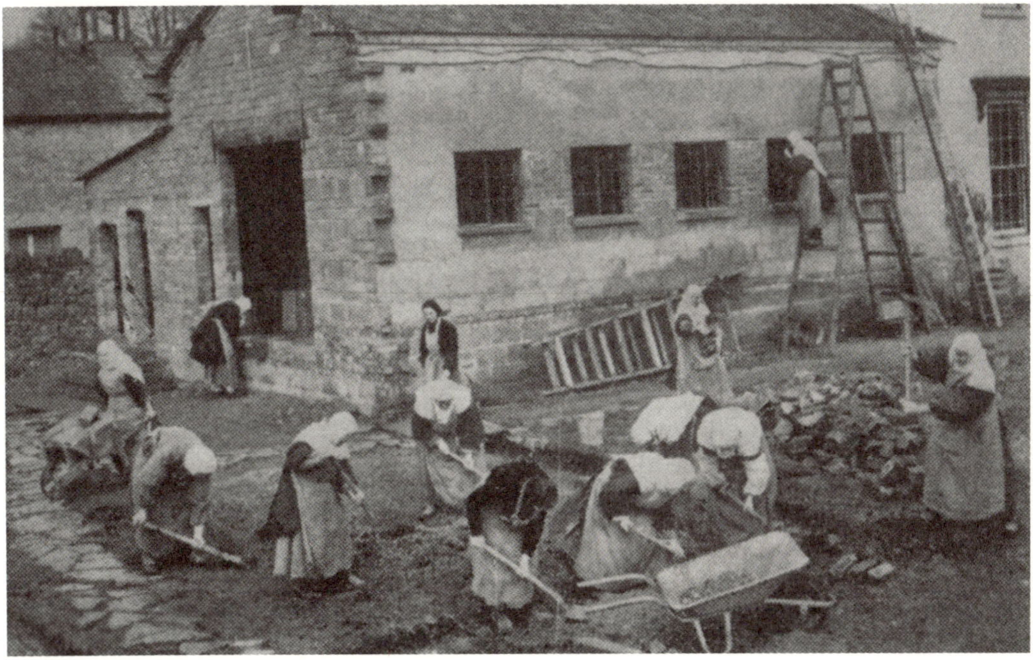

Graduating Students

Dr Kate Jordan
Ordered Spaces, Separate Spheres: Women and the Building of British Convents, 1829-1939
Principal Supervisor: Dr Barbara Penner
Second Supervisor: Dr Jan Birksted
Honorary Supervisor: Dr Carmen Mangion (Birkbeck)

Dr Torsten Lange
Komplexe Umweltgestaltung [complex environmental design]: Architectural Theory and the Production of the Built Environment in the German Democratic Republic (GDR), 1960-1990
Principal Supervisor: Professor Jane Rendell
Secondary Supervisor: Dr Peg Rawes

Dr Amy Thomas
A Material History of the City of London, 1945-1993: Architecture, Planning and Finance
Principal Supervisor: Professor Murray Fraser
Second Supervisor: Professor Iain Borden

Dr Danielle Shea Willkens
Thomas Jefferson, Sir John Soane, and Maria Cosway: The Transatlantic Design Network, 1786-1838
Principal Supervisor: Dr Barbara Penner
Second Supervisor: Professor Jonathan Hill

Image: Carmelite nuns on the building site of the Church Of Our Lady of the Assumption, Presteigne, c.1952

MPhil/PhD Architectural Space & Computation

Programme Tutor: Professor Laura Vaughan

Current Students
Andre Afonso, Marcela Aragüez Escobar, Moritz Behrens, Deborah Do Rosario Benros, John Bingham-Hall, Tom Bolton, Pheereeya Boonchaiyapruek, Giulio Brugnaro, Cauê Capillé, Frosso (Efrosini) Charalambous, Blerta Dino, Francesca Froy, Paul Goodship, Evan Greenberg, Emma Gribble, Abril Herrera Chavez, Fani Kostourou, Petros Koutsolampros, Kimon-Vincent Krenz, Stephen Law, Athina Lazaridou, Velina Mirincheva, Nurulhuda Mohammad Isa, Rosica Pachilova, Stamatios Psarras, Yao Shen, Dimitrie Stefanescu, Frederik Weissenborn.

Graduating Students
David Andreen, Ashley Dhanani, Sadaf Sultan Khan, Samuel Wilkinson, Laura Narvaez Zertuche

Leading to a PhD in Architecture, the MPhil/PhD Architectural Space & Computation (PhD ASC) programme is associated with the world-renowned Space Syntax Laboratory. The lab has an interdisciplinary research ethos, seeking to advance knowledge by studying the relations between spatial patterns and social outcomes, and between architectural design knowledge and computation.

——The PhD ASC has two principal streams: *Space and Society in Buildings and Cities* – here students use space syntax theories and methods to study the effects of spatial design on aspects of social, organisational and economic performance of buildings and urban areas; and *Architectural Computation* – here students apply technology to research into the built environment, bringing innovative computational analytical methods to the heart of the design process.

——The PhD ASC offers the ideal intellectual environment to develop interdisciplinary research from an architectural perspective. Whilst the programme is intended primarily for students from an architectural or urban design background wishing to pursue a programme that involves empirical research, many of our students hold degrees from other disciplines, such as geography, philosophy, anthropology, urban history, crime science, physics and computer science.

——Students pursue independent research projects supervised by a principal and secondary supervisor, culminating in a doctoral thesis of up to 100,000 words. Student topics are aligned to staff members' research interests, which range from media architecture and design interaction, architectural computation, urban form and society, workplace design and organisational behaviour, spatial narratives, space syntax and evidence-based design, urban design, spatial cultures and urban spatial history.

——Research supervision is complemented by a programme of fortnightly seminars throughout the academic year – some student-led, others led by leading experts from UCL and around the world. In the past year these have included Professor Howard Davis from the University of Oregon and Justin De Syllas of Avanti Architects.

——In their first year, students will commonly audit selected modules from the lab's MSc programmes in Spatial Design or Architectural Computation, benefiting from the rigorous training in theories and methods that these provide. The PhD ASC programme is also associated with the InnoChain European research network and the Engineering Doctorate in Virtual Environments, Imaging & Visualisation. Students on these programmes will typically take some of their taught modules jointly with the PhD ASC.

Current Supervisors
Dr Martin Zaltz Austwick, Ava Fatah, Dr Duncan Brumby, Jorge Fiori, Professor Murray Fraser, Dr Sam Griffiths, Dr Sean Hanna, Dr Kayvan Karimi, Dr Liora Malki-Epshtein, Dr Paul Marshall, Peter McLennan, Dr Anna Mavrogianni, Professor Alan Penn, Dr Sophia Psarra, Dr Kerstin Sailer, Dr Tasos Varoudis, Professor Laura Vaughan

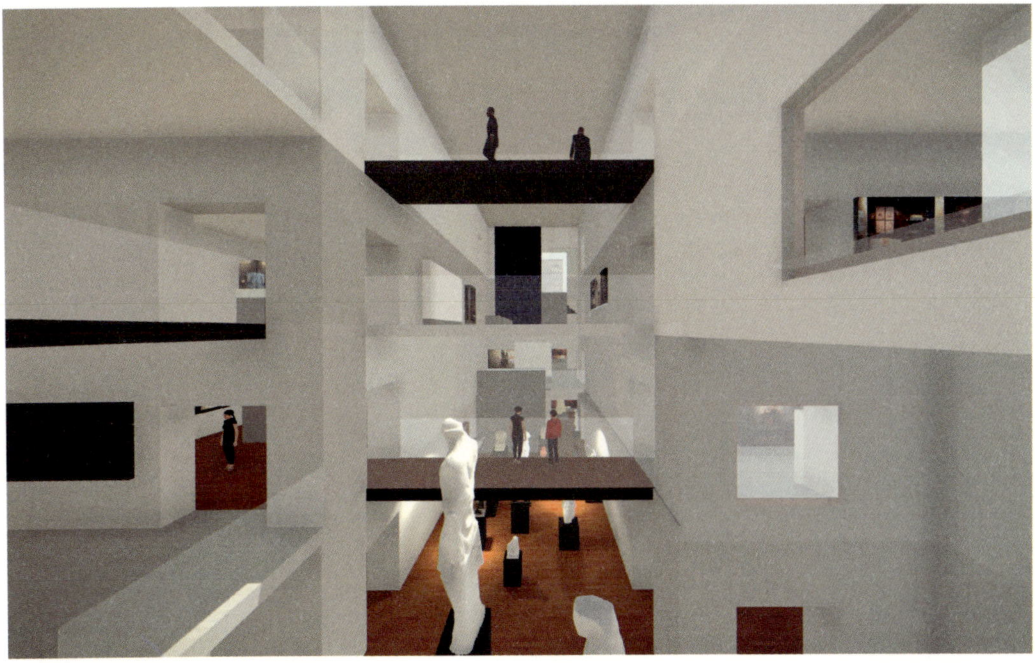

Athina Lazaridou
Spatial Navigation in Real and Virtual Museums in Two and Three Dimensions
Principal Supervisor: Dr Sophia Psarra
Subsidiary Supervisor: Dr Sean Hanna

Architecture embodies the human effort to structure space in meaningful ways. Designers often need to know how changes in the architectural design of museum environments can potentially affect human experience. This thesis explores how the three-dimensional layout of space shapes emergent patterns of navigation and spatial exploration.

——This subject is explored through real-time observations, space syntax analysis, agent-based models and virtual reality (VR) experiments. Most space syntax studies on human navigation focus on spatial characteristics and route choices in two dimensions and are consequently unable to address the effect of the third dimension on spatial behaviour. Here, three-dimensional spatial and navigational tools are used to enrich the two-dimensional space syntax approach in order to contribute to a better understanding of how the architectural design of museums shapes user experience.

——The thesis is framed around three European atria museums: the Ashmolean Museum of Art and Archaeology in Oxford, the Museum of Scotland in Edinburgh and the Acropolis Museum in Athens. The broad similarities between the three museums allow for exploration of critical differences in their spatial layout, human and simulated navigation patterns. The analysis outcomes are then appropriated to create systematic redesigns in the virtual reality experiments of the Ashmolean Museum, testing the degree of correspondence between users' experience in the real and virtual environments.

——The outcomes demonstrate significant analogies between real and virtual behaviour in these multi-level cultural environments. Further findings show that the museums' three-dimensional architectural design impacts significantly on navigational processes. Atria act as compositional devices of architectural expression, structuring relationships between exhibition spaces and the three-dimensional organisation of buildings while aiding spatial navigation. Spatial alterations in the vertical properties and three-dimensional visibility of the museums create variability in navigation patterns, pause points and gaze direction. This thesis has potential to inform three-dimensional architectural design processes with the ultimate goal of creating more user-friendly buildings.

Image: Athina Lazaridou, 'Virtual Reality navigational model of the Ashmolean Museum in Oxford, UK'. Design generated through the incorporation of mixed techniques: 3D modelling, 3D scanning, Game Design tools and geometry optimisation processes

New Programme

MEng Engineering & Architectural Design

Affiliated practices and institutes
AKT II, Arup, Buro Happold, CIBSE (Chartered Institution of Building Services Engineers), EI (Energy Institute), Feilden Clegg Bradley Studios, Foster + Partners, Hoare Lea Consulting Engineers, ICE (Institution of Civil Engineers), IStructE (Institution of Structural Engineers), Laing O'Rourke, Price & Myers, the RIBA

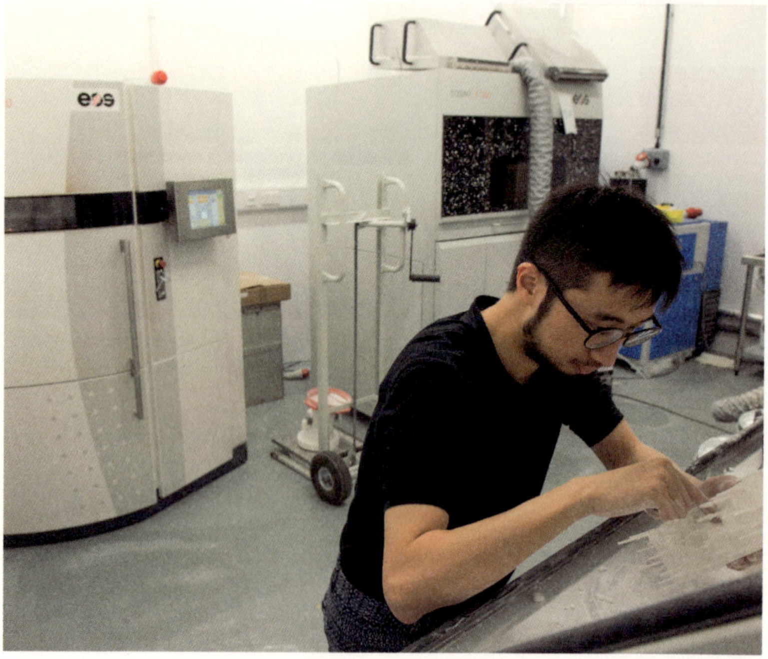

This new four-year integrated Masters in Engineering & Architectural Design aims to challenge students to develop a critical, independent, experimental and technically rigorous approach to architectural, environmental and structural design and engineering in buildings. The programme is delivered by experts drawn from The Bartlett School of Architecture, the UCL Institute for Environmental Design and Engineering and UCL Civil Environmental and Geomatic Engineering.

——Placing creativity and design at the centre of engineering education, the programme challenges conventional models, providing students with the opportunity to understand and develop advanced design methodologies whilst acquiring expertise on how they are augmented and resolved through engineering knowledge. Students will learn how to imagine, design and deliver resilient buildings that incorporate lifelong environmental and social responsibility.

——Graduates will be armed with the knowledge and expertise to undertake a project from inception to brief development through to design, and to advocate for their designs whilst engaging in robust, informed interdisciplinary discussion. Our MEng Engineering & Architectural Design graduates will be the future leaders of a collaborative and organisationally complex industry.

Image: 3D Model Making in the B-made workshop. Photo by Stonehouse Photographic

MA Situated Practice

New Programme

Affiliated practices and institutes
The Slade School of Fine Art, UCL Urban Laboratory

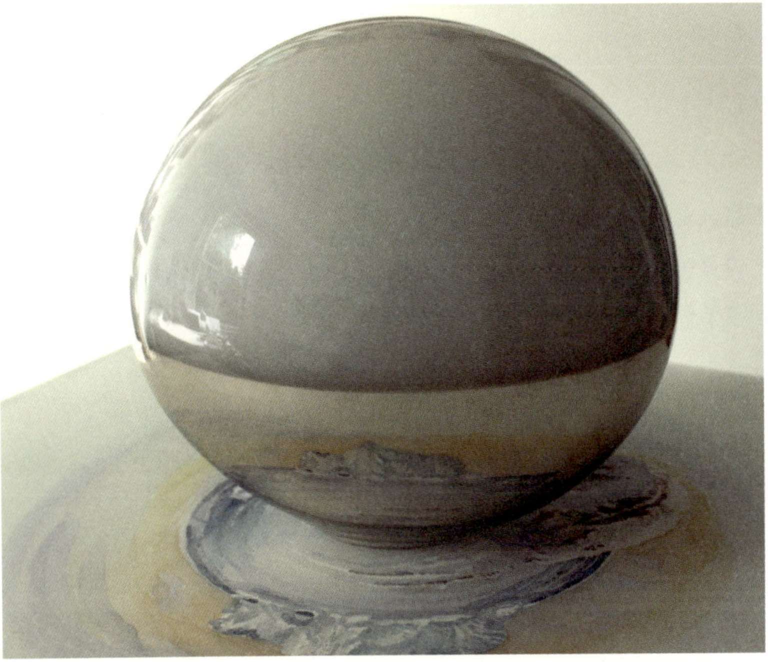

This new 15-month Masters provides knowledge and training in the principles and skills of situated practice in relation to conceptual spatial theories in art, architecture, performativity, urbanism and writing. On this programme, students will develop a strong understanding of appropriate research methodologies in art and design practice-led research, specifically relating to approaches to criticality, performativity and textuality. They will also make 'situated practice' projects that are site-related, from physical installations to digital interventions to site writings.

——This pioneering course examines the fertile territories where the discipline of architecture cross-pollinates with the other creative arts. Students will make work that is situated physically and engages with contemporary social, cultural and political conditions. Outcomes will combine media – comprising site-specific and performative installations, interventions, designs and events – that engage with their contexts and particular publics. Graduates from the MA Situated Practice will be highly equipped to pioneer new forms of hybrid practice between art and architecture in the domains of urban design, spatial design, event design, critical and theoretical writing, performance and craft.

Image: Polly Gould, 'Berg off Cape Evans'. 2013 (hand-blown coloured and mirrored glass, watercolour on sand-blasted glass, 40 x 40 x D.18 cm)

New Programme

MArch Design for Performance & Interaction

Affiliated practices and institutes
Arup, Bompass & Parr, Ciminod Studio, Jason Bruges Studio, Intel, Marshmallow Laser Feast, onedotzero, Rose Bruford College of Theatre and Performance, Royal Central School of Speech and Drama, ScanLAB Projects, Shobana Jeyasingh Dance Company, Stufish, Troika, Twitter, Soundform, Umbrellium

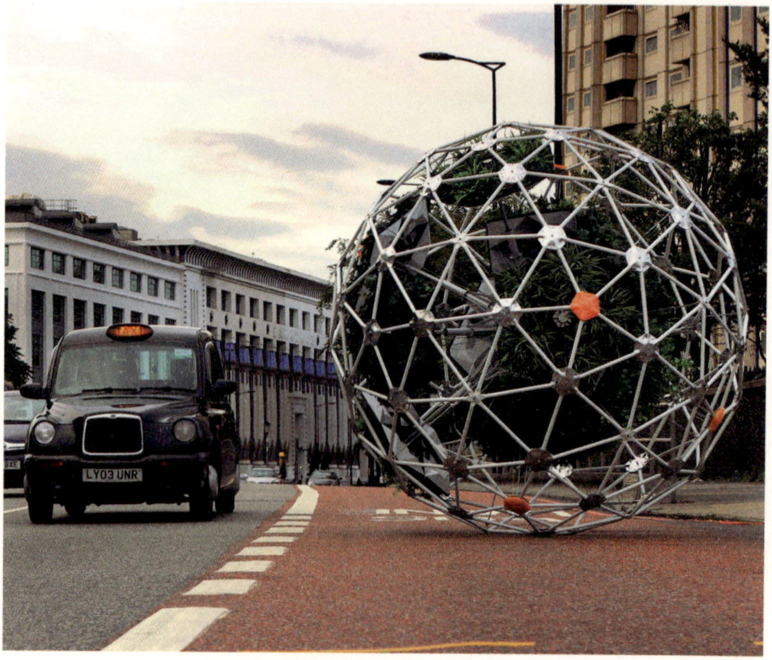

This new 15-month Masters teaches design in four dimensions. Students will design the performance and interaction of objects, environments and people using the latest fabrication, sensing, computation, networked and responsive technologies. Emphasis is placed on prototyping, from interactive objects and installations to staged events and performance architecture.

——The MArch Design for Performance & Interaction is a new programme which attracts students from a wide range of artistic and technical backgrounds. There are very few UK institutions that offer anything similar, and none have the access to cross-disciplinary expertise provided by both The Bartlett and UCL. The core of the programme is the belief that the creation of spaces for performance, and the creation of performances within them, are symbiotic activities. Design using interactive technologies enables us to consider objects, space, people and systems as potential performers. Design for performance and interaction has relevance across spatial and urban design, interface and systems design, auditoria and scenographic design, lighting and sound installation, physical and virtual environments and performance and event design. At The Bartlett School of Architecture, we believe this provides an unprecedented opportunity for informed, skilled and multi-disciplinary designers to define – and also deliver – spaces and systems for performance and interaction in the 21st century. Our new studio facilities at Here East offer unprecedented opportunities and resources for groundbreaking design work.

Image: William Victor Camilleri and Danilo Sampaio, 'Hortum Machina B', Interactive Architecture Lab

MArch Design for Manufacture

New Programme

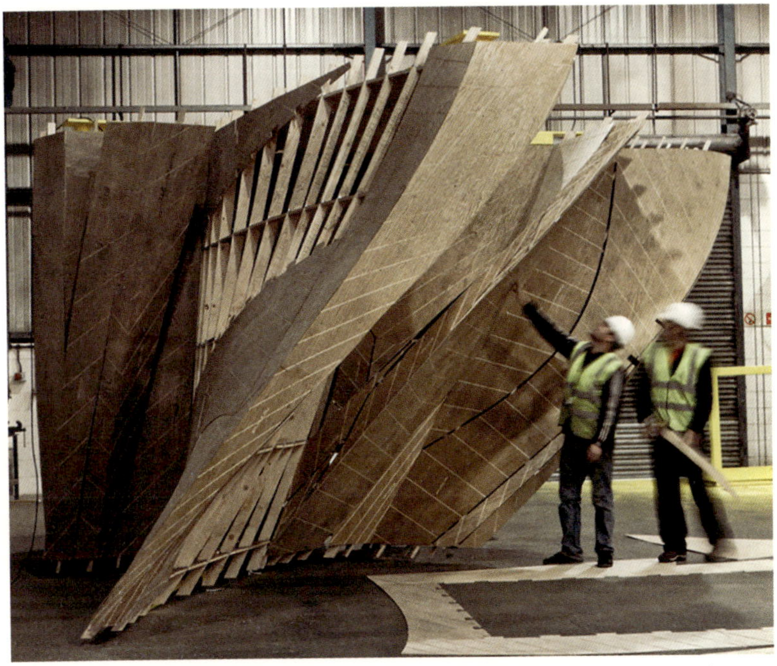

Affiliated practices and institutes
Arup, Buro Happold, Foster + Partners, Laing O'Rourke, Price & Myers, ScanLAB Projects, UCL Civil, Environmental and Geomatic Engineering (CEGE), UCL Institute for Environmental Design and Engineering (IEDE)

Starting in September 2017, this new 15-month Masters will teach students how to place their design skills in the context of pioneering developments in construction, fabrication, assembly, and automation, including robotics.

——There is an abundance of advanced design and engineering tools in the UK that an elite workforce develop and deploy to export their expertise worldwide. Yet there is a shortage of skilled workers at the point of production, tasked with delivering increasingly sophisticated and challenging projects by clients in line with rising expectations on quality and regulation. The Design for Manufacture Masters course aims to prepare a new professional workforce of highly skilled, creative and adaptable experts, with knowledge in design, engineering, material behaviour, analogue and digital craft, and advanced systems operations. This course will expose students to new forms of advanced design and engineering methodologies – such as robotics and 3D scanning – that are currently reinventing core approaches to shaping, making and refitting the built and manufactured environment.

Image: Tim Lucas, Price & Myers and Bartlett School of Architecture Lecturer in Structural Design. Photo by Maarten Kleinhout.

Bartlett Short Courses

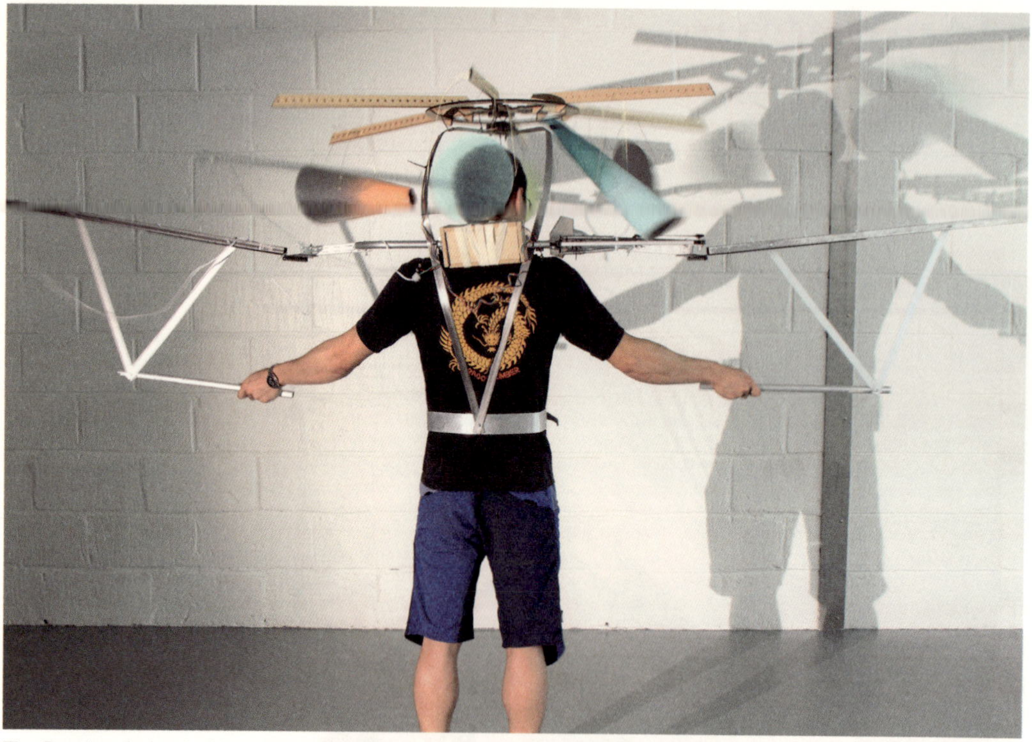

The Bartlett School of Architecture's short courses are aimed at school leavers, university students and professionals wishing to hone their skills. The courses give students a chance to experience life within the UK's leading architecture school, as well as access to cutting-edge facilities and staff. Courses include:

Summer School

This 10-day design-based course gives participants a first taste of studying architecture at UCL. The course attracts both young people still in their secondary education and school leavers considering creative careers.

Summer Studio

This tailored short course offers students already studying architecture at different universities, or undertaking similar creative programmes, the chance to diversify their skills in a range of areas.

Summer Skill-ups

The Summer Skill-ups are intensive five-day courses offering a wide range of computer and portfolio training to hone existing skills and develop new ones. These can be taken in conjunction with the longer Bartlett Summer School or Summer Studio.

Sir Peter Cook Masterclass

A new intensive masterclass specifically designed for architects who wish to extend the range of their work under the guidance of Professor Sir Peter Cook RA.

Pop-Up Collaboration

A series of tailor-made programmes offered to schools and universities wanting to gain an insight into the design approaches taught at The Bartlett School of Architecture.

UCL Pre-Masters Certificate in Architecture

A six-month course beginning in January 2016 for students holding a conditional offer on The Bartlett's MArch Architecture (ARB/RIBA Part 2).

Postgraduate Certificate in Advanced Architectural Research (pgCAAR)

This programme enables postgraduate students to take their work to a higher level of design and theoretical development in preparation for further study.

bit.ly/b-shortcourses

Image: Bartlett Summer Studio, from the workshop 'The Typology of your Life and the Life of Others'

Open Crits

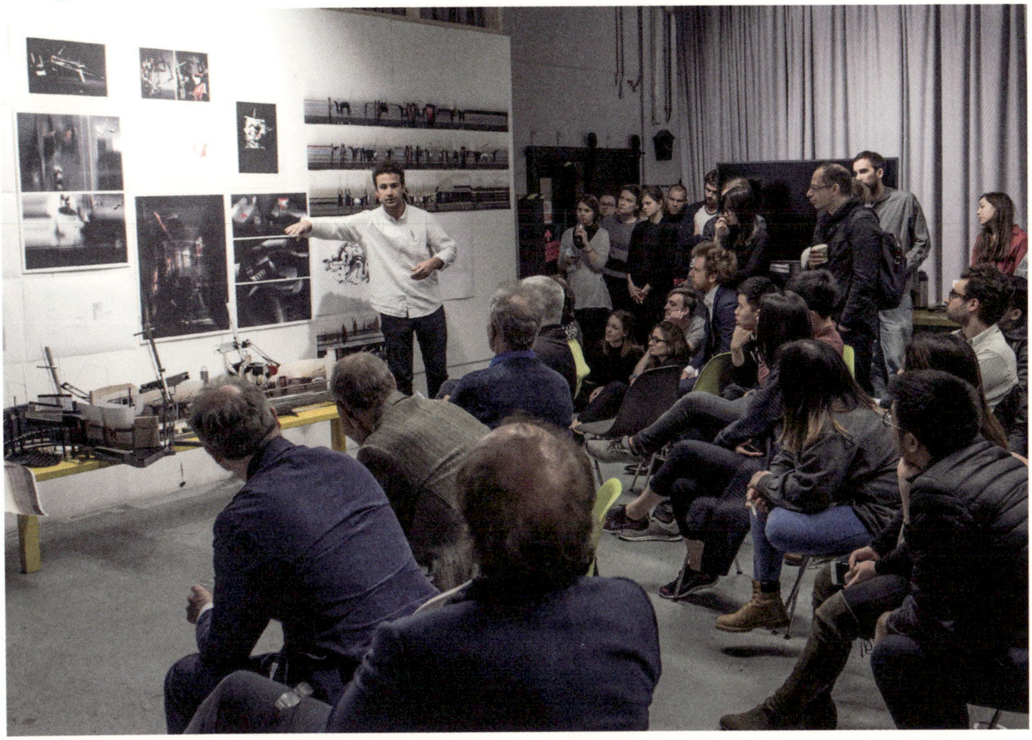

Curated by Professors Frédéric Migayrou, Sir Peter Cook and Bob Sheil, this year, a group of distinguished external critics reviewed a selection of BSc Architecture Year 3 and MArch Architecture Year 5 design projects over three days.

Critics

Alisa Andrasek | The Bartlett
Teresa Borsuk | Pollard Thomas Edwards
Andy Bow | Foster + Partners
Mark Burry | University of Melbourne
Peter Cook | CRAB Studio
Mario Carpo | The Bartlett
Izaskun Chinchilla | The Bartlett
Tom Dyckhoff
Ivan Harbour | Rogers Stirk Harbour + Partners
Simon Herron | University of Greenwich
Asif Khan
Jeremy Melvin
Frédéric Migayrou | The Bartlett
Alan Penn | The Bartlett
Frosso Pimenides | The Bartlett
Bob Sheil | The Bartlett
Mike Tonkin | Tonkin Liu
Sophy Twohig | Hopkins Architects
Mark Whitby | The Bartlett
Finn Williams | Common Office

Participating Students

Michael Arnett, Anthony Awanis, Amy Begg, Felicity Barbur, James Bradford, Amelia Black, Flavie Caroukis, Che-Hung Chien, Sam Davies, Tahmineh Emami, Chris Falla, Lucca Ferrarese, Rania Francis, Freddie Hong, Emma Jurczynski, Syafiq Hassan Jubri, Emma Kitley, Giota Kotsovinou, Luke Lupton, Elliot Mayer, Ben Mehigan, Adam Moqrane, Afrodite Moustroufi, Michelle Wang, Agata Murasko, Lily Papadopoulos, Calvin Po, Charlie Redman, Isaac Simpson, Ken Sheppard, Ben Sykes-Thompson, Matthew Turner, Tony Zhao, Han Zheng

Special Guests

Benjamin Ferns, Douglas Miller, Boon Yik Chung

Image: Luke Lupton presents his work at the 2016 Open Crits. Photo by Stonehouse Photographic

Bartlett Lectures

The Donaldson Lecture

The Donaldson Lecture is a major new annual lecture that aims to draw links between the built environment and the wider world. The lecture has been named after Thomas Leverton Donaldson, who in 1841 became UCL's first Chair in Architecture, one of the first in the UK, founding what later became The Bartlett School of Architecture.

The inaugural Donaldson Lecture was delivered by award-winning artist Grayson Perry CBE in January 2016 at Conway Hall.

The Bartlett International Lecture Series

The Bartlett International Lecture Series features speakers from across the world. Lectures in the series are open to the public and free to attend. This year's speakers included:

Fabrizio Barozzi + Alberta Veiga
Caroline Bos
Mario Carpo
James Corner
Sou Fujimoto
Adam Greenfield
Charles Jencks
Mitchell Joachim
Asif Khan
Amanda Levete
María Langarita + Víctor Navarro
Níall McLaughlin
Sheila O'Donnell + John Toumey
Dave Pigram
Peg Rawes
Jenny Sabin
Michael Silver
Endo Shuhei
Richard Wilson
Pier Vittorio Aureli

The Bartlett International Lecture Series is generously supported by the Fletcher Priest Trust

A range of smaller lecture series' attracted a wide range of speakers, including:

Bartlett Plexus

Isaïe Bloch, Shajay Bhooshan, Carlos Conceição, Alessio Erioli, Ruairi Glynn, Evan Greenberg, Hyunchul Kwon, Daniel Köhler, Alicia Nahmad, Filippo Nassetti, Raffael Petrovic, Sille Pihlak + Siim Tuksam, Davide Quayola, Gilles Retsin, Aleksandrina Rizova, Kristina Schinegger, David Sheldon-Hicks, Kibwe Tavares, Thomas Tvarijonas, Adam Vukmanov, Anouk Wipprecht

Situating Architecture

Adrian Forty, Hélène Frichot, Michelle Provoost, Peter Guillery, Colin Thom, Rodrigo Firmino, Daniel M Abramson

Sir Banister Fletcher Visiting Professorship

Sir Banister 'Flight' Fletcher (1866–1953) was an English architect and architectural historian. He trained at King's College London and University College London, and joined his father's practice (also Sir Banister Fletcher) in 1884, also studying at the Royal Academy Schools, the Architectural Association, and the École des Beaux-Arts, Paris. Father and son co-authored the seminal textbook *A History of Architecture on the Comparative Method*. In his will, he left a bequest to The Bartlett School of Architecture inaugurating an annual student prize, the Sir Banister Fletcher Prize Medal, in memory of his father, brother and himself, and a bequest to provide funds for an academic chair, now inaugurated as a Visiting Professorship.

——This year's Sir Banister Fletcher Visiting Professors are Joseph Grima and Dan Hill. Dan Hill is an Associate Director at Arup, where he is Head of Arup Digital Studio. A designer and urbanist, Hill has previously held leadership positions at Fabrica in Italy, SITRA in Finland, Arup in Australia, and Future Cities Catapult, *Monocle* and the BBC in the UK. Dan is also an adjunct professor in Design and Communication at RMIT University (Melbourne) and in Architecture at UTS (Sydney), and has taught at Goldsmiths, University of London, Politecnico di Milano, University of Sydney, Aalto University, Karlsruhe Institute of Technology and many others. Published writing includes *Dark Matter & Trojan Horses: A Strategic Design Vocabulary* (Strelka Press, 2012), as well as numerous pieces for books, journals, magazines and websites, including *Architectural Design* journal, *Volume*, *Domus*, *A+U* and *Dezeen*. He has produced the groundbreaking and highly influential blog City of Sound since 2001.

——Joseph Grima is an architect, writer and researcher based between New York and Genoa. He is a partner at Space Caviar, an architecture and research studio based in Genoa, Italy, operating at the intersection of design, technology, politics and the public realm, and director of the Ideas City program at the New Museum of Contemporary Art in New York. He was previously the editor-in-chief of *Domus* magazine and director of Storefront for Art and Architecture. In 2014 he was appointed co-curator of the first Chicago Architecture Biennial, the largest exhibition of contemporary architecture in the history of North America. He has taught and lectured widely at universities in Europe, Asia and America, including Strelka Institute of Media, Architecture and Design in Moscow under the direction of Rem Koolhaas. He is currently a Unit Master at the Architectural Association.

——As part of their Visiting Professorship at The Bartlett School of Architecture Joseph Grima and Dan Hill will give two Sir Banister Fletcher Lectures and run two week-long studios with MArch Urban Design students, around the theme of 'The Incomplete City' with Marco Ferrari, exploring adaptive, iterative approaches to urban design, planning and development.

Conferences

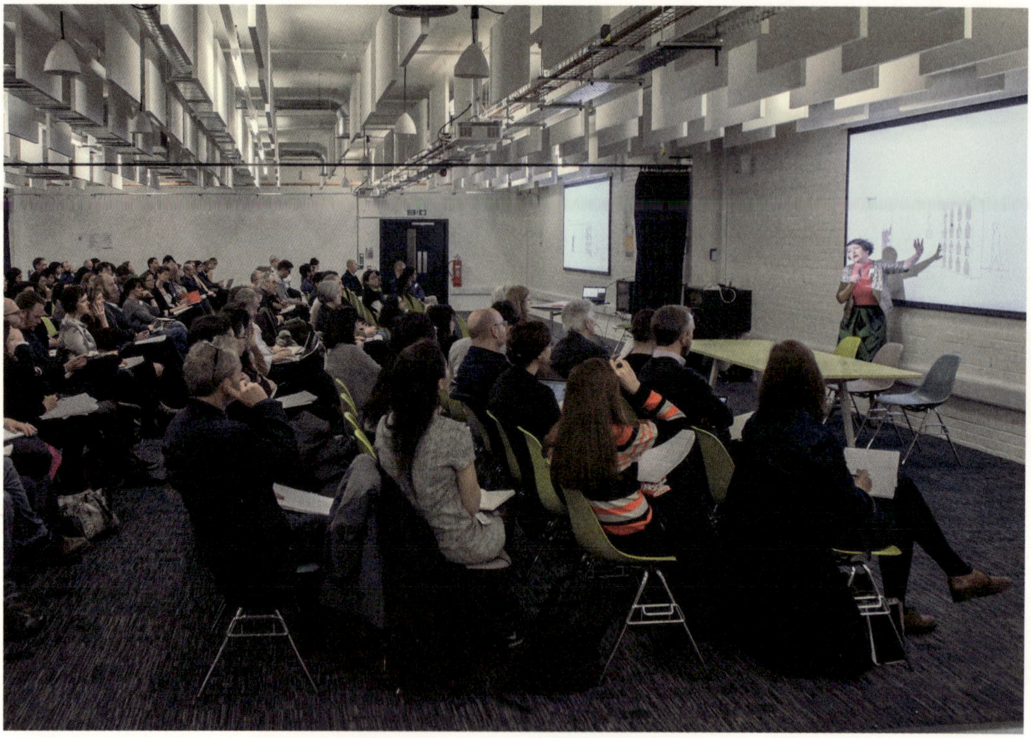

aae2016 conference on Research-Based Education

This year, in collaboration with the association of architectural educators (aae), we hosted aae2016, an international peer-reviewed conference on Research-Based Education.

——At a pivotal time for architectural education, the conference brought together global innovators in education, research and practice to interrogate the diverse natures and interrelationships between these realms as they relate to architecture, and to discuss how and why they might evolve over the coming century.

——The conference included sessions on the key themes of curiosity, risk, participation and production; whilst its keynote speakers included Izaskun Chinchilla Moreno, Lesley Lokko, Achim Menges and Etienne Wenger.

aae2016.org
Publication: bit.ly/aae2016book
Videos: bit.ly/aae2016videos

Drawing Futures

A new conference on speculative drawing for art and architecture, Drawing Futures will take place at The Bartlett School of Architecture on 11 – 12 November 2016. Chaired by Professor Frédéric Migayrou, Laura Allen and Luke Pearson, Drawing Futures explores how drawing is changing in relation to new technologies, and looks at how it still plays a central role as a vehicle for speculation.

——The conference's keynote speakers, Madelon Vriesendorp, Pablo Bronstein and Neil Spiller, will join leading practitioners to interrogate the state of contemporary drawing and its potential future directions as a critical tool for art and architecture.

drawingfutures.com

FABRICATE 2017

Held at the University of Stuttgart from 6 – 8 April 2017, FABRICATE discusses the progressive integration of digital design with manufacturing processes, and its impact on design and making in the 21st century.

——FABRICATE was conceived at The Bartlett School of Architecture, UCL, where its inaugural event was organised in 2011.

fabricate2017.org

Image: Keynote presentation by Izaskun Chinchilla Moreno on Curiosity during aae2016. Photo by Stonehouse Photographic

We are 175!

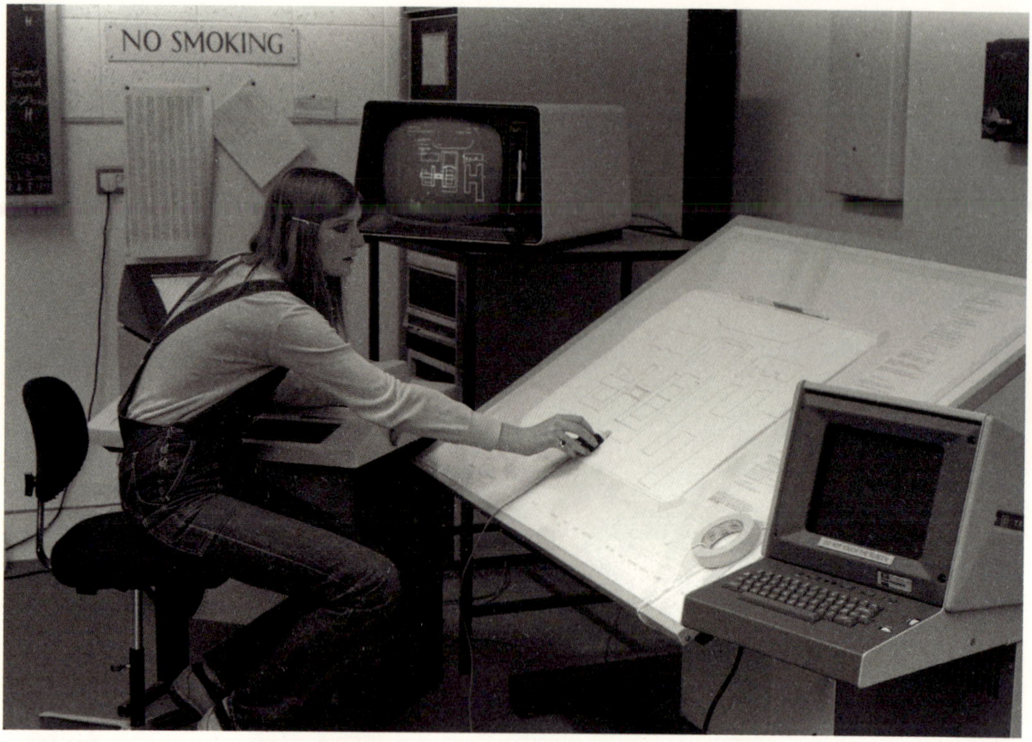

In 1841 Thomas Leverton Donaldson was appointed UCL's first Chair in Architecture, one of the first in the UK, founding what later became The Bartlett School of Architecture. Over its 175-year history, The Bartlett has established itself as one of the world's leading institutions for architectural education and research. To celebrate this milestone, 2016 has been a year of special events and activities:

——In January, we staged the inaugural Donaldson Lecture, a major new annual lecture by a household name, which aims to draw links between the built environment sector and the wider world. This year's speaker was award-winning artist Grayson Perry CBE.

——We produced a special Bartlett 175 publication together with the *Architectural Review*, celebrating the history of the School and the work of notable staff and alumni.

——We hosted aae2016, the conference of the association of architectural educators (aae), a major international conference on the theme of 'Research-Based Education', aae2016.

——We have launched a series of anniversary bursaries funded by alumni and supporters, to support promising students who may not otherwise be able to study with us.

Upcoming 175 Events

B-Pro Show

The annual exhibition of our groundbreaking post-professional advanced Architectural Design and Urban Design programmes, fast becoming a fixture on the architectural scene.
Opening Tuesday 24 September 2016

Drawing Futures

A new peer-reviewed conference exploring the critical role of drawing in relation to technology, contemporary architectural practice and beyond.
11-12 November 2016

22 Gordon Street Opening

Celebrate the return to our newly renovated home at 22 Gordon Street, formerly Wates House.
16 December 2016

For more information, go to
bit.ly/Bartlett175
#Bartlett175

Above: Computer technician Lindsay Wakeman in the computer room at Wates House (now 22 Gordon Street), c1981. Bartlett Archive
Right: Cover of 175 publication. Aiden Deng Ai, 'New York Automobile', 2015. MArch Architecture Unit 24

175

YEARS OF ARCHITECTURAL EDUCATION AT UCL

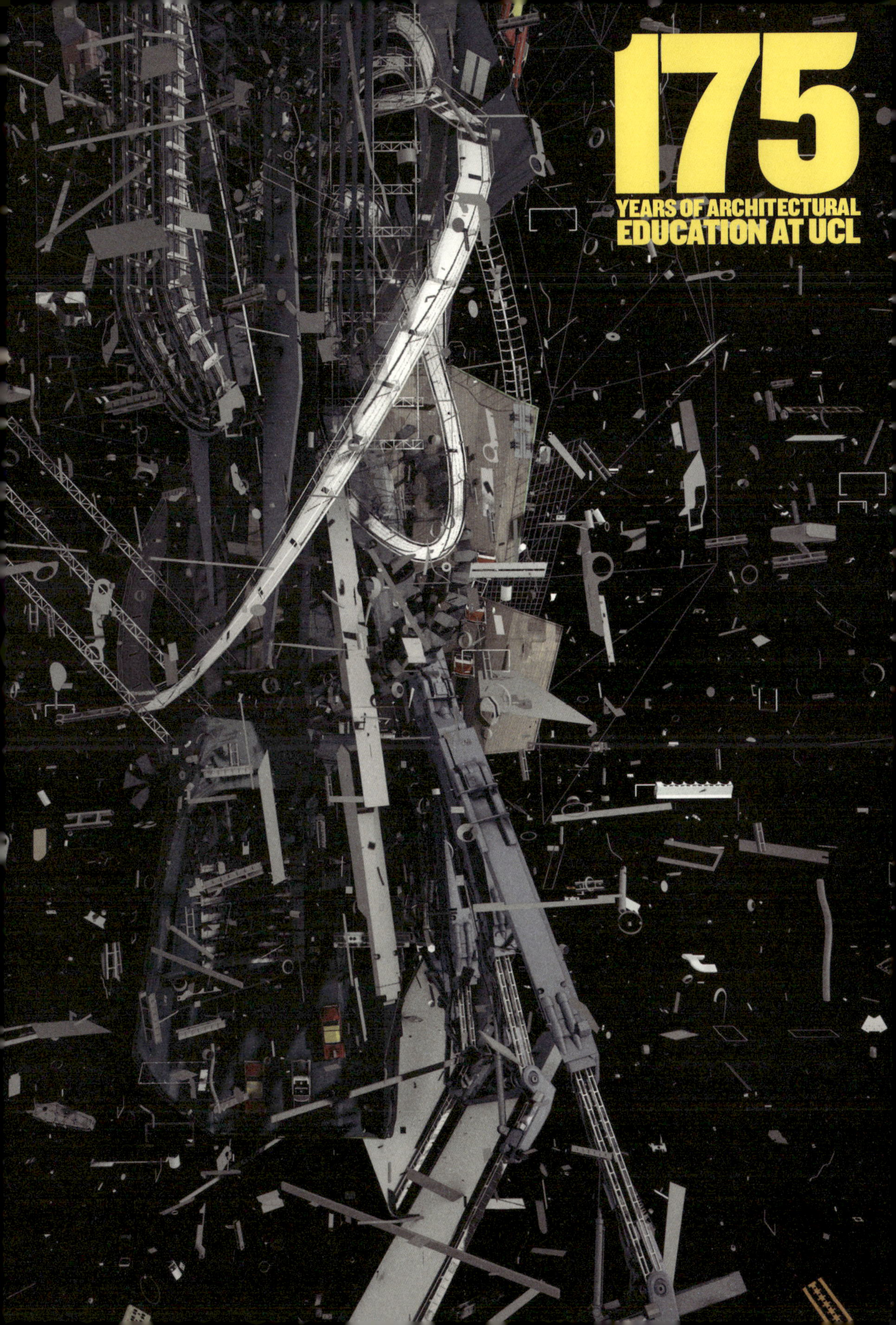

22 Gordon Street

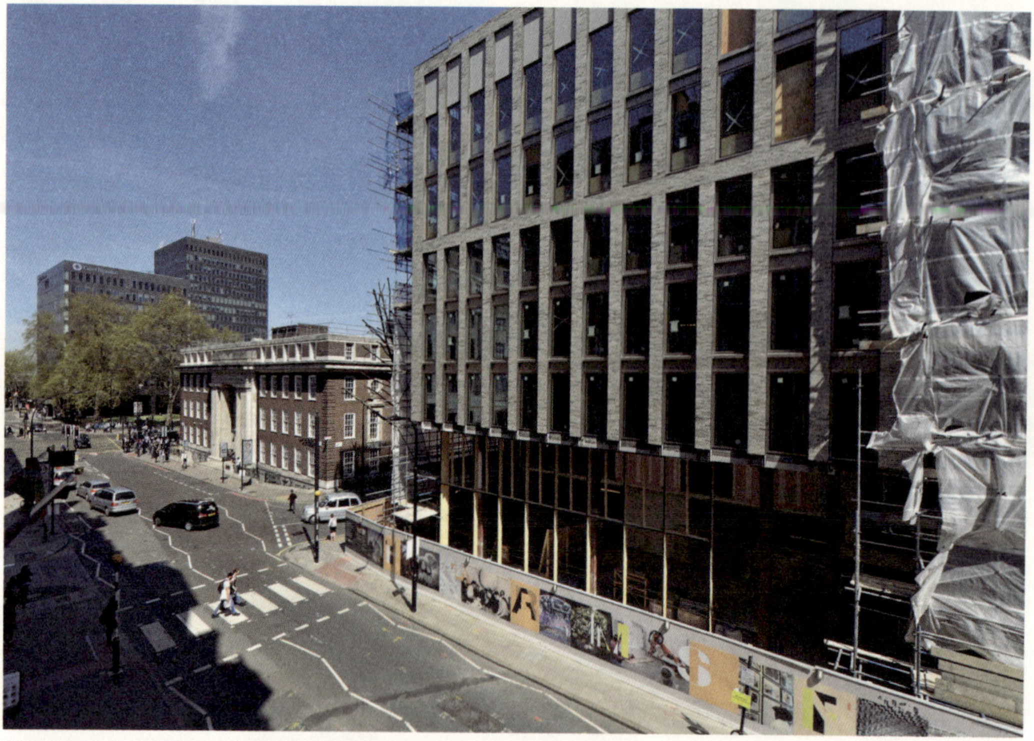

This autumn, The Bartlett School of Architecture will return to 22 Gordon Street (formerly Wates House) on UCL's Bloomsbury Campus. The £30 million refurbishment and extension, carried out as part of UCL's Bloomsbury Campus Refurbishments project, will provide additional space and a completely new environment and home for the School. The new building will have additional floors, an expansion to the south side of the building, brand new studios, new social and cafe areas, a contemporary exhibition space and expanded workshops.

Architect: Hawkins\Brown
Contractor: Gilbert Ash

An official Opening Party is planned for December 2016 as part of the School's Bartlett 175 celebrations.

For more information about the 22 Gordon Street refurbishment, visit the Bartlett Space website.
bit.ly/bartlettspace
#Bartlettspace

Image: 22 Gordon Street. Photo by Paul Smoothy

Here East

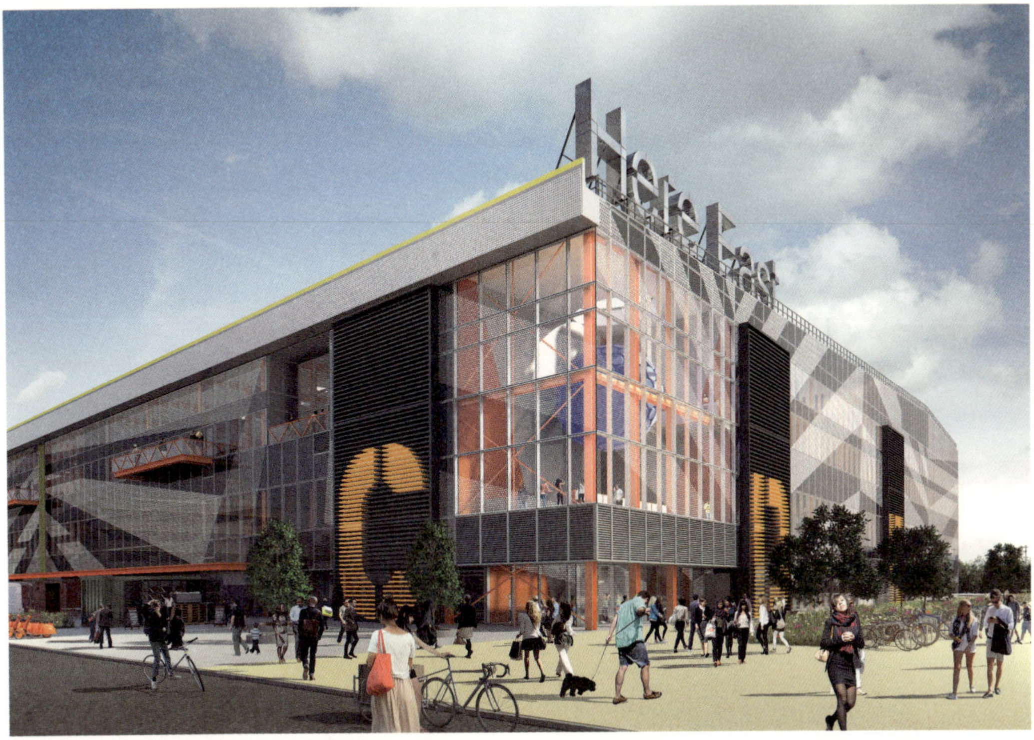

At 1.2 million square foot in London's Queen Elizabeth Olympic Park, Here East is one of London's most exciting new developments. A home for individuals and companies that range from start-ups to some of the most well-known organisations both in the UK and globally, Here East offers unparalleled new infrastructure for both innovation and excellence.

——In 2016, UCL took over 4,000 square metres of studio space at Here East, which will be used to undertake groundbreaking research in areas including architecture, infrastructure, transport, robotics, healthcare, manufacturing and environmental measurement. The Bartlett, UCL's Faculty of the Built Environment, and UCL Engineering will be expanding into these premises in mid-2017.

Here East will be the base for four exciting new programmes:

MArch Design for Manufacture
MArch Design for Performance & Interaction
MA Situated Practice
MEng Engineering & Architectural Design

The scale of The Bartlett at Here East will enable UCL to strengthen its interdisciplinary research and teaching, as well as promote greater engagement with the local community, in advance of the opening of UCL East at Queen Elizabeth Olympic Park in 2019.

Image: Here East at Queen Elizabeth Olympic Park.
CGI by Hawkins\Brown

Staff, Visitors & Consultants

A

Wes Aelbrecht
Ala Alfakara
Visiting Prof Robert Aish
Dr Kinda Al Sayed
Abeer Al Said
Laura Allen
Kit Allsopp
Gregoria Astengo
Sebastian Andia
Alisa Andrasek
Sabina Andron
Edwina Attlee
Bartek Arendt
Abigail Ashton

B

Julia Backhaus
Mark Ballard
Stefan Bassing
Scott Batty
Paul Bavister
Richard Beckett
Johan Berglund
Dr Doreen Bernath
Prof Peter Bishop
Izzy Blackburn
Isaïe Bloch
William Bondin
Prof Iain Borden
Shumi Bose
Roberto Bottazzi
Andy Bow
Matthew Bowles
Eva Branscome
Thea Brezank
Pascal Bronner
Giulio Brugnaro
Mark Burgess
Bim Burton
Matthew Butcher

C

Dr Graham Cairns
Dağhan Cam
Blanche Cameron
Ben Campkin
Tina Di Carlo
William Camilleri
Prof Mario Carpo
Dr Brent Carnell
Martyn Carter
Eray Cayli
Martyn Carter
Megha Chand
Prof Nat Chard
Laura Cherry
Izaskun Chinchilla Moreno
Dr Evengelia Chrysikou
Mollie Claypool
Dr Marjan Colletti
Emeritus Prof Peter Cook RA
Roger Courtney
Paul Crudge
Prof Marcos Cruz

D

Dr Edward Denison
Bernadette Devilat
Dr Ashley Dhanani
Paul Dobraszczyk
Inigo Dodd
Oliver Domeisen
Elizabeth Dow

E

Dr Eve Eylers

F

Ava Fatah gen Schieck
Bernd Felsinger
Peter Ferguson
Pedro Font Alba
Zachary Fluker
Emma Flynn
Prof Adrian Forty
Colin Fournier
Sara Franceschelli
John Fraser
Prof Murray Fraser
Daisy Froud

G

Prof Stephen Gage
Jean Garrett
Stelios Giamarelos
Visiting Prof Nicholas Grimshaw
Visiting Prof Joseph Grima
Emer Girling
Ruairi Glynn
Dr Jon Goodbun
Kevin Green
Adam Greenfield
Dr Sam Griffiths
Kostas Grigoriadis
Peter Guillery

H

Michael Hadi
Soomeen Hahm
James Hampton
Dr Sean Hanna
Tamsin Hanke
Usman Haque
Dr Penelope Haralambidou
Prof Christine Hawley
Colin Herperger
Prof Jonathan Hill
Visiting Prof Dan Hill
Prof Bill Hillier
Thomas Hillier
Bill Hodgson
Tom Holberton
Stephen Howson
Beth Hughes
Dr Anne Hultzsch
Francesca Hughes
Vincent Hughe
Maxwell Hutchinson

I

Damjan Iliev
Jessica In
Platon Issaias

J

Michal Jablonksi
Nannette Jackowski
Carlos Jiménez Cenamor
Manuel Jimenez Garcia
Steve Johnson
Helen Jones
Mikella Johnson

K

Dr Kayvan Karimi
Mara-Sophia Kanthak
Jonathan Kendall
Simon Kennedy
Anne Kershen
Xavier de Kestelier
David Kirsch
Fani Kostourou
Gergely Kovács
Sofia Krimizi
Dirk Krolikowski

L

Chee-Kit Lai
Felipe Lanuza
Justin Lau
Eli Lee
Dr Guan Lee
Stefan Lengen
Lucy Leonard
Dr Christopher Leung
Ifigeneia Liangi

Prof CJ Lim
Olga Linardou
Enriqueta Llabres
Andy Lomas
Alvaro Lopez
Tim Lucas
Michelle Lukins Segerström

M
Visiting Prof John Macarthur
Dr Abel Maciel
Dr Yeoryia Manolopoulou
Jonathan Martin
Maximo Martinez
Adriana Massidda
Emma-Kate Matthews
Prof Níall McLaughlin
Jeremy Melvin
Josep Miàs
Stoll Michael
Bartlett Prof Frédéric Migayrou
Jeffrey Miller
Tom Mole
Ana Monrabal-Cook

N
Jack Newton

O
Jamie O'Brien
Brian O'Reilly
James O'Leary
Bernie Ococ
Luke Olsen
Ricardo de Ostos
Jakub Owczarek

P
Dr Garyfalia Palaiologou
Igor Pantic
Jacob Paskins
Claudia Pasquero
Thomas Pearce
Luke Pearson
Prof Alan Penn
Dr Barbara Penner
Godofredo Pereira
Victoria Perry
Frederik Petersen
Mads Petersen
Simon Pilling
Frosso Pimenides
Maj Plemenitas
Kim van Poeteren
Andrew Porter
Arthur Prior
Sophia Psarra

R
Robert Randall
Eva Ravnborg
Dr Peg Rawes
Luis Rego
Dr Aileen Reid
Sophie Read
Prof Jane Rendell
Gilles Retsin
Harriet Richardson
Eduardo Rico
Ian Ridley
Aleksandrina Rizova
Gavin Robotham
Indigo Rohrer
Dr Jonathan Rokem
Javier Ruiz
Stefan Rutzinger

S
Dr Kerstin Sailer
Dr Sahed Saleem
Prof Andrew Saint
Kristina Schinegger
Carina Schneider
Peter Scully
Dr Tania Sengupta
Dr Miguel Serra
Sara Shafiei
Prof Bob Sheil
Naz Siddique
Colin Skeete
Paul Smoothy
Mark Smout
Vicente Soler
Camila Sotomayor
Brian Stater
Emmanouil Stavrakakis
Dr Kimberley Steed German
John Steadman
Dimitri Stefanescu
Tijana Stevanovic
Rachel Stevenson
Catrina Stewart
Chris Stutz
Sabine Storp
Michiko Sumi

T
Martin Tang
Dr Lusine Tarkhanyan
Huda Tayob
Philip Temple
Colin Thom
Michael Tite
Victor Torrance
Freddy Tuppen
Tomas Tvarijonas

V
Dr Angie Vanhoozer
Dr Tasos Varoudis
Melis Van Den Berg
Viktoria Viktorija
Nina Vollenbröker
Prof Laura Vaughan

W
Susan Ware
Barry Wark
Bill Watts
Peter Webb
Patrick Weber
Nick Westby
Mark Whitby
Andrew Whiting
Daniel Widrig
Finn Williams
Graeme Williamson
Meredith Wilson
Dr Robin Wilson
Oliver Wilton
Katy Wood

Y
Umat Yamac
Michelle Young

Z
Paolo Zaide
Emmanouil Zaroukas
Stamtios Zografos

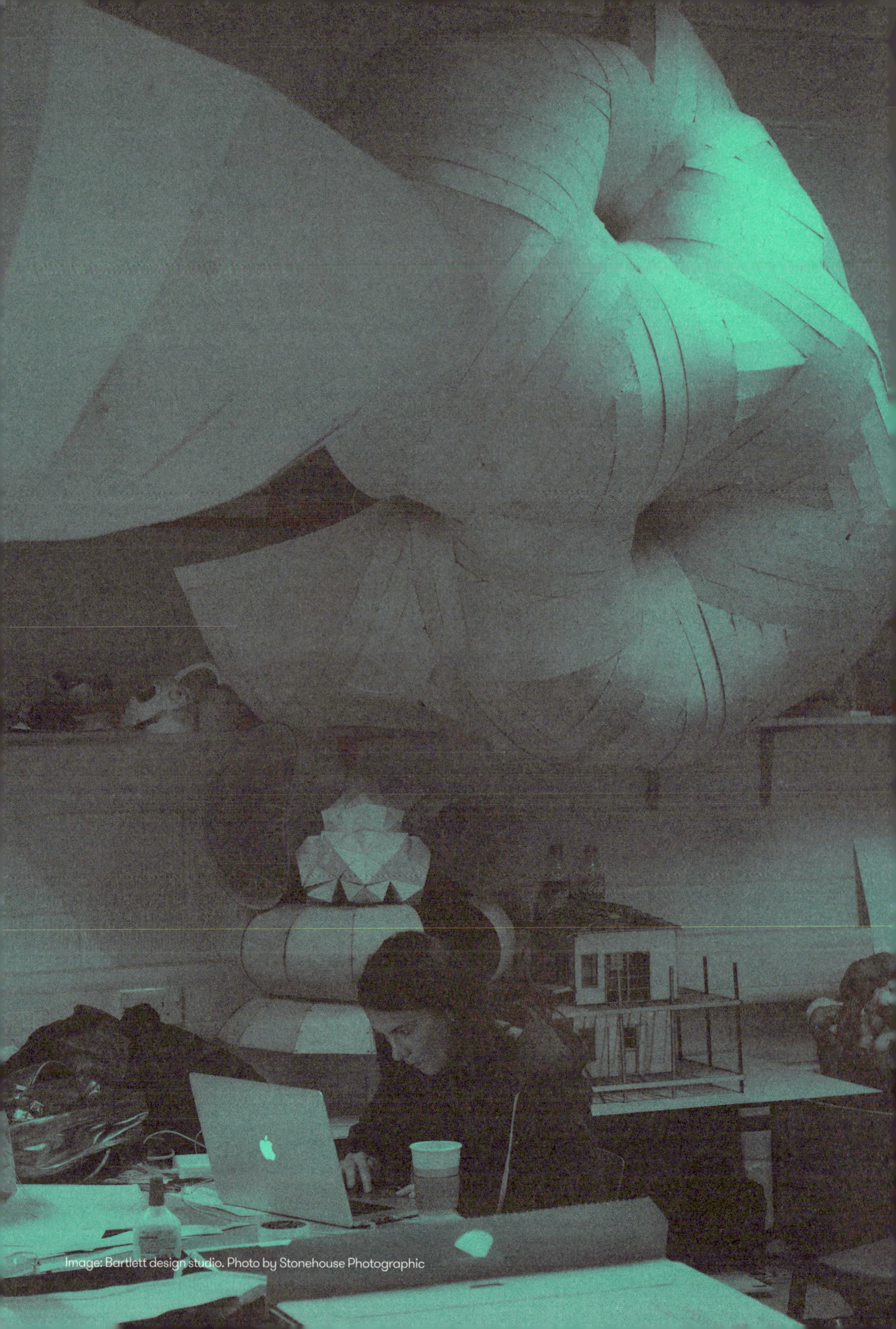

Image: Bartlett design studio. Photo by Stonehouse Photographic

Supporters

We are grateful to our generous supporters

Summer Show Main Title Supporter 2016
Foster + Partners

Lighting Supporter
iGuzzini

Prizes
Saint-Gobain
Max Fordham
iGuzzini

Bartlett Book 2016
Allford Hall Monaghan Morris

Private Reception
Adrem
Haines Watts

Bartlett International Lecture Series
Fletcher Priest Trust

MArch Architecture Bursaries
ImaginationAcademy
Kohn Pedersen Fox Associates
Rogers Stirk Harbour + Partners
Hawkins\Brown

Supporters of the Summer Show
Laing O'Rourke

Summer Show Opener's Prize, awarded by Liz Diller
Wilkinson Eyre

Bartlett 175 Sponsors

Gold
Allford Hall Monaghan Morris
Foster + Partners
Saint-Gobain
Rogers Stirk Harbour + Partners
Hawkins\Brown
ImaginationAcademy

Silver
Scott Brownrigg

Bronze
Derwent London
Duggan Morris Architects
Hopkins Architects
Piercy & Co
Pollard Thomas Edwards

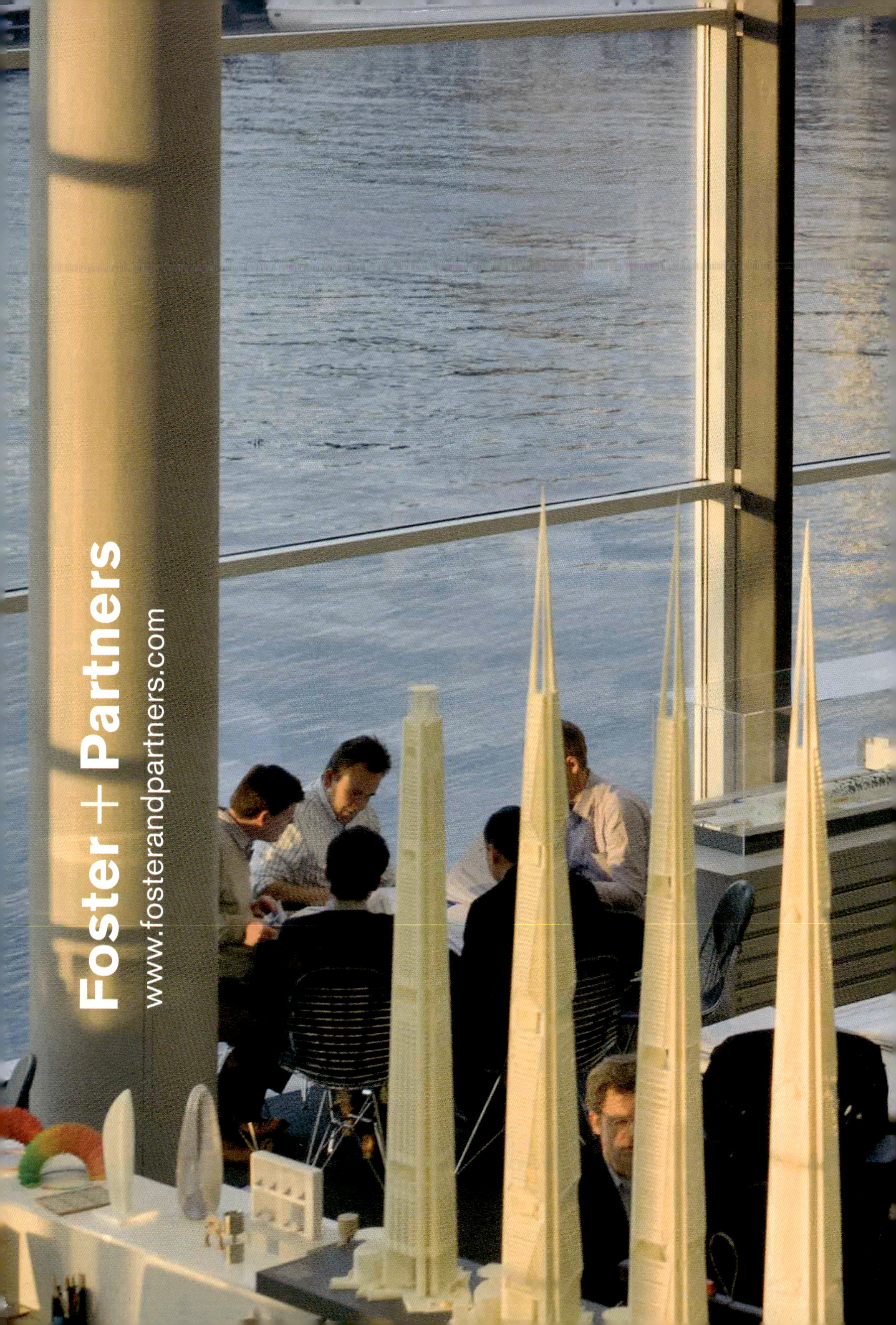
Foster + Partners
www.fosterandpartners.com

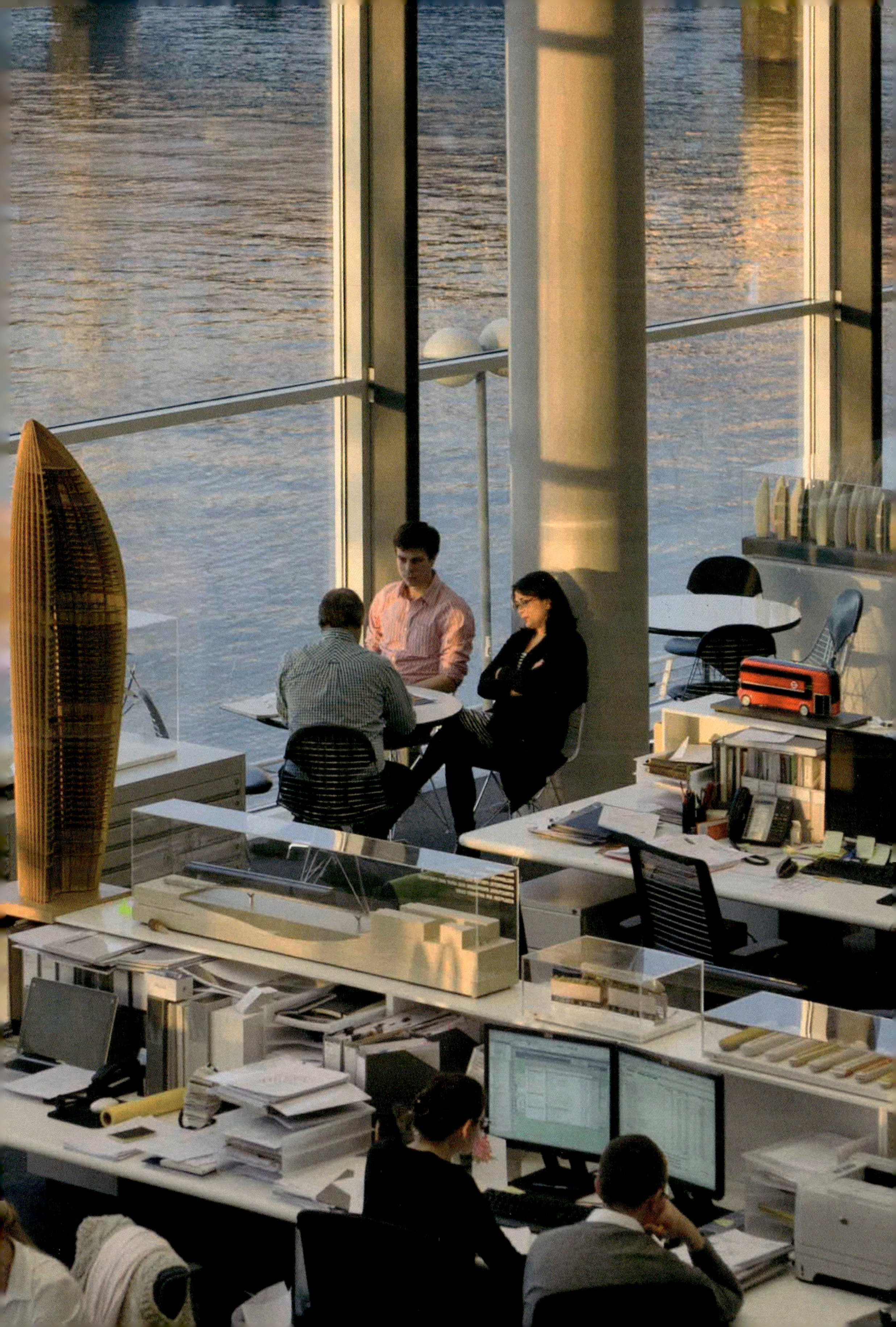

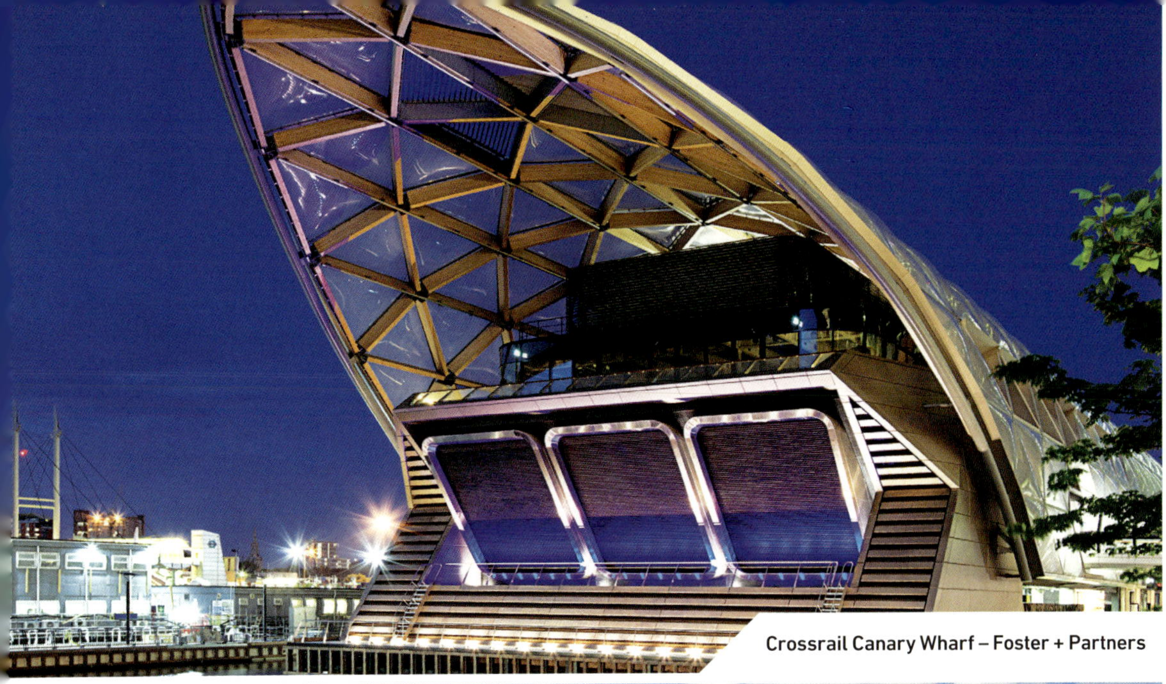

Crossrail Canary Wharf – Foster + Partners

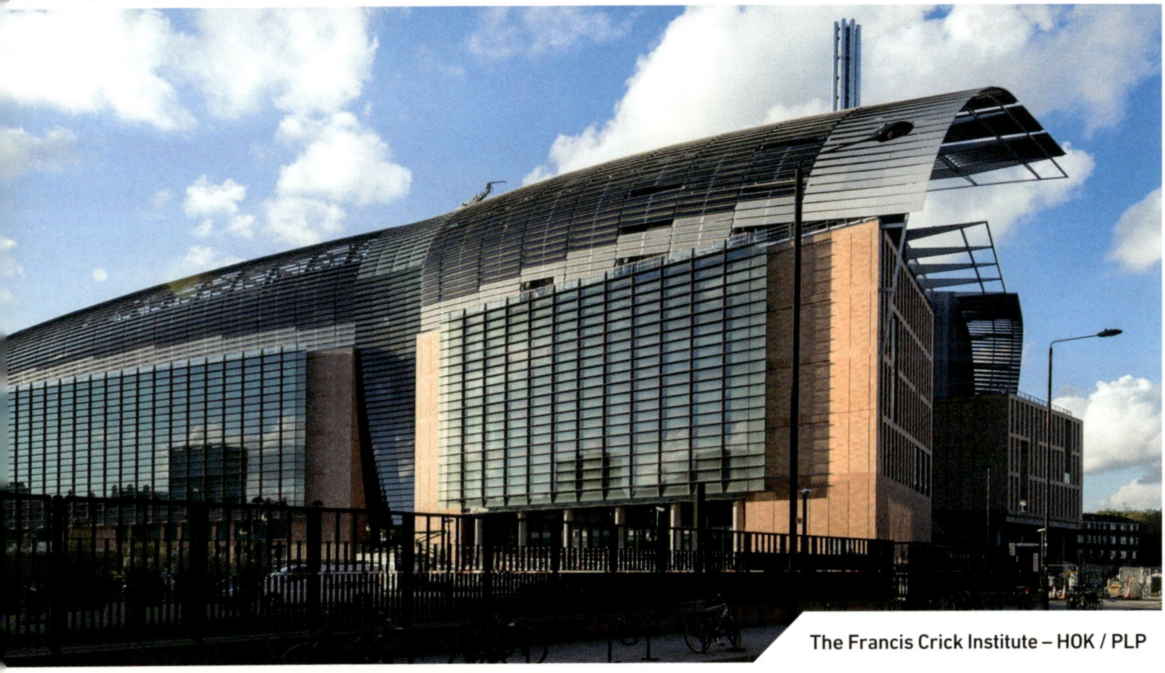

The Francis Crick Institute – HOK / PLP

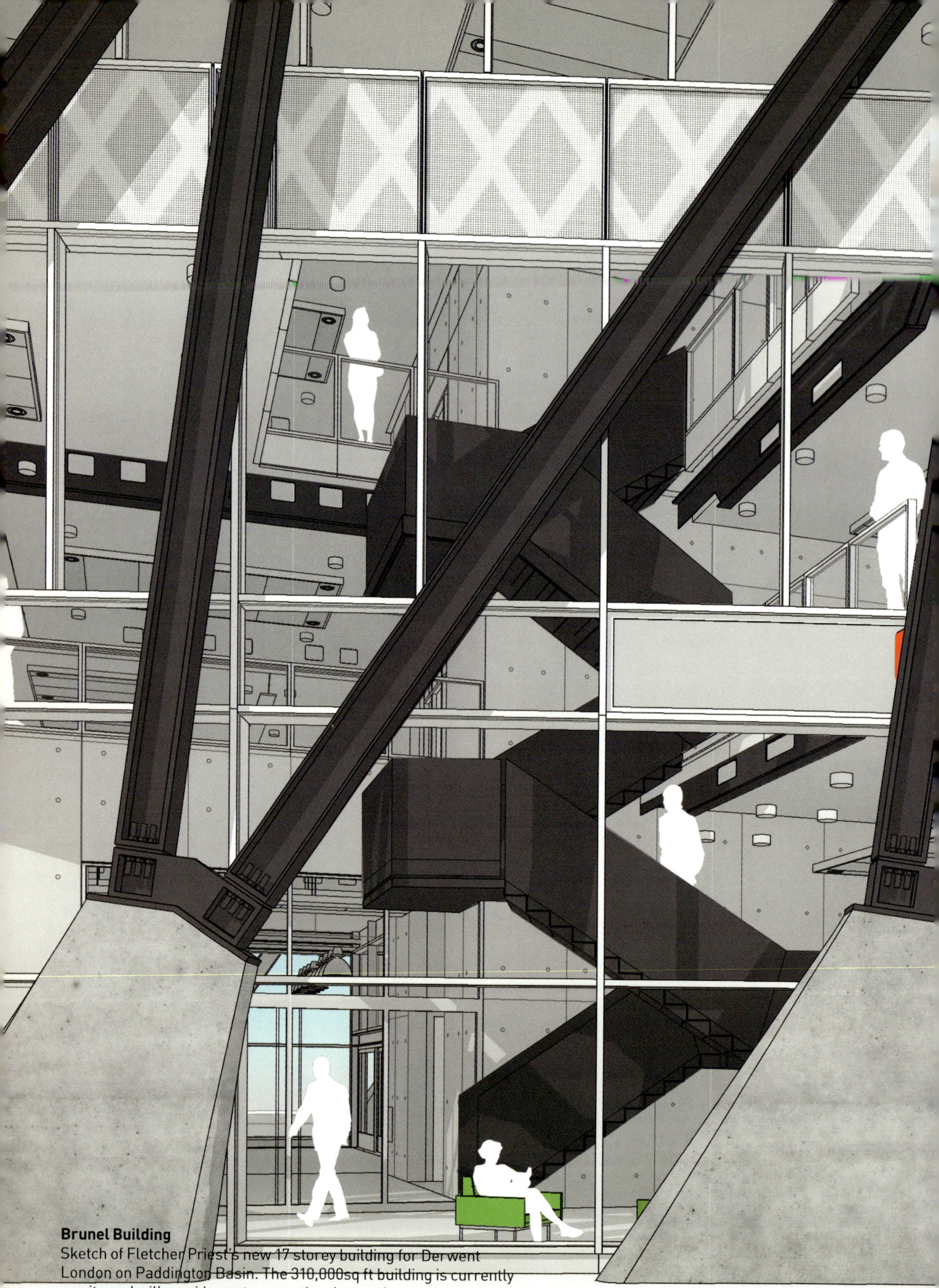

Brunel Building
Sketch of Fletcher Priest's new 17 storey building for Derwent London on Paddington Basin. The 310,000sq ft building is currently on site and will provide next generation, innovative work space with a unique external structure producing 3.5m high column free space.

bartlett.ucl.ac.uk/architecture

Publisher
The Bartlett School of Architecture, UCL

Editors
Eli Lee, Michelle Lukins Segerström

Graphic Design
Patrick Morrissey, Unlimited
weareunlimited.co.uk

Executive Editors
Laura Allen, Frédéric Migayrou, Bob Sheil

ISBN 978-0-9954819-0-9

For more information on all the programmes and modules at The Bartlett Faculty of the Built Environment, UCL, visit bartlett.ucl.ac.uk

The Bartlett School of Architecture, UCL
140 Hampstead Road
London NW1 2BX

+44 (0)20 3108 9646
architecture@ucl.ac.uk

Twitter: @BartlettArchUCL
Facebook: facebook.com/BartlettArchitectureUCL
Instagram: bartlettarchucl
Vimeo: vimeo.com/bartlettarchucl